Man
and the
Environment

This book is printed on paper containing a substantial amount of recycled fiber. The paper has been supplied by the Wausau Paper Company of Wausau, Wisconsin.

In addition to making considerable use of recycled fiber, Wausau is one of the first major paper mills to develop the high temperature recovery process of paper making chemicals. Their recovery process has contributed greatly to pollution abatement of the Wisconsin river—a problem of grave concern to environmentalists.

Man
and the
Environment

Third Edition

Wes Jackson
The Land Institute
Salina, Kansas

wcb
William C. Brown
Company Publishers
Dubuque, Iowa

Credits

"Overcrowding in Mice," from "Not with a Bang but with a Whimper," in *Science News*, Feb. 3, 1973. Reprinted by permission.

Richard L. Clinton, "The Specter of Starvation." Agency for Internal Development.

Robert Claiborne, "The Tehuacan Story," from "Digging Up Prehistoric America" by Robert Claiborne, Harper's Magazine 232:69-74. April 1966. Copyright 1966 by Harper's Magazine, Inc. Permission granted by the Julian Bach, Jr., Literary Agency.

Stephen H. Schneider, "The Green Revolution in Tropical Agriculture: Panacea or Disaster?" *The Genesis Strategy* by Stephen H. Schneider, pp. 259-264, 1976. Copyright 1976 by Plenum Publishing Corporation. Reprinted by permission.

Frances Moore Lappe and Joseph Collins, "More Food Means More Hunger," from *Development Forum*, published by the Centre for Economic and Social Information. All rights reserved.

Jean Mayer, "Starvation Patterns," from a letter by Jean Mayer in *Science* 152:291. 15 April 1966. Copyright by the American Association for the Advancement of Science.

Philip H. Abelson, "Malnutrition, Learning and Behavior," from "Malnutrition, Learning, and Behavior," an editorial by Philip H. Abelson. *Science* 164:17. 4 April 1969. Copyright 1969 by the American Association for the Advancement of Science.

Darryl G. Cole, "The Myth of Fertility Dooms Development Plans." *The National Observer* 7:10. 22 April 1968. Copyright 1968 by Dow Jones and Co., Inc.

William E. Moran, Jr., "Will the Amazon Basin Become a Desert?" from "Brazil: A Prodigy of Growth" by William E. Moran, Jr. *Population Bulletin* 25:89-90. September 1969. Copyright 1969 by the Population Reference Bureau, Inc.

Garrett Hardin, "Nobody Ever Dies of Overpopulation." *Science* 171:527. February 12, 1971. Copyright 1971 by the American Association for the Advancement of Science.

James Bonner, "The Starving as a Race Apart," from *The Next Ninety Years*. Copyright 1967 by California Institute of Technology.

Garrett Hardin, "Parenthood: Right of Privilege?" *Science* 169:427. 31 July 1970. Copyright 1970 by the American Association for the Advancement of Science.

Medcom, "From Magic to Science: A History of Contraception," *The Case for Population Control*. Copyright 1971, Medcom, Inc.

Garrett Hardin, "Coping with Contraceptive Failure," reprinted from *Perspectives in Biology and Medicine*, August 1966, by permission of The University of Chicago Press. Copyright 1966 by the University of Chicago Press.

Jon Tinker, "Democracy Versus the Breeder?" *New Scientist*, 28 October 1976. Copyright 1976 by Jon Tinker.

Fred Hoyle, "A Consequence of Fusion Energy?" from pp. 180-183 in *October the First is too Late* by Fred Hoyle. Copyright 1966 by Fred Hoyle. Reprinted by permission of Harper & Row, Publishers, Inc.

Erik P. Eckholm, "The Other Energy Crisis: Firewood," Worldwatch Paper 1. Copyright 1975 by Worldwatch Institute.

Edmund Faltermayer, "Metals: The Warning Signals Are Up." *Fortune* October, 1972. Copyright 1972 by Time, Inc.

John F. Henahan. "Whatever Happened to the Cranberry Crisis?" *Atlantic Monthly* 239:29-36 March 1977. Copyright 1977 by the Atlantic Monthly Company, Boston, MA. Reprinted with permission.

William A. Neiring, "The Effects of Pesticides." *Bioscience* 18:869-875. September 1968. Copyright 1968 by the American Institute of Biological Sciences.

Robert W. Holcomb, "Oil in the Ecosystem." *Science* 166:204-206; 10 October 1969. Copyright 1969 by the American Association for the Advancement of Science.

S.W.A. Gunn, "Oil Spills—An Old Story," from a letter to *Science* 165:967. 5 September 1969. Copyright 1969 by the American Association for the Advancement of Science.

David E. Elrich, "Soil Pollution," from a letter in *Science* 154:1275. 6 December 1966. Copyright 1966 by the American Association for the Advancement of Science.

"Shock at Sea." *Time* 94:40. 15 August 1969. Copyright by Time, Inc.

Environment Magazine, "What Happens to Ozone," reprinted by permission of the Scientists' Institute for Public Information. Copyright 1975 by Scientists' Institute for Public Information.

R.A. Brink, J.W. Densmore, and G.A. Hill, "Soil Deterioration and the Growing World Demand for Food," from *Science*, Vol. 197, pp. 625-630, 12 August 1977. Copyright 1977 by the American Association for the Advancement of Science.

Aldo Leopold, "Odyssey," from *A Sand County Almanac with other Essays on Conservation from Round River.* Copyright 1949, 1953, 1966, and renewed 1977 by Oxford University Press, Inc. Reprinted by permission.

Don Marquis, "What the Ants Are Saying," copyright 1935 by Doubleday & Company, Inc. from *The Lives and Times of Archy and Mehitabel* by Don Marquis. Used by permission of Doubleday & Company, Inc.

Lee Merriman Talbot, "The Wail of Kashmir," from *Wildlands in our Civilization*, ed. David Brower. Copyright 1964 by the Sierra Club.

U.P. Hedrick, "Passenger Pigeons," from *Land of the Crooked Tree* by Ulysses Prentiss Hedrick. Copyright 1948 by Oxford University Press, Inc., renewed 1976 by Ulysses Prentiss Hedrick, III. Reprinted by permission.

To Ben W. Smith

Contents

Contents

Preface

The environmental movement can be conveniently, and I think accurately, organized into four phases: development of a checklist, analysis of the problems, the search for alternatives, and the evolution of an environmental or ecological ethic.

The checklist developed during the early part of the 70's when the first edition of this book was published. Scholars who wrote about environmental concerns were engaged in defining and categorizing the numerous environmental problems.

Beginning during the checklist phase, but peaking sometime afterwards, an attempt was made by concerned scholars to analyze the environmental crisis. Why did we overpopulate the earth? Why do we pollute and waste resources? Of course our wasteful consumerism was linked to the age-old problems of greed and envy, but the Western attitude toward Nature was also blamed. Indeed we have and do regard Nature as an object, "out there," and us as the separate subject. This subject-object dualism, at least as old as Aristotle, had led us to a dangerous point in our history. But this analysis phase, reflected in the second edition of *Man and the Environment,* peaked in the mid-70's, and we are now firmly into the third period of the movement, the search for alternatives.

In this third phase we can observe people who once stood immobilized in despair now offering compelling alternatives in both lifestyles and technology to a culture whose momentum of exploitation seems to have no end. This third part of the movement has its frustrations. Many of the alternatives which have surfaced have not been, nor are they likely to become, part of the mainstream of American life. This is an experimental period in which we can expect to look hard for new options without expecting many of the seemingly desirable alternatives to compete with the expedient and wasteful ways of the time.

Since we have progressed to this third point in the evolution of the movement, I fully expect that by the end of the decade we will be moving very rapidly toward the fourth and final phase—the development of an ecological or environmental ethic. Some progress has already been made in that direction, but the wave of interest and discussion has not yet peaked.

The readings in this third edition are arranged according to the four phases of the environmental movement. By devoting only one section to the checklist of environmental problems, I have not chosen to provide material for a thorough understanding of the problems, but only to list some of the main areas of concern. This is still a major portion of the book, but is not as extensive as in the other two editions. The second phase of the environmental movement, the attempt to analyze the problems, is represented by some selections which are now "classics" in the environmental literature, two of them being "The Tragedy of the Commons" by Garrett Hardin and "The Historical Roots of our Ecologic Crisis" by Lynn White. Though often reprinted in anthologies, I include these once again as important touchstones in our attempts to analyze the problems. Most of the selections of this section however, are not widely recognized as classics but are fine readings nevertheless.

This edition differs substantially from the second, and for that matter from other environmental readers, in that the last two phases of the movement receive considerable emphasis. The reader may be surprised that the readings in the search for alternatives section have little to do with hardware such as solar collectors and wind generators and more to do with points of view which can ultimately change the direction of society. Readings cover such areas as politics, education, land use and science.

Finally, there is the fourth and last section which contains readings selected because I think they can contribute to our understanding and development of an environmental ethic.

During this effort I have tried to keep in mind the instructors who seek an integrative approach in the teaching of environmental studies. I think I know their main problem. Most of their students now have not all thoroughly experienced the first and second phases of the environmental movement. At the same time, most instructors are now weary of simply dealing with the checklist and analysis of problems one more time, at whatever stage we may be. I hope this book will help us all sharpen our focus and better understand the large dimension of the problems and their necessary solution.

Acknowledgments

I thank the numerous publishers and authors of articles for consent to reprint their materials in this edition. I am grateful to my former associates at California State University, Sacramento and recent associates with The Land Institute, Salina, Kansas for calling to my attention various writings and sharing their views on matters of environmental concern.

Much appreciated help came from Nancy Miller, Assistant Director of the Center for Environmental Studies at Bowling Green State University. Ms. Miller spent several days suggesting articles and books and finding references which had been published during several months of intellectual drought when my time was devoted to the physical construction of The Land Institute.

Ms. Louise Barrett of Wm. C. Brown Company Publishers deserves special thanks for her encouragement and patience over the past months. Finally, I wish to thank my wife and daughter for their help during the preparation. My wife, Dana strengthened the message through her critique of article organization and inclusion. Our daughter Laura spent an entire summer obtaining permission from publishers and authors and offered helpful critique of materials from time to time.

A Checklist of Environmental Issues

The Population-Food Problem

Introduction

No where in our recent past has it been necessary for humans to feel the significance of the number four billion, three hundred sixty-five million, the estimated standing crop of humans on the earth by mid-1978. The number begins to take on some significance when we calculate that for each 1,000 people, 30 are being born and 12 are dying. The population is doubling every 38 years. Before we put our pencils or hand-held calculators to rest, we usually try to determine the number of people living on earth by the year 2000, scarcely 20 years from now. As a number over six billion blinks on, we are amazed. There is little left but to shake our heads in anticipation of the future. The number climbs from over four billion to slightly over six billion mainly because 36 percent of the current population is under 15 years old, which means that within the 20 year period, well over a third of the population of the earth will have moved into the reproductive years. Even now, one infant in ten world wide dies in the first year. How many out of ten will die in the first year by century's end?

We of the United States tend to think that we have turned the corner on population growth. Our birth rate, which reached its peak in 1957, could rise after a steady decline,[1] in spite of the fact that ten to fifteen percent of college students want no children and a very large majority want only one or two.[2] It is that large number moving into the reproductive years which sustains the momentum of growth.

Conditions seem the most bleak, however, in the third world. Africa's population alone could very well reach 800 million by 2000, and *the first priority of this continent is not to limit population.*[3] In Latin America, the population is now doubling every 26 years. The current population of 336 million will likely have swelled to over 600 million if they can manage to be fed. The pressure to feed the ever-increasing biomass of humans will force the reduction of both biotic and cultural variety. Brazil's interior ecosystem is certainly threatened, and even now the aborigines experience genocide as the government pushes development. The Amazonian Indian can survive only through the loss of his identity.[4]

India, that sub-continent most of us think about when we discuss world hunger, imposed strict birth control measures under Indira Gandhi to slow population growth. Government employees and Delhi residents were threatened with such coercive measures as no jobs, medical care, drinking water, school or housing if families were not restricted to two children.[5] This issue contributed to the defeat of Mrs. Gandhi in the election.

The Peoples' Republic of China already has a population of over one billion. The population is currently doubling every 43 years because great achievements in birth control have been integrated in China through family planning.[6] Nevertheless, one-third of the people are 15 and under. Therefore, the momentum of the present is certain to impose a large number of people on that continent within a single generation.

For other places in the world, the story is similar. Zero population growth will not be achieved within several generations without an enormous increase in the death rate. A simple restriction of birth rate through humane methods won't do it alone.[7]

A search for optimism yields very little about which to be optimistic. In the United States we can point to the decline in birth expectations of young American wives[8] or to research going on to develop new hormonal methods to regulate male fertility.[9] But on a global scale these are but scant signs for optimism. The somber implications of the mathematics offsets any small bits of optimism. Simply stated, what do we do with those babies which seem certain to be born to those 36 percent of the earth's people now 15 and under? They will have to be clothed, housed and fed every day.

When we come to the food side of the crisis, the problem remains complex, if not bleak. Though famines have been with us, probably since civilization began, the most recent famine seems to occupy our thoughts. Right now, nowhere is the specter of an inadequate supply of food more pronounced than in the African Sahel, certain parts of India and Bali.[10, 11] The food problem in Singapore and Mexico is becoming increasingly acute because of the growing dependence on food imports.[12]

The controversy among experts as to the seriousness of the problems has to do with the fact that so many dimensions of the problem manifest themselves. Some countries simply lack the purchasing power to buy the products of a bountiful harvest in such food producing countries as the United States.[13] Furthermore, one group of experts on the Green Revolution is optimistic about world food production and its potential,[14] while others insist that the Green Revolution is over, having ended on the sour notes of famine and failure.[15]

Doubtlessly, there is some cushion in the earth's ability to supply food for the millions. On the one hand there is still some wild nature to be destroyed. In the United States, hundreds of miles of hedgerows and trees in small drainages were bulldozed out in 1975-76 to increase the numbers of acres to grow wheat and sorghum. Such swampy areas as the Albermarle-Pamlico peninsula in North Carolina are being eyed as a potential farming area to produce corn and soybeans.[16] In Africa, wild animals are being killed for food, thus threatening the extermination of several wild species.[17] At sea, the bluefin tuna is being pushed to the edge of extinction by American fishermen.[18] On the other hand, human cleverness is a bountiful source of hope. Scientists have discovered a source of liquid wax, formerly found only in the sperm whale oil, to also exist in the Sonoroan Desert plant, jojoba.[19] Pressure on the sperm whale can now be relaxed the optimists say. Our cleverness may produce new food supplies. We may be on the verge of widespread commercial production of single-celled protein[20] through the use of mixed bacterial cultures. The United States Department of Agriculture has estimated that as much protein as is found in the entire soybean crop[21] could be produced from the manure of U.S. livestock alone.

The list of clever methods to increase food production could go on and on.

Some have advocated that we seed salmon in the Antarctic Ocean to harvest the huge protein supplies in the krill.[22] Others have advocated the management of green sea turtle farms. An acre of salt water five feet deep is supposedly capable of producing 200,000 pounds of protein. Compared to the 800 pounds of beef produced on a single acre of land, the 2,000 fold difference seems attractive.

The population-food crisis is placed first on the checklist of environmental problems for a very good reason. Unless we learn to control our numbers and provide enough food for the hungry, the other problems will be increasingly difficult to manage. This is not to deny that an annual increase in the level of consumption of the affluent contributes more to the draw down of our finite resources and impacts the sinks of nature more than the extra humans who are born in poor nations each year. While the developed world screams "contraception" to the poor, leaders of poor nations scream "contrasumption" at us. Unless all nations soon begin to implement both contraception and contrasumption, thinking people have good reason to fear the future.

The thirteen readings of this section have been selected and grouped according to the categories which deal with some of the basic questions associated with the problem. The problem has many dimensions, and this section does not begin to cover even a small fraction of them. It is earnestly hoped, however, that the readings herein will help us strengthen our resolve to work on many fronts almost all at once.

REFERENCES

1. The American Birth Rate: Evidences of a Coming Rise, June Sklar, (Univ. of California, Berkeley) and, Beth Berkou (California State Dept. of Health). Science, Aug. 29, 1974, v 189, n 4204, p 693.
2. Family Planning and Health: Congruent Objectives of Malthus and Spock, Helen D. Cohn (Harvard Univ.) and E. James Lieberman (Children's Hospital, Hillcrest, Wash. D.C.), American J. Public Health, Mar. 1974, v 64, n 3, p 225.
3. Africa and Its Population Growth, Leon F. Bouvier, Univ. of Rhode Island, Population B, Jan. 1975, v 30, n 1.
4. How Can We Make Fewer Children More Attractive? J. H. Fremlin, Univ. of Birmingham, U.K., Intl. J. Env. Studies, Nov. 1974, v 7, n 1, p 57.
5. Delhito Penalizes Couples for Not Limiting Births, New York Times, Feb. 26, 1976, p. 1.
6. The Limitation of Human Population. A Natural History, Don E. Dumond, Univ. of Oregon, Science, Feb. 28, 1975, v 187, n 4178, p 173.
7. Human Population and Environmental Problems, Paul R. Ehrlich, Stanford Univ., Env. Conservation, Spring 1974, v 1, n 1, p 15.
8. Can We Believe Recent Data on Birth Expectations in the United States? Judith Blake, Univ. of California, Demography, Feb. 1974, v 11, n 1 p 25.
9. The Regulation of Male Fertility: The State-of-the-Art and Future Possibilities, D. M. de Kretser, Monash Univ., Australia, Contraception, June 1974, v 9, n 6, p 561.
10. Bali, Microcosm for Third World Agriculture, Albert Ravenholt, Common Ground, July 1975, v 1, n 3, p 13.
11. Drought in West Africa: Temporary Famine or Chronic Deficiency? Victor D. Du Bois, Common Ground, July 1975, v 1, n 3, p 35.
12. Japan and the World Food Problem, Charles F. Gallagher, Common Ground, July 1975, v 1, n 3, p 75.

13.   Brighter Forecasts for the World's Food Supply, Henry B. Arthur, (Harvard Business School) and Gail L. Cramer (Montana State Univ.), Harvard Business Review, May-June 1976, v 54, n 3, p 161.

14.   Green Revolution: Creators Still Quite Hopeful on World Food, Nicholas Wade, Science, Sept. 6, 1974, v 185, n 4145, p 844.

15.   The Green Revolution Is Over, Jon Tinker, New Scientist, Nov. 7, 1974, v 64, n 922, p 388.

16.   Agriculture: A New Frontier in Coastal North Carolina, Luther J. Carter, Science, July 25, 1975, v 189, n 4199, p 271.

17.   Wildlife as a Source of Protein in Africa South of the Sahara, Emmanuel O. A. Aisibey, Ghana Dept. of Game and Wildlife, Biological Conservation, Jan. 1974, v 6, n 1, p 32.

18.   Season Could Be Cruicial for Atlantic Tuna, William G. Walker, National Fisherman, June 1974, v 55, n 2, p 4A.

19.   Products from Jojoba: A Promising New Crop for Arid Lands, NAS Report, 1975.

20.   Single-Cell Protein Comes of Age, Martin Sherwood, New Scientist, Nov. 28, 1974, v 64, n 925, p 634.

21.   Fantasies of Famine, Frances Moore Lappe, Harpers Magazine, Feb. 1975, v 250, n 1497, p 51.

22.   Salmon—Future Harvest from the Antarctic Ocean? Timothy Joyner, *et al,* NOAA, Marine Fisheries Review, May 1974, v 36, n 5, p 20.

Not By Bread Alone

Overcrowding in Mice

Science News

One of the most dramatic demonstrations of the disastrous effects of over crowding has come to a quiet end. In July 1968 John B. Calhoun of the laboratory of brain evolution and behavior at the National Institute of Mental Health put four pairs of healthy mice in an eight-foot-square habitat. Given all the comforts and none of the problems of home, the mice prospered and proliferated. By February 1970 there were 2,200 mice in the cage. But the effects of overcrowding were beginning to show and not one newborn mouse survived after March 1970. Last month the lone survivor of the experiment, a female, died.

While the experiment was ongoing, a variety of abnormal activities were reported and attributed to overcrowding. Once the upper optimum limit of population—620—was reached, strange things began to happen. Normal animals became aggressive and began to attack other mice. Some even turned to cannibalism of immature rats. Mothers deserted their young and sexual activity became perverted. Some males made advances toward juveniles and females who were not in estrous. Others made no sexual advances at all. One group of rats became hyperactive while another group, says Calhoun, became "passive blobs of protoplasm, physically healthy but socially sterile."

Halsey Marsden, who worked with Calhoun on the project, explained some of its implications. With all adverse conditions, such as weather and disease, removed, he says, the original mice were given the opportunity to exploit a perfect universe. They did until there were no more territories to establish and no more social roles to fill. Healthy young mice attempted to enter the system and were frustrated by the lack of social opportunities. They turned to aggression, conflict and perversion. These abnormalities became so predominant that the chain of events could not be reversed, even after the mouse population had reduced itself to its former optimum levels. Near the end Calhoun separated out some healthy individuals and put them in a new environment. They mated but produced an abnormally low number of young, none of which survived. It was then obvious that the situation would become progressively worse until the animals completely destroyed their whole world.

An Overview of The Human Problem

The Specter of Starvation

Richard Lee Clinton

> *I sit on a man's back, choking him, and making him carry me, and yet assure myself and others that I am very sorry for him and wish to ease his lot by any means possible, except getting off his back.*
>
> LEO TOLSTOY

The question is increasingly asked, "Can mass starvation be prevented by 2000 A.D.?" The answer is no. Yet such an answer provides no warrant for despair and inaction. Recognizing that things will get worse before they get better is the first step toward a realistic grasp of the situation confronting humankind at this crucial point in history. And a realistic assessment of the situation, in turn, is the *sine qua non* of devising fruitful approaches for coping with what lies ahead. Moreover, realizing how drastic the crisis will be and the scale of human suffering that will accompany them is the best way to impress upon ourselves the urgency of committing all our energies to the task of meeting the challenges facing us with the least possible delay. Because we are the world's most optimistic people, however, the task of forcing ourselves to accept the sombre prospect before us will require as Herculean an effort of will as the subsequent mobilization of our resources to seek to minimize the suffering that can no longer be avoided.

While the origins of mankind's current dilemma are multiple, for present purposes we can limit our discussion of the underlying causes of the problems soon to become worse to the most immediate cause—the unprecedented magnitude and rapidity of global population growth.

A glance at the data in Table 1 should suffice to demonstrate the validity of this approach. Regardless of why human populations have so exploded, the fact is that they have, and the overriding consideration thus becomes how can this unsustainable growth be curtailed most expeditiously yet in the most humane way?

Crucial to an adequate understanding of this problem is the demographic concept of the inertia or momentum of population growth. This concept simply describes the tendency of a fast growing population to continue to grow for decades even after measures are taken to reduce its growth. Growth continues because a fast growing population is, by definition, a young population, i.e., one with a high proportion of its people below the age of 15 or 20. The potential for further growth is literally built into a fast growing population because, regardless of how birthrates might decline, large numbers of females already born would be entering their reproductive years each year for the next 15 to 20 years. Having entered the child-bearing years, moreover, the human female remains there for at least 30 years. Thus, as Table 2 indicates, even if conditions of extremely low birthrates could be reached in the next few years, the world's current population of four billion will still be signifi-

TABLE 1: Growth of World Population

Date	Millions	Doubling Time (years)
8000 B.C.	5	
1650 A.D.	500	1,500
1850 A.D.	1,000	200
1930 A.D.	2,000	80
1975 A.D.	4,000	45
(2010) A.D.	(8,000)	(35)

Source: *In The Human Interest* by Lester R. Brown. Copyright © 1974 by W. W. Norton & Company, Inc. Reprinted with the permission of the publisher and Curtis Brown, Ltd.

TABLE 2: Total World Population in the Year 2000 Assuming a Linear Decline of Fertility to NRR* of One by the Years Indicated

NRR = 1	Population in 2000 (millions)
1980-85	5,116
2000-05	5,923
2020-25	6,422
2040-45	6,670

Source: Reprinted with the permission of the Population Council from *Reference Tables to the Future of Population Growth: Alternative Paths to Equilibrium* by Tomas Frejka, 1973, p. 18.
*Note: A net reproduction rate of one means that on the average each woman would have only one daughter—or two children—during her entire reproductive period. Each couple would, therefore, just replace themselves; hence the term replacement level fertility.

cantly larger by the end of the century. In fact, it seems most unlikely that such low fertility rates could be achieved within this century, hence the population of the world in the year 2000 will probably be at least 50 percent larger than at present.

At present it is estimated that from 400 million to 1 billion of the world's people are inadequately nourished. Many place the number closer to 2 billion. No one disputes, however, that hundreds of thousands die each year from minor disorders they could have recovered from if their bodies had not been weakened by undernourishment (calorie deficiencies) or malnourishment (protein deficiencies). (See George Borgstrom, *The Food and People Dilemma,* North Scituate, Mass.: Duxbury Press, 1973.) In practically every poor country of the world, population is growing faster than per capita agricultural output, so the outlook is for even higher proportions of the human race to be receiving inadequate diets in the years ahead. When people are living under such marginal circumstances, shifts in weather patterns or prolonged social disruptions produce disastrous consequences, as the recent experience of the Sahelian region so tragically demonstrated. Moreover, when people are so poor that as much as 80 percent of their total annual income must be spent on food—not an uncommon percentage for many in the poor countries—what happens when food prices double?

It is with the question of food prices that the socio-economic and political aspects of the population-food crisis begin to emerge most clearly.

The first fact to keep in mind is that only the poor starve. No one with money goes hungry anywhere in the world. Thus the problem may not yet be one of absolute shortages of food so much as of maldistribution of purchasing power. A similar situation obtains with regard to the nations of the world. The major importers of foodstuffs are not India, Bangladesh, Pakistan, or Zaire but the wealthy Western European countries and the U.S.S.R. Not need but capacity to pay determines the destination of the major part of the world's exportable surpluses of food, most of which are produced by only three countries—Australia, Canada, and the United States. Table 3 gives a rough idea of the discrepancies that exist in per capita income among the major world regions and the outlook for these discrepancies by the year 2000.

TABLE 3: Estimates of Per Capita GNP for 1965 and 2000 (1965 Dollars)

	1965	2000
Developing Countries	145	388
Africa	144	281
Asia	118	324
South America	379	928
Developed Countries	1,729	6,126
Europe	1,377	5,087
Japan	866	8,656
North America	3,023	7,921
Oceania	1,641	3,344
World	646	1,769

Source: Reprinted with permission of Macmillan Publishing Co., Inc. from *Economics and World Order* edited by Jagish N. Bhagwati.

Not conveyed in Table 3 is the desperate balance of payments position in which most poor countries have found themselves since the recent quadrupling of petroleum prices. Imports must be paid for in dollars or some other acceptable foreign exchange currency and a country earns its foreign exchange by selling its exports abroad. Thus when the prices of imported products rise precipitously with no corresponding increase in the prices received for exports, a country's balance of payments position deteriorates and eventually forces a restriction of imports.

Clearly, if the capacity to pay continues to determine the destination of food exports, it does not appear that the poor countries are likely to become major recipients of food imports in the foreseeable future. Someone, of course, must pay the farmer for producing the food, so the question is really whether that source of payment will be foreign importers or the taxpayers of the affluent countries who might authorize their governments to purchase available food surpluses for shipment to the poor countries. Since the latter action would almost certainly contribute to increases in food prices for the citizens of affluent nations in addition to higher taxes, it seems rather far-fetched to expect such self-inflicted sacrifices from that quarter—unless a profound alteration of their world view were to occur.

All of the foregoing leads us to the second point to be kept in mind in seeking to understand the socio-economic and political implications of the time of troubles we are entering, namely, that the solution to the population-food imbalance cannot be sought through food shipment from food surplus regions to food deficit areas. The obstacles to such an approach, including the sheerly logistical ones, are too pervasive to be overcome and, even were they nonexistent, the approach could never succeed on a long-term basis anyway. As the Reverend Thomas Robert Malthus pointed out in 1798, "the power of population is indefinitely greater than the power in the earth to produce subsistence for men." (*An Essay on the Principle of Population,* Baltimore: Penguin, 1970, p. 71.) The only viable long term solution to the population-food imbalance is for the poor countries themselves to increase their food production and to decrease their rates of population growth.

That said, however, the impression often drawn is that there is little the wealthier countries can or perhaps even should do to help further these two interrelated processes. No impression could be more mistaken. It is, on the contrary, unlikely that the poor countries could make very rapid or significant progress in pursuing these ends without generous, massive, and judicious assistance from the rich countries. Such assistance, moreover, if it is to be effective, must be of two kinds: direct and indirect. The direct assistance would consist of such measures as technical advice, technology transfers, lenient credit terms, favorable pricing for the poor countries' exports, and lowering of tariff barriers to these exported products. The indirect assistance, of even greater importance than the direct, would imply sweeping changes in the life styles, consumption patterns, and politics of the populations of the affluent countries.

Within the direct approach, emphasis would need to be given to promoting a new style of development—ecodevelopment—a mode of production and consumption that fosters and maintains a sustainable relationship between a population and the ecosystem of which it forms a part. (See Richard Lee Clinton, *"Ecodevelopment,"* paper prepared for delivery at the International Studies Association annual meeting, Toronto, Ontario, February, 1976). The technical assistance, therefore, would be oriented largely toward increasing agricultural productivity in a labor-intensive way that would simultaneously reduce the need for costly imports of machinery and fuels while providing employment for the rural masses. The technological transfers would be of intermediate technologies that could be widely disseminated throughout the population (see E. F. Schumacher, *Small Is Beautiful: Economics As If People Mattered,* New York: Harper Torchbooks, 1973, pp. 161-179.) and of such large scale operations as fertilizer plants and industrial enterprises particularly suited to the area.

The indirect approach would revolve around the theme of "setting our own house in order" and would emphasize conservation, recycling, a shift to mass transportation, and a rejection of the bigger-is-better and growth-is-good assumptions that have become synonymous with the use-it-once-and-throw-it-away American way of life. (See Herman E. Daly, ed., *Toward a Steady-State Society,* San Francisco: W. H. Freeman, 1973.) Another essential component of the indirect approach would entail a reversal of our past and present counterrevolutionary stance vis-a-vis Third World countries. Only revolutionary regimes can effect the profound structural, attitudinal, and behavioral changes that must take place in practically every one of the poor countries if viable coping mechanisms are to be devised. Too often the United States has prevented revolutionary governments from coming to power in poor countries or has undermined those that were able to gain control, even when this was done democratically. Our leaders and the American public must come to understand that our form of government is ill suited to the conditions that prevail in most Third World countries; we must let those countries work out their own forms of governance without interference. We must recognize that the central aim of our politics—the limitation of power—is precisely the opposite of that of Third World politics, where political systems have to be capable of mobilizing their citizens and marshalling their scarce resources for their most effective use.

Somehow the American public must become aware of the radical interdependence that increasingly characterizes all nations and peoples on "Spaceship Earth". They must come to see that we who have the most also have the most to lose and that our highly technical and intricately organized modern society could be paralyzed by relatively minor but carefully planned disruptions. We are more vulnerable than we realize, and it is simply folly to allow ourselves to become the object of the majority of the world's animosity.

Moreover, in a moral sense, what will it mean for our own self-image as a humane and decent people if we continue to waste and overconsume while others starve? In a world of instant communication we could not escape seeing what was happening. As we continued to spend hundreds of billions on the instruments of death, we could not disguise from ourselves where our priorities lay; we could not console ourselves or assuage our consciences with the rationalization that, after all, it simply was not within our power to help. Would we not be killing off our own humanness? Would we not be creating a situation that, in Darwinian terms, would select for the more callous and unfeeling and against the more altruistic and sensitive? Can a society that does this survive? Would it be worth surviving in?

Perhaps the greatest need at present in the Western "modernized" countries, and particularly in America, is for political leaders who will bring these questions into the realm of public debate. (See Richard Lee Clinton, *"Politics and Survival,"* World Affairs, Vol. 138, No. 2, Fall, 1975, pp. 108-127.) Until the seriousness and urgency of the situation confronting us begin to be grasped by mass publics, there is little hope that the necessary measures can be undertaken. These measures will require sacrifice and painful adjustments in values; they can only be effectively implemented on a voluntary basis. Coercion, either political or economic, would be so resented that noncompliance would probably be more common than compliance. But before people would voluntarily incur the discomforts, inconveniences, and psychic stresses accompanying the early stages of the turning away from consumerism and materialism, they would have to understand why it is necessary to do so, and they would have to be convinced that the authority of the state would be enforcing the new rules of the game so that no one's sacrifice would be vitiated by someone else's failure to comply. (See Garrett Hardin, *"The Tragedy of the Commons"*).

Obviously, what is being called for here is a social revolution. Given the universal tendency for those with economic power to acquire political power, or the means to influence it, and to use that power to protect and enhance their economic interests, such a social revolution would also imply profound changes in political and economic arrangements.

As the era of cheap energy within which modern Western society evolved its way of life draws to a close—a trend that will continue for at least the next half-century, by which time fusion may possibly, but only possibly, become available—profound changes in nearly every aspect of our lives will be forced upon us, willy nilly. The plea here is for us to anticipate the constraints we will have to adjust to and to begin making the changes sooner rather than later, when alternative approaches will have been foreclosed.

The coal miners in Wales in the early days of the Industrial Revolution used to take caged birds into the mine shafts while they worked, not to hear their cheerful singing but to see if they remained alive in the often poisonous atmosphere of the mines. The birds were more sensitive to the poison gases than were the men, so they served as an early warning system. If the birds began to die, the miners made for the surface.

The populations of the poor countries are now in the unenviable position of serving as an early warning system for the populations of the rich countries. We ignore their plight at our own peril.

Food Abundance and Technology: Past and Present

The Tehuacan Story

Robert Claiborne

The Tehuacan story begins around 10,000 B.C. Then and for some 3000 years thereafter, the valley was occupied by a few families of nomadic hunters, totaling perhaps twenty men, women, and children. Their lives resembled those of today's South African Bushmen. Season by season, each family group wandered from one camp to another, hunting game with stone weapons and collecting the fruits, seeds, and roots of wild plants. Their meat diet came chiefly from small game—jackrabbits, gophers, rats, birds, and turtles. These people were not the "mammoth hunters" whose remains have been found elsewhere in North America. The first Tehuacanos, commented one expert, "probably found one mammoth in a lifetime and—like some archaeologists—never got over talking about it."

Slowly, these primitive people evolved a slightly more complex culture. The valley's population increased, though by 7000 B.C. it still numbered less than 100. Meat was scarcer, perhaps because there were more people, perhaps because the valley, growing drier, had become less hospitable to animal life. When the spring rains came, the families now congregated in somewhat larger bands to gather the briefly burgeoning wild plants. To prepare these increasingly important plant foods, they hammered out a variety of stone scrapers, choppers, and grinding stones. Their diet now included a kind of squash, amaranth, tiny avocadoes with pea-sized pits, and chili peppers—all of which were subsequently cultivated in Mexico, and still are. They wove nets, perhaps for snaring animals, and baskets, as well as colorful blankets of dyed wild cotton.

Along with these richer material goods, they had developed a fairly complex ceremonial and spiritual life. They may have practiced human sacrifice (a motif that crops up repeatedly in Middle American culture) and unquestionably buried their dead elaborately.

Though the Tehuacanos had clearly progressed beyond the bare subsistence level, by Old World standards they were still terribly primitive. Their contemporaries in Mesopotamia and Asia Minor were already full-time farmers, raising grain and vegetables and herding cows, sheep, goats, and pigs.

Sometime around 5500 B.C. these ancestral Mexicans seem to have conceived the notion that if you drop a seed in the ground at the proper time, a plant will grow up. The archaeological record shows that by that date the avocado pits are no longer pea-sized but acorn-sized, presumably as a result of cultivation. A little later, a new type of squash has appeared in the valley—and one that had no wild counterpart there. The prevalence of its seeds leaves little doubt that the ''import'' was sown and harvested in Tehuacan.

Around 5000 B.C. corn makes its first appearance among the relics. It was far from the corn we know today. Its skinny cobs, most of them less than an inch long, bore some fifty small kernels. These were rather loosely attached to the cob, and, unlike modern corn, were not completely enclosed in a husk, so that at maturity they could be jarred loose by a gust of wind and scattered to reproduce themselves. (Modern corn could not survive if it were not sown by man.) These remnants are true wild corn. Gathering it must have been a rather unprofitable business. The open husk gave free rein to birds and rodents, and the loosely attached kernels could too easily be scattered by a careless harvester.

By 4000 B.C. the Tehuacanos are quite definitely growing two kinds of squash, gourds, beans, and several other food plants. And they are growing corn. But this corn hardly differs from the wild variety. Its cobs are merely a little bigger.

Altogether, these cultivated plants supply only about a quarter of the Tehuacanos' diet. Though the people can now gather in large groups during the growing season, in the dry season they must still hit the foraging trail in small, family bands. The valley's population, in 300 generations, has grown only to about 200. (In Mesopotamia, men are already living in towns and building mud temples; before very long they will invent writing and the wheel.)

Now the pace of progress in Tehuacan begins to speed up a little. As the people harvested their corn patches, they must have selected the larger, more productive ears for next year's seed. Moreover, a new variety of corn makes its appearance. Called "early tripsacoid," it seems to represent a cross between corn and related wild grasses. The hybrid yielded ears considerably larger than those of the original Tehuacan strain; moreover, its kernels were more firmly attached to the cob, making for easier harvesting.

By 2000 B.C., the valley is dotted with half-a-dozen little villages, each surrounded by patches of corn, beans, squash, and pumpkins; dogs scavange among the refuse heaps (and are doubtless served up as the *piece de resistance* on feast days). The population still raises less than half its food, but it is a considerably bigger population—800 or so. It is also more skilled—its basketry, weaving, and stonework are more sophisticated, and it has learned how to make pottery, albeit still crude and poorly fired.

The corn crop continues to improve. The tripsacoid strain has crossed with the original Tehuacan strain, and some of the crosses are yielding fat ears, three inches or more long, bearing several hundred kernels. The ears are beginning to reach maturity enclosed in tight husks, which help ensure that men, rather than animals, will reap the crop—and which also make corn wholly dependent on man for propagation. It was this strain of corn that eventually replaced its wild ancestor.

By 1500 B.C. Tehuacan's transition toward an agricultural way of life is nearly complete. The population, farmers all, has passed the 2,000 mark, and is grouped in permanent villages of perhaps 200 souls. Before many generations have passed, these villages will begin to group together around small towns, each with its mud or mud-brick temple.

Around 800 B.C.—about the time that Homer was writing the Iliad—the Tehuacanos reach another milestone: they begin to irrigate their fields, constructing earth dams and crude ditches. With this systematic use of water, plus continued improvement in crop strains, the food supply leaps, and with it the population, to perhaps 8,000. The villages are larger, the temples are beginning to be built in stone rather than mud. Moreover, the valley is now in regular contact with other peoples. Chief among these—judging from the new patterns of tools and pottery—are the already-civilized Olmecs, who live several hundred miles to the east along the Gulf of Mexico.

By the time of Christ, other peoples have contributed additional food resources: peanuts, sunflowers, tomatoes, guavas, and turkeys. Agriculture is almost certainly regulated by some sort of calendar. One of the irrigation dams is now a masonry structure 70 feet high and a quarter-mile long. Anticipating the design of the most sophisticated modern dams, it is curved against the pressure of stored water, and has stone breakwaters upstream to protect it from the summer's flash floods. The population has swelled to around 20,000, and some of the villages have grown into sizable hilltop towns.

In the reigns of Charlemagne and Alfred the Great, the Tehuacanos number close to 100,000, supported by an agriculture based on large-scale irrigation. The valley is divided up into four or five littel city-states, each consisting of a half-dozen farming villages centered around a city. The states may already be—as they certainly become later—feudal dependencies of the Mixtec Empire. Trade is thriving. Specialist craftsmen produce cotton textiles, pottery, and salt for export.

To coordinate and enforce this complex social structure, other classes of specialists have grown up: professional priest-bureaucrats who keep records in picture writing, professional soldiers of a standing army, and perhaps a god-king or emperor over all. These, in turn, were undoubtedly supported by some system of taxation. Tehuacan has become thoroughly civilized.

The Green Revolution in Tropical Agriculture: Panacea or Disaster?

Stephen H. Schneider

In 1965 a great wave of optimism arose over the future of the Green Revolution. After many years of work a number of scientists—Norman Borlaug, who received the Nobel Peace Prize, is probably the best known—finally achieved success in breeding high-yielding varieties of corn, wheat, and rice that could be adopted by the agricultural systems in the developing world. Special institutes were set up to improve and implement the Green Revolution methods, and a great improvement in food productivity was achieved.

Yet, while the Green Revolution was being touted, the well-traveled agricultural specialists William and Paul Paddock argued in their book *Famine 1975* that it would not prevent the onset of "times of famines," which they predicted in 1967 would begin around 1975:

. . .synthetic foods will not turn aside man's hunger a decade from now, nor fish from the sea, nor irrigation with water from desalinization, nor culture by hydroponics, nor fertilizer, nor the cultivation of new land in the vast, untapped jungles or arid wastelands, nor land reforms, nor socialistic controls, nor capitalistic initiatives. Nor will research produce in time new seeds, new techniques, new plants for the farmers to sow and reap. All of these combined can be the salvation of the twenty-first century. Any one of these could achieve a sudden leap forward in progress before the end of this century. Yet none, alone or in combination with each other, will have major effect on the food crises of the 1970s.

The fact that famine became a real threat in the mid-1970s is not a full vindication of the Paddocks' position, for the Green Revolution techniques were able to increase dramatically the wheat yields in Mexico and India, for example, and rice yields in Asia; and food security and reserves were at reasonably high levels by 1972. But, despite the progress of the Green Revolution, the weather troubles of 1972 and 1974 and the agricultural policy of nations with food surpluses (primarily the United States and Canada) wiped out the optimism of many Green Revolution boosters and recalled the Paddocks' original contention that "overnight miracles . . .do not happen in agriculture."

Robert Chandler, who has directed the International Rice Research Institute in the Philippines, commented in defense of Green Revolution methods:

Those who take a more gloomy view of the future should consider the relatively short time during which the new technology has been available and the fact that it is still actively being improved. . . .Rice yields are so low now that there is much room for improvement. I believe it is entirely possible to double average rice yields in South and Southeast Asia within the next two decades.

But this will take large quantities of fertilizer, among other things. The principal problems with fertilizer are not only its expense and scarcity (or its potential to pollute waterways or create by-products that could destroy the ozone shield), but also convincing farmers to use it—particularly subsistence farmers in the developing countries. In *Famine 1975* the Paddocks also attacked fertilizer as a "panacea," arguing that farmers will not use it unless they know that they can make money doing so, if their government even permits them to make money. They also pointed out that to be economically profitable, the fertilizer must be correct for the soil, crop, and climate with which it is used.

Another important element of the Green Revolution is irrigation: Water may well be a fundamental limiting factor. And there is concern about the long-term effects of uncontrolled well-digging on the total supply of ground water.

In a more recent book, Green Revolution critics William and Elizabeth Paddock argue that irrigation has been the "lifeblood of the new cereals" and that "on nonirrigated land the new varieties do no better than the standard ones. . . .Ford Foundation's Lowell S. Hardin says that 'if one looks at a map the land where this new technology, this Green Revolution, applies is a postage stamp on the face of the earth.' "

Rice, which accounts for 40 percent of Asia's total food-energy supply, depends heavily on irrigation and is grown almost entirely on irrigated or rain-fed paddy fields. Together, China and India have nearly half the earth's irrigated land, and, not surprisingly, rice is the mainstay of the diets in those countries. The advantages of irrigation for rice and other crops are manifold: It contributes directly to higher yields, expands the possibility for profitable use of other yield-raising inputs (particularly fertilizer), and is essential for increasing multiple cropping in many areas of the world.

"Like many of man's other interventions in natural cycles, his reshaping of the hydrological cycle has had unwanted side effects," cautions Lester Brown while describing a well-known difficulty of technological farming. Diversion of river water onto land can raise the underground water table. As the irrigation water percolates downward, it accumulates and can gradually rise to within a few inches of the surface, inhibiting the growth of plant roots by waterlogging and making the surface soil salty.

Brown points out that such a situation occurred in Pakistan after decades of irrigating with water from the Indus River. Pakistan was losing twenty thousand acres of fertile cropland annually by 1960, and its population was growing 2.5 percent yearly. At Pakistan's request, an interdisciplinary team of researchers went there in 1961 to study the seriousness of the problem. After careful analysis they recommended a system of tubewells to lower the water table by tapping the water underground. Implementation of this solution brought large quantities of fresh water to the surface, which, as it percolated back into the ground, also washed the salt downward. The plan was a considerable success. "By 1966 the amount of abandoned land being brought back into production began to exceed that being lost. The continuing progress made since then, bringing the problem under control, constitutes one of the most exciting successes in the short history of international technical assistance."

In sum, much of the success of the Green Revolution depends on the breeding of new high-yielding plant varieties, varieties whose seeds often require carefully controlled but massive doses of both irrigation water and fertilizer to live up to their high potential. As a result, the Green Revolution methods can directly help only those who can afford them or who know how to employ them. As D. B. Singh, vice chancellor of the G. B. Pant University of Agriculture and Technology in Pantnagar, India, said:

Nobody has been able to invent a cow which will milk without being fed. How can we have bumper crops if rains fail, irrigation doesn't come, electricity is not available and fertilizer is scarce and available at abnormally high prices?

Once, when I mentioned my impression that Green Revolution strains, despite their high yields under optimal environmental conditions, could produce lower yields than conventional strains unless adequate supplies of fertilizer and irrigation water were available, I encountered strong opposition from a number of agriculturalists and a plant physiologist. Miracle crops are not necessarily more sensitive to environmental inputs than conventional varieties, they said; we were at a conference on food—climate interactions in Sterling Forest, New York, in December, 1974. I was informed that any knowledgeable plant breeder can usually pick a strain that yields more than conventional varieties *even without irrigation and fertilizer.* So why, then, I was asked by these Green Revolution supporters, do so many people attack the Green Revolution?

I argued that an important distinction had to be made between absolute yield and yield variability. Let us consider a hypothetical case, employing the best current methods, where the yield of a miracle crop is substantially higher than those of the conventional varieties—but only within a narrow range of environmental factors such as temperature, irrigation, or fertilizer. We can see that the yields of these environmentally sensitive miracle varieties can be even lower when the environmental factors are not favorable, such as in a stress environment. But plant breeding, I was told, has progressed to the point that yields need not be lower in most instances. Rather, by careful selection of miracle crops, some insensitive varieties can have higher *absolute yields* than conventional species over a wide variety of environmental factors—including stress conditions. Pest resistance, however, is not among the environmental conditions envisioned in this schematic figure.

Given that some miracle crops do better under fertilizer or water stress than some conventional varieties, why have I not yet abandoned the contention that miracle strains, even the insensitive ones, are still more environmentally sensitive than conventional ones? The reason is simply this: Both miracle and conventional strains exhibit yield variability when the environmental factors change, but miracle crops vary more. For instance, if the normal environment were suddenly changed to a stress environment because of drought, irrigation failure, or a fertilizer shortage, for example, the crucial question would be, Which variety would have a larger drop in expected yield—conventional or miracle? Obviously, the *variability* of yields with differing environmental factors is greater for the miracle strains than for the conventional ones. However, these insensitive miracle varieties are still more productive overall than conventional ones since they have higher absolute yields even in environmental stress conditions. The danger, however, of such insensitive miracle crops, assuming that they really do exist, is that their higher variability of yield may well produce much larger *fluctuations* in total food production than is found with conventional crops. And if food reserves are already low, as we know they are, then the world population becomes dangerously vulnerable to the high variability of these high-yielding strains. The lesson here is not to abandon these high-yielding miracle crops, but rather to be prepared for their potentially high variability by maintaining adequate food reserves as a cushion—a cushion that can be more easily built up in good years by use of these miracle strains.

A look at world history recounts an important example of the danger confronted by relatively large human populations depending on a few high-yielding varieties, and shows that the Green Revolution started long before the mid-twentieth century. We can go back to the Irish potato famine in 1846, for example. Because of the introduction and cultivation of a miracle crop, the potato, both the Irish population and the *temporary* carrying capacity of the land grew rapidly during the late eighteenth and early nineteenth centuries. Then, in the summer of 1846, weather conditions favorable for the initiation of a potato blight hit the country, and some 1.5 to 2 million of the 8 million Irishmen starved to death. In the following decades, another 2 million emigrated, mainly to the United States, and 4 million remained, most living in poverty. Even though part of the problem in Ireland was related to the distribution of food, which was controlled by the English landlords, the sudden collapse accompanying the potato famine proves that potential disasters from undiversified agriculture are more than speculative theories. "When such a thing as Green Revolution occurs," say William and Elizabeth Paddock, "its name will be Disaster if it arrives ahead of a Population Control Revolution."

More Food Means More Hunger

Frances Moore Lappe and Joseph Collins

> Appropriate technology might help to feed the world's hungry. In the following article, two food specialists offer the challenging thesis that many of the world's people are going hungry because they have been deprived of the means of feeding themselves. This provocative article is by the Co-Directors of the Institute for Food and Development Policy. Frances Lappe is widely known for her book *Diet for a Small Planet*.

Hunger is continually defined for us as a problem of inadequate production. Therefore, if people are hungry, the reason must be that there is not enough food. For at least 30 years, the fundamental goal of the "war on hunger" has been to produce more food.

Thus, we are treated almost daily to the "news release" approach to hunger. We learn of one new breakthrough after another—protein from petroleum, harvests of kelp, extracts from alfalfa—all to expand the food supply. Even pleas to cut consumption in rich countries are narrowed down to "eating one less hamburger a week" in order to increase the food supply for the hungry.

For many, the production approach is working. Today, more food is, in fact, being produced. The green revolution now adds an estimated 20 million tons annually to the grain larders of Asia. In Mexico, wheat yields tripled in only two decades.

But wait. There are now more hungry people than ever before. Since there is also more food than ever before, we are left with only two possible conclusions:

• Either the production focus is correct, but soaring numbers of people simply overrun even these dramatic production gains;

• Or the diagnosis is incorrect—scarcity is not the cause of hunger, and production increases, no matter how great, can never solve the problem.

Enough to Feed Everyone

The simple facts of world grain production make it clear that the overpopulation/scarcity diagnosis is actually incorrect. Present world grain production could more than adequately feed every person on earth. Even during the "scarcity" year, 1972 to 1973, there was 9% more grain per person than in an "ample" year like 1960. Inadequate production is clearly not the problem.

In fact, as ironic as it may sound, a narrow focus on increased production has annually compounded the problem of hunger. Because it goes against the popular wisdom, we found ourselves wanting to verify and re-verify this conclusion in our research at the Institute for Food and Development Policy.

What have we found? The production focus quickly becomes synonymous with "modernizing" agriculture—the drive to supply the "progressive" farmer with imported technology: fertilizer, irrigation, pesticides and machinery. The green revolution seeds only reinforce this definition of development because their higher yields depend heavily on these inputs. Agricultural progress is thus transformed into a narrow technical problem instead of the sweeping social task of releasing vast, untapped human resources.

Governments, international lending agencies and foreign assistance programmes pushing for greater production "at all costs" willingly subsidize the heavy financial expense of this type of modernization.

The result? This influx of public funds quickly turns farming into a place to make money—sometimes big money. To profit, however, one needs some combination of land, money, credit-worthiness and political influence. This alone eliminates most of the farmers throughout the world.

Ignoring substantial evidence from around the world that small, carefully farmed plots are more productive per acre than large estates and use fewer costly inputs, government production programmes invariably pass over small farmers (not to mention the landless). The common rationalization is that working with bigger production units is a faster road to increased production.

Competition for lands suddenly made profitable by this official production strategy has brought rising land values. Not atypically, land values have increased by 300 to 500% in the green revolution areas of India, setting off spiralling land speculation and even "land grabs."

The lure of greater profits tempts large landlords to take back land they formerly rented out. Many use their now higher profits to buy out small neighbouring farmers. Throughout the under-developed world, the landless now comprise 30 to

60% of the agrarian population. This does not even take into account the millions of landless refugees who are the human products of the production strategy. Finding no farm work, they join an equally hopeless search for work in urban slums.

The Big Farming Business

At the same time as the number of landless seeking work steadily grows, the number of jobs is shrinking. Mechanization enables the large landholder to cultivate more land himself without having to share the produce with sharecroppers or labourers. Despite mounting unemployment, governments encourage mechanization by subsidizing imported machinery and exempting mechanized farms from land reform.

Agricultural production based on purchased inputs—fertilizers, hybrid seeds, pesticides, machinery—inevitably means that money-based relationships come to replace rent and wages traditionally paid in farm produce. To pay a cash rent, however, the tenant must go into debt even before planting—and often at exorbitant interest rates. While rent in kind meant that a bad harvest was shared by both landlord and tenant, payment in cash means that the tenant must come up with the same rent no matter how the harvest is.

We are thus witnessing the radical transformation of the control of food resources—both in the industrialized and throughout the non-socialist underdeveloped world. Agriculture, once the livelihood for millions of self-provisioning farmers in the Third World, is being turned into a profit base for a new class of "farmers." Traditional landed elites, money-lenders, military officers, city-based speculators, foreign corporations and even African tribal chieftains are now becoming agricultural entrepreneurs.

In the course of this transformation, the hungry are being severed from the production process. At best, they become insecure wage labourers with seasonal jobs. To be cut out of the production process is to be cut out of consumption.

There *is* more food, but people are still hungry—in fact, more hungry. The process of creating more food has actually reduced people's ability to grow or to buy food. Where is the increased production? Did it mysteriously disappear? No.

● Some of it goes to urban middle income groups. The Governments of the U.S. and Pakistan collaborated with the New Jersey-based Corn Products Corporation to improve yields of Pakistani maize—historically, the staple food of the rural poor. Hybrid seeds and other inputs did increase yields. The maize, however, now grown by a relatively few large farmers, is processed into corn sweetener for soft drinks for the urban middle and upper classes.

● Some of it gets fed to livestock. The corn yields that were the pride of the green revolution in the U.S. have ended up in the stomachs of livestock. By 1973, two thirds of the green revolution rice in Colombia was going to feedlots and breweries.

● Some of it gets exported. Having based an agricultural strategy on imported inputs, countries become locked into production for export to earn foreign exchange to pay for those inputs. Despite the malnutrition of 80% of its rural population, Mexico in the late 1960s began to export its green revolution wheat. Central America exports between one third and one half of its beef to the United States.

● Some of it gets dumped. Fruits and vegetables produced in Central America for export to the United States are frequently either shut out from an over-supplied market or fail to meet U.S. "quality" standards—size, colour, smoothness. Since the local population—mostly landless—are too poor to buy anything, fully 65% of production is fed to livestock (which, in turn, are exported) or literally dumped.

A "Global Supermarket"

As food production is taken out of the hands of self-provisioning farmers and tied more and more into a worldwide marketing system, local food resources go less and less to feed local people. We see emerging a "global supermarket" in which the poorest in Central America or Africa must now compete for food with millions of Americans, Japanese and Europeans whose incomes are many times greater. Our "inter-dependent world" may be leading us to the same supermarket, but most have neither money to buy nor even welfare food stamps.

Development pegged to sheer production increases is taking us backward, not forward. It is more than just a diversion from the real task of reconstructing society to enable the majority of people to control and participate in the food production process. It is entrenching a new class of local and international profiteers who are better positioned than ever to fight against the slightest change.

If producing more food is the wrong solution, what then is the right one? In order to answer that question, we first have to understand that there is no developing country in which the food resources could not feed the local people. More importantly, because the under-developed countries are portrayed to us as helpless and pitifully in need of our aid, we lose sight of the simple truth that hungry people can and will feed themselves, if they are allowed to do so.

If people are not feeding themselves, you can be sure powerful obstacles are in the way. These obstacles are not, however, the hunger myths—over-population, too little land, laziness, religious taboos, inhospitable climate, lack of technology, unequal terms of trade, and so forth. In our research, we found that the most fundamental constraint to food self-reliance is that the majority of the people are not themselves in control of the production process and, therefore, more and more frequently they are not even participants.

How do we remove the obstacles preventing people from taking control of the production process and feeding themselves? What we have learned is that the path we are suggesting—the path of people taking control of food—is the *only* guarantee of long-term productivity and food security. It is the land monopolizers—both the traditional landed elites and corporate agribusiness—that have proven themselves to be the most inefficient, unreliable, and destructive users of agricultural resources.

Struggling for Control

Many, who have come to see that the problem of hunger is not simply a problem of production, conclude that instead it is a problem of distribution—getting the food to the hungry instead of the well-fed. We are saying something else. The issue of distribution is only a reflection of the more basic problem of control and participation in the production process itself.

Once we grasp these fundamentals, we will then begin to see that the "poor, hungry masses" whom we are repeatedly being told to fear are in reality our allies. Consciously or not, we are all joined in a common struggle for control of the most basic human need—food. "More food," or even redistribution programmes like food aid and food stamps, will continue to mean more hunger until we first come to grips with the problem of who controls and who takes part in the production process.

Overpopulation: A Disease With Some Predictable Patterns

The Three Choices

The Bible, II Samuel 24:1-2, 8-15

Again the anger of the Lord was kindled against Israel, and he incited David against them, saying, "Go, number Israel and Judah." So the king said to Joáb and the commanders of the army, who were with him, "Go through all the tribes of Israel, from Dan to Beer-sheba, and number the people, that I may know the number of the people." So when they had gone through all the land, they came to Jerusalem at the end of nine months and twenty days. And Joáb gave the sum of the numbering of the people to the king: in Israel there were eight hundred thousand valiant men who drew the sword, and the men of Judah were five hundred thousand.

But David's heart smote him after he had numbered the people. And David said to the Lord, "I have sinned greatly in what I have done. But now, O Lord, I pray thee, take away the iniquity of thy servant; for I have done very foolishly." And when David arose in the morning, the word of the Lord came to the prophet Gad, David's seer, saying, "Go and say to David, 'Thus says the Lord, Three things I offer you; choose one of them, that I may do it to you.' " So Gad came to David and told him, and said to him, "Shall three years of famine come to you in your land? Or will you flee three months before your foes while they pursue you? Or shall there be three days' pestilence in your land? Now consider, and decide what answer I shall return to him who sent me." Then David said to Gad, "I am in great distress; let us fall into the hand of the Lord, for his mercy is great; but let me not fall into the hand of man."

So the Lord sent a pestilence upon Israel from the morning until the appointed time; and there died of the people from Dan to Beer-sheba seventy thousand men.

Starvation Patterns

Jean Mayer

As a nutritionist who has seen famines on three continents, one of them Asia, and as a historian of public health with an interest in famines, I can say flatly that there has never been a famine or a food shortage—whether created by lack of water (droughts, often followed by dust storms and loss of seeds, being the most frequent), by plant disease (such as fungous blights), by large-scale natural disturbances affecting both crops and farmers (such as floods and earthquakes), by disruption of farming operations due to wars and civil disorders, or by blockade or other war measures directly aimed at the food supply—which has not first and overwhelmingly affected the small children.

It is very clear that death from starvation occurs first of all in young children and in the elderly, with adults and adolescents surviving better (pregnant women often abort; lactating mothers cease to have milk and the babies die). Children under five, who in many parts of the world are often on the verge of kwashiorkor (a protein-deficiency syndrome which often hits children after weaning and until they are old enough to eat "adult" food) and of marasmus (a combination of deficiency of calories and of protein), are the most vulnerable. In addition, a general consequence of famine is a state of social disruption (including panic). People who are starving at home tend to leave, if they can, and march toward the area where it is rumored that food is available. This increases the prevailing chaos. Families are separated and children are lost—and in all likelihood die. Adolescents are particularly threatened by tuberculosis; however, finding themselves on their own, they often band together in foraging gangs, which avoid starvation but create additional disruption. The prolonged and successful practice of banditry makes it difficult to rehabilitate members of these gangs.

Malnutrition, Learning, and Behavior

Philip H. Abelson

Children reared in poverty tend to do poorly on tests of intelligence. In part this is due to psychological and cultural factors. To an important extent it is a result of malnutrition early in childhood.

It seems likely that millions of young children in developing countries are experiencing some degree of retardation in learning because of inadequate nutrition, and that this phenomenon may also occur in the United States.

Because of complex social and psychological factors associated with malnutrition, it is not easy to assess the effects of dietary deficiencies in man. However, observations in underdeveloped countries, coupled with studies on animals, provide substantial evidence. In rats and pigs the brain reaches 80 percent of adult size by normal weaning time. At that stage, body weight is 20 percent of that at maturity. During the period of rapid growth the brain is vulnerable to nutritional damage. A relatively short period of undernutrition results in smaller brain size at maturity even if the animals are maintained on a good diet after weaning. Changes in brain size are accompanied by persistent anatomical and biochemical changes.

In humans, the brain of the infant attains 80 percent of adult weight by age 3, when the body weight is about 20 percent of that at maturity. Thus the animal experiments suggest that good nutrition during the first 3 years of life is particularly important.

The Future of the Tropics: Abundant Fertility or Impending Sterility?

The Myth of Fertility Dooms Development Plans

Darryl G. Cole

Not long ago Adrian Alfaro came to our home to tell us that his wife had been in labor for a week and could not give birth to her baby. Adrian owns a small farm near our coffee plantation at Canas Gordas in southwestern Costa Rica. A young man, he had been married a little more than a year. Now he was haggard and distraught. His wife was dying, he said.

My wife and I went to Adrian's farm and found Mrs. Alfaro resting on a bed of boards in a hut with a dirt floor and walls fashioned of split saplings. A white flour sack had been spread on the floor by an elderly midwife to receive the baby. We carried Mrs. Alfaro on a stretcher to our pickup truck. Adrian, two brothers, and his father held the stretcher in the back of the truck to ease the jolting of travel, and we began the trip to the regional medical station at San Vito de Jaba. It was in the middle of the wet season, a light rain was falling, and Adrian covered Mrs. Alfaro with a large sheet of plastic. The road to San Vito, 13 miles distant, was in bad condition. With heavy chains on its tires, and with a front-mounted winch, our truck would get through the mud. But as the rain fell over the soggy land, and the truck churned on, I felt immeasurably depressed.

Great Expectations

My family and I had come to Canas Gordas 13 years earlier. It was a frontier settlement then, emergent in the highland rain forest. We proposed to establish a diversified farm, employing the latest techniques of modern agriculture. Over the years my parents and my wife and I devoted a considerable amount of money and effort to the project. But our venture has yielded only a small measure of the rewards we expected. The emergency involving Adrian Alfaro and his wife underscored for me how mistaken those early expectations were.

I am frequently dismayed by articles appearing in the Costa Rican press asserting that agriculture in this country must be diversified and that the rich bounty and natural fertility of new land must be harvested. Such assertions seem to be made with all of the best intentions and with an eagerness from their writers suggesting that with this or another government program, with a loan or technical assistance, with the right attitude on the part of farmers, the new lands would yield prodigiously. Well-being and even prosperity would follow. I would like to submit that such hopes have not been realized in the Canas Gordas-San Vito area, that they are not being realized in other areas of Costa Rica, and that, on the basis of our present knowledge of tropical agriculture, they will not be realized in similar new lands in underdeveloped nations.

The Myth Persists

The myth of the fertility of these virgin lands has been too long in dying. It has long been dead for the farmers like Adrian Alfaro, whose subservience to a meager soil leaves them few illusions about the "untapped riches" of virgin lands. But the myth persists, and even thrives, among sectors of government and the public where misinformation has been accepted as fact.

When we came to Canas Gordas we purchased a tract of rain forest in an area widely acclaimed at that time as a future center of farming progress and development. An Italian colony had been started two years earlier in San Vito de Jaba, a project eventually involving the investment of about $2,000,000. We looked at the rain forest on our land, at the moist, dark soil supporting it, and concluded that anything would grow in soil so apparently fertile.

Fertility Restricted to Forest

We felled the forest, cleared the land, and planted the first crops. They were a failure from the beginning. We weren't discouraged; we began experimenting—using fertilizers, lime, manure, insecticides, fungicides, varieties of seed, cover crops, various methods of tillage. We consulted agronomists, farm-research and extension agencies, and farmers' publications, and called upon the experience that has enabled us to farm successfully in the United States. We discovered that other settlers in our area were making similar efforts with equally unsatisfactory results.

Finally, we learned what we might have been told at the beginning, had we been less adamant about our ability to succeed where others had demonstrated no remarkable success. We learned that the fertility of these virgin lands is mostly in the forest and in the thin layer of humus carpeting the forest floor.

The soil nutrients needed to sustain plant life are circulated from the soil through plant tissues. Drawn from the humus and top soil by the roots of the forest vegetation, the nutrients return to the soil in falling leaves and dead branches. At any given time the forest itself is a storehouse of soil fertility.

Cut down, the forest ceases to hold nutrients in suspension; violent rains drive over the land, leaching nutrients below root levels; sunlight invades shade-loving retreats; and, unwittingly, the farmer, by tilling and exposing the soil to the sun and rain, outrages its microbiotic order. Fertility vanishes in a sudden, stunning conflagration.

Diversity Is No Solution

Much can be done, of course, to supplement soil fertility with fertilizers. However, where rain drives month after month through loose, permeable soil, where terrain is hilly and erosion carries soil away, where sunlight burns fiercely into the land, it requires an art beyond the ability of most farmers to grow crops well over sustained periods, even with fertilizers and modern techniques. What is more to the point, such methods applied to soils divested of their original forest cover are seldom profitable.

There is a good deal of discussion today in Costa Rica about agriculture diversification. Hardly a week goes by without a pronouncement by someone on the important subject. It is evident that the traditional mainstays of the Costa Rican economy—coffee, cacao, bananas, sugar, which are embroiled in market surpluses or in rising production costs—cannot be relied upon.

What to do? The solution, most frequently advanced, to diversify, is little better than a restatement of the problem. It too frequently ignores the harshness of the land.

Farmers whose livelihood is dependent upon a monoculture crippled by the woes of international overproduction do not continue to rely upon that monoculture by choice; their dependence on the economic loser is largely the product of conditions that at no time have offered any significant measure of flexibility. Planners and economists, serving up the latest potpourri of diversification, might well consider that, where agriculture has seized upon one or two successful crops over a period of years, diversification has probably been tried and been found to be competitively impractical.

Enthusiasm Fades

The enthusiasm and confidence that characterized the beginning steps in development in the Canas Gordas-San Vito area have languished. They have been replaced by a lean skepticism, more closely defined by a need to survive than by a will to succeed. Under the circumstances of these latter years success has become merely the ability to subsist. Yet, what is more disturbing are the repeated assertions made publicly purporting that the limitations of this area either do not exist or can be eliminated with relatively simple measures.

Such arguments abet a form of social irresponsibility. They suggest that solutions to basic problems hinge on but a few steps that, if taken, would lead shortly to sweeping remedies.

Too often the standard of living in more-developed nations is used as an example of what can be accomplished by pursuing this or that technique. This point of view ignores the basic differences between the ingredients of agriculture in the developed nation and those in the nation seeking development. It would be preferable in underdeveloped nations to work within the limits of the environment and recognize that the blessings of fertility and productivity are not everywhere evenly distributed.

Mrs. Alfaro returned to her home not long ago with a baby boy, Adrian Alberto. I would like to believe that when Adrian Alberto goes to school he will follow a road no longer beset with the quagmires that made his arrival in the world the subject of an emergency, that as a man with a family he would enjoy the benefits his father has been denied. I would like to believe this, but 13 years of work in Canas Gordas have left me doubtful.

Will the Amazon Basin Become a Desert?

William E. Moran, Jr.

Few areas of the world have provoked greater agricultural fantasies than the Amazon Basin, which is itself larger than any other Latin American country. Various schemes have been advanced to turn this steaming jungle into a "breadbasket" for the continent. Few of these master-plans have adequately taken into account the fragile ecosystem of the tropical rain forest, which supports a profusion of plant and animal species but which erodes with stunning suddenness under the slash-and-burn cultivation that is now so tragically on the increase. While scientists have not yet defined the precise relationship between mycorrhizal fungi and tree roots which enables the jungle to thrive on very poor laterite soil, they do agree on one vital point: this incredibly lush jungle, where the rainfall averages over 80 inches a year, is ecologically only a few steps removed from a wasteland. If the forest vegetation were to be cleared, says Colombian geologist Carlos Eduardo Acosta, the Amazon Basin would become "a desert like the Sahara."

Living With The Problem: Deny The Cause And Regard The Victims As Different

Nobody Ever Dies of Overpopulation

Garrett Hardin

Those of us who are deeply concerned about population and the environment—"econuts," we're called—are accused of seeing herbicides in trees, pollution in running brooks, radiation in rocks, and overpopulation everywhere. There is merit in the accusation.

I was in Calcutta when the cyclone struck East Bengal in November 1970. Early dispatches spoke of 15,000 dead, but the estimates rapidly escalated to 2,000,000 and then dropped back to 500,000. A nice round number: it will do as well as any, for we will never know. The nameless ones who died, "unimportant" people far beyond the fringes of the social power structure, left no trace of their existence. Pakistani parents repaired the population loss in just 40 days, and the world turned its attention to other matters.

What killed those unfortunate people? The cyclone, newspapers said. But one can just as logically say that overpopulation killed them. The Gangetic delta is barely above sea level. Every year several thousand people are killed in quite ordinary storms. If Pakistan were not overcrowded, no sane man would bring his family to such a place. Ecologically speaking, a delta belongs to the river and the sea; man obtrudes there at his peril.

In the web of life every event has many antecedents. Only by an arbitrary decision can we designate a single antecedent as "cause." Our choice is biased—biased to protect our egos against the onslaught of unwelcome truths. As T. S. Eliot put it in *Burns Norton:*

Go, go, go, said the bird: human kind
Cannot bear very much reality.

Were we to identify overpopulation as the cause of a half-million deaths, we would threaten ourselves with a question to which we do not know the answer: *How can we control population without recourse to repugnant measures?* Fearfully we close our minds to an inventory of possibilities. Instead, we say that a cyclone caused the deaths, thus relieving ourselves of responsibility for this and future catastrophes. "Fate" is *so* comforting.

Every year we list tuberculosis, leprosy, enteric diseases, or animal parasites as the "cause of death" of millions of people. It is well known that malnutrition is an important antecedent of death in all these categories; and that malnutrition is connected with overpopulation. But overpopulation is not called the cause of death. We cannot bear the thought.

People are dying now of respiratory diseases in Tokyo, Birmingham, and Gary, because of the "need" for more industry. The "need" for more food justifies overfertilization of the land, leading to eutrophication of the waters, and lessened fish production—which leads to more "need" for food.

What will we say when the power shuts down some fine summer on our eastern seaboard and several thousand people die of heat prostration? Will we blame the weather? Or the power companies for not building enough generators? Or the econuts for insisting on pollution controls?

One thing is certain: we won't blame the deaths on overpopulation. No one ever dies of overpopulation. It is unthinkable.

The Starving as a Race Apart

James Bonner

We will, I suspect, begin to regard the starving populace of the underde-veloped nations as a race or species apart, people totally different from us, as indeed they will be. "They are just animals," we will say, "and a serious reservoir of disease." The inevitable culmination of the two cultures will be that one culture will devour the other. I would think that it would turn out that the rich and strong will devour the poor and weak.

A Contemporary Moral Question

Parenthood: Right or Privilege?

Garrett Hardin

Birth control is not population control. Individual goals, not community needs, motivate individual actions. In every nation women want more children that the community needs.

How can we reduce reproduction? Persuasion must be tried first. Tomorrow's mothers must be educated to seek careers other than multiple motherhood. Commu-nity nurseries are needed to free women for careers outside the home. Mild coercion may soon be accepted—for example, tax rewards for reproductive nonproliferation.

But in the long run a purely voluntary system selects for its own failure: non-cooperators outbreed cooperators. So what restraints shall we employ? A policeman under every bed? Jail sentences? Compulsory abortion? Infanticide?...Memories of Nazi Germany rise and obscure our vision.

We need not titillate our minds with such horrors, for we already have at hand an acceptable technology: sterilization. The taboo on this subject is fast dissolving, thanks to Arthur Godfrey and Paul Ehrlich, who have confessed their sterilizations in public. Fear (mostly unjustified) about the safety of the "pill" has motivated multitudes to follow in their footsteps.

It should be easy to limit a woman's reproduction by sterilizing her at the birth of her nth child. Is this a shocking idea? If so, try this "thought-experiment": let n = 20. Since this is not shocking, let n diminish until population control is achieva-ble. The Women's Liberation Movement may not like it, but control must be exerted through females. Divorce and remarriage play havoc with assigning respon-sibility to couples or to men. Biology makes women responsible.

Many who want no third child would fight resolutely for the freedom to have that which they do not want. But what is freedom? Hegel said that "Freedom is the recognition of necessity." People need to recognize that population control is needed to protect the quality of life for our children.

The "right" to breed implies *ownership* of children. This concept is no longer tenable. Society pays an ever larger share of the cost of raising and educating children. The idea of ownership is surely affected by the thrust of the saying that "He who pays the piper calls the tune." On a biological level the idea of ownership of children has not been defensible for almost a century, not since August Weismann drew his celebrated diagram of the relationship of germ plasm to somatoplasm.

Biologically, all that I give "my" child is a set of chromosomes. Are they *my* chromosomes? Hardly. Sequestered in the germinal area long before *my* birth, "my" gonadal chromosomes have lived a life of their own, beyond my control. Mutation has altered them. In reproduction, "my" germ plasm is assembled in a new combination and mixed with another assortment with a similar history. "My" child's germ plasm is not *mine;* it is really only part of the community's store. I was merely the temporary custodian of part of it.

If parenthood is a right, population control is impossible. If parenthood is only a privilege, and if parents see themselves as trustees of the germ plasm and guardians of the rights of future generations, then there is hope for mankind.

Contraception: History and Failure

From Magic to Science: A History of Contraception

Medcom

Primitive man believed that with prayer and magic he could control the fertility of his fields, livestock, and the animals he hunted. Even before he made the connection between sexual intercourse and human babies, he probably tried to control his own fertility, too.

Out of magic and out of trial and error came hundreds of gadgets, concoctions, spells, amulets to induce conception or to prevent it.

Most of the magic stayed in folklore—but some of it, and some results of trial and error, found their way into early philosophic and medical writings. These are our first records of contraceptives.

Until only 20 years ago, contraceptive measures all fell into a few types:

Potions taken by mouth—animal, vegetable, or mineral products, often harmful, usually ineffective, and usually based on magic or superstition or erroneous medicine.

Sheaths for the penis—made of various materials, to prevent sperm from reaching the womb.

Pessaries and tampons—objects placed in the vagina to absorb or block sperm or obstruct the entrance to the uterus. Pessary literally means "oval pebble."

Timing of intercourse—to coincide with various periods considered to be safe. The actual "safe" period was not determined until this century.

Lubricants, spermicides, and presumably spermicidal concoctions—believed to inhibit or destroy spermatozoa when introduced into the vagina or applied to the penis before, during, or after coitus.

The Egyptians

Egyptian papyri dating back to 1850 BC provide the earliest records of contraceptive efforts. One papyrus from that time includes a prescription for a pessary made of crocodile dung, and another for irrigating or plugging the vagina with honey and natron (sodium carbonate). Sticky material presumably was expected to catch sperm.

A papyrus dated 1550 BC describes a medicated lint tampon. The recipe for the medication includes fermented acacia tips, which release lactic acid—acid was a common ingredient of spermicides into the 20th century. In the history of contraception, because of trial and error, the right thing was occasionally done—for the wrong reasons.

The Hebrews

The Old Testament, which reports an oral tradition much more ancient than the text, condemns "the sin of Onan"—coitus interruptus—a prime contraceptive measure. The story of Onan has long been used as a religious argument against contraception, and against masturbation as well.

Herbs, and especially the mandrake plant, were used both to induce and to prevent conception, as well as to cause abortion. The mandrake has some chemical similarity to the Mexican yams which are now important in synthesizing hormones for drugs that are used both to induce and to prevent conception.

The ancient Hebrews also used the "cup of roots" to render women sterile. This may have consisted, among other things, of liquid alum and garden crocus. Taken with two cups of beer, it was said to cause female sterility—and cure jaundice. With wine, it was said to cure gonorrhea. From at least the 3rd century AD until the 20th, a sponge inserted in the vagina was a popular type of pessary. Among the Jews, female contraceptives were considered to be more "moral" than coitus interruptus, since, according to the rabbis, only men were enjoined by God to propagate, whereas women could bypass the commandment.

The Greeks and Romans

Aristotle comments that conception can be prevented by "anointing that part of the womb where the seeds fall with oil of cedar, ointment of lead, or with frankincense commingled with olive oil"—oil does reduce the motility of sperm. Cedar gum, alum, and crushed willow leaves, taken orally or spread on the genitals, were also believed to prevent conception.

Roman women wore asparagus amulets as insurance.

In his *Natural History,* written in the first century AD. Pliny the Elder suggested that two worms extracted from the hairy body of "the spider called Phalangium" should be attached to a piece of deerskin before sunrise, and then to a woman's body. Just how this contraceptive operated is unclear.

During the second century AD. Soranus, a Greek gynecologist practicing in Rome, distinguished clearly between contraceptives and abortifacients. He listed the indications and contraindications for both, and added a list of well-selected contraceptive measures: occlusive pessaries, vaginal plugs of wool and gummy substances, astringent solutions, and acidic fruits.

He also suggested abstention from coitus at the "dangerous" time—"directly before and after menstruation." It is possible, though not proven, that the Romans knew how to use animal membranes as condoms.

Other Ancient Societies

An ancient French cave painting in the Dordogne has been interpreted by some viewers as showing a man's penis covered by a sheath during coitus.

A 6th century Byzantine physician mentions the use of vinegar and brine, both highly spermicidal, for washing the genitals before intercourse. Like many bits of useful knowledge that survived in folklore, this one seems to have been forgotten by medicine until the 19th century.

Indian erotic literature includes many contraceptive hints—herbs and amulets, anointment with honey and oil, passivity in the female during coitus. Coitus obstructus, or the prevention of ejaculation, physically or magically, was also recommended.

Chinese women fried quicksilver in oil and drank it. They also believed it useful to swallow 14 live tadpoles three days after menstruation.

The wives of North African desert tribesmen mixed gunpowder solution and foam from a camel's mouth and drank the potion—proving that birth control can always be attempted with the materials at hand.

Islam knew pills or pessaries made of "cabbage, tamarisk dew, pitch, ox gall, pomegranate, animals' ear wax, elephant dung . . .used either alone or in combination," to prevent conception.

A Mohammedan writer recommended jumping seven or nine times—jumping forward to increase fertility, and backward to decrease it.

A 12th century physician at Saladin's court declared that eating beans on an empty stomach would cause female sterility, but also suggested tampons and pessaries and anointing the penis with oil or onion juice.

European ladies prevented pregnancy by spitting three times into the mouth of a frog or by eating bees. Others associated sterile animals, such as mules, with human infertility. One formula called for fumigating the vulva with the smoke resulting from holding a mule's hoof over burning prunes. Still others ate pieces of a mule's uterus or kidneys.

An appetizing instruction was to place roasted walnuts in the bosom, one nut for every barren year a bride desired. Or the bride might sit on her fingers while riding in a coach—one finger per barren year. The Middle Ages were not a time of progress for birth control.

The Renaissance

The first known published description of the condom, by the Italian anatomist Gabriel Fallopius, appeared in 1564. The renaissance of science naturally affected contraception along with other medical fields. Fallopius recommended a linen sheath to guard against syphilis, which had recently invaded Europe from the New World. It may be that some medieval slaughterhouse worker actually invented the condom made of the thin membranes of an animal. The origin of the name condom is also mysterious, but item and name became notorious in England in the 17th and 18th centuries. It was soon used for contraception as well as protection against disease. A British bishop's son wrote a poem celebrating the liberation of women by the condom. A comparable achievement is today attributed to the pill.

The Age of Reason

In the 18th century condoms were made of linen or of dried sheep gut, and the bottom was "generally bound round with a scarlet ribbon" for ornament.

Boswell, the companion of Dr. Johnson, described himself as in "complete armour" and "safely sheathed" for an amatory adventure.

But Madame de Sévigné called the sheaths "armour against enjoyment, and a spider web against danger."

The great lover Casanova sided with Boswell and used condoms to prevent infection as well as impregnation. He tested the merchandise by making sure each sheath held air. Casanova also suggested to his paramours the use of one of three gold balls he bought as pessaries for their protection.

Through the microscopic lens he developed, Anton van Leeuwenhoek studied semen, and, in 1677, discovered "animaliculi" therein.

These were sperm cells, and being able to see them made it possible for others to experiment and understand their nature—and work scientifically on chemical contraceptives. It was soon learned that seminal fluid could be diluted, with adverse effect on the animaliculi. They could be filtered and rendered impotent. Acids like vinegar, and the salts of certain heavy metals, were found to inactivate them.

Now that birth control was becoming feasible, puritanism, propaganda, and politics began to affect the development of contraceptives.

In the late 18th century Jeremy Bentham and others began to advocate birth control as a way of reducing poverty. Thus far, the rich had had access to what contraceptives there were, while the poor were left with folklore, dangerous abortions, and the pressures of large families. Now contraception became a social issue.

In 1798 Thomas Malthus introduced his theory that population tends to multiply faster than means of subsistence. He advocated "moral restraint" as the solution to overpopulation, feeling that the dole only increased the problem, and that poverty was inevitable for the poor, who deserved no better. Nevertheless his theory and name became watchwords for later advocates of family planning, and Malthus is remembered with more affection than he deserves.

The Victorians

Humanitarian reformers began to spread the word about contraception, birth control, and population control. In the early 19th century these "freethinkers" were recommending the sponge, condoms, coitus interruptus, and tampons of lint, wool, cotton, or flax. A manual called *Every Woman's Book* gave contraception snob appeal with such examples as "the Prudent English Duchess who never goes out to dinner without being prepared with the sponge."

Queen Victoria with her nine children did not set a good example as far as the birth control movement was concerned. But the 19th century contributed other suggested solutions to the poverty and population problem—infanticide, surgery for men with insufficient income to support families, and eugenics and euthenics. Contraception still seemed the most practical solution.

In 1838 a gynecologist, F. A. Wilde, published a treatise promoting a rubber pessary, fitted to the individual lady and completely covering the cervix, as the only effective means of contraception. Rubber diaphragms were not yet available, and he was probably right—but his contribution was forgotten until nearly a hundred years later.

Coitus reservatus. At this time, intercourse without male ejaculation came into some vogue. It is one of the few "contraceptive" measures acceptable even today to the Roman Catholic Church.

The rhythm method. The Greeks and various societies after them had tried to discover and compute the "safe" period as a means of contraception, but until the 1920s most of the guesses were wrong, the right guesses went unheard, and no safe period for the menstrual cycle was ever established.

During the mid-19th century ovulation was believed to coincide with menstruation. Later the unsafe period was thought to last for 12 days after menstruation, though some observant physicians noted that this couldn't be quite accurate.

The birth control issue continued to simmer quietly all over the world—with some hot moments when writers or reformers were too direct, or when pamphlets and products were "too inexpensive" and therefore "too easily available" to the masses. Anthony Comstock took up the cudgel against the reformers. His Society for the Suppression of Vice pushed through the New York law named after him. It permitted prosecution and punishment of anyone who tried to disseminate knowledge about contraception. Atheism and obscenity, in his opinion, "occupied the same bed," and birth control, the epitome of both, was the Devil's work.

But in England in 1877 the "New Malthusian League" sprang up, and other organizations devoted to family planning were formed thereafter in many countries—France, the Netherlands, Spain, Brazil, Cuba, Switzerland, Sweden, Belgium. Clinics were opened to give advice on infant care as well as on contraception to working-class women. The first diaphragms were given to women in a Netherlands clinic; the device had been invented in the 1880s by a German, Dr. Mensinga.

The 20th Century

In this country the long hard struggle for family planning was led by Margaret Sanger (1883-1966). Her dedication was based on her experience as a public health nurse in poor neighborhoods, where she saw fatally botched abortions and the effects of overcrowding and large families. Mrs. Sanger became an ardent feminist, believing it was a woman's basic right to decide how many children she would have, and when she would have them, for economic, social, and medical reasons. Mrs. Sanger opened the first U.S. clinic in New York City; it was closed after nine days by the Vice Squad. Released on bail, she reopened it, and was promptly sent to jail for 30 days. Her career included many such incidents and culminated in the formation of the Planned Parenthood Federation. All over the world birth control movements experienced similar ups and downs, but by the 1930s contraception had become legal in many countries and states and tacitly accepted in many others.

Contraception remains part of the age-old search for control over our destinies—the chance to choose.

Coping with Contraceptive Failure

Garrett Hardin

Every unintended pregnancy represents a failure of birth control. It is important to state this truism explicitly so that we can get on with the business of studying the system of birth control. Every system has its failures; what do we do about them? In general, we react in two ways: (1) we study the system and seek to improve it; and (2) we employ remedial actions for the failures we cannot avoid.

Let us take up the second aspect first. Of remedial measures for the unwanted child, there are only two important ones: infanticide and adoption. Infanticide has been practiced openly in many societies, though not in ours:—not openly, that is. The historical studies of William Langer have shown that infanticide was institutionalized in a cryptic way in the Western world, being particularly important in the nineteenth century. The institution was that of the "baby farmer," the obliging person of flexible conscience who took care of your unwanted child for a fee, with the implicit understanding that it would not be for long. It is this understanding that gives new meaning to the scene in Gilbert and Sullivan's *H.M.S. Pinafore* in which Little Buttercup reveals the dread secret she had hinted at earlier:

> A many years ago
> When I was young and charming,
> As some of you may know
> I practised baby-farming.

To which the chorus replies:

> Now this is most alarming!
> When she was young and charming,
> She practised baby-farming,
> A many years ago.

Why did they say "this is most alarming"? Because "alarming" rhymes with "charming," of course; and to create the mood for the coming revelation that Buttercup had mixed two babies up. But Langer's study suggests that the "alarm" had another source: Baby-farming in the Victorian world was no more respectable than bootlegging was in Prohibition days. It was an institutionalized way of dealing with failures in birth control. Many of the "best people" knew this; but they didn't speak of it. It was under taboo. In writing this scene, Gilbert was drawing on an ambiguous feeling of dread than no longer exists. He was not *merely* being funny.

Does baby-farming, in this sense, still exist? I have been informed by some who lived in Germany in the pre-Hitler days that they still had their "angelmakers," as they were called. I suspect the profession has declined since. It used to be easy to make angels: All you had to do was crowd the babies together, underfeed them somewhat, expose them a bit, and let "nature" (that is, crowd diseases) take over. With the coming of antibiotics and government inspection of nurseries, baby-farming on the old scale is hardly possible.

What used to be done professionally is now done by amateurs, less efficiently and more brutally. Parents have now taken over the executioner's role—not many parents, but *too* many. Child-ridden, impoverished, and desperate parents are responsible for thousands of "battered babies" every year and perhaps some hundreds of dead ones. Statistics are hard to come by because it is difficult to distinguish between accidents and homicides in this population.

The United States Energy Problem

Introduction

The United States may well be at the most important pivotal point in its history. If we take all the trends of economic growth, all the conventional indicators of "progress" and strong national defense, plot them on a graph and extrapolate by applying a ruler, rather than graphing the more disastrous exponential curve, we discover that the resources necessary to sustain this growth for a very long time are not likely to be available at a price we can afford. There must be a scaling down before these limits are reached or a crash is inevitable. We have what David Brower calls "strength through exhaustion."

Many environmentalists are now calling for an alternative path and an end to physical growth as we know it. The future we face is highly uncertain whatever we do, but rather than despair, we might regard this time as an opportunity for our culture to achieve growth in other directions. An individual grows from the fertilized egg to the mature adult, and none of us supposes that the continuation of such growth is either desirable or inevitable. When full height has been reached, intellectual, emotional and religious dimensions continue to expand. The individual moves toward other heights totally independent of more physical growth. If it be true of an individual, should it not also be true of society?

If now is the time for our culture to move toward the enrichment phase of our history, we have some blueprints available showing how this might be achieved. The best known architect for this alternative phase in our culture development is the London representative for Friends of the Earth, Amory Lovins. His now classic paper, "Energy Strategy: The Road not Taken," identifies two separate paths, one "hard" and the other "soft."[1] Lovins writes that "the first path resembles present federal policy and is essentially an extrapolation of the recent past. It relies on rapid expansion of centralized high technologies to increase supplies of energy, especially in the form of electricity. The second path combines a prompt and serious commitment to efficient use of energy, rapid development of renewable resources matched in scale and in energy quality to end-use needs, and special transitional fossil fuel technologies. This path, a whole greater than the sum of its parts, diverges radically from incremental past practices to pursue long-term goals."

For Lovins, "hard path" equals high technology equals centralized systems. The "soft path" leads to less capital-intensive technologies and decentralization. The conventional solutions invariably mean more of the "hard road" and less of the "soft" in meeting energy requirements. Lovins notes that "the usual proposed solution is rapid expansion of three sectors: coal (mainly strip-mined, then made into electricity and synthetic fluid fuels); oil and gas (increasingly from Arctic and offshore wells); and nuclear fission (eventually in fast breeder reactors)." This leads to a squeeze of our domestic resources. Furthermore, there is a disincentive to conserve.

There is another serious problem which Lovins believes the "hard" path promotes, "thermodynamic mis-match," its classic example being "cutting butter with a chain saw." Electricity is good for running motors and lighting. But because only some thirty percent of the energy in a lump of coal reaches the consumer's wall plug, that precious amount should be used to do thermodynamically appropriate work. It should not be used for resistance heating. That's "cutting butter with a chain saw." Much of Lovins' thesis is devoted to stressing that eventually the economics of scarcity will automatically discriminate against those who do not match the *source* of energy to its *end use*. Therefore, the power companies now promoting the "hard" path of centralized power plants will face financial disaster. The increasing cost of investment to supply more oil will be an awesome burden. In order to protect the huge capital investment, the government will have to subsidize the utilities. In short, the people will be asked to throw good money after bad.

Lovins presents other considerations besides the "mismatch" argument. The "hard path," he contends, localizes the risk and increases the likelihood of power failures which have already affected millions. The "soft path" counts on low technology of a diverse nature. "The soft path relies on smaller, far simpler supply systems entailing vastly shorter development and construction time, and on smaller, less sophisticated management systems...the soft path relies mainly on small, standard, easy-to-make components and on technical resources dispersed in many organizations of diverse size and habits; thus everyone can get into the act."

Because our technology is ultimately at the service of a dominating social organization, we need some sense of (1) how our society has responded historically, (2) what our society thinks now and how it compares to the attitudes of the federal government, and (3) some feeling of the social risk associated with "hard path" development.

The "hard path" is already well-worn, so much in fact, that even now we scarcely have to look down, just immediately ahead to the steady stream of people who follow this path. On the other hand, the "soft path" has scarcely been tried, and doubtless there will be many times when we lose our way. I think there are three main categories of consideration as we contemplate the need for a technical and social organization more characterized by "soft path" permanence than expediency. First of all, we need to consider how we have historically responded to leaders who have called for restraint and alternative strategies of resource management. As early as 1939, President Franklin D. Roosevelt, in a message to Congress, urged that a responsible policy regarding resource use be developed (reading 16). It wasn't, and of course there was World War II which shortly followed, but why did we not respond to this consideration after the war? That might be a good question for a class to consider.

The second and perhaps most obvious consideration has to do with what the American people think now (reading 17) and how the present administration views our current energy problem (reading 18). Finally there is a third and least-considered dimension associated with the "hard path," the social peril resulting from the extensive development of fission and fusion. Jon Tinker (reading 19), taking the entire fuel cycle into consideration, questions whether our democratic way of life can be sustained. Beyond fission, if we can imagine it, there is the physical growth afforded by fusion. If enough breakthroughs in fusion occur, our technology could grow to tottering dimensions (reading 20). On this latter point, I do not know whether the famous astronomer, Fred Hoyle, had fusion in mind when he wrote this message in a science fiction book, but it does seem that the pattern of events he details could only happen if we have an "unlimited" supply of energy.

REFERENCE

1. *Foreign Affairs,* October, 1976, reprinted by Friends of the Earth in *Not Man Apart.* A more detailed explanation of the thesis is outlined in his subsequent book, *Soft Energy Paths* (F.O.E., Ballinger Pub. Co., Cambridge, Mass., 1977).

What's New?

1939: The President Speaks to Congress

Franklin Roosevelt

To the Congress: Feb. 19, 1939

This report represents the joint effort of many specialists both within and outside the Federal Government. It suggests policies, investigations, and legislation necessary to carry forward a broad national program for the prudent utilization and conservation of the Nation's energy resources.

Our resources of coal, oil, gas and water power provide the energy to turn the wheels of industry, to service our homes, and to aid in national defense. We now use more energy per capita than any other people, and our scientists tell us there will be a progressively increasing demand for energy for all purposes.

Our energy resources are not inexhaustible, yet we are permitting waste in their use and production. In some instances, to achieve apparent economies today, future generations will be forced to carry the burden of unnecessarily high costs and to substitute inferior fuels for particular purposes. National policies concerning these vital resources must recognize the availability of all of them; the location of each with respect to its markets; the costs of transporting them; the technological developments which will increase the efficiency of their production and use; the use of the lower grade coals; and the relationships between the increased use of energy and the general economic development of the country.

In the past the Federal Government and the States have undertaken various measures to conserve our heritage in these resources. In general, however, each of those efforts has been directed toward the problems in a single field: toward the protection of the public interest in the power of flowing water in the Nation's rivers; toward the relief of economic and human distress in the mining of coal; or toward the correction of demoralizing and wasteful practices and conditions in the industries producing oil and natural gas. It is time now to take a larger view: to recognize—more fully than has been possible or perhaps needful in the past—that each of our great natural resources of energy affects the others.

It is difficult in the long run to envisage a national coal policy, or a national petroleum policy, or a national water-power policy without also in time a national policy directed toward all of these energy producers—that is, a national energy resources policy. Such a broader and integrated policy toward the problems of coal, petroleum, natural gas, and water power cannot be evolved overnight.

The widening interest and responsibility on the part of the Federal Government for the conservation and wise use of the Nation's energy resources raise many perplexing questions of policy determination. Clearly, there must be adequate and continuing planning and provision for studies which will reflect the best technical experience available, as well as full consideration for both regional and group interests.

Some Federal legislation affecting the energy resources will expire at the end of this fiscal year, other legislation at the end of a few more years. This report sets forth a useful frame of reference for legislative programs affecting these resources and illustrates another approach to the systematic husbandry of our natural resources. Specific recommendations are advanced for solution of the most pressing problems.

The Shaping of a Comprehensive Energy Plan

What the American People Think

Executive Office of the President

Soon after his inauguration, President Carter requested that a serious effort be launched to seek comments and recommendations from the public for a comprehensive national energy plan. In March, the effort was launched, using three simultaneous approaches to reach the public:

- A Federal Register and direct mailing request for written comment drew nearly 28,000 responses.
- Ten regional town meetings were conducted by the Federal Energy Administration. Some 800 persons spoke at the meetings which were attended by 2600 persons.
- Twenty-one small conferences were conducted by the Energy Policy and Planning Office in the Executive Office of the President for a broad spectrum of groups and individuals to address concerns about energy policy. Approximately 400 persons participated.

From the public participation effort three emerged certain themes, both explicit and implicit:

- Individuals, groups, and organizations regard the energy problem, and the need for national solutions, as a matter of high importance, and overwhelmingly appreciated being asked for their views and recommendations.
- In spite of some definite skepticism about the impact that their views would have, both the organized and unorganized public in large numbers came forward to express their views.
- Many comments were made to the effect that participation and discussion should be an ongoing process, and that such efforts to consult the American people should reach beyond Washington into the Nation's communities with their unique as well as their common problems.

From the standpoint of substance, the public participation effort produced a great diversity—indeed in some instances, a clash—of views and judgments when desirable, but competitive, goals and actions were weighed. While more detail follows in the individual sections, certain central themes and issues were evident:

● Most participants felt that the energy problem was real, and looked to the government to do a much better job of defining the problem and providing reliable and useful information about it. The need for better education on energy problems and their solutions came up time and again.

● Conservation was a theme which came up consistently with enormous general support, but with differing views as to how to achieve it. The dominant view favored voluntary means and incentives, but substantial support for regulation and standards was also expressed.

● The use of market place pricing as necessary for conservation provoke controversy, with strong support expressed for all conflicting views.

● Most of those expressing opinions saw an increasing dependence on imported energy as undesirable and regarded stockpiling as a sound approach to reduced vulnerability.

● The priorities for domestic supply development provided strong reactions. The concerned energy industries advocated policies in support of their views, while environmentalists took strong exception to many of those policies. Consumers warned about prices, and industries worried about the availability of supply as well as price. More use of coal received the most support; with enthusiastic and widespread interest in the development of solar energy. The much more controversial issue of nuclear energy received vigorous support from some, and substantial opposition on safety, environmental, and proliferation grounds from others.

● The comments also suggested that the federal government should play a substantial and vigorous role in research and development. Many also strongly urge long range national policies which would provide stable energy sources for the future.

The Administrative Overview

Executive Office of the President

The diagnosis of the U.S. energy crisis is quite simple: demand for energy is increasing, while supplies of oil and natural gas are diminishing. Unless the U.S. makes a timely adjustment before world oil becomes very scarce and very expensive in the 1980's, the nation's economic security and the American way of life will be gravely endangered. The steps the U.S. must take now are small compared to the drastic measures that will be needed if the U.S. does nothing until it is too late.

How did this crisis come about?

Partly it came about through lack of foresight. Americans have become accustomed to abundant, cheap energy. During the decades of the 1950's and 1960's, the real price of energy in the U.S. fell 28 percent. And from 1950 until the qadrupling of world oil prices in 1973-1974, U.S. consumption of energy increased at an average annual rate of 3.5 percent. As a result of the availability of cheap energy, the

U.S. developed a stock of capital goods—such as homes, cars, and factory equipment—that uses energy inefficiently.

The Nature of the Problem

The most critical increase in demand has been for oil, the most versatile and widely used energy resource. To meet that growing demand, the U.S. has turned increasingly to imports. In January and February of 1977, the U.S. imported about 9 million barrels of oil per day, half of total domestic oil consumption. By 1985, U.S. oil consumption could equal 12 to 16 million barrels per day.

U.S. domestic oil production has been declining since 1970. New production from Alaska, the deep Outer Continental Shelf, and new recovery methods should reverse the decline, but will be unable to satisfy the projected growth in U.S. demand. Other major additions to domestic oil supply are unlikely.

The principal oil-exporting countries will not be able to satisfy all the increases in demand expected to occur in the U.S. and other countries throughout the 1980's. In 1976, the 13 OPEC countries exported 29 million barrels of oil per day. If world demand continues to grow at the rates of recent years, by 1985 it could reach or exceed 50 million barrels per day. However, many OPEC countries cannot significantly expand production; and, in some, production will actually decline. Thus, as a practical matter, overall OPEC production could approach the expected level of world demand only if Saudi Arabia greatly increased its oil production. Even if Saudi Arabia did so, the highest levels of OPEC production probably would be inadequate to meet increasing world demand beyond the late 1980's or early 1990's.

There are physical and economic limits on the world's supply of oil. A widely used geological estimate of total recoverable world oil resources, past and present, is about 2 trillion barrels. More than 360 billion barrels have already been consumed. Current proved crude reserves are 600 billion barrels. World consumption of oil has grown at an average annual rate of 6.6 percent since 1940, and it grew by as much as 8 percent annually during the 1960's.

If it could be assumed that world demand for oil would grow at an annual rate of only 3 percent, and if it were possible (which it is not) that production would keep pace with that rate of growth, the world's presently estimated recoverable oil resources would be exhausted before 2020. At a conjectural growth rate of 5 percent, those resources would be exhausted by 2010. Despite some uncertainty about the exact size of recoverable world oil resources, and about the rate of increase of productive capacity, this fundamental fact is clear: *within about four generations, the bulk of the world's supply of oil, created over hundreds of millions of years, will have been substantially consumed.*

Of course, actual physical exhaustion of oil resources will not occur. Even today, well over half the oil in existing fields is being left in the ground because additional recovery would be too expensive. As production by conventional methods declines and oil becomes more scarce, its price will rise and more expensive recovery methods and novel technologies will be used to produce additional oil. As this process continues, the price of oil will become prohibitive for most energy uses. Eventually the nations of the world will have to seek substitutes for oil as an energy source, and oil will have to be reserved for petrochemical and other uses in which it has maximum value.

The world now consumes about 20 billion barrels of oil per year. To maintain even that rate of consumption and keep reserves intact, *the world would have to discover another Kuwait or Iran roughly every three years, or another Texas or Alaska roughly every six months.* Although some large discoveries will be made, a continuous series of such finds is unlikely. Indeed, recent experience suggests that, compared to world oil consumption, future discoveries will be small or moderate in size, will occur in frontier areas, and will yield oil only at very high cost. Obviously, continued *high rates of growth* of oil consumption simply cannot be sustained.

Natural gas supplies are also limited. In the U.S., natural gas constitutes only 4 percent of conventional energy reserves, but supplies 27 percent of energy consumption. Gas consumption grew about 5.7 percent per year between 1960 and 1970. From 1970 to 1974, however, consumption dropped 1.3 percent. The demand for gas is considerably higher than the amount that can be supplied. Hence, gas is rationed by prohibitions on hook-ups for new homes in many areas.

Gas is not only in short supply, but its allocation across the country is distorted, and its distribution among end-uses is unsatisfactory. Federal regulation of the wellhead price of natural gas in interstate commerce has discouraged its distribution from gas producing States to other States, and has encouraged consumption of this premium fuel for less essential uses. Industry and utilities currently consume almost 60 percent of U.S. natural gas, despite the fact that other fuels could be used in a majority of cases.

During the 1973-75 period, only 19 percent of new gas reserve additions were made available to the interstate market, and much of that gas was from the Federal domain. Since the price of intrastate gas is not regulated, there are strong economic incentives to sell gas within the producing States. *The existing distinction between intrastate and interstate sales has given intrastate users first claim to natural gas.*

Strategies and Objectives

The U.S. has three overriding energy objectives:

1. as an immediate objective that will become even more important in the future, to reduce dependence on foreign oil and vulnerability to supply interruptions;
2. in the medium term, to keep U.S. imports sufficiently low to weather the period when world oil production approaches its capacity limitation; and
3. in the long term, to have renewable and essentially inexhaustible sources of energy for sustained economic growth.

The U.S. and the world are at the early stage of an energy transition. Previous energy transitions in the U.S. were stimulated by new technologies, such as the development of the railroad and the mass production of automobiles, which fostered the use of coal and oil, respectively. The latest transition springs from the need to adjust to scarcity and higher prices.

To make the new transition, the U.S. should adhere to basic principles that establish a sound context for energy policy and provide its main guidelines. The energy crisis must be addressed comprehensively by the Government and by a public that understands its seriousness and is willing to make necessary sacrifices. Economic growth with high levels of employment and production must be maintained. National policies for the protection of the environment must be continued. Above all, the U.S. must solve its energy problems in a manner that is fair to all regions, sectors and income groups.

The salient features of the National Energy Plan are:

1. conservation and fuel efficiency;
2. rational pricing and production policies;
3. reasonable certainty and stability in Government policies;
4. substitution of abundant energy resources for those in short supply; and
5. development of nonconventional technologies for the future.

Conservation and fuel efficiency are the cornerstone of the proposed National Energy Plan. Conservation is cheaper than production of new supplies, and is the most effective means for protection of the environment. It can contribute to international stability by moderating the growing pressure on world oil resources. Conservation and improved efficiency can lead to quick results. For example, a significant percentage of poorly insulated homes in the United States could be brought up to strict fuel-efficiency standards in less time than it now takes to design, build, and license one nuclear powerplant.

Although conservation measures are inexpensive and clean compared with energy production and use, they do sometimes involve sacrifice and are not always easy to implement. If automobiles are to be made lighter and less powerful, the American people must accept sacrifices in comfort and horsepower. If industry is required to make energy-saving investments and to pay taxes for the use of scarce resources, there will be some increases in the cost of consumer products. These sacrifices, however, need not result in major changes in the American way of life or in reduced standards of living. Automobile fuel efficiency can be greatly improved through better design and use of materials, as well as by producing lighter and less powerful cars, without inhibiting Americans' ability to travel. With improved energy efficiency, the impact of rising energy prices can be significantly moderated.

Energy conservation, properly implemented, is fully compatible with economic growth, the development of new industries, and the creation of new jobs for American workers. Energy consumption need not be reduced in absolute terms; what is necessary is a slowing down in its rate of growth. By making adjustments in energy consumption now, the U.S. can avoid a possibly severe economic recession in the mid 1980's.

The U.S. has a clear choice. If a conservation program begins now, it can be carried out in a rational and orderly manner over a period of years. It can be moderate in scope, and can apply primarily to capital goods, such as homes and automobiles. If, however, conservation is delayed until world oil production approaches its capacity limitation, it will have to be carried out hastily under emergency conditions.

It will be sudden, and drastic in scope; and because there will not be time to wait for incremental changes in capital stock, conservation measures will have to cut much more deeply into patterns of behavior, disrupt the flow of goods and services, and reduce standards of living.

Pricing policies should encourage proper responses in both the consumption and the production of energy, without creating any windfall profits. *If users pay yesterday's prices for tomorrow's energy, U.S. resources will be rapidly exhausted. If producers were to receive tomorrow's prices for yesterday's discoveries, there would be an inequitable transfer of income from the American people to the producers, whose profits would be excessive and would bear little relation to actual economic contribution.*

Currently, Federal pricing policy encourages overconsumption of the scarcest fuels by artificially holding down prices. If, for example, the cost of expensive foreign oil is averaged with cheaper domestic oil, consumers overuse oil, and oil imports are subsidized and encouraged. Consumers are thus misled into believing that they can continue to obtain additional quantities of oil at less than its replacement cost.

Artificially low prices for some energy sources also distort interfuel competition. The artificially low price of natural gas, for example, has encouraged its use by industry and electric utilities, which could use coal, and in many areas has made gas unavailable for new households, which could make better use of its premium qualities.

These misguided Government policies must be changed. But neither Government policy nor market incentives can improve on nature and create additional oil or gas in the ground. From a long-term perspective, prices are an important influence on production and use. As long as energy consumers are misled into believing they can obtain energy cheaply, they will consume energy at a rate the U.S. cannot afford to sustain. Their continued overuse will make the nation's inevitable transition more drastic and difficult.

A national energy policy should encourage production. The energy industries need adequate incentives to develop *new* resources and are entitled to sufficient profits for exploration for *new* discoveries. But they should not be allowed to reap large windfall profits as a result of circumstances unrelated to the marketplace or their risk-taking.

The fourfold increase in world oil prices in 1973-74 and the policies of the oil-exporting countries should not be permitted to create unjustified profits for domestic producers at consumer's expense. By raising the world price of oil, the oil-exporting countries have increased the value of American oil in existing wells. That increase in value has not resulted from free market forces or from any risk-taking by U.S. producers. *National energy policy should capture the increase in oil value for the American people.* The distribution of the proceeds of higher prices among domestic producers and consumers must be equitable and economically efficient if the United States is to spread the cost fairly across the population and achieve its energy goals.

The pricing of oil and natural gas should reflect the economic fact that the true value of a depleting resource is the cost of replacing it. An effective pricing system would provide the price incentives that producers of oil and natural gas need by focusing on harder to find new supplies. The system should also moderate the adjustment that households will have to make to rising fuel costs. It should end the distortions of the intrastate-interstate distinction for new natural gas, which is a national resource. It should also promote conservation by raising the ultimate price of products made by energy-intensive processes.

Reasonable certainty and stability in Government policies are needed to enable consumers and producers of energy to make investment decisions. A comprehensive national energy plan should resolve a wide range of uncertainties that have impeded the orderly development of energy policy and projects. Some uncertainties are inherent in a market economy, and Government should not shelter industry from the normal risks of doing business. But Government should provide business and the public with a clear and consistent statement of its own policies, rules, and intentions so that intelligent private investment decisions can be made.

Resources in plentiful supply should be used more widely as part of a process of moderating use of those in short supply. Although coal comprises 90 percent of United States total fossil fuel reserves, the United States meets only 18 percent of its energy needs from coal. Seventy-five percent of energy needs are met by oil and natural gas although they account for less than 8 percent of U.S. reserves. This imbalance between reserves and consumption should be corrected by shifting industrial and utility consumption from oil and gas to coal and other abundant energy sources.

As industrial firms and utilities reduce their use of oil and gas, they will have to turn to coal and other fuels. The choices now for electric utilities are basically coal and nuclear power. Expanding future use of coal will depend in large part on the introduction of new technologies that permit it to be burned in an environmentally acceptable manner, in both power plants and factories. Efforts should also be made to develop and perfect processes for making gas from coal.

Light-water nuclear reactors, subject to strict regulation, can assist in meeting the United States energy deficit. The 63 nuclear plants operating today provide approximately 10 percent of U.S. electricity, about 3 percent of total energy output. That contribution could be significantly increased. The currently projected growth rate of nuclear energy is substantially below prior expectations due mainly to the recent drop in demand for electricity, labor problems, equipment delays, health and safety problems, lack of a publicly accepted waste disposal program, and concern over nuclear proliferation. The Government should ensure that risks from nuclear power are kept as low as humanly possible, and should also establish the framework for resolving problems and removing unnecessary delays in the nuclear licensing process.

To the extent that electricity is substituted for oil and gas, the total amounts of energy used in the country will be somewhat larger due to the inherent inefficiency of electricity generation and distribution. But conserving scarce oil and natural gas is far more important than saving coal.

Finally, *the use of nonconventional sources of energy must be vigorously expanded.* Relatively clean and inexhaustible sources of energy offer a hopeful prospect of supplementing conventional energy sources in this century and becoming major sources of energy in the next. Some of these nonconventional technologies permit decentralized production, and thus provide alternatives to large, central systems. Traditional forecasts of energy use assume that nonconventional resources, such as solar and geothermal energy, will play only a minor role in the United States energy future. Unless positive and creative actions are taken by Government and the private sector, these forecasts will become self-fulfilling prophecies. Other technologies that increase the efficiency of energy use should also be encouraged, such as cogeneration, the simultaneous production of industrial process steam and electricity.

A national energy plan cannot anticipate technological miracles. Even so, nonconventional technologies are not mere curiosities. Steady technological progress is likely, breakthroughs are possible, and the estimated potential of nonconventional energy sources can be expected to improve. Some nonconventional technologies are already being used, and with encouragement their use will grow. Because nonconventional energy sources have great promise, the Government should take all reasonable steps to foster and develop them.

The National Energy Plan is based on this conceptual approach. It contains a practical blend of economic incentives and disincentives as well as some regulatory measures. It strives to keep Government intrusion into the lives of American citizens to a minimum. It would return the fiscal surpluses of higher energy taxes to the American people.

Finally, the Plan sets forth goals for 1985 which, although ambitious, can be achieved with the willing cooperation of the American people. These goals are:

1. reduce the annual growth of total energy demand to below 2 percent;
2. reduce gasoline consumption 10 percent below its current level;
3. reduce oil imports from a potential level of 16 million barrels per day to 6 million, roughly one-eighth of total energy consumption;
4. establish a Strategic Petroleum Reserve of 1 billion barrels;
5. increase coal production by two-thirds, to more than 1 billion tons per year;
6. bring 90 percent of existing American homes and all new buildings up to minimum energy efficiency standards; and
7. use solar energy in more than 2½ million homes.

The Plan would reverse the recent trend of ever-rising oil imports and ever-increasing American dependence on uncertain foreign sources of supply. It would prepare the United States for the time when the world faces a limitation on oil production capacity and consequent skyrocketing oil prices. It would achieve substantial energy savings through conservation and increased fuel efficiency, with minimal disruption to the economy, and would stimulate the use of coal in a manner consistent with environmental protection.

The United States is at a turning point. It can choose, through piecemeal programs and policies, to continue the current state of drift. That course would require no hard decisions, no immediate sacrifices, and no adjustment to the new energy realities. That course may, for the moment, seem attractive. But, with each passing day, the United States falls farther behind in solving its energy problems. Consequently, its economic and foreign policy position weakens, its options dwindle, and the ultimate transition to scarce oil supplies and much higher oil prices becomes more difficult. If the United States faces up to the energy problem now and adopts the National Energy Plan, it will have the precious opportunity to make effective use of time and resources before world oil production reaches its capacity limitation.

The energy crisis presents a challenge to the American people. If they respond with understanding, maturity, imagination, and their traditional ingenuity, the challenge will be met. Even the "sacrifices" involved in conservation will have their immediate rewards in lower fuel bills and the sense of accomplishment that comes with achieving higher efficiency. By preparing now for the energy situation of the 1980's, the U.S. will not merely avoid a future time of adversity. It will ensure that the coming years will be among the most creative and constructive in American history.

Fission, Fusion and Social Institutions

Democracy vs. the Breeder

Jon Tinker

Public and scientific debate on the fast breeder reactor has centered on the technical issues, notably on the question whether storage methods for the hot wastes can remain foolproof for tens of thousands of years. An important new pamphlet by Dr. Michael Flood and Robin Grove-White (Friends of the Earth, 9 Poland St., London, W1: £1 post free) concentrates by contrast on the political implications.

Official UK projections suggest that soon after AD 2000 Britain could have about 50 breeders, which Flood and Grove-White calculate would involve 1700 cross-country shipments of upwards of 80 tonnes of plutonium per year. About 12 kg would suffice for a crude nuclear device, and smaller quantities could be used in a lethal dispersal weapon. The FOE pamphlet considers what level of security would be required to protect 50 reactors against sabotage and 1700 shipments against hijacking and subsequent use by terrorists. Their conclusions include the extension of positive vetting to 20,000 electrical supply workers; an armed and extra-legal nuclear police force at least one third the present size of the Metropolitan Police; surveillance and infiltration of conservation and amenity groups; police powers of house-to-house search without a warrant; and the authorisation of torture.

If these suggestions seem hysterical, consider the situation if the IRA or some other terrorist group announced it had concealed a plutonium device in central London, and the authorities knew that a few kg of fuel was indeed missing. Potential deaths would range from 2000 to 50,000; geiger counters would not detect such a bomb from the street; the area would have to be evacuated and searched on foot. Whether or not the device existed, and whether or not it was exploded, popular reaction would demand stringent counter-measures. It may be recalled, for comparison, that Parliament enacted the Prevention of Terrorism Act within a few days of the November 1973 Birmingham pub bombing, which involved only a score of casualties.

The damage posed to civil liberties by nuclear power does not all lie in the future. Already, this report claims, M15 is involved; press and parliament alike are denied all information about plutonium movements between Windscale and Dounreay; and the Atomic Energy Authority's 400-strong private police force, operating outside parliamentary scrutiny, is armed and has the right to arrest on suspicion. Flood and Grove-White do not argue that these measures are unjustified; on the contrary they contend that a plutonium economy would be incompatible with an open society.

Of course, democracies have for decades tolerated substantial and permanent infringements of liberty on grounds of military security, a term which has already extended far from the armed services themselves—to munitions workers, for example. Why could we not accommodate extensions of the same approach to electricity? The prime difference lies perhaps in the consequences of failure. Society has accepted—even laughed at—successive shortcomings in military security. It would be unlikely to feel the same way about plutonium. Moreover, it is not in the nature of policemen to use new powers with discretion: although 1330 people were arrested in the UK up to January 1976 under the Prevention of Terrorism Act, only 65 charges were preferred.

Once the breeder programme got under way, a major extension of police powers could hardly wait for the first act of nuclear terrorism. Plutonium could provide a would-be totalitarian government, or a weak government pretending to be tough, with impeccable and popular ground for a "temporary" but irreversible putsch.

A Consequence of Fusion Energy?

Fred Hoyle

The showing took upward of four hours. It was the longest documentary film I had ever seen, naturally enough for it dealt with a time span of six thousand years. We covered time at an average rate of a century to each four minutes. There was no place here for intricate involvements, or for the niceties of politics. Yet it was all too easy to follow. The black record of the human species swept remorselessly on as the minutes and hours ticked away.

It was a shock at the beginning to be very quickly out of both the twentieth and the twenty-first centuries. The first quick point was a transition from poverty to affluence in the undeveloped continents of the twentieth century, Africa and Asia. A homogeneous civilization swept with incredible speed over the whole Earth. There were brief flashes of the people, of their machines, their customs, their political leaders. It was all done visually. We sat in silence watching, our ears free of the cacophonous uproar of the usual sound track. It was easy to comment to each other on what we saw, not that we had much to say beyond the occasional exclamation.

Earth teemed with people. Cities spread out farther and farther until they became joined to each other. Urban populations covered an increasing fraction of the land surface. At first it was only one per cent, then five per cent, then twenty-five per cent. The technological drive went irresistibly on. Land became of more and more value. There was no room any longer for any animal save man. So we watched the gradual extinction of the whole animal world. Even the bird population declined and withered away.

We saw something of domestic life. We saw the standardized little boxes in which almost everybody was now living. The insistent question formed in your mind, what was it all good for? What conceivable reason could there be to prefer a thousand little boxes to one dignified house? The same of course for the people. What was the advantage of this appalling fecundity of the human species?

Soon we were in the twenty-fifth century. Angry voices began to be heard. The pressures were mounting, competing with the technology. The technology itself was kept going by the most rigorous demands on individual freedom. It was indeed a veritable ant-heap. The average person became restricted to a life that lay somewhere between the freedom of the twentieth century and the lack of freedom of a man serving a life sentence in prison. Nobody travelled now, except on official business—I mean travelled to distant parts. Everything was provided in one's own locality, food, amusements, work. The work itself demanded little initiative. The people were leading what can only be described as a punched-card life.

The technology wasn't working too well any more. Food was mostly of poor quality, mostly factory produced. At that stage, in the twenty-fifth century, the seas were essentially swept clean of fish. The land animals had been the first to go, then the birds, now last the fish.

The first disaster happened with amazing suddenness. What had seemed a more or less homogeneous civilization split into two, like the division of an amoeba.

"It's a point of instability," whispered John. "Look, the whole thing's going to grow exponentially."

Whatever he meant, this vast gargantuan, sprawling, tasteless, in every way appalling, civilization exploded in a flash. It started with bombs and rockets, with fire. The film, so far silent, now came alive, not with any synthetic sound track, but with the crackling of the actual fire, with the shriek, instantly cut short, of a woman enveloped in a cloud of burning petrol. Then it was all over. It was quiet everywhere. Death and decay swept at an incredible speed, like some monstrous fungus, everywhere over the Earth. There was no movement, no transport, no food distribution. The intricate organization which had itself fed on the efforts of a large fraction of the whole population was dead. Everything which had depended on it, including the lives of the people, now died too. We could hear the whine of infants, the despairing cries of children. The abomination came at last to an end. It seemed as if the human species, having wiped everything else from the face of the planet, had now itself become extinct.

Miraculously this did not happen. A dozen or more specially favoured, especially lucky, small centres of population managed to survive. They were already beginning their recovery by the time we saw them, I suppose because no camera had been there to record the worst moments. Indeed the technique of photography suddenly became very crude, almost the way it had been when photography was first invented.

We saw the slow steady expansion of one centre after another. The population increased, the technology improved. We saw the people happy and smiling again. We heard them talking in a new language. We saw them attempting to recover the relics and treasures of the past, particularly books and manuscripts. We saw how they made every effort as they improved to absorb the culture of the past. Amazingly, a great deal survived.

By now we were almost a thousand years on. The new civilization was becoming exuberant. There was nothing of the deathly, machine-like quality of the situation before the first upheaval, the Great Disaster as it came to be known. People were individuals again. There was hope for the future once more.

The different centres were by now overlapping each other. They were in argument. There was a period of war, astonishingly short it seemed to us on this kaleidoscopic record. The war turned out to be no more than a kind of lubricant that allowed the hitherto separate regions to join up with each other into a coherent whole. With a growing sense of horror I realized it was all going to happen again. There was going to be a second disaster. It became so completely inevitable as one watched. Century after century went by. Each brought its contribution to the elephantine growth. Gone was the zip and zest of the first pioneers of this new civilization. We were back again in a punched-card era. It all happened with horrible predictability. The first and second catastrophes might have been interchanged and you couldn't have told the difference.

Energy for the Poorest One-Third

The Other Energy Crisis: Firewood

Erik P. Eckholm

Dwindling reserves of petroleum and artful tampering with its distribution are the stuff of which headlines are made. Yet for more than a third of the world's people, the real energy crisis is a daily scramble to find the wood they need to cook dinner. Their search for wood, once a simple chore and now, as forests recede, a day's labor in some places, has been strangely neglected by diplomats, economists, and the media. But the firewood crisis will be making news—one way or another—for the rest of the century.

While chemists devise ever more sophisticated uses for wood, including cellophane and rayon, at least half of all the timber cut in the world still serves in its original role for humans—as fuel for cooking and, in colder mountain regions, home heating. Nine-tenths of the people in most poor countries today depend on firewood as their chief source of fuel. And all too often, the growth in human population is outpacing the growth of new trees—not surprising when the average user burns as much as a ton of firewood a year. The results are soaring wood prices, a growing drain on incomes and physical energies in order to satisfy basic fuel needs, a costly diversion of animal manures from food production uses to cooking, and an ecologically disastrous spread of treeless landscapes.

The firewood crisis is probably most acute today in the countries of the densely populated Indian subcontinent and in the semi-arid stretches of central Africa fringing the Sahara Desert, though it plagues many other regions as well. In Latin America, for example, the scarcity of wood and charcoal is a problem throughout most of the Andean region, Central America, and the Caribbean.

As firewood prices rise, so does the economic burden of the urban poor. One typical morning on the outskirts of Kathmandu, Nepal's capital city, I watched a steady flow of people—men and women, children and the very old—trudge into the city with heavy, neatly chopped and stacked loads of wood on their backs. I asked my taxi driver how much their loads, for which they had walked several hours into the surrounding hills, would sell for. "Oh wood, a very expensive item!" he exclaimed without hesitation. Wood prices are a primary topic of conversation in Kathmandu these days. "That load costs twenty rupees now. Two years ago it sold for six or seven rupees." This 300 percent rise in the price of fuel wood has in part been prompted by the escalating cost of imported kerosene, the principal alternative energy source for the poor. But firewood prices have risen much *faster* than kerosene prices, a rise that reflects the growing difficulty with which wood is being procured. It now costs as much to run a Kathmandu household on wood as on kerosene.

The costs of firewood and charcoal are climbing throughout most of Asia, Africa, and Latin America. Those who can, pay the price, and thus must forego consumption of other essential goods. Wood is simply accepted as one of the major expenses of living. In Niamey, Niger, deep in the drought-plagued Sahel in West Africa, the average manual laborer's family now spends nearly one-fourth of its income on firewood. In Ouagadougou, Upper Volta, the portion is 20 to 30 percent. Those who can't pay so much may send their children, or hike out into the surrounding countryside themselves, to forage—if enough trees are within a reasonable walking distance. Otherwise, they may scrounge about the town for twigs, garbage, or anything burnable. In many regions, firewood scarcity places a special burden on women, who are generally saddled with the tasks of hiking or rummaging for fuel.

In some Pakistani towns now, people strip bark off the trees that line the streets; thus, meeting today's undeniable needs impoverishes the future. When I visited the chief conservator of forests in Pakistan's North West Frontier Province at his headquarters in the town of Peshawar, he spoke in a somewhat resigned tone of stopping his car the previous day to prevent a woman from pulling bark off a tree. "I told her that peeling the bark off a tree is just like peeling the skin off a man," he said. Of course the woman stopped, intimidated by what may be the most personal encounter with a senior civil servant she will have in her lifetime, but she doubtless resumed her practice shortly, for what else, as the chief conservator himself asked, was she to do?

It is not in the cities but in rural villages that most people in the affected countries live, and where most firewood is burned. The rural, landless poor in parts of India and Pakistan are now feeling a new squeeze on their meager incomes. Until now they have generally been able to gather free wood from the trees scattered through farmlands, but as wood prices in the towns rise, landlords naturally see an advantage in carting available timber into the nearest town to sell rather than allowing the nearby laborers to glean it for nothing. This commercialization of firewood raises the hope that entrepreneurs will see an advantage in planting trees to develop a sustainable, labor-intensive business, but so far a depletion of woodlands has been the more common result. And the rural poor, with little or no cash to spare, are in deep trouble in either case.

With the farmland trees and the scrubby woodlands of unfarmed areas being depleted by these pressures, both the needy and the ever-present entrepreneurs are forced to poach for fuel wood in the legally protected, ecologically and economically essential national forest reserves. The gravity of the poaching problem in India has been reflected in the formation of special mobile guard-squads and mobile courts to try captured offenders, but law enforcement measures have little effect in such an untenable situation. Acute firewood scarcity has undermined administrative control even in China, where trees on commune plantations are sometimes surreptitiously uprooted for fuel almost as soon as they are planted.

Trees are becoming scarce in the most unlikely places. In some of the most remote villages in the world, deep in the once heavily forested Himalayan foothills of Nepal, journeying out to gather firewood and fodder is now an *entire day's* task. Just one generation ago the same expedition required no more than an hour or two.

Because those directly suffering its consequences are mostly illiterate, and because wood shortages lack the photogenic visibility of famine, the firewood crisis has not provoked much world attention. And, in a way, there is little point in calling this a world problem, for fuel wood scarcity, unlike oil scarcity, is always localized in its apparent dimensions. Economics seldom permit fuel wood to be carried or trucked more than a few hundred miles from where it grows, let alone the many thousands of miles traversed by the modern barrel of oil. To say that firewood is scarce in Mali or Nepal is of no immediate consequence to the boy scout building a campfire in Pennsylvania, whereas his parents have already learned that decisions in Saudi Arabia can keep the family car in the garage.

Unfortunately, however, the consequences of firewood scarcity are seldom limited to the economic burden placed on the poor of a particular locality, harsh as that is in itself. The accelerating degradation of woodlands throughout Africa, Asia, and Latin America, caused in part by fuel gathering, lies at the heart of the profound challenges to environmental stability and land productivity reviewed in this book—accelerated soil erosion, increasingly severe flooding, creeping deserts, and declining soil fertility.

The Dust Bowl years in the Great Plains of the thirties taught Americans the perils of devegetating a region prone to droughts. The images provided by John Steinbeck in *The Grapes of Wrath* of the human dislocation wrought by that interaction of people, land, and climate could easily describe present-day events in large semi-arid stretches of Africa along the northern and southern edges of the Sahara, and around the huge Rajasthan Desert in northwest India. Overgrazing by oversized herds of cattle, goats, and sheep is the chief culprit, but gathering of fuel wood is also an important contributor to the destruction of trees in these regions. Firewood is a scarce and expensive item throughout the Sub-Saharan fringe of Africa, all the way from Senegal to Ethiopia, but citizens in towns like Niamey are paying a much higher price than they realize for their cooking fuel. The caravans that bring in this precious resource are contributing to the creation of desert-like conditions in a wide band below the desert's edge. Virtually all trees within seventy kilometers of Ouagadougou have been consumed as fuel by the city's inhabitants, and the circle of land "strip-mined" for firewood—without reclamation—is continually expanding.

In the Indian subcontinent, the most pernicious result of firewood scarcity is probably not the destruction of tree cover itself, but the alternative to which a good share of the people in India, Pakistan, and Bangladesh have been forced. A visitor to almost any village in the subcontinent is greeted by omnipresent pyramids of hand-molded dung patties drying in the sun. In many areas these dung cakes have been the only source of fuel for generations, but now, by necessity, their use is spreading further. Between three hundred and four hundred million tons of wet dung—which shrink to sixty to eighty million tons when dried—are annually burned for fuel in India alone, robbing farmland of badly needed nutrients and organic matter. The plant nutrients wasted annually in this fashion in India equal more than a third of the country's chemical fertilizer use. Looking only at this direct economic cost, it is easy to see why the country's National Commission on Agriculture recently declared that "the use of cow dung as a source of non-commercial fuel is virtually a crime." Dung is also burned for fuel in parts of the Sahelian zone in Africa, Ethiopia, Iraq, and in the nearly treeless Andean valleys and slopes of Bolivia and Peru, where the dung of llamas has been the chief fuel in some areas since the days of the Incas.

Even more important than the loss of agricultural nutrients is the damage done to soil structure and quality through the failure to return manures to the fields. Organic materials—humus and soil organisms which live in it—play an essential role in preserving the soil structure and fertility needed for productive farming. Organic matter helps hold the soil in place when rain falls and wind blows, and reduces the wasteful, polluting runoff of chemical nutrients where they are applied. Humus helps the soil absorb and store water, thus mitigating somewhat the impact on crops of drought periods. These considerations apply especially to the soils in tropical regions where most dung is now burned, because tropical topsoils are usually thin and, once exposed to the burning sun and torrential monsoon rains, are exceptionally prone to erosion and to loss of their structure and fertility.

Peasants in the uplands of South Korea have adopted a different, but also destructive way to cope with the timber shortage. A United Nations forestry team visiting the country in the late 1960s found not only that live tree branches, shrubs, seedlings, and grasses were cut for fuel; worse, many hillsides were raked clean of all leaves, litter, and burnable materials. Raking in this fashion, to meet needs for home fuel and farm compost, robs the soil of both a protective cover and organic matter, and the practice was cited by the UN experts as "one of the principal causes of soil erosion in Korea." Firewood scarcity similarly impairs productivity in eastern Nigeria, where the Tiv people have been forced to uproot crop residues after the harvest for use as fuel. Traditionally, the dead stalks and leaves have been left to enrich the soil and hold down erosion.

The increasing time required to gather firewood in many mountain villages of Nepal is leading to what the kingdom's agricultural officials fear most of all. For once procuring wood takes too long to be worth the trouble, some farmers start to use cow dung, which was formerly applied with great care to the fields, as cooking fuel. As this departure from tradition spreads, the fertility of the hills, already declining due to soil erosion, will fall sharply. In the more inaccessible spots, there is no economic possibility whatsoever of replacing the manure with chemical fertilizers.

And so the circle starts to close in Nepal, a circle long completed in parts of India. As wood scarcity forces farmers to burn more dung for fuel, and to apply less to their fields, falling food output will necessitate the clearing of ever larger, ever steeper tracts of forest—intensifying the erosion and landslide hazards in the hills, and the siltation and flooding problems downstream in India and Bangladesh.

Firewood scarcity, then, is ultimately linked in two ways to the food problem facing many countries. Deforestation and the diversion of manures to use as fuel are sabotaging the land's ability to produce food. Meanwhile, as an Indian official put it, "Even if we somehow grow enough food for our people in the year 2000, how in the world will they cook it?"

B. B. Vohra, a senior Indian agricultural official who has pushed his government ahead on numerous ecological causes, shook his head as we talked in his New

Delhi office. "I'm afraid that we are approaching the point of no return with our resource base. If we can't soon build some dramatic momentum in our reforestation and soil conservation programs, we'll find ourselves in a downward spiral with an irresistible momentum of its own." Without a rapid reversal of prevailing trends, in fact, India will find itself with a billion people to support and a countryside that is little more than a moonscape. But the politicians, in India and other poor countries, will take notice when they realize that, if people can't find any firewood, they will surely find something else to burn.

The firewood crisis is in some ways more, and in others less, intractable than the energy crisis of the industrialized world. Resource scarcity can usually be attacked from either end, through the contraction of demand or the expansion of supply. The world contraction in demand for oil in 1974 and early 1975, for example, helped to ease temporarily the conditions of shortage.

But the poor, like the rich, are faced with the necessity of energy conservation. Millions of families cook over wood or charcoal stoves that are extremely inefficient in the use of heat; many cook over open fires. The dissemination of cheap, simple woodstoves that waste less heat could substantially reduce per capita firewood consumption.

Even if more efficient stoves are adopted, however, future firewood needs in developing countries will, in the absence of alternative energy sources, be heavily influenced by population growth.

If the demographers are surprised by quick progress on the population front over the next few decades, the demand for basic resources like firewood will still push many countries to their limits. Fortunately trees, unlike oil, are a renewable resource when properly managed. The logical immediate response to the firewood shortage, one that will have many incidental ecological benefits, is to plant more trees in plantations, on farms, along roads, in shelter belts, and on unused land throughout the rural areas of the poor countries. For many regions, fast-growing tree varieties are available that can be culled for firewood inside of a decade.

The concept is simple, but its implementation is not. Governments in nearly all the wood-short countries have had tree-planting programs for some time—for several decades in some cases. National forestry departments in particular have often been aware of the need to boost the supply of wood products and the need to preserve forests for an habitable environment. But several problems have generally plagued tree-planting programs.

One is the sheer magnitude of the need for wood and the scale of the growth in demand. Population growth, which surprised many with its acceleration in the post-war era, has swallowed the moderate tree-planting efforts of many countries, rendering their impact almost negligible. Wood-producing programs will have to be undertaken on a far greater scale than most governments presently conceive if a significant dent is to be made in the problem.

The problem of scale is closely linked to a second major obstacle to meeting this crisis: the perennial question of political priorities and decision-making time-frames. With elections to win, wars to fight, dams to build, and hungry people to feed, it is hard for any politician to concentrate funds and attention on a problem so multi-dimensional and seemingly long-term in nature. Some ecologists in the poor countries have been warning their governments for decades about the dangers of deforestation and fuel shortages, but tree-planting programs don't win elections. This phenomenon is, of course, quite familiar to all countries, not just the poorest. In the United States, resource specialists pointed out the coming energy crisis throughout the 1960s, but it took a smash in the face in 1973 to wake up the government, and, as of late 1975, the country still can hardly be said to have tackled the energy challenge head-on.

Despite these inherent political problems, India's foresters made a major breakthrough a few years back as the government drew up its five-year development plan for the mid-to-late seventies. Plans were laid for the large-scale establishment of fast-growing tree plantations, and for planting trees on farms and village properties throughout the country. A program is going ahead now, but there have been some unexpected events since the projects were first contemplated two or three years ago: the quintupling of the world price of petroleum, the tripling in price and world shortages of grains and fertilizers, and the subsequent wholesale diversion of development funds to maintenance and emergencies in order to merely muddle through 1974 without a major famine and a total economic breakdown. India's development efforts have been set back several years by recent events, and forestry programs have not been immune to this trend.

Even with the right kind of political will and the necessary allocation of funds, implementing a large-scale reforestation campaign is a complex and difficult process. Planting millions of trees and successfully nurturing them to maturity is not a technical, clearly defined task like building a dam or a chemical-fertilizer plant. Tree-planting projects almost always become deeply enmeshed in the political, cultural, and administrative tangles of a rural locality; they touch upon, and are influenced by, the daily living habits of many people, and they frequently end in failure.

Most of the regions with too few trees also have too many cattle, sheep, and goats. Where rangelands are badly overgrazed, the leaves of a young sapling tempt the appetites of foraging animals. Even if he keeps careful control of his own livestock, a herdsman may reason that if his animals don't eat the leaves, someone else's will. Marauding livestock are prime destroyers of tree-planting projects throughout the less developed world. Even if a village is internally disciplined enough to defend new trees from its own residents, passing nomads or other wanderers may do them in. To be successful, then, reforestation efforts often require a formidable administrative effort to protect the plants for years—not to mention the monitoring of timber-harvesting and replanting activities once the trees reach maturity.

Village politics can undermine a program as well. An incident from Ethiopia a few years back presents an extreme case, but its lessons are plain. A rural reforestation program was initiated as a public works scheme to help control erosion and supply local wood needs. The planting jobs were given to the local poor, mostly landless laborers who badly needed the low wages they could earn in the planting program. Seedlings were distributed, planting commenced, and all seemed to be going well—until the overseers journeyed out to check the progress. They found that in many areas the seedlings had been planted upside down! The laborers, of course, well knew the difference between roots and branches; they also knew that given the feudal land-tenure system in which they were living, most of the benefits of the planting would flow one way or another into the hands of their lords. They were not anxious to work efficiently for substandard wages on a project that brought them few identifiable personal returns.

In country after country, the same lesson has been learned: tree-planting programs are most successful when a majority of the local community is deeply involved in planning and implementation, and clearly perceives its self-interest in success. Central or state governments can provide stimulus, technical advice, and financial assistance, but unless community members clearly understand why land to which they have traditionally had free access for grazing and wood-gathering are being demarcated into a plantation, they are apt to view the project with suspicion or even hostility. With wider community participation, on the other hand, the control of grazing patterns can be built into the program from the beginning, and a motivated community will protect its own project and provide labor at little or no cost.

An approach like this—working through village councils, with locally mobilized labor doing the planting and protection work—is now being tried in India. There are pitfalls; Indian villages are notoriously faction-ridden, and the ideal of the whole community working together for its own long-term benefit may be somewhat utopian. But if it can get underway on a large scale, the national program in India may succeed. Once given a chance, fast-growing trees bring visible benefits quickly, and they just could catch on. The Chinese have long used the decentralized, community labor-mobilizing approach to reforestation, apparently with considerable success.

A new program of global public education on the many benefits of reforestation, planned by the United Nations Environment Program, will hopefully direct more attention to the tremendous global need for tree planting. Whatever the success of reforestation projects, however, the wider substitution of other energy sources for wood can also contribute greatly to a solution of the firewood problem. A shift from wood-burning stoves to those running on natural gas, coal, or electricity has indeed been the dominant global trend in the last century and a half. As recently as 1850, wood met 91 percent of the fuel needs of the United States, but today in the economically advanced countries, scarcely any but the intentionally rustic, and scattered poor in the mountains, chop wood by necessity anymore. In the poor countries, too, the proportion of wood users is falling gradually, especially in the cities, which are usually partly electrified, and where residents with any income at all may cook their food with bottled gas or kerosene. Someone extrapolating trends of the first seven decades of this century might well have expected the continued spread of kerosene and natural gas use at a fairly brisk pace in the cities and into rural areas, eventually rendering firewood nearly obsolete.

Events of the last two years, of course, have abruptly altered energy-use trends and prospects everywhere. The most widely overlooked impact of the fivefold increase in oil prices, an impact drowned out by the economic distress caused for oil-importing countries, is the fact that what had been the most feasible substitute for firewood, kerosene, has now been pulled even farther out of reach of the world's poor than it already was. The hopes of foresters and ecologists for a rapid reduction of pressures on receding woodlands through a stepped-up shift to kerosene withered overnight in December, 1973, when OPEC announced its new oil prices. In fact, the dwindling of world petroleum reserves and the depletion of woodlands reinforce each other; climbing firewood prices encourage more people to use petroleum-based products for fuel, while soaring oil prices make this shift less feasible, adding to the pressure on forests.

The interconnections of firewood scarcity, ecological stress, and the broader global energy picture set the stage for some interesting, if somewhat academic, questions about a sensible disposition of world resources. In one sense it is true that the poor countries, and the world as a whole, have been positively influenced by the OPEC countries, which, through price hikes and supply restrictions, are forcing conservation of a valuable and rapidly disappearing resource, and are not letting the poor countries get dangerously hooked on an undependable energy supply. In a word in which energy, ecology, and food were sensibly managed, however, the oil distribution picture would look far different. The long-term interest in preserving the productive capacity of the earth and in maximizing welfare for the greatest number of people might argue for lower prices and a rapid *increase,* not a halt, in the adoption of kerosene and natural gas in the homes of the poor over the next two decades. This, in turn, would be viable for a reasonable time period only if the waste and comparatively frivolous uses of energy in the industrial countries, which are depleting petroleum reserves so quickly, were cut sharply. It is not so far-fetched as it might first seem to say that today's driving habits in Los Angeles, and today's price and production-level decisions in the Persian Gulf, can influence how many tons of food are lost to floods in India, and how many acres of land the Sahara engulfs, in 1980.

Fossil fuels are not the only alternate energy source under consideration, and, over the coming decades, many of those using firewood, like everyone else, will have to turn in other directions. Energy sources that are renewable, decentralized, and low in cost must be developed. Nothing, for example, would be better than a dirt-cheap device for cooking dinner in the evening with solar energy collected earlier in the day. But actually developing such a stove and introducing it to hundreds of millions of the world's most tradition-bound and penniless families is another story. While some solar cookers are already available, the cost of a family unit, at about thirty-five to fifty dollars, is prohibitive for many, since, in the absence of suitable credit arrangements, the entire amount must be available at once. Mass production could pull down the price, but the problem of inexpensively storing heat for cloudy days and evenings has not been solved. The day may come in some countries when changes in cooking and eating habits to allow maximum use of solar cookers will be forced upon populations by the absence of alternatives.

Indian scientists have pioneered for decades with an ideal-sounding device that breaks down manures and other organic wastes into methane gas for cooking and a rich compost for the farm. Over eight thousand of these bio-gas plants, as they are called, are now being used in India. Without a substantial reduction in cost, however, they will only slowly infiltrate the hundreds of thousands of rural villages, where the fuel problem is growing. Additionally, as the plants are adopted, those too poor to own cattle could be left worse off than ever, denied traditional access to dung, but unable to afford bio-gas. Still, relatively simple and decentralized devices like solar cookers and bio-gas plants will likely provide the fuel sources of the future in the poor countries.

In terms of energy, Nepal is luckier than many countries in one respect. The steep slopes and surging rivers that cause so many environmental problems also make Nepal one of the few remaining countries with a large untapped hydroelectric potential. The latent power is huge, equaling the hydroelectric capacity of Canada, the United States, and Mexico combined. Exploitation of this resource will be expensive and slow, but will relieve some of the pressures being placed on forests by the larger towns of Nepal and northern India. On the other hand, cheap electricity will only partly reduce firewood demands, since the electrification of isolated villages in the rugged Himalayas may never be economically feasible.

The firewood crisis, like many other resource problems, is forcing governments and analysts back to the basics of human beings' relationship with the land—back to concerns lost sight of in an age of macro-economic models and technological optimism. Awareness is spreading that the simple energy needs of the world's poorest third are unlikely ever to be met by nuclear power plants, any more than their minimum food needs will be met by huge synthetic-protein factories.

Firewood scarcity and its attendant ecological hazards have brought the attitude of people toward trees into sharp focus. In his essay "Buddhist Economics," E. F. Schumacher praises the practical as well as esoteric wisdom in the Buddha's teaching that his followers should plant and nurse a tree every few years. Unfortunately, this ethical heritage has been largely lost, even in the predominantly Buddhist societies of Southeast Asia. In fact, most societies today lack a spirit of environmental cooperation—not a spirit of conservation for its own sake, but one needed to guarantee human survival amid ecological systems heading toward collapse.

This will have to change, and fast. The inexorable growth in the demand for firewood calls for tree-planting efforts on a scale more massive than most bureaucrats have ever even contemplated, much less planned for. The suicidal deforestation of Africa, Asia, and Latin America must somehow be slowed and reversed. Deteriorating ecological systems have a logic of their own; the damage often builds quietly and unseen for many years, until one day the system falls asunder with lethal vengeance. Ask anyone who lived in Oklahoma in 1934, or Chad in 1975.

Metal Depletion

Metals: The Warning Signals Are Up

Edmund Faltermayer

From the time that men in ancient Mesopotamia learned to smelt copper, metal has been synonymous with civilization. The very words bronze and iron denote human epochs. Today an incredibly vast array of objects—from electric appliances to skyscrapers to transportation systems—would be unthinkable without metal, and industry's appetite for it is insatiable. The U.S. has used more metal in the last thirty years than the whole human race had used until then, and demand keeps right on increasing. Yet many essential metals are found in the earth's crust in only limited quantities. One U.S. mining executive puts today's odds against finding a commercially exploitable metallic ore body at 10,000 to 1. Nor is there any way to synthesize metals, short of achieving sustained superhigh temperatures on a scale found only on exploding stars.

To be sure, a variety of nonmetallic substances are also vital to the world economy. Demand for a few of them, notably helium gas, fluorine, and potash, could begin to outrun supply in the generations just ahead. But the supply of most nonmetallic materials, including such basic items as sand, clay, gravel, stone, glass, and cement, can be considered limitless. Another basic material, wood, is renewable and can be made more plentiful through more advanced forestry. The world also has a lot of underused land despite the high population densities of some countries. Aside from the energy resources needed to make barren acreage productive and to drive the whole industrial process, therefore, the chief limit to growth is the availability of metal.

Has the U.S. been "creamed"?

A growing chorus of experts and study groups has been saying that this limit is closer than we think. The recent M.I.T. study sponsored by the Club of Rome, *The Limits to Growth,* warns that the world's known reserves of zinc can support the present pattern of growth for only eighteen more years, that copper and lead reserves will be exhausted in twenty-one years, bauxite for making aluminum in thirty-one years, and nickel in fifty-three years. New discoveries might postpone the day of reckoning, the M.I.T. study conceded. But, it added, even a fivefold increase in the reserves of all five metals would be eaten up by compound growth within a century.

There is certainly abundant physical evidence that the U.S., at least, may already have creamed off its *best* metallic resources. The easily accessible, high-grade iron ore of the Mesabi Range is mostly gone. Before World War I, copper companies hesitated to mine ore containing less than 2 percent metal; today they would be overjoyed to find new deposits half that rich. The U.S. Bureau of Mines warned in a massive 1970 study that "the rate of new discoveries and development of reserves is declining for a wide range of minerals."

As a consequence, American industry has been turning increasingly to foreign sources. A net exporter of raw materials until World War II, the U.S. has been an importer ever since, and the trade gap is widening. In 1970 the U.S. metal industry met less than 60 percent of its primary demand with domestic ores. The growing use of foreign ore places the U.S. in competition for the available supply with the rest of the world, where demand for metal has been soaring. With Japan's metal-hungry economy setting the pace, consumption of key minerals outside the U.S. rose 158 percent between 1950 and the late 1960's, compared to a 38 percent increase in this country.

Reserves Versus Resources

From all this, one might easily conclude that America's great industries are increasingly at the mercy of foreign lands, including some unfriendly ones, and that growing imports are merely a transitional phase to the time when all the world will enter an era of metal famine. Fortunately, the picture is not nearly so bleak.

For one thing, the concept of *reserves*—meaning discovered bodies of ore that can be profitably mined at current prices with existing methods—refers only to a part of the mineral *resources* in the earth's crust. It excludes both undiscovered deposits and known ore bodies of an inferior grade that might someday become exploitable with further improvements in mining and beneficiation techniques or with an increase in prices. With no new discoveries whatever, in fact, reserves of some metals would rise geometrically if prices increased by, say, 50 percent, because low-grade deposits might then be worth mining.

For a variety of reasons, including the high cost of exploration and property taxes, mining companies have little reason at present to hunt for or reveal reserves that exceed their requirements for more than about two decades ahead. Reserves, says a government geologist, "are just a working inventory." Figures on reserves permit inferences to be drawn about the total resources that will eventually place a ceiling on growth, but they understate the metal available to mankind.

The growing importation of foreign ore, moreover, does not mean that this country will be dependent on overseas sources from now on. The U.S. still has large deposits of many of the metals that it now imports; in a future emergency it could work these deposits just as it did during World War II and the Korean conflict. Industry has turned to foreign ores because they are cheaper or of a higher grade than domestic ones, or because they can be transported inexpensively by sea.

Nevertheless, metal consumption cannot go on doubling and redoubling indefinitely into the future. At some point the availability even of abundant metals, such as steel and aluminum, may be limited by lack of the energy needed to mine, concentrate, and smelt their ores. For less abundant metals such as copper, lead, and zinc, the sheer finiteness of the supply could begin to place a limit on global consumption in another hundred years or so, regardless of the availability of energy.

Several developments could alter the future supply of metal, however. The growing concern for the environment might constrict the supply. But the available supply might be increased by the development of advanced techniques for locating ore, and by stepped-up recycling of the billions of tons of metal already extant in the advanced countries.

Before these possibilities are examined, let's look briefly at what's currently known about the prospective supply of twenty important metals.

Iron, the raw material for steelmaking and the work-horse metal of the industrial age, constitutes nearly 6 percent of the earth's crust. Iron ores suitable for making steel at the prevailing price of 9 cents a pound, of course, are found only in specific deposits. But the number of known deposits has expanded rapidly. Since 1952, when the presidential commission headed by C.B.S. Chairman William S. Paley looked at natural resources, world reserves of iron ore have increased threefold.

As in the case of so many metals, a big new factor is Australia, which formerly banned the export of iron ore in the belief that its deposits were very limited. Reserves containing ten billion tons of iron have been identified in Australia, New Zealand, and nearby New Caledonia, and Australia's potential iron resources are characterized by the U.S. Bureau of Mines as "vast."

Though its easily accessible high-grade ore is almost gone, the U.S. has a fair amount of magnetic taconite, and domestic mines have been able to hang on to two-thirds of the American ore market through pelletizing techniques that produce blast-furnace feed that is superior to natural high-grade ores. With a 50 percent rise in the price of ore, the amount of available taconite could be expanded greatly. Meanwhile, a technique has been developed for using a type of nonmagnetic taconite that until recently defied concentration techniques. Cleveland-Cliffs Iron Co. will beneficiate the nonmagnetic ore from a big mine in Michigan through a new flotation process.

Aluminum is even more abundant than iron, making up about 8 percent of the earth's crust; it is literally right under our feet. However, the bauxite ore from which the metal is most economically processed is found in only a limited number of places, many of them in the tropics, so the U.S. has long been heavily dependent upon imports. World reserves of bauxite have increased greatly over the last two decades. Current Australian reserves alone—including a bauxite outcrop 300 miles long—are equal to the known total of the globe in 1950.

The U.S. has ample clays and other minerals that could substitute for bauxite if foreign supplies were ever cut off. But it would cost more to produce the metal, and entail an increase in the large energy input already required to make a pound of aluminum. Recently the Aluminum Co. of America purchased 8,000 acres of land in Wyoming to get a deposit of an aluminum-bearing mineral, anorthosite, that is larger than all the world's bauxite reserves combined.

A Bit of Reverse Malthusianism

Conceivably, the world could be *paved* with iron and aluminum if economics, energy, and environment imposed no constraints. Few other metals are present in anything approaching such abundance.

Copper, for example, constitutes only about one part in twenty thousand of the earth's crust. Yet despite the inroads of aluminum and plastics in recent years, demand for copper keeps rising, and it ranks third in industrial importance. It is indispensable in electric motors—motors with aluminum-wound armatures would be extremely bulky—in indoor wiring, for strong and corrosion-resistant tubing, and in making brass and bronze.

Until now, discoveries of new copper deposits have kept well ahead of demand. While some uncertainty clouds the future accessibility of high-grade copper ores in Chile, Zambia, and Zaïre (formerly the Belgian Congo), scores of low-grade deposits in porphyry rock are being developed in British Columbia, Iran, Panama, Bougainville in the Solomon Islands, and elsewhere. The U.S., which relies almost entirely on low-grade ores, is the world's largest producer of copper, with nearly one-fourth of world reserves. Yet the average grade of U.S. ore keeps declining, and ores containing as little as 0.4 percent copper are now being mined in the Southwest.

That trend may not be as ominous as it sounds. The late American geologist Samuel G. Lasky, a sort of Malthus-in-reverse, said that each arithmetic reduction in the grade of porphyry copper ore mined would open up vast marginal reserves, so that the amount of available metal would actually increase geometrically. That would mean that the steady decrease in the grade of ore presages more copper, not less. Another optimistic theory holds that the Western Hemisphere's entire mountain chain from Alaska through the Andes is sprinkled with copper deposits waiting to be found and worked.

Nevertheless, the Bureau of Mines believes that before the end of this century world demand for copper will exceed "by substantial margins" the supply available at the current price. If this rather gloomy prediction is borne out, the price will have to go up and more substitution of other metals for copper will occur. Men in the copper business, however, think it most unlikely that the world will run out of the metal even in a hundred years. We may use it more selectively, they say, but it will be available.

Lead is less abundant in the earth's crust than copper, but in recent years deposits of the metal have turned up in such places as Ireland and New Brunswick, Canada, as well as Missouri. Missouri's new lead belt, the so-called Viburnum Trend discovered in the mid-1950's by St. Joe Minerals Corp. and now worked by several companies, has reserves of up to 25 million tons of the metal. That looks like an adequate supply for a long time to come, especially when it is borne in mind that a lot of lead is recycled.

Zinc is a somewhat different story. More than a fourth of it goes for the galvanizing of steel, a "dissipative" use that does not easily lend itself to recycling. Over-all, less than 6 percent of the country's zinc comes from old scrap. U.S. reserves increased with new discoveries during the 1950's and 1960's, but some mines that serve obsolete smelters, incapable of meeting new antipollution standards, have shut down. Despite Texas Gulf Sulphur's big discovery at Timmins, Ontario, in 1964, world reserves seem inadequate to meet demand over the next three decades. The Bureau of Mines says that barring big new discoveries, higher prices, or more recycling, other materials will increasingly have to take the place of zinc. Metal experts are sure that more zinc will be found, and note that it is somewhat more abundant in the earth's crust than copper.

Nickel supplies seem ample for at least a century, even though worldwide usage has been growing at a relatively rapid 7 percent a year. International Nickel's underground deposits of high-grade ore in Ontario's Sudbury district are still the world's largest, but the opening up of low-grade nickel-bearing laterite ores in New Caledonia, the Philippines, Indonesia, and the Dominican Republic has greatly increased nickel reserves. U.S. reserves at current prices amount to a mere 200,000 tons, or about one year's consumption in this country. However, if the price were to rise 50 percent, domestic reserves would increase twenty-five-fold.

Scavengers and Tougheners

Four other essential metals used in large quantities (more than 100,000 tons a year) in the U.S. are magnesium, titanium, manganese, and chromium. While *magnesium* ranks just behind aluminum and iron in its abundance in the earth's crust, this country extracts its entire supply from seawater. One cubic mile of the ocean contains more of the metal than has been used up to now.

Titanium, used as a metal alloy as well as for paint pigment, is also a relatively abundant element, though the rutile ore favored by industry is found only in scattered locations. A lower grade of titanium-bearing ore called ilmenite, on the other hand, is virtually limitless in the U.S. and elsewhere. The chief limitation on consumption could turn out to be the supply of energy; titanium production requires about twice as much energy per ton as aluminum.

The U.S. has sizable resources of low-grade *manganese,* but industry has long chosen to import the metal. Close to irreplaceable in steelmaking, manganese acts as a "scavenger"; it combines with and removes the sulphur that contaminates iron. Most U.S. manganese comes from Brazil and Gabon, though the biggest reserves are in South Africa and the Soviet Union. The supply looks adequate for at least a century.

Chromium is essential for making corrosion-resistant and stainless steels. Indeed, it is possible to make stainless without nickel, but not without chromium. Despite chromium's critical importance, U.S. mines have not supplied a ton of it since 1961; our low-grade ores cannot compete with imports. Fortunately, world reserves are large. Even the Club of Rome study sees nothing to worry about for at least ninety-five years. But these reserves are of varying grades, and this fact is currently causing the U.S. some embarrassment. The biggest reserves of "metallurgical-grade" ore are in Rhodesia, and Congress has defied United Nations sanctions by authorizing continued importation of the ore. A lower "chemical-grade" ore, used in pigments and the chemical industry, is found in many foreign lands, but industry shuns it for making stainless steel because of the high costs involved in utilizing it. If new technology lowered these costs, the whole picture would change.

Besides chromium, industry depends on a whole family of other specialty metals that give desired properties to steel. Four important steel "vitamins," all used in modest but growing amounts, are molybdenum, vanadium, cobalt, and columbium. World reserves of molybdenum, which imparts strength and corrosion resistance, are considered adequate through at least the end of this century. Half of these reserves are in the U.S., which exports the metal. In contrast, the U.S. has few high-grade deposits of *vanadium,* which among other things increases the strength of structural steel. But vanadium is actually more abundant in the earth's crust than copper, and if necessary the U.S. could rely on low-grade domestic supplies.

This may never be the case with *cobalt,* a rare metal seldom found in this country. Cobalt is essential for electromagnets, and it is also used in heat-resistant turbine blades as well as in paints and ceramics; the world's biggest source is Zaïre, where the metal is a byproduct of copper mining. If no new sources are developed, cobalt could become scarce before the end of this century. But chances are good that the new laterite nickel mines, where cobalt is also present, will be able to make up any deficiency.

Columbium, also called niobium, is used in turbine blades and rocket nozzles as well as other heat-resistant applications. If the electric-utility industry ever switches to the compact cryogenic generating plants and underground transmission systems now being developed, demand for the metal could soar. The U.S. imports all its columbium—Brazil is the largest source—but a doubling of price could make this country self-sufficient because low-grade deposits do exist here. World reserves are adequate well beyond the year 2000.

What Platinum Does for Air Pollution

Unless there are some pleasant surprises, the world may become pinched for six other metals during the next hundred years. According to the Bureau of Mines, worldwide *gold* reserves will be adequate to the end of the century only if total demand is at the low end of its range of forecasts. World *platinum* reserves, at first glance, seem more than sufficient to meet prospective demand for that period. But this prognosis excludes two developments that could greatly expand usage. One is the development of economically competitive fuel cells for making electricity, and the other is the use of platinum to reduce air pollution in automobile exhausts. Ford Motor Co. already has signed up with South Africa for a large amount of platinum to assure a supply if it is needed for emission-control systems. For the same reason, Chrysler Corp. has been in discussions with South Africa and the Soviet Union.

The situation in *silver* looks more worrisome. World reserves may prove "seriously deficient" during the next three decades, the Bureau of Mines warns. Aside from its uses in silverware, jewelry, and coinage, silver is increasingly used by the electronics industry and in photography. At the moment there is no satisfactory substitute for silver in photographic film and papers: this use accounts for a fourth of U.S. silver consumption. Some of the photographic silver is recycled in developing laboratories, but more than half is dissipated to photo albums and wallets across the land. Domestic mines supply only a fourth of U.S. needs.

At the moment, the market is glutted with *mercury.* Since the mid-1960's, the price of a seventy-six-pound flask in New York has fallen from $725 to as low as $150. One reason is that the chlorine-making industry, whose use of mercury in its production process has accounted for a fourth of U.S. consumption, has been switching away from it because of the controversy over water pollution and the poisoning of marine life.

But the fact remains that mercury is one of the rarest of the commonly used base metals, and it is irreplaceable in many uses. No other metal combines its high specific gravity, its electrical conductivity, and its ability to flow at ordinary temperatures. Sometime around the turn of the century, world demand might very well get ahead of supply. Mercury, says M.I.T. geologist Patrick Hurley, "is really scarce and there is no way to expand reserves of this metal. When it's gone it's gone."

Tin may also become troublesome. Present world reserves, mainly in Thailand, Malaysia, Indonesia, and Bolivia, could turn out to be inadequate before the year 2000. Substitution could stretch the supply, of course. Over a third of the metal is used in making tin-plated steel, mainly for cans, and the U.S. can industry has begun marketing a tin-free container for beverages. But there is no satisfactory substitute for tin in making solder, and tin is essential in making bronze and pewter. Hardly any has been found in the U.S.

World reserves of *tungsten,* another vital metal, have increased over the past two decades, but only modestly. Used in steel armor plate since World War I, tungsten is also the most heat-resistant of all metals. Only 10 percent of tungsten is used for light-bulb filaments in the U.S. By far the major use is for the cutting edges of machine tools and drill bits. Titanium carbide might substitute for tungsten in the event of future scarcity. But in some tools, at least, there would be a loss of machining speed and, as a result, lower productivity. Recently, about half of this country's tungsten has come from domestic sources, but U.S. reserves are not large. World reserves, three-quarters of which are in mainland China, also seem far too low to meet anticipated global demand, and the U.S. Government foresees a possible "tight supply situation" as early as the mid-1980's.

What Do You Do With All That Rock?

The world's exploitable metal resources may eventually turn out to be far larger than any current figures on reserves suggest. This is an especially strong possibility for metals to which the Lasky theory—i.e., greater abundance as lower-grade ores are tapped—may apply. These include lead, zinc, nickel, columbium, and titanium as well as copper. But there are ominous possibilities of environmental devastation in moving more and more rock to produce a given amount of metal. David B. Brooks, a mineral economist in Canada's Department of Energy, Mines and Resources, considers the potential pollution of air and water and the general disturbance of the landscape "frightening."

Unless environmental damage is minimized, therefore, public opinion may bar the way to a lot of metal. Even with today's grades of ore, such as the 0.7 percent copper ore mined in the American Southwest, the environmental impact can be enormous. The most conspicuous effect is the creation of a huge man-made canyon that keeps getting wider and deeper as the years go by. The volume of rock blasted and moved is staggering. In an older mine, it is not uncommon to remove more than two and a half tons of overburden for each ton of ore. All together, the mine may move more than 500 pounds of rock in order to wind up with one pound of copper.

Much of the waste material winds up in huge overburden dumps around the fringes of these man-made canyons. About 99 percent of the rest winds up as tailings after the metal-bearing particles are removed in the concentration process that precedes smelting. The water used in this process can pollute streams. The tailing dumps themselves can be huge eyesores, and wind can blow their powdery material about. Nor does the potential damage stop there. Like nickel, zinc, lead, and some other metals, copper occurs as a sulphide compound, and this means that large amounts of sulphur oxides can be emitted into the air by smelters.

The important news, however, is that much of this environmental damage can be mitigated at an acceptable cost. A visit to Kennecott Copper Corp.'s Bingham Canyon mine in Utah, biggest in North America, and to its nearby concentrators, smelter, and refinery, illustrates some of the possibilities. Many environmentalists would be surprised to find the pit itself far from ugly. Its concentric tiers, with electric ore trains moving to and fro, suggest a mammoth version of an ancient Greek amphitheatre carved into a hillside. The over-burden dumps are ugly, but could someday be regraded and planted. The pit itself could possibly become a recreational lake.

At the concentrators fifteen miles away, Kennecott takes considerable care with tailings. These are carried in slurry form to a 5,300-acre pond that is sprayed, when dust threatens to blow, by aircraft carrying a polymer or other chemicals that coat the powdery material. In an experimental program, the Bureau of Mines has been making bricks from the tailings, and the Utah highway department plans to take some of the material for fill. No eyesore, the tailings pond looks like a drained extension of nearby Great Salt Lake.

The real environmental challenge is posed by the copper smelter. Kennecott says that it already removes 60 percent of the sulphur dioxide. But it claims not to know at this time how it can modify its smelter, at a bearable cost, to achieve the further reduction that the federal Environmental Protection Agency has proposed. The copper industry has warned that it may cost $600 million to comply with EPA criteria, which it calls excessively strict. If all else fails, says President Frank R. Milliken, Kennecott might have to ship its copper concentrates to smelters outside the U.S. Some copper companies are shifting to new processes, such as "flash-smelting," and experimenting with processes in which the metal is chemically leached from the ore. The change-over to new technologies, assuming they work, will not be cheap.

Someday, leaching might eliminate both the mine and the smelter, and thereby remove most of the objections of environmentalists. Copper men envision so-called *in situ* extraction in which the metal-bearing rock would never leave the ground. Instead, treated water would be pumped in, and the metal would be pumped out in a chemical solution from which it could be separated electrolytically. Some industry spokesmen caution, however, that large-scale mining *in situ* is a long way off.

Stepping Up the Ore Hunt

Today's geologists have an armamentarium of techniques and ore-sensing devices unknown a generation ago. Many of the devices, of course, are refinements of the airborne magnetometers, gravity meters, and spectroscopic equipment that have been in use for some time. One of the most important innovations is induced polarization, a method of passing an electrical current through the ground to detect sulphides of various metals. Where previous methods detected only sulphides in high concentrations, induced polarization has helped geologists locate lower concentrations, including the new copper deposits in British Columbia.

Despite all the improved techniques, there is some evidence that metallic ores are becoming harder to find, at least in this country. Ian MacGregor, chairman of American Metal Climax, says there are three times as many people looking for metal in the western U.S. as there were in 1955. He adds, however, that the estimated value of all the minerals discovered has been running only about 50 percent greater than in the late 1950's.

In many parts of the world, however, the new theory of continental drift may make some metals easier to find in the years to come. During the last decade geology has been revolutionized by the notion, increasingly borne out by evidence, that the earth's crust is composed of large plates slowly moving about. These plates collide to produce mountains like the Himalayas or slide under one another to form the deep ocean trenches that occur around the rim of the Pacific and elsewhere.

The whole theory is too new to be credited with any specific ore discoveries. But Philip W. Guild of the U.S. Geological Survey, who has studied the relationship of metallic deposits to continental drift, sees great significance in the fact that the copper deposits found off Southeast Asia in recent years happen to be near so-called "consuming" areas, where thin oceanic plates are slowly sliding beneath the plates on which Indonesia, the Philippines, and other island chains rest. Nobody knows exactly how these copper deposits were formed. One possibility, Guild believes, is that as the lower plate plunged deep beneath the upper one, part of it melted. The heated rock, being lighter in weight, rose through the upper plate carrying metallic compounds with it. While porphyry copper seems to fit most neatly into the new theory, other studies show that the continental-drift theory may also help in finding other metals, including tin and tungsten.

Billions Worth of Mud

A different kind of payoff is possible in "accreting" zones such as the Red Sea, where continental plates are slowly moving apart. There, new material has been extruded from below to fill the gap between plates, creating sediments rich in iron, zinc, copper, lead, silver, and gold. Studies of the feasibility of dredging these sediments are being carried out by West Germany's Preussag A.G. Not counting iron, the metals under the Red Sea may be worth $2.5 billion.

Continental drift may also account for the deposit of manganese nodules on the deep floors of the oceans over millions of years. Commercial mining of these deposits, which has aroused a lot of excitement for a decade, may become a reality before long. At two U.S. companies, Tenneco and Kennecott, officials say they expect to be selling metal made from the nodules by the end of the decade. The interest lies not so much in the manganese that is the most prominent metal in the potato-sized nodules, but in the nickel and copper that are also present, along with cobalt and up to thirty other metals.

"Contrary to much of the romantic reporting of the past," says John F. Flipse, president of the Tenneco subsidiary that has been studying the nodules for a decade, "the deep ocean floor is not uniformly coated with untold riches." But it does possess, Flipse says, "specific deposits of high-quality ores in realistic concentrations." The Tenneco subsidiary, Deepsea Ventures, has developed a method of collecting the nodules from depths as great as 20,000 feet, as well as a process for separating the various metals. Both Tenneco and Kennecott expect to mine beneath the Pacific Ocean off the West Coast.

The biggest problem may be international law rather than technology or economics; there is no clear-cut international or domestic body of law to protect a particular company's claim in international waters. The United Nations has scheduled a conference next year to take up the problem. The companies say they may go ahead with their deep-sea mining plans if the U.N. fails to come up with a satisfactory solution—provided the U.S. Congress will enact some sort of interim protection for them. Some metal companies are pointedly staying out of deep-ocean mining until they see firmer financial evidence that it can compete with land mining.

Incentives For Using Scrap Metal

There is another metal "mine" all around us, of course: the myriad used objects that we dump somewhere instead of recycling. The Scandinavian countries, Britain, West Germany, and Japan all melt down a larger portion of their old metal than the U.S. does. For all the attention it receives, the ecology movement has done little to improve our performance. All the aluminum beer and soft drink cans brought into voluntary recycling centers, for example, represent about a tenth of current production.

Economic incentives, rather than ecological zeal, are probably the way to get more used metal back into the system. For such items as beverage containers, a mandatory deposit system would bring back a lot more cans, or, alternatively, induce the public to use returnable bottles that need only to be cleaned and refilled. But the biggest hope may lie in revising the unfair freight rates and tax laws that put recycled metal at a disadvantage in competing with virgin metal made from ore. For example, virgin metal benefits from depletion allowances of 15 or 22 percent given to the mining industry. M. J. Mighdoll, executive vice president of the National Association of Secondary Materials Industries, which represents scrap processors and users, does not advocate repeal of these allowances. Instead, he has proposed an equivalent tax credit for scrap processors, which would be passed on to customers in the form of lower prices. "If economic impediments were changed," says Mighdoll, "it could turn things around."

Some authorities believe a big increase in recycling is merely a question of time. The Club of Rome study contains an "alternative" computer model under which world industry would become sustainable for the long-range future provided certain criteria were met. These include a curb on pollution, stabilization of population, and recycling programs that would reduce by three-quarters the virgin resources needed per unit of industrial output. No country today comes near meeting the recycling criterion. But Carl Rampacek, who heads research on recycling processes in the Bureau of Mines, believes it "quite likely" that the U.S. would be able to recycle three-quarters of its metal in another ten or fifteen years if necessary. One of the biggest metal mines, he notes, is municipal waste.

But long before cities get around to installing mechanized systems for recovering metal from trash, a better job could be done on such easily recyclable objects as automobiles. Shredders that chew up old cars and magnetically separate out steel scraps have proliferated around the U.S. since the mid-1960's. Now scrap processors are showing interest in a low-cost system, under development by the Bureau of Mines, for mechanically separating other metals from the nonferrous material rejected by the shredders.

It seems almost utopian to talk of an entire world economy organized to recycle at least three-fourths of its metal. To some geologists who worry about impending shortages of metallic ore, it also sounds visionary to talk of achieving high living standards in underdeveloped countries that now use relatively little metal. Even with a lot of recycling, says Preston Cloud of the University of California at Santa Barbara, it would take a huge "standing stock" of metal in circulation to bring the entire world up to, say, a Western European living standard.

According to Cloud's calculations, the world population of seven billion foreseen by around the year 2000 would need a pool of 60 billion tons of steel, or 140 times as much as the entire globe now produces in a year. Cloud sees no great difficulty in finding enough iron in the ground to create that pool, but he finds the prospects dimmer with copper, lead, zinc, and tin. For these, he says, the "standing stock" would have to be far larger than total world reserves at the present time—fifteen times as large in the case of tin.

"Running Without a Governor"

But there are more optimistic voices, too. Vincent E. McKelvey, director of the U.S. Geological Survey, believes that mankind can meet its mineral needs for "millennia" to come. McKelvey concedes that an eventual cutback in industrial production might prove necessary if mankind fails to develop an abundant new source of energy. But he also believes there are vast mineral deposits that remain undiscovered, as well as huge quantities of "paramarginal" and "submarginal" resources that could also be tapped if necessary.

The optimists' strongest argument, of course, is that enough metal has always turned up until now, at prices that usually have risen no faster than prices in general. "We have never run out of any mineral, though some have become a little scarcer," says James Boyd, executive director of the National Commission on Materials Policy. Established by a 1970 act of Congress, the commission is studying the nation's entire materials needs in the years ahead, and next June will produce recommendations on how the country can meet them.

For the rest of this century, it is fairly clear, the world will somehow get most of the metals it needs. But this is scant comfort to those who take a longer view. Even if energy imposes no constraint, worldwide metal consumption cannot go on increasing for very many centuries at its present rate. Joseph Fisher, president of Resources for the Future, Inc., a nonprofit research organization based in Washington, refuses to count himself among the alarmists. But, he adds, "there's a feeling, which I share, that the thing may be running without a governor."

Pollution

Introduction

The Toxic Substances Control Act requires the Environmental Protection Agency to "compile, keep current, and publish a list of each chemical substance which is manufactured, imported, or processed in the United States." The April, 1977, list included in three volumes, contains over 30,000 chemical substances with their registry numbers. One can imagine that these three volumes are much less interesting for most of us to read than is a very large phone book. But behind those names and formulae are countless stories of utmost interest and concern. Increasingly, industrialized societies are becoming forced to deal with the uncertainties of various types of chemical contamination.

The direct toxic effect on humans is where our concern usually begins and ends. But the indirect effects, in the long run, may be worse. Chemicals with which our cells have had no evolutionary experience now reach from pole to pole and all the way around the globe. But as ubiquitous as pollutants are, the environments of industrialized nations tend to be polluted the most. Even now in the U.S., huge quantities of drinking water are loaded with carcinogens from both the industrial processes and their products. The environments of underdeveloped countries, on the other hand, have problems long associated with civilization—lack of technology or the will to provide adequate waste disposal and healthful water supplies.

The economic costs of pollution can only be estimated. In 1970 air pollution damage was estimated at $12.3 billion. Of this total, the damage to plant life cost around $132 million. The health cost estimate ranged widely, between $62 and $311 million. This seems high, but it is really insignificant when one considers the health costs for the most intimate type of air pollutant, cigarette smoke. In 1970 the health cost due to smoking was estimated to be $4.23 billion. This included heart as well as lung problems, for the heart is the most vulnerable organ to low level exposure to carbon monoxide.

But how does one put a money cost on an acid rain or a temperature inversion in Fairbanks or kepone in the James River? For that matter, what price tag can be attached to the anxiety surrounding the two pack smoker whose lung has just been removed or whose second heart attack has occurred? Of course there is no meaningful price tag.

Checklists of pollutants and their price tags could be extended far beyond the 30,000 listed chemicals. The readings in this section merely touch on some of the major categories of concern: pesticides, oil, heat pollution and the degradation of ozone. But there is no reading about the ultimate polluting activity, which we seldom acknowledge—war. I suspect we tend to put the destruction and the pollution potential of war to the backs of our minds for a very simple reason—it is too horrible to think about for very long. Barry Commoner once described a cartoon he had seen of an old lady in an art gallery seated before a painting which depicted a scene of immense destruction. The old lady was copying from the original, except that her canvas was filled with a small bird from one corner of the painting. Her copy ignored the utter destruction all around. We tend to "paint the little bird" in these times, which is quite understandable, for with the horrible balance of nuclear terror, not to mention the chemical and biological warfare arsenal, all forms of life on earth are threatened.

The first reading of this section (reading 23) is a report on the status of some of the various environmental crises both past and present. The remaining five readings deal with some specific problems: problems of pesticides (reading 24), of oil (25 and 26) of soil pollution (27) and even the assortment of trash at sea (28). Finally, there is a specific account of what happens to our upper protective layer, the ozone, when certain fluorocarbons are set free (29).

In all likelihood, lists of toxic chemicals will get longer, estimates of monetary costs, including health costs, will go up, and cost/benefit analyses will be developed and debated. In the long run Americans will have to face the fact that industrialized societies are fresh out of sinks and that the externalized costs of industry will have to be paid. But in the final analysis, we need to remind ourselves that our insatiable appetites as consumers, however much those appetites have been whetted by advertising, place the responsibility for our fate and that of our children squarely on our own shoulders.

Whatever Happened to the Cranberry Crisis?

A Status Report on the Great Environmental Controversies

John F. Henahan

Just before Thanksgiving in 1959, Americans were told that the cranberries they expected to serve with the holiday turkey might be contaminated by a chemical weed killer known to cause cancer in animals. Hardly anyone remembers that the name of the chemical was aminotriazole, but nearly everyone remembers the "cranberry crisis."

It was the first of a series of potential environmental catastrophes which have popped via the news media into the public consciousness with increasing and relentless frequency. For example, attendees at a meeting of the American Chemical Society in San Francisco last August heard a University of California scientist warn that a fireproofing chemical used in large amounts in children's pajamas might cause cancer in those children. At the same meeting, scientists alerted their colleagues to the fact that some California wines were laced with large concentrations of poisonous and possibly cancer-causing arsenic, and that cancer-causing chemicals (carcinogens) were found in several commercial lawn and garden sprays.

As each of these new and potentially deadly encroachments on our health and environment works its way up the scare scale, it supplants—in the public's mind at least—other crises that have emerged in the last twenty years or so. In 1964, the discovery of DDT's toxicity caused Rachel Carson's fears of a silent spring. In the early 1970s, mercury was revealed as threatening serious damage to the brains and bodies of this and future generations, and the frightening dangers of asbestos were publicly acknowledged. What about those crises of yesteryear? Can we stop worrying about them? Or are they still around, silently threatening us and our children with premature death? What, for example, ever happened to the cranberry crisis?

In retrospect, it doesn't look nearly so frightening as it did when then Secretary of Health, Education and Welfare Arthur Flemming announced that two shipments of cranberries from the states of Washington and Oregon contained possibly harmful levels of aminotriazole. Because animal tests showed that the weed killer caused thyroid cancer, he recommended that cranberries from those states be taken off the supermarket shelves. The move seemed reasonable enough from a bureaucratic and health point of view, but it left shoppers with no way of telling whether their Thanksgiving cranberry sauce originated in Oregon or in a "safe" state, such as New Jersey. Then, just three days before the holiday, Flemming announced that the Department of Health, Education and Welfare had developed techniques for certifying cranberry batches as good or bad. By that time, however, much of the public had decided either to abstain from cranberries until the fuss blew over or to take their chances with the risk of cancer.

The cranberry scare now seems more of a nuisance than an environmental crisis. Cranberry growers felt a slight decline in their business for several months after the aminotriazole ban, but by the following Thanksgiving, Americans had

John F. Henahan is a free-lance science reporter who lives in California.

gotten over their cranbery phobia. And although the herbicide could no longer be used on food crops of any type, the growing demand for it as a weed control for roadsides, parks, and railroad rights-of-way easily offset the temporary losses experienced by aminotriazole's two manufacturers. In fact, the cranberry crisis might never have occurred if farmers in Washington and Oregon had followed the instructions on the aminotriazole bags and applied the weed killer *after* the berries were removed from the bushes instead of *before*.

Verdict: *The cranberry crisis is over.*

Was Rachel Carson Right?

Whether Rachel Carson was right when she warned about the perils of the insecticide DDT in *Silent Spring* has still not been completely resolved. But she might as well have been. Since her book appeared in 1962, use of DDT in this country has dwindled to a few select applications. Previously it had been sprayed indiscriminately from one end of the biosphere to the other. The series of actions against DDT, which began even before the book appeared, were based on findings that in some cases went well beyond Carson's predictions.

Unassailable evidence suggested that DDT was being carried by air, sea, and living organisms to areas as remote from the original spray site as the South Pole. The persistence of DDT, which made it so useful for the long-term control of mosquitoes in malaria areas, was also causing a long-term buildup in the fatty tissues of man and animals. The buildup started early: infants received their first taste of DDT in their mother's milk. Insects, on the other hand, were developing resistance to DDT, and each time a larger killing dose was aimed at the insects in the fields, the potential threat to man and animals also increased.

Researchers soon found that virtually all terrestrial organisms had to some extent been touched by DDT. It decreased photosynthetic processes in phytoplankton and they could no longer produce enough oxygen for fish to breathe. It blocked hatching in fish and sometimes built up to lethal levels in the brains of migrating birds. DDT, by reducing the thickness of bird's eggshells, threatened the existence of ospreys, sparrowhawks, pelicans, and other birds that feed on animals contaminated with DDT.

No proof is yet available that DDT is an immediate threat to human health. A few successful suicide attempts and a number of accidental deaths have been attributed to the injection of large amounts of DDT; there have also been a few cases that indicate that large doses will cause tremors and other symptoms of nerve damage. Yet, although millions of people in malaria areas and many workers in DDT plants were exposed to relatively high concentrations of DDT for as long as twenty years, the increased exposure has apparently had no adverse health effects to date. Critics of the DDT ban, including Dr. Thomas Jukes of the University of California at Berkeley, point out that for many years some chemical plant workers were taking in a daily dose of DDT approximately 1250 times greater than what the average American was absorbing in the late sixties.

Whether DDT can or will cause cancer in man is still very difficult to pin down. Some evidence suggests that it causes tumors in rats, but probably not in other animals, including monkeys and chickens. Like other chemical carcinogens, DDT may require an incubation period of twenty years or more before the cancer it produces becomes evident. If so, those cancers may just now be starting to appear. We may *never* know if DDT causes cancer in man, because everyone's fatty tissue contains some of the insecticide. Thus, we have no uncontaminated control population against which to measure its cancer-causing effect. Also, many of those most extensively exposed to DDT in farm and orchard were migrant workers who have now scattered beyond the reach of adequate medical follow-up.

Dr. Jukes says that the DDT boycott was chiefly an expression of "environmental chic" on the part of prosperous urban dwellers whose concern about the demise of the songbirds ignored the need for DDT among "the inarticulate majority of the world's people . . .who are struggling against disease and hunger." He argues that while DDT is not demonstrably harmful to human health, it *has* saved 5 million lives in underdeveloped areas and prevented 100 million illnesses since it was introduced in 1942. Dr. Jukes cites recent evidence from Cornell University that the thinning of eggshells was probably caused not by DDT but rather by other environmental contaminants, including mercury, or by one of the more recent worldwide pollutants, the polychlorinated biphenyls (PCBs).

The ban has not only lowered the environmental hazard associated with DDT; it has also left its mark on the manufacturers who produced it as well as on the farmers who saw it as a cheap and efficient way to kill pests and increase crop yields. Production of DDT in the United States dropped from a peak of 188 million pounds in 1963 to about 40 million pounds in 1974, and most of that is exported to malaria zones. Cotton producers, by far the largest users of DDT in this country, now complain that since they have been forced to control the boll weevil and other cotton pests with other, more expensive insecticides, cotton prices have risen and crop yields have gone down. Farm workers in California and other large agricultural areas are equally unhappy about the DDT ban because they know that the organophosphate insecticides that have replaced it are far more toxic than DDT. Although the organophosphates are quickly destroyed by rain and other environmental factors, they come from the same molecular family as the nerve gases in this country's chemical weapons stockpile. Not surprisingly, misuse of the organophosphates has sickened or killed children, spray-plane pilots, and farm workers who inadvertently absorbed them by mouth or through the skin.

In spite of those considerations, and the continuing objections to the ban by Dr. Jukes and Nobel Prizewinner Norman Borlaug (of Green Revolution fame), DDT will probably never again be used except on a spot basis in the United States. That happened recently in Colorado, when the Environmental Protection Agency said the state could use DDT to eliminate an outbreak of plague-carrying rat lice. Nevertheless, each time a community decides that a quick attack with DDT is needed to wipe out an invasion of gypsy moths or other pests, it must fight its way past local environmentalists and government restrictions. On that basis, a DDT revival on a national scale is almost inconceivable.

Verdict: *Rachel Carson may have been right. But while DDT's effects on human health seem negligible, its long-term effects may still be felt.*

The Cyclamate Scare

Artificial "cyclamate" sweeteners were banned by the Food and Drug Administration ten years after the cranberry crisis. Before the federal proscription, cyclamates generated a $500 million-a-year industry in the United States and were being ingested at a rapid rate in diet drinks, jams, jellies, children's vitamin preparations, desserts, ice cream, canned fruits, and other products. The ban was emphatic, but the FDA ruling softened the blow by allowing supermarkets, as well as food and beverage producers, to use up their backlog of cyclamate-containing products.

The sweetener, manufactured largely by Abbott Laboratories in Chicago, had come under suspicion well before the actual ban; animal studies carried out by the FDA suggested that it caused "teratogenic" abnormalities in chick embryos similar to those observed in children of pregnant women who had been taking the tranquilizer thalidomide. In addition, evidence had accumulated that cyclamate might have long-range genetic effects, since the substance apparently damaged chromosomes in the cells of animals and human beings. What ultimately led to the ban, however, was Abbott's own report to the FDA that bladder tumors developed in rats consuming the sweetner in daily amounts equivalent to what would have been found in 500 eight-ounce bottles of a typical diet cola.

Since then, both Abbott Laboratories and independent scientists have begun to question whether the evidence was sufficient. Abbott has been asking the FDA to lift the ban since 1973, arguing that its more recent long-term studies with various laboratory animals indicate that, at reasonable intake levels, cyclamates are perfectly safe.

The company was further encouraged in February of 1976 when a careful and critical analysis of all available data, by a panel of scientists commissioned by the National Cancer Institute, concluded that *"the present evidence does not establish the carcinogenicity of cyclamate or its principal metabolite cyclohexylamine."* The "cyclohexylamine" alluded to studies which indicated that after the cyclamate is broken down in the body to cyclohexylamine, the latter substance might also cause cancer or other adverse effects on health.

In its critique of several inconclusive animal tests, the NCI panel noted that although the earlier Abbott studies showed bladder tumors occurring in 12 of 80 rats, cyclamate alone was not necessarily the cause. Abbott scientists fed the rats mixtures of cyclamate, cyclohexylamine, and saccharin. Saccharin was added because it was contained in Abbott's commercial cyclamate formulations. The scientists on the NCI panel also noted the absence of conclusive evidence that cyclamate caused bladder tumors in hamsters, dogs, or monkeys, or in diabetics who consumed more of the artificial sweetener than average individuals. Rats, the scientists suggested, might be especially susceptible to its effects. They did not, however, ask that the cyclamate ban be lifted, pointing out that major uncertainties remained about the possible genetic or teratogenic effects of cyclamate or cyclohexylamine.

The NCI report was strong enough in some areas and vague enough in others so that each side in the controversy interpreted it as vindication of its own position. Convinced that the FDA would finally rescind the ban, Abbott petitioned the agency again, and the company was fairly confident that the sweetener would be back on the market before the end of 1976. But, in October, the FDA formally rejected the Abbott petition on grounds that cyclamate was still not safe enough for large-scale use as a sweetener. Abbott asked for a hearing before the FDA, and will go to the courts if that doesn't work.

Not that the company's fortunes will rise or fall on the basis of what the FDA finally decides. Just before the ban, annual sales of cyclamate reached about $8.5 million, or roughly one percent of the company's business. In addition, Abbott still has a "small slice" of the 5 to 8 million pounds of cyclamate being sold in thirty other countries, where it is considered safe. In Canada, cyclamate can be sold only as a table sweetener, but in Germany and other European countries, cyclamate appears in beverages and food products, just as it did in the United States before the ban.

Verdict: *The cyclamate crisis is over in the United States, and the sweetener may eventually win a clean bill of health. If the cyclamates do cause cancer or genetic defects in human beings, they are probably doing so in Germany and other countries where they are now being sold.*

The Mercury Crisis

In August 1976, twenty-five Indians who fished in the James Bay area of Quebec showed definite signs of mercury poisoning, proof that the mercury crisis of the early 1970s is still with us. It first made itself known in North America when a chemist from the University of Western Ontario found that fish from Lake St. Clair (near Detroit) contained mercury levels close to the levels found in fish eaten by mercury-poisoned residents of the two Japanese villages of Minimata and Niigata. The mercury in the Japanese incident was a byproduct of a plastics plant, and before the source was cut off scores of Japanese men, women, and children died, became insane, or developed neurological symptoms of mercury poisoning. The same findings in fish and other foodstuffs from lakes, rivers, and farms throughout the United States prompted quick controls on mercury pollution in those areas and, in some cases, fishing bans in the affected waters. The mercury crisis also inspired federal regulations on the mercury content of tuna and swordfish, both of which were found to contain abnormally high levels of the metal.

As the mercury crisis has disappeared from the headlines, earlier control measures seem to have been forgotten or deliberately overlooked. Most California fish markets sell swordfish containing higher than permissible levels of mercury. The government has moved with only limited success against the use of agricultural fungicides containing mercury, and in March 1976, the Environmental Protection Agency backed off from banning use of such fungicides in paints. Part of their reason was that the three manufacturers involved said that the ban would cost the jobs of forty employees and wipe out expected sales of $4 million in 1976.

But even if stringent controls on all sources of mercury pollution were strictly enforced, many scientists suspect that mercury already in the water supply will remain a threat for years to come. The reason is that when "inorganic" mercury salts enter a lake or river, they sink to the bottom, where they are slowly converted by microbial action into the "organic" methyl mercury form which killed scores of Japanese twenty years ago and poisoned the Quebec Indians last year. Once converted to the organic methyl mercury form, the poisons move up the food chain from phytoplankton to fish to man. That could mean that microbes will be converting the 200,000 pounds of mercury now resting on the bottom of Lake St. Clair alone into methyl mercury for the next 5000 years. And the mercury now there cannot be easily removed, since dredging operations would disseminate it more widely.

Verdict: *The mercury crisis may be forgotten, but it is not over.*

The Ozone Layer Controversy

"We can no longer be so easily described as environmental kooks," said Dr. F. Sherwood Rowland last fall, in response to a series of scientific findings and federal actions that seemed to vindicate his earlier warning that the stratospheric layer of ozone which normally shields us from harmful solar radiation was gradually being eaten away by the aerosol propellants known as chlorofluorocarbons.

Scientific backing for the controversial prediction that Dr. Rowland and his colleague Dr. Mario Molina made more than two years ago on purely theoretical grounds came last August from a committee appointed by the National Academy of Sciences to study the problem. Their report was followed within weeks by a statement from the Food and Drug Administration which proposed an "orderly phaseout of all non-essential uses of chlorofluorocarbon propellants in food, drug and cosmetic products." Soon after that, the Environmental Protection Agency called for a similar ban on pesticides which contained chlorofluorocarbon propellants.

The ozone layer controversy really began when Rowland and Molina, chemists at the University of California at Irvine, learned from other scientists that most chlorofluorocarbons produced so far are ending up in the atmosphere and will probably stay there for quite some time. That information set them to wondering what would happen if the relatively inert substances worked their way up into the ozone-rich stratosphere—some twenty miles above the earth—where they would be subject to attack by the sun's ultraviolet radiation. Rowland and Molina were particularly interested in the fate of chlorofluorocarbon-11 and chlorofluorocarbon-12, both of which are used as refrigerants and as the gaseous propellants for spray-can products.

Rowland and Molina were startled by the implications of their theoretical calculations, which indicated that when a chlorofluorocarbon molecule reaches the stratosphere and is attacked by ultraviolet radiation, it is broken down chemically and releases a chlorine atom. That in turn reacts with a single ozone molecule (composed of three oxygen atoms), setting off a chain reaction which doesn't stop until hundreds of thousands of other ozone molecules are destroyed.

Rowland and Molina theorized that if chlorofluorocarbon production were maintained at 1974 levels (about half a million tons a year), it would deplete the ozone layer from 7 to 14 percent by the year 2000. And if that trend should continue, the added ultraviolet radiation that got through to the earth's surface would destroy crops and probably interfere with world weather patterns. In addition, solid biological evidence suggested that an ozone depletion on that scale could increase skin cancer incidence among light-skinned individuals by 14 to 28 percent.

After the University of California at Irvine calculations appeared in *Nature* magazine in the summer of 1974, manufacturers of aerosols and aerosol products responded vigorously. They wouldn't hear of a chlorofluorocarbon ban, as Rowland had suggested, because the calculations were nothing more than a paper exercise in the industry's eyes. Further, they said, no real evidence had been offered that the heavy chlorofluorocarbon molecules ever reached the stratosphere, or, if they did, that they were destroying the ozone layer.

Industry's concern was understandable. In 1974, the chlorofluorocarbon and satellite industries employed more than a million people, and if the calculations of the two chemists were correct, they could seriously wound an industry that contributed an estimated $100 billion to the economy. Corporate giants, such as E. I. duPont de Nemours & Company, which sold $183 million worth of the propellants in 1974 (2.6 percent of its total sales), would undoubtedly weather the loss, but Racon, a smaller company, which derived 36 percent of its revenues from the chlorofluorocarbons, would not fare nearly as well if a ban were suddenly declared.

To counter the Rowland-Molina projections, the aerosol industry—most noticeably represented by duPont—came up with its own models of what might be happening to the chlorofluorocarbons. One alternative, now more or less debunked by laboratory findings and stratospheric measurements, proposed that after the aerosols are broken down by ultraviolet light, they react preferentially with other atmospheric components, rather than with the molecules of the ozone layer. However, after looking at all the evidence accumulated over the last two years, the NAS panel concluded that the chlorofluorocarbons were doing just about what the two California chemists predicted they would do.

The NAS committee report stopped short of recommending a ban on the aerosol propellants, suggesting that since the ozone layer would be depleted by only 0.2 percent in the next two years, and because many questions about the chemistry of the ozone layer were still unanswered, it would be safe to wait that long before implementing such a ban. However, the FDA and EPA actions, which are still subject to several months of public hearings on both sides of the question, make a ban a near certainty even before two years. Meanwhile, both government agencies call for interim warning labels on all products containing the chlorofluorocarbon propellants.

Even without the compulsions of a formal ban, a steady dropoff in chlorofluorocarbon production within the last year indicates that the industry has already been affected by what may be happening in the stratosphere. The American Can Company saw its spray can sales decline by 25 percent, while a company which made a billion valves for aerosol cans in 1975 cut production in 1976 by 40 percent. The scramble away from the chlorofluorocarbons is also evident in the trend toward roll-on deodorants and new kinds of dispensers, including pump tops and squeeze sprays. The switchover has meant increased profits for many other companies, including the Thiokol Corporation of Newton, Pennsylvania, which recently took orders for 25 million of its new non-pressurized trigger spray cans. Recognizing that the chlorofluorocarbons were no longer good business, the S. C. Johnson Company in Racine, Wisconsin, jumped the gun on the competition and announced with full-page newspaper ads that it was switching to hydrocarbon propellants, which presumably have no effect on the ozone layer. Finally, a duPont scientist recently conceded that his company is also looking for replacements for chlorofluorocarbons, but that the two most likely candidates discovered so far are too toxic to be considered for human use.

Verdict: *Look for a ban on chlorofluorocarbon aerosol propellants within two years. The detrimental effects of the millions of pounds of chlorofluorocarbons already en route to the stratosphere may not be felt for several decades.*

The Asbestos Time Bomb

Lodged in the lungs of nearly everyone breathing in today's industrial world are tiny fibers of asbestos which may represent one of the most frightening health hazards yet uncovered. Based on what has been learned from studies of asbestos workers over the last fifty years, the fibers could be the harbingers of a large-scale epidemic of lung cancer and an even more devastating malignancy known as mesothelioma.

Credit for sounding the asbestos alarm in this country goes to Dr. Irving Selikoff of the Mount Sinai School of Medicine of the City University of New York. About eight years ago, several studies carried out in this country, England, and South Africa convinced him that asbestos was not as inert and biologically harmless as originally believed.

Since the 1920s, we have known that asbestos workers employed in the industry for long periods of time were dying of asbestosis, a kind of pneumonia associated with a buildup of fibers in the workers lungs. Although asbestosis is not considered a malignant disease, the prognosis for asbestos workers began to look even worse in the 1930s, when physicians in several countries found that asbestos workers had about ten times the lung cancer risk other workers did. Lung cancer is extremely difficult to treat and is almost invariably fatal if not detected and treated at a very early stage. More bad news was yet to come. Asbestos workers were also dying of mesothelioma, a rare but deadly cancer which affects the lining surrounding the lungs and body cavity. Until it cropped up in asbestos workers, physicians infrequently encountered the disease.

Dr. Selikoff's own recent studies of 632 asbestos workers employed for various periods between 1943 and 1974 clearly implicate asbestos as a major cause of cancer. He found that 89 of the workers died of lung cancer, compared to an expected 12 deaths from the disease in the "normal" population. And in a group of 632, where *no* case of mesothelioma was expected, 35 died of the disease. More significant was the fact that even though many of the workers had been exposed to asbestos for periods of as little as a few months, they had apparently inhaled the seeds of cancerous conditions that flowered twenty to thirty years later. In spite of these ominous statistics, accumulated over a period of fifty years, the asbestos problem is only now beginning to be taken seriously.

"I can't explain that quiet period," Dr. Selikoff says. "The industry grew fivefold, but nothing was done to warn or protect the workers. No asbestos dust counts or other precautions were taken in asbestos plants. Unfortunately, now that we are finally aware of the dangers involved, we find that instead of a small problem, we have a huge problem."

What makes the asbestos problem so huge is that nearly everyone's body has been invaded by fibers from an industry which mines 3 to 4 million tons of asbestos every year. Asbestos is used in insulation for walls and furnaces, in fireproofing sprays for large skyscrapers, in floor and ceiling tiles, in automobile brake linings, in cement piping, for filtering beer and wine, and in scores of other applications.

The possibility that asbestos is contaminating people who never worked in the industry comes from studies in South Africa which clearly show that people who live near asbestos plants, or close relatives of employees who work there, have developed lung abnormalities and in some cases cancer. The circle of contamination may be widening still further. Asbestos fibers have been found in the air and water many large cities and almost universally in the lungs of their inhabitants.

Dr. Selikoff is concerned that even more asbestos will be spewed into the air we breathe as old buildings containing an estimated 25 million pounds of the mineral fibers are torn down or subjected to routine maintenance. Also, he says, another million workers in some 300,000 brake maintenance garages throughout the United States are exposed to daily doses of asbestos. After six years of litigation, Reserve Mining in Minnesota has been forced to stop dumping asbestos-containing tailing from its taconite iron ore mines into Lake Superior, as it has been doing at a 67,000-ton-a-day clip since 1955. Because of the company's contamination of 2000 square miles of Lake Superior with asbestos, Dr. William Nicholson, Dr. Selikoff's colleague at Mount Sinai, estimates that "the fibers ingested by persons in the Duluth area over a period of 15 to 17 years can be as many as workers inhale in their occupational experience."

To counter the rising levels of asbestos in the air both inside and outside asbestos plants, the EPA and other federal agencies have established new standards that limit asbestos concentrations to two fibers per cubic centimeter of air. However, Dr. Selikoff is disturbed that in spite of the large-scale contamination of Lake Superior, similar standards for water are being delayed by a debate now under way as to whether asbestos is as harmful when taken in with water as it is when inhaled into the lungs.

Further, he says that even with the new federal recommendations for "dust counts" and other protective measures, "virtually no inspections are carried out in asbestos working areas by the agencies who should be routinely doing those inspections."

Hit by a number of potentially costly lawsuits which hold that Johns-Manville Corporation, a major producer of asbestos products, failed to protect its employees and warn them about the hazards of asbestos, that company has initiated many stringent procedures which Selikoff says are the best in the business. They include ventilation hoods and air filters for catching asbestos fibers, protective masks and clothing, and other safety measures. The company also labels its asbestos products with warnings to the consumer of the potential hazard involved. Confident that the company can handle the asbestos problem, Johns-Manville has no plans to cut back production. In fact, spurred by an increasing demand for their products, they spent $75 million last year to expand mining and milling facilities in Asbestos, Quebec. But the asbestos time bomb has a long fuse, and the company's problems may not be over. As Roy Steinfurth, head of the Asbestos Workers and Insulators health hazard program, puts it: "We expect to see many more claims, because more people are dying of asbestos disease. We're just now starting to hear of cancer and asbestosis among guys who started working around World War II."

Dr. W. Clark Cooper, the California scientist who headed a National Academy of Science panel on asbestos five years ago, says that a shift to new insulation and fireproofing materials, along with recent government attempts to regulate asbestos emissions in plants, construction sites, and other chancy areas, have considerably improved things for the worker and the population at large in the period since the report was issued. However, he points out, we won't know how seriously the asbestos problem affects the rest of the population until scientists learn more about the effects of the lesser amounts of asbestos inhaled by non-asbestos workers or leached into the water supply from natural asbestos deposits. That will involve performing many autopsies, measuring the amount and location of the asbestos fiber, and then attempting to make some correlation between those levels and the cause of death.

Verdict: *The asbestos time bomb is still ticking.*

New Crises

The PCBs, used as coolants in electrical transformers and in other ways, permeate the earth and threaten afflictions ranging from acne to cancer. Toxic fire retardant PBBs were inadvertently mixed with animal feeds and may have contaminated much of the population of the State of Michigan, said Dr. Selikoff. Allied Chemical Corporation faces many multimillion-dollar suits because its insecticide Kepone has poisoned workers and contaminated the James River and other waterways. Recently the FDA saw fit to ban Red Dye No. 2 and Red Dye No. 4 as potential health hazards. Both have already been used widely as coloring agents in many foods, including margarine, maraschino cherries, and jelly beans. Also guilty or suspected of harming health and environment are chloroform, the dry-cleaning agent trichloroethylene, the plastic starting materials styrene and vinyl chloride, and the nitrosamines, compounds found as contaminants in several garden weed killers, and in several meat products.

All of the crises have many things in common. They usually involve chemicals found to be dangerous only after dissemination to the public at million- and even billion-pound levels. The Toxic Substances Control Act, signed last fall by President Ford, may change that situation. Before any substance is sold to consumers, companies will now be forced to show that it does not cause cancer. Each crisis usually reaches a point where environmental and health factors must be balanced against the need for the product in question. Is the elimination of body odor with aerosol sprays more important than keeping the ozone layer intact? Is maintaining the bird population as important as feeding the hungry and eliminating malaria in the jungles of Asia and India? Those answers, when complicated by the economic losses involved if a product is suddenly banned, do not come easily, but priorities must certainly be established.

Like asbestos, mercury, and DDT, the newly emerging crises are not to be dismissed lightly; but is the threat they pose diluted in the public's mind by a kind of crisis overkill? Possibly, says Dr. Selikoff, observing that when he walks through the halls of Mount Sinai, he is occasionally asked, "Well, what's the carcinogen of the week, doc?" Or is the awareness that so many things in our environment may cause cancer just too horrible to contemplate? Maybe, Dr. Selikoff says, but he believes that the crisis headlines underscore a hopeful new trend:

"We're in a new phase of research in which for the first time we're beginning to identify the causes of cancer. Whereas at one time cancer was thought to be an inevitable accompaniment of old age, we now realize that each cancer has a cause, environmental or otherwise. Any new cause of cancer may seem like bad news to some people, but it's the kind of bad news we have to have in order to get the good news."

The Effects of Pesticides

William A. Niering

The dramatic appearance of Rachel Carson's *Silent Spring* (1962) awakened a nation to the deleterious effects of pesticides. Our technology had surged ahead of us. We had lost our perspective on just how ruthlessly man can treat his environment and still survive. He was killing pesty insects by the trillions, but he was also poisoning natural ecosystems all around him. It was Miss Carson's mission to arrest this detrimental use of our technological achievements. As one might have expected, she was criticized by special vested industrial interests and, to some degree, by certain agricultural specialists concerned with only one aspect of our total environment. However, there was no criticism, only praise, from the nation's ecosystematically oriented biologists. For those who found *Silent Spring* too dramatic an approach to the problem, the gap was filled two years later by *Pesticides and the Living Landscape* (1964) in which Rudd further documented Miss Carson's thesis but in more academic style.

The aim of this chapter is to summarize some of the effects of two pesticides—insecticides and herbicides—on our total environment, and to point up research and other educational opportunities for students of environmental science. The insecticide review will be based on representative studies from the literature, whereas the herbicide review will represent primarily the results of the author's research and experience in the Connecticut Arboretum at Connecticut College. Although some consider this subject controversial, there is really no controversy in the mind of the author—the issue merely involves the sound ecological use of pesticides only where necessary and without drastically contaminating or upsetting the dynamic equilibrium of our natural ecosystems. I shall not consider the specific physiological effects of pesticides, but rather their effects on the total environment—plants, animals, soil, climate, man—the biotic and abiotic aspects.

Environmental science or ecosystematic thinking should attempt to coordinate and integrate all aspects of the environment. Although ecosystems may be managed, they must also remain in a relative balance or dynamic equilibrium, analogous to a spider's web, where each strand is intimately interrelated and interdependent upon every other strand.

The Impact of Insecticides

Ecologists have long been aware that simplifying the environment to only a few species can precipitate a catastrophe. Our highly mechanized agricultural operations, dominated by extensive acreages of one crop, encourage large numbers of insect pests. As insurance against insect damage, vast quantities of insecticides are applied with little regard for what happens to the chemical once it is on the land. Prior to World War II, most of our insecticides were nonpersistent organics found in the natural environment. For example, the pyrethrins were derived from dried chrysanthemum flowers, nicotine sulphate from tobacco, and rotenone from the tropical derris plants. However, research during World War II and thereafter resulted in a number of potent persistent chlorinated hydrocarbons (DDT, dieldrin, endrin, lindane, chlordane, heptachor and others) to fight the ever-increasing hordes of insects, now some 3000 species plaguing man in North America.

In 1964, industries in the United States produced 783 million lb. of pesticides, half insecticides and the other half herbicides, fungicides, and rodenticides. The application of these chemicals on the nation's landscape[1] has now reached the point where one out of every ten acres is being sprayed with an average of 4 lb. per acre (Anonymous, 1966).

Positive Effects of Target Organisms

That market yields and quality are increased by agricultural spraying appears to have been well documented. Data from the National Agricultural Chemical Association show net increased yields resulting in from $5.00 to $100.00 net gains per acre on such crops as barley, tomatoes, sugar beets, pea seed, and cotton seed. However, Rudd (1964) questions the validity of these figures, since there is no explanation just how they were derived. His personal observations on the rice crop affected by the rice leaf miner outbreak in California are especially pertinent. The insect damage was reported as ruining 10% to 20% of the crop. He found this to be correct for some fields, but most of the fields were not damaged at all. In this situation, the facts were incorrect concerning the pest damage. It appears that not infrequently repeated spraying applications are merely insurance sprays and in many cases actually unnecessary. Unfortunately, the farmer is being forced to this procedure in part by those demanding from agriculture completely insect-free produce. This has now reached ridiculous proportions. Influenced by advertising, the housewife now demands perfect specimens with no thought of a regard for how much environmental contamination has resulted to attain such perfection. If we could relax our standards to a moderate degree, pesticide contamination could be greatly reduced. Although it may be difficult to question that spraying increases yields and quality of the marketable products, there are few valid data available on how much spraying is actually necessary, how much it is adding to consumer costs, what further pests are aggravated by spraying, and what degree of resistance eventually develops.

---

1.   Dr. George Woodwell estimates that there are 1 billion lbs. of DDT now circulating in the biosphere.

Negative Effects on Nontarget Organisms

Although yields may be increased with greater margins of profit, according to available data, one must recognize that these chemicals may adversely affect a whole spectrum of nontarget organisms not only where applied but possibly thousands of miles from the site of application. To the ecologist concerned with the total environment, these persistent pesticides pose some serious threats to our many natural ecosystems. Certain of these are pertinent to review.

1. *Killing of nontarget organisms.* In practically every spray operation, thousands of nontarget insects are killed, many of which may be predators on the very organisms one is attempting to control. But such losses extend far beyond the beneficial insects. In Florida, an estimated 1,117,000 fishes of at least 30 species (20 to 30 tons), were killed with dieldrin, when sand flies were really the target organism. Crustaceans were virtually exterminated—the fiddler crabs survived only in areas missed by the treatment (Harrington and Bidlingmayer, 1958).

In 1963, there was a "silent spring" in Hanover, New Hampshire. Seventy per cent of the robin population—350 to 400 robins—was eliminated in spraying for Dutch elm disease with 1.9 lb. per acre DDT (Wurster et al., 1965). Wallace (1960) and Hickey and Hunt (1960) have reported similar instances on the Michigan State University and University of Wisconsin campuses. Last summer, at Wesleyan University, my students observed dead and trembling birds following summer applications of DDT on the elms. At the University of Wisconsin campus (61 acres), the substitution of methoxychlor has resulted in a decreased bird mortality. The robin population has jumped from three to twenty-nine pairs following the change from DDT to methoxychlor. Chemical control of this disease is often overemphasized, with too little attention directed against the sources of elm bark beetle. Sanitation is really the most important measure in any sound Dutch elm disease control program (Matthysse, 1959).

One of the classic examples involving the widespread destruction of nontarget organisms was the fire ant eradication program in our southern states. In 1957, dieldrin and heptochlor were aerially spread over two and one-half million acres. Wide elimination of vertebrate populations resulted; and recovery of some populations is still uncertain (Rudd, 1964). In the interest of science, the Georgia Academy of Science appointed an ad hoc committee to evaluate this control-eradication program (Bellinger et al., 1965). It found that reported damage to crops, wildlife, fish, and humans had not been verified, and concluded, furthermore, that the ant is not really a significant economic pest but a mere nuisance. Here was an example where the facts did not justify the federal expenditure of $2.4 million in indiscriminate sprays. Fortunately, this approach has been abandoned, and local treatments are now employed with Mirex, a compound with fewer side effects. Had only a small percentage of this spray expenditure been directed toward basic research, we might be far ahead today in control of the fire ant.

2. *Accumulation in the food chain.* The persistent nature of certain of these insecticides permits the chemical to be carried from one organism to another in the food chain. As this occurs, there is a gradual increase in the biocide at each higher trophic level. Many such examples have been reported in the literature. One of the most striking comes from Clear Lake, California, where a 46,000-acre warm lake,

north of San Francisco, was sprayed for pesty gnats in 1949, 1954, and 1957, with DDD, a chemical presumably less toxic than DDT. Analyses of the plankton revealed 250 times more of the chemical than originally applied, the frogs 2000 times more, sunfish 12,000, and the grebes up to an 80,000-fold increase (Cottam, 1965; Rudd, 1964). In 1954 death among the grebes was widespread. Prior to the spraying, a thousand of these birds nested on the lake. Then for 10 years no grebes hatched. Finally, in 1962, one nestling was observed, and the following year three. Clear Lake is popular for sports fishing, and the flesh of edible fish now caught reaches 7 ppm. which is above the maximum tolerance level set by the Food and Drug Administration.

In an estuarine ecosystem, a similar trend has been reported on the Long Island tidal marshes, where mosquito control spraying with DDT has been practiced for some 20 years (Woodwell et al., 1967). Here the food chain accumulation shows plankton 0.04 ppm, shrimp 0.16 ppm, minnows 1 to 2 ppm, and ring-billed gull 75.5 ppm. In general, the DDT concentrations in carnivorous birds were 10 to 100 times those in the fish they fed upon. Birds near the top of the food chain have DDT residues about a million times greater than concentration in the water. Pesticide levels are now so high that certain populations are being subtly eliminated by food chain accumulations reaching toxic levels.

3. *Lowered reproductive potential.* Considerable evidence is available to suggest a lowered reproductive potential, especially among birds, where the pesticide occurs in the eggs in sufficient quantities either to prevent hatching or to decrease vigor among the young birds hatched. Birds of prey, such as the bald eagle, osprey, hawks, and others, are in serious danger. Along the northeast Atlantic coast, ospreys normally average about 2.5 young per year. However, in Maryland and Connecticut, reproduction is far below this level. In Maryland, ospreys produce 1.1 young per year and their eggs contain 3 ppm DDT, while in Connecticut, 0.5 young ospreys hatch and their eggs contain up to 5.1 ppm DDT. These data indicate a direct correlation between the amount of DDT and the hatchability of eggs—the more DDT present in the eggs, the fewer young hatched (Ames, 1966). In Wisconsin, Keith (1964) reports 38% hatching failure in herring gulls. Early in the incubation period, gull eggs collected contained over 200 ppm DDT and its cogeners. Pheasant eggs from DDT-treated rice fields compared to those from unsprayed lands result in fewer healthy month-old chicks from eggs taken near sprayed fields. Although more conclusive data may still be needed to prove that pesticides such as DDT are the key factor, use of such compounds should be curtailed until it is proved that they are not the causal agents responsible for lowering reproductive potential.

4. *Resistance to sprays.* Insects have a remarkable ability to develop a resistance to insecticides. The third spray at Clear Lake was the least effective on the gnats, and here increased resistance was believed to be a factor involved. As early as 1951, resistance among agricultural insects appeared. Some of these include the codling moth on apples, and certain cotton, cabbage, and potato insects. Over 100 important insect pests now show a definite resistance to chemicals (Carson, 1962).

5. *Synergistic effects.* The interaction of two compounds may result in a third much more toxic than either one alone. For example, Malathion is relatively "safe" because detoxifying enzymes in the liver greatly reduce its toxic properties.

However, if some compound destroys or interrupts this enzyme system, as certain organic phosphates may do, the toxicity of the new combination may be increased greatly. Pesticides represent one of many pollutants we are presently adding to our environment. These subtle synergistic effects have opened a whole new field of investigation. Here students of environmental science will find many challenging problems for future research.

6. *Chemical migration.* After two decades of intensive use, pesticides are now found throughout the world, even in places far from any actual spraying. Penguins and crab-eating seals in the Antarctic are contaminated, and fish far off the coasts of four continents now contain insecticides ranging from 1 to 300 ppm in their fatty tissues (Anonymous, 1966).

The major rivers of our nation are contaminated by DDT, endrin, and dieldrin, mostly in the parts per trillion range. Surveys since 1957 reveal that dieldrin has been the main pesticide present since 1958. Endrin reached its maximum, especially in the lower Mississippi River, in the fall of 1963 when an extensive fish kill occurred and has since that time decreased. DDT and its cogeners, consistently present since 1958, have been increasing slightly (Breidenbach et al., 1967).

7. *Accumulation in the ecosystem.* Since chlorinated hydrocarbons like DDT are not readily broken down by biological agents such as bacteria, they may not only be present but also accumulate within a given ecosystem. On Long Island, up to 32 lb. of DDT have been reported in the marsh mud, with an average of 13 lb. presumed to be correlated with the 20 years of mosquito control spraying (Woodwell et al., 1967). Present in these quantities, burrowing marine organisms and the detritis feeders can keep the residues in continuous circulation in the ecosystem. Many marine forms are extremely sensitive to minute amounts of insecticides. Fifty per cent of a shrimp population was killed with endrin 0.6 parts per billion (ppb). Even 1 ppb will kill blue crabs within a week. Oysters, typical filter feeders, have been reported to accumulate up to 70,000 ppb. (Loosanoff, 1965). In Green Bay along Lake Michigan, Hickey and Keith (1964) report up to 0.005 ppm wet weight of DDT, DDE, and DDD in the lake sediments. Here the accumulation has presumably been from leaching or run-off from surrounding agricultural lands in Door County, where it is reported that 70,000 pounds of DDT are used annually. Biological concentration in Green Bay is also occurring in food chain organisms, as reported at Clear Lake, California. Accumulation of biocides, especially in the food chain, and their availability for recycling pose a most serious ecological problem.

8. *Delayed response.* Because of the persistent nature and tendency of certain insecticides to accumulate at toxic levels in the food chain, there is often a delayed response in certain ecosystems subjected either directly or indirectly to pesticide treatment. This was the case at Clear Lake, where the mortality of nontarget organisms occurred several years after the last application. This is a particularly disturbing aspect, since man is often the consumer organisms accumulating pesticide residues. In the general population, human tissues contain about 12 ppm DDT-derived materials. Those with meatless diets, and the Eskimos, store less; however, agricultural applicators and formulators of pesticides may store up to 600 ppm DDT or 1000 ppm DDT-derived components. Recent studies indicate that dieldrin and lindane are also stored in humans without occupational exposure (Durham, 1965). The possibility of synergistic effects involving DDT, dieldrin, lindane, and

other pollutants to which man is being exposed may result in unpredictable hazards. In fact, it is now believed that pesticides may pose a genetic hazard. At the recent conference of the New York Academy of Science, Dr. Onsy G. Fahmy warned that certain chlorinated hydrocarbons, organophosphates and carbamates were capable of disrupting the DNA molecule. It was further noted that such mutations may not appear until as many as 40 generations later. Another scientist, Dr. M. Jacqueline Verrett, pointed out that certain fungicides (folpet and captan) thought to be non-toxic have chemical structures similar to thalidomide.

We are obviously dealing with many biological unknowns in our widespread use of presumably "safe" insecticides. We have no assurance that 12 ppm DDT in our human tissue, now above the permissible in marketable products for consumption, may not be resulting in deleterious effects in future generations. As Rudd warns (1964): " . . .it would be somewhat more than embarrassing for our 'experts' to learn that significant effects do occur in the long term. One hundred and eight million human guinea pigs would have paid a high price for their trust."

Of unpredicted delayed responses, we have an example in radiation contamination. In the Bravo tests on Bikini in 1954, the natives on Rongelap Atoll were exposed to radiation assumed to be safe. Now more than a decade later, tumors of the thyroid gland have been discovered in the children exposed to these presumably safe doses (Woodwell et al., 1966). Pesticides per se or synergisms resulting from their interaction could well plague man in now unforeseen or unpredictable ways in the future.

The Sound Use of Herbicides

In contrast to insecticides, herbicides are chemical weed-killers used to control or kill unwanted plants. Following World War II, the chlorinated herbicide 2, 4-D began to be used widely on broadleaf weeds. Later, 2, 4, 5-T was added, which proved especially effective on woody species. Today, over 40 weed-killers are available. Although used extensively in agriculture, considerable quantities are used also in aquatic weed control and in forestry, wildlife, and right-of-way vegetation management. Currently, large quantities are being used as defoliators in Vietnam.

Although herbicides in general are much safer than insecticides in regard to killing nontarget organisms and in their residual effects, considerable caution must be exercised in their proper use. One of the greatest dangers in right-of-way vegetation management is their indiscriminate use, which results in habitat destruction. Drift of spray particles and volatility may also cause adverse effects on nontarget organisms, especially following indiscriminate applications. In the Connecticut Arboretum, shade trees have been seriously affected as a result of indiscriminate roadside sprays (Niering, 1959). During the spring of 1957, the town sprayed the marginal trees and shrubs along a roadside running through the Arboretum with 2, 4-D and 2, 4, 5-T (1 part chemical: 100 parts water). White oaks overarching the road up to 2 feet in diameter were most seriously affected. Most of the leaves turned brown. Foliage of scarlet and black oaks of similar size exhibited pronounced leaf curling. Trees were affected up to 300 feet back from the point of application within the natural area of the Arboretum. White oak twigs near the sprayed belt also developed a striking weeping habit as twig elongation occurred—a growth abnormality still conspicuous after 10 years.

The effectiveness of the spray operation in controlling undesirable woody growth indicated a high survival or unwanted tree sprouts. Black birch and certain desirable shrubs were particularly sensitive. Shrubs affected were highly ornamental forms often planted in roadside beautification programs. The resulting ineffectiveness of the spray operation was indicated by the need for cutting undesirable growth along the roadside the following year.

In the agricultural use of herbicides, drift effects have been reported over much greater distances. In California, drift from aerial sprays has been reported up to 30 miles from the point of application (Freed, 1965).

Although toxicity of herbicides to nontarget organisms is not generally a problem, it has been reported in aquatic environments. For example, the dimethylamine salt of 2, 4-D is relatively safe for bluegill at 150 ppm, but the butyl, ethyl, and isopropyl esters are toxic to fish at around 1 ppm (R. E. Johnson, personal communication). Studies of 16 aquatic herbicides on *Daphnia magna,* a microcrustacean, revealed that 2, 4-D (specific derivation not given) seemed completely innocuous but that several others (Dichlone, a quinone; Molinate, a thiolcarbamate; Propanil, an anilide; sodium arsenite and Dichlopenil, a nitrile) could present a real hazard to this lower food chain organism (Crosby and Tucker, 1966).

Effects of rights-of-way. The rights-of-way across our nation comprise an estimated 70,000,000 acres of land, much of which is now subjected to herbicide treatment (Niering, 1967). During the past few decades, indiscriminate foliar applications have been widespread in the control of undesirable vegetation, erroneously referred to as brush (Goodwin and Niering, 1962). Indiscriminate applications often fail to root-kill undesirable species, therefore necessitating repeated retreatment, which results in the destruction of many desirable forms. Indiscriminate sprays are also used for the control of certain broadleaf weeds along roadsides. In New Jersey, 19 treatments were applied during a period of 6 years in an attempt to control ragweed. This, of course, was ecologically unsound, when one considers that ragweed is an annual plant typical of bare soil and that repeated sprayings also eliminate the competing broadleaved perennial species that, under natural successional conditions, could tend to occupy the site and naturally eliminate the ragweed. Broadcast or indiscriminate spraying can also result in destruction of valuable wildlife habitat in addition to the needless destruction of our native flora—wildflowers and shrubs of high landscape value.

Nonselective spraying, especially along roadsides, also tends to produce a monotonous grassy cover free of colorful wildflowers and interesting shrubs. It is economically and aesthetically unsound to remove these valuable species naturally occurring on such sites. Where they do not occur, highway beautification programs plant many of these same shrubs and low-growing trees.

Recognizing this nation-wide problem in the improper use of herbicides, the Connecticut Arboretum established, over a decade ago, several right-of-way demonstration areas to serve as models in the sound use of herbicides (Niering, 1955; 1957; 1961). Along two utility rights-of-way and a roadside crossing the Arboretum, the vegetation has been managed following sound ecological principles, (Egler, 1954; Goodwin and Niering, 1959; Niering 1958). Basic techniques include basal and stump treatments. The former involves soaking the base of the stem for 12 inches; the stump technique involves soaking the stump immediately after cutting. Effective formulations include 2, 4, 5-T in a fuel oil carrier (1 part chemical: 20 parts oil). Locally, stem-foliage sprays may be necessary, but the previous two techniques form the basic approach in the selective use of weed-killers. They result in good root-kill and simultaneously preserve valuable wildlife habitat and aesthetically attractive native species, all at a minimum of cost to the agency involved when figured on a long-range basis. In addition to these gains, the presence of good shrub cover tends to impede tree invasion and to reduce future maintenance costs (Pound and Egler, 1953; Niering and Elger, 1955).

Another intriguing use of herbicides is in naturalistic landscaping. Dr. Frank Egler conceived this concept of creating picturesque natural settings in shrubby fields by selectively eliminating the less attractive species and accentuating the ornamental forms (Kenfield, 1966). At the Connecticut Arboretum we have landscaped several such areas (Niering and Goodwin, 1963). This approach has unlimited application in arresting vegetation development and preserving landscapes that might disappear under normal successional or vegetational development processes.

Future Outlook

Innumerable critical moves have recently occurred that may alter the continued deterioration of our environment. Secretary Udall has banned the use of DDT, chlordane, dieldrin, and endrin on Department of the Interior lands. The use of DDT has been banned on state lands in New Hampshire and lake trout watersheds in New York State; in Connecticut, commercial applications are limited to dormat sprays. On Long Island, a temporary court injunction has been granted against the Suffolk County Mosquito Control Board's use of DDT in spraying tidal marshes. The Forest Service has terminated the use of DDT, and in the spring of 1966 the United States Department of Agriculture banned the use of endrin and dieldrin. Currently, the Forest Service has engaged a top-level research team in the Pacific Southwest to find chemicals highly selective to individual forest insect pests and that will break down quickly into harmless components. The Ribicoff hearing, which has placed Congressional focus on the problem of environmental pollution and Gaylord Nelson's bill to ban the sale of DDT in the United States are all enlightened endeavors at the national level.

The United States Forest Service has a selective program for herbicides in the National Forests. The Wisconsin Natural Resources Committee has instituted a selective roadside right-of-way maintenance program for the State. In Connecticut, a selective approach is in practice in most roadside and utility spraying.

Although we have considerable knowledge of the effects of biocides on the total environment, we must continue the emphasis on the holistic approach in studying the problem and interpreting the data. Continued observations of those occupationally exposed and of residents living near pesticide areas should reveal invaluable toxicological data. The study of migrant workers, of whom hundreds have been reported killed by pesticides, needs exacting investigation.

The development of more biological controls as well as chemical formulations that are specific to the target organism with a minimum of side effects needs continuous financial support by state and federal agencies and industry. Graduate opportunities are unlimited in this field.

As we look to the future, one of our major problems is the communication of sound ecological knowledge already available rather than pseudoscientific knowledge to increase the assets of special interest groups (Egler, 1964; 1965; 1966). The fire ant fiasco may be cited as a case in point. And as Egler (1966) has pointed out in his fourth most recent review of the pesticide problem: " . . .95% of the problem is not in scientific knowledge of pesticides but in scientific knowledge of human behavior. . . .There are power plays . . .the eminent experts who deal with parts not ecological wholes."

One might ask, is it really good business to reduce the use of pesticides? Will biological control make as much money? Here the problem integrates political science, economics, sociology, and psychology. Anyone seriously interested in promoting the sound use of biocides must be fully cognizant of these counter forces in our society. They need serious study, analysis, and forthright reporting in the public interest. With all we know about the deleterious effects of biocides on our environments, the problem really challenging man is to get this scientific knowledge translated into action through the sociopolitical pathways available to us in a free society. If we fail to communicate a rational approach, we may find that technology has become an invisible monster as Egler has succinctly stated (1966).

Pesticides are the greatest single tool for simplifying the habitat ever conceived by the simple mind of man, who may yet prove too simple to grasp the fact that he is but a blind strand of an ecosystem web, dependent not upon himself, but upon the total web, which nevertheless he has the power to destroy.

Here environmental science can involve the social scientist in communicating sound science to society and involve the political scientist in seeing that sound scientific knowledge is translated into reality. Our survival on this planet may well depend on how well we can make this translation.

REFERENCES

Ames, P. L. 1966. DDT residues in the eggs of the osprey in the northeastern United States and their relation to nesting success. *J. Applied Ecol.,* (suppl.): 87-97.
Anonymous. 1966. Fish, wildlife and pesticides. U.S. Dept. of Interior, Supt. of Doc. 12 p.
Bellinger, F., R. E. Dyer, R. King, and R. B. Platt. 1965. A review of the problem of the imported fire ant. *Bull. Georgia Acad. Sci.,* Vol. 23, No. 1.
Breidenbach, A. W., C. G. Gunnerson, F. K. Kawahara, J. J. Lichtenberg, and R. S. Green. 1967. Chlorinated hydrocarbon pesticides in major basins, 1957-1965. *Public Health Rept.* 82: 139-156.
Carson, Rachel. 1962. *Silent Spring.* Houghton Mifflin, Boston, 368 p.
Cottam, C. 1965. The ecologists' role in problems of pesticide pollution. *Bio-Science,* 15: 457-463.
Crosby, D. G., and R. K. Tucker. 1966. Toxicity of aquatic herbidies to *Daphnia magna. Science,* 154: 289-290.
Dill, N. H. 1962-63. Vegetation management. *New Jersey Nature News,* 17: 123-130; 18: 151-157.
Durham, W. F. 1965. Effects of pesticides on man. *In* C. O. Chichester, ed., *Research in Pesticides.* Academic Press, Inc., New York.
Egler, F. E. 1954. Vegetation management for rights-of-way and roadsides. *Smithsonian Inst. Rept. for 1953:* 299-322.
——. 1964a. Pesticides in our ecosystem. *Am. Scientist,* 52: 110-136.
——. 1964b. Pesticides in our ecosystem: communication II: *BioScience,* 14: 29-36.

————. 1965. Pesticides in our ecosystem: communication III. *Assoc. Southeastern Biologist Bull.*, 12: 9-91.

————. 1966. Pointed perspectives. Pesticides in our ecosystem. *Ecology*, 47: 1077-1084.

Freed, V. H. 1965. Chemicals and the control of plants. *In* C. O. Chichester, ed., *Research in Pesticides*, Academic Press, Inc., New York.

Goodwin, R. H., and W. A. Niering. 1959. The management of roadside vegetation by selective herbicide techniques. *Conn. Arboretum Bull.*, 11: 4-10.

————. 1962. What is happening along Connecticut's roadsides. *Conn. Arboretum Bull.*, 13: 13-24.

Harrington, R. W., Jr., and W. L. Bidlingmayer. 1958. Effects of dieldrin on fishes and invertebrates of a salt marsh. *J. Wildlife Management*, 22: 76-82.

Hickey, J. J., and L. Barrie Hunt. 1960. Initial songbird mortality following a Dutch elm disease control program. *J. Wildlife Management*, 24: 259-265.

Hickey, J. J., and J. A. Keith. 1964. Pesticides in the Lake Michigan ecosystem. *In* The Effects of Pesticides on Fish and Wildlife. U.S. Dept. Interior Fish and Wildlife Service.

Keith, J. A. 1964. Reproductive success in a DDT-contaminated population of herring gulls, p. 11-12. *In* The Effects of Pesticides on Fish and Wildlife. U.S. Dept. Interior Fish and Wildlife Service.

Kenfield, W. G. 1966. *The Wild Gardner in the Wild Landscape*. Hafner, New York. 232 p.

Loosanoff, V. L. 1965. Pesticides in sea water. *In* C. O. Chichester, ed., *Research in Pesticides*. Academic Press, Inc., New York.

Matthysse, J. G. 1959. An evaluation of mist blowing and sanitation in Dutch elm disease control programs, N.Y.

Oil in the Ecosystem

Robert W. Holcomb

Oil pollution has been a human problem for most of this century, but it took the grounding of the tanker *Torrey Canyon* and the blowout of the well off the coast of Santa Barbara to draw public attention to the major problems that can arise in the production and shipping of petroleum. A five-fold increase in oil production is expected by 1980, and the potential for large-scale pollution can increase even faster because of changes in drilling location and shipping practice. Knowledge of how oil affects the environment is fragmentary and gives only dim clues about what to expect in the future.

The problems involved in oil studies are complex. Crude oil is not a single chemical but a collection of hundreds of substances of widely different properties and toxicities. Paul Galtsoff of the Bureau of Commercial Fisheries at Woods Hole, Massachusetts, stated recently that "oil in sea water should be regarded not as an ordinary pollutant but as a dynamic system actively reacting with the environment."

Viewing the problem of oil this way, one finds that biologists present an essentially unified account of how oil came to be an important part of the environment and that they can give a rough outline of the way oil interacts with the rest of the ecological system. However, it is still impossible to predict the behavior of specific oil spills, and little is known about the long-term effects of oil in the marine environment.

Most current research is directed toward the immediate problem of handling oil spills. There is little prospect that detailed ecological studies will increase dramatically in the near future, but plans are being considered for the establishment of broad-based environmental-monitoring programs.

Oil at Sea

In 1966, 700 million tons of oil—about half the world's total ocean tonnage—were shipped in 3281 tankers. In the best of worlds, this oil would remain in that part of the "ecological" system of interest only to humans—wells, tankers, refineries, and, finally, furnaces and machines. It is difficult to estimate just how far short we are of living in the best of worlds, but Max Blumer of Woods Hole Oceanographic Institute estimates that somewhere between 1 million and 100 million tons of oil are added to our oceans each year.

The major sources of this oil are handling errors, leaks from natural deposits, tanker and barge accidents, and illegal tanker bilge washings. Normal techniques of transferring oil to small coastal tankers, barges, and shore facilities result in a chronic source of coastal oil. The total amount of oil from this source is unknown, but the Massachusetts Division of Natural Resources says that, in Boston Harbor alone, a spill involving several tons of oil can be expected every third week. Less frequent, but more spectacular, are leaks from offshore deposits. These can occur naturally, but they have been associated with drilling operations since the 1930's, when fields in the Gulf of Mexico were opened. The biggest loss associated with the more than 9000 offshore wells was the million-gallon blowout early this year off the California coast near Santa Barbara. Tanker accidents are similar to well blowouts in that an occasional major catastrophe highlights a constant source of contamination. The grounding of the *Torrey Canyon* off the southwest coast of England in March 1967 was simply the most dramatic example of a type of accident that, on a worldwide basis, occurs more than once a week. Finally, deliberate dumping of bilge washings adds a considerable, but unknown, amount of oil to the oceanic environment. In 1962 Shell Oil Company developed a method to separate oil from such washings, and there is a tacit international agreement to use the method; however, shipmasters find the procedure inconvenient, and the dumping practice continues.

Although our oil resources are not unlimited, a quick look to the future indicates that pumping and shipping operations will continue to expand for the next few decades. The continental shelves of North and South America, Africa, and Australia all have oil. Seismic profiling has indicated the probable presence of oil in the North Sea, Persian Gulf, and Indonesia, and large deposits have been discovered in Alaska and Canada.

Oil from these new sources will be transported through pipelines and by gigantic tankers. Construction has already begun on a road that will be used to build the 800-mile, 48-inch, 900-million dollar pipeline from Alaska's North Slope to Valdez Bay, an ice-free port on the Gulf of Alaska. The large United States merchant vessel S.S. *Manhattan* was specially strengthened for travel in ice and fought her way through the Canadian Arctic in September. If such trial runs are judged successful, a fleet of six, quarter-million-ton vessels will be built for year-round service. (The *Torrey Canyon,* considered a large ship at the time of her grounding, had a displacement of 127,000 tons.)

The proposed drilling activities will involve greater risks of major losses because work must be done at sea or in inhospitable northern latitudes. The use of large tankers will reduce the probability of collisions and groundings, but there are few port facilities for these giants, so the possibility of spills during transfers to smaller tankers or barges will be increased. Major accidents, of course, will be of colossal proportions.

Behavior in Water

After coming in contact with water, crude oil rapidly spreads into a thin layer and the lighter fractions evaporate. In protected areas the oil often becomes adsorbed on particulate matter and sinks, but in open sea it tends to remain on the surface where wind and wave action aid in further evaporation. Some oil dissolves in seawater and some is oxidized but the hundreds of species of bacteria, yeasts, and molds that attack different fractions of hydrocarbons under a variety of physical conditions are primarily responsible for oil degradation.

Bacteria found in open seas tend to degrade only straight-chain hydrocarbons of moderate molecular weight, so branched-chain hydrocarbons of high molecular weight in the form of tarry chunks may persist for a long time. In still waters, a series of complex events results in almost complete degradation. In 1950, Soviet microbiologists showed that, after the lighter fractions of oil spilled on the Moskva River evaporated, the remaining oil was adsorbed by particles and sank. Bottom-dwelling microorganisms produced a new mixture of organic substances that were carried to the surface with bubbles of methane and other light gases. The new compounds again were adsorbed, sank, and the cycle was repeated. A number of cycles, repeated over several months, were necessary to degrade most of the oil.

Studies on the thoroughness of degradation have produced conflicting results. Research at Terrebonne Bay, Louisiana, in 1966 showed that essentially complete degradation occurs within a period of several months. Oil has been a consistent pollutant in the Bay since the 1930's, but analysis of bottom mud showed that significant concentrations of petrochemicals could be found only in areas that had received oil relatively recently. However, studies in the French Mediterranean, which will be discussed later, indicate that important chemicals are persistent in bottom sediments.

There is now a considerable body of literature on the interactions of microorganisms and petroleum products, most of it based on laboratory studies and much of it dating back to Soviet work in the 1930's and American work in the 1940's. However, these studies are scarcely past the descriptive stage, and, even when combined with field studies, they are not adequate for predicting the course of degradation of an oil spill.

Oil and Marine Life

The most visible victims of ocean oil are sea birds. It is impossible to even guess how many are killed each year, and about the only thing known for sure is that, once oiled, very few birds survive. After the *Torrey Canyon* disaster, 5711 oiled birds were cleaned off; apparently 150 of them returned to health and were released, but banding counts of these indicate that at least 37 died within the first month after release. Similar figures were obtained from French efforts at bird rehabilitation after the same disaster, and few of the 1500 diving birds cleaned after the Santa Barbara blowout survived.

It is believed that most deaths are the result of diseases, such as pneumonia, which attack the birds after they are weakened by the physical effects of the oil (feather matting, loss of buoyancy, flying difficulty, and others). However, the high death rate of cleaned birds is unexplained, so long-term toxicity of the oil cannot be ruled out.

The major studies of the effects of oil spills on species other than birds have produced a wide variety of results. Dr. Robert Holmes, the first director of a major study after the Santa Barbara blowout, has stated that plankton populations were unaffected, and, although his remark was challenged at the Massachusetts Institute of Technology symposium where it was made, it is generally agreed that visible damage to organisms other than birds has been relatively light.

On the other hand, in what is probably the best "before and after" study of a major spill, it was conclusively shown that almost the entire population of a small cove was killed by dark diesel oil from the tanker *Tampico Mara*. In March 1957, the tanker grounded at the mouth of a small, previously unpolluted cove on the Pacific coast of Baja California, Mexico, and, until destroyed by the sea, it blocked most of the cove's entrance. All signs of oil disappeared sometime between November 1957 and May 1958, but the ecology of the cove was radically changed. A few species returned within 2 months, but 2 years had elapsed before significant improvements were noted. Four years after the accident, sea urchin and abalone populations were still greatly reduced; and, at the last observations in 1967, several species present 10 years earlier had not returned.

Although toxicity studies in the ocean have been limited to a few large spills, considerable laboratory work has been done to determine the lethal concentrations of a number of chemicals on various species. Most toxic are the aromatic hydrocarbons (for example, benzene, toluene, and the xylenes), and investigators have recently shown that the low-boiling, saturated hydrocarbons are more toxic than formerly believed. The destructiveness of the *Tampico Mara* grounding was probably due to the saturated hydrocarbons, and it has been shown that aromatic hydrocarbons used to dissolve detergents in the effort to disperse oil from *Torrey Canyon* caused much of the damage. When a spill occurs at sea, a large portion of both these classes of compounds evaporates before reaching shore. This is probably the main reason that the Santa Barbara blowout was not more disastrous to shore life other than birds.

Biochemical Studies

Just enough is known about the higher-boiling, saturated hydrocarbons and the high-boiling, aromatic hydrocarbons to indicate that more study is needed. Saturated, higher-boiling compounds occur naturally in both crude oil and marine organisms, so they are probably not toxic; but work reported this year indicated that these compounds may affect the behavior of sea animals.

Blumer points out that very small amounts of certain chemicals are used by many species of sea animals as behavior signals in the vital activities of food finding, escaping from predators, homing, and reproduction. He has shown, for example, that starfish are attracted to their oyster prey by chemicals in concentrations of a few parts per billion. The responsible chemicals have not been identified, but Blumer believes that in many cases they may resemble the high-boiling, saturated hydrocarbons found in petroleum products. Because of the extreme sensitivity of the response and the similarity of the animal and petroleum chemicals, he thinks it is possible that pollution interferes with chemically stimulated behavior ''by blocking the taste receptors and by mimicking natural stimuli.''

Studies on chemically stimulated behavior of marine animals are in such an early stage that ideas about the role of sea oil in the process can only be considered speculative. However, the speculation indicated that the consequences—altered behavior of entire populations of commercially valuable species—are so serious that the matter deserves early attention.

Another matter still in the speculative stage, but with potentially hazardous consequences, is the significance of high-boiling, aromatic hydrocarbons. Crude oil and crude oil residues contain alkylated 4- and 5-ring aromatic hydrocarbons similar to those found in tobacco tars, but little is known about their role in the marine environment.

In 1964 Lucien Mallet, a French marine chemist, reported the presence of 3,4-benzopyrene, a known carcinogen, in sediments of the French Mediterranean. Concentrations ranged from 5.0 parts per million at a depth of 8 to 13 cm to 0.016 part per million at 200 cm. Similar concentrations have been found in other waters that had been polluted for a long time. Near the port of Villefranche, 3,4-benzopyrene in concentrations from 0.025 to 0.04 part per million have been found in plankton.

Benzopyrenes can be formed by algae, and they occur naturally in many soils in concentrations ranging from parts per million to parts per billion; thus their presence in marine sediments may not be cause for concern. However, the detection in sea cucumbers of concentrations that were slightly greater than those in the bottom sediments where these animals feed indicated that benzopyrenes in the marine environment may find their way into the food chain.

Pollutants tend to enter the food chain more easily and to pass through it with fewer changes in aquatic environments than they do in terrestrial environments. They can be introduced in solution through bottom sediments and even in dispersed droplets that are ingested by the numerous filter feeders that constitute an important part of aquatic food.

The presence of DDT in Lake Michigan's coho salmon drew public attention to the fact that some hydrocarbons pass through the aquatic food chain relatively unchanged. Work at Woods Hole has demonstrated that the ratios of olefinic hydrocarbons in zooplankton to those in livers of basking sharks and herring that feed on the plankton are so constant that they can be used to determine the feeding grounds of these species.

Obviously, studies should be conducted to see what concentrations of 3,4-benzopyrene and other potentially dangerous hydrocarbons must be in seawater or sediments before they are introduced into the food chain and whether the chemicals persist as they pass through the chain.

Priorities

Although the possible ill effects of long-term oil pollution point to the need for more studies on the complex chemical-biological relationships of oil and the environment, there is still work to be done on the immediate effects of oil spills. Dale Straugh, who now directs the large Santa Barbara study, said in a telephone interview that oil spills will undoubtedly continue and that much of the research effort should concentrate on methods of handling them.

Present alternatives are (i) to "corral" the oil and hold it at sea, (ii) to pick it up mechanically, or (iii) to treat it chemically so it will emulsify, dissolve, or sink. None of these methods is particularly successful, and research on all of them is continuing. The major requirement for further development is engineering and chemical knowledge, but biological expertise is necessary in some areas.

It is primarily biological studies, especially those after the *Torrey Canyon* incident, that precipitated the government decision not to use chemical treatment when the shore area is used as a source of fresh water or as a beach, or when it is necessary for commercially valuable species. Toxicity tests of chemicals developed to treat oil are now routinely conducted, and the Federal Water Pollution Control Administration is developing a standard procedure for such tests. This action was prompted in part by reports that a dispersal agent, Corexit, used at Santa Barbara was more toxic than earlier tests indicated.

The step beyond toxicity tests is a giant one of determining subtle and long-term effects of sunken, dissolved, or dispersed oil. Biological knowledge has advanced far enough to rule them out or to provide unquestionably safe alternatives. This task would require difficult, long-term studies on the complex interactions of oil, seawater, and marine life, and there is nothing on the horizon to indicate that these studies will progress rapidly enough to play a large role in decisions about methods of handling oil spills.

Another area in which biological knowledge could be helpful is in simply monitoring the oil that enters the oceans and determining, at least by sampling, its effects. On this horizon there seems to be some light. Several studies designed to determine the feasibility of establishing broad-based centers for environmental study are now in progress.

The systematic monitoring of the oceans, including their oil content, is a necessary step toward development of the capability of determining the worldwide consequences of effects that at present can be measured only in the laboratory or in relatively small field studies.

Oil Spills—An Old Story

S. W. A. Gunn

After charting the coastline of what is now Alaska, British Columbia, and Washington, the great English seaman, Captain George Vancouver, visited California in the *Discovery* in 1793, and made this entry in his log for Sunday, 10 November (1):

The surface of the sea, which was perfectly smooth and tranquil, was covered with a thick slimy substance, which, when separated, or disturbed by any little agitation, became very luminous, whilst the light breeze that came principally from the shore, brought with it a very strong smell of burning tar, or of some such resinous substance. The next morning the sea had the appearance of dissolved tar floating upon its surface, which covered the ocean in all directions within the limits of our view; and indicated that in this neighbourhood it was not subject to much agitation.

By coincidence, this was in the very area of Santa Barbara where the undersea oil well blew up recently, and following which the Department of the Interior stated that "there is a lack of sufficient knowledge of this particular geological area"!

REFERENCE

1.   J. S. Marshall, *Vancouver's Voyage* (Mitchell Press, Vancouver, 1967), p. 112.

Soil Pollution

David E. Elrick

Fertilizers are applied to the soil and it is the behavior of these chemicals both on or in the soil that will determine any subsequent transport which could lead to water pollution. Under normal conditions small amounts of some nutrients are transported. For example, fall applications of nitrogen fertilizers in the temperate climates will probably lead to an increased leaching of nitrogen as both nitrate (and nitrite) nitrogen are mobile and will move in some manner associated with the percolating water. Under normal growth conditions, microbial mineralization and nitrification will convert some of the organic and ammonium forms of nitrogen in the upper layers of the soil to the nitrate form. Phosphorus compounds are relatively immobile within the soil (movement is generally of the order of centimeters).

All of North America is involved because nitrate nitrogen is mobile within the soil and the real problem involves the long range effects of slowly increasing the nitrogen content of our groundwater supplies throughout the continent.

Shock at Sea

Time Magazine

When the Norwegian author-explorer Thor Heyerdahl sailed across half the Pacific on a balsawood raft 22 years ago, he recalls, "We on *Kon Tiki* were thrilled by the beauty and purity of the ocean." During his recent attempt to sail from Africa to Central America in a boat made of papyrus reeds, which he was forced to abandon last month 600 miles from his goal, Heyerdahl's old thrill was replaced by shock. In Manhattan he reported to the Norwegian Mission at the United Nations: "Large surface areas in mid-ocean as well as nearer the continental shores on both sides were visibly polluted by human activity."

Heyerdahl and his six-man crew were astonished and depressed by the quantity of jetsam bobbing hundreds of miles from land. Almost every day, plastic bottles, squeeze tubes and other signs of industrial civilization floated by the expedition's leaky boat. What most appalled Heyerdahl were sheets of "pelagic particles." At first he assumed that his craft was in the wake of an oil tanker that had just cleaned its tanks. But on five occasions he ran into the same substances covering the water so thickly, he told *Time* Researcher Nancy Williams, that "it was unpleasant to dip our toothbrushes into the sea. Once the water was too dirty to wash our dishes in."

The particles, some of which Heyerdahl collected for later analysis, are roughly the size of a pea. Oily and sometimes encrusted with tiny barnacles, they smell like a combination of putrefying fish and raw sewage. Heyerdahl hopes that his experience will stir the U.N. to propose new international regulations to keep the oceans clean. "Modern man seems to believe that he can get everything he needs from the corner drugstore," says the explorer. "He doesn't understand that everything has a source in the land or sea, and that he must respect those sources. If the indiscriminate pollution continues, we will be sawing off the branch we are sitting on."

What Happens to Ozone?

Environment Magazine

Ozone is simultaneously formed and destroyed in the upper atmosphere by several naturally occurring chemical reactions. The introduction into the stratosphere of certain fluorocarbons, man-made substances used as aerosol propellants and as refrigerants, will tend to accelerate the destruction process which, it is predicted, will lead to a net loss of stratospheric ozone.

Ozone Formation

When oxygen molecules (O_2) absorb sunlight, they dissociate into free oxygen atoms (O) which may then combine with O_2 to form ozone (O_3). Short-wavelength ultraviolet radiation (below 240 nanometers) is the most important form of light energy involved. Ozone formation is shown in the following reactions:

$O_2 + h\nu \rightarrow 2O$ ($h\nu$ = light energy)
$O + O_2 \xrightarrow{M} O_3$ (M = other gases)

Ozone Destruction

On the other hand, ozone concentrations in the atmosphere are reduced by several naturally occurring mechanisms:

Sunlight. While solar energy helps bring about production of ozone, sunlight is also responsible for its destruction. Sunlight dissociates the ozone molecule into free ozone and an oxygen molecule; the free oxygen then reacts with a molecule of ozone to form two additional molecules of oxygen, as shown here:

$O_3 + h\nu \rightarrow O + O_2$
$O + O_3 \rightarrow 2O_2$

Nitrogen Oxides. Nitric oxide (NO) interacts with ozone. Nitric oxide is principally formed from atmospheric nitrous oxide (N_2O) which in turn has been produced by certain species of bacteria which live in the soil. Smaller quantities of nitric oxide can be formed from ammonia, as well as from the breakdown of nitrogen gas molecules by cosmic rays. The overall reaction of nitrogen oxides with ozone is as follows:

$N_2O + O \rightarrow 2NO$
$NO + O_3 \rightarrow NO_2 + O_2$
$NO_2 + O \rightarrow NO + O_2$

Although this reaction occurs naturally, injection of large amounts of nitrogen oxides into the stratosphere, for example by the supersonic transport aircraft, could significantly increase the rate of ozone destruction.

Hydroxide Radicals. Of somewhat less importance in the breakdown of ozone is one form of the hydroxide (OH) molecule, called an hydroxide radical. Hydroxide radicals are formed in the stratosphere principally by the reaction of free oxygen with a water molecule. Hydroxide radicals can also be formed by the oxidation of both hydrogen and methane gas molecules.

Sunspots. It also appears that the ozone content in the stratosphere may be affected by events that occur on the surface of the sun. According to P. J. Crutzen at the National Center for Atmospheric Research in Boulder, Colorado, there is a correlation between atmospheric ozone concentrations and the sunspot cycle, with a lag period of about two and one-half years. That is, increases in ozone levels follow by two and one-half years the activities on the sun's surface. Also, events that lead to intense solar proton emissions have been noted to dramatically increase nitric oxide content in the stratosphere, the last such event occurring in August 1972. (Other similar events occurred, for example, in July 1966 and numerous times between 1958 and 1961.) It has recently been speculated that nearby supernova explosions could significantly reduce atmospheric ozone concentration by a cataclysmic bombardment of the earth by x rays and cosmic radiation. Fortunately, such events occur only every few hundred million years.

Fluorocarbons. The following reactions show how fluorocarbon gases lead to the destruction of ozone. Dichlorodifluoromethane (CF_2Cl_2) and trichloro-monofluoromethane ($CFCl_3$), Propellant-12 and Propellant-11 (commonly known by the DuPont trade name Freon), are first dissociated, under the influence of ultraviolet radiation below 230 nanometers.

$$CF_2Cl_2 + h\nu \rightarrow CF_2Cl + Cl$$
$$CFCl_3 + h\nu \rightarrow CFCl_2 + Cl$$

The chlorine atom (Cl) formed in these reactions, which occur at altitudes between 12 and 25 miles above the earth's surface, can lead to a chain of events that results in a net destruction of ozone molecules in the stratosphere:

$$Cl + O_3 \rightarrow ClO + O_2$$
$$ClO + O \rightarrow Cl + O_2$$
$$Net: O_3 + O \rightarrow 2O_2$$

Land Destruction

Nuclear war aside, the number one environmental problem may well be the loss of our soils. How land should be used is an old problem which has been discussed all the way from ancient civilizations to the present. Isaiah warned of the consequences of the corporate farm in ancient Israel (reading 30). Four centuries before Christ, Plato was lamenting the demise of the mountains of Attica (reading 31). In the third century A.D., Tertullian commented on mankind's role in changing the face of the earth (reading 32). The history of civilized man's destruction of the land and the resulting decline of great civilizations has been well-documented by many scholars, but perhaps most powerfully by Paul B. Sears in *Deserts on the March,* written in 1935 (reading 33).

We Americans tend to think that soil loss and desertification are the exclusive problems of the third world. Certainly they are third world problems. In scarcely half a century, the Sahara Desert has grown on its southern fringe encompassing 250,000 square miles of farm and grazing land. Almost every mountainous region of Latin America, Asia and Africa experiences an ever-accelerating rate of crumbling. Forests are cleared, then follows flooding and the inevitable soil erosion and silting. Nevertheless, land destruction is not the exclusive problem of either the past or the third world. In our own country, according to the Soil Conservation Service, an average of nine tons of topsoil per acre is lost each year. Any able-bodied person can see for himself by digging post holes and measuring the depth of the topsoil along railroad rights-of-way, along the old public roads, or in small country cemeteries and comparing these measurements to those taken in adjacent fields. This comparison will clearly show that the economic basis of our nation is being lost to the sea. Though careful studies of these losses continue (reading 34), the reasons they happen are made clear in Aldo Leopold's "Odyssey" which eloquently describes the travel of atoms under two systems, nature's and agricultural man's (reading 35).

Will our generation act any differently than our ancestors did? The ants, extrapolating from the record of humanity, don't think so. They are waiting to inherit the earth (reading 36).

Warning in Israel
Isaiah

Woe unto them that join house to house, that lay field to field, till there be no place, that they may be placed alone in the midst of the earth!''

Lament in Greece
Plato

There are mountains in Attica which can now keep nothing but bees, but which were clothed, not so very long ago, with...timber suitable for roofing the very large buildings...The annual supply of rainfall was not lost, as it is at present, through being allowed to flow over the denuded surface to the sea...''

An Observation in Early Rome
Tertullian

All places are now accessible...cultivated fields have subdued forests; flocks and herds have expelled wild beasts....Everywhere are houses, and inhabitants, and settled governments, and civilized life. What most frequently meets the view is our teeming population; our numbers are burdensome to the world...our wants grow more and more keen, and our complaints bitter in all mouths, whilst nature fails to afford us her usual sustenance. In every deed, pestilence, and famine, and wars, and earthquakes have to be regarded for nations, as means for pruning the luxuriance of the human race.

Deserts on the March (1935)
Paul B. Sears

By the time of Charlemagne, who was an enlightened ruler, the onslaught against the forests of western Europe was under way, to continue through the thirteenth century. By the end of the Middle Ages the land was largely divested of its trees, as the Mediterranean region had been before the Christian era, and stringent laws against cutting came into being. Whatever advanced ideas had been inherited from Rome were soon lost to sight. Fields were used, then abandoned. Feudal lords

From *Desserts on the March*, by Paul B. Sears. Copyright 1935 by the University of Oklahoma Press.

shifted their headquarters from one castle to another, to get away, it has been said, from the accumulated filth. But the coefficient of toleration of filth was so high in those days that the moving was more likely to have been for the purpose of tapping new sources of food as the old sections of the fief played out. Eventually, after a period of rest, the abandoned fields had to be used again. Such a system is unsound. Recuperation takes too long, and too much of the land at a time remains idle. Paintings and sculptured figures of the period portray human beings who are wan and rickety, and since these portrayals were commonest in sacred art, most of us still have the feeling that anaemia and sainthood are inseparable. Actually the trouble was due to inadequate diet and malnutrition on a huge scale, such as we find in backward rural communities.

Soil Deterioration and the Growing World Demand for Food

Soil losses by water erosion are estimated in five intensively farmed Wisconsin watersheds.

R. A. Brink, J. W. Densmore, G. A. Hill

> *Below that thin layer comprising the delicate organism known as the soil is a planet as lifeless as the moon.*
> —G. Y. JACKS and R. O. WHYTE (*1*).

A major contemporary problem in agriculture is how the mounting world need for food and livestock feed can be met in the face of an enormous and continuing increase in population without irreparably damaging the soil base on which their production depends. Soil losses due to water or wind erosion are coextensive with crop production on tilled land. Throughout much of human history deprivation has been largely kept at bay by shifting to other territory as the soils of the old were exhausted. In our time this evasion no longer works; there are now few, if any, virgin, high-quality soils in the world to turn to. Much of the remaining new land is of marginal quality and will require expensive improvements to be made agriculturally productive, or it is subject to other limitations. Meanwhile, the demand for food soars as the world's population increases by about 80 million persons per year.

More than a generation ago Jacks and Whyte (*1*) called attention to soil erosion by wind and water as a problem of global extent. Ecklund (*2*) recently described the increasingly serious degradation that is occurring in heavily populated Third World countries. The issue is of immediate domestic concern also. According to an inventory of conservation needs prepared by the U.S. Department of Agriculture (USDA) in 1974, additional soil protective measures are needed to ensure permanent agriculture on about two-thirds of the cropland and pasture in the United States (*3*). Pimentel *et al.* (*4*) recently called attention to the large losses of U.S. farmland that have resulted from urban expansion and highway construction as well as from soil erosion.

Expanding market forces in industrialized countries have significantly increased the pressure on U.S. soils for food and livestock feed. Even more serious are the rapidly growing food requirements of Third World countries, many of which are now only marginally able to feed themselves. Simultaneous, widespread crop shortfalls in these countries could result in calls for relief of unprecedented magnitude.

We have fallen behind in recent years in accommodating ourselves to such rapidly changing conditions. A comprehensive program of soil erosion control was inaugurated in the United States in the 1930's; it was one of the most important conservation developments in this nation's history. There are now unmistakable signs, however, that the program is becoming inadequate to protect our soils from unacceptable losses. As a result of mounting pressures on the land, the need for soil saving measures is outrunning the capacity of conservation agencies, as now financed, to assist farmers in meeting it. The first step in securing remedial action is arousing public recognition of this fact. Circumstances have greatly changed since organized soil conservation under public auspices was begun about 40 years ago.

In this article we present estimates of the soil damage that is occurring in one productive farming area in the United States under the impact of modern agricultural technology and in response to the current upsurge of international market forces affecting food supplies; the results of this local study are meaningful for a wide area northward from the central corn belt and elsewhere in the United States where row cropping is prevalent on sloping land. We then consider the general outlook for demands on U.S. agricultural exports, with particular reference to the food needs of Third World countries. Finally, research areas and conservation measures that should be emphasized for soil erosion control in the United States are discussed.

Soil Erosion Survey of Five Wisconsin Watersheds

The 1975 survey of crop acreages and soil erosion in Dane County is part of an ongoing study by the Dane County Soil and Water Conservation District and the Regional Planning Commission in developing a county water quality plan. Four of the five watersheds are located in the glaciated eastern section of the county, and one is in the unglaciated or "Driftless" area.

These watersheds are representative of a broad area of the northern Corn Belt. The Driftless area, represented in the survey by the Mount Vernon Creek watershed, covers 4,780,000 hectares in southwestern Wisconsin, but includes small adjoining parts of northwestern Illinois, northeastern Iowa, and southeastern Minnesota. The USDA Soil Conservation Service (SCS) calls this region the Northern Mississippi Valley Loess Hills (5). The glaciated portion of Dane County is an area of deep or moderately deep silt loam soils and undulating to rolling topography. The major land resources area of which it is a part is designated by SCS as the Southeastern Wisconsin Drift Plain, which covers southeastern Wisconsin and extends well into northern Illinois (6).

The 4160-ha Mount Vernon Creek watershed has ridge and valley topography. It has the steepest slopes and shallowest soils of the five watersheds surveyed and therefore has the greatest erosion potential. It does not, however, have the highest soil loss, as will be discussed later.

Sixmile Creek watershed (15,860 ha) and Pheasant Branch Creek watershed (5200 ha) are located in areas of terminal and recessional moraines with gentle to steep slopes and commonly irregular topography. Both drain into 3645-ha Lake Mendota. Door Creek watershed (3640 ha) and Maunesha River watershed (9100 ha) are located in a drumlin-marsh area, characterized by gently rolling hills separated by wetlands, many of which are now tile-drained.

All the watersheds support a large number of dairy and beef cattle and swine. Corn, alfalfa, and oats are the leading field crops. Canning crops, particularly peas and sweet corn, are also important in all but the Mount Vernon Creek watershed.

Four especially noteworthy changes have occurred in the farming pattern in Dane County in the past decade. First, there has been a 57 percent increase in corn acreage. Most of the increase has been at the expense of oats acreage, which has decreased 46 percent, and includes land that has been in the federal soil bank and diverted acres programs. Second, the number of dairy herds has decreased by nearly 46 percent and the number of dairy cows by 26 percent (6). Third, there are fewer farms, and the farming is now being done by fewer people. Fourth, the amount and size of the power equipment used have increased greatly.

Survey technique. A standard SCS technique was used in the soil erosion survey. Eighteen or more quarter-sections (65 ha each) were randomly chosen for study within each watershed. Soil type, degree of slope, length of slope, and current crop were recorded. Farmers were interviewed to learn the crop rotations and tillage practices employed.

Soil losses resulting from water erosion were estimated for each sampled area within a watershed by using the universal soil loss equation (7) employed by the SCS for predicting soil erosion and planning conservation. This multiterm equation, developed by the USDA Agricultural Research Service, is based on the results of more than 30 years of research at 48 stations in 26 states on the environmental factors that affect soil erosion (8, 9).

The number of blocks and the percentage of each watershed sample varied according to the size of the watershed. The percentages of the total area sampled in the respective watersheds to give uniform statistical reliability to the derived values for soil loss were: Pheasant Branch Creek, 22.8; Sixmile Creek, 8.6; Door Creek, 14.5; Maunesha River, 13.2; and Mount Vernon Creek, 28.0.

Distribution of land between crops. The data on crop acreages collected for the five watersheds are summarized in Table 1. As shown in column 2 of Table 1, two-thirds or more of the farmland is used for crops in four of the five watersheds. The value is only 57 percent for Mount Vernon Creek watershed, which has 14 percent in woodland and 21 percent in permanent pastures. A striking feature of the crop distribution in the area, as shown in column 3, is that corn now occupies one-half to three-fourths of the cropland in four of the watersheds. Based on countywide data, this is an increase of about 33 percent in the last 6 years and 57 percent in the last 10 years. The highest value, that for Maunesha River, is 76 percent. The lowest value for corn land in the series is 34 percent for Mount Vernon Creek watershed.

TABLE 1: Distribution of cropland and estimated soil losses in five Dane County watersheds. The values in parentheses in columns 7 and 8 are metric tons per hectare per year

Watershed	Cropland					Estimated soil losses (ton acre^{-1} year^{-1})	
	Percentage of total farmland	Corn (%)	Hay and rotation pasture (%)	Oats (%)	Other crops (%)	Average	Highest quarter-section
Maunesha River	80	76	12	8	1	5.9 (13.3)	13.7 (30.8)
Door Creek	66	70	12	4	4	8.6 (19.3)	24.8 (55.8)
Sixmile Creek	76	61	27	5	4	7.5 (16.9)	20.6 (46.3)
Pheasant Branch Creek	79	50	35	12	2	6.5 (14.6)	12.0 (27.0)
Mount Vernon Creek	57	34	57	7	0	5.2 (11.7)	16.0 (36.0)

The percentages of cropland used for hay and rotation pasture in the several watersheds are in reverse order to those for corn. Maunesha River and Door Creek devote only 12 percent to hay and rotation pasture. The proportion of cropland in hay and rotation pasture reaches its maximum in Mount Vernon Creek watershed, where the value is 57 percent. Countywide, oats acreage has decreased 46 percent in the last 10 years.

Estimated Soil Losses

Average soil losses from water erosion in the five watersheds, estimated from the universal soil loss equation, are shown in Table 1. The individual values vary widely from one sampled quarter-section to another in each watershed. Because of the high dispersion and the irregularity of the distributions, the soil loss value for each sampled area is entered separately in Fig. 1. The soil loss estimates for all the quarter-sections sampled ranged from 2.3 to 24.8 (short) tons per acre per year (5.2 to 55.8 metric tons per hectare per year).

The amount of soil lost by erosion that is considered tolerable varies with effective depth for each soil type, being higher for deep soils and lowest in the extreme case of a shallow soil over bedrock. Each soil in Dane County has been assigned a tolerated or allowable soil loss value by the SCS based on the amount of erosion it can tolerate and still remain productive. These so-called T factors ordinarily vary from 1 to 5 tons per acre per year (2.2 to 11.2 metric tons per hectare per year).

The five watersheds. Based on an analysis of the soil types on the cropland of the sample quarter-sections, an average T factor for the cropland in each of the five watersheds was determined. The average allowable soil loss for the Maunesha River and Sixmile Creek watersheds is 4 tons per acre per year. Mount Vernon Creek watershed, because of its somewhat more shallow soils, averages 2.8 tons per acre per year. The values for the Door Creek and Pheasant Branch Creek watersheds are 3.8 and 3.6 tons, respectively. The solid triangles on the soil loss scale in Fig. 1 mark the average T factors for the watersheds.

Of the 93 quarter-sections sampled in the five watersheds 65, or 70 percent, show estimated soil losses above the tolerated levels. Door Creek has the highest percentage of samples above the 4-ton level, namely 78 percent. The average T factor for the five watersheds is 3.6 tons per acre per year. Considering individual cases, the aggregate soil loss for the 65 individual entires in Fig. 1 that are above their respective allowable levels exceeds the value of 3.6 tons by 4.8 tons, on the average. That is, more than twice as much soil (3.6 + 4.8 tons) is being lost on 70 percent of the quarter-sections sampled than is consistent with proper land management.

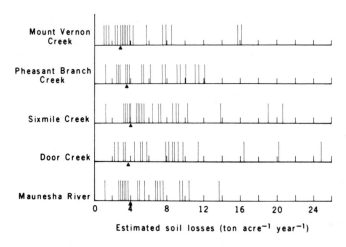

FIGURE 1. Estimated annual soil losses from erosion on cropland in five intensively farmed watersheds in Dane County. Each vertical line represents one randomly chosen quarter-section (65 ha) sampled area. (▲) Respective estimated amounts of erosion that the soils can tolerate and still remain productive. (Multiply by 2.25 to convert the baseline scale to metric tons per hectare per year.)

In the four glaciated watersheds contour strip-cropping has been eliminated on nearly 2000 acres since 1967. This estimate is based on a comparison of 1967 aerial photographs of the quarter-section samples with present field patterns. Most of the fields in question are still contoured, but the alternate strips of hay and cultivated crops have disappeared because of the conversion to continuous corn growing. This change could more than double the soil loss.

Mount Vernon Creek watershed. This watershed is a special case because it lies within the Driftless area, where the soils tend to be shallow and the slopes, in general, are steep. Of the five watersheds surveyed, it has the lowest average predicted annual soil loss, 5.2 tons per acre of cropland. Note from Fig. 1 that the soil loss values for cropland of the 18 quarter-sections sampled in this watershed are clustered toward the lower end of the scale. In only two of these quarter-sections are the losses severe—15.7 and 16.0, respectively.

Because of the steep topography of the area and the nearness of the bedrock to the surface, the soils in Mount Vernon Creek watershed are the ones most subject to destruction under row cropping. Why, then, does this watershed make the best showing among the five surveyed?

Since the establishment of the SCS, the Driftless area of southwestern Wisconsin has been the scene of a major research and educational effort in soil stabilization. This has transformed the region from one in which soil deterioration by sheet erosion and gully formation was widespread to one in which farming in accordance with sound conservation principles is now common.

The pressures to increase the acreage of row crops even in the Driftless area, however, must not be underestimated. A tabulation of data from the Wisconsin Department of Agriculture Statistical Reporting Service shows that the acreage of corn for grain and silage for the seven-county district in extreme southwestern Wisconsin, all in the Driftless area, rose from 420,000 to 520,000 in the period 1954 to 1974, a 24 percent increase.

Other areas. The estimated soil losses given above for five Dane County watersheds are probably indicative of what is happening over large areas of cropland in the United States. In a similar soil erosion study of the Obion–Forked Deer River Basin (1.2 million hectares) in northwest Tennessee, for example, the average erosion rate based on all cropland, bottomland as well as upland, was 9.1 tons per acre per year; for upland soils only it was 18.9 tons per acre per year (*10*). According to the study, erosion rates recently increased mainly because of a rise in soybean acreage.

Brune (*11*), the SCS state conservationist for Iowa, recently reported that the estimated average annual soil loss for unprotected sloping cropland in that state is 13 tons per acre. This is about two bushels of soil for each bushel of corn harvested on that land. Brune stated that in 1974, a disastrous erosion season in Iowa, soil losses of 40 to 50 tons per acre were not uncommon.

The severity and generality of the soil erosion problem on a national scale are further illustrated by the various additional instances cited by Pimentel *et al.* (*4*) of losses considerably exceeding the amounts consistent with the maintenance of agricultural productivity.

The Growing Demand for Food

Two factors are likely to keep the demand for cereals and soybeans grown in North America high in the years just ahead. They are (i) the large requirement at home and in other industrialized countries for food and especially for livestock feed, and (ii) the dependence of Third World countries mainly on the United States and Canada for relief in emergencies.

The average American uses about 1 ton of grain a year. Ninety-three percent of this is utilized indirectly as feed for cattle, hogs, and chickens, which supply our main protein sources, meat, milk, and eggs. Rising standards of living in other industrialized countries have led to increases in meat consumption. The amount of meat used in France, the United Kingdom, West Germany, Italy, and the Soviet Union, for example, increased 31 percent, on the average, between 1960 and 1970; in Japan the increase for the same period was 264 percent (*12*). Our much publicized grain sales to the Soviet Union in 1972 resulted from the Soviet government's decision to maintain the level of meat consumption in spite of a poor cereal crop at home. The United States and Canada are now the sources of about 80 percent of the food and feed grains imported by the industrialized nations.

The value of U.S. agricultural exports, as shown in Fig. 2, rose from about $5 billion in 1920 to $20 billion in 1974. Note that nearly all agricultural exports are now on a commercial rather than a government-aided basis under Public Law 480 (1954). In 1974 the United States supplied 85 percent of the soybeans, 60 percent of the feed grain (mostly corn and sorghum), 45 percent of the wheat, 30 percent of the cotton, and 24 percent of the rice moved in international trade (*13*).

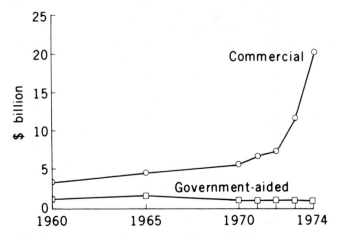

FIGURE 2. U.S. agricultural exports from 1960 to 1974 (*24*).

With massive shipments abroad and rising consumption at home, the cumbersome agricultural surpluses that accumulated after World War II have disappeared. Brown (*14*) estimates that the world's reserve stock of grain in 1974 was a 33-day supply. We are essentially dependent, therefore, on current production.

Until 200 years ago world population was low and comparatively stable. High birth rates were balanced by high death rates. Then an abrupt demographic change began as a result of falling death rates. It took man from his emergence as a distinct species, perhaps 3 million years ago, until 1830 to assemble the first billion people. As has been frequently pointed out, it required only 100 years (from 1830 to 1930) to add the second billion. The third billion arrived in 30 years, and the fourth billion followed in only 15 years. About 10 years hence, barring a catastrophe, there will likely be 5 billion people on the earth.

This enormous population expansion is new to human experience. Its implications for human welfare are profound. Of special concern here is the danger that the increased pressure for food will undermine our soil resources.

Demographers estimate that of the billion people who will be added to the world's population in the next decade, 90 percent will be in the economically underdeveloped nations of Asia, Africa, and Latin America. How are these 900 million additional mouths to be fed?

A realist has remarked that some problems do not have solutions, only consequences. The world population-food problem is one of them, in the sense that poverty and distress have become important components of it, as Malthus (*15*) foresaw. The technological problems involved are varied and often complex and the strains on people resulting from overcrowding and a dearth of the necessities for life threaten the political fabric of nations. The surging world population is pushing man in many places to the limits of his adaptability.

A general solution is not in sight, but we can visualize certain consequences of rapid population growth. Some that are particularly relevant to the subject of this article are mentioned below.

1. The prospect of feeding the world adequately is hopeless if the present rate of population increase (about 2.2 percent per annum) countinues. Exponential population growth cannot go on indefinitely. However, population control measures cannot solve the acute food problem that will develop in the decades just ahead. It would take about 75 years to obtain zero population growth even if a net reproduction rate of unity were achieved today. This is because of the age distribution in many underdeveloped countries. In Mexico, for example, not only is the growth rate very high, 2.4 percent, but 48 percent of the present population (60 million) is under 15 years of age. In Sweden, in contrast, where the growth rate is 0.2 percent, only 21 percent of the population (8.2 million) is under 15 years of age (*16*). Mexico's population would continue to surge even if the size of new families were reduced at once to 2.1, the replacement value. Sweden's would quickly decline under the same limitation.

2. The United States and Canada are the only remaining nations in the world with large surpluses of grain (*14*). Other nations that formerly either were self-sufficient or produced a surplus are now net importers. Rising prosperity and improved diets in the industrialized nations, especially Japan, European countries, and the Soviet Union, have used up the surplus stocks accumulated after World War II and have brought back into cultivation the idle cropland in the United States and Canada. The rising demand from the industrial nations means that there will be progressively less food available from the United States and Canada for poor countries. The inference is clear: the underdeveloped countries must look to themselves for the major portion of their additional food supply. Can they meet the demand, particularly in view of the fact that there will be about 900 million more people to feed within 10 years? Many with experience in the field are hopeful that food production can be greatly increased eventually in the underdeveloped countries, but this probably cannot take place rapidly enough to meet the shortages likely to develop in the decades just ahead. Apprehension arises from the fact that increasing agricultural production in much of the Third World involves not merely technical problems, but the political, social, and economic foundations of those nations.

3. Raising food production on a scale commensurate with population growth in the underdeveloped countries necessitates changing from subsistence farming to market agriculture. Growers need the purchasing power to obtain fuel, fertilizer, irrigation water, seed of improved varieties, pesticides, tools, machinery, storage facilities, and transportation and the management skills for a complex farming and marketing operation. This

involves a reordering of the national economy in many instances and radical changes in patterns of living.

4. If large food shortages become widespread, they will affect not only the Third World countries but also the industrialized nations. Tensions between the rich and the poor countries will mount with respect to (i) the donation of food for the relief of starving people, (ii) the terms of international trade in various raw materials on which industry is dependent, and (iii) greatly increased monetary and technical assistance for Third World development.

Responses to the Crisis

Since no general international plan for coping with the population-food problem is now in sight, the several consequences of explosive population growth will have to be dealt with separately as they become evident. Crucial questions will arise, including how to contain inflation in the face of persisting food scarcities. Many specialists are already concerned with the agricultural research and development needed in a world swarming with people (*17, 18*). A much less conspicuous problem, but one that is also vital for the national welfare, is how to protect our soils from degradation as a result of the growing pressures on them. In our judgment, this is a domestic problem which should have the highest priority.

During the last 30 years important gains have been made in controlling erosion on the U.S. cropland most subject to soil losses. Millions of acres less prone to damage but vulnerable over time still await adequate protection. The acreage of the two leading row crops, corn and soybeans, which already extend onto much unprotected sloping land, may rise further; market forces favoring such a trend are strong. Furthermore, corn growing has gained extraordinary momentum as a result of the development by intensive breeding of inherently high-yielding, fertilizer-responsive, and widely adapted hybrid strains, effective pest control, and complete mechanization. The demand for soybeans as an economical source of both high-quality protein and edible oil may drive U.S. acreage in this crop upward. Provision must be made, therefore, in the development of conservation plans, for the protection of a large acreage of row crops from excessive soil losses.

The national goal for soil conservation should now be soil security for all sloping cropland. This calls for wider application of all the familiar devices and procedures working toward this end, including contour farming, strip-cropping, terraces, sod waterways, interplanting, and conservation tillage practices.

Research

Two research areas particularly merit increased attention in an expanded soil erosion control program. One of these is forage crop breeding and management and the other is conservation tillage of row crops.

Forage plants are highly important for livestock feed; they are also of prime significance in protecting the soil against erosion (*19*). Row crops, except for the canopy developed from about midseason to harvest, leave much of the surface bare and thus subject to abrasion and scouring by wind and water. Small grains offer some protection by their uniform, although somewhat sparse, coverage of the soil. Only grasses and close-growing perennial forage legumes can afford complete vegetative cover and ensure against excessive soil losses even on relatively steep slopes.

Row crops and meadow crops are frequently grown in rotation in livestock farming. In the Great Lakes states, for example, corn is often followed by several years of alfalfa. In regions where much of the land is steeply sloping, the balance between the acreage of corn, an annual row crop, and alfalfa, a perennial, close-growing, meadow crop, is particularly important in soil erosion control. In seven Wisconsin counties within the hilly Driftless area, the ratio of harvested acres of meadow crops (mostly alfalfa) to those of corn declined from about 1.3 to 1.1, or about 15 percent between 1965 and 1974. The acreage of both corn and alfalfa increased during the period, mostly at the expense of oats, but corn increased more than twice as much as alfalfa (20). The steady gains in productivity of corn and the relative efficiency and convenience with which this crop is now handled with machines are major reasons for the larger corn increase.

Research support for forage crops lags far behind that for corn. Hodgson (21) stated that grasses and legumes now receive only about 4 percent of the funds provided for U.S. agricultural research, even though these crops, grown for livestock feed, are the mainstay of U.S. agriculture. More forage research funds could be of inestimable value for regions where erosion control calls for a high ratio of meadow crops to row crops in rotation farming.

Conservation tillage is a relatively new factor in soil protection (22). Revolutionary developments in chemical weed control since 1945 have stimulated changes in cropping systems and tillage practices that are significant for soil conservation. Conservation tillage reduces soil erosion by leaving residues from the preceding crop on the surface. Moldboard plows, which tend to bury these residues, are being replaced by machines that diminish soil displacement during and after preparation for row planting and also leave most of the plant debris in manageable form on top of the soil. These residues, if sufficiently dense, break the fall of raindrops, reduce splash and the detachment of small particles from the aggregated soil mass, and slow down the water runoff. A marked reduction in erosion can result. The practice is also adapted to large-scale farming with modern, specialized power equipment.

Research is already attacking some problems encountered in adapting conservation tillage to the diversity of soil, topographic, and weather conditions. Weeds, soil insects that impair seedling establishment, and pathogenic fungi associated with crop residues are hazards in a system that leaves much plant debris on the surface to decay slowly. Thus a variety of pest control problems are brought into focus in a new framework. Other problems, such as soil compaction, also emerge. The wide adoption of conservation tillage awaits the resolution of these problems.

Other Measures

Cost sharing, using public funds, is already a well-established procedure for encouraging farmers to adopt soil conservation measures. This economic incentive is essential to the success of any voluntary soil conservation program involving outlays substantially beyond ordinary farm costs. Much land in need of soil-saving measures remains outside organized programs because the public funds available for cost sharing are inadequate to attract the owners.

In our predominantly urban society, it may be difficult to gain the public support needed for funding an adequate soil conservation program. Many Americans still think in terms of abundance and steadily rising expectations. But shortages of various kinds, including the energy shortage, are now raising prices and pushing inflation. Public opinion will shift with the worsening of the world food crisis, and as famine abroad becomes more commonplace. Recognition of the need for conservation in general will grow, and with it appreciation that we depend on the soil for food.

An immediate problem is to overcome the delay in large-scale application of available conservation methods. An underlying reason for the delay is that man, as a species, has yet to understand his true place in nature. If he did, he would have accepted what Leopold (*23*) has termed a "land ethic." Leopold stated, "We abuse land because we regard it as a commodity belonging to us. When we see land as a community to which we belong, we may begin to use it with love and respect. There is no other way for land to survive the impact of mechanized man. . . ." The land ethic demands a harmonious balance between nature and all the works of man. Systematic cultivation in the public mind, in this critical period, of an ethical sense of man's relationship to the soil would facilitate the conservation of cropland which has now become more vulnerable to destruction than ever before.

Summary

A recent survey of five watersheds in south-central Wisconsin, where corn is now the dominant annual crop, illustrates the soil erosion damage that is occurring on sloping land under modern agricultural technology and prevailing market forces. In 70 percent of the 93 quarter-sections sampled, estimated soil losses, on the average, were more than twice the amounts considered compatible with permanent agriculture. Scattered studies by others indicate that the findings are meaningful for a large area in the United States when row cropping is prevalent on sloping soils.

Pressures on cultivated land, in general, are mounting rapidly because of the rising demand for meat in industrialized nations and the soaring numbers of marginally fed people in Third World countries. The world population–food problem makes increasing stress on U.S. soils inevitable in the foreseeable future. Adequate protection against excessive loss of productive topsoil requires that the level of publicly supported soil conservation activities be promptly adjusted to this circumstance.

REFERENCES AND NOTES

1.   G. V. Jacks and R. O. Whyte, *Vanishing Lands. A World Survey of Soil Erosion* (Doubleday, Doran, New York, 1939).
2.   E. P. Ecklund, *Losing Ground. Environmental Stress and World Food Prospects* (Norton, New York, 1976).
3.   "Our land and water resources. Current and prospective supplies and uses," *U.S. Dep. Agric. Misc. Publ. 1290 (1974).*

4. D. Pimentel *et al., Science* **194,** 149 (1976).
5. "Land resource regions and major land resource areas of the United States," *U.S. Dep. Agric. Agric. Handb. No. 296* (1965).
6. *Wisconsin Agricultural Statistics* (Wisconsin Statistical Reporting Service, Wisconsin Department of Agriculture, Madison, 1976).
7. The universal soil loss equation is usually expressed as $A = RKLSCP$, where A represents the average annual soil loss expressed in tons per acre per year; R is the rainfall factor, a measure of the erosive force of rainfall in a specific area; K is the soil erodibility factor (assigned to each soil type); L is the slope length factor; S is the slope gradient factor; C is the cropping-management factor, related to land use for crops and other purposes; and P is the erosion control practice factor, the ratio of soil loss with contouring, strip-cropping, or farming to that with straight row farming up and down the slope.
8. W. H. Wischmeir and D. D. Smith, "Predicting rainfall-erosion losses from cropland east of the Rocky Mountains," *U.S. Dep. Agric. Agric. Handb. No. 282* (1965).
9. *Control of Water Pollution from Cropland. A Manual for Guideline Development* (U.S. Department of Agriculture and Environmental Protection Agency, Washington, D.C., 1975).
10. *Interim Report, Obion–Forked Deer River Basin Study* (Soil Conservation Service, U.S. Department of Agriculture, Washington, D.C., 1972).
11. W. Brune, quoted from a report by L. C. Johnson, *Candid Conservationist* **26,** 1 (summer 1975).
12. B. Rensberger, in *Give Us This Day . . .A Report on the World Food Crisis,* prepared by the staff of the *New York Times* (Arno, New York, 1975).
13. *What Makes U.S. Farm Trade Grow. U.S. International Agricultural Trade: Its Growing Importance to the Nation's Economy* (Office of Communication, U.S. Department of Agriculture, Washington, D.C., 1974).
14. L. R. Brown, *Science* **190,** 1053 (1975).
15. C. W. Guillebaud, in *Encyclopaedia Britannica* (Benton, Chicago, ed. 14, 1940), vol. 14, pp. 744-745.
16. *World Population Estimates* (Environmental Fund, Washington, D.C., 1976).
17. S. H. Wittwer, *Science* **188,** 579 (1975).
18. N. Wade, *ibid.,* p. 585.
19. The initiation in 1926 by R. A.B. of the alfalfa breeding program that led eventually to the release in 1954 by the Wisconsin Agricultural Experiment Station, in cooperation with the U.S. Department of Agriculture and the Utah Agricultural Experiment Station, of the winter-hardy bacterial wilt–resistant 'Vernal' variety, since widely grown in the northern United States and Canada, was stimulated in part by the realization that a productive and highly persistent forage plant could be an important component in a soil erosion control program just then being started in the Driftless area of southwestern Wisconsin. The current interest of R.A.B. in soil conservation problems traces to that circumstance.
20. See the data in (6) for the period 1965 to 1974.
21. H. J. Hodgson, *Sci. Am.* **234,** 61 (February 1976).
22. *Conservation Tillage* (Soil Conservation Society of America, Ankeny, Iowa, 1973).
23. A. Leopold, *A Sand County Almanac* (Oxford Univ. Press, New York, 1966).
24. *How U.S. Farm Exports Have Grown* (U.S. Department of Agriculture, Washington, D.C., 1974).
25. *World Population: A Challenge to the United Nations and Its System of Agencies* (UNS-USA National Policy Panel in World Population, United Nations, New York, 1969).
26. We thank I. L. Baldwin, N. Clark, R. J. Muckenhirn, R. D. Powers, and E. C. Savage for helpful suggestions in the preparation of this manuscript or an earlier version of it.

Odyssey

Aldo Leopold

X had marked time in the limestone ledge since the Paleozoic seas covered the land. Time, to an atom locked in a rock, does not pass.

The break came when a bur oak root nosed down a crack and began prying and sucking. In the flash of a century the rock decayed, and X was pulled out and up into the world of living things. He helped build a catkin, which became an acorn, which fattened a deer, which fed an Indian, all in a single year.

From his berth in the Indian's bones, X joined again in chase and flight, feast and famine, hope and fear. He felt these things as changes in the little chemical pushes and pulls which tug timelessly at every atom. When the Indian took his leave of the prairie, X moldered briefly underground, only to embark on a second trip through the bloodstream of the land.

This time it was a rootlet of bluestem which sucked him up and lodged him in a leaf, which rode the green billows of the prairie June, sharing the common task of hoarding sunlight. To this leaf also fell an uncommon task: flicking shadows across a plover's eggs. The ecstatic plover, hovering overhead, poured praises on something perfect; perhaps the eggs, perhaps the shadows, or perhaps the haze of pink phlox which lay on the prairie.

When the departing plovers set wing for the Argentine, all the bluestems waved farewell with tall new tassels. When the first geese came out of the north and all the bluestems glowed wine-red, a forehanded deermouse cut the leaf in which X lay and buried it in an underground nest, as if to hide a bit of Indian summer from the thieving frosts. But a fox detained the mouse, molds and fungi took the nest apart, and X lay in the soil again, foot-loose and fancy-free.

Next he entered a tuft of side-oats grama, a buffalo, a buffalo chip, and again the soil. Next a spiderwort, a rabbit, and an owl. Thence a tuft of sporobolus.

All routines come to an end. This one ended with a prairie fire, which reduced the prairie plants to smoke, gas, and ashes. Phosphorus and potash atoms stayed in the ash, but the nitrogen atoms were gone with the wind. A spectator might, at this point, have predicted an early end of the biotic drama, for with fires exhausting the nitrogen, the soil might well have lost its plants and blown away.

But the prairie had two strings to its bow. Fires thinned its grasses, but they thickened its stand of leguminous herbs: prairie clover, bush clover, wild bean, vetch, lead-plant, trefoil, and baptisia, each carrying its own bacteria housed in nodules on its rootlets. Each nodule pumped nitrogen out of the air into the plant, and then ultimately into the soil. Thus the prairie savings bank took in more nitrogen from its legumes than it paid out to its fires. That the prairie is rich is known to the humblest deermouse; why the prairie is rich is a question seldom asked in all the still lapse of ages.

Between each of his excursions through the biota, X lay in the soil, and was carried by the rains, inch by inch, downhill. Living plants retarded the wash by impounding atoms, dead ones, by locking them to their decayed tissues. Animals ate the plants and carried them briefly uphill or downhill, depending on whether they died or defecated higher or lower than they fed. No animal was aware that the altitude of his death was more important than his manner of dying. Thus a fox caught a gopher in a meadow, carrying X uphill to his bed on the brow of a ledge where an eagle laid him low. The dying fox sensed the end of his chapter in fox-dom, but not the new beginning in the odyssey of an atom.

An Indian eventually inherited the eagle's plumes, and with them propitiated the Fates, whom he assumed had a special interest in Indians. It did not occur to him that they might be busy casting dice against gravity; that mice and men, soils and songs might be merely ways to retard the march of atoms to the sea.

One year, while X lay in a cottonwood by the river, he was eaten by a beaver, an animal which always feeds higher than he dies. The beaver starved when his pond dried up during a bitter frost. X rode the carcass down the spring freshet, losing more altitude each hour than heretofore in a century. He ended up in the silt of a backwater bayou, where he fed a crayfish, a coon, and then an Indian, who laid him down to his last sleep in a mound on the riverbank. One spring an oxbow caved the bank, and after one short week of freshet, X lay again in his ancient prison, the sea.

An atom at large in the biota is too free to know freedom; an atom back in the sea has forgotten it. For every atom lost to the sea, the prairie pulls another out of the decaying rocks. The only certain truth is that its creatures must suck hard, live fast, and die often, lest its losses exceed its gains.

It is the nature of roots to nose into cracks. When Y was thus released from the parent ledge, a new animal had arrived and begun redding up the prairie to fit his own notions of law and order. An oxteam turned the prairie sod, and Y began a succession of dizzy annual trips through a new grass called wheat.

The old prairie lived by the diversity of its plants and animals, all of which were useful because the sum total of their cooperatives and competitions achieved continuity. But the wheat farmer was a builder of categories; to him only wheat and oxen were useful. He saw the useless pigeons settle in clouds upon his wheat, and shortly cleared the skies of them. He saw the chinch bugs take over the stealing job, and fumed because here was a useless thing too small to kill. He failed to see the downward wash of over-wheated loam, laid bare in spring against the pelting rains. When soil-wash and chinch bugs finally put an end to wheat farming, Y and his like had already traveled far down the watershed.

When the empire of wheat collapsed, the settler took a leaf from the old prairie book: he impounded his fertility in livestock, he augmented it with nitrogen-pumping alfalfa, and he tapped the lower layers of the loam with deep-rooted corn. With these he built the empire of red barns.

But he used his alfalfa, and every other new weapon against wash, not only to hold his old plowings, but also to exploit new ones which, in turn, needed holding.

So, despite alfalfa, the black loam grew gradually thinner. Erosion engineers built dams and terraces to hold it. Army engineers built levees and wing-dams to flush it from the rivers. The rivers would not flush, but raised their beds instead, thus choking navigation. So the engineers built pools like gigantic beaver ponds, and Y landed in one of these, his trip from rock to river completed in one short century.

On first reaching the pool, Y made several trips through water-plants, fish, and waterfowl. But engineers build sewers as well as dams, and down them comes the loot of all the far hills and the sea. The atoms which once grew pasque-flowers to greet the returning plovers now lie inert, confused, imprisoned in oil sludge.

Roots still nose among the rocks. Rains still pelt the fields. Deermice still hide their souvenirs of Indian summer. Old men who helped destroy the pigeons still recount the glory of the fluttering hosts. Black and white buffalo pass in and out of red barns, offering free rides to itinerant atoms.

What the Ants Are Saying

Don Marquis

dear boss i was talking with an ant
the other day
and he handed me a lot of
gossip which ants the world around
are chewing over among themselves

i pass it on to you
in the hope that you may relay it to other
human beings and hurt their feelings with it
no insect likes human beings
and if you think you can see why
the only reason i tolerate you is because
you seem less human to me than most of them
here is what the ants are saying

it wont be long now it wont be long
man is making deserts of the earth
it wont be long now
before man will have used it up
so that nothing but ants
and centipedes and scorpions
can find a living on it
man has oppressed us for a million years
but he goes on steadily
cutting the ground from under
his own feet making deserts deserts deserts

we ants remember
and have it all recorded
in our tribal lore
when gobi was a paradise
swarming with men and rich
in human prosperity
it is a desert now and the home
of scorpions ants and centipedes

what man calls civilization
always results in deserts
man is never on the square
he uses up the fat and greenery of the earth
each generation wastes a little more
of the future with greed and lust for riches

north africa was once a garden spot
and then came carthage and rome
and despoiled the storehouse
and now you have sahara
sahara ants and centipedes

toltecs and aztecs had a mighty
civilization on this continent
but they robbed the soil and wasted nature
and now you have deserts scorpions ants and centipedes
and the deserts of the near east
followed egypt and babylon and assyria
and persia and rome and the turk
the ant is the inheritor of tamerlane
and the scorpion succeeds the caesars

america was once a paradise
of timberland and stream
but it is dying because of the greed
and money lust of a thousand little kings
who slashed the timber all to hell
and would not be controlled
and changed the climate
and stole the rainfall from posterity
and it wont be long now
it wont be long
till everything is desert
from the alleghenies to the rockies
the deserts are coming
the deserts are spreading
the springs and streams are drying up
one day the mississippi itself
will be a bed of sand
ants and scorpions and centipedes
shall inherit the earth

men talk of money and industry
of hard times and recoveries
of finance and economics
but the ants wait and the scorpions wait
for while men talk
they are making deserts all the time
getting the world ready for the conquering ant
drought and erosion and desert
because men cannot learn

rainfall passing off in flood and freshet
and carrying good soil with it
because there are no longer forests
to withhold the water in the
billion metriculations of the roots

it wont be long now it wont be long
till earth is barren as the moon
and sapless as a mumbled bone

dear boss i relay this information
without any fear that humanity
will take warning and reform

        archy

The Loss of Wild Things

Introduction

The histories of famines, land destruction and species extinctions share one thing in common: they read with appalling monotony. Interestingly enough, the three are related, almost in tandem. Carnivores and large herbivores are exterminated, the vegetation is plowed under, cut or burned. Ecological capital which had accumulated goes to support the human agricultural enterprise. In many parts of Africa and Latin America, human populations increase, land is worn out and famines result. The process begins with the loss of wild things, a signal of things to come. Since 1600, 226 animal species have become extinct. Currently there are 159 on the federal endangered species list.

Large animals, generally speaking, are the most vulnerable to the encroachment by man, and many of the largest could be gone by the year 2000. The African elephant, largest of all land dwellers, is threatened by poachers, overcrowding, starvation and drought. The two million elephants left in Africa have moved into the parks and wildlife preserves, leaving destruction in their wake. African lions have had their numbers reduced to 2000, half as many as there were in 1950. Their range has been reduced from four to two million square miles. Scarcely 2,000 Indian tigers are left, and fewer than 500 rhinos remain in the world (an amazingly high number considering the large number of people who believe the rhino horn contains aphrodisiac powers). Besides the elephants, cats and rhinoceroses, the hippopotami and great apes are also threatened. Lack of knowledge about these animals is not the problem, rather the political climate in the developing countries is such that economic expansion will be sought and further encroachment into animal habitats seems certain.

The large mammals of the deep are also in great trouble. Almost every country in the United Nations has pleaded to stop the killing of whales by calling for a ten year moritorium. Yet every fifteen minutes a whale is killed. The Japanese and Russian hunters are armed with explosive-tipped harpoons designed to bring sure death, and they continue to hunt the whale, in spite of protests by groups such as the Greenpeace Foundation, whose members placed themselves between the whales and their hunters and refused to move.

Americans fear the whale may suffer the fate of the buffalo. A million buffalo a year were slaughtered between 1872 and 1879, and ten years later the species was almost extinct. During the 1960's, one million kangaroos were slaughtered each year, but this has mostly stopped before the history of the buffalo is repeated in Australia.

The readings in this section illustrate three important principles: (1) The pattern of events from wilderness to desert involves human need and greed and a shortsighted view of the future (reading 37). (2) The abundance of a species is not necessarily an indication of its permanence, as in the cases of the passenger pigeon (reading 38), buffalo and maybe even *Homo sapiens.* (3) Wild things are a living gene bank carrying genetic sequencees which one day may be incorporated with the DNA of our domestic species to reduce the vulnerability of the current human food supply (readings 39 and 59).

The Wail of Kashmir

Lee Merriman Talbot

A striking example of man's growing impact on the land is the Great Thar Desert in western India. At the time of Christ, Indian rhinoceros roamed in grass jungles in the middle of what is now desert. And for the past 80 years the desert has been advancing into the rest of India at the rate of one-half mile a year along its whole long perimeter. That means that in 80 years, an estimated 56,000 square miles, or an area equal to that of Wisconsin, has been turned into shifting sand.

The mechanics of this land degradation seem clear. The starting point is the mature forest with its wildlife, fertile soil, and abundant water. The lumber is cut, often clear-cut with young growth destroyed. The land is then cultivated for a time, then grazed and overgrazed. There can be no replacement of trees or grass, for everything green is eaten by ravenous livestock. When there is nothing left for cattle, goats take over, and when the goats have left, nothing remains but sand or blowing dust. This story holds true, with the same plot and characters, but with different stage scenery and costumes, throughout much of the world.

To illustrate the effect of this land-use pattern on wilderness, let us consider Kashmir, the ancient Moguls' "paradise on earth." This is a lovely mountain land in northernmost India, lying at about the same latitude as San Francisco, and bordered by Tibet, China, and Pakistan. The British with the local maharajah set aside magnificent wild areas here. But when independence came, here as in most former colonies, the tendency during the first burst of nationalism was to reject all that smacked of the previous "imperialism" or "colonialism." Parks and wilderness areas were thought of as something kept away from the people by the former rulers rather than as a resource maintained for them, so the first reaction was to destroy them, to take "what was rightfully ours." On top of this came political and military unrest with a side effect of a large population suddenly armed but with little discipline. Among the results have been large-scale poaching leading to the virtual extermination of the Kashmir stag, heavy forest cutting, and overgrazing.

Through much of Kashmir up to and above timberline one runs into herders and livestock. In less than ten years much of this land changed from dense conifer forest or park lands like the best of our Sierra or Rockies, to what are approaching high-altitude deserts, with the vegetation pulled apart, cut, overgrazed, and burned out—and the soil, too.

Economic need, destructive land use, and destructive nationalism form a constantly recurring pattern deadly to wilderness. Until all three of these factors are somewhat ameliorated it is hard to be optimistic about the future of wilderness lands throughout the world.

As my last example I would like to mention an area not usually thought of as living wilderness—the Middle East. Much of it is arid desert, but when Moses led the children of Israel through the Sinai wilderness, it was a live wilderness with wildlife and trees. Today one can go for days through that country and never see a living thing. The mountains above the Promised Land were cloaked with dense forest, with pine, oak, and cedar; and in the more open areas, Asiatic lions stalked abundant wildlife. Today these mountains are largely dead stone skeletons, and the last small remnant of the Asiatic lions is to be found 3,000 miles to the east. There are still two more or less living wilderness areas left—in northern Lebanon and western Syria. Until recently, protected by inaccessibility and unsettled conditions, the forest here remained intact; but within the last few years, lumbering and cultivation have begun to move into these last forests. When the land's fertility has been cropped out and the trees have been cut off, the crops will give way to grazing. Once overgrazing has gone far enough, the starving animals preventing grass, brush, and tree reproduction, the area will assume the desert aspect of most of the Middle East.

This remnant biblical wilderness illustrates one of the very real economic values of wilderness that, perhaps, is not often thought of in our country. It would be easy to say, looking at most of the desert Middle Eastern lands, that this area never did support much life, or that the old records of forests and crops are wrong, or that if there were trees here once there has since been a climactic change. But in these remaining wild forest areas we have the living proof that this was not the case. North Lebanon and western Syria provide a point of reference by which one may judge the condition of the land as it was, see what man has done to the rest of the land, and therefore see what can be done with what land is left.

Passenger Pigeons

By U. P. Hedrick

Not in the forests of North America or in any other part of the world is there now a single live passenger pigeon. In my boyhood, in the Land of the Crooked Tree [at the northern tip of the Michigan lower peninsula], in pigeon years there were millions and millions. Their roosting place, in the season of which I am about to write, made a vast city in the air a few miles from my home. To this rookery a small army of pigeon trappers came to ply their vocation. The pigeon trapper, who did so much in the extermination of this bird, is another vanished species. The prey, the hunter, and the industry, all are gone.

My remembrance of pigeons and pigeon trappers can be summarized best by giving an account of a single day spent in a pigeon roost in one of the big pigeon years just before these birds disappeared.

The spring after the 'Arctic winter,' wild pigeons came in such countless numbers to the Land of the Crooked Tree that ever after we all spoke of that year as the 'great pigeon year.'

Spring in the land of our adoption, was always a time of scarcity of food, in which the whites were near starvation and the poor Indians were perishing from hunger. Pigeons came this spring as did manna to the Israelites. For six weeks before the young were of a size to eat, our whole population gorged themselves on the dark meat of old pigeons, eagerly waiting for the tender butterballs into which young squabs quickly developed.

Besides, there was money to be made in trapping pigeons to supply cities near the Great Lakes with the bountiful food from sky and woods. Adventurous men followed the pigeons that then existed in a few great conclaves. To these pigeon trappers, the hunt was a means of livelihood. To Indians and settlers it was an opportunity to make a little money as well as to supply their larders.

Father was anxious to see a pigeon roost the birds had established that year near the head of Little Traverse Bay, some four or five hours distant by land and water from the harbor village. Joutel, our trapper and trader friend, was employed to act as boatman and guide. A condition of my going was that Juliette, the half-breed girl, should go to take care of me, on the theory that I could not keep pace all day with the men.

Joutel, like many French Canadians of the woods, was a fountain of song, and now he started to make our voyage pleasant with melody, his first song suggested by a partridge drumming on the bluff along the shore. In after years I came to know the words and music as the Ottawan song of Clear Skies. There were repetitions and improvisations and a great volume of sound that bespoke a full heart and a blithe spirit in a happy man.

The day was perfect. A soft purple haze floated over the harbor, with too little breeze to carry it away or to move our boat at more than a snail's pace with all sails set. The haze, the languid air, the mayflies, the quiet water, the still forest, the magic of summer, all gave a feeling of peacefulness in strong contrast to the expectancy of adventure in our boat.

The morning flight of pigeons from the roost was nearly over, and I was fearful that they had taken wing to some distant forest region; or that the birds of prey, which hovered over them and shadowed the small flocks now in the sky, had destroyed all but these few. Joutel said that we should see pigeons in plenty as they returned to their roost in the afternoon, and I was comforted.

Joutel, his hunter's instinct aroused, repeatedly called attention to the pursuing hawks. Sometimes these marauders flew above the pigeons; sometimes abreast the van; again they loitered in the rear; and always there were goings and comings from the land where their catch was eaten. From the vantage point of the boat we were thrilled with the evolutions a large flock of pigeons made as they sought to escape from the pirates of the air. When the hawks pressed close upon the rear, they drove the flying multitude into a compact mass like an enormous swarm of bees, a movement accompanied by a noise like thunder from the fluttering wings. The most remarkable evolution was one in which, for some cause or other, the pigeons divided into columns and then ascended in a spiral like the coil of a long snake.

Our little party hurried into the woods. Joutel briskly led the way. For more than a mile our trail was through thick underbrush that dripped with dew. We followed a stream that leaped and roared over many-colored rocks. As we rested on its banks, Joutel showed me fingerling trout darting to and fro under forest wastage, and in some excitement pointed to a full-grown fish, its dim form vibrating in the shadow of a dark pool.

Some three to four miles inland we came to the roost. The birds had chosen for their season's nesting place alluvial lands about a long waterway of lakes and connecting streams. As we passed from the upland forests into these lower lands, we skirted a dreary waste of oozy swamp, on the banks of which were gardens of fern and clumps of whimsical white, yellow, and red toadstools. The red toadstools, Juliette told me, were 'ears of dead men,' and from their shape and texture so they might have been.

A little farther in this valley of vegetable succulence and sanctuary of wild life, we came to the pigeon roost. Pigeon dung covered the ground, looking like a heavy fall of grayish snow; flowers, shrubs, underwood, and small trees were dead as if fire had swept through the woods, and thousands of large trees might as well have been gridled by the ax; great limbs were scattered about as though a tornado had followed the fire. The ground was strewn with bodies of pigeons, killed by accident in the gathering of the great assemblage. Mingled with the dead pigeons were countless numbers of pure white eggs. The smell of dead birds and rotten eggs added to that of the dung, so that all that breathed were threatened with suffocation. The noise was so great that we could speak to one another only by shouting; cooings of pigeons were to my ears moans of pain; whirring wings sounded like the coming of a storm. These continuous noises were punctuated by the fall of limbs overweighted with pigeons.

Most of the pigeon hunters were Indians, armed with axes, poles, and bows. The men slashed down trees loaded with nests from which the young were about to fly. As the squabs fluttered from their cradles, they were caught by women and children, decapitated by a quick jerk, and their quivering bodies tossed to swell the family heap. Nests on low branches of large trees were knocked from the supports with long poles and blunt arrows. The squabs were covered with scalelike feathers, easily removed by rubbing, after which they were drawn and packed in receptacles to be taken to the camp where they were smoked for winter.

Besides the Indians there were professional pigeon trappers. With L'Arbre Croche as a center, the pigeons ranged for food over a radius of a hundred miles. In this vast territory white pigeon hunters, who captured their prey in nets, multiplied the catch of the Indians a thousandfold.

We came now to a road, the main artery of the traffic. It led from the roost some twelve or fifteen miles to a railroad, which recently had been extended to the southern boundary of our country. The road was a comfort to our tired feet, since holes had been filled with wings and feathers from pigeon-packing places, which had made a kind of carpet.

We passed several pigeon nets before coming to one that had been 'stuck.' Here we saw hundreds of glittering heads stretched upward through the meshes of the net, the fluttering birds putting forth frantic efforts to escape. Two hairy Esaus, plastered with mud, blood, and feathers, stood in the ooze of the pigeon bed, red-handed from the slaughter of the catch. One with a pair of pincers and the other with thumb and finger gave the necks of the pigeons a remorseless twist. Blood burst from the bird's eyes, the wings fluttered, the body quivered, and the bird was dead.

The pigeon netters chose for their nets low, marshy spots, from which they removed all growth and forest refuse. Pigeons have a liking for salt, and a bed was first saturated with salt; then the further bait of grain was scattered. Some netters added a perfume of sulphur, saltpeter, or anise seed. On this enticing bit of earth a stool pigeon, eyes punched out, was tied on a block, and a cord was so arranged that the fluttering bird could be raised and lowered to attract pigeons passing high overhead. A pigeon net is 8 feet wide and 30 feet long. The trap was set by an adjustment of a spring pole and rope at one edge of the net. Forty feet from an end of the net, the trapper secreted himself in a bough house and awaited the moment to 'strike' when the bed was azure blue with birds. Twenty dozen pigeons was a good catch.

It was then well toward noon, and Father looked for a spring where we might eat and drink. Luncheon over, Father and Joutel left to see more of the pigeon netters. I was to sleep while Juliette watched over me. When I awakened, Juliette suggested that we go pigeon-nesting, an amusement easily pursued since there were trees all about, small enough to climb, that held from one to a dozen or more nests. The nests were made of a few dry twigs so carelessly put together as scarcely to hold the single egg that each usually contained. According to Joutel, pigeons nested three or four times in a season.

Passing through open beech woods where nuts were very plentiful, we were overtaken by billows of young birds just learning to fly. They fed on nuts buried in leaves and every pigeon wanted to be in front, so that the scrambling multitude appeared to roll through the forest. They took no heed of Juliette and me, and as the birds struck us with body and wings we were forced to fight them off, as one does a swarm of gnats. We were glad when the waves of birds passed on, and we started back to our luncheon place to wait for our elders.

As we sat waiting, we were amused by pompous male pigeons making love to prospective spouses. A cock would spread his tail, trail his wings, puff his throat, and call a tender 'coo, coo, coo.' Now and then he rose for a short flight, and then returned to renew his wooing. The timorous females responded with cooing endearments. All around mated couples were jangling, so that the forest rang with their clamor. As they had filled their crops during the day, it was easy to approach either young or old. Even my child's eyes could distinguish the sexes, the differences being as marked as in chickens. The neck and breast of the males were vividly iridescent with the azure of the back and outer wings. The females were much less gaudy in color and their bodies smaller and trimmer.

The afternoon was beginning to wane and we made a hurried start for the beach. Father and Joutel each wore a festoon of squabs. Joutel had made these garlands by pulling out the four long tail feathers of cocks, which he knotted in twos. He then stuck the stiff quill ends through the tender lower mandibles of the squabs, and, to complete the festoon, tied together the feather ends of small strings until he had fifteen or twenty squabs in his wreath.

Suddenly the flow of day changed to twilight. The pigeons were returning to the roost after a day of foraging. The sun seemed to have left the heavens. High above the tallest treetops the pigeons flew, rapidly and steadily, several strata deep. The vast cloud of birds extended as far in every direction as the eye could reach. In the two hours it must have taken us to reach the beach there was no diminution in their numbers, nor was there until we had been at camp quite another hour and the sun had set. Now and then the cloud broke in undulation, whether from attacks of hawks or currents of air, I do not know. When they descended, they came in a Niagara-like cataract, eventually rising again to the general level of the flight. Black was the prevailing color in the thick cloud of birds, but at times, depending on sunlight or shadow, the numbers of strata, the height, or the angle of flight, the color was grayish white, a shimmering azure, or a rich deep purple.

At sundown we came to our landing-place of the morning. The shore now teemed with life. A dozen Indian families were on the beach. With appetites whetted by exertion and L'Arbre Croche air, Indian families were hurrying preparations for the evening meal. At last food was in sight, and Joutel struck up the hearty dinner *chanson des coureurs de bois,* which sounds the praise of a *pâté de trois pigeons.*

I was loathe to leave the gay and picturesque camp. Fires had been built on the hard-packed sand of the shore, about which the men sat on flotsam and smoked while the women cleared away the remains of the supper.

Night was well begun when our boat headed into the vast light of the lake. Behind us campfires lighted the shore with crimson radiance and intensified the blackness of the forest background. Running athwart the skies was the broad white road of the heavens. Far out in L'Arbre Croche waters, a steamboat, outlined by starlike lights, moved slowly along the horizon.

Loss Of Wild Genetic Stocks

Kenneth S. Norris

Naturalists are growing increasingly aware that to let any species become extinct is a deeply serious error. The mere presumption of humans obliterating other species is reason enough to avoid this error, but a practical reason also exists for saving species. Each organism contains within it a genetic code that has been buffeted, altered, and molded through long geologic time, fitting that organism to the subtle and varied complex of environmental stresses imposed by nature. Each organism is thus a magnificently intricate response system whose subsystems and structures mesh together for survival. Each is a marvel of adaptation.

Modern genetics has revealed so much of the living blueprint in recent years that one may predict with some confidence that our means for altering the genetic constitutions of our domestic animals and plants may increase manyfold in the coming years. The raw materials will most likely be these natural systems, tested and approved by nature. Already we often return to wild plants or animals for genetic materials to diversify and strengthen our in-bred food stocks. Genetic modification will probably become a much more sophisticated applied science, placing great power in human hands, and we will need nature as its basis. The use of such a "gene bank" will likely extend far beyond application to our present domestic animals and plants, to subtle use in bringing many organisms, now useless from the human standpoint, under our control. Crops may one day thrive on salt flats or on barren desert slopes as a result.

Some Attempts to Analyze the Problem

Introduction

While the red man watched the takeover of his continent by the white alien, he undoubtedly wondered at times what he had done to deserve such vicious displacement. It wasn't until very late in the conflict that the white scholar began to discover the introspection and eloquence of the despised "primitive" when the words of such notables as Crazy Horse, Black Elk, Chief Seathl and Sitting Bull were translated into English. The Indian's analysis of the white man's mind may, in the long run, be the last and most thorough-going analysis. The first two readings in this section are samples of both the eloquence and insight of the Indian. The first (reading 40) is a letter written to the President of the United States in 1855 by Chief Seathl of the Duwamish Tribe of Washington state, regarding the proposed purchase of the tribe's land. Sitting Bull's comments concerning the habits of the white settlers (reading 41) were made at the Powder River Council in 1877.

No scholarly attempt to unravel the threads of our contemporary crisis is considered complete without a mention of Lynn White's paper, "The Historical Roots of our Ecologic Crisis" (reading 42). White places the blame on the Judeo-Christian tradition. Whatever shortcoming White's analysis might have, it represents one of the first bold attempts in modern times to analyze the problem. It must be regarded as one of the environmental classics.

No scholar has given more thought to the relationship between the American Wilderness and the American mind than Roderick Nash. In the first edition of his book, *Wilderness and the American Mind,* Nash traced the Old World roots of opinion all the way back to the Judeo-Christian tradition and earlier still, "to classical mythology and the idea of paradise." But in his revision of that work, Nash acknowledges the rootedness of our species in the paleolithic past, and that our attitudes and conduct go beyond the "five-thousand-year veneer we call 'history.' " He explains this in the preface to the revised edition, part of which is reprinted here (reading 43).

Garrett Hardin is best known for his interest in the population-food problem and as a proponent of the lifeboat ethic. His classical paper, "Tragedy of the Commons" (reading 44) first appeared in 1968 and perhaps is reprinted more often than any other document in the area of human ecology. The "commons" concept is now a reference point as we attempt to pigeon-hole our various social and environmental problems.

Yi-Fu Tuan's article (reading 45) should discourage those who wish to believe that western civilization need only turn to an oriental ethos in order for us to get right with Nature. Many of the beautiful cosmic insights and poetry of the ancient Chinese were written by retired bureaucrats, living on estates trimmed and managed by others. There is wisdom in the East, but it is by no means the complete or last statement.

Finally, there is an additional view as to what constitutes the linchpin of our crisis, the scientific-technological revolution. Theodore Roszak, author of *Where the Wasteland Ends,* argues that Christianity paved the way for science by insisting that nature was devoid of spirits and excluded all other myths save its own. Once this was thoroughly accomplished, Roszak argues, it was inevitable that the "nothing buts'' of nature could be manipulated for our ends. Complete dominion arises when nature has been completely de-sacralized. Furthermore, proponents of science largely insisted that *the* way to the good life would only come through science. Not long ago I acquired a discarded copy of a beginning physics book which, it turned out, was published in 1946. The first two paragraphs of the text reflected the prevailing attitude of the time.

Millions of people go through life without knowing anything about physics. In spite of this ignorance, all the African natives do not starve; nor do all the Eskimos freeze; and the Indians, though they had none of our science, still managed to exist. But these people only exist; they do not really live. They could not live our way, for our world is entirely organized according to the principles of physics. You, yourself, must understand these principles, or you will be more or less like a barbarian in a modern city.

Without knowing physics we might still have some kind of food, shelter, and clothing; but we want a lot more than that. We want a variety of food brought from all parts of the world; we want safe houses, comfortably heated and lighted; we want different kinds of clothing for different uses and seasons. In addition, we have learned to expect quick and easy transportation by rail, airplane, boat, or motor; cheap and ready communication by radio, telephone, or telegraph; and hundreds of other things that increase our comfort, reduce our labors, and meet our demands in the way of sports, hobbies, and amusements. All these science helps us to produce.

In the introduction of *Where the Wasteland Ends*, Roszak comments on the condition of the times. The young are rejecting the tradition of reason and adopting mysticism as part of a massive salvage operation to see things in their roundness or wholeness, an experience denied those caught up in reductionistic science. ''I believe,'' Roszak continues, ''that it means we have arrived, after long journeying, at an historical vantage point from which we can at last see where the wasteland ends and where a culture of human wholeness begins. We can now recognize that the fate of the soul is the fate of the social order, that if the spirit within us withers so too will all the world we build about us. Literally so. What, after all, is the ecological crisis that now captures so much belated attention but the inevitable extroversion of a blighted psyche? Like inside, like outside. *In the eleventh hour, the very physical environment suddenly looms up before us as the outward mirror of our inner condition, for many the first discernible symptom of advanced disease within.*'' (Italics mine.)

Fred Hapgood (reading 46), while somewhat in agreement with Roszak's contention, does not believe the clock can be turned back, and that a ''reformation within the scientific church'' is in the making. Hapgood's contribution, which paints some of the history leading up to our alienation with the environment in broad brush strokes, does see the way to another stage in our cultural evolution. It is a positive note and appropriate for ending this section.

What Some "Primitives" Said

Chief Seathl's Letter of 1855

Chief Seathl

The Great Chief in Washington sends word that he wishes to buy our land. The Great Chief also sends us words of friendship and good will. This is kind of him, since we know he has little need of our friendship in return. But we will consider your offer, for we know if we do not so, the whiteman may come with guns and take our land. What Chief Seathl says, the Great Chief in Washington can count on as truly as our white brothers can count on the return of the seasons. My words are like stars—they do not set.

How can you buy or sell the sky—the warmth of the land? The idea is strange to us. Yet we do not own the freshness of the air or the sparkle of the water. How can you buy them from us? We will decide in our time. Every part of this earth is sacred to my people. Every shining pine needle, every sandy shore, every mist in the dark woods, every clearing and humming insect is holy in the memory and experience of my people.

We know that the whiteman does not understand our ways. One portion of the land is the same to him as the next, for he is a stranger who comes in the night and takes from the land whatever he needs. The earth is not his brother, but his enemy, and when he has conquered it, he moves on. He leaves his father's graves behind and he does not care. He kidnaps the earth from his children. He does not care. His father's graves and his children's birthright are forgotten. His appetite will devour the earth and leave behind only a desert. The sight of your cities pains the eyes of the redman. But perhaps it is because the redman is a savage and does not understand.

There is no quiet place in the whiteman's cities. No place to hear the leaves of spring or the rustle of insect's wings. But perhaps because I am a savage and do not understand—the clatter only seems to insult the ears. And what is there to life if a man cannot hear the lovely cry of a whippoorwill or the arguments of the frogs around a pond at night? The Indian prefers the soft sound of the wind darting over the face of the pond, and the smell of the wind itself cleansed by a mid-day rain, or scented with a pinon pine. The air is precious to the redman. For all things share the same breath—the beasts, the trees, the man. The whiteman does not seem to notice the air he breathes. Like a man dying for many days, he is numb to the stench.

If I decide to accept, I will make one condition. The whiteman must treat the beasts of this land as his brothers. I am a savage and I do not understand any other way. I have seen a thousand rotting buffalos on the prairies, left by the whiteman who shot them from a passing train. I am a savage and I do not understand how the smoking iron horse can be more important than the buffalo that we kill only to stay alive. What is man without the beasts? If all the beasts were gone, men would die from great loneliness of spirit, for whatever happens to the beasts also happens to man. All things are connected. Whatever befalls the earth befalls the sons of the earth.

Our children have seen their fathers humbled in defeat. Our warriors have felt shame. And after defeat, they turn their days in idleness and contaminate their bodies with sweet food and strong drink. It matters little where we pass the rest of our days—they are not many. A few more hours, a few more winters, and none of the children of the great tribes that once lived on this earth, or that roamed in small bands in the woods, will be left to mourn the graves of a people once as powerful and hopeful as yours.

One thing we know which the whiteman may one day discover. Our God is the same God. You may think now that you own him as you wish to own our land. But you cannot. He is the God of man. And his compassion is equal for the redman and the white. The earth is precious to him. And to harm the earth is to heap contempt on its creator. The whites, too, shall pass—perhaps sooner than other tribes. Continue to contaminate your bed, and you will one night suffocate in your own waste. When the buffalo are all slaughtered, the wild horses all tamed, the secret corners of the forest heavy with the scent of many men, and the view of the ripe hills blotted by talking wives, where is the thicket? Gone. Where is the eagle? Gone. And what is it to say good-bye to the swift and the hunt, the end of living and the beginning of survival.

We might understand if we knew what it was that the white man dreams, what hopes he describes to his children on long winter nights, what visions he burns into their minds, so that they will wish for tomorrow. But we are savages. The white man's dreams are hidden from us. And because they are hidden, we will go our own way. If we agree, it will be to secure your reservation you have promised. There perhaps we may live out our brief days as we wish. When the last redman has vanished from the earth, and the memory is only the shadow of a cloud moving across the prairie, these shores and forest will still hold the spirits of my people, for they love this earth as the newborn loves its mother's heartbeat. If we sell you our land, love it as we've loved it. Care for it, as we've cared for it. Hold in your mind the memory of the land, as it is when you take it, and with all your strength, with all your might, and with all your heart—preserve it for your children, and love it as God loves us all. One thing we know—our God is the same God. This earth is precious to him. Even the white man cannot be exempt from the common destiny.

Sitting Bull, 1877

Sitting Bull

"They claim this Mother Earth of ours for their own and fence their neighbors away from them. They degrade the landscape with their buildings and their waste. They compel the natural earth to produce excessively and when it fails, they force it to take medicine to produce more. This is evil."

Some Scholarly Attempts
to Analyze the Problem

The Historical Roots of our Ecologic Crisis

Lynn White, Jr.

A conversation with Aldous Huxley not infrequently put one at the receiving end of an unforgettable monologue. About a year before his lamented death he was discoursing on a favorite topic: man's unnatural treatment of nature and its sad results. To illustrate his point he told how, during the previous summer, he had returned to a little valley in England where he had spent many happy months as a child. Once it had been composed of delightful grassy glades; now it was becoming overgrown with unsightly brush because the rabbits that formerly kept such growth under control had largely succumbed to a disease, myxamatosis, that was deliberately introduced by the local farmers to reduce the rabbits' destruction of crops. Being something of a Philistine, I could be silent no longer, even in the interests of great rhetoric. I interrupted to point out that the rabbit itself had been brought as a domestic animal to England in 1176, presumably to improve the protein diet of the peasantry.

All forms of life modify their contexts. The most spectacular and benign instance is doubtless the coral polyp. By serving its own ends, it had created a vast undersea world favorable to thousands of other kinds of animals and plants. Ever since man became a numerous species he has affected his environment notably. The hypothesis that his fire-drive method of hunting created the world's great grasslands and helped to exterminate the monster mammals of the Pleistocene from much of the globe is plausible, if not proved. For 6 millennia at least, the banks of the lower Nile have been a human artifact rather than the swampy African jungle which nature, apart from man, would have made it. The Aswan Dam, flooding 5000 square miles, is only the latest stage in a long process. In many regions terracing or irrigation, overgrazing, the cutting of forests by Romans to build ships to fight Carthaginians or by Crusaders to solve the logistics problems of their expeditions, have profoundly changed some ecologies. Observation that the French landscape falls into two basic types, the open fields of the north and the *bocage* of the south and west, inspired Marc Bloch to undertake his classic study of medieval agricultural methods. Quite unintentionally, changes in human ways often affect nonhuman nature. It has been noted, for example, that the advent of the automobile eliminated huge flocks of sparrows that once fed on the horse manure littering every street.

The history of ecologic change is still so rudimentary that we know little about what really happened, or what the results were. The extinction of the European aurochs as late as 1627 would seem to have been a simple case of overenthusiastic hunting. On more intricate matters it often is impossible to find solid information. For a thousand years or more the Frisians and Hollanders have been pushing back the North Sea, and the process is culminating in our own time in the reclamation of the Zuider Zee. What, if any, species of animals, birds, fish, shore life, or plants have died out in the process? In their epic combat with Neptune have the Netherlanders overlooked ecological values in such a way that the quality of human life in the Netherlands has suffered? I cannot discover that the questions have ever been asked, much less answered.

People, then, have often been a dynamic element in their own environment, but in the present state of historical scholarship we usually do not know exactly when, where, or with what effects man-induced changes came. As we enter the last third of the 20th century, however, concern for the problem of ecologic backlash is mounting feverishly. Natural science, conceived as the effort to understand the nature of things, had flourished in several eras and among several peoples. Similarly there had been an age-old accumulation of technological skills, sometimes growing rapidly, sometimes slowly. But it was not until about four generations ago that Western Europe and North America arranged a marriage between science and technology, a union of the theoretical and the empirical approaches to our natural environment. The emergence in widespread practice of the Baconian creed that scientific knowledge means technological power over nature can scarcely be dated before about 1850, save in the chemical industries, where it is anticipated in the 18th century. Its acceptance as a normal pattern of action may mark the greatest event in human history since the invention of agriculture, and perhaps in nonhuman terrestrial history as well.

Almost at once the new situation forced the crystallization of the novel concept of ecology; indeed, the word *ecology* first appeared in the English language in 1873. Today, less than a century later, the impact of our race upon the environment has so increased in force that it has changed in essence. When the first cannons were fired, in the early 14th century, they affected ecology by sending workers scrambling to the forests and mountains for more potash, sulfur, iron ore, and charcoal, with some resulting erosion and deforestation. Hydrogen bombs are of a different order: a war fought with them might alter the genetics of all life on this planet. By 1285 London had a smog problem arising from the burning of soft coal, but our present combustion of fossil fuels threatens to change the chemistry of the globe's atmosphere as a whole, with consequences which we are only beginning to guess. With the population explosion, the carcinoma of planless urbanism, the now geological deposits of sewage and garbage; surely no creature other than man has ever managed to foul its nest in such a short order.

There are many calls to action, but specific proposals, however worthy as individual items, seem too partial, palliative, negative: ban the bomb, tear down the billboards, give the Hindus contraceptives and tell them to eat their sacred cows. The simplest solution to any suspect change is, of course, to stop it, or, better yet, to revert to a romanticized past: make those ugly gasoline stations look like Anne Hathaway's cottage or (in the Far West) like ghost-town saloons. The "wilderness area" mentality invariably advocates deep-freezing an ecology, whether San Gimignano or the High Sierra, as it was before the first Kleenex was dropped. But neither atavism nor prettification will cope with the ecologic crisis of our time.

What shall we do? No one yet knows. Unless we think about fundamentals, our specific measures may produce new backlashes more serious than those they are designed to remedy.

As a beginning we should try to clarify our thinking by looking, in some historical depth, at the presuppositions that underlie modern technology and science. Science was traditionally aristocratic, speculative, intellectual in intent; technology was lower-class, empirical, action-oriented. The quite sudden fusion of these two, towards the middle of the 19th century, is surely related to the slightly prior and contemporary democratic revolutions which, by reducing social barriers, tended to assert a functional unity of brain and hand. Our ecologic crisis is the product of an emerging, entirely novel, democratic culture. The issue is whether a democratized world can survive its own implications. Presumably we cannot unless we rethink our axioms.

The Western Traditions of Technology and Science

One thing is so certain that it seems stupid to verbalize it: both modern technology and modern science are distinctly *Occidental*. Our technology has absorbed elements from all over the world, notably from China; yet everywhere today, whether in Japan or in Nigeria, successful technology is Western. Our science is the heir to all the sciences of the past, especially perhaps to the work of the great Islamic scientists of the Middle Ages, who so often outdid the ancient Greeks in skill and perspicacity: al-Razi in medicine, for example; or Ibn al-Haytham in optics; or Omar Khayyam in mathematics. Indeed, not a few works of such geniuses seem to have vanished in the original Arabic and to survive only in medieval Latin translations that helped to lay the foundations for later Western developments. Today, around the globe, all significant science is Western in style and method, whatever the pigmentation or language of the scientists.

A second pair of facts is less well recognized because they result from quite recent historical scholarship. The leadership of the West, both in technology and in science, is far older than the so-called Scientific Revolution of the 17th century or the so-called Industrial Revolution of the 18th century. These terms are in fact outmoded and obscure the true nature of what they try to describe—significant stages in two long and separate developments. By A.D. 1000 at the latest—and perhaps, feebly, as much as 200 years earlier—the West began to apply water power to industrial processes other than milling grain. This was followed in the late 12th century by the harnessing of wind power. From simple beginnings, but with remarkable consistency of style, the West rapidly expanded its skills in the development of power machinery, labor-saving devices, and automation. Those who doubt should contemplate that most monumental achievement in the history of automation: the weight-driven mechanical clock, which appeared in two forms in the early 14th century. Not in craftsmanship but in basic technological capacity, the Latin West of the later Middle Ages far outstripped its elaborate, sophisticated, and esthetically magnificent sister cultures, Byzantium and Islam. In 1444 a great Greek ecclesiastic, Bessarion, who had gone to Italy, wrote a letter to a prince in Greece. He is amazed by the superiority of Western ships, arms, textiles, glass. But above all he is astonished by the spectacle of waterwheels sawing timbers and pumping the bellows of blast furnaces. Clearly, he had seen nothing of the sort in the Near East.

By the end of the 15th century the technological superiority of Europe was such that its small, mutually hostile nations could spill out over all the rest of the world, conquering, looting, and colonizing. The symbol of this technological superiority is the fact that Portugal, one of the weakest states of the Occident, was able to become, and to remain for a century, mistress of the East Indies. And we must remember that the technology of Vasco da Gama and Albuquerque was built by pure empiricism, drawing remarkably little support or inspiration from science.

In the present-day vernacular understanding, modern science is supposed to have begun in 1543, when both Copernicus and Vesalius published their great works. It is no derogation of their accomplishments, however, to point out that such structures as the *Fabrica* and the *De revolutionibus* do not appear overnight. The distinctive Western tradition of science, in fact, began in the late 11th century with a massive movement of translation of Arabic and Greek scientific works into Latin. A few notable books—Theophrastus, for example—escaped the West's avid new appetite for science, but within less than 200 years effectively the entire corpus of Greek and Muslim science was available in Latin, and was being eagerly read and criticized in the new European universities. Out of criticism arose new observation, speculation, and increasing distrust of ancient authorities. By the late 13th century Europe had seized global scientific leadership from the faltering hands of Islam. It would be as absurd to deny the profound originality of Newton, Galileo, or Copernicus as to deny that of the 14th century scholastic scientists like Buridan or Oresme on whose work they built. Before the 11th century, science scarcely existed in the Latin West, even in Roman times. From the 11th century onward, the scientific sector of Occidental culture has increased in a steady crescendo.

Since both our technological and our scientific movements got their start, acquired their character, and achieved world dominance in the Middle Ages, it would seem that we cannot understand their nature or their present impact upon ecology without examining fundamental medieval assumptions and developments.

Medieval View of Man and Nature

Until recently, agriculture has been the chief occupation even in ''advanced'' societies; hence, any change in methods of tillage has much importance. Early plows, drawn by two oxen, did not normally turn the sod but merely scratched it. Thus, cross-plowing was needed and fields tended to be squarish. In the fairly light soils and semiarid climates of the Near East and Mediterranean, this worked well. But such a plow was inappropriate to the wet climate and often sticky soils of northern Europe. By the latter part of the 7th century after Christ, however, following obscure beginnings, certain northern peasants were using an entirely new kind of plow, equipped with a vertical knife to cut the line of the furrow, a horizontal share to slice under the sod, and a moldboard to turn it over. The friction of this plow with the soil was so great that it normally required not two but eight oxen. It attacked the land with such violence that cross-plowing was not needed, and fields tended to be shaped in long strips.

In the days of the scratch-plow, fields were distributed generally in units capable of supporting a single family. Subsistence farming was the presupposition. But no peasant owned eight oxen: to use the new and more efficient plow, peasants pooled their oxen to form large plow-teams, originally receiving (it would appear) plowed strips in proportion to their contribution. Thus, distribution of land was based no longer on the needs of a family but, rather, on the capacity of a power machine to till the earth. Man's relation to the soil was profoundly changed. Formerly man had been part of nature; now he was the exploiter of nature. Nowhere else in the world did farmers develop any analogous agricultural implement. Is it coincidence that modern technology, with its ruthlessness toward nature, has so largely been produced by descendants of these peasants of northern Europe?

This same exploitive attitude appears slightly before A.D. 830 in Western illustrated calendars. In older calendars the months were shown as passive personifications. The new Frankish calendars, which set the style for the Middle Ages, are very different: they show men coercing the world around them—plowing, harvesting, chopping trees, butchering pigs. Man and nature are two things, and man is master.

These novelties seem to be in harmony with larger intellectual patterns. What people do about their ecology depends on what they think about themselves in relation to things around them. Human ecology is deeply conditioned by beliefs about our nature and destiny—that is, by religion. To Western eyes this is very evident in, say, India or Ceylon. It is equally true of ourselves and of our medieval ancestors.

The victory of Christianity over paganism was the greatest psychic revolution in the history of our culture. It has become fashionable today to say that, for better or worse, we live in "the post-Christian age." Certainly the forms of our thinking and language have largely ceased to be Christian, but to my eye the substance often remains amazingly akin to that of the past. Our daily habits of action, for example, are dominated by an implicit faith in perpetual progress which was unknown either to Greco-Roman antiquity or to the Orient. It is rooted in, and is indefensible apart from, Judeo-Christian teleology. The fact that Communists share it merely helps to show what can be demonstrated on many other grounds: that Marxism, like Islam, is a Judeo-Christian heresy. We continue today to live, as we have lived for about 1700 years, very largely in a context of Christian axioms.

What did Christianity tell people about their relations with the environment? While many of the world's mythologies provide stories of creation, Greco-Roman mythology was singularly incoherent in this respect. Like Aristotle, the intellectuals of the ancient West denied that the visible world had had a beginning. Indeed, the idea of a beginning was impossible in the framework of their cyclical notion of time. In sharp contrast, Christianity inherited from Judaism not only a concept of time as nonrepetitive and linear but also a striking story of creation. By gradual stages a loving and all-powerful God had created light and darkness, the heavenly bodies, the earth and all its plants, animals, birds, and fishes. Finally, God had created Adam and, as an afterthought, Eve to keep man from being lonely. Man named all the animals, thus establishing his dominance over them. God planned all of this explicitly for man's benefit and rule: no item in the physical creation had any purpose save to serve man's purposes. And, although man's body is made of clay, he is not simply part of nature: he is made in God's image.

Especially in its Western form, Christianity is the most anthropocentric religion the world has seen. As early as the second century both Tertullian and Saint Irenaeus of Lyons were insisting that when God shaped Adam he was foreshadowing the image of the incarnate Christ, the Second Adam. Man shares, in great measure, God's transcendence of nature. Christianity, in absolute contrast to ancient paganism and Asia's religions (except, perhaps, Zoroastrianism), not only established a dualism of man and nature but also insisted that it is God's will that man exploit nature for his proper ends.

At the level of the common people this worked out in an interesting way. In antiquity every tree, every spring, every stream, every hill had its own *genius loci,* its guardian spirit. These spirits were accessible to men, but were very unlike men; centaurs, fauns, and mermaids show their ambivalence. Before one cut a tree, mined a mountain, or dammed a brook, it was important to placate the spirit in charge of that particular institution, and to keep it placated. By destroying pagan animism, Christianity made it possible to exploit nature in a mood of indifference to the feelings of natural objects.

It is often said that for animism the Church substituted the cult of saints. True; but the cult of saints is functionally quite different from animism. The saint is not *in* natural objects; he may have special shrines, but his citizenship is in heaven. Moreover, a saint is entirely a man; he can be approached in human terms. In addition to saints, Christianity of course also had angels and demons inherited from Judaism and perhaps, at one remove, from Zoroastrianism. But these were all as mobile as the saints themselves. The spirits *in* natural objects, which formerly had protected nature from man, evaporated. Man's effective monopoly on spirit in this world was confirmed, and the old inhibitions to the exploitation of nature crumbled.

When one speaks in such sweeping terms, a note of caution is in order. Christianity is a complex faith, and its consequences differ in differing contexts. What I have said may well apply to the medieval West, where in fact technology made spectacular advances. But the Greek East, a highly civilized realm of equal Christian devotion, seems to have produced no marked technological innovation after the late 7th century, when Greek fire was invented. The key to the contrast may perhaps be found in a difference in the tonality of piety and thought which students of comparative theology find between the Greek and the Latin Churches. The Greeks believed that sin was intellectual blindness, and that salvation was found in illumination, orthodoxy—that is, clear thinking. The Latins, on the other hand, felt that sin was moral evil, and that salvation was to be found in right conduct. Eastern theology has been intellectualist. Western theology has been voluntarist. The Greek saint contemplates; the Western saint acts. The implications of Christianity for the conquest of nature would emerge more easily in the Western atmosphere.

The Christian dogma of creation, which is found in the first clause of all the Creeds, has another meaning for our comprehension of today's ecologic crisis. By revelation, God had given man the Bible, the Book of Scripture. But since God had made nature, nature also must reveal the divine mentality. The religious study of nature for the better understanding of God was known as natural theology. In the early Church, and always in the Greek East, nature was conceived primarily as a symbolic system through which God speaks to men: the ant is a sermon to sluggards; rising flames are the symbol of the soul's aspiration. This view of nature was essentially artistic rather than scientific. While Byzantium preserved and copied great numbers of ancient Greek scientific texts, science as we conceive it could scarcely flourish in such an ambience.

However, in the Latin West by the early 13th century natural theology was following a very different bent. It was ceasing to be the decoding of the physical symbols of God's communication with man and was becoming the effort to understand God's mind by discovering how his creation operates. The rainbow was no longer simply a symbol of hope first sent to Noah after the Deluge: Robert Grosseteste, Friar Roger Bacon, and Theodoric of Freiberg produced startlingly sophisticated work on the optics of the rainbow, but they did it as a venture in religious understanding. From the 13th century onward, up to and including Leibnitz and Newton, every major scientist, in effect, explained his motivations in religious terms. Indeed, if Galileo had not been so expert an amateur theologian he would have got into far less trouble: the professionals resented his intrusion. And Newton seems to have regarded himself more as a theologian than as a scientist. It was not until the late 18th century that the hypothesis of God became unnecessary to many scientists.

It is often hard for the historian to judge, when men explain why they are doing what they want to do, whether they are offering real reasons or merely culturally acceptable reasons. The consistency with which scientists during the long formative centuries of Western science said that the task and the reward of the scientist was "to think God's thoughts after him" leads one to believe that this was their real motivation. If so, then modern Western science was cast in a matrix of Christian theology. The dynamism of religious devotion, shaped by the Judeo-Christian dogma of creation, gave it impetus.

An Alternative Christian View

We would seem to be headed toward conclusions unpalatable to many Christians. Since both *science* and *technology* are blessed words in our contemporary vocabulary, some may be happy at the notions, first, that, viewed historically, modern science is an extrapolation of natural theology and, second, that modern technology is at least partly to be explained as an Occidental, voluntarist realization of the Christian dogma of man's transcendence of, and rightful mastery over, nature. But, as we now recognize, somewhat over a century ago science and technology—hitherto quite separate activities—joined to give mankind powers which, to judge by many of the ecologic effects, are out of control. If so, Christianity bears a huge burden of guilt.

I personally doubt that disastrous ecologic backlash can be avoided simply by applying to our problems more science and more technology. Our science and technology have grown out of Christian attitudes toward man's relation to nature which are almost universally held not only by Christians and neo-Christians but also by those who fondly regard themselves as post-Christians. Despite Copernicus, all the cosmos rotates around our little globe. Despite Darwin, we are *not,* in our hearts, part of the natural process. We are superior to nature, contemptuous of it, willing to use it for our slightest whim. The newly elected Governor of California, like myself a churchman but less troubled than I, spoke for the Christian tradition when he said (as is alleged), "when you've seen one redwood tree, you've seen them all." To a Christian a tree can be no more than a physical fact. The whole concept of the sacred grove is alien to Christianity and to the ethos of the West. For nearly two millennia Christian missionaries have been chopping down sacred groves, which are idolatrous because they assume spirit in nature.

What we do about ecology depends on our ideas of the man-nature relationship. More science and more technology are not going to get us out of the present ecologic crisis until we find a new religion, or re-think our old one. The beatniks, who are the basic revolutionaries of our time, show a sound instinct in their affinity for Zen Buddhism, which conceives of the man-nature relationship as very nearly the mirror image of the Christian view. Zen, however, is as deeply conditioned by Asian history as Christianity is by the experience of the West, and I am dubious of its viability among us.

Possibly we should ponder the greatest radical in Christian history since Christ: Saint Francis of Assisi. The prime miracle of Saint Francis is the fact that he did not end at the stake, as many of his left-wing followers did. He was so clearly heretical that a General of the Franciscan Order, Saint Bonaventure, a great and perceptive Christian, tried to suppress the early accounts of Franciscanism. The key to an understanding of Francis is his belief in the virtue of humility—not merely for the individual but for man as a species. Francis tried to depose man from his monarchy over creation and set up a democracy of all God's creatures. With him the ant is no longer simply a homily for the lazy, flame a sign of the thrust of the soul toward union with God; now they are Brother Ant and Sister Fire, praising the Creator in their own ways as Brother Man does in his.

Later commentators have said that Francis preached to the birds as a rebuke to men who would not listen. The records do not read so: he urged the little birds to praise God, and in spiritual ecstasy they flapped their wings and chirped rejoicing. Legends of saints, especially the Irish saints, had long told of their dealings with animals but always, I believe, to show their human dominance over creatures. With Francis it is different. The land around Gubbio in the Apennines was being ravaged by a fierce wolf. Saint Francis, says the legend, talked to the wolf and persuaded him of the error of his ways. The wolf repented, died in the odor of sanctity, and was buried in consecrated ground.

What Sir Steven Ruciman calls "the Franciscan doctrine of the animal soul" was quickly stamped out. Quite possibly it was in part inspired, consciously or unconsciously, by the belief in reincarnation held by the Cathar heretics who at that time teemed in Italy and southern France, and who presumably had got it originally from India. It is significant that at just the same moment, about 1200, traces of metempsychosis are found also in western Judaism, in the Provencal *Cabbala*. But Francis held neither to transmigration of souls nor to pantheism. His view of nature and of man rested on a unique sort of pan-psychism of all things animate and inanimate, designed for the glorification of their transcendent Creator, who, in the ultimate gesture of cosmic humility, assumed flesh, lay helpless in a manger, and hung dying on a scaffold.

I am not suggesting that many contemporary Americans who are concerned about our ecologic crisis will be either able or willing to counsel with wolves or exhort birds. However, the present increasing disruption of the global environment is the product of a dynamic technology and science which were originating in the Western medieval world against which Saint Francis was rebelling in so original a way. Their growth cannot be understood historically apart from distinctive attitudes toward nature which are deeply grounded in Christian dogma. The fact that most people do not think of these attitudes as Christian is irrelevant. No new set of basic values has been accepted in our society to displace those of Christianity. Hence we shall continue to have a worsening ecologic crisis until we reject the Christian axiom that nature has no reason for existence save to serve man.

The greatest spiritual revolutionary in Western history, Saint Francis, proposed what he thought was an alternative Christian view of nature and man's relation to it: he tried to substitute the idea of the equality of all creatures, including man, for the idea of man's limitless rule of creation. He failed. Both our present science and our present technology are so tinctured with orthodox Christian arrogance toward nature that no solution for our ecologic crisis can be expected from them alone. Since the roots of our trouble are so largely religious, whether we call it that or not, we must rethink and refeel our nature and destiny. The profoundly religious, but heretical, sense of the primitive Franciscans for the spiritual autonomy of all parts of nature may point a direction. I propose Francis as a patron saint for ecologists.

The Prehistoric Roots of our Attitudes

Roderick Nash

The first point to be made is that wilderness was the home of protohumans until they created a civilization—for millions of years, in other words. Looked at another way, our kind has lived in wilderness at least one hundred times longer than it has lived in civilization. Certainly the influence of this immense background of collective experience would not disappear easily or completely.

Until roughly fifteen million years ago our prehuman ancestors dwelt in an arboreal environment. They were at home in jungles or forests primeval—"wilderness" in the usual sense of that term. At this distant point there was no dichotomy between prehumans and wild country: the creatures that evolved into men were part of the wilderness. The dark hiding places among trees and vines were sanctuaries. But approximately fifteen million years ago, geological and anthropological studies have revealed, climatic changes began to reduce the area of forest and jungle in central Africa, and other seedbeds of man. The primates that became man gradually left the shrinking arboreal environment and began to adapt to a life of hunting on the grasslands.

In this open, spacious environment of great distances, vision assumed an importance it lacked in the dense, dark wilderness. To cope with the requirements of life on the plains the protomen needed and developed, among other attributes, remarkable visual ability. In part this compensated for the superior sense of smell and hearing and the speed, size, and strength of other animals. Good vision was early man's competitive edge in the struggle for existence. Coupled with his brain it enabled him to anticipate, plan ahead, and survive. A lion a mile away, for example, presented an entirely different set of problems from one that sprung from a nearby thicket. With his eyes, early man bought time and the chance to think. Sight (and openness) meant security.

It followed that early man preferred an open environment, where he could employ his vision and his brain, to the shadowy wilderness. In the forest or jungle keen sight counted for little. There the race usually went to the smellers, the hearers, and the physically powerful, and man did not rank high in these categories. Thus once our ancestors left the wilderness, they were loath to return to an environment that neutralized their visual advantages. Indeed, when they could they burned forests in order to convert them to open grassland.

Early man feared the night for the same reasons he feared wilderness. With the setting of the sun, while other predators began their hunts, man sought the protection of a cave and, in time, of fire. I do not think fire has been sufficiently appreciated as an aid to vision as well as a means of warming and cooking. In that magic circle of light there was comfort and security. The darkness beyond, like the wilderness, was terrifying.

I have been arguing that millions of years of life in open environments, relying on vision in the struggle for existence, stamped a lasting bias against wilderness on the mind of protoman and man himself. If this is so, it should be possible to observe the bias lingering even after the advent of civilization. I believe we do find it in our continuing fear of the forest and the night. Unquestionably, some of this fear has seeped into the realms of the subconscious and instinctive. Yet its power remains. Take, for instance, the experience of North American pioneers. In the thick forest of the Atlantic coast they felt uneasy. Account after account describes how the wilderness hemmed man in, frustrating his vision and concealing a host of dangers, both real and imaginary. As my second chapter, below, attempts to show, the pioneers feared and hated this environment. Recognizing the root of their bias, they used visual metaphors to express their feelings. The wilderness was "dark" and "gloomy" or "nightmarish." The pioneers' obsession was to clear the land, to remove the vision-obscuring trees and vines, to bring light into darkness. Certainly there was an economic motive for this attitude. Religion also figured in it, since wilderness was construed by most frontiersmen to be in league with devils, demons, and the evil forces of darkness that civilization must overcome. But, I increasingly feel, the heart of the bias against wilderness was the ancient association between security and sight. The American pioneer re-experienced the situation and the anxieties of early man. Neither felt at home in the wilderness.

In this connection it is interesting to note that many accounts of westward migration in North America contain expressions of relief on emerging from the Eastern forest wilderness to the openness of the Great Plains. All at once the pioneers could *see,* and their spirits immediately brightened. In rhapsodic language, never applied to forests, accounts such as James Hall's *Notes on the Western States* (1838) described the waving grass, the profusion of flowers, the brilliant sunshine. The Midwestern plains, to be sure, were just as devoid of civilization as the Eastern forests, but from the pioneers' perspective they were a different kind of environment. This is evident from the fact that the term "wilderness" was seldom applied to the grasslands of the Middle West. "Garden," on the other hand, was frequently employed. In a high-speed rerun, the emergence from forest to plains in North America repeated the process of fifteen million years before, which resulted in arboreal primates becoming plains-dwellers and the ancestors of man. This same process stacked the deck of man's priorities against wilderness.

Despite the rise in appreciation of wild country, some of the ancient vision-oriented antipathy remains today. We find it in our environmental preferences, both conscious and unconscious. Consider, as a case in point, the reason why ridgetop and cliffside houses with views usually command the highest prices. One could simply explain this preference for a vantage point as a matter of aesthetics or prestige or happiness. But, probing deeper, perhaps the basic reason is the old relationship between sight and security. Remnants of the primordial dread of wilderness placed the nobleman's castle and the millionaire's split-level on the top of the hill.

The same preference for openness influences our choice of camping sites. Isn't it true that we prefer open places like meadows and lake shores and river banks? Don't we avoid camping in the dense forest, the classic "wilderness," if we can? Ancient impulses that we scarcely understand cause us to feel vaguely ill-at-ease in the deep woods.

The Tragedy Of The Commons

Garrett Hardin

At the end of a thoughtful article on the future of nuclear war, Wiesner and York (1) concluded that: "Both sides in the arms race are . . .confronted by the dilemma of steadily increasing military power and steadily decreasing national security. *It is our considered professional judgment that this dilemma has no technical solution.* If the great powers continue to look for solutions in the area of science and technology only, the result will be to worsen the situation."

I would like to focus your attention not on the subject of the article (national security in a nuclear world) but on the kind of conclusion they reached, namely that there is no technical solution to the problem. An implicit and almost universal assumption of discussions published in professional and semipopular scientific journals is that the problem under discussion has a technical solution. A technical solution may be defined as one that requires a change only in the techniques of the natural sciences, demanding little or nothing in the way of change in human values or ideas of morality.

In our day (though not in earlier times) technical solutions are always welcome. Because of previous failures in prophecy, it takes courage to assert that a desired technical solution is not possible. Wiesner and York exhibited this courage; publishing in a science journal, they insisted that the solution to the problem was not to be found in the natural sciences. They cautiously qualified their statement with the phrase, "It is our considered professional judgment . . ." Whether they were right or not is not the concern of the present article. Rather, the concern here is with the important concept of a class of human problems which can be called "no technical solution problems," and, more specifically, with the identification and discussion of one of these.

It is easy to show that the class is not a null class. Recall the game of tick-tack-toe. Consider the problem, "How can I win the game of tick-tack-toe?" It is well known that I cannot, if I assume (in keeping with the conventions of game theory) that my opponent understands the game perfectly. Put another way, there is no "technical solution" to the problem. I can win only by giving a radical meaning to the word "win." I can hit my opponent over the head; or I can drug him; or I can falsify the records. Every way in which I "win" involves, in some sense, an abandonment of the game, as we intuitively understand it. (I can also, of course, openly abandon the game—refuse to play it. This is what most adults do.)

The class of "No technical solution problems" has members. My thesis is that the "population problem," as conventionally conceived, is a member of this class. How it is conventionally conceived needs some comment. It is fair to say that most people who anguish over the population problem are trying to find a way to avoid the evils of overpopulation without relinquishing any of the privileges they now enjoy. They think that farming the seas or developing new strains of wheat will solve the problem—technologically. I try to show here that the solution they seek cannot be found. The population problem cannot be solved in a technical way, any more than can the problem of winning the game of tick-tack-toe.

What Shall We Maximize?

Population, as Malthus said, naturally tends to grow "geometrically," or, as we would now say, exponentially. In a finite world this means that the per capita share of the world's goods must steadily decrease. Is ours a finite world?

A fair defense can be put forward for the view that the world is infinite; or that we do not know that it is not. But, in terms of the practical problems that we must face in the next few generations with the foreseeable technology, it is clear that we will greatly increase human misery if we do not, during the immediate future, assume that the world available to the terrestrial human population is finite. "Space" is no escape (2).

A finite world can support only a finite population; therefore, population growth must eventually equal zero. (The case of perpetual wide fluctuations above and below zero is a trivial variant that need not be discussed.) When this condition is met, what will be the situation of mankind? Specifically, can Bentham's goal of "the greatest good for the greatest number" be realized?

No–for two reasons, each sufficient by itself. The first is a theoretical one. It is not mathematically possible to maximize for two (or more) variables at the same time. This was clearly stated by von Neumann and Morgenstern (3), but the principle is implicit in the theory of partial differential equations, dating back at least to D'Alembert (1717-1783).

The second reason springs directly from biological facts. To live, any organism must have a source of energy (for example, food). This energy is utilized for two purposes: mere maintenance and work. For man, maintenance of life requires about 1600 kilocalories a day ("maintenance calories"). Anything that he does over and above merely staying alive will be defined as work, and is supported by "work calories" which he takes in. Work calories are used not only for what we call work in common speech; they are also required for all forms of enjoyment, from swimming and automobile racing to playing music and writing poetry. If our goal is to maximize population it is obvious what we must do: We must make the work calories per person approach as close to zero as possible. No gourmet meals, no vacations, no sports, no music, no literature, no art . . .I think that everyone will grant, without argument or proof, that maximizing population does not maximize goods. Bentham's goal is impossible.

In reaching this conclusion I have made the usual assumption that it is the acquisition of energy that is the problem. The appearance of atomic energy has led some to question this assumption. However, given an infinite source of energy, population growth still produces an inescapable problem. The problem of the acquisition of energy is replaced by the problem of its dissipation, as J. H. Fremlin has so wittily shown (4). The arithmetic signs in the analysis are, as it were, reversed; but Bentham's goal is still unobtainable.

The optimum population is, then, less than the maximum. The difficulty of defining the optimum is enormous; so far as I know, no one has seriously tackled this problem. Reaching an acceptable and stable solution will surely require more than one generation of hard analytical work—and much persuasion.

We want the maximum good per person; but what is good? To one person it is wilderness, to another it is ski lodges for thousands. To one it is estuaries to nourish ducks for hunters to shoot; to another it is factory land. Comparing one good with another is, we usually say, impossible because goods are incommensurable. Incommensurables cannot be compared.

Theoretically this may be true; but in real life incommensurables are commensurable. Only a criterion of judgment and a system of weighting are needed. In nature the criterion is survival. Is it better for a species to be small and hideable, or large and powerful? Natural selection commensurates the incommensurables. The compromise achieved depends on a natural weighting of the values of the variables.

Man must imitate this process. There is no doubt that in fact he already does, but unconsciously. It is when the hidden decisions are made explicit that the arguments begin. The problem for the years ahead is to work out an acceptable theory of weighting. Synergistic effects, nonlinear variation, and difficulties in discounting the future make the intellectual problem difficult, but not (in principle) insoluble.

Has any cultural group solved this practical problem at the present time, even on an intuitive level? One simple fact proves that none has: there is no prosperous population in the world today that has, and has had for sometime, a growth rate of zero. Any people that has intuitively identified its optimum point will soon reach it, after which its growth rate becomes and remains zero.

Of course, a positive growth rate might be taken as evidence that a population is below its optimum. However, by any reasonable standards, the most rapidly growing populations on earth today are (in general) the most miserable. This association (which need not be invariable) casts doubt on the optimistic assumption that the positive growth rate of a population is evidence that it has yet to reach its optimum.

We can make little progress in working toward optimum population size until we explicitly exorcize the spirit of Adam Smith in the field of practical demography. In economic affairs, *The Wealth of Nations* (1776) popularized the "invisible hand," the idea that an individual who "intends only his own gain," is, as it were, "led by an invisible hand to promote . . .the public interest" (5). Adam Smith did not assert that this was invariably true, and perhaps neither did any of his followers. But he contributed to a dominant tendency of thought that has ever since interfered with positive action based on rational analysis, namely, the tendency to assume that decisions reached individually will, in fact, be the best decisions for an entire society. If this assumption is correct it justifies the continuance of our present policy of laissez-faire in reproduction. If it is correct we can assume that men will control their individual fecundity so as to produce the optimum population. If the assumption is not correct, we need to reexamine our individual freedoms to see which ones are defensible.

Tragedy of Freedom in a Commons

The rebuttal to the invisible hand in population control is to be found in a scenario first sketched in a little-known pamphlet (6) in 1833 by a mathematical amateur named William Forster Lloyd (1794-1852). We may well call it "the tragedy of the commons," using the word "tragedy" as the philosopher Whitehead used it (7): "The essence of dramatic tragedy is not unhappiness. It resides in the solemnity of the remorseless working of things." He then goes on to say, "This inevitableness of destiny can only be illustrated in terms of human life by incidents which in fact involve unhappiness. For it is only by them that the futility of escape can be made evident in the drama."

The tragedy of the commons develops in this way. Picture a pasture open to all. It is to be expected that each herdsman will try to keep as many cattle as possible on the commons. Such an arrangement may work reasonably satisfactorily for centuries because tribal wars, poaching, and disease keep the numbers of both man and beast well below the carrying capacity of the land. Finally, however, comes the day of reckoning, that is, the day when the long-desired goal of social stability becomes a reality. At this point, the inherent logic of the commons remorselessly generates tragedy.

As a rational being, each herdsman seeks to maximize his gain. Explicity or implicitly, more or less consciously, he asks, "What is the utility *to me* of adding one more animal to my herd?" This utility has one negative and one positive component.

1) The positive component is a function of the increment of one animal. Since the herdsman receives all the proceeds from the sale of the additional animal, the positive utility is nearly $+1$.

2) The negative component is a function of the additional overgrazing created by one more animal. Since, however, the effects of overgrazing are shared by all the herdsmen, the negative utility for any particular decision-making herdsman is only a fraction of -1.

Adding together the component partial utilities, the rational herdsman concludes that the only sensible course for him to pursue is to add another animal to his herd. And another; and another . . . But this is the conclusion reached by each and every rational herdsman sharing a commons. Therein is the tragedy. Each man is locked into a system that compels him to increase his herd without limit—in a world that is limited. Ruin is the destination toward which all men rush, each pursuing his own best interest in a society that believes in the freedom of the commons. Freedom in a commons brings ruin to all.

Some would say that this is a platitude. Would that it were! In a sense, it was learned thousands of years ago, but natural selection favors the forces of psychological denial (8). The individual benefits as an individual from his ability to deny the truth even though society as a whole, of which he is a part, suffers. Education can counteract the natural tendency to do the wrong thing, but the inexorable succession of generations requires that the basis for this knowledge be constantly refreshed.

A simple incident that occurred a few years ago in Leominster, Massachusetts, shows how perishable the knowledge is. During the Christmas shopping season the parking meters downtown were covered with plastic bags that bore tags reading: "Do not open until after Christmas. Free parking courtesy of the mayor and city council." In other words, facing the prospect of an increased demand for already scarce space, the city fathers reinstituted the system of the commons. (Cynically, we suspect that they gained more votes than they lost by this retrogressive act.)

In an approximate way, the logic of the commons has been understood for a long time, perhaps since the discovery of agriculture or the invention of private property in real estate. But it is understood mostly only in special cases which are not sufficiently generalized. Even at this late date, cattlemen leasing national land on the western ranges demonstrate no more than an ambivalent understanding, in constantly pressuring federal authorities to increase the head count to the point where overgrazing produces erosion and weed-dominance. Likewise, the oceans of the world continue to suffer from the survival of the philosophy of the commons. Maritime nations still respond automatically to the shibboleth of the "freedom of the seas." Professing to believe in the "inexhaustible resources of the oceans," they bring species after species of fish and whales closer to extinction (9).

The National Parks present another instance of the working out of the tragedy of the commons. At present, they are open to all, without limit. The parks themselves are limited in extent—there is only one Yosemite Valley—whereas population seems to grow without limit. The values that visitors seek in the parks are steadily eroded. Plainly, we must soon cease to treat the parks as commons or they will be of no value to anyone.

What shall we do? We have several options. We might sell them off as private property. We might keep them as public property, but allocate the right to enter them. The allocation might be on the basis of wealth, by the use of an auction system. It might be on the basis of merit, as defined by some agreed-upon standards. It might be by lottery. Or it might be on a first-come, first-served basis, administered to long queues. These, I think, are all the reasonable possibilities. They are all objectionable. But we must choose—or acquiesce in the destruction of the commons that we call our National Parks.

Pollution

In a reverse way, the tragedy of the commons reappears in problems of pollution. Here it is not a question of taking something out of the commons, but of putting something in—sewage, or chemical, radioactive, and heat wastes into water; noxious and dangerous fumes into the air; and distracting and unpleasant advertising signs into the line of sight. The calculations of utility are much the same as before. The rational man finds that his share of the cost of the wastes he discharges into the commons is less than the cost of purifying his wastes before releasing them. Since this is true for everyone, we are locked into a system of "fouling our own nest," so long as we behave only as independent, rational, free-enterprisers.

The tragedy of the commons as a food basket is averted by private property, or something formally like it. But the air and waters surrounding us cannot readily be fenced, and so the tragedy of the commons as a cesspool must be prevented by different means, by coercive laws or taxing devices that make it cheaper for the polluter to treat his pollutants than to discharge them untreated. We have not progressed as far with the solution of this problem as we have with the first. Indeed, our particular concept of private property, which deters us from exhausting the positive resources of the earth, favors pollution. The owner of a factory on the bank of a stream—whose property extends to the middle of the stream—often has difficulty seeing why it is not his natural right to muddy the waters flowing past his door. The law, always behind the times, requires elaborate stitching and fitting to adapt it to this newly perceived aspect of the commons.

The pollution problem is a consequence of population. It did not much matter how a lonely American frontiersman disposed of his waste. "Flowing water purifies itself every 10 miles," my grandfather used to say, and the myth was near enough to the truth when he was a boy, for there were not too many people. But as population became denser, the natural chemical and biological recycling processes became overloaded, calling for a redefinition of property rights.

How To Legislate Temperance?

Analysis of the pollution problem as a function of population density uncovers a not generally recognized principle of morality, namely: *the morality of an act is a function of the state of the system at the time it is performed* (10). Using the commons as a cesspool does not harm the general public under frontier conditions, because there is no public; the same behavior in a metropolis is unbearable. A hundred and fifty years ago a plainsman could kill an American bison, cut out only the tongue for his dinner, and discard the rest of the animal. He was not in any important sense being wasteful. Today, with only a few thousand bison left, we would be appalled at such behavior.

In passing, it is worth noting that the morality of an act cannot be determined from a photograph. One does not know whether a man killing an elephant or setting fire to the grassland is harming others until one knows the total system in which his act appears. "One picture is worth a thousand words," said an ancient Chinese; but it may take 10,000 words to validate it. It is as tempting to ecologists as it is to reformers in general to try to persuade others by way of the photographic shortcut. But the essense of an argument cannot be photographed: it must be presented rationally—in words.

That morality is system-sensitive escaped the attention of most codifiers of ethics in the past. "Thou shalt not . . ." is the form of traditional ethical directives which make no allowance for particular circumstances. The laws of our society follow the pattern of ancient ethics, and therefore are poorly suited to governing a complex, crowded, changeable world. Our epicyclic solution is to augment statutory law with administrative law. Since it is practically impossible to spell out all the conditions under which it is safe to burn trash in the back yard or to run an automobile without smog-control, by law we delegate the details to bureaus. The result is administrative law, which is rightly feared for an ancient reason—*Quis custodiet ipsos custodes?*—"Who shall watch the watchers themselves?" John Adams said that we must have "a government of laws and not men." Bureau administrators, trying to evaluate the morality of acts in the total system, are singularly liable to corruption, producing a government by men, not laws.

Prohibition is easy to legislate (though not necessarily to enforce); but how do we legislate temperance? Experience indicates that it can be accomplished best through the mediation of administrative law. We limit possibilities unnecessarily if we suppose that the sentiment of *Quis custodiet* denies us the use of administrative law. We should rather retain the phrase as a perpetual reminder of fearful dangers we cannot avoid. The great challenge facing us now is to invent the corrective feedbacks that are needed to keep custodians honest. We must find ways to legitimate the needed authority of both the custodians and the corrective feedbacks.

Freedom To Breed Is Intolerable

The tragedy of the commons is involved in population problems in another way. In a world governed solely by the principle of "dog eat dog"—if indeed there ever was such a world—how many children a family had would not be a matter of public concern. Parents who bred too exuberantly would leave fewer descendants, not more, because they would be unable to care adequately for their children. David Lack and others have found that such a negative feedback demonstrably controls the fecundity of birds (11). But men are not birds, and have not acted like them for millenniums, at least.

If each human family were dependent only on its own resources; *if* the children of improvident parents starved to death; *if,* thus, overbreeding brought its own "punishment" to the germ line—*then* there would be no public interest in controlling the breeding of families. But out society is deeply committed to the welfare state (12), and hence is confronted with another aspect of the tragedy of the commons.

In a welfare state, how shall we deal with the family, the religion, the race, or the class (or indeed any distinguishable and cohesive group) that adopts overbreeding as a policy to secure its own aggrandizement (13)? To couple the concept of freedom to breed with the belief that everyone born has an equal right to the commons is to lock the world into a tragic course of action.

Unfortunately this is just the course of action that is being pursued by the United Nations. In late 1967, some 30 nations agreed to the following (14):

The Universal Declaration of Human Rights describes the family as the natural and fundamental unit of society. It follows that any choice and decision with regard to the size of the family must irrevocably rest with the family itself, and cannot be made by anyone else.

It is painful to have to deny categorically the validity of this right; denying it, one feels as uncomfortable as a resident of Salem, Massachusetts, who denied the reality of witches in the 17th century. At the present time, in liberal quarters, something like a taboo acts to inhibit criticism of the United Nations. There is a feeling that the United Nations is "our last and best hope," that we shouldn't find fault with it; we shouldn't play into the hands of the archconservatives. However, let us not forget what Robert Louis Stevenson said: "The truth that is suppressed by friends is the readiest weapon of the enemy." If we love the truth we must openly deny the validity of the Universal Declaration of Human Rights, even though it is promoted by the United Nations. We should also join with Kingsley Davis (15) in attempting to get Planned Parenthood-World Population to see the error of its ways in embracing the same tragic ideal.

Conscience Is Self-Eliminating

It is a mistake to think that we can control the breeding of mankind in the long run by an appeal to conscience. Charles Galton Darwin made this point when he spoke on the centennial of the publication of his grandfather's great book. The argument is straightforward and Darwinian.

People vary. Confronted with appeals to limit breeding, some people will undoubtedly respond to the plea more than others. Those who have more children will produce a larger fraction of the next generation than those with more susceptible consciences. The difference will be accentuated, generation by generation.

In C. G. Darwin's words: "It may well be that it would take hundreds of generations for the progenitive instinct to develop in this way, but if it should do so, nature would have taken her revenge, and the variety *Homo contracipiens* would become extinct and would be replaced by the variety *Homo progenitivus*" (16).

The argument assumes that conscience or the desire for children (no matter which) is hereditary—but hereditary only in the most general formal sense. The result will be the same whether the attitude is transmitted through germ cells, or exosomatically, to use A. J. Lotka's term. (If one denies the latter possibility as well as the former, then what's the point of education?) The argument has here been stated in the context of the population problem, but it applies equally well to any instance in which society appeals to an individual exploiting a commons to restrain himself for the general good—by means of his conscience. To make such an appeal is to set up a selective system that works toward the elimination of conscience from the race.

Pathogenic Effects of Conscience

The long-term disadvantage of an appeal to conscience should be enough to condemn it; but has serious short-term disadvantages as well. If we ask a man who is exploiting a commons to desist "in the name of conscience," what are we saying to him? What does he hear?—not only at the moment but also in the wee small hours of the night when, half asleep, he remembers not merely the words we used but also the nonverbal communication cues we gave him unawares? Sooner or later, consciously or subconsciously, he senses that he has received two communications, and that they are contradictory: (i) (intended communication) "If you don't do as we ask, we will openly condemn you for not acting like a responsible citizen"; (ii) (the unintended communication) "If you *do* behave as we ask, we will secretly condemn you for a simpleton who can be shamed into standing aside while the rest of us exploit the commons."

Everyman then is caught in what Bateson has called a "double bind." Bateson and his co-workers have made a plausible case for viewing the double bind as an important causative factor in the genesis of schizophrenia (17). The double bind may not always be so damaging, but it always endangers the mental health of anyone to whom it is applied. "A bad conscience," said Nietzsche, "is a kind of illness."

To conjure up a conscience in others is tempting to anyone who wishes to extend his control beyond the legal limits. Leaders at the highest level succumb to this temptation. Has any President during the past generation failed to call on labor unions to moderate voluntarily their demands for higher wages, or to steel companies to honor voluntary guidelines on prices? I can recall none. The rhetoric used on such occasions is designed to produce feelings of guilt in noncooperators.

For centuries it was assumed without proof that guilt was a valuable, perhaps even an indispensable ingredient of the civilized life. Now, in this post-Freudian world, we doubt it.

Paul Goodman speaks from the modern point of view when he says: "No good has ever come from feeling guilty, neither intelligence, policy, nor compassion. The guilty do not pay attention to the object but only to themselves, and not even to their own interests, which might make sense, but to their anxieties" (18).

One does not have to be a professional psychiatrist to see the consequences of anxiety. We in the Western world are just emerging from a dreadful two-centuries-long Dark Ages of Eros that was sustained partly by prohibition laws, but perhaps more effectively by the anxiety-generating mechanisms of education. Alex Comfort has told the story well in *The Anxiety Makers* (19); it is not a pretty one.

Since proof is difficult, we may even concede that the results of anxiety may sometimes, from certain points of view, be desirable. The larger question we should ask is whether, as a matter of policy, we should ever encourage the use of a technique the tendency (if not the intention) of which is psychologically pathogenic. We hear much talk these days of responsible parenthood; the coupled words are incorporated into the titles of some organizations devoted to birth control. Some people have proposed massive propaganda campaigns to instill responsibility into the nation's (or the world's) breeders. But what is the meaning of the word responsibility in this context? Is it not merely a synonym for the word conscience? When we use the word responsibility in the absence of substantial functions are we not trying to browbeat a free man in a commons into acting against his own interest? Responsibility is a verbal counterfeit for a substantial *quid pro quo*. It is an attempt to get something for nothing.

If the word responsibility is to be used at all, I suggest that it be in the sense Charles Frankel uses it (20). "Responsibility," says this philosopher, "is the product of definite social arrangements." Notice that Frankel calls for social arrangements—not propaganda.

Mutual Coercion Mutually Agreed Upon

The social arrangements that produce responsibility are arrangements that create coercion, of some sort. Consider bank-robbing. The man who takes money from a bank acts as if the bank were a commons. How do we prevent such action? Certainly not by trying to control his behavior solely by a verbal appeal to his sense of responsibility. Rather than rely on propaganda we follow Frankel's lead and insist that a bank is not a commons; we seek the definite social arrangements that will keep it from becoming a commons. That we thereby infringe on the freedom of would-be robbers we neither deny nor regret.

The morality of bank-robbing is particularly easy to understand because we accept complete prohibition of this activity. We are willing to say "Thou shalt not rob banks," without providing for exceptions. But temperance also can be created by coercion. Taxing is a good coercive device. To keep downtown shoppers temperate in their use of parking space we introduce parking meters for short periods, and traffic fines for longer ones. We need not actually forbid a citizen to park as long as he wants to; we need merely make it increasingly expensive for him to do so. Not prohibition, but carefully biased options are what we offer him. A Madison Avenue man might call this persuasion; I prefer the greater candor of the word coercion.

Coercion is a dirty word to most liberals now, but it need not forever be so. As with the four-letter words, its dirtiness can be cleansed away by exposure to the light, by saying it over and over without apology or embarrassment. To many, the word coercion implies arbitrary decisions of distant and irresponsible bureaucrats; but this is not a necessary part of its meaning. The only kind of coercion I recommend is mutual coercion, mutually agreed upon by the majority of the people affected.

To say that we mutually agree to coercion is not to say that we are required to enjoy it, or even to pretend we enjoy it. Who enjoys taxes? We all grumble about them. But we accept compulsory taxes because we recognize that voluntary taxes would favor the conscienceless. We institute and (grumblingly) support taxes and other coercive devices to escape the horror of the commons.

An alternative to the commons need not be perfectly just to be preferable. With real estate and other material goods, the alternative we have chosen is the institution of private property coupled with legal inheritance. Is this system perfectly just? As a genetically trained biologist I deny that it is. It seems to me that, if there are to be differences in individual inheritance, legal possession should be perfectly correlated with biological inheritance—that those who are biologically more fit to be the custodians of property and power should legally inherit more. But genetic recombination continually makes a mockery of the doctrine of "like father, like son" implicit in our laws of legal inheritance. An idiot can inherit millions, and a trust fund can keep his estate intact. We must admit that our legal system of private property plus inheritance is unjust—but we put up with it because we are not convinced, at the moment, that anyone has invented a better system. The alternative of the commons is too horrifying to contemplate. Injustice is preferable to total ruin.

It is one of the peculiarities of the warfare between reform and the status quo that it is thoughtlessly governed by a double standard. Whenever a reform measure is proposed it is often defeated when its opponents triumphantly discover a flaw in it. As Kingsley Davis has pointed out (21), worshippers of the status quo sometimes imply that no reform is possible without unanimous agreement, an implication contrary to historical fact. As nearly as I can make out, automatic rejection of proposed reforms is based on one of two unconscious assumptions: (i) that the status quo is perfect; or (ii) that the choice we face is between reform and no action; if the proposed reform is imperfect, we presumably should take no action at all, while we wait for a perfect proposal.

But we can never do nothing. That which we have done for thousands of years is also action. It also produces evils. Once we are aware that the status quo is action, we can then compare its discoverable advantages and disadvantages with the predicted advantages and disadvantages of the proposed reform, discounting as best we can for our lack of experience. On the basis of such a comparison, we can make a rational decision which will not involve the unworkable assumption that only perfect systems are tolerable.

Recognition of Necessity

Perhaps the simplest summary of this analysis of man's population problems is this: the commons, if justifiable at all, is justifiable only under conditions of low-population density. As the human population has increased, the commons has had to be abandoned in one aspect after another.

First we abandoned the commons in food gathering, enclosing farm land and restricting pastures and hunting and fishing areas. These restrictions are still not complete throughout the world.

Somewhat later we saw that the commons as a place for waste disposal would also have to be abandoned. Restrictions on the disposal of domestic sewage are widely accepted in the Western world; we are still struggling to close the commons to pollution by automobiles, factories, insecticide sprayers, fertilizing operations, and atomic energy installations.

In a still more embryonic state is our recognition of the evils of the commons in matters of pleasure. There is almost no restriction on the propagation of sound waves in the public medium. The shopping public is assaulted with mindless music, without its consent. Our government is paying out billions of dollars to create supersonic transport which will disturb 50,000 people for every one person who is whisked from coast to coast 3 hours faster. Advertisers muddy the air-waves of radio and television and pollute the view of travelers. We are a long way from outlawing the commons in matters of pleasure. Is this because our Puritan inheritance makes us view pleasure as something of a sin, and pain (that is, the pollution of advertising) as the sign of virtue?

Every new enclosure of the commons involves the infringement of somebody's personal liberty. Infringements made in the distant past are accepted because no contemporary complains of a loss. It is the newly proposed infringements that we vigorously oppose; cries of "rights" and "freedom" fill the air. But what does "freedom" mean? When men mutually agreed to pass laws against robbing, mankind became more free, not less so. Individuals locked into the logic of the commons are free only to bring on universal ruin; once they see the necessity of mutual coercion, they become free to pursue other goals. I believe it was Hegel who said, "Freedom is the recognition of necessity."

The most important aspect of necessity that we must now recognize, is the necessity of abandoning the commons in breeding. No technical solution can rescue us from the misery of overpopulation. Freedom to breed will bring ruin to all. At the moment, to avoid hard decisions many of us are tempted to propagandize for conscience and responsible parenthood. The temptation must be resisted, because an appeal to independently acting consciences selects for the dissappearance of all conscience in the long run, and an increase in anxiety in the short.

The only way we can preserve and nurture other and more precious freedoms is by relinquishing the freedom to breed, and that very soon. "Freedom is the recognition of necessity"—and it is the role of education to reveal to all the necessity of abandoning the freedom to breed. Only so, can we put an end to this aspect of the tragedy of the commons.

<h2 style="text-align:center">References</h2>

1. J. B. Wiesner and H. F. York, *Sci. Amer.* 211 (No. 4), 27 (1964).
2. G. Hardin, *J. Hered.* 50, 68 (1959); S. von Hoernor, *Science* 137, 18 (1962).
3. J. von Neumann and O. Morgenstern. *Theory of Games and Economic Behavior* (Princeton Univ. Press, Princeton, N.J., 1947), p. 11.
4. J. H. Fremlin, *New Sci.,* No. 415 (1964), p. 285.
5. A. Smith, *The Wealth of Nations* (Modern Library, New York, 1937), p. 423.
6. W. F. Lloyd, *Two Lectures on the Checks to Population* (Oxford Univ. Press, Oxford, England, 1833), reprinted (in part) in *Population, Evolution, and Birth Control,* G. Hardin, Ed. (Freeman, San Francisco, 1964), p. 37.
7. A. N. Whitehead, *Science and the Modern World* (Mentor, New York, 1948), p. 17.
8. G. Hardin, Ed. *Population, Evolution, and Birth Control* (Freeman, San Francisco, 1964), p. 56.
9. S. McVay, *Sci. Amer.* 216 (No. 8), 13 (1966).
10. J. Fletcher, *Situation Ethics* (Westminster, Philadelphia, 1966).
11. D. Lack, *The Natural Regulation of Animal Numbers* (Clarendon Press, Oxford, 1954).
12. H. Girvetz, *From Wealth to Welfare* (Stanford Univ. Press, Stanford, Calif., 1950).
13. G. Hardin, *Perspec. Biol. Med.* 6, 366 (1963).
14. U. Thant, *Int. Planned Parenthood News,* No. 168 (February 1968), p. 3.
15. K. Davis, *Science* 158, 730 (1967).
16. S. Tax, Ed., *Evolution after Darwin* (Univ. of Chicago Press, Chicago, 1960), vol. 2, p. 469.
17. G. Bateson, D. D. Jackson, J. Haley, J. Weakland, *Behav. Sci.* 1, 251 (1956).
18. P. Goodman, *New York Rev. Books* 10 (8), 22 (23 May 1968).
19. A. Comfort, *The Anxiety Makers* (Nelson, London, 1967).
20. C. Frankel, *The Case for Modern Man* (Harper, New York, 1955), p. 203.
21. J. D. Roslansky, *Genetics and the Future of Man* (Appleton-Century-Crofts, New York, 1966), p. 177.

Rhetoric vs. Reality

Discrepancies between Environmental Attitude and Behaviour: Examples from Europe and China

Yi-Fu Tuan

Discrepancy between stated ideal and reality is a worrisome fact of our daily experience: in the political field one learns to discriminate between an orator's fulsome profession and what he can or will, in fact, carry out. The history of environmental ideas, however, has been pursued as an academic discipline largely in detachment from the question of how—if at all—these ideas guide the course of action, or how they arise out of it. Needless to say, there are many paradigmatic views of nature, such as those of science, that have great explicatory power and may, once they are applied, affect the lives of many people; but in themselves they do not enjoin a specific course of action. In contrast, the acceptance of certain specific environmental ideas can have a definite effect on decision and on behaviour. If it is widely held, for example, that a dry and sunny climate is a great restorer of health, we may suppose that an appreciable number of people will seek out these areas for health. But what of less specific ideas? We may believe that a world-view which puts nature in subservience to man will lead to the exploitation of nature by man; and one that regards man as simply a component in nature will entail a modest view of his rights and capabilities, and so lead to the establishment of a harmonious relationship between man and his natural environment. But is this correct? And if essentially correct, how direct or tenuous is the link? These are some of the questions I wish to explore with the help of examples from Europe and China. The discrepancies are noted here; their resolution must await another occasion.

I

To the question, what is a fundamental difference between the European and the Chinese attitude towards nature, most people with any opinion at all will probably make some such reply: that the European sees nature as subordinate to him whereas the Chinese sees himself as a part of nature. Taken as a broad generalization and with a grain of salt there is much truth in this distinction; a truth illustrated with diagrammatic force when one compares the formal European garden of the seventeenth century with the Chinese naturalistic garden. The geometric contrast reflects fundamental differences in environmental evaluation. The formal European garden in the style of the Le Nôtre was designed to produce a limited number of imposing prospects. It can be appreciated to the full only at a limited number of favoured spots where the onlooker is invited by the garden's design to gaze at distant vistas. Or, seen in another way, the European garden is a grandiose setting for man; in deference to him, nature is straitjacketed in court dress. The Chinese garden, on the other hand, is designed to produce almost constantly shifting scenes: there are no set prospects. The nature of the garden requires the perceiver to move along a winding path and to be more than visually involved with the landscape. It is not nature that is required to put on court dress in deference to man: rather, it is man who must lay aside his formalistic pretensions in order to enter nature.

This widely recognized distinction is valid and important. On the other hand, by the crude test of the total tonnage of earth removed there may not be so very much difference between the European formal and the Chinese naturalistic garden. Both are human artifacts. It is not widely known that some of the famous scenic areas of China are works of man rather than of geologic processes. The West Lake of Hang-chou, for example, was celebrated by T'ang and Sung poets and it remains to this day an adornment of China. To the casual visitor, the West Lake region may appear to be a striking illustration of how the works of man can blend modestly into the magistral context of nature. However, the pervasiveness of nature is largely an illusion induced by art. Some of the islands in the lake are man-made. Moreover, the lake itself is artificial and has to be maintained with care. In the thirteenth century, military patrols, under the command of specially appointed officials, looked after its policing and maintenance; it was forbidden, for example, to throw any rubbish into it or to plant in it lotuses or water-chestnuts. Peasants were recruited to clear and enlarge the lake, to keep it from being cluttered up by vegetation and silt.[1] Hang-chou's environs, then, owe much of their calm, harmonious beauty to human art and effort. The sense of open nature in Hang-chou is enhanced by its scale: the West Lake region is a cluster of public and semi-public parks. In the much smaller compass of the private garden the illusion of pervasive nature is far more difficult to achieve: nevertheless the aim of the Chinese gardener was to achieve it with cleverly placed, water-worn limestone whose jagged outlines denoted wildness, and by means of winding footpaths that give the stroller an illusion of depth and space. In this line the Oriental's ultimate triumph is symbolized by the miniature garden, where wild nature is reduced to the scale of a dwarf landscape that can be fitted into a bowl. Complete artifice reigns: in the narrow confines of a bowl, shrubs are tortured by human skill into imitating the shape and posture of pines, the limbs of which may have been deformed by winds that swept the China Seas.

II

I have begun with a contrast and then proceeded to suggest that, from another perspective, the contrast is blurred. The publicized environmental ethos of a culture seldom covers more than a fraction of the total range of environmental behaviour. It is misleading to derive the one from the other. Simplifications that can mislead have at times been made. For example, Professor Lynn White has recently said: ''What people do about their ecology depends on what they think about themselves in relation to things around them. Human ecology is deeply conditioned by beliefs about our nature and destiny—that is, by religion.''[2] He goes on to say that the victory of Christianity over paganism was the greatest psychic revolution in Western culture. In his view, despite all the talk of ''the post-Christian age'' and despite evident changes in the forms of modern thinking, the substance often remains amazingly akin to that of the Christian past. The Western man's daily habits of action are dominated by an implicit faith in perpetual progress which was unknown either to Greco-Roman antiquity or to the Orient. It is rooted in, and is indefensible apart from, Judeo-Christian teleology. Peoples of the Western world continue to live, as they have lived for about 1700 years, very largely in a context of Christian beliefs.

And what has Christianity told people about their relations with the environment? Essentially that man, as something made in God's image, is not simply a part of nature; that God has planned the universe for man's benefit and rule. According to White, Christianity is the most anthropocentric religion the world has seen. It has not only established a dualism of man and nature but has also insisted that it is God's will that man exploit nature for his proper ends.[3]

To press the theme further, it is said that Christianity has destroyed antiquity's feeling for the holiness of landscapes and of natural things. The Greek religious tradition regarded the land not as an object to be exploited, or even as a visually pleasing setting, but as a true force which physically embodied the powers that ruled the world. Vincent Scully, the architectural historian, has argued that not only were certain landscapes regarded by the ancient Greeks as holy and expressive of specific gods, but also that the temples and the subsidiary buildings of their sanctuaries were so formed in themselves and so placed in the landscapes and to each other as to enhance, develop, and complement the basic meaning of the landscape.[4]

Martin Heidegger, a modern philosopher whose insights have been greatly influenced by early Greek philosophy, characterized the Greek temple as disclosing the earth on which it stands. The whiteness of the temple discloses the darkness and the strength of the rock underneath; it reveals the height and blueness of the sky, the power of the storm and the vastness of the sea.[5] In the Christian tradition, on the other hand, holiness was invested not in landscapes but in man-made altars, shrines, churches, and basilicas that dominated the landscapes. Constantine and Helen are said to have built basilicas over caves in the Holy Land to celebrate the triumph of Christianity over the "cave cultus" of the pagan world. In the Christian view it was not emanation from the earth but ritual that consecrated the site; man not nature bore the image of God and man's work, the hallowed edifice, symbolized the Christian cosmos. In pagan antiquity, at the level of the common people, each facet of nature had its own guardian spirit. Before one ventured to cut a tree, mine a mountain, or dam a brook, it was important to placate the spirit in charge of that particular situation, and to keep it placated. By destroying animistic beliefs, Christianity made it possible to exploit nature in a mood of indifference to the feeling of natural objects.

Much of this is now Western folklore and Lynn White is among the more recent writers to give it eloquent expression. The thesis, then, is that Christianity has introduced a fundamentally new way of evaluating the environment, and that this new evaluation has strongly affected Western man's traffic with the natural objects around him. The generalization is very useful, although one should take note of facts that appear to contradict it. As Clarence Glacken has demonstrated, in the ancient world there was no lack of interest in natural resources and their quick exploitation. Economic activities such as mining, the various ways of obtaining food, canal building, and drainage are clear proof of man's incessant restlessness in changing the earth about him.[6] Glacken points out that in Sophocles' *Antigone* there are lines which remind one of the eulogies of science in the eighteenth century, and of contemporary enthusiasm for man's control over nature. At one point in the play the chorus declares how the earth has felt man's ungentle touch:

Oh, Earth is patient, and Earth is old,
And a mother of Gods, but he breaketh her,
To-ing, froing, with the plough teams going,
Tearing the soil of her, year by year.[7]

The tearing of soil has led to erosion. In Plato's *Critias* there is the well-known passage in which he describes how the soils of Attica have been washed down to the sea. "And, just as happens in small islands, what now remains compared with what then existed is like the skeleton of a rich man, all the fat and soft earth have wasted away, and only the bare framework of the land being left." Plato then describes the former arable hills, fertile valleys, and forested mountains "of which there are visible signs even to this day." Mountains which today have food only for bees could, not so long ago, grow trees fit for the largest buildings. Cultivated trees provided pasturage for flocks, and the soil was well watered and the rain was "not lost to it, as now, by flowing from the bare land to the sea."[8] Plato's comments sound remarkably modern; they remind us almost of the lamentations of latter-day conservationists.

If there is evidence of man's awareness of his power to transform nature—even destructively—in the time of Sophocles and Plato, there is evidence of much greater awareness of the almost limitless capabilities of man in Hellenistic times. Agriculture and related occupations such as cattle-breeding were then the most important source of wealth in the ancient world. Land reclamation was not a haphazard affair but one based on the science of mechanics and on practical experience with canal-digging, irrigation, and swamp drainage. It was a time of faith in progress. But far more than the Greeks, the Romans have imposed their will on the natural environment. And perhaps the most dramatic example of the triumph of the human will over the irregular lineaments of nature is the Roman grid method of dividing up the land. As Bradford puts it, centuriation well displayed the arbitrary but methodical qualities in Roman government. With absolute self-assurance and great technical competence, the Romans have imposed the same formal pattern of land division on the well-watered alluvium of the Po Valley as on the near-desert of Tunisia. Even today the forceful imprint of centuriation can be traced across some thousands of square miles on both sides of the central Mediterranean, and it can still stir the imagination by its scale and boldness.[9]

Against this background of the vast transformations of nature in the pagan world, the inroads made in the early centuries of the Christian era were relatively modest. Christianity teaches that man has dominion over nature. St. Benedict himself had cut down the sacred grove at Monte Cassino because it was a survival of pagan worship. And the story of how monks moved into the forested wilderness, and by a combination of work and prayer, had transformed them into cloistered "paradises" is a familiar one. But for a long time man's undisputed power over nature was more a tenet of faith than a fact of experience: to become a realized fact Europe had to wait for the growth of human numbers, for the achievement of greater administrative centralization and for the development and wide application of new technological skills. Fields that were cleared in heavy forests testified to the mediaeval farmer's great capacity for changing his environment: it was a change, however, that must continually be defended against the encroachments of nature.

Farmsteads and arable lands multiplied through the Middle Ages at the expense of forests and marshes, but these man-made features lacked the permanence, the geometric order, and the prideful assertion of the human will that one can detect more readily in the Roman road system, aqueducts, and centuriated landholdings. The victory of Christianity over paganism may well have been, as Lynn White says, the greatest psychic revolution in Western culture; but for lack of real, as distinct from theologically postulated, power the full impact of that revolution on ecology was postponed.

III

As to China, Western humanists commonly show bias in favour of that country's Taoist and Buddhist traditions. They like to point out the virtues of the Oriental's quiescent and adaptive approach towards nature in contrast to the aggressive masculinity of Western man. Support for the quiescent view is easily found in the Taoist classics. The *Tao Tê Ching,* for example, has a rather cryptic message of seven characters (*wei wu wei, tzu wu pu chih*) which James Legge has translated as: "When there is this abstinence from action, good order is universal." And Joseph Needham has recently interpreted it to mean: "Let there be no action (contrary to Nature), and there is nothing that will not be well regulated."[10] It is easy to see how these words might appeal to the modern man, who finds in his own environment the all-too-evident consequences of human action "contrary to nature." In another influential Taoist book of much later date *(T'ai shang kan ying p'ien),* one finds the belief that "even insects and crawling things, herbs and trees, may not be injured." These Taoist texts have been much translated into European languages; the latter, with its injunction against injuring even insects and crawling things, is believed to have had some influence on the thought of Albert Schweitzer.[11]

Another aspect of Chinese attitude towards nature, which has found favour among some Western humanists, is embodied in the concept of *feng-shui* or geomancy. This concept has been aptly defined as "the art of adapting the residences of the living and the dead so as to co-operate and harmonize with the local currents of the cosmic breath."[12] If houses and tombs are not properly located, evil effects would injure the inhabitants and the descendants of those whose bodies lay in the tombs. On the other hand, good siting would favour wealth, health, and happiness. Good siting involves, above all, taking proper note of the forms of hills and directions of watercourses since these are themselves the outcome of the moulding influences of winds and waters, that is, of *feng-shui;* but in addition one must also consider the heights and forms of buildings, the directions of roads and bridges. A general effect of the belief in *feng-shui* is to encourage a preference for natural curves—for winding paths and for structures that seem to fit into the landscape rather than to dominate it; and at the same time it promoted a distaste for straight lines and geometrical layouts. In this respect it is of interest to note the short life of China's first railway. This was built in 1876 and connected Shanghai with its port of Wu-sung. Although the venture was at first well received, the mood of the local people turned sour after a native was killed by the locomotive. The people in their hostility thought that the railway had offended the principle of *feng-shui.* On 20 October, 1877, the Chinese government closed the railway, and so a symbol of

Western progress was temporarily sacrificed to the local currents of the cosmic breath.[13]

An adaptive attitude towards nature has ancient roots in China. It is embodied in folklore, in the philosophical-ethical precepts of Taoism, and later, Buddhism, and it draws support from practical experience: the experience that uncontrolled exploitation of timber, for example, brings hurtful results. In ancient literature one finds here and there evidence of a recognition for the need to regulate the use of resources. Even as early as the Eastern Chou period (eighth century–third century B.C.), deforestation necessitated by the expansion of agriculture and the building of cities seems to have led to an appreciation of the value of trees. In that ancient compendium of songs the *Shi Ching,* we find the sentiment expressed in lines such as these:

On the hill were lovely trees,
Both chestnut-trees and plum trees.
Cruel brigands tore them up;
But no one knew of their crime.

Trees were regarded as a blessing. As another poem put it,

So thick grow those oaks
That the people never look for firewood.
Happiness to our lord!
May the spirits always have rewards for him.[14]

In the *Chou Li*—a work which was probably compiled in the third century B.C., but may well include earlier material—we find mentioned two classes of officials whose duties were concerned with conservation. One was the *Shan-yu,* inspector of mountains, and the other the *Lin-heng,* inspector of forests. The inspectors of mountains were charged with the care of forests in the mountains. They saw to it that certain species were preserved, and in other ways enforced conservation practices. Thus trees could only be cut by the common people at certain times; those on the south side in the middle of winter and those on the north side in the middle of summer. At other seasons the people were permitted to cut wood in times of urgent need, such as when coffins had to be made or dykes strengthened, but even then certain areas could not be touched. The inspectors of forests (in the *Lin-heng* office) had similar duties. Their authority covered the forests that lay below the mountains.[15] Another ancient literary reference to conservation practice was in the *Mencius.* The sage advised King Huai of Liang that he would not lack for wood if he allowed the people to cut trees only at the proper time.[16]

Through Chinese history perspicacious officials have from time to time warned against the dire consequences of deforestation. A scholar of the late Ming dynasty reported on Shan-hsi, a province in North China: "At the beginning of the reign of Chia-ching" (1522-66), he wrote, "people vied with each other to build houses, and wood from the southern mountains was cut without a year's rest. The natives took advantage of the barren mountain surface and converted it into farms. . . .If heaven sends down a torrent, there is nothing to obstruct the flow of water.

In the morning it falls on the southern mountains; in the evening, when it reaches the plains, its angry waves swell in volume and break embankments causing frequent changes in the course of the river.''[17]

Deforestation was deplored by the late Ming scholars not only because of its effect on stream flow and on the quality of the soil in the lowlands, but also—interestingly enough—because of their belief that the forests on mountain ridges were effective in slowing down the horse-riding barbarians. As one scholar put it, ''I saw the fact that what the country relies on as strategically important is the mountain, and what the mountain relies on as a screen to prevent advance are the trees.''[18] There was also recognition of the aesthetics of forested mountains. Wu-tai mountains in northern Shan-hsi, for example, were famous everywhere. But the question was asked: since they have become almost bare, what remained to keep them famous?

These brief notes suggest that there existed in China an old tradition of forest care. Officials encouraged the practice but the people engaged in it on their own initiative when it did not conflict with the urgent needs of the moment. Nearly forty years ago, the American conservationist W. C. Lowdermilk noted how thousands of acres in An-hui and Ho-non were planted with pine from local nurseries, a practice he recognized as ancient and independent of the modern forestry movement. Lowdermilk also found that the North China plain ''actually exports considerable quantities of logs of *Paulownia tomentosa* to Japan and poplar *(Populus tomentosa)* to match factories. It is true that no forests are to be found in this plain, but each village has its trees, which are grown according to a system.''[19]

In Communist China trees are extensively planted to control soil erosion, in answer to pressing economic needs but also for aesthetic reasons. Roadside planting, a practice dating back to the Eastern Chou period, uses the ''traditional'' trees *(Populus simonii, Pinus tabulaeformis, Salix babylonica, S. matsudana, Aesculus chinensis, Ulmus parvifolia),* but in particular the poplars. Afforestation proceeds in villages, and most conspicuously, in cities, new suburbs, and industrial districts where the trees hide a great deal of the raw ugliness of new construction.[20]

IV

Thus far I have sketched what may indeed be called the ''official'' line on Chinese attitude towards environment; it is widely publicized and commonly accepted. There is however another strain: the enlightened memorials to the emperor on the need for the conservation of resources are in themselves clear evidence of the follies that have already been committed. Unlike the Western man of letters the geographer is usually aware of China's frequent mistreatment of nature. He perceives that country, not through the refined sentiments of Taoist philosophy, Neo-Confucianism, and Oswald Siren, but through the bleak reports of Mallory, Lowdermilk, and Thorp. Deforestation and erosion on the one hand, the building of cities and rice terraces on the other are the common foci of his attention rather than landscape painting or poetry contests in the cool precincts of a garden. The two images of reality complement each other: in an obvious but not trite sense, civilization is the exercise of human power over nature, which in turn may lead to the aesthetic appreciation of nature. Philosophy, nature poetry, gardens, and orderly countryside are products of civilization, but so equally are the deforested mountains, the clogged streams, and, within the densely packed, walled cities, the political intrigue.

If animistic belief and Taoist nature philosophy lie at the back of an adaptive attitude towards nature, what conceptions and ideals—we may ask—have encouraged the Chinese, through their long history, to engage in gigantic transformation of environment—whether this be expressed positively in huge works of construction or negatively in deforested mountains? Several ancient beliefs and conceptions may be recognized and they, individually or together, have allowed the Chinese to express the "male" principle in human nature. Consider, for example, the fact that one of the greatest culture heroes of China was Yu, the legendary founder of the Hsia dynasty. He was famed primarily for his magnificent deeds: He "opened up the rivers of the Nine Provinces and fixed the outlets of the nine marshes"; he brought peace and order to the lands of Hsia and his achievements were of an enduring kind which benefited succeeding dynasties.[21] Chinese rulers were bidden to imitate the ancient culture heroes, and one way to imitate them was to ensure order and prosperity by large-scale engineering works. Another ancient idea of importance to the "male" principle of dominance was to see in the earthly environment a model of the cosmos. The regular motions of the stars were to be translated architecturally and ritually to space and time on earth. The walled city oriented to the cardinal directions, the positioning of the twelve city gates, the location of the royal compound and the alignment of the principal axial street were given a geometric pattern that reflected the order to be found in heaven. The key concept was built on the related notions of rectilinearity, order, and rectitude. This key concept acquired architectural and social forms which were then imposed on earth, for the earth itself lacked paradigms of perfect order. Indeed the experience of mountains and waters has led to such unaggressive prescriptions as the need to observe and placate the spirits of the earth, the need for man to understand the balance of forces in nature, to contemplate this harmony and to adapt himself to it. By contrast, the observation of the stars has inspired such masculine attitudes as geometric order, hierarchy, and authoritarian control over earth and men.

The two outlooks—celestial and terrestrial, masculine and feminine—are not easy to reconcile. Events in heaven affect events on earth but not in any obvious or dependable way: abnormal floods and droughts have traditionally been taken as warnings by those who derive their power from astronomy. Tension, if not contradiction, is also revealed when these two ideas find architectural and geographical substance. The construction of Ch'ang-an in the Sui and T'ang dynasties illustrates the triumph of the cosmic principle of order and rectilinearity over the earth principle of complex harmony and natural lines. Ch'ang-an was laid on new ground and on an unprecedented scale. The site in the Wei Ho valley was chosen for functional reasons but also because of its great historical links: the site received the sanction of the great men and deeds in the past. Geomantic properties of the site were studied; however, unlike villages and rural roads the topographical character of the region seems to have made little impact on the city's fundamental design. Astronomers had an important role in the laying out of the city: they measured the shadow of the noon sun on successive days and observed the North Star by night in order to arrive at accurate alignments of the city walls to the four directions.[22] In the course of building Ch'ang-an, which had an enclosed area of 31 square miles, villages were levelled and trees uprooted; broad straight avenues were laid out and then rows of trees planted. Thus, despite the geomantic gestures, in Ch'ang-an the superposition of man's and heaven's order on natural terrain was complete. Or rather not quite complete, if we accept the charming story of why one great old locust tree was not in line. It had been retained from the old landscape because the chief architect had sat under it as he supervised the construction, and a special order from the emperor in honour of his architect spared it from being felled.[23]

V

The natural environment of both Mediterranean Europe and China has been vastly transformed by man: constructively in the building of cities and roads, in the extension of arable land and the introduction of new crops: destructively in deforestation and erosion. Of any long-settled, thoroughly civilized part of the world, we can draw up a list of forces and the motives for their use that would more or less account for the transformation of the biotic mantle. Such lists may well agree in fundamentals: fire is widely used to clear vegetation; the forest is cleared to create more grazing and arable land; timber is needed for the construction of palaces, houses, and ships, for domestic and industrial fuel, or as raw material for paper mills. Then again the forest is pushed back because it may shelter dangerous wild animals or provide hiding places for bandits. Naturally, the means at hand and the motives for using them vary from region to region: in contrast to the Mediterranean world, for example, China's vegetation suffered less from sheep and goats, and less from the enormous demands of shipbuilding which flourished with the Mediterranean maritime powers. China's forests, on the other hand, suffered more from the demands of city building and the need for domestic fuel.

To illustrate further the kinds of force that work against conservation practices in China, consider some of the causes of deforestation. One is the ancient practice of burning trees in order to deprive dangerous animals of their hiding places. There exists a passage in the *Mencius* of how in ancient times the luxuriant vegetation sheltered so many wild beasts that men were endangered. The great minister Shun of legendary repute ordered Yih to use fire, and "Yih set fire to, and consumed the forests and vegetation on the mountains and in the marshes, so that the birds and beasts fled away to hide themselves."[24] Even in the early decades of the twentieth century non-Chinese tribes in Kuang-hsi and Kuei-chou provinces are known to burn forests to drive away tigers and leopards; and in North China, in such long-settled areas as central Shen-hsi province, fires were ostensibly started by Chinese farmers for no other purpose. It is not always easy to establish the real reason for setting fire to forest. When asked, the farmers may say that it is to clear land for cultivation, although the extent of burning far exceeds the need for this purpose; or it is to leave fewer places in which bandits may hide; or to encourage the growth of small-sized sprouts in the burnt over area, which would then save the farmers the labour of splitting wood![25] The last reason tends to upset any residual illusion we may have of the Chinese farmer's benign attitude towards nature. A fire can of course also be started accidentally. A risk that is special to the Chinese is the forest fire caused by the burning of paper money at the grave mounds, which, in the rugged parts of the South, are commonly located beyond the fields and at the edge of the forested hills.

Forests in North China were depleted in the past for the making of charcoal as an industrial fuel. Robert Hartwell has shown how, from the tenth century onward the expanding metallic industries had swallowed up many hundreds of thousands of tons of charcoal each year, as did the manufacture of salt, alum, bricks, tiles, and liquor.[26] By the Sung dynasty (A.D. 960–1279) the demand for wood and charcoal as both household and industrial fuel had reached a level such that the timber resources of the country could no longer meet it; the result was the increasing substitution of coal for wood and charcoal.

An enormous amount of timber was needed in the construction of the old Chinese cities, probably more than that required in building Western cities of comparable size. One reason for this lies in the dependence of traditional Chinese architecture on timber as the basic structural material. Mountains may be stripped of their cover in the construction of a large palace.[27] And if a large palace required much timber, a whole city would require much more, especially if it were of the size of Ch'ang-an, capital of T'ang dynasty, and Hang-chou, capital of the southern Sung dynasty. Both had populations of more than a million people. The great expansion in the size of Hang-chou in the thirteenth century led to the deforestation of the neighbouring hills for construction timber. The demand for timber was such that some farmers gave up rice cultivation for forestry.[28] Cities in which houses were so largely made of wood ran the constant danger of demolition by fire; and this was especially true of the southern metropolises where the streets tended to be narrow. The necessity of rebuilding after fire put further strain on timber resources. But of even greater consequence than the accidental burning of parts of cities was the deliberate devastation of whole cities in times of upheaval, when rebels or nomadic invaders toppled a dynasty. The succeeding phase of reconstruction was normally achieved in quick time by armies of men who made ruthless inroads upon the forest.

VI

The theme we have yet to trace is the involved interplay between environmental attitude and environmental behaviour, between the philosophy identified with a people and the actions that people may undertake. Besides the more glaring contradictions of professed ideal and actual practice, there exist also the unsuspected ironies: these derive from the fact that the benign institutions of a complex society, no less than the exploitative, are not always able to foresee all the consequences of their inherent character and action. For example, Buddhism in China is at least partly responsible for the preservation of trees around temple compounds, for the islands of green in an otherwise denuded landscape; on the other hand, Buddhism introduced to China the idea of the cremation of the dead; and from the tenth to the fourteenth century the practice of cremation was sufficiently common in the southeastern coastal provinces to have had an effect on the timber resources of that area.[29] The researches of E. H. Schafer provide us with another illustration of irony in Chinese life; for it would seem that the most civilized of arts was responsible for the deforestation of much of North China. The art was that of writing which required soot for the making of black ink. The soot came from burnt pine. And, as Schafer put it, ''Even before T'ang times, the ancient pines of the mountains of Shan-tung had been reduced to carbon, and now the busy brushes of the vast T'ang bureaucracy were rapidly bringing baldness to the T'a-hang Mountains between Shansi and Hopei."[30]

VII

I began by noting the contrast between the European formal garden and the Chinese naturalistic garden, and then suggested that these human achievements probably required comparable amounts of nature modification. To compare artworks and construction projects on the basis of the quantitative changes made on the environment is a useful exercise in so far as we wish to emphasize the role of man as a force for change along with other geophysical forces; but it is only the beginning in the interpretation of the meaning of these works and how they reflect cultural attitudes. It seems to me valid to see the European garden as an extension of the house: in the development of the European garden some of the formality and values of the house are taken outdoors in the form of courtyards, terraces, formal parterres, and avenues, and now the smooth, carpet-like lawn. The lawn displays the house; its sloping surfaces are a pedestal for the house. The Chinese garden, on the other hand, reflects a totally different philosophy from the orthogonal rectitude of the traditional Chinese house. In stepping through a circular gate, from the rectangular courtyard into the curvilinear forms of the garden, one enters a different world. Perhaps something of the difference in attitude towards outdoor spaces is retained to the present day. Simone de Beauvoir notes how a French family picnic is often an elaborate affair involving the transportation of a considerable portion of the household goods outdoors; it is not always a harmonious event for whatever tension that may exist in the house is carried to the less organized natural environment where it is exacerbated by entanglement with flies, fishing rods, and spilled strawberry jam. In Communist China, de Beauvoir spent an afternoon (1955) in the playgrounds of the Summer Palace outside Peking. She captures the peace of the scene with an anecdote: "In the middle of the lake I see a little boat: in it a young woman is lying down peacefully asleep while two youngsters are frisking about and playing with the oars. Our boatman cups his hands. 'Hey!' he calls. 'Look out for those kids!' The woman rubs her eyes, she smiles, picks up the oars, and shows the children how they work."[31]

REFERENCES

1. Gernet, Jacques, *Daily Life in China on the Eve of the Mongo! Invasion 1250–1276* (London, 1962), pp. 51-52.
2. White, Lynn, "The Historical Roots of Our Ecologic Crisis," *Science,* CLV (1967), 1205.
3. *Ibid.*
4. Scully, Vincent, *The Earth, The Temple, and The Gods* (New Haven, 1962), p. 3.
5. Vycinas, Vincent, *Earth and Gods: An Introduction to the Philosophy of Martin Heidegger* (The Hague, 1961), p. 13.
6. Glacken, Clarence, *Traces on the Rhodian Shore* (Berkeley and Los Angeles, 1967), p. 118.
7. Sophocles, *Antigone,* transl. by Gilbert Murray in Arnold Toynbee, *Greek Historical Thought* (New York, 1952), p. 128.
8. Plato, *Critias,* transl. by Arnold Toynbee in *Greek Historical Thought,* pp. 146-47.
9. Bradford, John, *Ancient Landscapes* (London, 1957), p. 145.

10. Needham, Joseph, *Science and Civilisation in China,* vol. II (Cambridge, 1956), p. 69.

11. Schafer, E. H., "The Conservation of Nature under the T'ang Dynasty," *Journ. Econ. and Soc. Hist. of the Orient,* v (1962), 282.

12. Chatley, H., "Feng shui" in *Encyclopaedia Sinica,* ed. by S. Couling (Shanghai, 1917), p. 175. See also Andrew March, "An Appreciation of Chinese Geomancy," *Journ. Asian Studies,* XXVII (1968), 253-67.

13. *Encyclopaedia Sinica,* p. 470.

14. *Shi Ching,* transl. by Arthur Waley as *The Book of Songs* (New York, 1960), pp. 138, 213.

15. *Chou Li,* transl. by E. Biot as *Le Tcheou-li* (Paris, 1851), vol. I, 371-74.

16. *Mencius,* Bk. I, pt. 1, 3:3.

17. Chi, Ch'ao-ting, *Key Economic Areas in Chinese History* (New York, 1963), p. 22.

18. Gazetteer (1596) written by Chen Teng and translated by W. C. Lowdermilk, and D. R. Wickes, *History of Soil Use in the Wu Tai Shan Area,* Monog., Roy. Asiatic Soc., NCB, 1938, p. 8.

19. Lowdermilk, W. C., "Forestry in Denuded China," *Ann., Amer. Acad. Pol. Soc. Sci.,* CLII (1930), 137.

20. Richardson, S. D., *Forestry in Communist China* (Baltimore, 1966), pp. 152-53.

21. Ssu-ma Ch'ien, *Shi Chi,* chap. 29.

22. Wright, A. F., "Symbolism and Functions: Reflections on Changan and Other Great Cities," *Journ. Asian Studies,* XXIV (1965), 670.

23. Wu, N. I., *Chinese and Indian Architecture* (New York, 1963), p. 38.

24. *Mencius,* Bk. III, pt. 1, 4:7.

25. Reported by A. N. Steward and S. Y. Cheo in "Geographical and Ecological Notes on Botanical Explorations in Kwangsi Province, China," *Nanking Journ.,* v (1935), 174.

26. Hartwell, R., "A Revolution in the Chinese Iron and Coal Industries during the Northern Sung, 960–1126 A.D.," *Journ. Asian Studies,* XXI (1962), 159.

27. See L. S. Yang, *Les aspects économiques des travaux publics dans la Chine impériale,* College de France, 1964. p. 37.

28. Gernet, (n. 1), p. 114.

29. Moule, A. C., *Quinsai* (Cambridge, 1957), p. 51.

30. Schafer, (n. 11), pp. 299-300.

31. de Beauvoir, Simone, *The Long March* (Cleveland, 1958), p. 77.

32. *The Canadian Geographer,* 12, no. 3 (1968), 176-191. Reprinted by permission of the author. The illustrations originally accompanying this article have been omitted.

Some Changes in the Wind

The Reformation in Science

Fred Hapgood

The time seems right for an ambitious young playwright, out to make a mark, to rewrite the story of Galileo's persecution by the Church, casting Galileo as the villain. The debates between the physicist, who would be depicted as driven to follow his curiosity with no consideration of social costs, and a suave prince of the Church, who would insist that Galileo take responsibility for the cultural impact of his science, might or might not make good theater, but they would have a very modern ring.

Galileo would argue that it is noble to move closer to reality, to voyage into it, to make one's grasp of the world deeper and more true. The cardinal would reply that a tree bears fruit whether or not one knows the exact number of leaves on its branches. What is important is a knowledge of the *point* of what one sees, of its human meaning, and that sense of significance is a grace from God, not something sifted out of piles of facts. "There are many," the cardinal would say, "who have an accurate sense of life and who neither read nor cipher. And tell me this: Where will you stop? When will you be satisfied? If your answer is 'never,' and you have no ends at all in view, why should you inflict your goal-lessness on mankind? And even if you will be satisfied—which we both know not to be the case—after you have solved ten or twenty more of these puzzles you set yourself, have you any reason to believe that you will then stand any closer to the meaning of the universe than you did as a child?"

If nothing else, such a play would give new dignity to the historical fact of Galileo's recantation, he would have throttled his science not from fear of torture but from genuine moral doubts. And potential producers might be enticed by pointing to the number of scientists who grapple, in their funding proposals and congressional testimony, with what our secular age can manage as the equivalent of these questions: Will your work bring us any closer to a cure for cancer or independence from Arab oil?

For some time now it has been obvious that profound changes are taking place in the public's attitude toward science. *Science* magazine reports that the words "basic research" have become a red flag to congressmen, who see no reason that someone should get thirty thousand a year for thinking about element abundances in interstellar dust grains when cities cannot afford to pay one quarter that sum to hire someone to work in a hospital. *The Atlantic* ran an article recently by a primatologist who wrote that he hoped that the last species of primate likely to be discovered, the abominable snowman, would forever remain out of reach. He meant by that out of science's reach: that the yeti would never be studied, classified, have its stomach contents analyzed, its dominance hierarchies and breeding systems charted, and the like. What the primatologist was expressing was the intuition that science tames and domesticates nature, that a wild and free quality goes out of those parts of the world that fall under its procedures. He was expressing the sense of doom we feel at the prospect of a world in which "everything is explained."

Taken literally, there seems very little risk of that. Science is far more accurately understood as an enterprise which creates ignorance and uncertainty rather than solid explanations. I have yet to meet a scientist who does not feel that a successful experiment is one that opens up six new questions, and that the sweetest triumph of the business is to illuminate a whole new field of ignorance, to ask a question of a kind that no one even thought of asking before. Scientists always pose their questions as sweepingly and inclusively as possible, and present their answers cribbed up by more cautions and qualifications than one would think a human mind could endure. No doubt if we simply count the facts in our textbooks, we do know far more than the Victorians did; but set those facts against our sense of what we need to know but do not, calculate it on a net basis, and we are far more ignorant. This has not happened in spite of modern science but as an inevitable result of its normal operation.

Still, the intuitions suggested above, that scientists are a self-indulgent, quasi-parasitic elite, demanding support from the public to pursue entirely private whims;

and that science itself is destroying the most precious of our nonrenewable resources—a sense of the world's wonder—are based on something real. What could it be?

For most of us—working scientists aside—science is one of those "senses of the intellect," like literature or religion, which give us a gut feeling of what sort of world we live in and how we ought to behave in it. What is the natural, harmonious way of relating to the world? Science gives us many little dramas, about the stars, and trees, and the movements of the earth, that feed this need. Literature conducts experiments into the realities of human nature, with plausibility the confirming test. Religion wraps both into one big drama.

The science that we were all brought up on instructed us in and stood for a view of nature that was not dissimilar from the Victorian's view of Africa. Both could be colonized, their secrets assaulted, their frontiers thrown back, without any fear that a trespass had been committed. Scientists explored and penetrated and mastered; they won victories over a nature that had been wastefully locked away in mystery until they came along, and penned up in a cage of determinist relations. We applauded and trusted this kind of achieving in all aspects of the culture.

Obviously the day of optimistic expansiveness is past. All our "intellectual senses," science very much among them, are blinking yellow or red, communicating the idea that the world of realities (defined by William James as those things which, like it or not, must be taken account of) is vast, complex, and threatening. The right attitude to take toward it is therefore one of great thoughtfulness, skill, and care, with an emphasis on coping with our present position and not rushing off to any new adventures. Science has therefore suffered, especially nuclear science, with its atom-smashing, and molecular biology, which is usually presented in such terms as "penetrating the secrets of life itself." The suspicion toward nuclear science has centered upon nuclear reactors; that toward "unrestrained biological research" upon recombinant DNA experiments, which involve transplanting a few genes from one organism into the genetic material of another.

Of course both the nuclear reactor and the recombinant issues are argued in terms of their effect on the public health, but one is never sure how seriously one should take such terms. We are a pragmatic society, suspicious of philosophy, which means only that we must translate metaphysical questions into issues of health and economics before we feel they can be properly raised. No one argues against the space program on the explicit grounds that it embodies the wrong assumptions about man and his correct relationship to the earth and the stars, but such grounds seem to me to lurk just below the surface of the debates about diverting funds from health care. We talk as though all that concerns us is the health of the body, but it is difficult for me to believe that we are not, in our own fashion, just as concerned with the health of our souls as the members of every other civilization have been.

Some analysts, pre-eminent among whom is the prolific Ted Roszak, have argued that what we need is a return to the "ancient gnosis," a rehabilitation of the more venerable, and directly theological, categories of spiritual mysteries and meanings. Perhaps unfairly, though, I cling to the typically American prejudice that the clock cannot be turned back. Rather, I think that what we need, and what is happening, is a reformation within the scientific church, splitting a world view that was once as seamless as the Catholic Church's before Luther into two, a Worms and a Rome.

One can see evidence of this change everywhere. First of all, scientific terminology has begun to move away from words which emphasize how nature can be trussed up. Particle physicists have been labeling the attributes of new particles they discover as "charm," "color," and "strangeness," words which set off a radically different set of vibes from those of terms like pion and K meson. Molecular biologists now tend to give to the phenomena they study names that frame functions and actions, such as "repressor," "operator," and "reverse transcriptase," rather than names (such as deoxyribonucleic acid) that highlight the dead world of chemical reactions.

Evolutionary biologists talk freely of animals "choosing" evolutionary strategies, and attempting to maximize their genetic representation in the next generation. Recently I attended a conference in which two virologists referred to their creatures not as "it" or "them," nor even as "he" or "she," but as "you" (as in "You might want to produce just so much of enzyme X and no more. Therefore what you could do is . . ."). There seems to be a virtual collapse of that stern deterministic discipline so rigorously imposed on the science students of a generation ago: that one must never speak of natural things as though they cooked up purposes on their own. Instead I find a flippant anthropomorphism everywhere.

Second, a whole new set of sciences has been developing. These new sciences are environmental and ecological. They are conducted in the field as much as in the laboratory. They observe more than manipulate; monitor and survey and watch and listen rather than rush into testing the simplest theoretical system. One thinks of ethology, or sociobiology; and people like Dian Fossey, who spent ten years living with the Eastern Mountain gorillas, or Lindauer, who watched a single worker bee for 176 hours. Another example might be the MODE project, a vast international effort, sponsored by a dozen nations, to chart ocean dynamics; or the burgeoning efforts to track down the composition and processes of the atmosphere; or the surprising interest in extraterrestrial communication.

Finally, there are signs of a new kind of science writing, one that will stress what is, after all, one of the basic qualities of science: the contemplative, quasimeditative relation of man to the universe which accepts the judgment attained from natural evidence as the supreme authority. In this writing (it can be found in Stewart Brand's new magazine, *CoEvolution Quarterly*) scientists do not triumphantly penetrate nature's secrets; they are given answers as a reward for managing to frame their questions on nature's terms. The emphasis is on illuminating new dramas, new phenomena, and less on flattening them into networks of cause-and-effect reactions. There is a very high tolerance for uncertainty, even a reveling in it.

By contrast, my daily newspaper recently carried a story about an experiment in which a cancerous mouse sperm was implanted in a mouse egg, and a normal embryo resulted. The story stressed the miraculous powers of the *scientists,* in such lines as "scientists announced today that they had mated a cancer cell with a mouse and produced a normal mouse." That is an example of the "old" school of science journalism: the scientist is the active agent; nature is the passive backdrop. A member of the "new" school would instead (assuming this was compatible with the facts) have stressed the marvelous powers of the egg in accepting a diseased sperm, returning it to health, and then continuing with it along the normal path of development. The role of the scientist would have been reduced to that of witness, or, at most, the architect of the stage on which the drama was presented.

I think the "scientist as hero" form of science writing (a good deal of which issues from the scientists themselves) is responsible for the near total inaccessibility of molecular biology to lay persons. This is not a trivial cultural deprivation. Nowhere else does one find such natural intelligence, such elaborate self-sufficiency, such a scale of complexity regulated with such a degree of precision, as one does in the cell. No doubt there is a general suspicion that all these molecules—amino acids, enzymes, and so on—are not natural, but artifacts, like gears and screws, developed by scientists as a way of expanding their "mastery" over nature. But—purely as a question of the public interest—to the extent that our culture needs a vision of nature as active, up to any number of contingencies, highly competent in pursuit of a very wide range of purposes, and entirely self-regulating, the parable of the cell ought to serve magnificently. That it has not suggests that the "new" science writing has, as one of its first orders of business, an act of cultural damage to repair. Ultimately, it is probably impossible to grasp the cell at all unless one begins with the assumption that nature is full of active purposes.

There is another theory for the trouble that science is now in: that is, that we have lost our self-confidence, and with it, our belief that we can do anything right. Science has just been caught up in the general failure of nerve, and the emphasis on preserving the natural order, the "balance of nature," stems from a willingness to hand over the reins to some other, more competent, authority.

The theory I favor is that we sense that the world has changed enough to make a search for new ways of addressing the realities necessary, and that what we are seeing now is both the signs of the search and the emerging answers. Man is a uniquely generalized species; not only have we adapted to the arctic, the jungle, the seashore, the mountains, the central plains, and the river deltas, but we have adapted to a life of continuous migration, and, at other times, to a stable life, bound to a given place for generations. We have coped with high and low population pressures, with rich and poor lands, with environments that were high in risk and danger and those that were benign and peaceful. It is reasonable to believe that such an animal must have evolved ways of grasping the nature of this situation at its most abstract and dealing with it.

Perhaps that was the evolutionary origin of religion. If this is true, then perhaps what we are doing now is listening: pulling away from those sense organs that seem to be likely to block nature off, developing others that are more sensitive and open, trying to learn, as we no doubt have thousands of times before, what it is, this time, that the world wants us to become.

The
Search for
Alternatives

Introduction

A small but growing number of individuals and groups are actively involved in a search for alternatives in this third phase of the environmental movement. Most are devoted to the idea that we are in need of a new utopian era. This era would be one in which decentralized, appropriate or ''soft'' technology, built and applied at the human scale would replace the system which thrives on the glut of mass-produced consumer goods. Technology would not disappear but would be a ''technology with a human face,'' as E. F. Schumacher called it. This is not a time for remorse. For with the reduction in economic growth, the society could develop its intellectual, spiritual and creative powers. With technology more at the service of humanity, art and work and technology would be integrated as one. René Dubos has thought of this new phase as a renaissance within a steady state (reading 47) and more of a time for challenge than despair.

The architects of this change, like all other humans have blind spots, but because those bent on change are the most visible, so are their blind spots. There is no way that numerous pitfalls can be avoided, but the three reminders presented here might be of some value. First of all, the ecologically-oriented should not forget the most important law of ecology—everything is connected to everything else. Therefore, we can never do *only* one thing (reading 48). The second consideration is that we should not deny that the attitudes which need to change might have had an adaptive value—in fact an adaptive value which possesses a subtle, but important residual component even today. The admonition is, that in our effort to do good, we can make matters worse (reading 49). Finally, there is a good chance that a backlash movement will rub out any progress made toward contrasumption if we push too far too quickly. The option of retreating to the consumerism afforded by affluence stands ready for the anxiety-ridden. China, under Mao, had a phrase which meant ''hurry slowly.'' I would suppose this means that while pressure must be maintained to bring about change, people still need time to adjust. An affluent society needs time to ''harden off'' (reading 50).

As we begin our search for alternative value systems, there is the appeal of the ''noble savage.'' Indeed the noble savage has produced some high poetry (readings 40 and 41), and in most cases he lived well within his environment, stepping softly on the earth. Nevertheless, much of the primitive existence has been rather drab and bleak and the anxieties rather cruel (reading 51). Furthermore, kindness to nature did not always prevail among all tribes at all times (readings 52 and 53).

After we have considered alternative ethical systems we might consider alternative accounting systems. Tom Bender has some useful suggestions on this topic (reading 54).

Political change will be necessary (readings 55 and 56), but we need to remember that more is necessary than the making of a law. Chief Justice William O. Douglas many years ago noted that considerable reform legislation had been inacted, but that enforcement of the laws had been placed in the hands of people with neither the vision nor the will to bring about reform. This is essentially the conclusion reached in reading 57 as it pertains to land ownership.

In our search for alternatives—alternatives in agriculture should probably be close to the top of the list. John Todd, director of The New Alchemists discusses the smooth integration of sun, wind, biology and architecture on behalf of humanity and the earth so that we might live within the earth's limits (reading 58). My article (reading 59) stresses the need for a sustainable agriculture rather than one which promotes the loss of our soils and other finite resources.

Karl Hess, now a bartering craftsman but formerly a speech writer for Senator Barry Goldwater, writes of an experiment in community technology and self-reliance in which he participated in Washington, D.C. In reading 60, he explains why this experiment has faltered. Finally, Maynard Kaufman, himself an experimenter in the new homesteading movement writes of this very movement in America today (reading 61).

The Renaissance Within the Steady State

Rene Dubois

The ecological constraints on population and technological growth will inevitably lead to social and economic systems different from the ones in which we live today. In order to survive, mankind will have to develop what might be called a "steady state" a phrase that I prefer to John Stuart Mill's "stationary state."

The "steady state" formula is so different from the philosophy of endless quantitative growth, which has governed Western civilization during the nineteenth and twentieth centuries, that it may cause public alarm. Many persons will mistakenly assume that the world is entering a period of stagnation, leading eventually to decadence. Yet, a steady state is compatible with creative changes. In fact, change within a closed system will probably offer intellectual possibilities much more challenging than those offered by the kind of rampant growth that prevails at present.

The ecological constraints on the growth of the world population and on the production of energy and of goods will generate new kinds of scientific problems. For example:

1. The drastic limitation of family size will probably create social, psychological, physiological, and perhaps even genetic disturbances concerning which little, if anything, is known.
2. The distribution and utilization of energy under controlled conditions will require sophisticated knowledge of regional and spaceship ecology.
3. Entirely new technologies, and therefore new kinds of scientific knowledge, will have to be developed to minimize pollution and to recycle the natural resources in short supply.

The steady state will thus compel a reorientation of the scientific and technologic enterprise. Indeed, it may generate a scientific renaissance. But this will not happen without a conscious, and probably painful, effort from the scientific community.

Three Reminders for
Those Bent on Change

You Can Never Do Only One Thing (Hardin's Law)

A. J. Sharp

In eastern Borneo there is a rainy, wet valley which had a high incidence of malaria. Officials of the World Health Organizations decided to use the insecticide, DDT, which definitely reduced the mosquito population and the number of malarial cases. The ever-abundant cockroaches also received the DDT which killed only a few but interfered with the movement of the survivors. As a result the geckos (the common house-lizards) caught more than the usual number of cockroaches with their loads of DDT, and in turn their movement was retarded by the ingested insecticide. House-cats there appreciate geckos just as our housecats relish rats and mice. DDT is poisonous to cats, and the subsequent decimation of the cat-population due to the ingestion of many geckos was followed by an increase in numbers of rats and fleas, and potentially, cases of other diseases including bubonic plague. All of this the local people understood, but the next event seemed to make no sense. Within about two years their thatch roofs began rapidly to disintegrate. They connected the problem with the mosquito-control program since it was limited to the treated area. Scientists were sent to find an explanation for the unusual destruction of roofs which was causing discontent among the natives. After a difficult study, it was discovered that the population of larvae which fed on the thatch had been kept under control by parasites which were killed by DDT (geckos may have helped too); but with less predation there was a population-explosion of larvae which literally ''ate the roofs off the houses''. An interesting side activity was known as ''Operation Cat Drop'' with cats flown in from other countries.

REFERENCE

Vol. LVL No. 3, *Phi Kappa Phi Journal*, Summer 1976.

Deeply Held Attitudes May be Rooted in Survival

Howard T. Odum

An example of a primitive agricultural system of man and nature is provided by the system of rice and cattle in India and in other monsoon climates where the severity of the dry season essentially forces all systems of vegetation, whether controlled by man or not, to recommence each year. There is a flow of energy through rice and some grass, man, and the sacred cattle (work animals) with loopback circuits of work control. Harris[1] opposes those who state that the sacred animals on the intensified, nonsubsidized farms are superfluous. He mentions that they glean from a different plant base than man, serve as a source of critical protein, and especially facilitate mineral cycling and work on the plots necessary for a fast start on crop production when the wet monsoon begins. Those who advocate removal of the sacred cows needed under the present agricultural system refer to the simple principle of shortening the food chain to save energy. In this case, a little knowledge about one process without understanding the complete system may be producing recommendations that endanger millions by upsetting a self-supporting system. Harris cites Gandhi's comment that cows are sacred because they are necessary. The more general principle may be that religion is the program of energy control necessary for survival encoded in behavioral language.

A Greenhouse Culture Requires Hardening Off

Wes Jackson

I once planted some seeds of a wild winter annual in small pots in a greenhouse. They were painstakingly watered and fertilized and produced a green, luxurious growth, surpassing in overall vegetative vigor their relatives in the field. From experience, it was known that if we moved these plants from the cozy greenhouse environment and left them outside, they would be vulnerable to the very environment which had shaped their ancestors. A high percentage would be unable to withstand the shock and might die, not because they lacked the genetic potential to resist the environmental extremes, but because the narrow greenhouse environment had not called forth the broad spectrum of genetic potential necessary to endure the adversity usually presented to wild populations.

The United States as a developed country might be regarded as a greenhouse culture. Lately we have been watching a gathering storm outside our comfortable environment and have become suddenly cognizant of how vulnerable our culture is. We lately anticipate that our cozy environment may fast disappear. In fact, only a few supporting sub-systems responsible for our affluence need falter, and we will find ourselves "out in the cold."

There is a way to gradually prepare greenhouse plants for a full life outside. It is called "hardening off." By placing the plants outside a few hours a day at the beginning and gradually increasing the amount of time they are left outside, eventually they can be safely left there. The first time they are placed outside, on a quiet, warm afternoon, the outside environment may appear to differ very little from the greenhouse environment. But it is an important first step, and somehow it seems different. What we are doing, during this "hardening off" period, is giving the plant the outside conditions and the time to "kick in" the genetic machinery it has and needs to cope physically and physiologically with the outside environment. The purpose of many of the new organizations such as The New Alchemists of Massachusetts, the Fallarones Institute of California, or The Land Institute of Kansas is to work on low resource consuming alternatives, especially in the areas of agriculture, energy, shelter and waste. We might say that these people are contributing to a cultural "hardening off" process. At this time, their experiments in organic agriculture, fish culture, construction of wind machines, solar collectors, composting toilets, etc. may be no more than moving plants from a warm, still greenhouse to the outside on a warm still day. But I expect most of their activity is a bit more than that. We know that if we jump too quickly into the world of the future, a world in which a healthy poverty (as Annie Dillard calls it) is cultivated, we might become so discouraged that we refuse to venture out again. It seems to be the hope of this small group of workers that one day we may regard being whipped by the wind as being touched by the earth, rather than threatened with wilt. From my point of view that can happen only if we have been properly "hardened off."

A Look to the Noble Savage

The Fuegian Inhabitants

Charles Darwin

At a subsequent period the Beagle anchored for a couple of days under Wollaston Island, which is a short way to the northward. While going on shore we pulled alongside a canoe with six Fuegians. These were the most abject and miserable creatures I any where beheld. On the east coast the natives, as we have seen, have guanaco cloaks, and on the west, they possess seal-skins. Amongst these central tribes the men generally possess an otter-skin, or some small scrap about as large as a pocket-handkerchief, which is barely sufficient to cover their backs as low down as their loins. It is laced across the breast by strings, and according as the wind blows, it is shifted from side to side. But these Fuegians in the canoe were quite naked, and even one full-grown woman was absolutely so. It was raining heavily, and the fresh water, together with the spray, trickled down her body. In another harbour not far distant, a woman, who was suckling a recently-born child, came one day alongside the vessel, and remained there whilst the sleet fell and thawed on her naked bosom, and on the skin of her naked child. These poor wretches were stunted in their growth, their hideous faces bedaubed with white paint, their skins filthy and greasy, their hair entangled, their voices discordant, their gestures violent and without dignity. Viewing such men, one can hardly make oneself believe they are fellow-creatures, and inhabitants of the same world. It is a common subject of conjecture what pleasure in life some of the less gifted animals can enjoy: how much more reasonably the same question may be asked with respect to these barbarians. At night, five or six human beings, naked and scarcely protected from the wind and rain of this tempestuous climate, sleep on the wet ground coiled up like animals. Whenever it is low water, they must rise to pick shell-fish from the rocks; and the women, winter and summer, either dive to collect sea eggs, or sit patiently in their canoes, and, with a baited hair-line, jerk out small fish. If a seal is killed, or the floating carcass of a putrid whale discovered, it is a feast: such miserable food is assisted by a few tasteless berries and fungi. Nor are they exempt from famine, and, as a consequence, cannibalism accompanied by parricide.

The tribes have no government or head, yet each is surrounded by other hostile ones, speaking different dialects; and the cause of their warfare would appear to be the means of subsistence. Their country is a broken mass of wild rock, lofty hills, and useless forests: and these are viewed through mists and endless storms. The habitable land is reduced to the stones which form the beach; in search of food they are compelled to wander from spot to spot, and so steep is the coast, that they can only move about in their wretched canoes. They cannot know the feeling of having a home, and still less that of domestic affection; unless indeed the treatment of a master to a laborious slave can be considered as such. How little can the higher powers of the mind be brought into play! What is there for imagination to picture, for reason to compare, for judgment to decide upon? to knock a limpet from the rock does not even require cunning, that lowest power of the mind. Their skill in some respects may be compared to the instinct of animals; for it is not improved by experience: the canoe, their most ingenious work, poor as it is, has remained the same, for the last two hundred and fifty years.

Whilst beholding these savages, one asks, whence have they come? What could have tempted, or what change compelled a tribe of men to leave the fine regions of the north, to travel down the Cordillera or backbone of America, to invent and build canoes, and then to enter on one of the most inhospitable countries within the limits of the globe? Although such reflections must at first occupy one's mind, yet we may feel sure that many of them are quite erroneous. There is no reason to believe that the Fuegians decrease in number; therefore we must suppose that they enjoy a sufficient share of happiness (of whatever kind it may be) to render life worth having. Nature by making habit omnipotent, and its effects hereditary, has fitted the Fuegian to the climate and the productions of his country.

How Some Indians Hunted Buffalo

Meriwether Lewis

today we passed on the Stard. side the remains of a vast many mangled carcases of Buffalow which had been driven over a precipice of 120 feet by the Indians and perished; the water appeared to have washed away a part of this immence pile of slaughter and still their remained the fragments of at least a hundred carcases they created a most horrid stench. In this manner the Indians of the Missouri destroy vast herds of buffaloe at a stroke; for this purpose one of the most active and fleet young men is selected and disguised in a robe of buffaloe skin, having also the skin of the buffaloe's head with the years and horns fastened on his head in form of a cap, thus caparisoned he places himself at a convenient distance between a herd of buffaloe and a precipice proper for the purpose, which happens in many places on this river for miles together; the other indians now surround the herd on the back and flanks and at a signal agreed on all shew themselves at the same time moving forward towards the buffaloe; the disguised indian or decoy has taken care to place himself sufficiently nigh the buffaloe to be noticed by them when they take to flight and runing before them they follow him in full speede to the precipice, the cattle behind driving those in front over and seeing them go do not look or hesitate about following until the whole are precipitated down the precepice forming one common mass of dead and mangled carcases: the decoy in the mean time has taken care to secure himself in some cranney or crivice of the clift which he had previously prepared for that purpose. the part of the decoy I am informed is extreamly dangerous, if they are not very fleet runers the buffaloe tread them under foot and crush them to death, and sometimes drive them over the precipice also, where they perish in common with the buffaloe.

Primitive Man's Relationship to Nature

Daniel A. Guthrie

In discussing the causes of our environmental crisis, many authors seem to consider modern man's relationship to his environment as somehow unnatural. This attitude is due, in part, to a belief that primitive man lived in harmony with nature, a harmony that has been lost by modern society. Both Christianity (White, 1967) and Christianity coupled with technology (Roszak, 1969) have been blamed for this loss of harmony with nature. Yi-Fu Tuan (1970) and Richard Wright (1970) have disputed this belief by showing that Christians are not alone in their exploitation of the environment but share this trait with other cultures. Still, the attitude persists that primitive man, especially the American Indian, was somehow attuned to nature. This belief appears in Stewart Udall's book *The Quiet Crisis* (1964) in which he speaks of the land wisdom of the Indians, and in Theodore Roszak's *The Making of a Counter Culture* (1969) in which the kinship of primitive man to nature, as reflected through his belief in spirits and magic, is taken as an indication of a primitive ability to live in harmony with the environment. More recently Fertig (1970) has attempted to show that "Indians were part of a natural order between whose people and other animal and plant life there was a well-nigh perfect symbiosis" and concluded that "the Indians' nearly forgotten land wisdom, his ecological sense, is indispensable to our survival." It is my contention that primitive man was no better in his attitude toward his environment than we are today and that the concept of primitive man living in harmony with nature is a serious distortion of the facts.

For the purposes of this discussion, primitive cultures can be viewed as differing from modern society in three significant ways. The first two of these are in population size and in the level of technological sophistication. The populations of primitive peoples were small and the waste products of their cultures were for the most part biodegradable and did not occur in such concentrations as to overwhelm the ability of natural systems to deal with them. The situation is far different today. Not only is our population density such that our wastes cannot be accommodated easily by natural processes, but we turn the resources of our environment into new synthetic forms that cannot be degraded by natural processes and that may actually poison them. Furthermore, our technological sophistication allows a much greater level of consumption than was possible for primitive man. This very real difference in ability to affect the environment between primitive people and modern society must not be confused with a difference in attitude toward the environment.

The other significant difference between modern society and primitive cultures is in the way that primitive people view nature. The flavor of this relationship is expressed by Simpson (1964) in the following story.

Years ago I lived for a time with a group of uncivilized Indians in South America. Their world is very different from ours: in space, a saucer a few miles across; in time, from a few years to a few generations back into a misty past; in essence, lawless, unpredictable, and haunted. Anything might happen. The Kamarakoto Indians quite believe that animals become men and men become stones; for them there is neither limitation nor reason in the flux of nature. There is also a brooding evil in their world, a sense of wrongness and fatality that they call *kanaima* and see manifested in every unusual event and object.

The level of invalid perceptions might be called the lower superstition. It is nevertheless superior in some respects to the higher superstitions celebrated weekly in every hamlet of the United States. The legendary metamorphoses of my Indian friends are grossly naive, but they do postulate a kinship through all of nature. Above all, they are not guilty of teleology. It would never occur to the Indians that the universe, so largely hostile, might have been created for their benefit.

The religions of primitive peoples, full of spirits and myths, often express a kinship with nature or what Cassirer (1944) calls a sympathetic view of nature. This view is often expressed by American Indians when speaking of nature. Roszak quotes a Wintu (California) Indian as saying:

The white people never cared for land or deer or bear. When we Indians kill meat, we eat it all up. When we dig roots, we make little holes . . . We shake down acorns and pinenuts. We don't chop down the trees. We only use dead wood. But the white people plow up the ground, pull up the trees, kill everything. The tree says "Don't. I am sore. Don't hurt me." But they chop it down and cut it up. The spirit of the land hates them. . . . The Indians never hurt anything, but the white people destroy all.

Similarly, Udall (1964) refers to many Indian sayings such as "the land is our mother" and "Our fathers received the land from God" to show the reverence that the Indians had for their environment.

While primitive man thus may view his relationship with nature quite differently from modern man (see also Kluckhohn and Murray, 1956), his actions toward nature are another matter. Tuan (1970) has pointed out that a wide gap may exist between a culture's ideals and their expression in the real world. This is not to deny that many Indian actions were and are ecologically sound. In order for primitive man to survive he, of necessity, had to develop a certain harmony with nature. To put it bluntly, those tribes that did not develop some "ecological consciousness" soon became extinct. However, I believe that this ecological consciousness was not arrived at through careful analysis of the environment, but rather through a trial and error approach. Harmony with nature, thus arrived at, did not prevent the existence of polluting habits, when these habits did not immediately threaten the survival of the society, nor did this harmony with nature prevent the acceptance of new inventions or ways of life that were ecologically disastrous.

Thus, the Sioux Indian, who would not drive stakes in his mother, the earth, or cut her with a plow, showed no qualms about driving a herd of buffalo over a cliff or about starting a range fire to drive the buffalo. The Indian, like the wolves, often ate only the choicest parts of the buffalo, the tongues, when game was plentiful, or left some of his kill unused (Wheat, 1967). Indeed, primitive man's hunting abilities are believed by Martin and Wright (1967) to have been the cause of widespread extinction of large mammals during the Pleistocene. Early man was nomadic in part because prolonged habitation in any one area depleted game and firewood and accumulated wastes to the extent that the region was no longer habitable. One wonders, looking at Mesa Verde cliff dwellings, how it was to live over a garbage dump. Was their custom of throwing all garbage over the edge of the cliff in front of their homes any different from our current civilized attitudes?

Finally, it has been shown that the American Indian was quite willing to take advantage of advances in technology to further exploit his environment. Farb (1968) has documented the effect of the horse on the lives of the Plains Indians. Long accustomed to hunting and traveling on foot, the horse caused a revolution in hunting ability. Buffalo robes were a sign of wealth to the Plains Indians and with the advent of the horse, the hunter could kill more buffalo than one woman could clean. The result was the spread of polygyny and even the acceptance of "squaw men," men who did women's work as wives, not for any sexual purpose but so that more hides could be processed. There is some feeling that even if the white man had not overhunted buffalo with firearms, the buffalo would soon have been exterminated by overhunting on the part of the Indians. Other examples of acceptance of new technologies without regard to their effect upon the environment are to be seen in the Navaho acceptance of sheep, and the subsequent overgrazing in the Southwest, and in the litter of bottles and junked cars to be found on Indian reservations today.

Perhaps there are some primitive peoples living in limited areas such as islands who have a clear view of the limitations of their resources and of the need to conserve them. Lyle's story (1967) of the Tikopian Islanders gives some indication of this. The American Indian, however, shared with the early white settlers of our continent a feeling that there were limitless horizons toward which he could expand. Despite his expression of a kinship with nature and his possession of a few ecologically sound practices, his actions show him to be no better than the early white settlers in his understanding of his basic dependence upon his environment.

A return to the "ecological intuitions and memories of the Red Man," as called for by some authors (Fertig, 1970), is not a solution to our current ecological problems. The Indian's actions toward nature were, and are, identical to those of modern man. What concern for the environment there was existed for the express purpose of guaranteeing human survival. A true reverence for nature, where nonhuman organisms are given a right to survival equal to that of man, has never been part of man's emotional makeup. Man shares with all other animals a basic lack of concern about his effect upon his surroundings. Grizzly bears tear up hillsides in search of ground squirrels and marmots and destroy trees and shrubbery in fits of anger. Herd animals cause erosion on the plains by wearing paths in the topsoil. Many animals, such as bears and wolves, are known to kill more than is necessary for their survival when game is plentiful. We tend to view these actions of animals as part of nature's plan and so they are, but these actions are on a limited scale destructive of the environment. Furthermore, they are no different in kind from the actions of primitive or modern man. Man's attitude toward the environment has not changed in the millennia since his evolution from lower animals. Only his population size and the sophistication of his technology are different.

I personally doubt that large numbers of people can ever develop a new emotion of concern for their environment in which animal life is considered equally as valuable as human life. However, there are signs that this may not be necessary. Unlike many undeveloped countries, most U.S. citizens are not primarily concerned with the basic survival issues of food and shelter. Our great wealth allows us to concern ourselves with the "quality" of our lives. Furthermore, as we become increasingly withdrawn from the land, our interest in its preservation increases. Meier (1966) has pointed out that the cities, repeatedly castigated for their pollution, are the sources of most of our concern about resources. The rancher in Wyoming, living at a population density similar to that of primitive man, is not worried about air pollution nor does he show concern about leaving rusting farm equipment lying about his land. Further, he, like primitive man, views coyotes and eagles as direct threats to his livestock, and prairie dogs and rabbits as threats to his crops. This frontier attitude toward nature is not seen in the reaction of Alaskans to conservationist's efforts to prevent the development of the North Slope oil fields. One wonders, too, if those who abandon the cities for rural communes in order to avoid pollution and to return to a life style in harmony with nature will develop this frontier attitude toward the environment when their crops and livestock are threatened? It is the city dweller, divorced from a direct dependence upon the land, who has taken the lead in conserving our wildlife and natural areas. Urban citizens can afford to view the eagle and coyote as beautiful creatures, not economic liabilities, and to view land they do not own or have an economic interest in as worthy of preservation in a natural state. Further, it is the urban resident who is most affected by overcrowding and pollution.

To be sure, this attitude of concern stems more from self-interest in recreational use of the environment and in the quality of the air and water that we use than from any true respect for the rights of nonhuman organisms. As such, we are likely to save "scenic wonders" and ignore swamps, or to favor oil production and boat marinas over natural areas. Still, much can be done through informing the public as to what is truly in their interest. Many swamps have been saved not out of a public interest in swamps, but because they were necessary wintering places for migratory game birds or spawning grounds for commercial shellfish.

Our population is becoming increasingly urban, and it will be the urban majority that will determine the nation's conservation policies and have a major voice in pollution and population control. As our population becomes increasingly divorced from the land, it is the duty of every scientist, working through every educational device available, to keep the urban American aware of the natural condition of his country and of his interest in its preservation.

REFERENCES

Cassirer, Ernst. 1944. An *Essay on Man*. Yale University Press, New Haven, Conn. 237 p.

Farb, Peter. 1968. Rise and fall of the Indian of the wild West. *Natur. Hist.*, 77:32-41.

Fertig, Fred. 1970. Child of nature, the American Indian as an ecologist. *Sierra Club Bull.*, 55:4-7.

Kluckhohn, Clyde, and Henry A. Murray. 1956. *Personality in Nature, Society and Culture*. Alfred A. Knopf, New York. 701 p.

Lyle, David. 1967. The Human race has, maybe, thirty-five years left. *Esquire*, 68:116-118.

Martin, Paul S., and H. E. Wright, Jr. (eds.). 1967. Pleistocene extinctions. *Proc. 7th Cong. Int. Assoc. for Quaternary Res.*, Vol. 6. Yale University Press, New Haven, Conn.

Meier, Richard L. 1966. Technology, resources and urbanism—the long view. In: *Future Environments of North America*, F. Frazer Darling and John P. Milton (eds.), Natural History Press, Garden City. P. 277-288.

Roszak, Theodore, 1969. *The Making of a Counter Culture*. Doubleday & Co., Garden City, N.Y. 303 p.

Simpson, George G. 1964. *This View of Life, the World of an Evolutionist*. Harcourt, Brace & World, Inc., New York, 308 p.

Tuan, Yi-Fu. 1970. Our treatment of the environment in ideal and actuality. *Amer. Sci.*, 58:244-249.
Udall, Stewart L. 1964. *The Quiet Crisis.* Avon Books, New York. 244 p.
Wheat, Joe Ben. 1967. A Paleo-Indian Bison kill. *Sci. Amer.*, 216:44-52.
White, Jr., Lynn. 1967. The historical roots of our ecologic crisis. *Science*, 155: 1203-1207.
Wright, Richard T. 1970. Responsibility for the ecological crisis. *Bio Science*, 20: 851-853.

Appropriate Accounting

Stolen Goods

Tom Bender

We often complain about having to pay too much for things, but do we ever complain because we have to pay too little for something?

Can things cost too little?

When someone stops us on the street and offers us a TV or watch or stereo at a really low price, the first thing that pops into our heads is: "Is it HOT?" Our intuition always warns us that when something costs a lot less than it's supposed to, there is probably something funny going on.

We think about stolen goods when someone offers us a "deal" on the street. But do we think about stolen goods when we find a "bargain" at a supermarket, a discount plaza or an import store? Do we think about stealing from our children when we go to the gas station? Yet we buy gasoline that is cheap because we're pumping out the energy savings of millions of years so rapidly that none will be left for our own future or for our children.

When we buy fresh produce from California in the supermarket, do we realize we are likely buying goods that are produced illegally? Is it less wrong to buy illegal goods from a "Safeway" than on the street? Much of California's produce comes from the Central Valley, where vast corporate farms operate with flagrant disregard of federal and state laws limiting use of irrigation water to 160-acre family farms. And much of the produce is picked by illegal immigrants in violation of immigration, tax and employment laws. Is it stealing when a company that monopolizes food processing sets impossible quality criteria for produce of small independent farmers, then buys their crop cheap because there are no other buyers to whom they can sell?

How do we know if prices for things are low because they are being *dumped*? It's not uncommon for large producers to sell some items below cost to drive out their small competitors who produce more efficiently but can't afford large losses. And how can small farmers compete with corporate farming that *wants* to operate at a loss for tax writeoffs?

Imports also can be too cheap when our trade arrangements and energy sources exploit the workers of other countries (RAIN, May 1976). How would we feel if our country had no source of cheap fossil fuels and another country started to sell fossil-fuel-produced goods in our country so cheaply that we were all put out of work? We would end up having to work for starvation wages to compete with such cheap energy sources and stay alive. Is it right to purchase goods that support such an exploitative relationship?

So what if we do buy stolen goods, or illegally-produced products, or goods that are produced by exploitation? The major problem, it seems, is that when someone loses, someone else gains. *Someone* gets rich off of "stolen goods"—either the buyer or an intermediary or both. When wealth accumulates, power accumulates—whether we speak of large corporations vs. individual Americans or U.S. citizens vs. the rest of the world. And the more that power is concentrated, the less possible it is to sustain the principles of democracy and equality that our country was founded upon and which are necessary to the kind of society we wish to live in. Buying stolen goods contradicts those principles we claim to believe in and follow, and either we must change or they must.

Whether or not we eventually buy a "hot" TV hinges not only on whether we will get caught, but also—on some level—on a realization that supporting a market for stolen goods increases the odds that sometime we may become the source for such stolen goods.

Chickens always come home to roost one way or another. Exploitation of others eventually comes full circle—if not through rebellion, then through disease—if not through disease, then from atrophy. Wealth insulates and isolates, and, removed from the continual probing and testing of real forces of life, our information and judgment fail to keep us within the limits of the game. (Our Drain America First energy policy is a good example of this kind of failure.) While we become wealthy off of other countries, we are in turn exploited and controlled by the power and wealth of our large institutions.

Though we claim and often act otherwise, our purchasing decisions are never based on economics alone. Our so-called economic decisions always occur within limits set by ethics, morals and other social values. We require things to be Union Made. We don't allow child labor. We set the rules on corporate taxes, patents and monopoly that become the rules of the game within which economic trade, survival and success occur. Such ethical frameworks are essential and are more basic than profit or economics because they enable the continued survival and health of the resources, environment, social fabric and personal judgment necessary for our survival and well-being.

The separation of our ethics and our actions has occurred in part because our production and exchange processes are so complex and large that we are isolated and distant from where goods may have been "stolen." Without knowing what occurs or sensing the effects, we have less and less reason to trust our ethical judgment. We're also so wealthy ourselves, as a country, and so unused to doing things ourselves that we often have little sense of value and costs.

"Marked" prices, standardized goods, changing prices, take-it-or-leave-it buying, and prices totally determined by someone else are so universal that we have very little sense of what we're getting for what we pay or what is fair exchange. We don't know *what* we're getting (poly-epoxyl who?), if profit on it is excessive, if taxes were paid, if someone was unfairly paid for making it, if externalized costs were accounted for in its price. And things really *have* been changing so rapidly it's difficult to judge prices. New technical processes produce things more cheaply, but inflation and exhaustion of resources cause prices to swing erratically upwards.

Not only do our economics become confused as a result of all this, but our relationships with other people are harmed. Because we don't know what a fair deal would be, we can only assume that the less we can get something for, the better deal we got. But even then we're uncertain that the other person knows something we don't and we might get taken. And *someone,* it seems, is supposed to get the best deal out of an exchange. Our exchanges rarely give us good feelings towards the people we exchange with. We never end up thankful to other people or wishing to do something nice for them in the future in exchange for what they did or gave us.

All these things tie back to our not knowing what's happening, and so do ways of changing the situation. There are lots of things we can do:

- Reduce the scale of organizations. A small and knowable scale of production is the best insurance against not knowing what's happening. Present regulations discriminate heavily against small but efficient producers.

- Open financial records. Seeing how much a merchant or producer pays and gets for their products pinpoints avoidable expense and profit. More businesses are feeling more comfortable with people knowing rather than wondering. People act differently, too, when they know!

- Encourage local auctions, exchanges, flea markets, used goods sales. They will be more and more valuable in the future, are fun, and are good places to learn what things are worth. They have been regulated away in many communities.

- Exchange with friends and people you know—and *give* more than required. It will usually come back with interest. Remember the baker's dozen.

- Make and do things ourselves instead of purchasing them. Do real and varied work. We can save money, taxes and reduce the GNP while learning the worth of things.

- Get poor—live simply—and avoid the rush later. Reducing desires instead of satisfying them helps get us closer to reality and to the worth of things.

- Learn and share the energetics and economics of our foreign trade and our national economy.

- Regulate foreign trade of items not produced at equal wage rates or with careful energetics. The only trade that is socially affordable is trade of surpluses, not necessities.

- Prevent passing the buck, the costs and the damages caused by our activities on to people who don't profit from those activities.

- Give legal standing to trees, future generations and our shared surroundings so that passing on of costs to them and exploiting them can be controlled.

The more people know about something, the less chance there is of monkey business. There are ethical dimensions to exchange. Their importance to society is greater than the economic dimensions of exchange, and it is up to us to ensure their observance.

Political Changes

Politics and Survival

Richard Lee Clinton

> . . .our political leaders have failed us in three major areas: in challenge, in faithfulness, and in candor. . . . There is, however, a second half to the equation, for citizens—followers—owe their country something that they too have failed to give. All too often our people look for the easy answer and for leaders who, in the words of Sidney Harris, will "reconcile the irreconcilable . . .and promise us a society where we can continue to be as narrow and envious and shortsighted as we like without suffering the consequences." So as citizens we have some obligations to fulfill, too, and foremost among them is an honest assessment of where we are heading.[1]
>
> Morris K. Udall

Toward the end of his new book, *An Inquiry into the Human Prospect,* Robert Heilbroner captures precisely the mood against which I am struggling in writing the present essay when he says, "With the full spectacle of the human prospect before us, the spirit quails and the will falters. We find ourselves pressed to the very limit of our personal capacities, not only in summoning up the courage to look squarely at the dimensions of the impending predicament, but in finding words that can offer some plausible relief in a situation so bleak."[2]

As a basically unfriendly reviewer of the book remarked, "The spectacle that Heilbroner's thesis represents is almost as distressing as his prospect for the race. Here is no Spengler taking sardonic pleasure in declines and falls. Here is a man of practical intelligence and good will, a man equipped by temperament and upbringing to hope. Yet his book is an epitaph on liberalism and written with conspicuous pain by an author who includes himself in the epitaph."[3]

In this brief space I cannot begin to demonstrate the factual basis for the conclusions upon which my remarks will be predicated. Nor can I, except in the most abbreviated way, suggest the measures required if we are to preserve any approximation of our present quality of life for our children and their descendants. These matters have been covered by others more qualified than I and can be pursued by reference to the sources cited throughout this essay. The tasks I shall attempt here are the limited ones of, first, seeking to establish the desperateness of our situation by pointing out some of the difficulties involved in our recognition of it and inherent in trying to deal with it, given the perspective and value commitments we are locked into; and, second, suggesting the scope of the response the situation requires. Even this is too ambitious a goal for an essay of this compass, but if I can succeed in motivating some of my readers to seek further understanding of the issues and to begin reflecting on what they can do in their own individual lives to contribute to solutions, my purpose will have been well served.

I feel uncomfortably presumptuous in appearing to have any special insight into matters of such overarching significance, so let me acknowledge at the outset that few of the ideas in this essay are original. My thinking, as I will try to show, is largely an amalgam of the thoughts of the scores, indeed hundreds, of other scholars, scientists, and informed citizens whose writings have stimulated my concern for the set of interacting issues I shall be discussing. That these issues and the implications of their interactions are still not widely recognized, at least not in proportion to their importance, bespeaks the overspecialization, heavy demands, and incessant distractions of modern life as well as the complexities of the issues themselves.

I

The set of interacting issues to which I refer can best be described in terms of the unprecedented stress being placed on our global life-support system; on the nonrenewable resource stocks of the planet; and on our political, administrative, and problem-solving capacities by the combined effects of rapid population growth, new technologies, increasing disparities in wealth, and heightened interdependence. In recent books the situation has been variously referred to as "the world problematique,"[4] "the predicament of mankind,"[5] and "the macroproblem."[6] Whatever the preferred designation, the essence of the situation is clearly that the quantity and quality of man's activities have reached levels at which, for the first time in the planet's history, their interactions are producing impacts on a global scale, some of which are potentially disastrous.

On a finite planet with randomly distributed resources and a global life-support system, continued population growth eventually results in a radical new form of interdependence. People in one area of the world depend on fossil fuels or grain or metals or sugar or a variety of other commodities and manufactured products from other parts of the world. No longer can any country or region pretend to independence, if only because pollutants cannot be detained at national frontiers and weather patterns in some areas can be drastically altered by interference with climate-influencing factors in other areas.

Such radical interdependence can produce either of two reactions among human populations organized in nation-states: competition or cooperation. Competition for the dwindling resource reserves of the planet will, of course, eventually lead to conflict, which will inevitably submerge concern for and attention to preserving both environmental amenities and crucial aspects of the planet's ecological balance as scarcities become more acute and the threat of thermonuclear Armageddon looms larger. Yet very little in man's history since the onset of civilization some five millenia ago suggests that he is capable of suppressing competition and conflict in favor of cooperation.

It is this simultaneous approach toward various types of limits—the limits of the ecosystem to reprocess wastes, the limits of nonrenewable resources, the limits of man's capacities for overcoming the obstacles to effective organizational responses to these and other accompanying problems—which makes our present situation so desperate, for our common sense should tell us that we are simply not able to handle problems of such magnitude and with so many unknown and counterintuitive interrelations all at the same time. In addition to the inadequacy of our intelligence gathering and organizational capacities and our inability to transcend short-term perspectives and expeditiously to override vested interests, there are further obstacles to cooperative information sharing, rational problem solving, and coordinated planning inherent in our present ideological commitments and racial, religious, and ethnic prejudices. Overlooking or discounting these barriers, none of which is entirely absent when human beings are involved, can result from simple naïveté, Panglossian optimism, reckless self-delusion, or unbounded arrogance; in any case the consequences will eventually be the same—catastrophic.

In short, while it has been obvious to the more insightful for centuries that our fecundity, technological cleverness, and greed were in excess of our foresight, wisdom, and virtue, the new and determining factor in the survival equation is that the synergistic interactions of our fecundity, technology, and greed have now begun to surpass even nature's prodigious capacities to absorb our wastes and to supply us with the basic elements of life.

II

The implications of this altered state of affairs could not be more profound, for they mean that the basic conditions within which we exist are undergoing a drastic alteration, hence our values, beliefs, and behavior must be modified accordingly. Values, beliefs, and behavior, it should be recalled, are not immutable. They have changed in the past; in fact, they have been in a constant state of flux throughout man's history. They have changed as the conditions to which they were a response changed; and since the changes in those conditions were usually gradual, the modifications in values, beliefs, and behavior have traditionally also been gradual. The conditions under which man lives are being transformed now, however, with unprecedented rapidity; and the modification of our values, beliefs, and behavior must be accomplished with corresponding haste.

William Ophuls, one of the relatively few political scientists to bring an ecological perspective to the study of politics, has succinctly stated the crux of the changed conditions within which man now exists: "Things which used to be free goods [for example, water]...now become common property resources subject to the dynamics of competitive overexploitation.... What was free has become scarce and must therefore be placed under political and economic controls to prevent mutual ruin."[7] Lynton Caldwell, also in the vanguard of ecologically aware political scientists, explains the altered state of affairs with his characteristic lucidity: "When the fit between man and milieu is loose, voluntary individual adaptations are possible. When social pressures on the environment are severe and the man/milieu relationship is tight, politics replaces individual choice, and priority, rationing, or some other form of social decision overrides voluntary behavior."[8] Yet another of the handful of political scientists who have written on these topics, Victor Ferkiss, puts the matter more dramatically: "An existential revolution is under way that may destroy the identity of the human race, make society unmanageable, and render the planet uninhabitable. Bourgeois man is incapable of coping with this revolution."[9] Ophuls sums up the matter concretely for Americans in this way: "The individualistic basis of society, the concept of inalienable rights, the purely self-defined pursuit of happiness, liberty as maximum freedom of action, and laissez faire itself all require abandonment or major modification if we wish to avoid inexorable environmental degradation and perhaps extinction as a civilization. . . .In the face of deep crisis, democracy may simply not be a valid system of politics.''[10]

Few Americans are ready yet to accept such a sweeping indictment of their most cherished values, and the great danger is that too few can be convinced that the situation is really so serious in time to devise and implement more viable alternatives that still contain as many of the best features of our present system as possible. As Richard Falk, one of the earliest pioneers in political research on environmental problems, has put it, ''There is not yet any appropriate sense of the magnitude of the task and of its urgency, and there is no understanding of the extent to which the protection of the environment will require an organizational and attitudinal revolution of a global scale.''[11]

Our reluctance to embrace such a dire assessment of the state of the world is simply enough explained, for our historical experience, cultural biases, and psychological make-up enable us—perhaps compel us—to believe that things will go on more or less as usual, without major discontinuities and generally in the direction of ''progress,'' and that man's ingenuity will provide solutions to any problems that might arise along the way. Are we not, after all, as David Potter has characterized us, ''the people of plenty''?[12] Have we not come to rely on continuous economic growth to handle for us what has correctly been called the most difficult political challenge of all—the crisis of distribution? (Don't worry about the fact that your share is so much smaller than mine; look how much larger it is than it was last year or the year before. Just keep the wheels of industry turning; as long as the whole pie is getting larger, we'll all have bigger pieces.) Do we not derive solace—some degree of psychic security—in this kaleidoscopically changing world from our unarticulated, perhaps largely unconscious, faith in an underlying continuity; in certain basic premises; in the timeless, unchanging verities such as ''growth is good,'' ''bigger is better,'' ''always look out for number one,'' ''good fences make good neighbors,'' and ''that government is best which governs least''? Yet the conditions which determine our continued existence are requiring us to recognize the limits to growth; the finiteness of the earth; the essential brotherhood of all mankind, all of whom are passengers on the same fragile spacecraft; the possibility of the community welfare's taking precedence over the individual within the hierarchy of values of each member of the community; and the wisdom of Nietzsche's paradoxical assertion that ''freedom is the recognition of necessity.''

The shift this implies in our thinking, in our outlook toward and expectations from life, in our view of man and his place in nature, and in our self-images could scarcely be more sweeping and profound. This radically altered way of looking at the world finds parallel in its impact on mankind as a whole perhaps only in the rise of monotheism, in the Copernican revolution, and in the adjustments attendant on Darwin's theory of evolution.

Kenneth Boulding grasped the essence of our position over a decade ago when he wrote:

The twentieth century marks the middle period of a great transition in the state of the human race. . . .It may be called the transition from civilized to postcivilized society. . . .The word post-civilized . . .bring[s] out the fact that civilization is an intermediate state of man dividing the million years or so of precivilized society from an equally long or longer period which we may expect to extend into the future postcivilization.

.

We must emphasize [however] that there is no inevitability and no determinism in making this great transition. . . . There are a number of traps which lie along the way and which may either prevent man and his planet earth from making the transition altogether or delay it for many generations or even thousands of years.[13]

André Malraux echoed Boulding when he recently said, "We are actually between civilizations. . . . "[14] William Irwin Thompson considers us at the climax of human cultural evolution, a point from which we "will now either slide back into a new Dark Age or evolve into a higher, more spiritual being."[15] Lester Brown, writing in 1974, perceives the situation thus: "There are numerous indications that we may be on the verge of one of the great discontinuities in human history—economic, demographic, political. . . . Changes in attitudes and values are required of people everywhere. The needed changes may far exceed those any generation has been called upon to make. . . . "[16] A year earlier, Frederick C. Thayer put it this way: " . . . whether we describe the transcendent experience ahead of us as a revisioning of history, a transformation, a paradigm change, or something else—the conventional wisdom of politics and economics can have no part to play in that experience."[17]

Surely by the end of 1974 the inadequacy of "the conventional wisdom of politics and economics" had become all too "perfectly clear"—more than a year having elapsed since the "energy crisis" and still no semblance of an energy policy; inflation and recession worsening simultaneously; corporate profits at record highs yet the stock market hovers uncertainly at a twelve-year low and unemployment rises daily; a "cap" negotiated on the strategic arms race with the USSR which allows for continued strategic expenditures on our part of $1,500,000,000 per year for the next ten years; and the majority of Americans continuing to overeat, while many of their aged countrymen subsist on dog food, and millions of people in the poorest countries face the spectre of famine.

III

One hopes that the broad range of scholars and scientists whose assessments were cited above add credence to my assertion that our situation is desperate. It is amazing, though, how many experts and opinion leaders can still be found who not only reject this assertion but who disparage as "doomsdayers" and "alarmists" those who dare make it. Why this occurs should be fully understood, for it confuses and baffles both policy makers and the public, who consequently are able to convince themselves that, since the problems are obviously too difficult for them to comprehend, they might as well not worry about them. Thus, in the wake of conflict among the experts, those whose responsibility is management of the society at large—our political leaders—find renewed warrant for ignoring long-term considerations in favor of more immediate ones, although quite obviously a society is quintessentially a long-term project.

This cacaphony of discord among experts can be traced to a number of factors. In the first place, only over the past decade or so have many of the second- and third-order effects and counterintuitive interactions among exponential population growth, new technologies, rising affluence, and finite, natural life-support systems come to be recognized and understood by ecologists, oceanographers, medical researchers, and other specialists who devote themselves to the study of these interactions. Because they are so complex and because of the way scientific investigation is done, these problems have to be broken down into simpler, more homogeneous sub-areas, amenable to the techniques of different specialists. In today's world of exploding knowledge, however, it has become almost impossible for a well-trained specialist to keep abreast of areas beyond his own narrow field of expertise; hence, it is rare to find specialists who are able to visualize the overall context within which the particular problem they are studying occurs in the real world. The result is that the solutions prescribed by the various specialists studying different aspects of the same problem, although adequate perhaps for the limited aim for which they were designed, often create serious difficulties in other not always obviously related areas. These conflicting prescriptions, and the lack of any holistic view of the overall system within which the problems are interacting, account for a large part of the disagreement among experts.

Similarly, within the universities, which might reasonably be expected to be far ahead of other societal institutions in responding to such complicated problems, it seems that academic curricula and the people who design them are often too constrained by their disciplinary rigidities, departmental structures, and high levels of specialization to be able to react rapidly to new fields of knowledge or emerging problem areas, particularly when they do not fit neatly into a single already established field of inquiry or lack a vociferous self-interested constituency. Perhaps it is as an acerbic *Time* reviewer once remarked, "The implications of great societal upheavals like the Industrial Revolution were first grasped by 'crazies' like William Blake, whose ideas gradually percolated down to artists, savants, and finally pedants."[18]

Moreover, without implying a full-blown conspiratorial theory of power elites, it is obvious that there are powerful groups whose short-term interests are served by not calling too much attention to the growing number and seriousness of problems with which present economic, social, and political arrangements are unable to deal effectively, lest people begin to question those arrangements. Richard Falk has joined this issue and its implications with admirable directness:

The need for drastic change suggests the likelihood of struggle between those who operate and benefit from the present political system and those who support the creation of an increasingly powerful world government. Good education, as always, should pursue a strategy of subversion, weakening confidence in existing arrangements, and even converting the old elite to the new vision; but it seems likely that the defenders of the status quo will condemn and suppress those who work visibly and effectively toward a new world system based on an ecological vision of wholeness.[19]

Of course, not everyone who refuses to accept the seriousness and urgency of the situation is a defender of the status quo or in the employ of self-interested parties. Many are simply inadequately informed, others have an almost religious faith in either technology or man's ingenuity, some have so trained their minds to skepticism that they doubt everything, some have overreacted to the premature cries of wolf of earlier decades, not a few are merely incorrigible optimists, and a sizable proportion are, as John Graham has insightfully noted, "engaged . . . in repressing the fear that our world is slipping out of human control." Addressing himself particularly to his fellow medical scientists, but with obvious relevance for all professionals, he added, "We repress this fear, in part, by burying ourselves more deeply in technical preoccupations."[20]

Another aspect of the difficulty of perceiving the seriousness of the consequences of rapid population growth, resource depletion, environmental deterioration, and the overload on human problem-solving capacities is the gradualness and indirectness with which these problems manifest themselves. While the growth of global population from one billion in 1850 to two billion in 1930 to four billion today is anything but gradual in terms of man's three or four million years of existence as a species, it has been gradual and, perhaps just as important, continuous, and, therefore, "normal" in our lifetimes; hence, we seldom pause to question it. Similarly, it is hard to grasp the lethal nature of the process, both because its major effects occur in faraway lands and because no one ever seems to die of overpopulation.[21] The cause of death of millions of children who die each year is listed as diphtheria, measles, dysentery, or some other disease, but it is rarely mentioned that malnutrition and/or undernourishment had so weakened their resistance that they succumbed to an illness that a well-fed child might easily have shaken off. When a tidal wave took the lives of more than three hundred thousand men, women, and children in Bangladesh in 1970, few noted that they were in fact victims of overpopulation. These miserable people knew that the lowlands they inhabited were subject to tidal-wave flooding, but population densities were so high in safer areas that they were forced to settle wherever they could find empty space. Yet we think of their having drowned rather than having died of overpopulation.

The depletion of resources is also difficult to perceive because of the way the growing scarcity is filtered through the economic system. As the increasing scarcity, of, say, a given metal drives its price up, another metal or alloy with similar properties, which might formerly have been considered too expensive for many uses to which the now scarce metal was put, becomes price competitive and is substituted for the increasingly scarce metal. All the public, and apparently most policy makers, notice is the higher price of the finished product, not the steady depletion of the unrenewable resource. The science of economics further contributes to disguising the seriousness of the depletion of nonrenewable resources by assuming that such substitution can continue to take place indefinitely, as long as increased costs of a superior grade of ore make it "economical" to refine an inferior grade. No physical limits—for instance, the availability of energy or water or the capacity of the environment to process wastes—are taken account of in economists' calculations.[22]

In like fashion, the overall impact on the environment, that is, on our global lifesupport system, goes largely unmonitored and unreported. We hear about the results of the more shocking insults to the environment when chemical-laden rivers catch fire, whole cities are endangered by smog or by carcinogenic drinking water, and our national symbol, the bald eagle, is threatened with extinction; but we have little comprehension of the myriad ways in which the day-to-day activities of industrial civilization are steadily poisoning the ecosystem. How many of us are aware that the level of DDT is higher in the milk of American mothers than the law allows in cow's milk? that mercury concentrations have already made some types of ocean fish unsafe for human consumption? that one of the most basic components of plastics, vinyl chloride, has in some circumstances produced an incurable and always fatal form of cancer of the liver in human beings? that our use of aerosol products last year alone resulted in the release of a million tons of fluorocarbon gases into the stratosphere where they may be destroying the ozone layer which protects us from cancer-inducing ultraviolet radiation? that generation of electricity by nuclear reactors produces as a waste product vast quantities of plutonium-239, a material so deadly that inhalation of one-millionth of a gram induces lung cancer and so long-lived that it must be kept sealed off from the biosphere for tens, perhaps hundreds, of thousands of years? or that the only major obstacle in the path of terrorists, criminal elements, or crackpots who might seek their nefarious ends through nuclear blackmail has been the difficulty of acquiring fissionable material such as plutonium-239, which is now becoming ever more accessible as "peaceful" nuclear reactors are built all around the world?

IV

What, then, is to be our response to this unprecedented conjunction of events? No one, of course, can say, although a probable range of alternatives can be inferred and a preference for some rather than others expressed and defended.

In attempting to guess the proximate future, the least risky procedure is to assume a continuation of the present. This was the course followed by the Meadows' team in their seminal study *The Limits to Growth*. The projections their computer simulations generated by extrapolating from present trends were not pleasant to contemplate, the basic behavioral mode being one of "overshoot and collapse." As their myriad critics invariably insisted, as if the Meadows and their collaborators had not been at pains to make the point themselves, such a more-of-the-same strategy has obvious inadequacies when used for long-term forecasting, since new variables are likely to enter the picture as time passes and events occur. It is in regard to those new variables that I would like to speculate, for it is in them that whatever hope we may have lies.

Desperate situations have, of course, been confronted by man at many points throughout history, and much can be learned by referring to these examples as long as the differences between them and likely future situations are kept clearly in mind. While the possibility of a uniquely innovative response cannot be ruled out, it seems reasonable to suppose that any new variables that enter into the equation will resemble to some degree one or another of these past responses. Generally speaking, these responses have been of three kinds: (1) more-of-the-same approaches or new but ineffective innovations were attempted, with chaos and anarchy eventually resulting from their failure to cope with the new challenges; (2) either just prior to the disruption of society or after some period of it an authoritarian regime might arise either through conquest or revolution with the power to force compliance with rules— usually very unpleasant ones—designed to meet the challenges; or (3) a religious or moral revitalization movement might sweep the population, often as the result of the appearance of a Messiah, prophet, or spiritual leader, changing the people's values, beliefs, or patterns of behavior in a way allowing for adjustment to the challenges.

Probably other types of responses have occurred, but most seem to fit within one or another of these three basic categories. Of the three, the last has been perhaps the least frequent, yet it is some variation on that theme which must be forthcoming if we are to avert human misery on an unprecedented scale and the perhaps total destruction of our biosphere inherent in either the chaos and turmoil accompanying the gradual breakdown of our institutions or the titanic struggles sure to emerge along with totalitarian regimes. Nothing less than such dire consequences seems realistic to contemplate when it is recalled that global population has reached levels which cannot be sustained without massive worldwide transfers of resources and commodities and that we continue to live under a nuclear sword of Damocles.

Thus, while some version of alternatives (1) or (2) would seem more likely, the great task of our times is to attempt to bring about a functional equivalent of alternative (3). I recognize how unfashionable such a suggestion is and, indeed, how it seems to fly in the face of several centuries of steady secularization of society. Let me hasten to explain, therefore, that the sort of functional equivalent of alternative (3) I have in mind involves philosophical innovation and political leadership, not a return to mysticism or state religions.

As Gregory Bateson wrote in 1972 ''...the next five to ten years will be a period comparable to the Federalist period in United States history. New philosophies of government, education, and technology must be debated....''[23] One might quibble with Bateson's estimate of when it will begin or how long it will go on, but the necessity for such a debate is incontestable. What must issue from that debate is a global Declaration of Interdependence and a revised national Constitution with principles of law and governance congruent with the new realities of life on a spaceship with too many passengers.

For this to occur, however, the crucial catalyst is enlightened political leadership, a resource ever in short supply and seemingly already depleted on this continent. Mercifully, however, such leadership is not a nonrenewable resource. Like that most elusive of political concepts—power—leadership exists only in a relational sense, depending on the responsiveness of those led as well as on the qualities of the leaders. Thus, altering the consciousness of an electorate—making them responsive to issues and challenges which they had been ignoring—may reveal the existence of leaders who formerly had gone unnoticed.

By good fortune, the United States enjoys four salient advantages of incalculable importance in the race with time to effect such a change in consciousness on the part of the public: (1) a literate population; (2) our First Amendment freedoms of speech, press, and peaceful assembly; (3) our institutions of higher learning and the tradition of free inquiry and expression upon which they rest; and (4) a mass media system that reaches into the home of practically every citizen of the country.

If these formidable advantages can be utilized astutely enough by the increasing number of thoughtful and respected people who are becoming aware of the dimensions of the menace that threatens and of the magnitude of the changes which must be brought about, there is hope that the American public can be sensitized in a relatively short period of time to the type of political leadership needed. When this occurs, and the events of the next few years should help the process along considerably, the possibility is enhanced that enlightened leaders will appear—men and women with integrity and vision, dedicated to serving humanity rather than special interests; men and women who now reject political careers because of the hypocrisy and moral compromise which presently are part and parcel of the American political process.

Ah, it is argued, but that process and its symbiont, the free enterprise economic system, have served us well for, lo, these two hundred years! They have given us, as our business leaders are wont to proclaim, the highest standard of living in the world. Certainly they have faults, their apologists concede, but withal they have functioned better than any other system, and, anyway, it's an imperfect world; it would be unrealistic to demand perfection. Such arguments ring true for the pragmatic American, reared in traditions of original sin, patriotism, competitiveness, and laissez faire, but they overlook a number of crucial considerations.

In the first place the longevity of our political system is hardly solid evidence of its intrinsic resilience and workability. We should recall that it proved incapable of dealing, without recourse to war, with the two most severe trials it has undergone; I refer, of course, to the separatist movement of the South and to the Great Depression. Moreover, the vast wealth and wide-open spaces of the territory over which it rules provided the system with wide margins of error, enabling it to write off mistakes, miscalculations, and neglected opportunities for which most political regimes and economic orders would surely have been held accountable and probably transformed. The natural richness of the North American continent and its original sparseness of population also acted as a lubricant for the political system in another important way, since the potential for seemingly unlimited growth kept the people busy pursuing their personal goals of upward social mobility and affluence, virtually guaranteeing the smooth functioning of the largely unmonitored and almost superfluous government.

Of course, government provided the law and order, monetary system, and some of the infrastructural underpinnings essential to economic development and even made more active contributions in a variety of ways, but, by and large, economic development took care of itself in this country. Under the kinds of conditions which existed during the first century and a half of our history, minimal governmental interference and often generous governmental cooperation with commerce and industry meant that economic growth could proceed apace, unplanned and largely unregulated. We tend to give our political and economic systems major credit for this accomplishment, and unquestionably they were a help, but does it make sense to expect the same political and economic arrangements to serve us equally well in achieving very different goals under radically altered circumstances?

The 75 per cent of our population now concentrated on 2 per cent of the national territory in and around our metropolitan areas is totally dependent on the uninterrupted production and flow of goods—particularly water, energy, and agricultural produce—and removal of wastes. Can a political system be called responsible if it does not plan for coping with as wide a range of adverse contingencies as possible to keep disruptions of such production and flows to a minimum? Is a political system which leaves most production and allocation decisions in private hands and is philosophically committed to a minimum of regulation capable of devising such plans?

As the web of our interdependence becomes ever more elaborate and complicated; as the depletion of resources results in more frequent shortages, soaring prices, widespread unemployment, and other economic dislocations; as every group capable of organization seeks to protect its own interests in ways often inimical to the public welfare; and as environmental limits are approached and ever more perilously strained, the demands on our political system are multiplied manyfold. Can a system dedicated to the proposition that "that government is best which governs least" successfully cope with such an avalanche of demands? Can a system which has relied on continuous economic growth to resolve its most difficult problems suddenly grasp the nettle and begin to make hard political decisions on its own? In short, can a system geared to affluence continue to function under conditions of scarcity without major modification?

The cruel prank which history has played on us is that just as it is becoming clear to the most thoughtful that we must cease continuous growth and learn to live in harmony with our environment if we are to survive, it is becoming far more difficult for our government to attempt such a policy, since only through continued growth can the fast-multiplying demands on the system be accommodated without completely restructuring the system. Needless to say, there are vested interests within and without any ongoing political-economic system which oppose any such restructuring, so as things get worse—as growth-related problems multiply—the prospect is for most governments, including our own, to reject appeals to limit growth and instead to redouble their efforts to promote it. Indeed, the United States government's response to the energy shortage of 1973-74 has followed precisely this pattern, with environmental protection measures being relaxed and national forests, oil shale mountain ranges, and offshore areas being opened up for exploitation by the oil companies.

Another argument of the proponents of continued reliance on our tried and true political and economic institutions rather than risking experimentation with radical new approaches is that old saw about "the highest standard of living in the world" and its corollary "no other system has done as well." It is not my intention to denigrate the truly remarkable achievements made to date under our present system, but it is impossible to overlook how disproportionately material these achievements have been and how little attention has been paid to other vital aspects of human welfare and development—e.g., national health and dental care; equal opportunities for all races and classes (and both sexes) in education, employment, political participation, and recreation; quality public education; efficient mass transportation; preservation of the environment; etc. It is equally impossible to overlook the growing number of social pathologies which stain the reputation of our society and threaten the quality of our lives—e.g., crime; violence; narcotic addiction and alcoholism; mental illness; child abuse; broken homes; neglect of the aged; alienation; and an enervating sense of powerlessness, frustration, and fatalism which increasingly pervades even the better-off in the society.

To point to these uncomplimentary aspects of the system is not to deny its accomplishments but to question its priorities and the use it has made of the resources it has had available to it. As these resources dwindle, the way the priorities of their use is decided and precisely what these priorities are become increasingly important to society as a whole, which is to say they become increasingly important *political* questions that can no longer be left to private interests or to an assumed "invisible hand" to resolve.

Finally, those opposed to new and radical methods for handling the new problems which face us always seem to return to the truism that it's a far from perfect world as grounds for asserting that we should be satisfied with a system that has worked, however imperfectly, for two centuries. They label us utopian and vision-ary, if not Socialist or pinko-Communist, efforts to equalize opportunities, to regu-late business activities in the public interest, and to relieve people of the fear and insecurity of not being able to provide a minimum level of income and medical care for themselves and their families.

Of course, not everyone in our society reacts so negatively to ideas such as these, but a disappointingly high proportion do, and many others who favor the ideas in principle consider them unworkable or infeasible in practice. Both reactions are curiously at odds with our deeply internalized approval of and faith in technolog-ical innovation. It would be ''un-American'' indeed to suggest that we be satisfied with our present level of technology and cease to strive for continued advances. And it would be almost unthinkable for an American to dismiss out of hand the possibil-ity of a new technological breakthrough enabling us to perform even the most dif-ficult feat. After all, a nation that can put men on the moon . . .! Yet our expecta-tions for improvement in social technologies—in the capacity of our public institutions to manage social problems—are at a self-fulfilling low. We suddenly become literal interpreters of the Bible, piously subscribing to the view, ''The poor ye have with ye always.''

It is tempting to try to trace the origins of this pessimism about our ability to improve our social technologies, but the point to be made here is that with en-lightened political leadership the possibility exists that we could break through that pessimism and restore our faith in ourselves. Political leaders who respect our intel-ligence by being straightforward and truthful might find their constituents less con-fused, better informed, more trusting, and more tolerant when mistakes are made. Political leaders who inspire us by calling our attention to what could, indeed what must, be done instead of what has been done in the past might find a public more willing to postpone immediate gratification. Only political leaders who help us to understand the problems confronting us, who explain all the options open to us and the likely costs of each, who stimulate our imaginations and mobilize our energies can move us away from the competitive, materialistic, exploitative, individualistic ethic to which we are inured and toward a set of values based on cooperation, full human development, respect for the natural systems of which we are a part, and the solidarity of all mankind.

And only such a metamorphosis of our values will suffice if we are to succeed in preserving a quality of life at all comparable to that we have enjoyed to date. Anything less than such an unparalleled shift in values will find us first in the straits which Japan has reached already and eventually in a world which we of today could hardly recognize and in which we would probably be psychologically and perhaps physiologically incapable of surviving. Whether our grandchildren would be able to survive in such a world is, of course, moot, but the opinion they will hold of us if they do can be surmised with considerable certainty: they will excoriate us for our unpardonable perversity, for the quarrelsome, vainglorious, moral midgets which each evening's news report shows us to be.

Our primordial need, in Benjamin DeMott's words, is ''for a politics of institu-tional transformation''[24] that can create the conditions for the kind of moral and political leadership our current situation demands by giving meaning to our lives, restoring our faith in ourselves and in our fellow man, and rebuilding trust in our capacity to meet the challenges which confront us, if not with complete success at least with rationality and justice. This is not to imply that we should expect the state to solve our problems for us—only that we must realize that no other institution is even theoretically capable of making a credible attempt.[25] We will still be plagued with all the inefficiencies and dysfunctional emergent properties of bureaucracies. There will still be corruption and mismanagement to contend with. Frustration, alienation, and apathy will hardly disappear. The point is not to make things perfect, however, but to make them better.

In pursuing this limited goal we are greatly favored by how bad our habits have become, for even modest changes in them can show immediate positive results. Simply limiting the size of automobiles to a maximum of 2,500 pounds would (1) substantially cut our energy import requirements, thereby lowering our dependence on foreign powers and improving our balance of payments; (2) reduce the rate of depletion of scores of raw materials; (3) improve the quality of our air; (4) lessen the carnage on our highways; and (5) even make it easier to find a parking place. Construction of an adequate system of mass transportation, besides providing thousands of jobs, would multiply these benefits many times over. Further substituting vegetable oils for animal fats, poultry and pork for beef, and soya and pulses for animal protein, would not only free up vast quantities of grain for export to the world's hungry but would reduce many of the diet-related disorders Americans currently suffer from. Better insulation, less commercial lighting, more sensible pricing policies by utility companies, and other relatively simple measures could result in a 30 per cent improvement in the efficiency with which we use electricity, thus conserving our fossil fuel supplies and weakening the case for strip mining, offshore drilling, and nuclear reactors. Transferring the fertilizer we use on our lawns, golf courses, and cemeteries to the less developed countries would result in significant increases in the crops grown in those chronically malnourished areas, with immeasurable benefits for their developmental efforts and a lessening of the pressures on our food-producing capacity which have lately driven food prices so high. A return to the frugality and simplicity that once characterized Americans would, of course, prolong for decades or longer the resources which at current rates of consumption will be exhausted in a few years, in addition to ameliorating our devastating impact on our ecosystem and perhaps restoring our ability to enjoy the little things in life which those we have called wise have always told us are the most important.

At a minimum, individual efforts at conservation and recycling would enhance our badly eroded sense of personal efficacy and sensitize us to the unconscionable waste and environmental damage being caused by certain corporate interests and governmental entities such as the Army Corps of Engineers and the various branches of the military—and growing public intolerance of such practices is the stuff of which enlightened political leaders are made.

To repeat, the relationship between a people and their leaders is reciprocal; the better leaders we deserve, the better we will get, but also vice versa—hence, the necessity of doing everything we as individuals can to make our system responsive, to make it live up to the spirit of the timeless ideals expressed in our Declaration of Independence:

That to secure these [unalienable] rights, Governments are instituted among Men, deriving their just powers from the consent of the governed,—That whenever any Form of Government becomes destructive of these ends, it is the Right of the People to alter or to abolish it, and to institute new Government, laying its foundation on such principles and organizing its powers in such form, as to them shall seem most likely to effect their Safety and Happiness.

What is needed is to restore the primacy of politics in our social life. We must learn again what the ancient Greeks knew well, that the highest virtue is the ability to participate wisely in public affairs. We must learn to accord our greatest esteem to those of our fellow citizens who dedicate themselves to public service rather than to those who manage to amass the largest material accumulations. At present we are expected, indeed it is demanded of us, to spend most of our time working in our own individual interest, and we honor those who can show the most for their efforts. By necessity, we delegate responsibility for public affairs to elected representatives, yet they are usually as much a part of our self-centered cult of the individual as are we and are equally as caught up in the materialism of our present societal reward structures. Is it any wonder, then, that they often pay disproportionate attention to the rich and powerful interests which court their favor and that they occasionally succumb to the temptation to feather their own nests? The wonder is that so many resist this temptation and strive to serve the public interest fairly, even though so few of their constituents follow their actions or ever bother to communicate their approval.

Perhaps the greatest intellectual challenge of the moment is to help people regain the insight that we neglect involvement in political choices at our peril, that when politics is widely considered "a dirty business" many of the potentially best leaders are lost to the process, and that without effective and enlightened political leadership there is no possibility of minimizing the traumas of the period of profound changes we are entering.

The sense of personal powerlessness which pervades American society today is more easily explained than dispelled, yet it is one of the principal obstacles to creating conditions conducive to the emergence of enlightened political leadership. Being one of more than 212,000,000 citizens inevitably dwarfs one's sense of efficacy in being able to make one's voice heard, but the American genius for organization is making it possible for us to do just that. Public interest groups and citizens' lobbies such as Common Cause, Public Citizen, the Environmental Defense Fund, and dozens of more specialized organizations have been formed for precisely the purpose of channeling the voice of the people into the halls of power. These and many other groups also perform the invaluable service of monitoring the decisions and actions of our representatives and leaders and communicating this crucial information to us so that our votes can be informed and discriminating choices rather than empty symbolic gestures. These organizations, even in their early years and with limited finances, have proved in case after case how effective they can be. With enlarged and active memberships, their potential for making the system more responsive and responsible is enormous. We have not earned the right to resign ourselves to cynicism or despair until we have supported these new institutions and found them wanting.

What is required, however, goes far beyond these first steps, indispensable though they are. What is required is an effort comparable to but probably exceeding that of the mobilization this nation underwent in the context of World War II. Every activity must justify itself in terms of its potential for contributing to our ability to manage the crises ahead and to foresee and avoid as many of them as possible.

Unlike in World War II, however, the enemy against whom we fight will not be so easily perceived nor so readily portrayed as vicious and hateful. In Pogo's immortal words, "We have met the enemy, and they is us." The difference between the two situations is not trivial, for the burden placed on our political leaders will be infinitely greater as they struggle to convince us that we and many of our most basic values are our own most dangerous foes.

V

I hope I have succeeded in conveying the awesomeness and urgency of the situation we face without overpowering the reader's resolve to struggle against it. This is the Scylla and Charybdis I navigate between each semester in my courses on population and politics, and I'm afraid I have yet to pass the straits unscathed. It is so easy, especially when one is young, to convince oneself that everything will work out for the best, that someone else will take care of it, or even that, if things are so bad, I might as well enjoy myself while I can. Only political leaders supported by the authority, legitimacy, and mystique of the nation, and one hopes by some charisma of their own, can possibly convince a critical mass of citizens that the situation is as desperate as it is and thus requires daring measures to meet it.

I recognize the dilemma of the chicken-or-egg relationship between the quality of the citizenry and the quality of the leadership which emerges to guide them. All I can say is that the two are mutually reinforcing and in a kind of dynamic equilibrium. It would be tragically self-defeating to abdicate our individual responsibility and simply sit back and hope that enlightened political leaders will come forth; the only truly human alternative is to do everything we as individuals can to make the system open and responsive and thus conducive to their emergence.

Revolutionaries will scoff at such apparent naïveté, while reactionaries will redouble their efforts to suppress such subversive doctrines. Neither group has anything to offer in resolving the dreadful problems we are beginning to confront until they shed their ideological lenses and recognize whence our most imminent threats derive, namely, from (1) the addiction to unending growth, (2) the assumption that man can continue to dominate nature with impunity, and (3) the conviction that sovereign nation-states are the only proper form of organization for human populations. These traits are common to all present political systems and regimes, to all social strata and economic classes, indeed to almost all people everywhere. Current ideologies of the left or of the right give us no purchase on these sorts of problems. Only a political philosophy informed by ecological consciousness and ecological understanding can provide such a purchase. And only an ethics founded on an ecological vision of wholeness, interconnectedness, and mutual obligation can bring us to reject the values which have fostered our superaffluence and unbalanced overdevelopment that now exacerbate the problems of our planet and so obstruct efforts at resolving them.

As Lynton Caldwell has said, "The ultimate outcome of the [ethical and institutional] changes that are required can be hardly less than a new phase in the development of human society.''[26] It may seem utopian to expect so much in the short time left before it is too late, when we have evolved so little in this regard in preceding centuries, but the truly quixotic course would be to attempt unabated growth of population and material goods in a finite world already straining many of its natural limits. The early warning indicators are flashing ''system overload'' from every direction; to persist in our present patterns of incessant strife and wanton destructiveness is to invite certain retribution from the instruments of death we have amassed or from our ravaged ecosystem. To welcome a slowing of growth in Gross National Product does not, however, mean freezing all economic sectors at their present levels of output, with the obviously unacceptable unemployment and other disruptions this would entail. Our unmatched productive capacity must be utilized to the fullest for decades to come to provide the food, tools, and equipment that can facilitate the development of Third-World nations. Such uses of our productivity will simultaneously cushion our gradual transition toward a steady-state economy while enabling Third World peoples to bring themselves to a level of material well-being at which they can begin to accept the idea of following our example.

Nor would a shift from our present energy-intensive life styles to a simpler less wasteful way of life expose us to undue hardship, if such a shift could be made before too much more time elapses. True, many of the conveniences we have come to expect and many of the luxuries we may have enjoyed—or aspired to—will have to be foregone, but these sacrifices will be insignificant compared with those we would soon be forced to endure should we refuse to make them, and, moreover, they are often the sorts of sacrifices which turn out to be blessings in disguise, as when riding a bus to work instead of driving enables one to get to know one's neighbors.

Similarly, a slowing down and eventual cessation of economic growth need not imply any parallel reduction in the growth of opportunities available or in the rate of scientific and technological advance. On the contrary, as less time and energy are expended in needlessly competitive and unproductive pursuits, such as advertising and excessive packaging, to cite two seemingly trivial but pervasive examples, more service-oriented and research activities could be encouraged. As populations stabilized, a spur to technological innovation and automation would be provided by the declining numbers of new entrants into the labor force, and as improved technologies resulted in greater efficiency and less demand for labor, more service jobs could be created to meet the needs of a population with greater and greater amounts of leisure time.

Again, the magnitude of the value changes required is enormous, for people must learn to want to use their leisure time in productive and non-resource-intensive ways—for instance, in broadening their education and skills, in cultural pursuits, in sports, in time-intensive activities such as deepening friendships and child rearing. Merely to allude to the magnitude of the challenge, however, is also to suggest the scope of the opportunities and fascinating areas for involvement which will accompany movement toward a steady-state economy. These challenges and opportunities are the truly unlimited frontiers which man can explore and conquer infinitely.

Far from any connotation of stagnation or indication of antipathy toward science and technology, the idea of a steady-state economy is predicated on never-ending intellectual and moral growth and scientific progress. As Philip Handler, president of the National Academy of Sciences, recently noted, "The fruits of science did much to make our civilization worthwhile; now only political leadership combined with yet more science can save that civilization."[27] But as Caldwell reminds us, "The problem of applying science is not primarily a matter of knowledge, but of public will. . . ."[28]

Perhaps the reason our ethical and political evolution has not kept pace with our scientific and technological advances is that our survival never seemed to depend on it. This has not been the case at least since the success of the Manhattan Project, but only with the aid of more recent ecological insights are the less prescient of us coming to take seriously the altered circumstance that henceforth our survival does depend almost entirely on our ethical and political maturation. If this realization can be generalized in time, there is no predicting man's response, for, among the examples of the grandeur of the human spirit which history holds, most have shown man to be at his best when undergoing his direst tests.

In the nightmarish tragedy which seems to be inexorably building to its climax about us, two straws of hope remain yet to be grasped. Warren Wagar perceived them both over a decade ago, and I can do no better than to appeal to his eloquent statement of them. On the one hand,

All through history, men have responded to the collapse of old social orders by creating new social orders extensive enough to secure civil peace and humane values within the geographical limits of the society. In the present crisis, since here on earth geographical limits no longer exist, the only possible response true to man's nature as a social animal is the building of a world civilization. If the response has succeeded before, on a continental scale, it can succeed again, on a planetary scale.[29]

And on the other hand,

No sober assessment of our chances, not even the soul-sickness endemic in our times, can rob us of the Nietzschean joy of confronting with courage a world in disintegration. . . .and Albert Camus tells us . . . "The struggle itself toward the heights is enough to fill a man's heart."
. . .We are the link between the traditional civilizations of a well remembered past and the emergent world civilization. We stand between. . . .Such a task against such towering odds joins man to man and weaves meaning into the vast fabric of confusion. It can be the difference between the life and death of the soul.[30]

What must be done, then, is to make people understand the gravity of our plight while at the same time inspiring them with the confidence that they still can affect their destiny. In accomplishing this task, shallow optimism is as out of place and counterproductive as either fatalistic despair or reliance on faith that some supernatural power will deliver us. What must be inculcated is trust in ourselves, if not to solve every problem or to prevent every disaster, at least to prove again the magnificence of the human spirit. It may well be that we will learn that human dignity thrives better in the harsh climate of adversity than in the lush warmth of affluence.

NOTES

1. Robert L. Peabody, ed., *Morris K. Udall: Education of a Congressman* (Indianapolis: Bobbs-Merrill Co., 1972), p. 351.
2. Robert L. Heilbroner, "The Human Prospect," *The New York Review of Books* (January 24, 1974), p. 33.
3. Melvin Maddocks, "Quo Vadis," a review of *An Inquiry into the Human Prospect, Time* (April 1, 1974), p. 82.
4. Donella H. Meadows, Dennis L. Meadows, Jorgen Randers, and William W. Behrens, III, *The Limits to Growth* (New York: Universe Books, 1972), p. x.
5. *Ibid.*
6. Kan Chen, *et al., Growth Policy: Population, Environment, and Beyond* (Ann Arbor: University of Michigan Press, 1974), p. 1.
7. William Ophuls, Locke's Paradigm Lost: The Environmental Crises and the Collapse of Laissez-Faire Politics, paper delivered at the Annual Meeting of the American Political Science Association, New Orleans (September 4-8, 1973).
8. Lynton K. Caldwell, *Environment: A Challenge to Modern Society* (Garden City, N.Y.: Doubleday and Co., 1970), p. 115.
9. Victor C. Ferkiss, *Technological Man: The Myth and the Reality* (New York: George Braziller, Inc., 1969), p. 245.
10. Ophuls, *op. cit.*
11. Richard A. Falk, "Adapting World Order to the Global Ecosystem," pp. 245-257 or John Harte and Robert H. Socolow, eds., *Patient Earth* (New York: Holt, Rinehart and Winston, 1971), p. 253.
12. David M. Potter, *The People of Plenty: Economic Abundance and the American Character* (Chicago: University of Chicago Press, 1954).
13. Kenneth E. Boulding, *The Meaning of the 20th Century: The Great Transition* (New York: Harper and Row, 1965), pp. 1, 2, and 24.
14. Paul Ress, "Malraux: The End of a Civilization," *Time* (April 8, 1974), p. 34.
15. Philip Herrera, "Waiting for Godlings," a review of *Passages about Earth, Time* (April 8, 1974), p. 86.
16. Lester R. Brown, *In the Human Interest: A Strategy to Stablize World Population* (New York: W. W. Norton and Co., 1975), p. 172.
17. Frederick C. Thayer, *An End to Hierarchy! An End to Competition: Organizing the Politics and Economics of Survival* (New York: Franklin Watts, Inc., 1973), p. 116.
18. Herrera, *op. cit.*
19. Falk, *op. cit.,* p. 256.
20. John B. Graham, "The Relation of Genetics to Control of Human Fertility," *Perspectives in Biology and Medicine,* Vol. 14, No. 4 (Summer, 1971), p. 626.
21. Garrett Hardin, "Nobody Ever Dies of Overpopulation," *Science,* Vol. 171, No. 3971 (February 12, 1971), p. 527.
22. Three notable exceptions are E. J. Mishan, Herman Daly, and Nicholas Georgescu-Roegen, all of whom have argued for a restructuring of economics on the basis of the second law of thermodynamics. See E. J. Mishan, *Technology and Growth: The Price We Pay* (New York: Praeger, 1969); Herman Daly, ed., *Toward a Steady State Economy* (San Francisco: W. H. Freeman, Inc., 1973); and Nicholas Georgescu-Roegen, *The Entropy Law and the Economic Process* (Cambridge: Harvard University Press, 1971).
23. Gregory Bateson, *Steps to an Ecology of Mind* (New York: Ballatine Books, 1972), p. 493.
24. Benjamin DeMott, "The New Sexistentialism," *Saturday Review* (July 10, 1971), p. 51.
25. For a full development of the logic behind this assertion, see Garrett Hardin, "The Tragedy of the Commons," *Science,* Vol. 162, No. 3859 (December 13, 1968), pp. 1243-1248.
26. Caldwell, *op. cit.,* p. 204.
27. Philip Handler, "On the State of Man," remarks before the Annual Convocation of Markle Scholars (September 29, 1974), p. 17.
28. Caldwell, *op cit.,* 165.
29. W. Warren Wagar, *The City of Man: Prophecies of a World Civilization in Twentieth Century Thought* (Boston: Houghton Mifflin Co., 1963), p. 8.
30. *Ibid,* pp. 9-10.

Land Reform Declarations

First National Conference on Land Reform

Land is a precious and finite resource and the birthright of the people. Its ownership and control, and the associated economic and political power, must be widely distributed.

A sound land policy should regulate the use of the land in the public interest; keep the land in the hands of those who live and work on it; put the land in trust for the public good; and prevent it from falling into the hands of large corporations and wealthy individuals who are absentee owners. It should preserve and strengthen the family farm, make it possible for people on the land to earn a decent living, and provide conditions that revitalize rural communities. Government policies that encourage absentee ownership, the corporate takeover of agriculture, and the exodus of people from rural areas to the cities must be reversed.

A broad range of Americans have a vital interest in regaining control of land from absentee corporations in which it is unduly concentrated. We urge environmental organizations, labor unions, independent bankers, small business groups, farmers and farm organizations, cooperative members, consumers, and low-income and minority groups to join forces in shaping and implementing policies that preserve land and jobs, create parks and housing, provide recreational and economic opportunities, and protect legitimate land ownership and use while discouraging the abuses of concentrated absentee ownership and irresponsible economic and political power.

Energy resources on public lands should be developed by public entities in the public interest and the give-away of public resources to large corporations must cease.

We urge national officials responsible for law observance to enforce national policy as expressed in acreage limitations and residency requirements for receivers of federal irrigation water. We also favor government purchase of excess lands at the pre-water price specified by law.

Timber on public lands should be made available on a preferential basis to independent woodcutters and cooperatives.

Absentee corporations with non-farm interests should be barred from agriculture.

Tax laws that encourage ownership of land by speculators, corporations, and absentee landlords should be repealed. "Tax loss" farming, preferential treatment for capital gains, depletion allowances, and underassessment of corporate landholdings must be eliminated. Large landholdings should be discouraged through the use of progressive property taxes, taxes on the unearned increment in land value and increases in severance taxes. The proceeds of taxes on large landholdings should be used to provide human social services such as schools and health care for rural people, to preserve wilderness land, and to encourage small-scale farming, timber, and other rural enterprises through the financing of land banks and trusts.

Indians have been stripped of their historic claims to land. Shameful violations now occurring should be halted and the Indian land base preserved. In any land reform policy the Indian trust relationship with the federal government and Indian water rights should remain undisturbed. Treaties, executive orders, and hunting and fishing rights should be upheld. To provide for economic growth the tax-free status of Indian lands should be maintained. The policy of individual allotment was designed to alienate the land and break up the reservations; a positive government program should be initiated to consolidate these allotments under tribal control where the tribe so requests.

Land granted to railroads by federal and state governments other than rights-of-way presently retained by railroads should revert to original Indian tribes now on those lands. Mineral rights claimed or appropriated should also revert to said tribes. Remaining land not needed for rights-of-way should revert to the public domain. Additional mineral rights claimed or appropriated by railroads should also revert to the public domain.

Hispanic-Americans have been robbed of common and private lands on a massive scale throughout the Southwest in gross violation of the Treaty of Guadalupe-Hidalgo of 1848. These legitimate land claims must be resolved.

In any distribution or disposal of surplus lands, Indians and Hispanic-Americans with historic claims, along with low-income people generally, should receive priority.

The technical and financial assistance programs of the U.S. Department of Agriculture and the land grant colleges should be completely restructured. Their services should be offered exclusively to family farmers, farmworkers, and consumers. Moreover, the USDA should promote the development of new technologies that enable people to earn a decent living on family-sized farms. The crop supply-management program should be restored to its original objective of helping family farmers remain on the land by assuring that they receive a fair return for their labor and investment. New efforts, such as providing long-term, low-interest loans, should be given high legislative priority to allow able and willing young people to enter family farming.

The exploitation of rural labor must be halted immediately. We support the efforts of farmworkers, woodcutters, and other rural workers to organize effective unions and associations. Decent minimum wages, unemployment compensation and union protection similar to the provisions of the original Wagner Act should be extended to all rural workers and the exploitation of child labor must be abolished. We support the non-violent struggle of the United Farm Workers and the boycott of non-union lettuce and grapes.

Abuse of the land must also be halted at once. Strip mining should be prohibited. Severe penalties should be applied to corporate offenders in all cases of excessive water and air pollution and irresponsible timber and mining operations. A shift away from monoculture which depletes the natural fertility of the soil should be a long-range goal of national farm policy.

We condemn the monopolistic market power of big corporations like General Mills, Del Monte, International Paper, Tenneco, Consolidation Coal and ITT in food, timber, coal and other land-based industries. We call for the vigorous enforcement of anti-trust laws in these industries.

To achieve these policies aimed at reclaiming America's land for the benefit of her people, we conferees resolve to carry on the work begun at this First National

Conference on Land Reform. We resolve to return to our regions and localities to help educate and organize a network of people committed to a redirection of the nation's land policies at the local, state and federal levels.

Public Policy and the Shaping of Rural Society

Paul S. Taylor*

This article traces the social and economic history of the family farm, concentrating on relevant governmental actions. The author examines the Homestead Act of 1862 and the Reclamation Law of 1902 and their administrative interpretations. He determines that although the intention of the acts was to support the family farm, the administrators have failed to carry out this purpose. The author concludes that political and economic realities demand that Congress declare and administrators enforce a policy favorable to the family farm or this institution will be lost as a way of life.

Introduction

[I]n the absence of any national policy or regional plan, the agribusiness corporations have simply availed themselves of technological change to maximize profits and have left society to cope with the human consequences.
NEW YORK TIMES EDITORIAL, DECEMBER 27, 1971.[1]

Is declaration of public policy toward rural society, and its effective implementation, necessary? Or can the outcome be left safely to the unrestrained forces of technology and the market?

Answers to these questions lie in the historical development of the farming culture in the United States. Study reveals the conflicting characters of an industrialized farm or plantation society and a family farm society. In recognition of this conflict, the United States Congress, since the Homestead Act of 1862, has consistently declared when disposing of public land or authorizing public development of public waters that an essential element of sound rural society is the family farm operated by actual residents upon their own land. Unfortunately, Congress has often failed to support its own policy. Furthermore, the implementation of policy often has been frustrated by bureaucratic misinterpretation if not defiance of congressional mandate.

Backdrop of History

"The magic of property turns sand into gold," the classic saying of Arthur Young, has been widely accepted, yet some of its market place decisions have been

*Professor of Economics Emeritus, University of California, Berkeley. Martha Chase assisted in preparation of this paper, and the Institute of Business and Economic Research and Committee on Research of the University of California aided.

challenged from time immemorial. Not least among these have been decisions resulting in landownership by the few and landlessness among the many. "Woe unto them that join house to house," said the prophet Isaiah, "that lay field to field till there be no place, that they may be placed alone in the midst of the earth."[2] The Roman Pliny voiced an identical concern in 77 A.D. Peasant revolts spotted the Middle Ages and surfaced in the French Revolution. Control over land tends to give control over the labor that makes it productive, and to shape the very foundations of rural society.

Our own twentieth century has witnessed both revolution founded on landlessness, and land reform intended to draw the fires of such extremism. In its second decade revolutions almost simultaneously overturned the governments of Mexico in the New World and Russia in the Old. The slogan of the former was "Land and Liberty," and of the latter, "Peace, Bread, and the Land."

In the fifth decade, under General Douglas MacArthur, commander of an army of occupation, Japan administered a thorough land reform on the principle that "to the tiller belongs the soil." At almost the same time and in rapid succession, Mainland China and North Vietnam went through Communist revolutions grounded on peasant dissatisfactions.[3]

The United States, too, has experienced both the stabilizing and the divisive influences of differing relationships of man to land. From earliest settlements in the seventeenth century, opposed patterns of rural society—the family farm and the plantations—spread over the lands of the North and the South. Eventually these societies clashed in bitter warfare.

In the New England colonies, farmers as a rule owned the land they tilled by their own labor and the labor of their families. Celebrating the bicentennial of the landing of the Pilgrims, Daniel Webster drew these conclusions:

[Our New England ancestors] were. . .nearly on a general level in respect to property. Their situation demanded a parcelling out and division of the lands, and it may be said fairly, that this necessary act *fixed the future frame and form of their government.* . . . The consequence has been a great subdivision of the soil, and a great equality of condition; the true basis most certainly of popular government.[4]

As settlement spread across the Middle West, the New England pattern expanded with it. A century after Webster, the superintendent of the Wisconsin State Historical Society defined the prevailing rural character in terms now well familiar:

[S]tudy. . .reveals agriculture as one of the main supports of American democracy because it is an occupation embracing millions of freemen who own property and cultivate land on a somewhat equal basis. . . . A farm represents a "living," . . .but neither an actual nor a potential modern "fortune." . . .[T]he family-sized farm is the American ideal and means in effect that the owner and his son or sons can perform the actual work of tillage, the female members of the household smoothing the way by providing home comforts, assisting about chores, or in field or meadow as pressure of work may dictate. Hired men are rather the exception than the rule in this typical agriculture. So far as they are employed, it is usually with the instinctive purpose of raising the labor force to the normal family plane rather than in the hope of abnormally expanding the business beyond the family-farm norm.[5]

The distribution of landownership pattern that came to characterize the South contrasted sharply with that of the North. Large plantations rather than family farms came to dominate the South. Plantations produced commodities such as tobacco or cotton for export rather than for local markets or to provide food and fiber for the farm family. They were worked by slave laborers belonging to often absentee masters, and under the immediate supervision of local overseers and drivers.

The plantation system was challenged unsuccessfully as early as 1732 by the British founders of Georgia, last of the Thirteen Colonies. Disapproving of the plantation societies as they had developed in Virginia and the Carolinas, the Georgia Trustees in London decided instead to place a 500 acre ceiling on landownership, to settle their new colony with families on generally fifty acre farms and to forbid slave labor.

South Carolina planters and aspiring planters in Georgia, however, brought pressure in Parliament, and ultimately succeeded in terminating the Trustees' family farm plan. When it came to an end in 1752, plantations of up to 2000 acres appeared quickly, and slaves poured in to work them.[6] From these beginnings along the eastern seaboard, plantation society spread westward over the southern black belt of Alabama, the delta lands of Mississippi and Louisiana, and onto the Brazos River bottoms of eastern Texas.

A century after defeat of Georgia's planned family farm society and on the eve of civil war, South Carolina's Senator Hammond gave Congress the Southern view of the plantation system:

In all social systems there must be a class to do the mean duties, to perform the drudgery of life. That is, a class requiring but a low order of intellect and but little skill. Its requisites are vigor, docility, fidelity. Such a class you must have, or you would not have that other class which leads progress, refinement, and civilization. It constitutes the very mud-sills of society and of political government; and you might as well attempt to build a house in the air, as to build either the one or the other, except on the mud-sills.[7]

As the war moved into its later stages, President Abraham Lincoln, too, noted the contrast between Southern and Northern rural societies. In his second inaugural address he said:

One eighth of the whole population were colored slaves, not distributed generally over the Union, but localized in the southern part of it. These slaves constituted a peculiar and powerful interest. All knew that this interest was somehow the cause of the war.[8]

In the Far West even before the Civil War, a distinctive pattern of man's relation to land was being laid down. At the conclusion of the war with Mexico a variant of the South's plantation appeared quickly in California. Slave labor was rejected, but concentrated landownership and dependence upon landless laborers were accepted. In 1854 the *California Farmer* expressed the prospect in these words:

California is destined to become a large grower of cotton, rice, tobacco, sugar, tea and coffee and where shall the laborers be found? Americans will not become the working men of our . . .rice and our cotton plantations. . . .At the south, this is the work of the slave, but...California is a free state....Then where shall the laborers be found? The Chinese!...that population, educated, schooled and drilled in the cultivation of these products are [*sic*] to be to California what the African has been to the south. This is the decree of the Almighty, and man cannot stop it.[9]

A generation of land grabbing followed this early forecast.[10] The land and labor pattern of rural society that resulted was described by James Bryce in the 1880's:

When California was ceded to the United States, land speculators bought up large tracts under Spanish titles, and others, foreseeing the coming prosperity, subsequently acquired great domains by purchase, either from the railways which had received land grants, or directly from the government. Some of these speculators...made it difficult for immigrants to acquire small freeholds, and in some cases checked the growth of farms....[O]thers established enormous farms, in which the soil is cultivated by hired labourers, many of whom are discharged after the harvest—a phenomenon rare in the United States....Thus the land system of California presents features both peculiar and dangerous, a contrast between great properties, often appearing to conflict with the general weal, and the sometimes hard pressed small farmer, together with a mass of unsettled labour, thrown without work into the towns at certain times of the year.[11]

This pattern of rural society has persisted in California and spread to Arizona, Florida and scattered areas where fruits and vegetables are intensively produced.[12] The operators of these agricultural industries were well aware of the contrast between their methods and those of the North and Middle West. In 1939 the *Western Grower and Shipper* declared, "The incidents of husbandry, the family-sized farm with all its glamor, is a lovely idyll—elsewhere than most sections of California."[13] The dependence of this type of industrialized farming upon landless laborers was attested to before Congress by the spokesman for the California Agricultural Legislative Committee. Opposing legislation to restrict free entrance of immigrants from Mexico, he said:

Somebody, somewhere, has to do hard physical labor because it is here to be done....Under our present system of education, we must either bring somebody in here to do our hard work or we must go elsewhere for our foodstuffs and clothing.[14]

As in the Southern plantation belt, Far Western industrialized agriculture has proved productive of crops for distant markets. It is marked by large landownerships, large-scale operating units, and by recurrent and apparently unending friction between growers and farmworkers.[15]

Thus the period from the first settlement to the 1860's saw the emergence of three types of American rural society—the Northeastern family farm, the Southern plantation, and the Far Western pattern falling in between. The three types grew relatively uninfluenced by government regulation but rather in response to economic forces of the time. It was in this context that Congress moved to spread the Northern pattern as it deliberated on the Homestead Act.

Homestead Act of 1862

Slavery cannot exist except with the system of large farms, and your homestead bills establish the system of small farms with which free labor is inseparably connected.
—CARL SCHURZ' PARAPHRASE OF SLAVEHOLDERS'
OPPOSITION TO HOMESTEAD BILLS 1860[16]

In years preceding the Civil War, national land policy was under recurrent congressional debate. The nation's frontier was moving westward, and an underlying issue was whether national land policy should favor expansion of the New England family farm pattern or the southern plantation-slave-labor system. The family farm pattern won out when Congress passed and President Abraham Lincoln signed the Homestead Act in 1862.[17] The new law was designed to favor the actual settler on the land, and was passed after southern representatives had left Washington with the outbreak of war. Historian Benjamin H. Hibbard has described the Homestead Policy:

Settlers finally could acquire farms of 160 acres free of all charges, except a minor fee to be paid when filing the claim. To insure permanency of settlement the law specified that before title to the land was gained the individual must live on the homestead for five years.[18]

Although the intent to insure permanency was clear, the device to achieve it was inadequate. Pointing to the critical weakness, Hibbard notes that the public policy controls ended once title had passed from the government to a landowner:

With the feeling that all land should be made private property as rapidly as possible...that *laissez faire* is the best guide in deciding questions...there was little opportunity for the development of a conscious, workable, vigorous land policy. A land policy means social control over one of the greatest instruments of production....

That the land issue is not settled once for all by and through private ownership is demonstrated in the history of most countries of which we have knowledge, and conspicuously in the struggles going on around us to-day [1924]. Not only do Russia and Mexico furnish evidence of the persistence of the land problem long after land has once been put into private hands, but countries much more stable exhibit tendencies almost as pronounced and not greatly different in character. For example, within a quarter century there has been a virtual revolution in the land system of Ireland, supervised and financed through government...in Denmark...in New Zealand...Australia....[19]

As the nation's agricultural frontier moved westward across the hundredth meridian, the insufficiency and undependability of rainfall began to impede successful homesteading by family farmers under the terms of the Homestead Law. Congress thereupon passed a succession of measures designed to encourage private or state development of water resources, in part by allowing larger farms in the arid and semiarid belt than the 160 acres practicable in the humid belt.

Yet as it turned out, these statutes failed to achieve either substantial irrigation or establishment of actual settlers on the land. As to the latter, historian Arthur B. Darling concluded that "in spite of every measure yet devised, the nation's resources in land were accumulating in large tracts owned by a few wealthy individuals and corporations."[20] Allowing settlers to acquire full ownership in less than five years by paying the regular price "was to prove a loophole in the law through which many worked their way into possession of large areas of the public land."[21] Acquisition of full title by homesteading for five years briefly retarded but did not prevent this process.

Reviewing the effect of the Homestead Act in 1937, a Presidential committee reported that tenancy in the United States grew from 25.6 percent in 1880 to 42.1 percent in 1935.[22] "While aggravated by the depression," said President Franklin D. Roosevelt, "the tenancy problem is the accumulated result of generations of unthinking exploitation of our agricultural resources, both land and people."[23] The Report noted that "In some of our States, among them a number settled under the homestead system little more than a generation ago, it is estimated that the equity of operating farmers in their lands is little more than one-fifth; nearly four-fifths is in the hands of landlords and mortgage holders."[24] The Report continued, "The land policy adopted by this country, under which title to practically all of the agricultural land of the Nation passed to private owners in fee simple absolute, has proved defective as a means of keeping the land in the ownership of those who work it."[25] The Report recommended placing restrictions upon the too rapid transfer of property in fee.

These recommendations received general, although not unanimous, support. As a member of the committee, E. A. O'Neal, President of the American Farm Bureau Federation, gave only limited approval. Recording specific dissent, he said:

I cannot approve . . .withholding the transfer of title to any purchaser who is able to pay the principal indebtedness for which he obligated himself. . . .I regard restriction on alienation of lands as contrary to sound American jurisprudence. . . .By and large, I am of the conviction that a man who owns a proper equity in a farm . . .is capable of the responsibilities of . . .ownership. Other policies relating to the use of agricultural land should be approached from the standpoint of education and demonstration rather than through limitations on the right of ownership.[26]

Limitations on the right of land ownership, to which O'Neal objected, are neither new nor few. The Virginia Legislature in 1776 abolished primogeniture and entailed estates. Thomas Jefferson, sponsor, said:

In the earlier times of the colony, when lands were to be obtained for little or nothing, some provident individuals procured large grants . . .desirous of founding great families for themselves. . . .To annul this privilege, and instead of an aristocracy of wealth, of more harm and danger, than benefit, to society, to make an opening for the aristocracy of virtue and talent, which nature has wisely provided for the direction of the interests of Society, and scattered with equal hand through all its conditions, was deemed essential to a well-ordered republic.[27]

Long after Jefferson, the Homestead Act explicitly expressed ownership of land by actual settlers as its policy goal. However, by making its protections little more than threshold requirements, it failed to achieve sustained success for its declared policy. Public controls ended when title passed to the first landowner, opening the door to subsequent purchase of large blocks by speculators. In light of this experience Congress deliberated carefully over the conditions it would attach to appropriations of public funds to finance western water development.

National Reclamation Act of 1902

Lord Macauley said we never would experience the test of our institutions until our public domain was exhausted and an increased population engaged in a contest for the ownership of land. That will be the test of the future, and the very purpose of this bill is to guard against land monopoly and to hold this land in small tracts for the people of the entire country. . . .Convey this land to private corporations and doubtless this work would be done, but we would have fastened upon this country all the evils of land monopoly which produced the great French revolution which caused the revolt against church monopoly in South America, and which in recent times has caused the outbreak of the Filipinos against Spanish authority.

—CONGRESSMAN FRANCIS G. NEWLANDS, 1902[28]

The next major land legislation following the Homestead Law of 1862 was the National Reclamation Act of 1902. This time Congress sought to close the loopholes that left public policy with merely threshold rather than enduring support. The statute specifies simply that

No right to the use of water for land in private ownership shall be sold for a tract exceeding 160 acres to any one landowner, and no such sale shall be made to any landowner unless he be an actual bona fide resident on such land, or occupant thereof residing in the neighborhood of said land. . . .[29]

Furthermore Congress expressly forbad "commutation" of the residence requirement on reclamation projects in return for cash payment.[30]

The language of this reclamation statute contains no hint that its controls over monopoly and absentee ownership were intended to expire at any time. In addition, the legislative history of the reclamation bills confirms that Congress intended to permanently close the loopholes that had become visible when the Homestead Act left the family farm exposed to the forces of the marketplace. With a long look into the future, Senator Hansbrough of North Dakota said in 1902:

It is argued by some that as wealth grows larger in a few hands the opportunities of the laboring classes to secure employment are multiplied. . . .[B]ut looking a little beyond immediate benefits, it appears that the tendency under such a condition is to dwarf self-reliance in the masses and to make the mere service of opulent employers by the great army of breadwinners the fulfillment of all human ambition. I think it is the duty of the legislator to pursue a policy under which the greatest possible number of our people may be provided with the means of independent employment, by which the aspirations of the individual may be encouraged and developed.[31]

In similar vein, Congressman Martin of South Dakota said, "The policy of the Government is to build up communities of many settlers with small holdings, and not to encourage the prosecution of agriculture by large corporations."[32]

Congressman Frank W. Mondell of Wyoming emphasized that the strictness of the reclamation bill as compared to the Homestead Act would assure achievement of public policy goals:

No law ever presented to any legislative body has been so carefully drawn with a view of preventing the possibility of speculative ownership in lands. . . .[W]e have thrown further safeguards around the public lands than . . .[the author of the Homestead Law] felt necessary in his act. . . .[33]

Congressman Francis G. Newlands of Nevada told how President Theodore Roosevelt, who was personally familiar with North Dakota, had taken a hand during consideration of the reclamation bill to tighten its language:

It passed in the Senate . . .and then President Roosevelt, who is entirely familiar with that region and knows its wants, invited in consultation some members of the Irrigation Committee of the House, regardless of party. He was somewhat in doubt as to whether the bill was sufficiently guarded in the interest of homeseekers.

It was a question simply of construction. We all wanted to preserve that domain in small tracts for actual settlers and homebuilders. We all wanted to prevent monopoly and concentration of ownership, and the result was that certain changes were made absolutely satisfactory both to the Executive and to the Irrigation Committee, and intended only to carry out the intentions of both.[34]

A statute, however, has only the effect given it by its administrators. Notwithstanding the unqualified language of the Reclamation Act and its legislative history, administrators have limited the duration of residency requirement. According to a Reclamation Decision of 1917: "After approval of the application further residence is not required of such applicant," and upon transfer of ownership of the land receiving water "it is immaterial whether or not the transferee be 'an actual bona fide resident on such land or occupant thereof residing in the neighborhood.' "[35] Thus since 1917 administrators have treated the residency requirement as no more than a threshold requirement expiring with the acquisition of a water right.

This early administrative determination opened loopholes which allowed for absenteeism and tenancy under reclamation law. Such loopholes were comparable to the Homestead Act's statutory termination of residency requirements upon completion of five years in residence or earlier commutation cash payment.

Judicial review of this administrative interpretation came only after more than a half century. In 1971 federal district Judge William D. Murray held that administrators

cannot repeal an Act of Congress. . . .The fact that residency has not been required by the Department of Interior for over 55 years cannot influence the outcome of this decision. Failing to apply the residency requirement is contrary to any reasonable interpretation of the reclamation law as a whole, and is destructive of the clear purpose of a valid law.[36]

This decision is currently under review by the Ninth Circuit Court of Appeals.

Limitation of water received by an individual landowner to an amount sufficient to irrigate 160 acres is the companion requirement of residency. As with residency, question has arisen among administrators whether at some time this condition terminates. In 1957 Secretary of the Interior Fred A. Seaton said that "The Department continues to recognize and support the basic concept of reclamation law that full and final payment of the obligation of a district to the Federal Government ends the applicability of the acreage limitations."[37]

The repayment obligation laid upon irrigators is normally discharged over forty years without interest. Such repayment, as discussed below, does not cover or terminate the subsidy to irrigators.[38]

Official challenge of the Secretary's termination of public policy upon repayment came quickly from a member of Congress. Senator Paul H. Douglas of Illinois stated in an open exchange of correspondence with the Secretary:

It seems plain to me that Congress reserved to itself the authority to make any modifications in application of the excess-land provisions and has not conferred on anyone else the power to declare any date at which the application of the provision terminates, whether upon completion of financial aspects of a transaction or otherwise.[39]

Then he repeated Secretary Seaton's own statement amazingly made in this same context: "What I am concerned about is the process by which inferences are based on inferences, and there is a whittling away at a principle until all that is left is a pile of shavings."[40]

Administrative termination of acreage limitation upon pay-out remains unchallenged in the courts, although failure to apply acreage limitation to particular projects is currently under judicial review.[41] Thus both requirements of the Reclamation Act intended to insure widespread ownership of the land—the absentee ownership provision and the acreage limitation—have been frustrated and circumvented by administrators who have a long and varied record of "whittling away" at national water policy rather than infusing it with life.[42]

Heritage

It has been demonstrated historically and is true in many countries today that those who control the land end up controlling the country.

—SENATOR GAYLORD NELSON OF WISCONSIN, 1968[43]

Corporations and big commercial farmers have the capital to introduce modern technology rapidly with consequences which are unplanned and unprovided for. . . .The entrance of diversified corporations into agriculture has not produced better or cheaper or more varied food. America does not become a healthier, more diversified, more self-reliant society by reducing farmers to the status of corporation dependents. . . .

—EDITORIAL, NEW YORK TIMES, DECEMBER 27, 28, 1971[44]

The legacy of the Homestead and Reclamation Acts, as explained above, included on the one hand, expression of a national policy favoring wide distribution of landownership among actual settlers, and on the other hand, the absence of statutory and administrative controls essential to make this policy effective and enduring. The net result was to leave the outcome largely to the play of private forces in the marketplace and the arena of politics.

The *New York Times* recently described the current situation, noting that

[a] million family-sized farms were consolidated out of existence in the 1950's and another million in the 1960's. . . .Small towns which live by serving farmers have also suffered. It has been estimated that one small town businessman goes under for every six farmers who quit farming.[45]

Land and water laws are not the only legislative expressions that shape actual public agricultural policy. Some of the other acts have also brought unfavorable results. For example, tax laws favor entry of nonfarm corporations into agriculture. A recent North Central States Agricultural Extension publication entitled *Who Will Control U.S. Agriculture?* summarizes the adverse effect of tax laws on family farms:

In principle, all kinds of farmers—small and large, part-time and full-time, operating farmers and so-called Wall Street investors—are equally eligible to use tax rules to their own gain. . . .However, the deductions and concessions have their greatest attraction and deepest impact for high-tax-bracket investors who have a sizeable nonfarm income in addition to their farm operations—irrespective of whether they are basically farmers or non-farmers. This is true because tax rates are graduated, and because losses in farming are deductible from income received from other sources.[46]

Agricultural subsidy legislation also has had the effect of displacing family farms. Conceived in the early 1930's as a program to relieve family farmers caught in the depths of depression, an elaborate system of farm subsidies has unfolded with generally unanticipated adverse effects upon them. Its practical impact on the nation's farms has been described in a Brookings Institution staff report:

Since farm subsidies accrue roughly in proportion to sales, it follows that the bulk of subsidies go to that fifth of farmers with the highest average income . . .[to that small group of farmers with incomes averaging $20,000]. [B]ecause the value of the subsidy tends to get reflected in farmland prices, the subsidies are gradually translated into capital gains for long-term holders of land, while recent purchasers and renters receive a much smaller benefit, losing at least part of the subsidy in higher carrying costs or rents.[47]

In the course of time extensive inequities appeared in the distribution of subsidies. At the top of the scale in 1968 a single corporation in Kings County, California, received payments of 3,010,042 dollars,[48] and in adjoining Fresno County 487 payees each received 5,000 dollars or more for a total of 16,392,595 dollars.[49]

This situation, including these extreme examples, has brought the subsidy program under critical legislative review. In two stages, Congress lowered the subsidies which could be paid to farmers. First, it reduced the ceiling to 55,000 dollars for each wheat, feed grains and cotton subsidy program.[50] It then lowered to 20,000 dollars "[t]he total amount of payments which a farm shall be entitled to receive under one or more of the annual programs. . . ."[51]

Nevertheless, for a generation the subsidy program has favored larger farms, whether corporate or not. Joined to inadequate statutory land law, administrative laxity in the enforcement of water law, the incidental effects of income tax law, and the increasing availability of technology, the subsidy program has contributed to the weakening of family farming and diminished widespread landownership by resident farmers.

Perennial Issue

I do not believe that we should concern ourselves only with trying to decide what the future of American agriculture is going to be—but what it should be. We should not accept any trend as inevitable. Trends are made by our public policy, not born of the wedding of inscrutable and uncontrollable forces.

—Tony T. Dechant, President, National
Farmers Union, 1968[52]

[T]he form of agricultural organization that maximizes profit may not necessarily be the form desired for society.

—Recent American Experience
in Agrarian Reform, 1966[53]

In the political arena strong interests oppose each other over the issue: what should be our agricultural structure? The character of our rural society depends upon the answer.

What difference does it make whether rural society is founded upon family-size farms or upon large-scale corporation farms? The most intensive documentation in search of an answer was made in the midst of congressional deliberation on proposals to exempt the Central Valley Project in California from acreage limitation and residency provisions of federal reclamation law.

Two communities were compared—Arvin, founded upon large-scale farms, and Dinuba, founded upon smaller family-size farms.[54] The small farm community supported separate business establishments in a ratio of two to one; retail trade was greater by sixty-one percent; expenditures for household supplies and building equipment were three times greater. It was found further that the small farm community supported about twenty percent more people and that there was a higher average standard of living.

The occupational composition of the two communities contrasted sharply:

Over one-half the breadwinners in the small-farm community are independently employed businessmen, persons in white-collar employment, or farmers; in the large-farm community the proportion is less than one-fifth. . . . Less than one-third of the breadwinners in the small-farm community are agricultural wage laborers (characteristically landless, and with low and insecure income) while the proportion of persons in this position reaches the astonishing figure of nearly two-thirds of all persons gainfully employed in the large-farm community.[55]

In the small-farm community schools, parks, churches and civic organizations were more plentiful; there were two newspapers with many times the news space, compared to the single newspaper in the large-farm community.

Notwithstanding the finding that small farm communities are substantially healthier, *i.e.,* culturally richer and better balanced economically and socially, than large farm communities, opposition to legislative controls over landownership favoring family farms remains strong on both state and federal levels. In 1968 the Task Force on the Acreage Limitation Problem appointed by Governor Ronald Reagan of California recommended giving owners of lands exceeding 160 acres the option of avoiding the provisions of reclamation law by repaying a minor portion of the subsidy conferred on them by construction of the project.[56] Two years later the federal Public Land Law Review Commission recommended complete abandonment of legislative controls intended to check land monopoly and speculation:

The allocation of public lands to agricultural use should not be burdened by artificial and obsolete restraints such as acreage limitations on individual holdings, farm residency requirements, and the exclusion of corporations as eligible applicants.[57]

A third government board, the National Water Commission, also examined the Reclamation Act of 1902 and dismissed the concept of the family farm as "Agrarian Myth." More specifically, in 1973 the Commission recommended that "Congress should abolish the 160-acre limitation in reclamation projects constructed in the future; provided, however, that direct project beneficiaries pay the full costs of the projects allocated to irrigation."[58] The Commission did not apply the same financial standard to existing reclamation projects. It suggested termination of acreage limitation upon either pay-out after forty years without interest or lump-sum prepayment, the alternatives to be at the option of either irrigation districts of individual owners of excess lands. It also proposed payment of an interest charge. These options have long been favored by large landowners and administrators cool toward the law.[59]

Mere payment of interest charges, however, does not assure elimination of subsidy. In the Small Reclamation Projects Act, for example, the interest rate is well below market rate.[60] Furthermore, interest-free money is only one among the subsidies. On the Central Valley Project in California receivers of water from the Friant-Kern Canal were asked to pay only twenty-five percent of the rate that "would be necessary if subsidies and special benefits under reclamation law were eliminated."[61] On the project as a whole, "Irrigation represents 63% of the reimbursable costs but will repay only 17%."[62]

In addition to placing a low estimate on the importance of subsidization of past projects, the Commission failed to recognize a meaningful relationship between acreage limitation and residency provisions and the quality of rural life. According to the Report, "the acreage limitation has little to do with the nature of rural life or the mode of farming."[63] Furthermore, its "effect on land tenure and corporate farming would seem to be miniscule."[64] The Commission thus made no mention that administrators over a half-century ago had construed the residency requirement out of existence, and that only in 1971 had a federal district judge, as discussed above, declared it to be nevertheless valid.[65]

The Commission also noted that the "average size of the American farm has been on the increase as economies of scale are achieved with improved technology,"[66] and expressed the view that enforcement of acreage limitation might be "at the cost of a less efficient irrigation industry."[67] The Commission ignored contemporary testimony before Congress that

[i]n this structure of large and small farms, the large farm appears to be efficient, cost-conscious, and the source of much of our efficiency in agricultural production. But this could well be a transitional phase. If there are only large farms, the potentials for collusion, market sharing, restrictions on entry of new firms, and outright supply control are enormously increased. It is part of our mythology of large firms that they are efficient. For very large farms, the answer is clear: At the exercise of market power.[68]

Neither did the Commission take note of the observations of the *California Farmer* on efficiency and the quality of life on lands recently developed under the 160 acreage limitation law in Central Valley, California.[69] Posing the question of whether the 160 acre limitation helps or hinders, the *Farmer* answered:

Short term financing has become almost routine. Methods to make agriculture profitable are working. Economies of big production are in evidence. Also, the economies of the small producer are there. Farm planning has been brought to engineering perfection. Production costs have been held if not actually reduced.

In short, farming in southeast Tulare County has taken on a new glamor under the 160 acre limitation rule, or so it would seem. This has been done even in the face of the accusation that the limitation was throttling, rather than helping, agriculture.

[Ray Cawelti] is a skilled mechanic and green thumb artist, as well as a beginning owner of 20 acres of producing trees. This, too, may be an advantage of many ownerships and cooperative farm management. Capable persons . . .can have ownership hopes and ambitions which large acreage owners deny their workers.

The quality of living, too, in this new water area is good and has become available to many people. . . .

[E]fficiencies usually attributed to large acreages can be met and perhaps surpassed for an owner of less than 160 acres, while the quality of country living is increased.[70]

Nevertheless, powerful forces within state and federal governments, exemplified by the Public Land Law Review and National Water Commissions, have been indifferent to preservation of the family farm and a balanced rural society.

Questions of the quality of rural life and stability of the place of individuals within it are not confined to the reclamation belt. Awareness of the relevance of the California Arvin-Dinuba study has spread eastward. In recent years, notably from the 1960's, spokesmen for family farmers on the fringes of the arid region and in the humid belt east of the hundredth meridian have voiced acute concern over their buffeting amid the forces of the marketplace and in the arena of politics. In 1968 the president of the South Dakota Farmers Union described the extreme impact on rural society:

The exodus of our farm people . . .has produced economic and social decay in small towns and cities throughout the Nation. You can drive almost anywhere in the rural areas and see the results of our failure to weigh social consequences in determining our economic objectives: the weathered, abandoned farmhouse, a curtain flapping through a broken window; the soaped-up plate glass of the store front with the "closed" sign taped to the door; the weeds standing tall around the vacant service station, and the growing ratio of older people on our main streets in areas like South Dakota.[71]

At the same Senate hearing the economist of the Fond du Lac, Wisconsin Pure Milk Products Cooperative, pointed to the farmers' hard alternative in leaving the land:

We cannot afford to force more of our farm population into urban slum areas as they are squeezed off farms. Many are trained, skilled, and experienced in agriculture with a lifetime on the farm, but would be qualified in the city only for the unskilled jobs at the bottom of the income ladder . . .and . . .will only add to the ranks of poverty.[72]

This concern for family farmers in both the humid and dry belts is a repetition of concerns for "actual settlers" stretching back for over a century. Expressed originally in federal policy-making legislation in the Homestead and Reclamation Acts, this concern has been evident more often in the deliberations of legislative or administrative committees than in enactment of supporting statutes to make the policy effective. Administrative initiative gave birth to the Resettlement Administration under the New Deal, but legislative attack from Farm Bureau opponents ultimately curbed its support of the family farm in the 1940's.[73] In the early fifties Congress, which had declined in the forties to exempt the big Central Valley Project from acreage limitation and residency requirements, approved giving owners of excess lands on "small" projects the option of conforming to reclamation law or of paying a modest sum.[74] These are the cross-current winds of politics.

In perspective, it becomes clear that the survival of widespread family farming is as much a question of politics as of economics, if not more so. Some threats to family farming appear to have no relation to the issue, but do, *e.g.*, tax-loss loopholes that encourage investment of nonagricultural capital in land purchase and operation, and the search for monopoly market power through vertical integration raising antitrust questions. Therefore, the tactics relevant to family farm survival need to be broadly conceived.

Remedies

In the last half century those friendly to the family farm have produced numerous studies and proposed much legislation to shield it from the continuing trend towards industrialized or agribusiness farming. Most of this legislation, however, has not been enacted. For example, in 1939 and 1940 the LaFollette Committee carried out investigations focused on violations of free speech and rights of labor within western industrialized agriculture. A relationship between dependence on disadvantaged laborers in industrialized agriculture and disadvantaged working family farmers became evident. Senator Robert M. LaFollette, Jr., told Congress:

This same disadvantaged [labor] status appeared to have spread to large numbers of family farms, affecting owner and tenant alike. They were persistently faced with the competition of cheap farm labor, mechanization, drought, debt, and the movement toward large-scale commercialized agriculture.

I wish to point out . . .that the tendency toward commercialized or industrial farming is not confined to any one section of the country. It is manifesting itself all over the United States.[75]

The Senator then introduced five bills designed to raise standards of labor in industrialized agriculture to reduce industrialized agriculture's differential advantage over family farmers from the use of cheap labor. He made his committee report during the first year of World War II, and—whether because of that timing or other reasons—Congress took no action upon LaFollette's recommendations.[76]

Other congressional surveys related to family farming followed. Between studies of the acreage limitation provisions of reclamation law in 1947[77] and 1958[78] that produced no action, a House committee reported on the family farm itself. This Report, too, despite its strongly expressed sentiments, and like other hearings from the forties through 1972, produced no family farm legislation:[79]

The free-enterprise system grew out of an early dream of a nation sustained chiefly by and for devout, free, independent, and home-owning farmers. . . .Disturbing reports have come from the broad agricultural domain of America, telling of increasing numbers of farm families leaving the soil because of the deterioration of their competitive position, with their acreages becoming consolidated by purchase into larger holdings where hired labor supplants the family unit enterprise.[80]

Government purchase of farm lands also has been proposed nationally. In 1971 Congressman Robert W. Kastenmeier of Wisconsin introduced a Reclamation Lands Authority bill. It proposed government purchase of excess lands above the 160 acre limit of irrigated lands contained in the reclamation law; the administrators would resell or lease such lands. The present law requires the Secretary of the Interior to set the sale price of excess lands so as to relieve the purchaser of the burden of paying windfall profits to the dry land owner. The price is to be set "on the basis of its actual bona fide value . . .without reference to the proposed construction of the irrigation works."[81] Thus by adding government administration to present price controls, the prospect for effective and enduring achievement of policy goals would be substantially enhanced. The author of the bill has described its purposes as follows:

One, to enact a long overdue, and long recommended, method for enforcing the public interest provisions of reclamation law effectively;

Two, to finance public education by grants of revenues created from public water development, just as grants of 94 million acres of public lands financed public education at an earlier point in our history; and

Three, to enable the public itself, through a newly established authority, to plan the environment that public water development creates.[82]

Although the bill is in the tradition of retention of national forest and grazing lands in public ownership, with government supervision of their use, no hearings were held.

Another proposal is the Nelson-Abourezk amendment to the Clayton Act which would limit participation in farming and farmland ownership by persons engaged ''in a business other than farming, whose nonfarming business assets exceed $3,000,000. . . .''[83] The proposal makes specific exemptions for farm cooperatives and charitable organizations. A land divestiture provision is also included in the proposal which would require sale of any farmland held by a violating corporation within five years of passage of the act. In the spirit of the Reclamation Lands Authority bill, the Nelson-Abourezk proposal would empower the Farmers Home Administration to purchase such land if the corporation could not divest by itself. The bill was introduced but not enacted in the ninety-third Congress; it was recently reintroduced.

The federal government is not lacking in expressions favoring family farming or in experience supporting it. The Farmers Home Administration and the Agricultural Extension Service were designed originally to make financial and educational assistance available to family farmers in need of them. These instruments, however, are presently wholly inadequate to meet the spread of industrialized agriculture.[84] Thus neither Congress nor federal administrators have been effective so far in checking the decline of the family farm.

A wide variety of measures more directly aimed at discouraging absorption of family farms has been passed or proposed on the state level. Some of these seek to limit or to bar corporate ownership or operation, in general only if beyond family membership in the corporation.[85] They vary widely in detail. For example, the South Dakota Family Farm Act of 1974 prohibits the use of the corporate form but allows exceptions when members of a family are a majority of the stockholders, own a majority of the stock, and one of the family members resides on the farm.[86] In contrast, North Dakota law prohibits any corporation from entering into farming and excepts only farmer owned cooperatives.[87] The effectiveness of these statutes is in dispute.[88] Another approach was proposed by California Assemblyman (now Congressman) John Burton. In 1972 he introduced a graduated land tax bill in the California Legislature. No action was taken.[89]

The search for remedies is not limited to securing the passage of laws. In California, for example, landless persons are actively seeking remedies through action on their own part. This is done sometimes by operating modest plots of land to raise labor intensive crops, seeking outside financial help to accomplish it. Sometimes the remedy sought is by initiating litigation in the courts to secure observance of acreage limitation and residency law by its administrators.

In the San Joaquin Valley a pilot community development program with public and private financing was initiated in 1973. It reports:

One group of six families was loaned $5,000 to cover out-of-pocket crop expenses for growing cherry tomatoes on six rented acres, a labor intensive, low energy consuming operation. They grossed $65,000, enough to repay their loan, buy 40 acres, level the land and sink a well. They owed about $4,000 on the 40 acres at the end of their first year. WSPG provided, in addition to the loan, legal and accounting services and consultation on supply sources and marketing outlets.[90]

In Imperial Valley, California, 123 landless persons, inspired by a physician, have brought suit to enforce reclamation law's acreage limitation and residency provisions. Final outcome doubtless awaits decision by the Supreme Court, since neither side is likely to accept an adverse decision by a lower court.[91]

So far, persons in other states—farmers and would-be farmers—have shown little awareness that success in these endeavors in California could open access to farm lands for themselves as well as for Californians.

Conclusion

Since the earliest settlements in the seventeenth century, America has experienced both the stabilizing and the divisive influences of differing relationships of man to the land. The small family farms of New England contrasted greatly with the vast Southern plantations. The farms of the Middle West and Far West had elements of both systems, the former leaning strongly towards the New England pattern and the latter towards the Southern. In the middle of the nineteenth century Congress declared in favor of the farm worked by the actual settler by adopting the Homestead Act of 1862, and later by reaffirming its choice in the Reclamation Act of 1902.

These declarations of national policy, however, often are at odds with other congressional actions. It has turned out, for example, that apparently neutral tax and agricultural subsidy laws have seriously undermined the declared policy and the position of the smaller farmer.

Furthermore, even when the congressional intent to favor family farmers is clear from the legislative history, administrators all too often have failed to carry out that intent. Perversion of the 160 acre limitation and residency requirements of the reclamation law is a prime example.

A result of these inconsistencies between announced policy and actuality is that the small farmer has suffered greatly. As noted above, 2,000,000 farms were eliminated through consolidation in the 1950's and 1960's.

The human and social costs have been tremendous. The Arvin-Dinuba study of 1946 demonstrated that residents of rural communities based on the family farm have a higher average standard of living than those of a community based on large-scale farming, and that the small farm community is much more socially balanced and less class-divided. Further, there is little hard evidence that, in the long run, the conglomerate corporate farm will be more productive, efficient and advantageous to the consumer than the smaller family farm; indeed, some suspect that the contrary might well be true.

The question posed at the beginning was whether a declaration of public policy towards rural society and its effective implementation were necessary, or whether the fate of that society could safely be left to the forces of technology and the marketplace. The political and economic realities discussed herein demand that Congress declare and administrators consistently enforce a policy favorable to the working farmer. In the past, failure to do so has led to the accelerating destruction of the small farm community by corporate conglomerates, with concomitant social disruption and narrowing control over the food supply. An internally consistent program supporting the family farm system is necessary to its survival as a way of life and as a foundation of a democratic society.

REFERENCES

1. N.Y. Times, Dec. 27, 1971, at 26, col. 1 (Editorial).
2. *Isaiah* 5:8.
3. House Government Operations Comm., Foreign Operations and Government Subcomm., Communist Strategy and Tactics of Employing Peasant Dissatisfaction over Conditions of Land Tenure for Revolutionary Ends in Vietnam, 91st Cong., 2d Sess. (Comm. Print 1970).
4. D. Webster, *First Settlement of New England,* in The Life, Eulogy, and Orations of Daniel Webster 113-14 (1854).
5. J. Schafer, The Social History of American Agriculture 289-90 (1936).
6. P. Taylor, Georgia Plan 1732-1952, at chs. 8, 9 (1972).
7. Cong. Globe, 35th Cong., 1st Sess. 962 (1858).
8. 8 A. Lincoln, The Writings of Abraham Lincoln 329-30 (A. Lapsey ed. 1888).
9. California Farmer, May 26, 1854, at 164, *quoted in* Fuller, *The Supply of Agricultural Labor as a Factor in the Evolution of Farm Organization in California, in Hearings Before a Subcomm. of the Senate Comm. on Education and Labor on Violations of Free Speech and Rights of Labor,* 76th Cong., 2d, 3d Sess. pt. 54 (1940).
10. Gates, *The Homestead Law in an Incongruous Land System,* 41 Am. Hist. Rev. 652, 668-69 (1936); Cooper, Land, Water, and Settlement in Kern County, California, 1850-1890, 1954 (dissertation, University of California, Berkeley).
11. II J. Bryce, The American Commonwealth 427 (1924) (footnote omitted). *See also* R. Fellmeth, Politics of Land (1973).
12. Taylor, *Migratory Farm Labor in the United States,* 44 Monthly Labor Rev. 537-49 (March 1937).
13. Western Grower & Shipper (Oct. 1939). *See also Hearings Before a Subcomm. of the Senate Comm. on Education and Labor on Violations of Free Speech and Rights of Labor,* 76th Cong., 2d, 3d Sess. pts. 47, 54 (1940).
14. *Hearings Before the House Comm. on Immigration & Naturalization on H.R. 6465: Immigration from Countries of the Western Hemisphere,* 70th Cong., 1st Sess. 307 (1928) (testimony of Ralph H. Taylor).
    Seasonal dependence upon migratory labor prevailed on the Great Plains wheat belt from the late 1860's until the middle 1920's when mechanical harvesting ended the necessity for hand labor. P. Taylor, Origins of Migratory Labor in the Wheat Belts of the Middle West and California: Second Half of Nineteenth Century in *Hearings Before the Subcomm. on Migratory Labor of the Senate Comm. on Labor and Public Welfare on Migrant and Seasonal Farmworker Powerlessness,* 91st Cong., 1st, 2d Sess. pt. 8C at 6258-98 (1970).
15. R. De Toledano, Little Cesar (1971); E. Galarza, Merchants of Labor (1966); E. Galarza, Spiders in the House and Workers in the Field (1970); Senate Comm. on Education and Labor, Violations of Free Speech and Rights of Labor, Employers' Associations and Their Labor Policies in California's Industrialized Agriculture, S. Rep. No. 1150, 77th Cong., 2d Sess. pt. 4 (1942).
16. *Quoted in* B. Hibbard, A History of the Public Land Policies 382 (1924) [hereinafter cited as Hibbard].
17. Ch. 75, 12 Stat. 392.
18. Hibbard, *supra* note 16, at 385.
19. *Id.* at 562-63.
20. Darling, *Irrigation,* in I The Public Papers of Francis G. Newlands 54-55 (A. Darling ed. 1932).
21. *Id.* at 52.
22. National Resources Comm., Farm Tenancy 96 (1937) [hereinafter cited as Farm Tenancy]. The Committee's findings of fact were reprinted as H.R. Doc. No. 149, 75th Cong., 1st Sess. (1937) [hereinafter cited as H.R. Doc. No. 149]. In North Dakota the percentage of tenancy had increased from 2.1 to 39.1 and in South Dakota from 4.4 to 48.6. Farm Tenancy, *supra* at 96; H.R. Doc. No. 149, *supra,* at 96.
23. Farm Tenancy, *supra* note 22, at 26; H.R. Doc. No. 149, *supra* note 22, at iii.
24. Farm Tenancy, *supra* note 22, at 3; H.R. Doc. No. 149, *supra* note 22, at 2.
25. Farm Tenancy, *supra* note 22, at 6; H.R. Doc. No. 149, *supra* note 22, at 6.
26. Farm Tenancy, *supra* note 22, at 23; H.R. Doc. No. 149, *supra* note 22, at 27.

27. T. Jefferson, Autobiography (1821), *reprinted in* I The Writings of Thomas Jefferson 36 (A. Bergh ed. 1907). Congress limited corporate landownership in territories in 1887 to 5,000 acres. Act of March 3, 1887, ch. 340, 24 Stat. 476. Corporate landownership in Puerto Rico was limited to 500 acres in 1900. Act of May 1, 1900, ch. 23, § 3, 31 Stat. 716. Congress continued this limitation in 1917. Act of March 2, 1917, ch. 145, 93 Stat. 964, 48 U.S.C. § 752 (1970).

28. 35 Cong. Rec. 6734 (1902).

29. 43 U.S.C. § 431 (1970).

30. 43 U.S.C. § 432 (1970); *see* Taylor, *Excess Land Law: Execution of a Public Policy,* 64 Yale L.J. 477, 513 (1955).

31. 35 Cong. Rec. 1386 (1902).

32. *Id.* at 6750.

33. *Id.* at 6678. Likewise, in the Senate, Senator William A. Clark of Wyoming said, "The present proposed bill is far more stringent in its operation than was the homestead law. . . ." *Id.* at 2222.

34. *Id.* at 6674.

35. *In re* J. W. Merritt (Truckee-Carson), I Fed. Reclamation Laws Ann. 67 (Reclamation Decision July 25, 1917).

36. Yellen v. Hickel, 335 F. Supp. 200, 207-08 (S.D. Cal. 1971). *See also* Taylor, *Water, Land, and Environment, Imperial Valley: Law Caught in the Winds of Politics,* 13 Natural Resources J. 1 (1973).

37. *Hearings Before a Subcomm. on Irrigation and Reclamation of the Senate Interior and Insular Affairs Comm. on S. 1425, S. 2541, and S. 3448* at 26, 27 (1958) (Appendix C) [hereinafter cited as *S. 1425 Hearings*].

38. *See* text accompanying notes 60-62 *infra. See also* Page, *Acreage Limitation: Policy Considerations,* 38 Calif. L. Rev. 728, 730 n.13 (1950).

39. *S. 1425 Hearings, supra* note 37, at 20-25.

40. *Id.*

41. Bowker v. Morton, No. C-70-1274 (1973) (appeal pending 9th Cir.); United States v. Tulare Lake Canal Co., 340 F. Supp. 1185 (E.D. Cal. 1972) (appeal pending 9th Cir.); Yellen v. Hickel, 335 F. Supp. 200 (S.D. Cal. 1971) (appeal pending 9th Cir.), *joined with,* United States v. Imperial Irrigation Dist., 322 F. Supp. 11 (S.D. Cal. 1971) (appeal pending 9th Cir.).

42. *Hearings Before a Subcomm. of the House Comm. on Government Operations on the Nation's Estuaries: San Francisco Bay and Delta, Calif.,* 91st Cong., 1st Sess. 229-33 (1969) (statement of Paul S. Taylor); Taylor, *Excess Land Law: Calculated Circumvention,* 52 Calif. L. Rev. 978, 1008-14 (1964); Taylor, The 160-Acre Law, 114 Cong. Rec. 24142-146 (1968); Taylor, The 160-Acre Limitation, 119 Cong. Rec. 5343-46 (1973).

43. *Hearings Before the Subcomm. on Monopoly of the Senate Select Comm. on Small Business on the Effects of Corporation Farming on Small Business,* 90th Cong., 2d Sess. 199 (1968) [hereinafter cited as *1968 Hearings*].

44. The mechanical cotton picker, the Times notes, in addition to displacing marginal farmers, swept most sharecroppers, laborers paid a share of the crop, into the cities where "their migration contributed significantly to the welfare and housing crisis." N.Y. Times, Dec. 27, 1971, at 26, col. 1-2 (Editorial). From three-quarters of a million in 1930, the number of sharecroppers shrank so rapidly that by 1969 the census no longer separately reported them. United States Dep't of Commerce, Bureau of the Census, 15th Census of the United States, vol. 7, at 156, table 7 (1930).

45. N.Y. Times, Dec. 28, 1971, at 28, col. 1-2 (Editorial).

46. University of Illinois (Champaign-Urbana), College of Agriculture, Cooperative Extension Service, How Federal Income Tax Rules Affect Ownership and Control of Farming 1 (North Central Regional Publication 37, Special Publication 32, July 1974). *See also Hearings Before the Subcomm. on Migratory Labor of the Senate Comm. on Labor and Public Welfare on Land Ownership, Use, and Distribution: Farmworkers in Rural America, 1971-1972,* 92d Cong., 1st, 2d Sess. pt. 3A, at 1065 (1972) [hereinafter cited as *Farmworkers in Rural America*].

    A recent study concludes that in California's Westlands Water District,

    [a]lthough the Reclamation law was designed to preserve the family farm, there is much evidence that the administration of the Reclamation Law is such that the small farmer is not the major beneficiary of the lower water costs. . . . Altogether the interpretation and administration of the Reclamation Law has substantially favored the large landowner, while the initial objec-

tives of the Reclamation Law—to assist the small-scale farmer and foster the family farm—are not being achieved. J. Jamieson, S. Sonenblum, W. Hirsch, M. Goodall, & H. Jaffe, Some Political and Economic Aspects of Managing California Water Districts 277-78 (1974).

47. C. Schultze, The Distribution of Farm Subsidies 3 (1971).
48. *Hearings Before the Subcomm. of the Senate Comm. on Appropriations on H.R. 11612, Department of Agriculture and Related Agencies Appropriations for Fiscal Year 1970*, 91st Cong., 1st Sess. pt. 3, at 114 (1969).
49. *Id.* at 126.
50. Agricultural Act of 1970, Pub. L. No. 91-524, 84 Stat. 1358.
51. 87 Stat. 221, 7 U.S.C. § 1307 (1970).
52. Forward to Ray, Corporate Invasion of Agriculture v (1968).
53. United Nations Food and Agricultural Organization, World Land Reform Conference, Country Paper: United States of America 3 (1966).
54. Senate Special Comm. to Study the Problems of American Small Business, Small Business and the Community, 79th Cong., 2d Sess. (Comm. Print 1946) [hereinafter cited as Arvin-Dinuba Study], *reprinted in 1968 Hearings, supra note 43, at 295-441 (1968) and reprinted in Hearings Before the Subcomm. on Monopoly of the Senate Select Comm. on Small Business on the Role of Giant Corporations in the American and World Economies*, 92d Cong., 1st, 2d Sess. pt. 3A, at 4465-4590 [hereinafter cited as *Senate Hearings*]. *See also* Kirkendall, *Social Science in the Central Valley of California: An Episode*, 43 Calif. Hist. Soc'y Q. 195-218 (1964), *reprinted in Senate Hearings, supra*, pt. 3, at 3897-920.
55. Arvin-Dinuba Study, *supra* note 54, at 5; *1968 Hearings, supra* note 40, at 307; *Senate Hearings, supra* note 54, at 4476.
56. Report of the Governor's Task Force on the Acreage Limitation Problem 23 (Calif. 1968). For a critical comment by the author, see Letter from Dr. Paul S. Taylor to California State Board of Agriculture, March 5, 1968, *reprinted in* 114 Cong. Rec. 7420-21 (1968).
57. Public Land Law Review Commission, One Third of the Nation's Land 182 (1970). Representative Wayne N. Aspinall and Senator Henry M. Jackson, Chairmen of the House and Senate Interior Committees, were among the signers; Representative Aspinall was Chairman of the Commission. *Id.* at iii-iv.
58. National Water Comm'n, Water Policies for the Future 149 (1973) [hereinafter cited as National Water Comm'n].
59. *E.g.*, correspondence between Senator Paul H. Douglas of Illinois and Secretary of Interior Fred A. Seaton, *reprinted in S. 1425 Hearings, supra* note 37, at 20-25.
60. Taylor, *Excess Land Law: Legislative Erosion of Public Policy*, 30 Rocky Mt. L. Rev. 1, 20-29 (1958).
61. *Hearings Before a Subcomm. of the Senate Comm. on Public Lands on S. 912: Exemption of Certain Projects From Land-Limitation Provisions of Federal Reclamation Laws*, 80th Cong., 1st Sess. 869, at plate 8 (1947) (statement of Paul H. Johnstone, Regional Economist, Bureau of Reclamation) [hereinafter cited as *S. 912 Hearings*]. This estimate did not include the flood control subsidy. *Id.*
62. Page, *Acreage Limitation: Policy Considerations*, 38 Calif. L. Rev. 728, 730 n.13 (1950).
63. National Water Comm'n, *supra* note 58, at 147.
64. *Id.* at 148.
65. Yellen v. Hickel, 335 F. Supp. 200 (S.D. Cal. 1971).
66. National Water Comm'n *supra* note 58, at 147.
67. *Id.*
68. *Senate Hearings, supra* note 54, pt. 3, at 3966 (statement of Philip. M. Raup).
69. Porteous, *Is This a New Era in California Agriculture?*, California Farmer, Sept. 18, 1971, *reprinted in Farmworkers in Rural America, supra* note 46, at 824.
70. *Id.* at 824-25.
71. *Senate Hearings, supra* note 54, at 21 (statement of Ben H. Radcliffe); *1968 Hearings, supra* note 43.
72. *1968 Hearings, supra* note 43, at 275-76 (statement of Arthur Miller).
73. S. Baldwin, Poverty and Politics 341-46 (1968) [hereinafter cited as Baldwin].
74. Taylor, *Excess Land Law: Legislative Erosion of Public Policy*, 30 Rocky Mt. L. Rev. 1, 20-29 (1958).

75. 88 Cong. Rec. 8317 (1942).
76. *Id.* at 8317-38 (1942).
77. *S. 912 Hearings, supra* note 61.
78. *S. 1425 Hearings, supra* note
79. The Small Reclamation Projects Act did emerge. Its concealed aim is to enable larger farmers to escape acreage limitation. *See* text accompanying note 74 *supra.*
80. Subcomm. on Family Farms of the House Agriculture Comm., The Family Farm, 84th Cong., 2d Sess. 1 (1956),
81. 43 U.S.C. 423e (1970).
82. 117 Cong. Rec. 11201 (1971). Six California Congressmen co-authored the bill, and four Senators introduced identical bills.
83. S. 1458, 94th Cong., 1st Sess. (1975). *See* Abourezk, *Agriculture, Antitrust, and Agribusiness: A Proposal for Federal Action,* 20 S.D.L. Rev. 499 (1975).
84. *1968 Hearings, supra* note 43, at 91-101 (statement of Howard Bertsch, Administrator, Farmers Home Administration). *See also* Baldwin, *supra* note 73.
85. Wisconsin Legislative Council, Corporate Farming and State Legislation (Staff Brief 73-4, July 5, 1973).
86. S.D. Compiled Laws Ann. § 47-9A-14 (Supp. 1974).
87. N.D. Cent. Code § 10-06-01, 04 (1960).
88. For a critical analysis of this matter and an analysis of the South Dakota Family Farm Act, *see,* Comment, *The South Dakota Family Farm Act of 1974: Salvation or Frustration for the Family Farmer?,* 20 S.D.L. Rev. 575 (1975).
89. Oakland Tribune, April 17, 1972. *See also* California Legislative Assembly S.B. No. 679 (1973) (introduced by Mr. Roberti), the intent of which is "to promote possessory interest in small farms." The bill pro-to be rented back to the farmer for annual fee of one dollar per acre, the fee to go to the local school district. Should the lessor die or cease to lease, the option is to be given, in order of priority, to the spouse, to children of the lessor in descending order of their age, and finally to another qualified farmer. The land, once acquired by the state, is not to be sold without specific legislative enactment.
90. Westside Planning Group, Inc., Farms for Families. A strawberry cooperative organized among landless pickers near Watsonville, California, reports similar success. *Farmworkers in Rural America, supra* note 46, at 158.
91. Kinsley, *Ben Yellen's Fine Madness,* 2 Washington Monthly 38 (Feb. 1971).

Alternatives in Agriculture

A Modest Proposal: Science for the People

John Todd

> I HAVE been assured by a very knowing *American* of my Acquaintance in *London;* that a young healthy Child, well nursed, is, at a Year old, a most delicious, nourishing, and wholesome Food....I GRANT this Food will be somewhat dear, and therefore very *proper for landlords;* who, as they have already devoured most of the Parents, seem to have the best Title to the Children.
>
> —JONATHAN SWIFT, 1729
> *A Modest Proposal*

John Todd is a director and cofounder of the New Alchemy Institute, Woods Hole, Mass.

A single overview is increasingly dominating human affairs while diversity and indigenous approaches are being set aside with the flourishing of modern science and technology. If the present trend continues, the world community will be shaped into a series of highly planned megalopolises that are regulated by an advanced technology and fed by a mechanized and chemically sanitized agriculture.[1] This future course is countered largely by the tenacity of many peoples throughout the world, including many indigenous peoples, marginal and peasant farmers, traditional craftsmen, and new generations seeking alternatives to the modern industrial state. However, national and international agencies and business enterprises are vigorously attempting to "raise the standard of living" of most of these peoples and to incorporate them into the framework of the dominant societies. The rapid influx of populations into urban areas indicates that these attempts are successful in at least one respect—namely, that the numbers and impact of those who live apart from the mainstream of society are constantly being reduced. The world is rapidly becoming more homogeneous, and therein may lie one of the most serious problems confronting modern societies.

Most current solutions to the immense problems facing us utilize the latest techniques of systems engineering and involve resource and social management on a previously unattainable scale.[2] Increasingly, governments and international agencies are coping FAO's (Food and Agricultural Organization of United Nations) ambitious plan known as the Indicative World Plan for Agricultural Development exemplifies this approach and will strongly influence, if not dictate, agricultural development in many of the poorer nations over the next quarter century.[3] There are a number of dangers built into top-down management at national or supra-national levels as progressively fewer people are going to be making more and more of the recommendations. This could lead to a lessening of the representation of people and points of view involved in shaping society, particularly if systems-specialists take it upon themselves to select the inputs and come up with the answers to future planning. Unfortunately, there is no guarantee that the methods currently in vogue will do any more than identify the crises which are piling up, and if important social or environmental variables are omitted, then these plans may actually aggravate our problems.

It is my contention that we are in danger of losing an important amount of social variability in the human community at the same time that we are losing the required amount of biological variability in our life-support bases. If we continue on our present path, at the present rate, then our chances of maintaining healthy communities and environments will be reduced dramatically before the year 2000, perhaps beyond a point where society as we know it will be capable of functioning.

A few years ago a group of scientists and humanists began a search for ways in which science and the individual could come to the aid of people and the stressed planet. We all shared the uneasy feeling that modern science and technology have created a false confidence in our techniques and abilities to solve problems. We were also disturbed that most futurology seemed to jeopardize the continued survival of man by displaying a real ignorance of biology. It was clear from the outset that social and biological diversity needed to be protected and, if at all possible, extended.

We felt that a plan for the future should create alternatives and help counter the trend toward uniformity. It should provide immediately applicable solutions for small farmers, homesteaders, native peoples everywhere, and those seeking ecologically sane lives, enabling them to extend their uniqueness and vitality. Our ideas could also have a beneficial impact on a wider scale if some of the concepts were incorporated into society at large. This modest and very tentative proposal suggests a direction that society might well consider.

At the foundation of the proposal is the creation of a biotechnology which by its very nature would

1. function most effectively at the lowest levels of society;
2. be comprehensible to and utilizable by the poorest of peoples;
3. be based upon ecological as well as economic realities, leading to the development of local economies;
4. permit the evolution of small decentralist communities which in turn might act as beacons for a wiser future for much of the world's population; and
5. be created at local levels and require relatively small amounts of financial support. This would enable poorer regions or nations to embark upon the creation of indigenous biotechnologies.

Unnatural Selection: Loss of Diversity

It is necessary, before describing a way of reviving diversity at all levels, to evaluate how its loss threatens the future of man. Suppose some wise alien from another planet were commissioned to investigate earth. He would no doubt be dismayed at the outset by the tendency of the dominant societies, whether "communist" or "capitalist," to be constantly selecting the most efficient or profitable ways of doing things. Our visitor would ascertain clearly that our narrow approaches are reducing our options and that people are being conditioned and habituated to the options that remain. To him it would represent an evolutionary trap, and after his survey of energy use and agriculture was completed, he would confidently predict a major catastrophe. There would be no need to go on to industry, the university, or government, despite the fact that much ecological insanity resides in them also.

Examples of unnatural selection are everywhere.

For hundreds of years prior to the industrial revolution a wide variety of energy resources were used by man. Besides animal power and human toil there was a subtle integration of resources such as wind and water power, and a variety of fuels including peat, wood, coal, dung, vegetable starches, and animal fats.[4] This approach of integration through diversity in providing the energy for society has been replaced by an almost exclusive reliance on fossil fuels and nuclear power. Energy sources are often linked together into huge transmission grids which provide electric power over large sections of the country. The industrial revolution took place only where there was a large-scale shift to fossil fuels as an energy source. The costs resulting may yet overshadow its benefits. The production of air pollutants and highly dangerous radioactive wastes continues to increase rapidly, and no downward trend is immediately in sight, despite an increased environmental awareness. Modern society, by reducing the variety of its basic energy sources while increasing its per capita energy needs, is now vulnerable to disruption on an unprecedented scale. It would be fool-hardy to disregard the very real possibility of a small group of people destroying our power transmission systems. Tragically, there are no widely disseminated backup sources of power available to help the majority of people in a nation hooked on massive amounts of electricity. Our society was not as precariously based as this in 1776, or even 1929.

On this country's farmlands changes have taken place over the last fifty years that have not yet had their full impact on the nation. The majority of the population has been displaced from relatively self-sufficient farms by large monoculture farm industries. That many of the displaced farm people are on welfare or adding to the ghetto's problems is not usually considered by agricultural planners. Unfortunately, the trend is world-wide as former colonial regimes and the present economic involvement by powerful industrial nations have created a climate of uncontrolled urbanization in Third World countries. There is a contemporary theory that contends that the industrial powers have contributed directly to the conditions that led to their dangerously high population levels.[5]

Proselytizers on behalf of modern agribusiness rarely consider the key role of numerous and diverse small farms as a social buffer during periods of emergency or social breakdown. This oversight could well be the result of a lack of civilian research into the needs of a major industrial nation under the stress of severe crises, despite the fact that a disaster could occur.[6] A depression like that which befell the country in 1929 could well take place; but if one should happen in the 1970s the social consequences would be much more severe. In 1929, a large percentage of Americans had friends or relatives on farms that could operate on a self-sufficient basis during lean periods. Today the situation is alarmingly different, as the rural buffer is largely gone and far fewer people have access to the land. The problem is compounded by the fact that today's farms have little resemblance to those of forty years ago; the modern farm is in no way independent, and like other businesses requires large amounts of capital, machinery, and chemicals to maintain its operations.

The replacement of rural populations and cultures by agribusiness operated primarily on the basis of short-term incentives rather than as legacies for future generations, is resulting in a tremendous loss of biological and social diversity in the countryside. When the land and landscapes become just another commodity, society as a whole suffers. It would not be so serious if the loss of a viable countryside were all that was threatened by modern agriculture, but a closer look at present agricultural methods suggests that many of them are causing a severe loss of biological variability, so vital to any sound and lasting agriculture.

The Green Revolution: Unnatural Selection

Over the past several decades the agricultural sciences have created a number of major advances in food raising, and the widely acclaimed green revolution has come to symbolize the power of applied science and technology working on behalf of all people. Our confidence has been renewed that mushrooming populations can be fed if only Western agriculture can be spread rapidly enough throughout the world.[7] But the green revolution has not been shaped by an ecological ethic, and its keenest enthusiasts are usually manufacturers of chemicals and agricultural implements backed by government officials, rather than farmers and agricultural researchers who are generally aware of the immense complexity of stable agricultural systems. A brief examination of the ads in a wide variety of American journals and magazines would lead one to believe that the agricultural revolution is actually a chemical revolution, and perhaps it basically is.

A number of biologists and agricultural authorities are cautious about the future, as they foresee environmental decimation which will offset the agricultural gains before the turn of the century.[8] Among some of them, there is a disquieting feeling that we are witnessing the agricultural equivalent of the lauching of the *Titanic,* only this time there are several billion passengers.

The modernization of agriculture has resulted in the large-scale use of chemical fertilizers upon which many of the new high-yielding strains of grains depend. Coupled with this is a basic emphasis on single cash crops which are grown on increasingly larger tracts of land. The dependency on fertilizers for successful crops has created depressed soil faunas and an alarming increase in nitrates in the ground waters of some areas. The nitrate levels are often above the safety limits set by the U.S. Public Health Service for infants' drinking water.[9]

Accompanying the widespread use of chemical fertilizers has been the rapid increase of biocides to control pests and weeds. These, in turn, have reduced the number of species of soil animals in many farm fields, with subsequent reductions in the quality of humus, which is essential to the sustained health of soils.[10] Unfortunately, these changes are occurring just as we are beginning to discover how much the soil fauna, particularly the earthworms, contribute to plant growth and health.[11] The use of biocides has triggered a vicious cycle: soils decline in quality, which in turn makes crops more vulnerable to attack by pests or disease organisms. This creates a need for increasingly large amounts of pesticides and fungicides for agricultural production to be sustained.

The full impact of biocides has yet to come. It is as if ecology and agriculture represent a modern Janus in their antithetic stances. While a team of ecologists has recently announced that the full impact of DDT often does not show up in long-lived birds, predatory animals, and humans for twenty-five years after application,[12] agricultural planners confidently predict a 600-percent increase in the use of pesticides in Third World countries over the next few years.[13] By the year 2000 the developing nations, as the beneficiaries of an uncontrolled experiment, will have reason to resent the blessings of modern technology.

The most notable achievement of the green revolution has been the creation of new high-yield strains of rice, wheat, and corn.[14] World agriculture has in the space of a few years been made more efficient, and in the short run, more productive because of these supergrains, particularly the Mexican semidwarf varieties of wheat. They represent a triumph of the modern plant breeder's art, but are in no way a panacea to the world food shorage. The grain revolution has an Achilles' heel; the new varieties, grown on increasingly vast acreages, are causing the rapid extinction of older varieties and a decline in diversity of the germ plasm in nature. The genetic variability which initially enabled the new types to be created is threatened, and the very foundation of the new agriculture is being eroded. In Turkey and Ethiopia thousands of local wheats have become extinct over the last several decades, and the phenomenon is widespread.[15] It is possible that the genetic variability of wheats could be irreplaceably lost. Erna Bennett of FAO has stated that "the world is beleaguered as far as its genetic resources are concerned."[16] Some of the most influential agricultural experts are deeply aware of the problem and are attempting to create the necessary "gene banks" before it is too late. It has been suggested that the race to save our genetic resources may be hampered by another biological fact of life, namely that seed storage may not be enough since "reserves" of the original microclimates and ecosystems may also be required if the viability of the local strains is to be maintained.[17]

The trend away from cultivating local varieties to a few higher-yielding forms is placing much of the world's population out on a limb. If the new varieties are attacked by pathogens the consequences could be world-wide rather than local, and plant breeders may not be able to create new strains before it is too late. Such events are not without precedent. An earlier counterpart of the green revolution occurred in Ireland in the eighteenth century, with the introduction of the Irish potato from the western hemisphere.[18] Production of food dramatically increased, and by 1835 a population explosion had taken place as a result of the land's increased carrying capacity. During the 1840s a new fungal plant disease appeared, destroying several potato crops, and one-quarter of the Irish people died of starvation.[19] The recent devastation of coffee plants in Brazil is partly the result of their narrow genetic base and their consequent vulnerability to leaf rust disease.[20] The 1970 corn leaf blight in the U.S. was caused by a fungus which attacks plants that carry the T gene for male sterility, and 70–90 percent of the corn hybrids carry this gene.[21] Despite heavy applications of fungicides, corn blight spread with heavy crop losses.

Clearly, a modern agriculture frantically struggling to right the wrongs of its single vision is not ecologically sane, no matter how productive, efficient, or economically sound it may seem.

There are other hidden perils associated with the modernization of agriculture,[22] but the loss of genetic diversity is perhaps the most obvious example of general changes taking place at every level of society. Since a scientific or technological advance on one level (e.g., the supergrains) may be pushing us closer to disaster, on another, it is time to look carefully at the roots of the alternatives before these avenues have disappeared behind us.

Psychic Diversity and the Human Experience: A Narrowing Path?

The environmental dilemma is mirrored by comparable changes in people themselves. Unnatural selection is causing a loss of diversity in the human sphere, and this loss may lead toward social instability. The roles of most individuals are becoming ever more reduced as they relinquish the various tasks of living and governing to myriads of machines and specialists. Unlike our ancestors we have little direct control over the creation of our power and energy, food, clothing, or shelter. Claude Lévi-Strauss has shown how far this narrowing of roles has progressed, particularly with regard to our direct experience of the world around us. People fly faster, travel farther, and partake of more of the world, and yet in doing so, the world, sampled widely but without depth, becomes more elusive and farther from their grasp.[23]

It is highly probable, although difficult to prove, that the simplification and impoverishment of the lives of most of us lie close to the roots of much of the chaos threatening modern society. Erich Fromm has suggested that violence particularly is related to boredom:[24] It seems highly likely that boredom is one result of impoverishment or retreat from function.

Retreat from function is a negative trend since it removes the individual from the totality of his world. Restoring and extending genuine interaction with the life processes is the only lasting way to reverse this course, and this should begin at the basic functional levels of society, within the life-spaces of the individual or the small group. Fraser Darling, in his perceptive studies of remote Scottish peoples, showed how self-sufficiency was a positive force in their lives.[25] The most independent communities were far more diverse and socially vital than single-industry towns heavily dependent on a lifeline to the outside. He also came to realize that they coped far better in their dealings with the world at large. Equally important, the independent communities cared for their environment and were less prone to despoil it for short-term monetary gain. Another study of two California farm communities (Arvin–Denuba) revealed a comparable story.[26]

Modern science and its technologies have shaped industrially based societies that dominate the world today. These societies have an almost unlimited capacity to manipulate and destroy nature and men. In the long run they will not prove adaptive: as our options narrow, the specter of a future which is inhumane and in violation of nature looms larger. To reverse this trend, a moral, intellectual, and scientific renaissance will be required. Fortunately the basis for an adaptive view of society in nature is beginning to emerge, and an attendant science and philosophy exists in embryonic form today.

New Alchemy and a Reconstructive Science: An Alternative Future

The direction of contemporary science is powerfully influenced by its patrons: the military and large corporations with their governmental cohorts. If a major scientific project or discipline does not hold out some promise of profit or military supremacy, it is not usually supported. The driving wheel of science in industrial societies is not a dispassionate seeking of knowledge. Science rarely addresses itself to the needs of human beings at the level of the individual or small group. With a sprinkling of notable exceptions, particularly in medicine, modern science and its technologies affect the majority of mankind in a negative or oppressive way, if at all. Science ignores, rather than addresses itself to, the richness and range of human potential. Knowledge is being replaced by hardware, not so much because hardware is superior to knowledge, but because it is more profitable. Unfortunately, technology as we know it cannot be expected to correct its own ills. These must be replaced with wisdom and practices that are fundamentally restorative rather than destructive.

An alternative science must seek to act on behalf of all people by searching for techniques and options that will restore the earth and create a new sense of community along ecological lines. Many talented people are working in the cities on urban problems, trying to make the cities livable and human, but very few are interested in making the countryside and farmlands livable by providing viable alternatives to the present rural destruction. Tools and techniques for individuals or small groups, however poor, must be sought to enable rural dwellers to work toward recapturing and extending their biological and social diversity. This new science must also link social and scientific purpose with the aim of creating a reconstructive knowledge that will function at the basic levels of society. If it did address itself to social and environmental microcosms, any group of people would be able to create its own indigenous biotechnic systems, gain more control over its own lives, and become more self-sufficient.

The ideal is to find ways of living that will help alleviate oppression at all levels, against the earth as well as against people. Ecology and personal liberation together have the potential to create environments within which people can gain increasing control over the processes which sustain them. This philosophy, call it "New Alchemy," in seeking modes of stewardship, attempts to fuse ethics with a scientific commitment to microcosms, because in caring for the immediate, a dynamic may be born that will ultimately lead to a saner tomorrow.

Centers for New World Research

The New Alchemy Institute has established a few small independent centers in a variety of climates and environments, including the tropics. In this way we hope to induce a high degree of diversity into research and approaches to land stewardship. However, there does run within the organization a common thread, namely a holistic view of the task ahead. No research is undertaken in a vacuum. Energy is linked to food production, food production to the larger questions of environment and communitas. Where possible, wastes, power, gardens, aquaculture, housing, and surrounding ecosystems are studied simultaneously. In the foreseeable future all elements of the systems will be linked in a variety of ways so that the most viable living environment can evolve. Thus a holistic view becomes possible at the level of the social microcosm.

The New Alchemy farm on Cape Cod in Massachusetts typifies our research approach to the rural problems of tomorrow. The fundamental strategy has been to integrate an array of low-cost yet sophisticated and efficient biological and solar energy systems. This has created a productive and self-contained microcosm— stewardship responsive to local conditions.

With respect to our *preliminary* model at Cape Cod, windmills, solar heaters, intensive vegetable gardens, field crops, and fish cultures are linked together in mutually beneficial ways. Brief descriptions follow.

The Wind Generator: A wind generator is a streamlined windmill that generates enough power to run an electric generator. It was once popular in rural areas during the 20s and 30s, before the advent of rural electrification. Our wind generator, which cost very little, was assembled primarily from scrap auto parts.[27] However, it is by no means perfected, and a great deal still needs to be learned about producing electricity inexpensively from the wind. Recent designs and new gearing systems, discoveries of solid-state power converters, and efficient storage batteries and airfoil blade designs, coupled with a dwindling supply and increased cost of fossil and nuclear fuels are making wind generators increasingly practical as an alternative energy source.

Fish Ponds: Below the windmills, at the entrance to the gardens, are two small solar-heated aquaculture minifarms. One is covered with a dome having a clear plastic skin and curved surface to trap the sun's heat and store it in a "tropical" pond fashion.[28] The other covered pond of more conventional design uses a solar heater for additional warming of the water. Both ponds are maintained around 80°F throughout the late spring and summer months. Within the 25-foot-diameter pools, *Tilapia,* a tropical fish of high food value, is raised. These fish derive their feed primarily from massive algae blooms whose growth is stimulated in waters warmed by the sun and enriched by small amounts of animal manure. Edible-size fish have been cultured in as brief a time as ten weeks.

Other food sources will come from research involving the production of high-protein insect-food in polluted waters. In order to accomplish this, insects with an aquatic larval stage are being reared in large numbers in the tiny ponds. These provide an ecological food source for *Tilapia* and other fish.[29] The insects currently being cultured are midges or Chironomids, tiny nonbiting mosquitolike insects which commonly swarm on summer evenings. The larval stage, normally found in the bottom muck in ponds, is cultured on burlap mats suspended in the fertilized ponds. The problems of food production and water purification are interconnected at the point of fertilization. At present, in order to obtain high yields, animal manures are used as fertilizer. The ponds are, in fact, polluted to increase production. While growing, the larval midges help to purify the ponds. They accomplish this by feeding on microscopic organisms whose populations are increased by the manure, and perhaps also by direct assimilation of nutrients in the enriched waters. At this stage the insect-rearing ponds use only manure, but there are plans to shift some of the culture over to human sewage, thereby linking sewage purification with the rearing of insects for fish culture.

The sun and the wind are coupled in the backyard fish system to optimize productivity. It is a self-sufficient approach to the rearing of aquatic foods and there is little in the way of capital involved. It requires only labor and a large array of ecologically derived ideas, many of which have yet to be completely elucidated.

Household Purification System: Human sewage is being partially purified in one practical experiment. A small glass-sided A-frame structure is used to elevate temperatures over a series of pools that purify household sewage and wastes, through the culture of aquatic plants, live-bearing fishes, and insects of a variety of species. The produce from the household waste purification system is fed in turn to a flock of chickens. The wastes, partially purified by the living organisms, are subsequently used for irrigating the lawn and tree crops. Sewage, ordinarily an expensive and awkward problem for society, becomes a beneficial source of energy when dealt with on a small scale. New animal feeds are found and local soils enriched.

Intensive Vegetable Gardens: The birthplace of much of our agricultural research is in the gardens below the ponds. Several experiments intended to help find ways of culturing plants and animals without using expensive and harmful biocides have been initiated. One large project, is a systematic search for varieties of vegetables that may have some built-in genetic resistance to insect pests. Most modern plant breeders have assumed that pesticides are an inevitable tool in agriculture; consequently, knowledge is scant concerning vegetable varieties with an intrinsic ability to resist pest attacks. In another research project the efficacy of interplanting vegetables with herbs and flowers that have a suspected ability to trap or repel pests is being tested, along with techniques for performing reliable yet simple experiments in highly productive vegetable gardens.[30] Each of the experimental gardens, regardless of the research taking place, is treated as a miniature ecosystem, and many of the biological processes are monitored to determine aspects of diversity and "stability" in each of the systems.

Integrating Gardens—Fish Ponds: Ideas for future research projects are being tested in gardens. For example, one experimental plot is being used to look into the value of using nutrient-laden water from the small fish ponds for irrigating crops. Some fish species, when cultured in high densitites, apparently secrete a fatty substance that tends to reduce evaporation. Consequently, pond water containing moisture-conserving substances as well as nutrients may be highly useful for irrigating crops, especially under arid conditions. Early laboratory trials with lettuce and parsley indicated that the water from tanks containing fish has a "hermetic" quality that conserves moisture around the roots of the plants. Field trials conducted in 1973 demonstrated the agricultural value of using aquaculture wastes. Lettuce yields were increased up to 112 percent over controls.

Already we can begin to envisage closely linked aquatic and terrestrial food systems suited to regions where water is seasonal and limited. Vegetation for food and for shelter from the sun could be nurtured from water stored and enriched in aquaculture ponds. Many of the earth's arid regions may one day sustain small communities within microenvironments that are biologically complete without the need to import large amounts of food, energy, and capital.

Ecologically Derived Structures: The investigations of a small group of people at a single New Alchemy center are coming together most completely in a project initiated in 1973. A direct involvement in process has drawn us toward the idea of creating living structures that are ecologically derived and reflect all that we have learned. Our initial approach to such housing is to have the structures evolve directly out of the ongoing aquaculture, waste, greenhouse, and solar and wind energy research. On a microscopic scale such a strategy seems to make good sense, as the threads of each person's investigations are spun together to create a structure that mimics nature and perhaps will enable us to live in, rather than apart from, her. These structures will be self-regulating and eventually will provide inhabitants with shelter and a wide variety of aquatic plant and animal feeds as well as vegetables and fruits.[31] Such systems have the potential to provide the majority of food needs as well as housing for their inhabitants. Only the essential grains would need to come from outside.

The Ark: Our first structure, just started, is called the "ark." It is a solar-heated greenhouse and aquaculture complex adapted to the rigorous climates of the northeast. If suitable internal climates can be maintained, we will eventually attach living quarters to the structure. The prototype will include a sunken greenhouse, an attached aquaculture pond, and a diversity of light and heat conservation and distribution components (see Figures 3 and 4). It will be an integrated self-regulating system requiring the sun, power for water circulation, waste materials, and labor to sustain its productivity. The electricity to drive the circulation pump will be provided by a windmill. The heat storage-climate regulation component will be a

13,500-gallon aquaculture pond. Solar heat will be trapped directly by the covered pond and by water circulating through the solar heater. The attached greenhouse will be built below the frost line and will derive its heat from the earth, direct sunlight, and from the warmed pond water passing through pipes in the growing beds within the structure.

The intensive fish-farming component will be comparable to those already pioneered by New Alchemists. Several crops of *Tilapia* fish will be cultured through the warm months and a single crop of perch and trout during the cooler seasons. The aquaculture system may prove productive enough to underwrite the construction and maintenance costs of similar food-growing complexes in the future.

The greenhouse will be used to raise high-value vegetables and greens fertilized by wastes from the aquaculture pond. If our solar-heated ark should prove successful, then ecologically derived low-energy agricultures may thrive in northern climates.

So far, while building our models, we have learned that incredibly little is known about devising and caring for small-scale systems for communities that are both ecologically complete and restorative of environments. The contemporary colossal sense of scale, combined with the fragmentation of knowledge by the scientific establishment, has effectively blocked the development of an alternative for the future that is humble and yet ecologically wise. There are as many mysteries to be explored in the workings of the wind, the sun, and the soil on a tiny plot of ground as exist in the grandiose schemes of modern science. The totality of the human experience becomes available to each of us as we begin to learn to function at the level of the microcosm.

Beyond Ourselves: A People's Science

A few people working at a handful of centers cannot alone affect the course of human events. The elitism underlying contemporary science must be eliminated and a reconstructive science created. Knowledge should become the province of many, including all those struggling to become pioneers for the twenty-first century. If responsibility and diversity are to be established at the level of the individual, then individuals with a wide array of backgrounds and experiences should take part in the discovery of the knowledge and techniques required for the transformation ahead. A lay science, addressing itself to problems at basic levels of society, could restore diversity to the human sphere and establish an involvement for many in the subtle workings of the world around them.

Already a number of lay scientists are working with us investigating the backyard fish farm concept, experimenting with the raising of *Tilapia* under intensive culture conditions.

Other lay researchers are involved in experiments to determine the value of ecologically designed food gardens. One of the experiments is a systematic search for varieties of vegetables that may have some genetic resistance to insect pests. Another is a search to determine the techniques of interplanting vegetables with herbs and flowers with a suspected ability to trap or repel pests and to nurture natural control agents of those pests.

Only with the help of hundreds of earth scientists could this kind of information be acquired on a country-wide scale, in a relatively short period of time. The research on resistance and ecological design must take into account soils, environments, and climates from a diversity of regions in order to comprehend the forces underlying a balanced and restorative agriculture. Such a study has not been attempted by orthodox research organizations, nor is it likely to be attempted.

It is too soon for us to have developed much experience in guiding a lay science that will create its own independent dynamic. If we are at all successful, individuals and groups will within a few years branch out and explore the questions that seem most relevant to them and their own lives. Indigenous centers for learning through direct involvement in the process of reconstruction will spring up, providing an alternative to the colonization and fragmentation of knowledge by the universities.

Our initial approach was to compile two working manuals covering the research that is now part of the peoples' research program.[32] One of the manuals deals with agricultural research and the other is a guide to the fish farm project. The agricultural manual attempts to show the garden as an experimental system and leads the potential investigator through problems often faced by ecologists. After working with the manual in an experimental garden the problems and concepts gradually become comprehensible. The aquaculture investigator's manual uses a somewhat different method, following more of a "cook book" approach, with a step-by-step guide through the fish culture experiment.

There is a strong tendency in the academic world of modern science to publish more and more (usually about less and less) to be considered a successful scientist. To peruse most research publications is an almost absurd experience. The contents are dreary, fragmented, and usually border on irrelevancy. What a far cry from the scientific writings of men like Charles Darwin, who would not publish his theory of evolution without years of intensive labor. Today, a Darwin would probably be sacked from even the most progressive college. Despite almost a lifetime of illness, his intense intellectual activity ultimately resulted in the publication of books on evolution and natural selection, earthworms, the formation of coral reefs, and the behavior of humans and animals which remain of real value to this day.

Although the criticism of scientific publishing is usually valid, it still seems clear that publishing will have to remain a cornerneed for publications that are readily understandable, relevant, and directly applicable to the needs of the new pioneers. They should reflect education in the broadest sense, in which individuals, society, and the biosphere are seen in holistic and meaningful terms.

Already it is apparent that an alternative science is evolving on a world-wide scale, and will continue to grow. There are common threads weaving the tapestry that underlies the lives of the new pioneers and scientists; among these are a strong sense of the human scale, a desire to comprehend the forces of communitas, and a passion for ecology and its teachings, which imply ethics and awakened sensibility and morality. These are forces in their own right, and though pitted against the shadow of technological man destroying man and nature, and a science operating in a moral vacuum, they may still represent the beginning of a hopeful path along which we may one day travel.

NOTES

1. R. B. Fuller, *Operating Manual for Spaceship Earth* (New York: Pocket Books, 1970). See also J. B. Billard, "The Revolution in American Agriculture," *National Geographic* 137, no. 2 (February 1970). Both works represent the prevailing views in global engineering, city design, and agriculture.
2. J. Platt, "What We Must Do," *Science* 162 (1969): 1115.
3. A. H. Boerman, "World Agricultural Plan," *Scientific American* 223, no. 2 (1970).
4. Murray Bookchin, "Ecology and Revolutionary Thought," *Anarchos* 1 (1968). This essay is also in "Post-Scarcity Anarchism"—a much more accessible source.
5. Barry Commoner, *The Humanist,* November–December 1970.
6. Platt, "What We Must Do."
7. Boerman, "World Agricultural Plan"; L. R. Brown, *Seeds of Change* (New York: Praeger, 1970).
8. Barry Commoner, "Soil and Fresh Water: Damaged Global Fabric," *Environment* 12, no. 3 (1970); W. C. Paddock, "How Green Is the Green Revolution?" *BioScience* 20, no. 16 (1970); John H. Todd, Editorial, The New Alchemy Institute Bulletin 1 (1970), Box 432, Woods Hole, Mass. 02543.
9. Commoner, "Soil and Fresh Water."
10. C. R. Malone, A. G. Winnett, and K. Helrich, "Insecticide-Induced Responses in an Old Field Ecosystem," *Bulletin Environ. Contam. Toxicol.* 2, no. 2 (1967).
11. R. Rodale, ed., *The Challenge of Earthworm Research* (Emmaus, Pa.: Soil and Health Foundation, 1961).
12. H. L. Harnson et al., "Systems Studies of DDT Transport," *Science* 170 (1970): 503.
13. Paddock, "How Green Is the Green Revolution?"; President's Science Advisory Committee, *The World Food Problem* 1 (1967). See also *Chem. Eng. News* 49, no. 2 (1971).
14. L. P. Reitz, "New Wheats and Social Progress," *Science* 169 (1970): 952.
15. G. Chedd, "Hidden Perils of the Green Revolution," *New Scientist* 48 (1970): 724.
16. Ibid.
17. John E. Bardach, personal communication.
18. *World Food Problem.*
19. Redcliffe N. Salaman, *The Influence of the Potato on the Course of Irish History,* Tenth Findlay Memorial Lecture, University College, Dublin, 27 October 1943 (Dublin: Brown & Nolan).
20. Chedd, "Hidden Perils."
21. N. Gruchow, "Corn Blight Threatens Crop," *Science* 169 (1970): 961.
22. N. Pilpel, "Crumb Formation in the Soil," *New Scientist* 48 (1970): 732.
23. Claude Lévi-Strauss, *The Savage Mind* (Chicago: Univ. of Chicago Press, 1966).
24. Erich Fromm, *The Revolution of Hope: Toward a Humanized Technology* (New York: Harper & Row, 1968).
25. F. F. Darling, "The Ecological Approach to the Social Sciences," *Amer. Sci.* 39, no. 2 (1951).
26. W. Goldschmidt, *As You Sow* (Glencoe, Ill.: Free Press, 1947).
27. E. Barnhart, "A Windmill for Generating Electricity," *The Journal of the New Alchemists* 1 (1973): 12–15.
28. W. McLarney, "An Introduction to Aquaculture on the Organic Farm and Homestead," *Organic Gardening and Farming,* August 1971, pp. 71–76; J. H. Todd and W. O. McLarney, "The Backyard Fish Farm," *Organic Gardening and Farming,* January 1972, pp. 99–109. W. McLarney, *The Backyard Fish Farm Working Manual,* Readers Research Project No. 1, New Alchemy Institute (Emmaus, Pa.: Rodale Press, 1973). See also *Journal of the New Alchemists* 2 (1974) New Alchemy Institute, Woods Hole, for more recent work with endemic aquaculture systems in cool-temperature climates.
29. W. McLarney, S. Henderson, and M. Sherman, "The Culture of Chironomids," *Journal of the New Alchemists* 2 (September 1974).
30. J. Todd and R. Merrill, "Insect Resistance in Vegetable Crops," *Organic Gardening and Farming,* March 1972; R. Merrill, "Companion Planting and Ecological Design in the Organic Garden," *Organic Gardening and Farming,* April 1972; R. Merrill, *Designing Experiments for the*

Organic Garden: A Research Manual, Readers Research Project, New Alchemy Institute, Woods Hole, Mass. 1973.

31. J. Todd, R. Angevine, and E. Barnhart, *The Ark: An Autonomous Fish Culture—Greenhouse Complex Powered by the Wind and the Sun and Suited to Northern Climates* (Woods Hole, Mass.: New Alchemy Institute, 1973).

32. McLarney, *Backyard Fish Farm Working Manual;* Merrill, *Designing Experiments for the Organic Garden.*

Soil Loss And The Search For A Sustainable Agriculture

Wes Jackson

> ''. . .not content with the authority of either former or present day husbandmen, we must hand down our own experiences and set ourselves to experiments as yet untried.''
>
> Columella, On agriculture in 1st century A.D.[1]

Nowhere is the human-nature split more dramatic than the manner in which land is covered by vegetation. To maintain the "ever-normal" granary, agricultural man's pull historically has been toward the monoculture of annuals. Nature's pull is toward a polyculture of perennials. This is not to say that we humans exclude perennials from our agricultural endeavors, just as nature does not exclude the annual plant as part of her strategy to keep vegetation on the ground. Certainly the numerous nut and citrus trees, grapes and berries (be they blue, black, rasp or straw), along with other perennial plants, are important to this agricultural species of ours. As for nature, no naturalist need remind us that her annuals are widely dispersed in natural ecosystems.

The main purpose of this paper is to consider the implications of these opposite tendencies on our earth with an eye to the serious work involved in healing the split. Nature is at once uncompromising and forgiving, but we do not precisely know the degree of her compromise and the extent of her forgiveness. I frankly doubt that we ever will. But we can say with a rather high degree of certainty that if we are to heal the split, it is the human agricultural system which must grow more toward the ways of nature rather than the other way around.

Nature rewards enterprise on a limited scale. A weedy annual is enterprising. Not only will it cover bare ground quickly, but it will yield an excess of potential energy besides. This is probably the reason our most important crops are weedy annuals. A small amount of annual vegetative biomass promotes the production and survival of a rather large number of seeds during a growing season. This is usually assured by one of three ways or even a combination of all three: (1) the storage of plenty of food in the seed, (2) the set on of many seeds and (3) the ability to colonize a disturbed area. Many perennials may have these three characteristics, but it is less critical for them to come through in a particular season, for there is always another year. For that matter, there is always another year for many annuals too, as their seed will remain viable for more than one year. But overall the colonizing annual has had to rely on *enterprise*. The ancestors of our current crops may well have been camp followers, that is, colonizers of the disturbed ground around the campsite. They were obvious candidates for selection by humans because of their availability and their inherent ability to produce an excess of potential energy. They are the enterprisers of the higher plants.

We don't know whether the early agriculturists were faced with famine or not. But when they began to plant annuals in fields, they were beginning to *reward* enterprise. The monoculture of annuals, the enslavement of enterprising species, was a big new thing in the history of the earth. The face of the earth was changed. Is it possible that enterprising plant species taught humans enterprise?

By and large, the patient earth has rewarded patient ecosystems, but it would seem that enterprise has probably always been rewarded too, though on a very limited scale. It would seem to be a good strategy for an ecosystem to have enterprising species present, for these quick colonizers could rapidly cover the ground made naked by a migrating buffalo which had wallowed and dusted himself, or an excessive flood or an insistent wind. The ecological capital which had been sucked from parent rock material or stolen from the air could be retained to promote more life for future generations of all species in the system.

The selection of enterprising plant species has rewarded all humans bent on enterprise in food production. But there is a second consideration. Humanity also has long been armed with a psyche to take without thinking. After all, life and sustenance itself have forever been gifts of nature. It was the juxtaposition of these two psychological characteristics, however, enterprise and the taking without thought, which resulted in a rub which is yet to be reckoned with in the four hundred generations since humanity started seed time and harvest. The problem is this: to maintain any system, agricultural or natural, bills must be paid eventually. In nature's prairie, the bills are paid automatically and with amazing regularity. The wild forms have evolved methods for dispersing seed, recycling minerals, building soil, maintaining chemical diversity, promoting new varieties and even controlling weeds, e.g. through a shading system. The prairie has been successful because close attention has been paid to seeing that these jobs get done. Most biologists believe that natural selection alone was up to these tasks, and that purpose was not necessary.

This "no-free-lunch law" applies just as much to man's culture as it does to the biotic cultures of nature. For when agricultural man substitutes his annual monoculture on this prairie land, be it corn, wheat, milo sorghum, rye, oats or barley, the same bills have to be paid or failure is inevitable. Mechanical and commercial preparation of the seed and planting, the application of fertilizer, chemical and power weeding, mechanical soil preparation, pesticides and fungicides and plant breeding are all the clumsy inventions we have devised for paying the same bills nature pays.

In contrast to the system of nature which relies solely on the daily allocation of solar energy, in the industrialized world our inventions for the successful monoculture of the annuals require the stored light of the geologic past. Efficiency in energy use is the way of nature, not of industrialized man.

I mentioned at the beginning that the human-nature split was the most dramatic in the matter in which land is covered with vegetation. Aside from nuclear proliferation, soil loss ranks along side the death of our oceans and contamination and loss of our fresh waters. If soil loss were not such a reality, it would be much more difficult to argue that the way of nature is inherently better than the way of agricultural man in the developed world. Energy use is not the major consideration.

We are back again to an examination of the consequences of the human-nature split. I have mentioned that the monoculture of annuals leads to soil erosion. The methods almost inherent in the monoculture of annuals require that ground be devoid of vegetation for too long a time, often during critical periods of the year. The forces of wind and rain can now rapidly move soil seaward. Even during the growing season, especially for the row crops, the loss is substantial. Crops such as corn, cotton and soybeans have much of their holding power destroyed between the rows as the farmer loosens the earth to cultivate. For this reason, J. Russell Smith called corn, "the killer of continents . . . and one of the worst enemies of the human future."[2]

The polyculture of perennials is another matter, however. The more elaborate root system is an excellent soil binder. It has been estimated that before the white man, fires were sufficiently common and any given area became burned at least once in a decade.[3] Though the top organic matter may have been absent for brief periods, the roots at least were alive and binding the soil.

What Will Nature Require of Us?

It seems doubtful that nature will uncompromisingly insist that the polyculture of perennials is the only way humans can peacefully co-exist with her. As I mentioned earlier, she employs some annuals in her own strategy. One might begin a limited systematic inquiry into the nature of a high-yielding and permanent agriculture by asking whether it is the annual versus perennial condition of the plant or monoculture versus polyculture we need to investigate first.

In a more thorough-going systematic study, we may have to contrast, not just annual versus perennial, or monoculture versus polyculture, but the woody versus the herbaceous condition and whether the human interest is in the fruit/seed product or the vegetative part of the plant. When we consider these four contrasting considerations, in all possible combinations, we have sixteen categories for assessment.

We can eliminate four of these sixteen categories listed in the table for they involve woody annuals, an unknown phenomenon in nature. This leaves us with twelve categories for consideration. Eleven of these remaining combinations are currently employed in the human enterprise. But there is one, category seven, which involves the polyculture of the herbaceous perennials for seed/fruit production. This category is almost opposite of our current high-yielding monoculture of annual cereals and legumes.

Fruit/seed material is the most important plant food humans ingest. This is so because of the readily storable, easily handled, highly nutritious nature of the seeds we call grains. Unfortunately, none of our important grains are perennial. If a few of them had been, we might not have so thoroughly plowed from the edge of the eastern decidous forest to the Rockies. Where we did not plow or where we did plant back nature's herbaceous perennials in polyculture, our livestock have become fat on the leaf and seed products. Throughout this entire expanse, the mixed herbaceous perennials have not been cultured for the purpose of harvesting the seed except for the occasional times when collections were made to plant more mixed pasture.

In the eastern tall grass region, the white settler substituted the domestic tall grass- corn. In the middle or mixed grass region, he substituted a domestic middle-sized grass-wheat. Part of the problem of the dust bowl is that we tried to substitute the middle-sized grass wheat in what was short grass prairie.

The Dust Bowl followed the great plowing of the teens and twenties. When the dry winds blew in the thirties, the bad reputation for the region became firmly implanted on the American mind. We have had other severe droughts in the area since, and the wind has blown just as strong. All the work done by the Soil Conservation Service and others to prevent this major loss of our ecological capital should be applauded. It is truly the work of thousands of diligent and dedicated people who have spent most of their productive lives thinking and working on the problem, but a most sober fact can not be ignored. The soil is going fast. On some flat land there may be very little loss, but on rolling land the loss can be as high as sixty tons per acre per year. According to the General Accounting Office, the average yearly loss is nine tons per acre. Based on a random sample, eighty-four percent of the farms are losing more than five tons of soil per acre each year.[4] Furthermore, there is little difference between farms participating in USDA programs and those which do not.

TABLE I

Poly vs. monoculture	Woody vs. Herbaceous	Annual vs. Perennial	Fruit/Seed vs. Vegetative	Current Status
1. Polyculture	Woody	Annual	Fruit/Seed	Not Applicable
2. Polyculture	Woody	Annual	Vegetative	Not Applicable
3. Polyculture	Woody	Perennial	Fruit/Seed	Mixed Orchard
4. Polyculture	Woody	Perennial	Vegetative	Mixed Wood Lot
5. Polyculture	Herbaceous	Annual	Fruit/Seed	Dump Heap Garden*, Companion Planting
6. Polyculture	Herbaceous	Annual	Vegetative	
7. Polyculture	Herbaceous	Perennial	Fruit/Seed	
8. Polyculture	Herbaceous	Perennial	Vegetative	Pasture & hay (Native or Domestic)
9. Monoculture	Woody	Annual	Fruit/Seed	Not Applicable
10. Monoculture	Woody	Annual	Vegetative	Not Applicable
11. Monoculture	Woody	Perennial	Fruit/Seed	Orchard
12. Monoculture	Woody	Perennial	Vegetative	Managed Forest or Woodlot
13. Monoculture	Herbaceous	Annual	Fruit/Seed	High-Producing Agriculture
14. Monoculture	Herbaceous	Annual	Vegetative	Ensilage for Livestock
15. Monoculture	Herbaceous	Perennial	Fruit/Seed	Seed Crops for Category 16
16. Monoculture	Herbaceous	Perennial	Vegetative	Hay Crops (Legumes & Grasses) & grazing

*See *Plants, Man & Life* by Edgar Anderson for the splendid chapter on Dump Heap Agriculture.

Unless the pattern of agriculture is changed, our cities of this region will stand as mute as those near the Great Wall of China, along the fertile crescent or the region of Egypt which once hosted grain fields that supplied the empire of ancient Rome.

If we are serious in our intentions to negotiate with nature while there is still time for the American to heal the split, are we not being forced to ask if nature will uncompromisingly require us to put vegetation back on the ground with a promise that we are not to plow except for the occasional replanting? If that is nature's answer from the corn belt to the Rockies, will it require that we develop an agriculture based on the polyculture of herbaceous perennials which will yield us seeds not too unlike our cereals or legumes? This category, so glaringly blank in our table, needs filling desperately; and yet to contemplate the research, breeding, establishment of the crops, the harvest and separation of seeds is mind boggling. All this effort must go hand in hand with the transportation, milling and ultimately, the eating of this "instant granola in the field."

Is it too much to expect plant scientists to come up with such perennials, either through some inter-generic crossing of our high-producing annuals with some perennial relatives, or by selecting some wild perennial relatives which show promise of a high yield of a product that is at once abundant and tasty? Any scenario surrounding such an agriculture does seem to be truly in a fantasy world. For mechanized agriculture it would mean either a minimum amount or a complete absence of plowing, disking, chiseling and mechanical power weeding. There would be only harvest, some fertilizing, pest control, genetic selection and the occasional replanting.

How about Fruit or Nut Trees for Saving our Soils?

The virtues of orchards need little promotion. Trees have many advantages over their herbaceous relatives. Propogation by twig or bud through grafting allows the multiplication of any useful mutant by the millions. Because of their deep rootedness and woody nature, trees are better able to withstand fluctuations between drought and rainfall. Trees provide shade and fuel and are altogether handsome on the landscape. Because of their numerous attributes, I would encourage any lover of trees to commit all the acres he or she could to their culture.

In spite of all the gifts trees offer, the sober fact remains that year in and year out they do not compete with wheat, rice, corn and soybeans either in ease of production and harvest of yield. Even if we discount how long it takes for trees to bear fruit, any compelling substitute must lend itself to machine harvest and high production.

Trees can compete in saving soil, however. There is a wide range of slopes, from the extreme of steep, rocky land all the way to the flat alluvial, with soils which can best be protected by orchard trees, if not returned to the wild. A land ethic stronger than a short-run production ethic will favor trees over high-yield annuals on sloping ground.

How Feasible is the Development of High-Yielding, Seed-Producing Herbaceous Perennials for This Century?

The answer to this question hinges on settling a fundamental question of plant science, the question of whether perennialism and high-seed yield are mutually exclusive or not. Some highly reputable plant geneticists I have asked, who have worked and thought on the question, not only have discouraging comments but lean toward a categorical "no" when asked about the possibility of co-existence of perennialism and high yield. Others felt there were some possibilities. However, essentially all the work on this problem has involved the crossing of important annuals with some of their wild perennial relatives. It is well known that perennials provide a fair to good stand the first year and often a pretty good stand the second, but by the third year, production is headed steeply down.

Nevertheless, the problem under discussion would seem to have more promise than the effort to convert cereals into legume-like, nitrogen-fixing plants. The high-yield crops at least have perennial close relatives. The base line for any encouragement in the development of nitrogen-fixing cereals are the few wild tropical grasses which are minimum nitrogen-fixers.[5]

In spite of all the discouraging efforts so far, if the relationship between high-yield and perennialism is not absolutely mutually exclusive, the development of only one new high-producing perennial crop could promote dividends for both developed and developing nations which could pay off forever. Such a crop could go a long way toward preventing erosion and desertification, problems common to both types of nations.

The important point for our consideration here is that no new breakthroughs are necessary for us to begin a very large program involving scores, if not hundreds, of crosses and selection experiments now in our universities and research organizations. Some incentive seed money is always needed to accompany policy change. But we need not wait for additional scientific and technological developments. These developments occurred the first half of our century as biologists sought to fuse Charles Darwin's ideas of evolution through natural selection with Gregor Mendel's principles of heredity, both of which had developed over thirty-five years before. This exciting period of history in biology, an excitement we too readily forget with our contemporary mania over such gee-whiz genetics as cloning and genetic surgery, began early in the century with attempts to establish the chromosome theory of heredity and by and large culminated with the elucidation of the chemical structure of the hereditary material, the DNA, by Watson and Crick. During this period, techniques were developed to count chromosomes and follow them through the various stages replication and division. Chromosomes were irradiated, broken and fused and some of their genes mapped. Sterility barriers between species came to be understood, and artificial hybrids, including some resulting from intergeneric crosses, were successfully made. We came to understand how species arose through chromosome numbers being doubled or reduced, and investigators learned to artificially induce these changes. Chromosome numbers have been successfully doubled through chemical agents to the point it has become a matter of routine. Numerous species have had their karyotypes or genetic fingerprints determined.

This work which linked the independent ideas of Darwin and Mendel is now a reservoir of practical knowledge. Interestingly enough, a relatively small amount of this information has been used in crop and livestock improvement. The plant scientist and the breeder did use some, but mostly they applied the tools from the newly-emerging field of statistics and made significant advances in crop production through improvement in experimental design and a better understanding of hybrid vigor. These assiduous experts were less interested in new crops than in their imaginative programs of "fine-tuning" the traditional crops. Thankfully, the same hardware (optical equipment, growth chambers, greenhouses etc.) and the basic research necessary for "fine-tuning" will be needed as we research the fundamental question of whether perennialism and high yield are mutually exclusive or not. The supporting fields of plant physiology, plant pathology, entomology and biochemistry have the necessary working bibliographies, equipment and experts to work in concert with the geneticists to gain information which has an impact on our number two national problem—soil loss.

This is a period in which we should encourage much wide-ranging imagination and speculation on new crop development. Numerous botanists and crop scientists will have various plant candidates in mind. I will suggest here one species and two groups of plants which should not be overlooked: (1) Eastern Gama Grass, (2) the perennial soybeans and (3) the wild perennial relatives of millet.

Eastern Gama Grass, *Tripsacum dactyloides* (L.) L. is a perennial relative of corn and a plant which cattle relish; which suggests that its seeds may be highly nutritious for humans. The virtues this species offers are numerous. (1) It has already been extensively studied, particularly by those interested in the evolution of corn.[6] Therefore, important basic information already exists. (2) The species is already at home in our corn belt for it nearly rivals corn in the extent of its distribution in North America ranging from Florida to Texas and Mexico north to Massachusetts, New York, Michigan, Illinois, Iowa and Nebraska.[7] (3) Because this tall, stout perennial has thick rhizomes, any desirable races could be propogated vegetatively from clumps. (4) The part of the flower that sets seed is localized and separate from the part which produces pollen. Therefore, no tedious effort is necessary for the breeder to emasculate before making crosses. (5) The species contains at least two, more or less true breeding chromosome races. These are five distinct advantages. One disadvantage this plant poses is that the seeds are enclosed in thickened boney joints which would have to be loosened up or softened, either in milling or breeding or both. This problem should not be insurmountable considering some of the amazing amount of genetic engineering with other species accomplished through ordinary plant breeding methods.

Perhaps just as promising as the above mentioned corn relative are the relatives of our high-yielding, leguminous, nitrogen-fixing crop, soybean. *Glycine max* (L.) Merr., as it is scientifically called, is an annual. But every other species in this genus is perennial. The genus itself consists of three subgenera which include 10 species and 18 genetic entities, i.e. subspecies or varieties. Furthermore, there are three closely related genera comprising some 12 additional species.[8] The variation within *Glycine* alone is truly remarkable. However, the entire American soybean industry which produces 75% of the world's supply, in the words of Professor Jack R. Harlan of the University of Illinois, "can be traced to six accessions introduced from the same part of Asia."[9] It would seem that something could be done to test our basic question concerning perennialism and high-yield with some of the other species of this genus or even the relatives of the closely related genera.

The third example involves a grass again, the Panicum complex, which includes broomcorn millet or Hog Millet, as it is sometimes called. Most species are perennials and the genus *Panicum* has a large range both in latitude and longitude, suggesting great genetic elasticity. A closely related genus *Setaria* includes the Common Millet as one of its species.

These are but three examples. The possibilities are there for other groups as well. All that is needed now is the interest on the part of potential investigators and some seed money from foundations and the government for researchers to redirect their efforts.

Why Have We not Developed Any New Herbaceous Perennial Seed Crops So Far?

As I have already mentioned, one explanation might be that it can't be done. Another might be that we have lacked, in the right places, the kind of holistic thinking which would link high-yield seed production of annuals with soil loss. Even if we have seen the problem, most of us must confine our breadwinning efforts to a narrowly-defined job description. In discussing the problem with colleagues, many, like myself, were aware that soil was probably being lost at an unacceptable rate, but were not aware until the release of the study that the problem was so accute and therefore had not concentrated their minds on the need for an agricultural solution.

New crop development has had relatively little attention in the history of our species since those centuries eight to ten thousand years ago when several generations of the most important revolutionaries ever to live on earth gave us essentially all of our crops and livestock. Of the thousands of seed-producing plant species known, fewer than one percent have been utilized by humans for food, clothing and shelter. By and large humans do the easy things first, and so our crop scientists have improved the plants which have already demonstrated their amenability to cultivation.

Because these plants have an economic history, there is a ready-made economic data base for evaluating market opportunities against cost for any breeding work to be done. After all, much of our culture is built around relationships involving the farmer, the processor and the consumer. There has always been plenty of work to do in crop improvement without looking for more. Of the hundreds of crops available in our inventory now, fewer than a dozen supply the huge bulk of food stuffs. I think I have read that the top four supply as much food as the next twenty-six. Therefore, we have logically questioned the wisdom of adding more plants when we are not fully utilizing many of the proven plants which are already available.

There is probably another reason why we have not looked to herbaceous seed producers to save our soils and yield high-quality food. Imagine the psychological climate of the scientific community forty years ago. We were still in a depression, and the dust storms had already become legend. In response to this national tragedy, the Roosevelt administration had recently established the Soil Conservation Service; and at its head was placed the energetic and imaginative Hugh Hammond Bennett, who quickly assembled the most able engineers, agronomists, nurserymen, biologists, foresters, soil surveyors, economists, accountants, clerks, stenographers and technicians of many backgrounds into the service of saving the soil. There was an anxious urgency on the part of nearly everyone involved. The Soil Conservation Service was, as Wellington Brink put it, ''born with pride and loyalty and a sense of high destiny—an inner element which was to persist and spread and animate the organization and weld it together with a spirit altogether unique in modern government."[10] Because of the high caliber of the people employed, the Service gained a good reputation fast. Scholars and laymen alike could now comfortably turn their attention to other matters, entirely confident that the effort to save the soil was in the best hands possible. It would simply be a matter of time before this problem was solved. Since the procedures were both practical and scientific, everyone felt comfortable. There was little incentive to look elsewhere for solutions to the soil loss problem.

What Environmental Benefits (other than reduced soil loss) Could We Expect from an Agriculture of Herbaceous Perennial Seed-Producers?

(1) Perennial culture could reduce energy consumption. The energy for traction in seed bed preparation and cultivation is significant, for it comprises the major fuel bill for the farmer year in and year out. (2) Perennial culture could reduce pesticide dependency resulting in both energy savings and healthier soil and food. The direct fossil fuel energy which goes into our pesticide program nation-wide amounts to at least eighty percent of the total of one billion pounds sprayed on our fields each year.[11] This amounts to around two million barrels of oil. (Not included in these figures is the energy cost for making the chemicals, nor the distribution to the farmer or his energy cost for application.) Because many of these new crops would presumably be the result of various inter-specific and inter-generic crosses, they would be represented by a broad genetic base of disease resistance. The current "hard agricultural path" promotes a genetic narrowing and therefore increased vulnerability to pests overall.

(3) Perennial culture would reduce our dependency on commercial fertilizer. I assume this because the application of fertilizer to perennial forage crops is, on the average, much less than to annual grain crops. The slow decay of plant materials from perennials releases nutrients at a rate that they can more efficiently be assimilated by new growth. This saving would be significant, for not only is commercial nitrogen fertilizer energy-intensive, it is toxic to children and farm animals.[12] It is not common for water tables to have high levels of nitrates and for aquatic ecosystems to be placed greatly out of balance. Besides, a real fertilizer crisis is not far ahead. The feed stock for much of our commercial fertilizer is natural gas, the fossil fuel in shortest supply. In 1976, twenty-two percent of the interruptable supply of natural gas was devoted to manufacture of fertilizer.[13]

(4) The development of new, high-yield, perennial, seed-producing crops could reverse the current decline of our domestic genetic reservoir. Population increase and intensive agriculture have reduced the amount of "waste land" where teosinte, the wild relative of corn, once lived. For wheat and rice, the old low-yielding but faithful varieties of various races and ethnic groups have been driven from the fields.[14] Many of these low performers by modern standards have been the genetic bank which breeders would tap now and then to introduce new germplasm into their crops made narrow by selection.

Even if we were not successful in establishing the compatability between perennialism and high yield, some unproductive new stocks might be established which would provide a bridge for introducing new, raw material into our current grain crops.

The cost for maintaining a very wide spectrum of genetic variation is prohibitive for most of the seed companies. The National Seed Storage Laboratory at Fort Collins, Colorado is charged with the expensive and difficult responsibility of keeping genes stored. The most efficient storage is in living organisms.

In summary, success in herbaceous perennial crop development would lead to a reduction in resource depletion for both fossil fuels and germplasm and reduced pollution of our waters, soils and ultimately ourselves. Even if we are not successful in our attempts to develop high-yielding perennial crops the low-yielding and otherwise useless new stocks may serve as a bridge for introducing new germplasm into our high-yielding annuals.

How Does the Proposal Discussed Here Relate to the Bigger Vision of the Environmentalist?

Because sunshine is dispersed rather evenly over the earth; because nature's three dimensional solar collectors called green plants, with an efficiency in the neighborhood of one to two percent, are also dispersed; because these collectors are so critical to the rest of life forms, including humans; because the land for growing these collectors in the U. S. is eroding at the rate of nine tons per acre per year on the average: any who advocate a sunshine future or soft energy path must ultimately adopt a land ethic which embraces an energy ethic.

The soft energy path or sunshine future advocated by Amory Lovins, it would appear, would ultimately require a decentralized society. Sunshine is dispersed. Nature's three dimensional solar collectors are dispersed. A major emphasis of Lovins' thesis is the thermodynamic match, i.e. energy source and energy end-use should be matched. Therefore, should not nature's people be dispersed?

The romantic back-to-the land movement, as minimal as it is thus far, is a faint sign that decentralization might be possible. But what happens when we all get there, after the first generation of back-to-the land romantics have been buried organically in their gardens? Will their children maintain the back-breaking work most humans have sought to avoid over the centuries? Isn't this one of the components of the human condition? It has yet to sink into our culture that we are still basically gatherers and hunters, and that the era of agriculture is but a thin veneer over an evolutionary past which tolerated a great deal of leisure. The appeal of the countryside is the appeal open space has always had to we gatherer-hunters. The appeal of the city is that it at least faintly suggests a mixture of leisure and stimulation most of us need.

Van Rensselaer Potter has pointed out that we all have a need for an optimum stressor level which varies for each of us.[15] On one side of this optimum is boredom, which can come from too long a period in the fields. At the other end is the problem of information overload which may come from being over-stimulated in the city. The only way I can see the decentralized culture joyfully surviving is if our technology allows us both stimulation and time for leisure, so that we might play out the longings of that gathering-hunting body and brain.

But what do perennial seed-producers have to do with an Utopian vision which includes an optimum mix of leisure and stimulation? In the Summer, 1949, issue of the now defunct *Land Quarterly* (a truly amazing journal published between 1940 and 1953) is an article entitled "Sweet Living at Yellow River" written by a Channing Cope. Mr. Cope describes a goal which he and his family had recently achieved on a farm in Georgia:

"At long last we have it. The result is far beyond our fondest dreams, for we never thought we would so utterly eliminate drudgery from farming through a combination of four basic plants working in natural unison to sustain life. These four plants are Kudzu, sericae lespedeza, Kentucky 31 fescue grass and ladino clover . . . Front porch farming calls for perennials to the greatest extent possible, and if these are not possible we court the annuals which have the habit of reseeding each year. Therefore, no plowing except to get the crop started."

Speaking of anyone who would have such a farm, he continued that such a person

"will pass it on to the next generation in better shape than he found it. He couldn't design a better monument than a weather-proof farm. It won't wash away. It won't wear out. It will furnish basic food. It gets better as the years move on. It makes a local, statewide and national contribution; and, to the extent of its influence, it helps prevent war."

Channing Cope's perennials, of course, are all plants devoted to the production of vegetative material. His personal dream could come true because he lived in a culture where the slack was taken up by the thousands of seed-producing farmers of our nation. Nevertheless, what he calls "front porch" farming as an appealing way of life brings to mind the need of the gatherer-hunter for sweet leisure. It also illustrates that such leisure has provided Channing the opportunity to reflect on the old religious questions and critical values necessary for a sustainable culture and agriculture when he speaks of building a "weather-proof farm" as his "monument." He saw in his individual action a positive chain of events, perhaps as part of a web, but certainly as a local response to large problems which even included the prevention of war!

The scientific-technological revolution has surely already provided us with enough recyclable hardware to keep a decentralized society stimulated. But the human-nature split remains. As immodest as it may sound, I think we can at once provide leisure and begin to close the split if the Channing Copes can be provided with high-yield, seed-producing perennials.

In Conclusion.

The depth of the human-nature split is not highly visible in modern agriculture. The chemotherapy treatments to the land promote a temporary vigor more impressive than our fields have ever known. Though the physician may rejoice with his cancer patient that he is feeling better in response to the treatment, he is also careful to monitor the telltale systems of the body. Similarly, those interested in the long-term health of the land need only stand on the edge of a stream after a rain and watch a plasma boil and turn in the powerful current below and then realize that the vigorous production of our fields is, unfortunately, temporary. Since we initiated the split with nature some 10,000 years ago by embracing enterprise in food production, we have yet to develop an agriculture as sustainable as the nature we destroy.

REFERENCES AND NOTES

1.   This first century writing is in Lucius Janius Moderatus Columella, On Agriculture, with English translation by Harrison Boyd Ash, Cambridge, Mass., 1942.
2.   Smith, J. Russell, 1953. *Tree Crops*. The Devin-Adair Company, New York.
3.   Dr. Lloyd Hulbert, Plant Ecologist at the Kansas Agriculture Experiment Station and Professor of Biology at Kansas State University, after observing the time in which woody vegetation encroaches when fire is not present, has supplied me with this number. In the eastern part of the prairie, it would be more frequent than 10 years. In the western third of the grasslands, 15 years or more could lapse without fire. Grasses have probably evolved to invite fire.
4.   In February, 1977, the General Accounting Office (GAO) released an analysis of the United States Department of Agriculture (USDA) Soil Conservation efforts. The GAO based its conclusions, in part, on visits to 283 farms in the corn belt, Great Plains, and the Pacific Northwest.
5.   Döbereiner, Joanna, 1977. "N Fixation Associated with Non-Leguminous Plants" in *Genetic Engineering for Nitrogen Fixation* edited by Alexander Hollaender. Plenum Press. Page 451.
6.   See, for example, the paper by J. M. J. de Wet and J. R. Harlan delivered at the Symposium on Origin of Cultivated Plants at the XIII International Congress of Genetics. There are numerous literature citations which give one a sense of the history of studies on *Tripsicum*.
7.   Steyermark, Julian A., 1963. *Flora of Missouri*. Iowa State University Press, Ames, Iowa. Pages 252-254.
8.   Herman, J. M., December 1962. "A Revision of the Genus *Glycine* and its Immediate Allies." U.S.D.A. Technical Bulletin No. 1268.
9.   Harlan, Jack R., 1972. "Genetics of Disaster." *Journal of Environmental Quality*, Vol. 1, no. 3.
10. Brink, Wellington, 1951. "Big Hugh's New Science." *The Land*, Vol. X, no. 3.
11. Jellinek, Steven D., December, 1977. "Integrated Pest Management from Concept to Reality." U.S. Env. Protection Agency.
12. Ehrlich, Paul R., Anne H. Ehrlich and John P. Holdren, 1977. *Ecoscience: Population, Resources, Environment*. W. H. Freeman & Co., San Francisco. Page 558.
13. Miles, Guy H., November 1974. "The Federal Role in Increasing the Productivity of the U.S. Food System." NSF—RA-N-74-271. Page 20.
14. Wilkes, Garrison, 1977. "The World's Crop Plant Germplasm—An Endangered Resource." *Bulletin of the Atomic Scientists*. See also "Our Vanishing Genetic Resources" by J. R. Harlan, reprinted in *Food: Politics, Economics Nutrition and Research*. AAAS edited by P. H. Abelson, 1975.
15. Potter, Van Rensselaer, 1971. *Bioethics: Bridge to the Future*. Prentice-Hall.

Experiments in Community Self-Reliance

Flight From Freedom

Memories of a Noble Experiment

Karl Hess

Adams-Morgan is a small country afloat in a great city. It is a 70-block neighborhood in the center—almost the exact center—of Washington, D.C. The population is 58 percent black, 18 percent white, 22 percent Latin, with the remainder mostly Middle Eastern. It is a neighborhood in transition; as a small country, it's in decline.

For a while, during a rash and wonderful tilt at making itself a true community, Adams-Morgan was a fascinating culture in which to live. More recently it has become a prime target for real estate speculators, a bullish market well beyond the means of the people who first made it a good neighborhood. Its nature is slowly changing to chic—from workshops to boutiques, from bars to cocktail lounges, from a heady whirl with community government to an enclave of town houses with barred windows, and residents whose concerns are global rather than local. If the present trend continues, the neighborhood will eventually disappear, and Adams-Morgan will be just another Washington address. A fancy one.

For almost five years, Therese Machotka and I worked with hundreds of people in the neighborhood striving for an entirely different future. Some are still at it. We quit two years ago and moved. What happened—and continues to happen—goes something like this:

I spent my childhood in the neighborhood, got my first haircut in a local barbershop that is now a locksmith's shop, kissed my first girl in the part of Rock Creek Park that borders Adams-Morgan. I had my first fistfight under the bridge that carries fashionable Connecticut Avenue safely past the northwest edge of the neighborhood, and I attended one of the two schools from which Adams-Morgan derives its name.

After 40 years or so I came back. What had been comfortably middle-class had become very lower-class, a shambles about to become a slum. But it was cheap—and it tolerated hippies both socially and economically. This was the mid-sixties. The hippies who moved in were mostly exiles, mostly useless, and the neighborhood slipped down another notch. Venereal disease went up. Panhandling became the local growth industry. Welfare blacks and zonked-out whites began to drink Ripple together and curse the dark night of colonialism, oppression, and shortages of good hash and sturdy H.

By the late sixties something began to stir in the debris. In the manner of the opening scene in *2001*, some dazed hippie got sick of the faucet dripping or the VW van not running—some minor calamity—and, wonder of wonders, got straight long enough to FIX IT. Perhaps the change began more subtly, a complex process susceptible to sociological jargon. My own experience is that it was fairly simple and direct. Somebody had to do something. Someone did. It worked. And the world changed a little. Odd jobs became more satisfying than panhandling. How-to books began sliding into shelves alongside the mystics and the revolutionaries. And something very important began to happen to the residential warrens in which the stoned citizens had compartmented themselves.

By the end of the sixties, there were probably 60 to 75 functioning communes in the neighborhood, and a burst of productive energy emanated from them. A worker-managed grocery store opened and thrived as a place to find good prices and good-natured advice about nutrition. Then a second one opened. A local newspaper popped up, reporting neighborhood news. Then a second one. A record store. Several bookstores. Crafts people, from potters to auto mechanics, began hawking their wares from community billboards, tree posters, street corners. Musicians rented a storefront and began nightly sessions of jazz, rock, country, classical. Several graphic arts shops opened. A community credit union was started. A community government proclaimed itself, called a meeting, and actually got off the ground.

The government arose, like everything else, from the rubble of failures immediately past. Until then, Adams-Morgan's neighborhood organizations had merely presented resolutions *to* the city government. None had dared to *be* a government.

At the first meeting to discuss something new, the pioneers were young, white products of the counterculture who proposed a breakthrough—not just another civic group, but a town meeting. In homely, practical terms, they argued that a town meeting would bring neighborhood people together to state their problems, discuss solutions, and decide what they could actually do themselves—without futile complaining to the sluggish, federally controlled city bureaucracy.

The thing was called AMO (Adams-Morgan Organization). At its first meeting, someone argued that the streets were dirty. Someone else suggested a clean-up day. The meeting agreed. Signs were mimeographed on a church duplicator, paper was donated by a man working in a print shop. The neighborhood was saturated with the information that AMO members (then only about 300) were going to sweep down the main street over the weekend. About 200 people actually got out and swept. Nearly all of the neighborhood's 40,000 residents heard about it. People began to perceive AMO as an organization more interested in doing than in talking. By the time we left, the membership exceeded 3,000.

The town meetings—or AMO Assemblies, as they were called—were the most exciting political experiences I have ever had. After sampling a participatory democracy, I would never trade it for a merely representative one. Still, there was a small problem: not everyone accepted the difference between participation and representation.

The counterculture people were looking for a new way to make social decisions without one group exploiting another. They were inspired by the idea that town meeting participants not only made decisions but also carried them out, rather than getting someone else to do it. As a result, counterculture types made up at least half of every Adams-Morgan meeting.

Blacks had a clearly different view. They accepted the rhetoric of participation, but they were mainly concerned with representation. In that neighborhood, at least, they were not interested in changing the way social decisions were made. What they wanted was the power to make those decisions—power *in* the system, not power to change it. Whites who do not understand this can make mistakes in assessing black-white alliances.

Therese and I had our own special interest. Although we were among the town meeting's most active participants, we were preoccupied with science and technology—not in the abstract, but in terms of helping the neighborhood. We had long worked with the Institute of Policy Studies on a project aimed at identifying ways of life and social agreements in which people are full participants. As advocates of political decentralization, we focused our IPS work on learning how to put science and technology at the service of a free society in which people are truly responsible for their actions. Such freedom, we felt, requires a system of mutual support, enabling people to join democratically in deploying the tools of everyday life and production. Our laboratory was our neighborhood—Adams-Morgan.

We began weekly talks with a couple of engineers we had met through the peace movement, some craft friends, and students. Others joined and soon tired of talking. Therese and I coaxed a neighborhood clinic, operated by Children's Hospital, into letting us have unused space in the warehouse building it rented. Therese agreed to put most of her salary as an editor into buying equipment and paying stipends for work. Our talk group became a project that we called Community Technology.

Our weekly meetings continued, sometimes crowded with 40 or 50 visitors, as an information-sharing process. A young physicist with superb general mechanical skills came on full time for a subsistence share of the money Therese made available. I covered our living expenses by writing, welding, selling metal sculpture, and occasionally lecturing. Our experiments began.

Food, it seemd to us, was the place to start. What could be more basic? Also, the idea of developing food production in a ghetto neighborhood seemed as stern a test of our general propositions as could be imagined. There's no land for growing food in a city. If there is any open space, it's too much trouble. Yet the land problem was easily solved. Food grows, not in an abstraction called land, but in a reality called someplace-nutritious-to-put-down-roots. Space for this reality need be only that—space. We located a lot of it.

First, the rooftops. Most of the neighborhood consists of three-story row houses and apartment buildings. Nearly all the roofs are flat. On very strong roofs, organic soil can be spread, or boxed, for growing vegetables. Therese and I grew such a garden. Less sturdy roofs accommodated the lighter demands of hydroponic growing—the cultivation of plants in tanks of liquid nutrients or in nutrient-soaked sand. Friends who began a companion enterprise called the Institute for Local Self-Reliance, still a prospering activity, operated a hydroponic garden with storybook success and wildly bountiful crops. They also managed to fill virtually the entire neighborhood's demand for bean sprouts from a single basement facility.

More traditionally, we worked with kids in the neighborhood to establish regular gardens in vacant lots and in any backyard space that people wanted to make available. The entire back lot of our warehouse was covered with dirt that we begged from local excavators and converted into a community garden. Also, using the vegetable wastes from several local grocery stores, leaves from suburban lawns, and horse manure from a park police stable, we maintained about 90 feet of compost pits behind the warehouse.

To supplement the vegetable crop we looked around for a suitable meat animal. Cows were out. Too big. Rabbits didn't make it. Too cuddly. Chickens wouldn't do. Too noisy. How about fish?

One of our group, an organic chemist, was experienced in trout farming and suggested that we work up some high-density indoor tanks for raising that fancy fish.

Plywood tanks sheathed in fiberglass were built by Jeff Woodside, our resident physicist and jack-of-all-trades, together with his immensely energetic friend Esther Siegal, our chemist Fernwood Mitchell, and Therese. To recirculate the water, they used pumps from discarded washing machines. To handle the fish waste, they contrived filters made of boxes filled with calcite chips (the standard marble chips sold in garden supply stores) and a couple of cups of ordinary soil. The soil provided nitrifying bacteria that fed on the ammonia in the fish waste.

The bacteria kept the water clean. The pumps and some well-placed baffles kept the tank water moving in a strong current. The fish (which we first reared from eggs in ordinary aquarium tanks) swam strongly, ate heartily of the commercial feed that we first used as a convenience, and grew as fast as fish in streams. In fact, they converted their feed to flesh at a rate of one ounce of fish per two ounces of food. This made them just as efficient as chickens and about 500 percent more efficient than beef cattle. Our installation, neatly tailored to urban basements, produced five pounds of fish per cubic foot of water. A typical basement in the neighborhood could produce about three tons annually at costs well below grocery store prices.

Other members of our group tried other projects:

A young stonemason began experimenting with small, completely self-contained bacteriological toilets. He had fair success demonstrating that any neighborhood can unhook itself from conventional sewer systems, with their inefficiency and pollution.

A marine engineer built a very effective solar cooker that tracked the sun automatically and cost under $300. Using energy collected by an outside mirror, in the shape of a three-foot-long trough, the device heated an indoor hot plate up to 400 degrees Fahrenheit.

The group generally began discussing the design of a shopping cart that could be built in the neighborhood; a self-powered platform that would handle most of the neighborhood's heavy moving chores; a neighborhood chemical factory to make household cleansers, disinfectants, insecticides, even aspirin; and a neighborhood methanol plant to convert local garbage into a fuel roughly similar to gasoline.

We sought a grant from the National Science Foundation to start a science center where local people could study the natural science of the neighborhood, possible tools and techniques, and the appropriate role of science and technology. The NSF sent a sociologist to look us over and turned our application down cold. We did not fit the government definition of a neighborhood self-help program. Even at NSF such programs are aimed at enhancing a group's ability to get more welfare—not to mold its own economic future.

Government programs aim at giving money to poor people. Our hope was that knowledge would, in the long run, be more useful, even provide more money, and eventually strike at the systemic causes of poverty. Government believes that poverty is actually a lack of money. We felt, and continue to feel, that poverty is actually a lack of both skill and the self-esteem that comes from being able to take charge of one's life and work.

It will not be denied that ours was and remains a middle-class attitude, quite classical and thoroughly Western. It stands opposed to the elitist notion of mandarins caring for benighted peasantry—an attitude that prevails today in various modern trappings, among them enlightened capitalism, state socialism, and welfare statism.

But so much for big notions. Reality was something else.

At Assembly meetings, reports of our work were always greeted with applause and great enthusiasm. We were a showcase bunch of wizards doing wonderful, far-out things. Our appeals for neighbors to join us in the work, to help improve the fish farm, to move the gardens along, to experiment with new ways of growing, to start stores and even factories based on our skills and tools, got choruses of right ons—and no participants.

Instead, the Assembly began to emphasize direct appeals to government agencies and foundations for grants. More and more people wanted to make complaints about landlord abuses, not make plans to buy them out.

At meeting after meeting, for instance, we discussed the idea of pooling money to establish neighborhood ownership of key properties, to provide homes for the evicted, to set new patterns of ownership for a new kind of neighborhood. Plenty of right ons. No cash. Was there any cash? Of course. Even people on welfare have disposable incomes. The pool of money needed to buy our neighborhood would have been relatively modest, the weekly equivalent of a carton of cigarettes or a bottle of whiskey from each member of the Assembly. Of course, it would have meant sacrifice. Some of us have little enough pleasure, and a smoke or a drink is to be treasured beyond all the promises of paradise.

There were, in fact, jobs aplenty in the neighborhood. The District of Columbia government, sternly charged by federal authorities with making the streets safe for visiting dignitaries, including congressmen and bureaucrats, had decided that bribery was the best tool available for getting young people off the streets. The District funded programs through which teenagers could draw a minimum of $1.75 an hour for the exertion of signing in each morning and signing out each afternoon. There is no convincing evidence that this did anything to halt incipient criminality. It seemed to me that it accomplished a great deal more in terms of separating young people from the possibilities of self-reliance. It anchored them more firmly to habitual dependence on unearned incomes and, thus, on the people who dispense them—be they welfare bureaucrats or those less willing providers, the victims of larceny.

A question began nagging a lot of our work and discussion: Was our vision of neighborhood self-help crumbling along racial lines? Are blacks particularly disabled when it comes to seeking alternatives to welfare programs?

The Adams-Morgan neighborhood, like Washington overall, is certainly black. The people who seemed to talk most about, and do the least in support of, our group's proposals were black. Young whites seemed to respond more to skill- and production-centered activities. Those are solidly middle-class values out of a

primarily European culture. Blacks have been the victims rather than the beneficiaries of both the values and the culture.

Blacks think black, as they continually say. In Adams-Morgan, at least, black
has come to mean poor and oppressed. Black demands have come to mean black
reparations: to be given something, rather than seeking the chance to do something.

Everyone in our largely white group abhorred racial discrimination. Some
went further and supported the implicit strategy for social redress through reparation
rather than community renewal.

My problems and doubts began with my conclusion (shared by Therese) that
such a strategy was not only useless: it was unjust, crippling, and ethically de-
bilitating.

As I nursed such doubts, the Community Technology work began to seem
quite different to me. I no longer thought it truly relevant to what was happening in
the neighborhood. The hope that people would want to fashion new lives, based
upon new knowledge and new skills, seemed now very romantic and very wrong.
Desirable, yes, but hopeless.

There was another problem. Crime. It too fell along racial lines.

At one AMO meeting, a young white man reported a particularly vicious hold-
up, beating, and rape that had occurred at a communal house. Before any discussion could get under way, he was asked the color of the victims. White. He was
asked the color of the attackers. Black. With blacks in the majority, that particular
meeting simply moved on to another topic.

This typified a particularly destructive, if fashionable, impulse among both
blacks and whites to dismiss all discussion of crime as oppressively racist despite
the fact that blacks are the principal victims of black crime.

Another major victim of unchecked (because unmentionable) crime has been
the AMO organization itself. Keeping a typewriter available in the office has always required a rigorous and none-too-successful exercise in security. Money
needed for important things is eaten up in replacing routine equipment, rather than
being devoted to attacking the roots of the problem—the need for self-reliance instead of welfare services.

Given a situation of rising, undiscussed crime, the inevitable result is
neighborhood deterioration—and, ironically, the arrival of more affluent but less
neighborly residents. These people can afford better security and don't mind living
in a small fortress so long as the address is fashionable. This is now happening in
Adams-Morgan.

Could neighborhood people have coped with crime? I certainly think so. It
would mean first coping with their own children, facing them down, creating
families that would absorb their energies and deserve their loyalties. Not easy. Not
likely. And particularly not likely when parents are opiated by a welfare existence,
and where schools are simply disciplinarian baby-sitters, offering young people no
creative alternative to violence as the way to get out, to get up, to get even.

It was the growing crime and violence that finally drove Therese and me from
Adams-Morgan. After being robbed every 60 days or so, Therese began to feel
terrified at night in the neighborhood. We both resented the constant loss of things,
particularly since our income was roughly at the poverty level. Being larger and a
male, I had not felt the terror. After a time, Therese felt it sharply enough to leave.

We moved to West Virginia. Having been raised in rural Wisconsin, Therese found the West Virginia hills immediately hospitable in ways the city's streets had never been. I still love the city, but I have experienced a homecoming in these hills that is richer than I anticipated.

I still believe from my experience with the small workings of Community Technology that science can thrive in a neighborhood. Ordinary people can get together to discuss physical principles just as well as they can discuss abstruse political principles in the fashion of young radicals and young conservatives.

But the culture of poverty is not easily weaned from the illusory "cure" of program handouts. If this culture of poverty is to be broken in any black neighborhood, I am convinced that it must be broken by black people, not by starry-eyed whites talking soul patter. But even the most adventurous blacks will have trouble. Coming from his Chicago base, Jesse Jackson lectured black Washington teenagers on the need to learn skills rather than gripe endlessly about feeling oppressed. He was virtually run out of town for his effort. Washington's blacks are still infected by the notion that their problems are mainly political and will disappear when black power surpasses white power. Many are less interested in a better world than in a black one.

When the Assembly focused on local problem solving, rather than conventional constituency politics, it was greatly effective. Shy people spoke out. Seemingly hopeless people sparked to new life. Now all this is fading as the old idea of representation begins to recover the ground lost to the experiment in community participation. The Assembly has become more a bandstand for aspiring politicians than a forum for people.

A similar malady afflicts some of the worker-managed enterprises that brought the neighborhood to life in the first place. The malady is ideology. For several years, the workers in those enterprises toiled hard at being useful to the neighborhood and good friends to each other. Now several of the key groups have begun to work equally hard at becoming friends, not of people, but of history. They spend hours, behind closed doors, thrashing out the correct line on this or that remote political issue or revolutionary posture. They have forfeited real social power in Adams-Morgan and become figments of history floating in clouds of rhetoric and theory.

Blacks, by and large, have moved wholly into the rat race of conventional politics and foundation grantsmanship. And upper-middle-class *arrivistes,* both black and white, share no concern for the neighborhood beyond the recent trendiness of its address.

Some of the original spirit persists, however. The people at the Institute for Local Self-Reliance go on doing what they can, but more frequently this entails reaching into other communities—which would be fine, except that it stunts the growth of neighborhood resources. With Therese gone and rent no longer provided, our Community Technology warehouse has been turned into a soap factory operated by Jeff and Esther, stalwarts of our group from the start. They make a living at it and they try to teach a few kids in the neighborhood how to read. They grin and bear the annual vandalism of the gardens by kids who think that vegetables are underclass food, while TV snacks, beer, and dope are the fare of real operators.

The weekly meetings have ended. Information is now swapped by phone and mail. But almost everyone who was involved in the effort retains faith that it was a right thing to do, and that someday the memory of it will finally inspire neighborhood people to take their culture, their lives, and their productive possibilities wholly into their own hands. Such a neighborhood will not change the world overnight, as in the fervid dreams of the young revolutionaries. But it will make a small part of the world much better.

The New Homesteading Movement: From Utopia to Eutopia

Maynard Kaufman

> . . .for, as Professor Patrick Geddes points out, Sir Thomas More was an inveterate punster, and Utopia is a mockname for either Outopia, which means no-place, or Eutopia—the good place.
> —Lewis Mumford, *The Story of Utopias* (1922), p. 267.

While it may not sound as though there is much difference between "utopia" and "eutopia," it is the theme of this essay that there is now a definite movement from "no-place" to "the good place" which is significant for what it reveals about the quest for the good life in America and important as an expression of the counter culture. This is the new homesteading movement, or the back-to-the-land movement, associated with agrarian communes and with the vogue for organic foods and gardening. Urban intellectuals have condemned this movement as a cop-out and warned against its atavistic tendency; they have derided its primitivism and denied the possibility of a subsistence economy. Perhaps such negative attitudes are justified; perhaps they reflect urban provincialism. In any event, judgments about a social phenomenon, if they are not to be merely pejorative, should be well-informed; and thus, even though I think this movement stands in need of support and encouragement at this time, my main purpose here is to mediate a better understanding of these new homesteaders and their motivations.

Critics of the homesteading movement seem to assume that it is a visionary and impractical dream in our highly industrialized society—that it is indeed "utopian." We shall see that such criticism is partly true, but it misses the important fact that as the utopian vision finds a local habitation, after the seeking is done and a good place is found, the practical problems of living on the land must be mastered. Thus the full title of a recent book is *The Ex-urbanite's Complete & Illustrated Easy-Does-It First-Time Farmer's Guide, A Useful Book.*[1] The literature which is generated by (and in turn helps to generate) the new homesteading movement consists almost entirely of practical, how-to-do-it information. Periodicals such as *The Mother*

Maynard Kaufman was born on a farm in South Dakota and received his graduate education at the University of Chicago Divinity School. He now lives on a farm and teaches in the Religion Department of Western Michigan University at Kalamazoo, Michigan.

Earth News, Countryside, and *The Green Revolution* are unofficial organs of the movement, while *Organic Gardening and Farming* has very recently discovered the proximity of its back-to-nature agriculture to the new back-to-the-land movement. The several editions of *The Whole Earth Catalog,* with its unique mixture of futurism and nostalgia, humanized technology and old-time tools and crafts, are also useful to the new homesteader.

This movement differs from the older homesteading movement of the 1930's in that it is not as strongly stimulated by an economic depression. The newer homesteaders are also less theoretical, less inclined to justify and rationalize their intention to "live off the land." Earlier drop-outs, such as Scott Nearing and Ralph Borsodi,[2] were social scientists concerned to demonstrate, both statistically and in practice, the possibility of their utopian visions. Like the newer homesteaders of today, however, they were sensitive to what we now call "ecology" and to the ecological aspects of homesteading. In his book of 1929, *This Ugly Civilization,* Ralph Borsodi already envisioned a new homesteading movement as an alternative to further environmental degradation.

To be able to abandon the buying of the products of our non-essential and undesirable factories, and still be comfortable, the home must be reorganized—it must be made into an economically creative institution. It must cease being a mere consumption unit. It must become a production unit as well. It must be as nearly as possible an organic home—house, land, machines, materials and a group of individuals organized not for mere consumption but for creative and productive living.[3]

Subsistence homesteading might thus be defined as living on a productive, self-sufficient small farm where needs and wants for boughten goods are reduced to a minimum. And we might emphasize that the aesthetic aspects of homesteading are at least as important as its economic aspects; it appeals to those who are in search of a simple, healthful, and satisfying way of life.

If the new homesteading movement is not stimulated primarily by economic necessity, it will be helpful to discern its origins and motivations. Let us try, then, to trace the movement from utopia to eutopia, even though it may require sweeping generalizations.

The utopian phase in the counter culture emerged gradually as the prevailing techno-culture became so total and all-encompassing that there was literally no place to go to escape except to drop out. Thus a "turned-off" generation becomes "down and out" instead of "up and coming," in the words of Gibson Winter, as it "embodies the antithesis of techno-man and his controlled world."[4] Having no place to go, however, the drop-out becomes, according to Winter, a mendicant who exists parasitically in the interstices of the techno-culture. He might, since he was spawned by a middle-class society that has made the manufacture of drugs a major industry, quite naturally turn to various drugs and hallucinogens to discover and explore his inner space. Such drugs are, as Gibson Winter goes on to point out, a threat to the older generation because they break up the controls that maintain the stability of the establishment: "they represent the breaking up of will, calculation and control which is the latter-day version of the Protestant ethic."[5] It is certainly true that drugs, and especially marijuana and LSD, have come to be associated with those who rebel against the techno-culture. Charles Reich claims that the widespread use of marijuana is an extremely important catalyst in precipitating a new consciousness. He points out that "in some less uptight society marijuana would be just a toy, a harmless 'high.' But in a society that keeps its citizens within a closed system of thought, that depends so much on systematic indoctrination and an imposed consciousness, marijuana is a maker of revolution, a truth-serum."[6] It would be a mistake to conclude from this that drugs are the cause of the cultural revolution or that the visions they promote serve as patterns for a new culture. Rather, just as drugs relax the controls of the prevailing techno-culture, so they are part of a larger cultural disintegration. Young people turn to drugs because they find nothing else worth doing; "doing" drugs is first a symptom of meaninglessness. Afterwards drugs may be appropriated as symbols of a new and liberated consciousness, after they have revealed the artificiality of cultural controls and thus exposed the mendacity of political and economic spokesmen.

It is important to reiterate the fact that young people "do" drugs because the socio-economic system offers them no meaningful work to do. Paul Goodman called attention to this problem *(Growing Up Absurd)* some ten years ago in relation to the drop-outs of the Beat Generation. Drop-outs are far more pervasive now, of course, but perhaps the situation is more hopeful than it was ten years ago. We can now recognize that the drop-out embodies a powerful critique of the established techno-culture, and this is especially obvious as the young begin to work out alternatives to it, such as homesteading. We can also now see the transience of the drop-out phase: "doing" drugs may lead on to hard drugs and destruction, or, by means of that intensified perception the psychedelic experience offers, to a holistic or "ecological" consciousness. This, again, should not be misunderstood. Drugs are surely no magical short-cut to knowledge. Rather, the psychedelic vision is often similar to the awareness of the ecologist. As Richard Underwood put it, "both thrust one into an awareness of the inter-connectedness of things and thus a deliverance from bondage to the dichotomy of inner and outer, mind and matter, subject and object."[7] If the word "ecology" is used among young people as a symbol to express this sense of totality which includes one's own body in the balance of nature, it does not necessarily imply that those who use the word have studied this aspect of biological science. But the ecological awareness, however mediated, is most significant as an enabling factor for the development of alternatives in the counter culture. With this new awareness goes a reassessment of priorities, and the drop-out begins to seek for a way of life in harmony with his natural environment and for a sense of internal balance. He may be led to macrobiotic food, to organic food, and, of course, to organic gardening.

Some of the utopian aspects of the counter culture are opposed to the prevailing techno-culture, but others are carried over directly from it. In *The Greening of America* Charles Reich has succeeded, more than other interpreters of youth culture, in bringing its utopian elements into focus. He maintains that the new consciousness will bring with it a non-violent revolution—some time, in the future. This revolution will not negate the culture built of technology but will humanize it and thus fulfill its promise. "We have all heard the promise," explains Reich: "affluence, security, technology make possible a new life, a new permissiveness, a new freedom, a new expansion of human possibility."[8] Most of us grow up to be skeptical about this promise, but many young people, according to Reich, drop out because they feel this promise has been betrayed. Reich's revolutionary "Consciousness III" thus turns out to be a more stubbornly believed version of the kind of utopian aspiration engendered by the Industrial Revolution. (Most utopian thought today, according to Northrop Frye, includes technological themes, "and, because technology is progressive, getting to the utopia has tended increasingly to be a journey in time rather than space, a vision of the future and not of a society located in some isolated spot on the globe."[9] Reich, however, may have projected his liberal aspirations into the youth culture movement. It is more likely that the widespread use of marijuana and the concentration of "nowness" it induces has helped to expose the vacuity of an abstract future (postponed gratification) and to undercut the rhetoric of progress.

The drop-out phase among "hippies" and people of the new or counter culture is intrinsically transitional. Many of those who find it difficult to give up the gadgets and material comforts of the techno-culture eventually get a job, however meaningless it may be, and are reabsorbed by the system. But an increasing number are deeply disillusioned with utopia either in the techno-culture or outside of it ("like, man, that's nowhere"). They literally move out in search of eutopia, but in doing so they seem to move in and together as well. In his very personal but beautiful story of today's communal movements Robert Houriet describes this process.

The first phase of the movement was *implosive,* that is, an escape from the all-pervasive influences of a plastic, fragmented mass society and a return to the primal center of being and man. In the classical utopian tradition, the commune was an island, a free space, a cultural vacuum. It was the ideal situation for spiritual revelation—for regaining the vision of a simpler, unified life and the pristine consciousness of uncomplicated, tribal man. But unlike the desert island, the communes were not naturally surrounded by an ocean to keep the "outside" society at bay. Exiles in their own country, they had to erect psychological defenses against the "outside" by drawing a "we/they" dichotomy that often verged on paranoia.[10]

The attempt to make a new beginning is almost invariably charged with the symbolism of a New Creation, Adam and Eve in Paradise, and it thus entails the substitution of an older or "classical" utopian tradition for the more recent utopian tradition. The communard may therefore be out in the wilderness, "grooving on nature," and working out a cooperative life style that is rich in interpersonal encounters, but if he is preoccupied with fighting the society he left he has not yet appropriated the good place. He has not yet created a new community or a new social reality. The homesteader knows that freedom from the "outside" is achieved in large measure when he becomes relatively self-sufficient on the land, and very few communes have yet achieved this.

One of the basic problems which faces communards and homesteaders is to learn how to handle technology. Robert Houriet observes that "those who sought exile in communes initially rejected technology *in toto,* making little discrimination between the tools that liberated and those that enslaved. They went back to the past for tools."[11] This is understandable in the light of the "we/they" dichotomy so pervasive in the communard's outlook, for "their" technology was to be distrusted. It was, after all, modern technology and the way of life it engendered that originally moved the communard to drop out. But at least two factors were at work to mitigate this uncompromising stand against modern technology. The first was practical; *some* modern tools and services, such as vehicles and roads, were found to be necessary, while others, such as electricity or chain saws, were useful in addition to the tools and skills of the past century. Considerations of modern technology are simply unavoidable. The other factor which led to a limited acceptance of modern technology in communes was, ironically, the ecological awareness which originally prompted the move into the country and back to nature. "All over the country," reports Robert Houriet, "communes talked enthusiastically of finding such new pollution-free sources of energy; they resurrected yellowed manuals of companies that had manufactured windmills in the 1920's, like the Le-Jay Corporation; they sent away for the designs of Pelton Wheels to harness water power; they read in *Mother Earth News* of how the methane in animal dung can be used to run electrical generators."[12] It is here that the practical orientation of the new homesteading movement is most relevant, for it is experimenting with ecologically sound alternatives to polluting forms of technology and to agribusiness, that bastard produced when farming was raped by the chemical industry.

There are indications that the new homesteaders will soon move beyond enthusiasm and superficial know-how to a deeper understanding and to a more scientific knowledge of their place in the ecosystem. Recent issues of *Organic Gardening and Farming* magazine include a "back to the land" section and greater emphasis on organic farming. In doing so it is moving beyond the interests of the back-yard hobby gardener to a recognition that organic gardening implies an organic way of life. The magazine's association with the New Alchemy Institute could be a hopeful sign too, for, as its director, John H. Todd, writes, "the tending and planting of ecologically sophisticated farms will require far more training, knowledge and labor than is now the lot of employees in specialized agribusinesses."[13] Thus the function of the New Alchemy Institute, says Todd, is to develop a "New Science" for the organic homestead.

The basic axiom of organic gardening, namely the creation of superb soils and the raising of high quality plants and animals, together in sophisticated polyculture schemes which imitate the processes of nature, will be emphasized. These farms will be totally unlike the farms that the Department of Agriculture promotes. They will not be the large, unstable monoculture enterprises which are so highly specialized that they often carry out only a single function. The organic farms of tomorrow will no longer be geared to displacing people from the land, but will reverse the trend by providing beautiful places to live for the people who tend and love the landscapes.[14]

From this statement we can infer that the difference between the new homesteading movement and commercial farming is equivalent to what Aldo Leopold called the "A-B cleavage": "one group (A) regards the land as soil, and its function as commodity-production; another group (B) regards the land as biota, and its function as something broader."[15] The new homesteader's romantic enthusiasm for getting back to the land and merging with it will very likely inhibit his tendency to exploit it. The farmer may be a conscientious steward in his use of the land, and many farmers surely are, but the image appropriate to the homesteader's attitude toward the land is husbandry rather than stewardship.

Is the affective or non-rational bias of the new homesteader an asset or a liability? The situation today is very similar to that projected by Kurt Vonnegut, Jr., in his futuristic novel of 1952, *Player Piano*. His slightly rebellious anti-hero, Paul Proteus, longs to escape from the rational and electronically automated world in which he is an elite manager.

Farming—now *there* was a magic word. Like so many words with a little magic from the past still clinging to them, the word "farming" was a reminder of what rugged stock the present generation had come from, of how tough a thing a human being could be if he had to. The word had little meaning in the present. There were no longer farmers, but only agricultural engineers.[16]

When Doctor Proteus sees his old-fashioned farm for the first time he is captivated by it. "With each new inconvenience, the place became more irresistible. It was completely isolated backwater, cut off from the boiling rapids of history, society, and the economy. Timeless."[17] Vonnegut apparently wrote to expose what he regarded as the futility and atavism of his hero's longing. The fact is that farms like the one described appeal to the new homesteaders of today for precisely the same reasons alluded to by Vonnegut, but because today's homesteaders emerged after a drop-out phase during which they learned to do without the gadgets and conveniences of our techno-culture, they can get along on the marginal land and buildings which today's agriculture abandons. And, as Robert Houriet explains, many of these drop-outs are, like Vonnegut's Paul Proteus, former affluent suburbanites.

Industrial engineers, corporate executives, research scientists, vice-presidents of advertising agencies—others of this stripe were joining the movement toward country and community. They shared a dissatisfaction with jobs repeatedly described as "meaningless," "abstract," and "boring"; and a thwarted yearning to return to a simpler rural existence. They could no longer tolerate commuting, the inflexibility of nine-to-five schedules, and the deteriorating quality and increasing cost of urban life.[18]

Is such a yearning for a simpler rural life an atavistic regression? It certainly is if the ex-urbanite fails to recognize that nature also imposes her discipline and her rigid time schedules. But if the new homesteader can accept this discipline, learn to work and plan with nature, he can help to work out a viable alternative to the prevailing techno-culture and its insane policy of infinite progress and growth on a finite planet.

Such alternatives are vitally important at this time, and the position which informs this essay is that any alternative is an alternative to some form of totalitarianism, however benign it may appear at this point. Theodore Roszak, along with other cultural critics such as Gibson Winter, Charles Reich, Paul Goodman, and Herbert Marcuse, has sought to unmask the subliminal aspects of technocratic control. "So subtle and so well rationalized have the arts of technocratic domination become in our advanced industrial societies that even those in the state and/or corporate structure who dominate our lives must find it impossible to conceive of themselves as the agents of a totalitarian control," writes Roszak.[19] The mass production of goods requires mass-man for their consumption, but this is an unhealthy situation. Ecologists warn that as an ecosystem is simplified it becomes increasingly unstable. The diversified mini-farm of the homesteader is an alternative to the monoculture which characterizes so much of commercial agriculture. And just as the durability of the ecosystem depends on diversity, so our social, economic, and political institutions could be strengthened by the "new" elements which the revolution in youth culture has introduced as alternatives to the prevailing techno-culture. The new homesteading movement provides alternatives to urban life and its sense of dispossession and meaningless labor, to the "need" to consume artificial goods and inferior products, to the ideology of progress and futurism, and to an economy based on the idea of scarcity. Let us examine these issues in greater detail.

The readers' letters in periodicals such as *Countryside* or *The Mother Earth News* make it perfectly obvious that the factors which push people back to the country are the over-crowding, the sense of rootlessness, the tensions and the deteriorating quality of city life. These "earth people" naturally want a place of their own in the country. Robert Ardrey suggests that this desire for land may be our genetic inheritance and thus more natural than we usually think.

As our populations expand, as a world-wide movement from countryside to city embraces all peoples, as problems of housing, of broken homes and juvenile delinquency, of mass education and delayed independence of the young rise about us in our every human midst, as David Riesman's phrase "the lonely crowd" comes more and more aptly to describe all humankind, have we not the right to ask: Is what we are witnessing, in essence, not the first consequence of the deterritorializing of man? And if man is a territorial animal, then as we seek to repair his dignity and responsibility as a human being, should we not first search for a means of restoring his dignity and responsibility as a proprietor?[20]

The Homestead Act of 1862 was an attempt to provide ownership of land with little or no cash investment, and thousands of family farms began in that way. Since then we have witnessed the decline of this family farm until today less than ten percent of the people in this country are farmers. And, of course, there are very few land-owners in our large cities.

In view of the fact that so few people in the inner city have real property (and the dignity and security of ownership that goes with it), an "Urban Homestead Act" has been proposed for America's cities.[21] It is a sensible proposal and it deserves support. People will continue to live in cities, and urban life must be humanized. But, given the absurd concentration of people in cities already, one must ask whether it would not be possible also to help in the resettlement of those who already want to move back to the land—especially at a time when increasing automation and/or economic recession threaten to create even greater unemployment. The fact that there are people who actually want to go back to the land should not be overlooked, for, as Ralph Borsodi pointed out, "history records almost no instance in which landless city dwellers abandoned city life until they were driven into the country by famine, pestilence or warfare."[22] Already in 1962 Russell Lord perceived a movement "outward from the jammed-up rim of suburbia toward modest country places and a certain amount of small-scale farming," and he argues that it could easily be given Federal support and encouragement. "If subsidies, inducement payments, and the mechanisms of government and private credit can serve, as they have in the main, to crowd families out of farming, changed laws and agencies with the power of the government behind them could surely stem such a trend and reverse it toward any designed measure of a more sensible and healthful farm and nonfarm ratio.''[23] If the notion of homesteading—the farm as home, the home as a productive unit—comes into vogue, even in Washington, a new era in sane and healthy living could result.

Private philanthropic efforts are being made to help small farmers remain on the land, especially in the South. The Rural Advancement Fund of the National Sharecropper's Fund, for example, aims to counteract discriminatory national agricultural policies by helping black farmers develop cooperative and organic farming methods so that they can live on the land with health and dignity. Such efforts should also be the concern of the Department of Agriculture, and they should be given priority over efforts to increase production.

But American Agribusiness, as promoted by the Department of Agriculture, is a division of the Corporate Technocratic State, and it is so production oriented that it seems capable only of bigness and growth. According to Mr. Lord, who had spent a lifetime in agricultural administration,

commercial farm interests and the cold-blooded school of economic statisticians alike are forever asserting that 90 percent of the American farm output comes from the ''top'' 50 percent of our farms, with the other percent producing a paltry dab of the total output. These efficiency experts, lay and professional, flinch at the very thought of such piddling producers and cry it forth that so many ''little'' operators working ''inadequate'' holdings, part time or full time, will surely reduce both unit and total crop yields and levels of productive efficiency.[24]

The question of efficiency is not just a matter of yield and production. It is obvious, given the embarrassing surpluses we already have, that we do not need a quantitative increase, but we do need ways to increase the production of healthy, quality food. Whether the methods of large-scale chemical farming produce better food is questionable. Moreover, increased bigness may actually curtial productivity. Robert Ardrey points out that ''private plots occupy about 3 percent of all Russian cultivated land, yet they produce almost half of all vegetables consumed, almost half of all milk and meat, three-quarters of all eggs, and two-thirds of that staff of Russian life, potatoes.''[25] This may prove something about private (not corporation) enterprise, to be sure, but Ardrey does also point out that the factory farm in Russia was simply inefficient in contrast to carefully tended small plots. Finally, statistics on production do not consider the fact that the farm homestead is not merely a production unit but a home, and this is the important thing about it.

The technological revolution in agriculture and food processing, ranging from chemically-stimulated growth to additives and preservatives, has kept pace with an unhealthy tendency in American life generally. As Alan Watts summed it up, ''we are living in a culture which has been hypnotized with symbols—words, numbers, measures, quantities, and images—and . . .we mistake them for, and prefer them to, physical reality.''[26] Or, as Charles Reich put it, ''the Corporate State draws its vitality by a procedure that impoverishes the natural world. It grows by a process we shall call 'impoverishment by substitution.' ''[27] He who complains about this strange kind of ''growth'' is asked, ''And what would you put in its place?'' The new homesteader has an answer: ''The natural thing.'' His alternative to eating processed or ''plastic'' food is to raise his own food and bake his own bread. The recent concern over the deleterious effects of some chemical additives in "store-bought" food indicates that the desire for organic food is not just the faddish quirk of a few quacks. Indeed, homesteaders here, as in Russia, are finding that they can sell their surplus organically-grown food at a premium and thus earn the cash they need.

Productive and self-sufficient homesteads in the countryside would serve the need for environmental improvement better than the suburban sprawl which now surrounds our cities. During the depression of the 1930's a project such as this was begun near Dayton, Ohio with the support of the Subsistence Homestead Division under the Secretary of the Interior—then Harold L. Ickes. The project did not succeed, according to Ralph Borsodi, who served as a consulting economist for it and helped to plan it, because "the palsied hand of bureaucracy has been laid upon it."[28] Perhaps the homesteading movement of today, which has emerged by choice rather than out of economic necessity, and independently of governmental support, stands a better chance of success.

The homesteading movement which is emerging out of the cultural revolution of the past decade is an alternative to the still dominant ideology of progress, with its future orientation. Philip Slater comments on this difference between the old and the new culture.

The hippie movement, for example, is brimming with nostalgia—a nostalgia peculiarly American and shared by old-culture adherents. This nostalgia embraces the Old West, Amerindian culture, the wilderness, the simple life, the utopian community—all venerable American traditions. But for the old culture they represent a subordinate, ancillary aspect of the culture, appropriate for recreational occasions or fantasy representations—a kind of pastoral relief from everyday striving—whereas for the new culture they are dominant themes. The new culture's passion for memoriabilia, paradoxically, causes uneasiness in old-culture adherents, whose future-oriented invidiousness leads to a desire to sever themselves from the past.[29]

There are surely many reasons why Americans have felt that they can move into the future only by severing themselves from the past (the immigrant's attempt to become Americanized, for example), but this tendency has so impoverished the quality and richness of our lives that we have begun to suffer the disease Alvin Toffler has called "future shock." And Toffler, even as he notices that the new culture in America is trying to ease the strains of future shock, is too infected with futurism himself to recognize the intrinsic value and significance of the new culture.

Most of today's "intentional communities" or utopian colonies . . .reveal a powerful preference for the past. These may be of value to the individuals in them, but the society as a whole would be better served by utopian experiments based on super- rather than pre-industrial forms. Instead of a communal farm, why not a computer software company whose program writers live and work communally?[30]

One answer could be that only the farm offers the possibility of meaningful physical work. It is important to notice, moreover, that communes seek utopia in the past rather than in the future, reversing a trend which began with the Industrial Revolution, when Western man began to look to the future for that which the present denied him. The fact that young people are now looking backward does not mean that they are trying to go back in time—on the contrary, the tactic of looking backward probably represents the wave of the future. But the recognition that time goes on does not entail the attempt to deliberately sever oneself from the past; indeed, it is this repudiation of the past that causes future shock, not the oncoming future. The communards and homesteaders are trying, as Philip Slater said, "to built a future that does not always look to the future."[31] It is not only possible but desirable that the future should be enriched with things of value and ways of life kept from the past. And if it is necessary to go "back" to nature to establish our relationship to it, let us by all means go "back." What use is our awareness of history if it does not free us from the tyranny of historical determinism or from continual and impoverishing change? And what good is affluence if it means that nothing can be treasured?

The true meaning of affluence, as Philip Slater so lucidly points out, is that one is freed from competitive striving and from the compulsion to invest oneself in possessions. The old culture's compulsion to buy and to compete rested on the assumption of scarcity. But the new culture, says Slater, "is founded on a rejection of scarcity assumptions."[32] This is obviously a psychological process and not just a matter of economics. There would hardly be an actual abundance of goods if they were properly distributed, at least not as long as many of them are wasted on war, but there are enough if we do not grasp and hoard. If we live with the confidence that there is plenty (a feeling that comes naturally to the organic gardener), we no longer need to accumulate more things. We thus recognize that growth for the sake of growth is, as they say, the ideology of the cancer cell. It may even be that the voluntary poverty of the subsistence homesteader would very likely not have emerged except in a society that has experienced a glut of consumer goods. This has created misunderstandings which will never be wholly resolved as long as artificially created scarcity is so real for so many Americans, for it is inevitable that the homesteader should be resented by the Black or by the Chicano, who very seldom in their history could experience the land as a benign and hospitable reality. The land is psychically available to young people of middle class background, and perhaps economically feasible for them too, as it is not available to the "other" Americans. Perhaps this "class conflict" will subside if it is recognized that some people are deprived of material goods while others are deprived of meaningful work. If the middle-class homesteader shows that he is sincerely dedicated to voluntary poverty and really serious about living and working on the land others may come to understand his motives. It has happened that when "hip" communards in the country have worked hard they have won the respect and even friendship of their sceptical old-culture rural neighbors.

When all is said and done it must be acknowledged that the movement back to the land is a trickle compared to the flood of those leaving the farm. Perhaps numbers are not important, since enough are going back to show that it is a real possibility. Close to a hundred thousand farms continue to be abandoned in the United States each year as the small farmers are being crowded out. The new homesteading movement will not reclaim all these farms; indeed, they are not even available except in areas of marginal agricultural potential where a large-scale operation is not profitable. And perhaps the most marginal land should be preserved as wilderness areas. But the new homesteading movement is a state of mind as well as a topographical reality. The movement has, after all, taken only the first step into eutopia; the other foot is still in utopia, and its state of mind is similarly divided. Although it is confused, some characteristics of this state of mind in more general terms can be ventured here, and in thus moving on to a more abstract level we shall also gain the perspective necessary to make a critique of the movement.

Nothing is more important, in the long run, than the values and ideals which serve as the ultimate sanctions of a culture. Since utopian thought is a very sensitive barometer of the pressures that create change, an examination of utopian theory and practice can help us ascertain the direction of current cultural trends.

We noticed earlier that utopian thought since the Industrial Revolution has been futuristic and technological, a tradition which is carried on today by thinkers like Buckminster Fuller. But it is important also to notice that the creative well-springs of this type of utopian thought have dried up, at least as far as the literary imagination is concerned. Chad Walsh almost belabors the obvious in his book *From Utopia to Nightmare* as he shows how contemporary "utopian" novels tend to be "dystopian." The Christianity of the major denominations in America, which has sanctioned this futuristic religion of progress, has also become secularized in the process. Although some religious thinkers defend the idea of a secular Christianity, in the perspective of the history of religions it can be seen as a fossilization. Thus it is not surprising that an older tradition of utopian thought has come back into currency. The shift from city to country and from future to past which we have discerned in the new homesteading movement can be seen as an expression of this older mythic strand in our utopian tradition. Northrop Frye has succinctly described these two archetypal structures.

In Christianity the city is the form of the myth of *telos,* the New Jerusalem that is the end of the human pilgrimage. But there is no city in the Christian, or Judaeo-Christian, myth of origin: that has only a garden, and the two progenitors of what was clearly intended to be a simple and patriarchal society. In the story which follows, the story of Cain and Abel, Abel is the shepherd and Cain a farmer whose descendants build cities and develop the arts. The murder of Abel appears to symbolize the blotting out of an idealized pastoral society by a more complex civilization. In Classical mythology the original society appears as the Golden Age, to which we have referred more than once, again a peaceful and primitive society without the complications of later ones. In both our main literary traditions, therefore, the tendency to see the ideal society in terms of a lost simple paradise has a ready origin.[33]

The utopian refuses to believe that paradise is really, irrecoverably lost. And the American experience, with its emphasis on beginning again, which R.W.B. Lewis has emphasized in his book *The American Adam,* has reinforced this strand in our mythic heritage. The idea of recovering paradise and making a new start is important here because it provides an archetype for the homesteader's movement to eutopia. Let us consider this movement, then, in relation to the notion of returning to origins and a new beginning. And since there can be no new beginning unless there has been an end, let us consider the ways in which the new homesteading movement is an end as well as a beginning.

One goes "back" to nature, or "back" to the country, mythically speaking, because one is returning to paradise, to the place of origin. Many urban Americans, incidentally, still have parents or grandparents on the farm, and the return to the country is for them infused with memories of childhood and personal origins. The return to origins in a temporal sense is expressed by the primitivism, the voluntary poverty, and the anti-technological bias which characterizes so many rural communes. A relaxation of sexual mores can similarly be seen as an attempt to return to a non-repressive style of life. A commune called "Greenfeel" was an example of the attempt to regain a polymorphous sexuality. In his brief discussion of its demise Ron Norman explained that "a major part of Greenfeel was sexuality—we would run naked in the woods, feel our bodies alive all day, sleep together at night, have sex anytime: men and women and kids, without feeling perverted and guilty. We would be a primitive animal tribe."[34] Here the paradisiacal aspects of the return to nature are strongly expressed. And since the commune is a less repressive kind of society, this return makes possible a reappropriation of the human body.

If the rural communards and homesteaders express a nostalgia for paradise, for a new beginning, we must go on to ask what has ended. In pursuing this question it is possible to sense the powerful religious seriousness which motivates the movement. It is an eschatological phenomenon. Several aspects of the rural commune, aspects which seem to emerge spontaneously, conform rather closely to the morphology of various millenary movements or cargo cults. In his essay on "Cosmic and Eschatological Renewal," Mircea Eliade suggests that the "eschatological nudism" and sexual freedom which characterizes several such cults is the ritual anticipation of paradise.

What Tsek [the cult founder] announces in his message is in fact the imminent restoration of Paradise on Earth. Men will no longer work; they will have no more need for tools, domestic animals or possessions. Once the old order is abolished the laws, rules, taboos will lose their reason. The prohibitions and customs sanctioned by tradition will give place to absolute liberty; in the first place to sexual liberty, to orgy. For, in human society, it is sexual life that is subject to the strictest taboos and constraints. To be free from laws, prohibitions and customs, is to rediscover primordial liberty and blessedness, the state which preceded the present human condition, in fact the paradisiacal state.[35]

Attitudes such as this are expressed by many contemporary communards, and their revolutionary thrust is obvious. The influence of neo-Freudian thought (Norman Brown and Wilhelm Reich, for example), the rediscovery of the body via LSD, various experiments in group marriage and pan-sexuality, Tantric non-orgasmic sexuality, all witness to the powerful desire to move beyond a repressive reality to the polymorphous sexuality of childhood and to the innocence of Adam before the Fall. Most communards have given up private possessions and hold all things in common. Thus Lou Gottlieb deeded his farm in California to God and freed it for Morning Star, an open-land commune. The "cargo" theme in this complex of paradisiacal attitudes is expressed in the widely-held belief that since production in an advanced industrial society is largely automated, and since prosperity depends on production and consumption, there will be free food and goods without working. The theme of free food also finds expression in the recent vogue for books like *Stalking the Wild Asparagus* by Euell Gibbons and in the enthusiasm for edible wild plants. It may be that such ideas are typical only of the "lunatic fringe" in the commune movement, but a reading of *Modern Man in Search of Utopia* or most other issues of *The Modern Utopian,* the comprehensive inter-commune periodical, will show that these are the kinds of ideas that find frequent literary expression.

It cannot be denied that the eschatological bias so prevalent in the commune movement, and especially in the so-called "hip" communes, is based on actual experience. The "end of the world" is experienced personally by the drop-out. As a former suburbanite matron in a commune explained to Robert Houriet, "I learned that you have to be completely busted and lose everything before you can become new and whole again. Praise the Lord."[36] Or the notion of the "end of the world" can be expressed and experienced through the imagery of environmental pollution and ecological catastrophe, racial strife, war and the demonic technocratic system that supports it—for a man-made system that has become autonomous and self-perpetuating is demonic. It is typical of a millenary movement that the old system is experienced as an evil and demonic reality that is about to collapse, while the "saving remnant" that has withdrawn from the system ritually anticipates, through drugs and music and dance, the paradise that will come after the old order has passed away.

The "hip" commune, then, probably expresses the most complete version of utopia as a regained paradise that has emerged in the West for a long time. Its eschatological and messianic aspects remain to be explored, though it is very likely that someone is hard at work right now on a study of "the Commune Movement as a Cargo Cult" or something like that.[37] The myth of a lost paradise, and nostalgia for it, is also quite naturally, though to a lesser degree, a part of the new homesteading movement as well. The eutopian is not yet free from utopian dreams and visions, nor should he be. But these utopian elements must be clearly recognized for what they are, and cherished as such, while the more practical business of establishing eutopia is going on. Nearly every group of cult that has been swept away by the full mythic power of its eschatological vision has also been led to disillusionment and destruction. It could happen again, though it is less likely to happen as the commune matures into a community.

One thing is certain: the pressures that generate a nostalgia for paradise and its peculiar eschatological orientation are real enough. The vitality of the old culture, urban technological civilization, is waning; it tries to maintain itself by force, dealing death instead of promoting life. The movement back to the land is a symptom of this social and political degradation and an alternative to it. "It should not surprise us," wrote Lewis Mumford, "if the foundations of eutopia were established in ruined countries; that is, in countries where metropolitan civilization has collapsed and where all its paper prestige is no longer accepted at its paper value." But the end of the old culture does not automatically generate the emergence of the new, and therefore, as Mumford went on to say, "the chief business of eutopians was summed up by Voltaire in the final injunction of Candide: Let us cultivate our garden."[38] God may have planted the first garden of Eden for man, but man has to plant and tend all others by himself.

In summary, then, we have seen that the movement from utopia to eutopia is a movement through *two* types of utopia. The first is the futuristic utopia of urban techno-culture where one tries to be at home in the world by finding one's "place" in the socioeconomic system. The second is the paradisiacal utopia exemplified by the "hip" commune with its extravagant expectation of eschatological renewal.

Although these utopians are drawn back to nature in their search for the lost paradise, they are uneasy about space, move about frantically, and dread the thought of being stuck in one place. The paradise they seek exists only in some mythical topography or in "middle earth." The new homesteader has moved beyond these utopias, for he remembers that the Earthly Paradise has already been found and needs only to be reappropriated. As Mircea Eliade explained in his essay on the mythical geography of paradise and utopia, the discovery and exploration of America was heavily freighted with the imagery of paradise—a New Beginning in a New World. Eliade goes on to point out that "the long resistance of American élites to the industrialization of the country, and their exaltation of the virtues of agriculture, may be explained by the same nostalgia for the Earthly Paradise."[39] Thus the mythic basis of essays such as the one I am now concluding is exposed! And given the fact that industrialization has triumphed, so that the earth and its resources are regarded as "raw materials" for the production of manufactured "goods," the resurgence of the myth of the Earthly Paradise may seem anachronistic. But the new homesteader has gone through every step of the modern experience; only after that did he rediscover the land and his place on it. As he becomes integrated with his physical environment and realizes his symbiotic relationship to the earth he encounters a reality which he recognizes as more primordial and more ultimate than the socio-economic system. It may even come to pass that the new homesteading movement will be seen as the beginning of a new or revitalized religious phenomenon which once again makes it possible to experience a sense of cosmic sacrality.

NOTES

1. Bill Kaysing, *First-Time Farmer's Guide* (San Francisco: Straight Arrow Books, 1971). This book contains a comprehensive and up-to-date bibliography of useful publications on the theory and practice of homesteading, pp. 297-310.
2. See Helen and Scott Nearing, *Living the Good Life* (Harborside, Maine: Social Sciences Institute, 1954, reprinted by Schocken Books in 1971), and Ralph Borsodi, *Flight from the City* (New York, 1933).
3. Ralph Borsodi, *This Ugly Civilization* (New York, 1929), p. 272. Borsodi's thought continues to be influential with the communal group at Heathcote Center where the School of Living publishes *The Green Revolution*.
4. Gibson Winter, *Being Free* (New York, 1970), p. 91.
5. Ibid., p. 105.
6. Charles Reich, *The Greening of America* (New York, 1970), p. 259.
7. Richard Underwood, "Ecological and Psychedelic Approaches to Theology," *Soundings*, 53 (Winter, 1960), p. 385.
8. Reich, p. 218.
9. Northrop Frye, "Varieties of Literary Utopias," in *Utopias and Utopian Thought*, ed. Frank E. Manuel (Boston, 1967), p. 28.
10. Robert Houriet, *Getting Back Together* (New York, 1971), p. 210.
11. Ibid., p. 215.
12. Ibid., p. 220.
13. John H. Todd, "Designing a New Science," *Organic Gardening and Farming* (October, 1971), 83-84.
14. Ibid., 83.
15. Aldo Leopold, "The Land Ethic," in *A Sand County Almanac* (New York, 1970), pp. 258-259.
16. Kurt Vonnegut, Jr., *Player Piano* (New York, 1970), p. 144.

17. Ibid., p. 147.

18. Houriet, *Getting Back Together,* p. 236.

19. Theodore Roszak, *The Making of a Counter Culture* (Garden City, New York, 1969), p. 9.

20. Robert Ardrey, *The Territorial Imperative* (New York, 1971), pp. 94-95.

21. James H. Davis, "The Urban Homestead Act," *Landscape,* 19 (Winter, 1970 [published July, 1971]), pp. 11-23.

22. Borsodi, *This Ugly Civilization,* p. 316.

23. Russell Lord, *The Care of the Earth* (New York, 1963), p. 344.

24. Ibid., p. 345.

25. Ardrey, *The Territorial Imperative,* p. 107.

26. Alan Watts, *Does it Matter?* (New York, 1971), pp. 36-37.

27. Reich, *The Greening of America,* p. 158.

28. Borsodi, *Flight from the City,* p. xviii. A description of this homesteading project is included as a postlude to the book, pp. 151-171. Russell Lord implied (in *The Care of the Earth,* pp. 280-281) that the project was aborted because it was thought to be communistic.

29. Philip Slater, *The Pursuit of Loneliness* (Boston, 1971), p. 109.

30. Alvin Toffler, *Future Shock* (New York, 1970), p. 414. Toffler's book reads like a book on pornography: while ostensibly showing the dangers of rapid social change, he appears to derive a perverse kind of enjoyment from presenting the data.

31. Slater, *The Pursuit of Loneliness,* p. 142.

32. Ibid., p. 139.

33. Frye, "Varieties of Literary Utopias," *op. cit.,* p. 40.

34. Ron Norman, "Greenfeel: Final Notes on an Intentional Community," *Alternatives Newsmagazine,* 1971, p. 17. This is a publication of Alternatives! Foundation, which also publishes *The Modern Utopian.*

35. Mircea Eliade, *The Two and the One* (New York, 1969), p. 127.

36. Houriet, *Getting Back Together,* p. 94.

37. Whether these "hip" communes do indeed reflect the pervasive eschatological consciousness of the typical cargo cult or whether they merely herald the beginning of a new religion or a revitalization movement, analogous to the new religions in Japan, for example, will have to be discussed by a scholar who is more competent than I am. H. Byron Earhart has been seeking to clarify the methodological issues involved in this kind of problem relative to the new religions of Japan. See, for example, "The Interpretation of the 'New Religions' of Japan as Historical Phenomena," *Journal of the American Academy of Religion,* XXXVII (September, 1969), 237-248.

38. Lewis Mumford, *The Story of Utopias* (New York, 1922), pp. 306-307.

39. Mircea Eliade, "Paradise and Utopia: Mythical Geography and Eschatology," in *Utopias and Utopian Thought,* ed. Manuel, p. 269.

Toward an
Ecological Ethic

Introduction

Presumably, *Homo sapiens* is the only species not only on this planet but in our entire solar system, which is capable of devising ethical systems. It seems likely that this very ability itself, however, is rooted in our biological nature. Perhaps this ability is one of a long string of adaptations which has yielded us continued survival. If this is so, it seems worthwhile to think about that biological nature (reading 62).

Though we may be characterized as an ethic-making species, our ethical systems may be very fragile. There are two selections presented here which illustrate this fragility—one written by D. H. Lawrence about The Great God Pan (reading 63). Pan, so important to generations of our European ancestors, became nothing more than a diminished comical figure as Christianity insisted on the truth of its myth to the exclusion of all other myths. The tragedy of the Ik and Kaiadilt described by John B. Calhoun, famous for his work on crowding in mice, is another example of the fragility of a highly sophisticated ethical system (reading 64).

If science has eroded much of our former ethical base, it has also taught us of the inter-relatedness of all living things and their physical environment. Now many scientists have moved toward the humanities in order to understand more of the totality of the human experience at the level of organization in which we ordinarily operate. It is afterall through the pre-suppositions of our religion, science, and social structures all acting as one which has allowed us to regard nature as a resource from which we receive our commodities. This happened partly because nature has been de-sacralized and the result is that both living and non-living nature has been regarded now as "nothing-but." There is some indication that this may be beginning to change.

Professor Carl Swanson, a biologist well-known for his work at the cellular level of organization, in a way most splendid describes some environmental literature that has traditionally been regarded as in the domain of the humanities (reading 65) and recommends it as important reading for the environmentalist. Since the natural world will not permanently respond to the needs of humans if it is treated solely as an economic entity, Swanson calls for a merger of the scientific and humanistic to mold a future of appropriate values to accommodate this value-guided species of ours.

The second paper of this section (reading 66) is an elaboration on another important dimension—the adoption of a *reliable* criterion of the value of species and communities. The author, Professor Ehrenfeld believes that economic or ecological justifications will not hold up and he therefore concludes that species should be conserved *because they exist and have existed for a long time*. This is essentially the same decision the Hebrew God made when he instructed Noah on taking living things onto the ark. The implications of this viewpoint are such that "non-significant" species become powerful enough through the agency of humans to stop the construction of multi-million dollar projects (reading 67). The kind of head change necessary for much of this conserving action to come about is well outlined in Aldo Leopold's essay on the "Ecological Conscience," (reading 68) written over 30 years ago.

My paper (reading 69), after some analysis of the problems discusses four specific proposals for helping us toward the development of an ecological ethic. Finally, we have the wise and learned perspective of Nobel Laureate George Wald who sees the present as a time for great decision on earth. As he thinks about the future he reflects on the past, a necessary type of symmetry, it seems, for meaningful discussion on the human enterprise (reading 70).

The Biological Roots
of an Ethic-Making Mammal

The Biological Nature of Man

> The answer to the ancient question "What is man?"
> must be based first on man's biological character.

George Gaylord Simpson

> It has often and confidently been asserted that man's origin can never be known:
> but ignorance more frequently begets confidence than does knowledge: it is those
> who know little, and not those who know much, who so positively assert that this
> or that problem will never be solved by science. (1)

Those words were written by Charles Darwin nearly 100 years ago and were published in 1871 in the introduction to his book on *The Descent of Man.* In his even better known work on *The Origin of Species* (2), which had appeared 12 years earlier, he had been content to say (somewhat coyly) that by that work "light would be thrown on the origin of man and his history." Others soon indicated the nature of that light. Thomas Henry Huxley's classic *Man's Place in Nature* (3) was published in 1863, and by 1871 numerous other naturalists of the first rank had already accepted the evolutionary origin of the human species. Darwin's own contribution to the problem of man's origin firmly established two points: first, *Homo sapiens,* like all other organisms, has evolved from prior, extremely different species by natural means and under the directive influence of natural selection; and second, man is the descendant of apes or monkeys of the Old World.

Darwin's first point, that man is the product of evolution involving natural selection, has been attacked on emotional grounds, but it was not and is not now honestly questionable on strictly scientific grounds and by anyone really familiar with the facts. The second point, of man's descent from an Old World ape or monkey, was for some time more open to scientific dispute. However, here, too, the debate was often more emotional than objective. In some pedagogic circles it became usual to maintain that man is not descended from an ape but from a common ancestor neither man nor ape nor, if one cared to go still further afield, monkey. Some went so far as to attempt to enlist Darwin posthumously in their own pussyfooting ranks by saying that he never maintained that man arose from an ape but only from a common ancestor . . .and so forth. In fact, although Darwin was slow to enter the dispute, when he did so he was more honest than those supposed defenders. He flatly said, "We must conclude, however much the conclusion may revolt our pride, that our early progenitors would have been properly . . .designated (as apes or monkeys)." The unscientific and really uncalled-for remark on pride does little to modify the forthrightness of the conclusion.

Darwin's conclusions in 1871 already covered what is most vital for consideration of man's biological status. Subsequent discovery and study have fully corroborated Darwin and have added an enormous amount of detail. That is interesting and important, and most of what I have to say here concerns it. At this point, however, the essential thing is that Darwin put the whole subject of the nature of man on a new and sound footing. To be sure, in the introduction of *The Descent of Man,* from which I have already quoted, Darwin went on to say that, "The conclusion that man is the codescendant with other species of some ancient, lower, and extinct form, is not in any degree new." He then cited Lamarck, Wallace, Huxley, Lyell, Vogt, Lubbock, Büchner, Rolle, Haeckel, Canestrini, and Barrago as "having taken the same side of the question." In fact, as regards this particular point, Darwin was doing too much honor to those worthies, some still famous and some now forgotten. It is true that they had all discussed the descent of man before Darwin himself did so in an explicit way, but with the sole exception of Lamarck they had done so after publication of *The Origin of Species* and on the basis of that work by Darwin. As for the few who really had postulated an evolutionary origin for man before *The Origin of Species,* their views were largely philosophical speculations inadequately or not at all supported by objective evidence and sometimes, as in the case of Lamarck, reaching a conclusion only approximately correct on grounds that were flatly wrong (4).

What Is Man?

The question "What is man?" is probably the most profound that can be asked by man. It has always been central to any system of philosophy or of theology. We know that it was being asked by the most learned humans 2000 years ago, and it is just possible that it was being asked by the most brilliant australopithecines 2 million years ago. The point I want to make now is that all attempts to answer that question before 1859 are worthless and that we will be better off if we ignore them completely. The reason is that no answer had a solid, objective base until it was recognized that man is the product of evolution from primeval apes and before that through billions of years of gradual but protean change from some spontaneously, that is, naturally, generated primordial monad.

It is the biological nature of man, both in his evolutionary history and in his present condition, that presents us with our only fixed point of departure. These are the facts we can find out for ourselves, in great, ever-increasing detail and soundness, open to all of us in irrefutable observations. Their interpretation is in some respects ambiguous and disputable, but interpretation at a given point becomes increasingly clear and undisputed as time goes on. Doubtfulness moves outward with the expanding frontier of knowledge.

I do not mean to say that the biological study of man or even that the scientific study of man in terms broader than biological can here and now—if ever—provide a satisfactorily complete answer to the question "What is man?" The other, older approaches through metaphysics, theology, art, and other nonbiological, nonscientific fields can still contribute, or can now contribute anew. But unless they accept, by specification or by implication, the nature of man as a biological organism, they are merely fictional fancies or falsities, however interesting they may be in those nonfactual categories. I am here concerned with man's biological nature in a rather broad sense, on the grounds that this is a necessary, even though it is not a completely sufficient, approach to comprehension of man's nature.

Already in Darwin's day it was clearly established that among living animals the great apes are anatomically most similar to man. Some anatomists, reluctant to acknowledge their poor relatives, stressed differences between man and any apes: the larger human brain, obviously; the longer and less divergent first toe of man; the absence or, more commonly, the only-sporadic presence in us of certain apish muscles and other structures. Such discussions completely missed the point. Of course men and apes differ. In itself, that means only that we belong to different species. The point at issue is not whether we differ, but in what way and how closely the different species are related.

All later study has corroborated the special relationship between men and apes and has made knowledge of it more precise. The evidence has lately been greatly increased in extent, in detail, and in its basic character. It now includes such fundamental points as the numbers and shapes of chromosomes, the exact molecular structure of hemoglobins, the resemblances and differences of serum proteins, and many others (5). All the evidence agrees and the conclusion is unequivocal. Man is not identical with apes in these or other respects. However, he is clearly related to the apes, and among the apes he is most particularly related to chimpanzees and gorillas, which are closely related between themselves. A necessary inference from this evidence is that the common ancestor of apes and men was itself a member of the ape family. Not only that; we had a common ancestor with gorilla and chimpanzee after their ancestry had become distinct from that of the other living apes (orangutan and gibbons). Our relationships to gorilla and to chimpanzee are about equal, although gorillas may have become somewhat more specialized with respect to the common ancestry.

Evidence from Fossils

More precise evidence as to relationships and as to the course of anatomical change in the human ancestry must come from fossils. There are special reasons why pertinent fossils are comparatively uncommon: Crucial stages apparently occurred in the tropics, where preservation and discovery of fossils are difficult and where exploration has generally lagged; populations of apes and of prehumans were always small, not at all comparable with the great herds of grazing animals, for example, common as fossils; and the habits and abilities of apes and pre-humans were such as to reduce chances of natural burial and preservation as fossils.

Nevertheless, a great many fossils have been recovered and discovery is active at present. We are far from having the whole story, but parts of it are increasingly clear.

In Darwin's time only one really distinctive kind of fossil ape *(Dryopithecus)* and only one really distinctive kind of fossil man (Neanderthal) were known. From the former, Darwin correctly inferred that by late Miocene, at least, the lineages of apes and monkeys had separated. He was not clear as to the possible implications for separation of the strictly human lineage, which he thought might have occurred much earlier. As regards Neanderthal man Darwin could only express surprise that in spite of their antiquity the Neanderthals had brain capacities probably greater than the average for modern man.

Now it is known that apes more or less similar to *Dryopithecus* were widespread and, as apes go, numerous through the Miocene and Pliocene of Europe, Asia, and Africa (6). Present estimates place the beginning of the Miocene at approximately 25 million years ago (7). The divergence of apes and Old World monkeys is thus at least that old. There is, in fact, some evidence that this divergence occurred in the Oligocene, which preceded the Miocene and began some 10 million years earlier. Divergence of apes and monkeys was identical with divergence of the human ancestry and monkeys, because the earliest apes were also ancestral to man. The time of the final split of the specifically prehuman lineage from that leading to gorilla and chimpanzee has not yet been closely determined. On present evidence it seems most likely to have occurred during the Miocene, that is, quite roughly between 10 and 25 million years ago. The earliest known forms that may be definitely on a prehuman line as distinct from a pre-gorilla-chimpanzee line are *Ramapithecus* from India and the closely similar, indeed probably identical supposed genus *Kenyapithecus* from Africa (8). Unfortunately those animals are known only from teeth and fragments of jaws, so that their affinities are somewhat uncertain and the anatomy of their skulls and skeletons is entirely unknown. The known specimens are approximately 10 million years old, give or take a few million.

The next significant group of fossils is that of the australopithecines, literally "southern monkeys" although they almost certainly were not exclusively southern and with complete certainty were not monkeys. They are surely and comparatively well known from East and South Africa, doubtfully and, at best, poorly known from elsewhere in Africa and from Eurasia. In Africa they are clearly divisible into two distinct groups. There is dispute as to whether those groups should not be subdivided still further and whether they should be called species or genera. Although the specialists can become enraged over those questions, they have no real importance for others, the important fact being simply that the two separate groups did exist, a point on which even the specialists now agree. Both groups resemble apes much more than we do now, but both are more nearly related to us than to the apes—another point on which the specialists have finally agreed after years of wrangling. They definitely belong to the human family, Hominidae.

One group, typified by *Australopithecus robustus* or, as it is also often called, *Paranthropus robustus,* retained some particularly primitive (more or less apelike) features and yet became somewhat aberrantly specialized. It cannot have been directly ancestral to modern man. The other group, typified by *Australopithecus africanus,* although also primitive within the human family, more closely resembles our own genus, *Homo.* Both groups are now believed to have appeared at least 2 million years ago. For a long time, perhaps 1½ million years, there were at least two distinct lineages of the human family living in Africa and probably throughout the warmer parts of the Old World. One, more primitive and aberrant, showed little progress and finally became extinct. The other, more progressive, evolved into *Homo.* A matter still under sharp dispute is whether the latter lineage included *Australopithecus africanus* as our direct ancestor, or whether for a time there were not actually three distinct lines: the two kinds of australopithecines and still another more directly related to *Homo.* The latter suggestion arises from Leakey's discovery of what he calls *Homo habilis* (9). However, some authorities believe that supposed species not to be on a distinct lineage but to belong to the line leading from *Australopithecus africanus* eventually to *Homo sapiens.*

That dispute is interesting and we hope it may soon be settled, but it is far less important than the fact that our ancestry passed through a stage closely similar to *Australopithecus africanus* if it was not that group itself. Our ancestors were then fully bipedal, ground-living animals, using their hands for manipulation as we do but perhaps not quite so skillfully. Their teeth were so like ours as to be hard to distinguish, but their brains were little larger than those of apes, and if we could see them alive their physiognomy, while distinctive, would probably strike us as more apelike than manlike.

By a time probably not later than 500,000 years ago and perhaps earlier, gradual evolution from australopithecines had reached a stage that was human in a more restricted sense, belonging not only to the human family. Hominidae, but also to the same genus as ourselves, *Homo.* Doting and ambitious discoverers have given many different names to such early fossil men, including *Pithecanthropus* and *Sinanthropus,* but most of them are now usually placed in a single species, *Homo erectus.* Bodily anatomy and even physiognomy were now almost fully human, but to our eyes there was still a coarse or brutish cast of countenance because of heavy brow ridges over the eyes and a low, small brain case. The brain size was neatly intermediate between australopithecines (or modern apes) and modern man.

Finally, and still gradually, our own species, *Homo sapiens,* emerged. Although not entirely certain, it is now the usual opinion that the quite varied fossils known collectively as Neanderthal men belonged to *Homo sapiens* and only represent ancient races that were at first primitive (not so far removed from *Homo erectus*) and later somewhat aberrant. The more aberrant late Neanderthals became extinct as such, although it is probable that some of their genes survive.

So much for more or less direct knowledge of man's physical, anatomical origin. The main points are these:

1. Man evolved from apes also ancestral to chimpanzees and gorillas, but less specialized than the latter.

2. The divergence of man's ancestry from the apes was early marked by bipedalism and upright posture, with extensive correlations and implications in anatomy, habits, and capabilities.

3. Also early was divergent dental evolution, again with other implications, for example as to diet and means of defense. It is not known whether posture and dentition diverged from the apes simultaneously or in which order.

4. Only after evolution of human posture and dentition was essentially complete did man's brain begin to enlarge beyond that of the apes. (Intelligence depends not only on size of the brain but also on its internal anatomy, and we do not know the internal anatomy of our fossil ancestors' brains. However, it is fairly certain that a species with average brain size as in apes could not be as intelligent as *Homo sapiens.*)

Systematics of Modern Man

Now let us briefly consider the taxonomic, biological systematic nature of mankind as it exists today. First and most important is the fact that mankind *is* a kind, a definite and single species. A biological species is an evolutionary unit composed of continuing populations that regularly interchange genes by interbreeding and that do not or cannot have such regular interchange with other species (10). The definition clearly applies to mankind: all human populations can and, as opportunity occurs, do interbreed, producing fertile offspring and thus continuing the species and keeping it bound together as a unit. It is unlikely that, for example, a Greenland Eskimo has ever interbred with a South African Bushman, but since all intervening populations can and do interbreed they are nevertheless members of the same species. That species, *Homo sapiens,* is not connected with any other species by interbreeding.

Comparison of Eskimo and Bushman brings up the obvious (although occasionally denied) fact that the human species includes quite diverse races. A race is simply a population (or group of populations) that is genetically distinguished from others. The distinction is not absolute. It is unlikely that Negroes, for example, have any genes that do not occur in some white populations, or that whites have any genes absent in all Negro populations. The usual situation is that a race has certain genes and gene combinations that are more frequent in it than elsewhere, and therefore typical in that sense, but not confined to the race. Races always grade into each other without definite boundaries. There is not now and never has been such a thing as a pure race, biologically speaking. Any two human populations, no matter how small or how large, differ in some respects, so that there is no fixed number of races. One could count thousands or two, and no matter how many are counted, there will be some populations and many individuals that do not clearly fit into one or another. Moreover, races are evanescent in the course of evolution. A given race may change, disappear by fusion with others, or die out altogether while the species as a whole simply continues its evolutionary course (11).

Races of man have, or perhaps one should say "had," exactly the same biological significance as the subspecies of other species of mammals. Widespread animals have local populations that live under diverse conditions and that may become temporarily and in part isolated from each other. They may then more or less accidentally have different proportions of genes (in stricter technical language, of alleles) from other such populations, and if the situation continues long enough, they will almost inevitably evolve somewhat different adaptations to local conditions. Primitive men were relatively few in number and relatively immobile, but they spread over enormous areas—the whole land area of the earth except for Antarctica and a few small islands. They evolved into races or, in better biological terms, into subspecies exactly as any other animal would have under those circumstances. Racial differentiation in man was originally geographic and, for the most part, adaptive.

That was the original biological significance of race. One must say that Negroes were biologically superior to whites, if reference is to prehistoric times, when the races were originating, and to African conditions, to which Negroes were biologically adapted and whites were not. At the present time race has virtually no strictly biological significance because of two crucial changes. First, human adaptation to different environments is now mostly cultural and is directly biological only in lesser part, so that the prehistoric biological adaptations have lost much of their importance. Second, tremendous increases in population size, in mobility, and in environmental changes brought about by man himself have the result that extremely few men are now living under the conditions to which their ancestors were racially adapted.

Evolution does not necessarily proceed at the same rate in different populations, so that among many groups of animals it is possible to find some species that have evolved more slowly, hence are now more primitive, as regards some particular trait or even over-all. It is natural to ask—as many have asked—whether among human races there may not similarly be some that are more primitive in one way or another or in general. It is indeed possible to find single characteristics that are probably more advanced or more primitive in one race than in another. For example, the full lips and kinky hair of some Negroes are almost certainly progressive traits in comparison with the more primitive, decidedly apelike thin lips and straight hair of most whites. However, that does not mean that whites in general are more primitive than Negroes or otherwise inferior to them. Overall primitiveness and progressiveness in comparison of different groups of animals is practically confined to cases in which the groups are of different species, so that genes of the more rapidly evolving species cannot be transferred to the lagging species. Human races all belong to the same species and have generally had enough interbreeding so that genetic progress, as distinct from local adaptation, could and evidently did spread through the entire species. Only if some race entirely ceased to interbreed with any other would it be likely for it to fall behind and become definitely inferior. Let us hope that will not happen.

Resemblances, Anatomical and Psychological

Regardless of the diversity of races, it is obvious that all men resemble one another much more than any of them differ from each other. They all share the basic qualities, anatomical, physiological and psychological, that make us human, *Homo sapiens,* and no other species that is or ever was. Something has already been said of anatomical peculiarities of *Homo sapiens* with respect to living apes and human ancestors. Here are some of the most striking human anatomical traits:

Normal posture is upright.

Legs are longer than arms.

Toes are short, the first toe frequently longest and not divergent.

The vertebral column has an S curve.

The hands are prehensile, with a large and strongly opposable thumb.

Most of the body is bare or has only short, sparse, inconspicuous hair.

The joint for the neck is in the middle of the base of the skull.

The brain is uniquely large in proportion to the body and has a particularly large and complex cerebrum.

The face is short, almost vertical under the front of the brain.

The jaws are short, with a rounded dental arch.

The canine teeth are usually no larger than the premolars, and there are normally no gaps in front of or behind the canines.

The first lower premolar is like the second, and the structure of the teeth in general is somewhat distinctive.

Given those characteristics, a museum curator could readily identify any specimen of *Homo sapiens* that was added to the collections, or that happened to walk into his office. However, we who are pondering the question "What is man?" must feel that these anatomical features, fully diagnostic as they are, yet do not amount to an answer adequate for our purposes. Even if we were defining, say, a species of mouse, the anatomical definition would not take us far toward understanding "What is mouse?" or, better, "What is mouseness?" unless we related the bodily mouse to the behaving mouse and the thinking mouse. Even thus, human anatomy reflects truly essential man-ness or human nature only to the extent that it is related to human activities and psychology. Already in *The Descent of Man* (1) Darwin discussed such traits in which man appears to be most distinctive. His points, here greatly abbreviated and paraphrased, were as follows:

In proportion with his higher intelligence, man's behavior is more flexible, less reflex or instinctive.

Man shares such complex factors as curiosity, imitation, attention, memory, and imagination with other relatively advanced animals, but has them in higher degree and applies them in more intricate ways.

More, at least, than other animals, man reasons and improves the adaptive nature of his behavior in rational ways.

Man regularly both uses and makes tools in great variety.

Man is self-conscious; he reflects on his past, future, life, death, and so forth.

Man makes mental abstractions and develops a related symbolism; the most essential and complexly developed outcome of these capacities is language.

Some men have a sense of beauty.

Most men have a religious sense, taking that term broadly to include awe, superstition, belief in the animistic, supernatural, or spiritual.

Normal men have a moral sense; in later terms, man ethicizes.

Man is a cultural and social animal and has developed cultures and societies unique in kind and in complexity.

The last point, which some students now consider the most important of all, was least emphasized by Darwin, who was here mainly concerned with the relationship of social evolution to the origin of the moral sense. Darwin's general purpose was not to characterize *Homo sapiens* as the unique species that he is. The purpose was to show that the characteristics that make him unique are nevertheless foreshadowed in other animals, and that the evolution of man from other, earlier, quite distinct species is therefore plausible. We are no longer concerned with *whether* man evolved, because we know that he did. We are still very much concerned with *how* he evolved, with what is most characteristically human about him and how those characteristics arose. The list of traits discussed by Darwin is still valid from this somewhat different point of view.

That list should not be taken as involving so many separate and distinct things. These are aspects of the behavior, capacities, and accomplishments of a species that is characterized by all of them together and not by each or any one separately. They

interact and interlock not only with each other but also with the previously mentioned physical or anatomical characteristics of man. For example, complex human
societies, especially the modern industrial civilization rapidly spreading to the
whole world, require specialization of activities by different members of society
further involving manipulation of complex machines. Such specialization, which is
nongenetic, requires individual flexibility and could not occur in a mainly instinctive animal. The machines are tools and could only have been devised by a reason-
ing, toolmaking animal. Invention also required manual deftness, which was provided by (and which also gave selective value to) the structure of the human hand,
which required upright posture and could not have been acquired by a quadruped.
Further evolution of the early cultural adaptations that led eventually to modern
industry also had increased intelligence as a necessary concomitant, and that eventually required larger brains, which in turn involved change in skull structure and in
stance—and so on. Even the changing pattern of the teeth can be related to this
unitary complex.

The Major Evolutionary Changes

Because all the specifically human traits are integrated within the whole that is
human, and because each of the traits as well as their integration must have arisen
gradually, it is somewhat questionable to speak of definite milestones or even of
particular critical phases in the evolution of man. Yet there are three among these
slow and coordinated changes that seem particularly basic for the concept of
human-ness. The most crucial single anatomical point is acquisition of upright posture and strictly bipedal locomotion. Most of the other main peculiarities of human
anatomy either follow from that or are coadapted with it. The other two major factors
are cultural, but are no less biological since both represent attainment and maintenance of biological adaptation by cultural means. They are tool making and language.

Extremely crude but unmistakable stone tools are found in the oldest rock
strata containing indisputable members of the human family, nearly, if not quite, 2
million years old. It will be difficult to authenticate still older and more primitive
stone tools, because they must have consisted of natural pebbles or rock fragments
picked up and used with little or no modification. It has long been maintained that
deliberate manufacture of a tool is the distinctive human trait, since many other
animals, even including some insects, use natural objects as tools but do not make
tools. Now it has been found that chimpanzees may trim and shorten twigs or straws
for use as tools (12), and although that simple behavior is almost too primitive to be
called tool making, it sufficiently demonstrates that the capacity for tool making is
biologically ancient and prehuman. If one wants a more diagnostic statement, it
probably is true that man is the only living animal that uses tools to make tools.
However, that trait would follow soon and inevitably once tool making really got
under way. A stone used to knock flakes off an incipient stone ax is already a
machine tool.

Ancient tools more perishable than stone are rarely preserved. Nevertheless, the
course of increasing diversity and complication of tools can be followed well enough to
demonstrate the gradual and inconstant but generally continual progress through
prehistory. The tremendously accelerated progress in historic times is very well

documented and is familiar to all of us in general outline, at least. The whole sweep from stone axes to electronic computers is a natural and comprehensible extension of the biological capacities of an unusual species. It is uniquely wonderful, and yet, lest we stand too much in awe of our own products, let us remember that a digital computer is merely a rapid and automated tool for what amounts to counting on fingers.

As posture is focal for consideration of man's anatomical nature and tools are for consideration of his material culture, so is language focal for his mental nature and his non-material culture (13). Language is also the most diagnostic single trait of man: all normal men have language; no other now-living organisms do. That real, incomparably important, and absolute distinction has been blurred by imprecise use of the word "language" not only in popular speech but also by some scientists who should know better, speaking, for example, of the "language of the bees" (14).

In any animal societies, and indeed in still simpler forms of aggregation among animals, there must be some kind of communication in the very broadest sense. One animal must receive some kind of information about another animal. That information may be conveyed by specific signals, which may be of extremely diverse kinds both as to form and as to modality, that is, the sensory mode by which it is received. The odor of an ant, the movements of a bee, the color pattern of a bird, the howl of a wolf, and many thousands of others are all signals that convey information to other animals and that, in these and many other examples, are essential adaptations for behavioral integration in the species involved.

Human language is also a system of interpersonal communication and a behavioral adaptation essential for the human form of socialization. Yet human language is absolutely distinct from any system of communication in other animals. That is made most clear by comparison with other animal utterances, which most nearly resemble human speech and are most often called "speech." Nonhuman vocables are, in effect, interjections. They reflect the individual's physical or, more frequently, emotional state. They do not, as true language does, name, discuss, abstract, or symbolize. They are what the psychologists call affective; such purely affective so-called languages are systems of emotional signals and not discourse. The difference between animal interjection and human language is the difference between saying "Ouch!" and saying "Fire is hot."

That example shows that the nonlanguage of animal interjection is still present in man. In us it is in effect not a part of language, but the negative of language, something we use in place of speech. In part we even use the same signals as do the apes, a fact already explored to some depth by Darwin in another of his basic works, *The Expression of the Emotions in Man and Animals* (15). Much more is now known about such expressions in animals, and particularly in our closer relatives the apes and monkeys, and it is not surprising to find that the non-linguistic, affective system is particularly complicated in them and has not progressed but may even have retrogressed in man. Still we do retain that older system along with our wholly new and wholly distinct system of true language. It is amusing that the human affective interjectional reaction to a bad smell is practically the same as in all other primates, down even to the most primitive.

Attempts To Trace Language

Darwin's study and many later studies sought to trace the evolutionary origin of language from a prehuman source. They have not been successful. As a recent expert in the field (16) has said, "The more that is known about it (that is, communication in monkeys and apes), the less these systems seem to help in the understanding of human language."

Many other attempts have been made to determine the evolutionary origin of language, and all have failed. Because language is so important for any concept of man and because this is an interesting example of methodology and limitations, it is worthwhile to consider some of these futile attempts. One, fairly obvious once the idea of linguistic evolution had arisen, was by comparison of living languages. One result was a supposed genetic sequence: (i) isolating languages, like Chinese, which string together invariable word roots; (ii) agglutinating languages, like Mongolian, which modify roots by tacking on prefixes and suffixes; and (iii) flexional languages, like Latin, which modify by (partly) internal changes in words. The trouble is that these categories are not really distinct and, especially, that they did not historically occur in this sequence. For example, Chinese was probably flexional at one time and is now becoming agglutinating with a possibility of becoming flexional again. English was flexional until quite recently and is now mostly isolating with a strong dash of agglutination. Moreover at the present time no languages are primitive in the sense of being significantly close to the origin of language. Even the peoples with least complex cultures have highly sophisticated languages, with complex grammar and large vocabularies, capable of naming and discussing anything that occurs in the sphere occupied by their speakers. Tales of tribal natives who cannot count beyond 4 and who have vocabularies of only two or three hundred words betray the shortcomings of gullible travelers, not of the natives (17).

Another approach is to follow back directly historical records, which cover several thousand years for some European, Asiatic, and north African languages. It is then possible to project still further and to reconstruct, for example, a proto-Indo-European anterior to Sanskrit. But this still leaves us tens or hundreds of thousands of years—perhaps even more—from the origin of language. The oldest language that can reasonably be reconstructed is already modern, sophisticated, complete from an evolutionary point of view.

Still another attempt, which now seems very naive, is through the ontogeny of language, that is, the acquisition of language by children. This relies on the famous but, as it happens, quite erroneous saying that ontogeny repeats phylogeny. In fact the child is not evolving or inventing primitive language but is learning a particular modern language, already complete and unrecognizably different from any possible primitive language. Moreover, the child is doing this with a modern brain already genetically constructed (through the long, long action of natural selection) for the use of complete, wholly nonprimitive language.

It is a tempting hypothesis that the time, at least, of the origin of language might be determined by structural characteristics in fossils. One rather elaborate attempt departed from the fact that all linguistic phonetic systems, varied as they are, depend in part on the shape of the lower jaw and the hard palate, anatomically quite different in typical members of the human and the ape families. It was postulated that speech began when these anatomical parts reached human form, which was in the australopithecines or somewhat earlier. But the postulate is clearly wrong. Audible signals capable of expressing language do not require any particular phonetic apparatus, but only the ability to produce sound, any sound at all. Almost all mammals and a great number of other animals can do that. Moreover, a number of animals, not only birds but also some mammals, can produce sounds recognizably similar to those of human language, and yet their jaws and palates are radically nonhuman. A parrot is capable of articulating a human word but is completely incapable of understanding what the word means.

Given any method of sound production, the capacity for language depends not on characteristics of the sound apparatus but on the central nervous system. Speech is particularly connected with the left temporal lobe of the human brain, as shown, for example, by the fact that ability to speak is generally lost if that lobe is severely damaged. The gross development of the lobe can be seen in plaster casts of the insides of fossil skulls, and that, too, has been proposed as a means of determining whether or not a given fossil individual could speak. But all mammals have left temporal lobes, some smaller and some larger. Those with smaller lobes do not speak just a little and those with larger lobes more. There is no graded sequence: normal men speak completely; other animals, whatever the relative size of their temporal lobes, do not speak at all.

The essential anatomical and physiological basis of speech is nevertheless in the structure and function of the brain (18). That basis is not fully known, but it evidently involves not just a language center, such as might be localized in the temporal lobe, but an intricate and widespread system of associative connections throughout much of the brain. (The nature or presence of these connections cannot be determined in fossils.) Thus sensations of any kind derived from an external object or event can be generalized according to similarities with others. Each kind can then be associated with a distinctive symbol, which does not resemble the object or event at all but which arbitrarily stands for it. That symbol, a supreme element in the nature of man, is the word, and it is not surprising that words meaning "word," abstraction and symbolization on still another level, have acquired such mystical and philosophical overtones. (Λόγος!)

It is still possible but it is unlikely that we will ever know just when and how our ancestors began to speak. Yet it is certain that this ability depends on physical, structural, and chemical characteristics of the nervous system which evolved from our nonspeaking ancestors under the force of natural selection. The capacity for this unique kind of symbolization is quite general. It does not determine what symbol will be used for a given concept, but that any symbol can be associated with any concept. Thus we are all using exactly the same genetic capacity and symbolizing the same concept when various of us say "woman," "Weib," "femme," "mujer," "zhenshchina," or "imra," depending on whether we happen to have been raised in England, Germany, France, Spain, Russia, or Egypt. The words do not resemble each other and even less resemble the concept they stand for. Moreover, they can be written in different ways, as in Latin, Arabic, or Chinese characters, that do not resemble each other and that have no physical resemblance to the spoken words. They can even be associated with some symbol that is not verbal at all, as in this example with the simplified representation of Venus's mirror that biologists use to designate females: ♀ .

Conclusion

Language has become far more than a means of communication in man. It is also one of the principal (although far from the only) means of thought, memory, introspection, problem-solving, and all other mental activities. The uniqueness and generality of human symbolization have given our mental activities not only a scope but also a quality far outside the range of other animals. It keeps us aware, to greater extent than can otherwise be, of past and future, of the continuity of existence and its extension beyond what is immediately sensed. Along with other peculiarly human capacities, it is involved in what I consider the most important human characteristic from an ethical point of view: foresight. It is the capacity to predict the outcome of our own actions that makes us responsible for them and that therefore makes ethical judgment of them both possible and necessary (19).

Above the individual level, language and related powers of symbolization make possible the acquisition, sharing, and preserving of knowledge far beyond what would be possible for any single individual. That is an indispensable element in all forms of human social organization and cultural accomplishment, even the most primitive.

It is obvious that I have by no means touched on all aspects of the biological nature of man. That would be impossible in one essay by one author. Those familiar with recent developments in biology may particularly miss reference to molecular biology and especially to the compound called DNA, now known to be largely involved in heredity and also in control of biochemical activities in cells. Those subjects are extremely fascinating at present and may be portentous for the future. However, in my opinion nothing that has so far been learned about DNA has helped significantly to understand the nature of man or of any other whole organism. It certainly is necessary for such understanding to examine what is inherited, how it is expressed in the developing individual, how it evolves in populations, and so on. Up to now the triumphs of DNA research have had virtually no effect on our understanding of those subjects. In due course molecular biology will undoubtedly become more firmly connected with the biology of whole organisms and with evolution, and then it will become of greater concern for those more interested in the nature of man than in the nature of molecules.

Finally, it should be pointed out that although man is a unique animal and although we properly consider his nature in the light of his peculiarities, he also has many non-peculiarities. Man is not *merely* an animal, that is, his essence is not simply in his shared animality. Nevertheless he *is* an animal and the nature of man includes and has arisen from the nature of all animals. Indeed if all the material characteristics of man could be enumerated, it would surely be found that the vast majority of them also occur in other animals. In fact at the level of molecular structure and interaction, information storage and transfer, energy transactions, and other defining characteristics of life, man is hardly significantly different from a bacterium—another illustration of the fact that that level of study is not particularly useful in considering the nature of man.

Like other animals, man develops, is born, grows, reproduces, and dies. Like other animals, he eats, digests, eliminates, respires, locomotes. He bends the qualities of nature to his own ends, but he is as fully subject to nature's laws as is any other animal and is no more capable of changing them. He lives in biological communities and has a niche and an ecology, just as do robins and earthworms. Let us not forget those aspects of man's nature. But let us also remember that man stands upright, builds and makes as never was built or wrought before, speaks and may speak truth or a lie, *worships and may worship honestly or falsely,* looks to the stars and into the mud, remembers his past and predicts his future, and writes (perhaps at too great length) about his own nature.

REFERENCES AND NOTES

1. C. Darwin, *The Descent of Man, and Selection in Relation to Sex* (Murray, London, 1871).
2. ———, *On the Origin of Species by Means of Natural Selection, or The Preservation of Favoured Races in the Struggle for Life* (Murray, London, 1859).
3. T. H. Huxley, *Evidence as to Man's Place in Nature* (Williams and Norgate, London, 1863).
4. Lamarck's view (unknown to most Neo-Lamarckians) was that *all* organisms are evolving toward and will eventually become human, after which they will degenerate through the inorganic world and eventually be spontaneously generated as lowly organisms and start again on the path to man. Today's amoeba is tomorrow's man, day after tomorrow's mineral, and still another day's amoeba once more. In the state of knowledge and philosophy of Lamarck's day it would perhaps be too strong to label his views as absurd, but they were certainly less sensible and less progressive than has often been claimed.
5. These new data are well exemplified in S. L. Washburn, Ed., *Classification and Human Evolution* (Aldine, Chicago, 1963).
6. E. L. Simons and D. R. Pilbeam, *Folia Primatol.* No. 46 (1965).
7. On this and other absolute (year) dates see D. E. Savage, J. F. Evernden, G. H. Curtis, G. T. James, *Am. J. Sci.* 262, 145 (1964).
8. E. L. Simons, *Postilla* (Yale Peabody Museum) No. 57 (1961); *Proc. Nat. Acad. Sci. U.S.* 51, 528 (1964).
9. L. S. B. Leakey, P. V. Tobias, M. D. Leakey, J. R. Napier, *Nature* 202, 3 (1964); P. V. Tobias, *Science* 149, 22 (1965). For discussion and dissent see P. L. DeVore, Ed., *The Origin of Man* (transcript of a symposium, Wenner-Gren Foundation, New York, 1965).
10. Age-long argument on the definition of species is perhaps sufficiently summarized in G. G. Simpson, *Principles of Animal Taxonomy* (Columbia Univ. Press, New York, 1961) and E. Mayr, *Animal Species and Evolution* (Harvard Univ. Press, Cambridge, 1963).
11. On animal races see especially Mayr (10). On the perennial, knotty problem of human races, a sensible general statement with many references is in Th. Dobzhansky, *Mankind Evolving* (Yale Univ. Press, New Haven, 1962).
12. J. Goodall, in *Primate Behavior,* I. DeVore, Ed. (Holt, Rinehart and Winston, New York, 1965). p. 425.
13. The literature on human culture and linguistics is as voluminous as that of any field of science. Some recent studies especially pertinent to my text are: A. L. Bryan, *Current Anthropol.* 4, 297 (1965); M. Critchley, in *Evolution after Darwin,* S. Tax, Ed. (Univ. of Chicago Press, Chicago, 1960), vol. 2, p. 289; A. S. Diamond, *The History and Origin of Language* (Philosophical Library, New York, 1959); E. L. DuBrul, *Evolution of the Speech Apparatus* (Thomas, Springfield, Ill., 1958); B. R. Fink, *Perspectives Biol. Med.* 7, 85 (1963); C. F. Hockett, in *The Evolution of Man's Capacity for Culture,* J. N. Spuhler, Ed. (Wayne State Univ. Press, Detroit, 1959), p. 32; C. F. Hockett and R. Ascher, *Current Anthropol.* 5, 135 (1964); A. Kortlandt, *ibid.* 6, 320 (1965). See also works cited in 16.
14. Misuses of the term "language" are too widely exemplified to need citation. The distinction is discussed by several of the authors cited in *13,* also (among other places) in J. B. S. Haldane and H. Spurway, *Insectes Sociaux* 1, 247 (1954) and J. B. S. Haldane, *Sci. Progr.* No. 171, 385 (1955).
15. C. Darwin, *The Expression of the Emotions in Man and Animals* (Murray, London, 1872).

16. J. B. Lancaster, in *The Origin of Man*, P. L. DeVore, Ed. (transcript of a symposium, Wenner-Gren Foundation, New York, 1965). See also discussions by A. R. Diebold, Jr., T. A. Sebeok, D. Slobin in the same volume, and bibliography on pp. 149-150.
17. I first began to appreciate the richness and complexity of "primitive" languages when I visited the Kamarakotos of Venezuela in 1939, and I commented on it in G. G. Simpson, *Los Indios Kamarakotos* (Ministerio de Fomento, Caracas, 1940).
18. N. Geschwind, *Brain* 88, 237 (1965).
19. G. G. Simpson, *Am. Psychologist* 21, 27 (1966).
20. During 1965 varying versions of this essay were presented as lectures at Randolph Macon College, the University of Paris, and the University of Washington. I have profited by discussions on those occasions.

The Fragility of
Our Ethical Dimension

Pan in America

D. H. Lawrence

At the beginning of the Christian era, voices were heard off the coasts of Greece, out to sea, on the Mediterranean, wailing: "Pan is dead! Great Pan is dead!"

The father of fauns and nymphs, satyrs and dryads and naiads was dead, with only the voices in the air to lament him. Humanity hardly noticed.

But who was he, really? Down the long lanes and overgrown ridings of history we catch odd glimpses of a lurking rustic god with a goat's white lightning in his eyes. A sort of fugitive, hidden among leaves, and laughing with the uncanny derision of one who feels himself defeated by something lesser than himself.

An outlaw, even in the early days of the gods. A sort of Ishmael among the bushes.

Yet always his lingering title: The Great God Pan. As if he was, or had been, the greatest.

Lurking among the leafy recesses, he was almost more demon than god. To be feared, not loved or approached. A man who should see Pan by daylight fell dead, as if blasted by lightning.

Yet you might dimly see him in the night, a dark body within the darkness. And then, it was a vision filling the limbs and the trunk of a man with power, as with new, strong-mounting sap. The Pan-power! You went on your way in the darkness secretly and subtly elated with blind energy, and you could cast a spell, by your mere presence, on women and on men. But particularly on women.

In the woods and the remote places ran the children of Pan, all the nymphs and fauns of the forest and the spring and the river and the rocks. These, too, it was dangerous to see by day. The man who looked up to see the white arms of a nymph flash as she darted behind the thick wild laurels away from him followed helplessly.

He was a nympholept. Fascinated by the swift limbs and the wild, fresh sides of the nymph, he followed for ever, for ever, in the endless monotony of his desire. Unless came some wise being who could absolve him from the spell.

But the nymphs, running among the trees and curling to sleep under the bushes, made the myrtles blossom more gaily, and the spring bubble up with greater urge, and the birds splash with a strength of life. And the lithe flanks of the faun gave life to the oak-groves, the vast trees hummed with energy. And the wheat sprouted like green rain returning out of the ground, in the little fields, and the vine hung its black drops in abundance, urging a secret.

Gradually men moved into cities. And they loved the display of people better than the display of a tree. They liked the glory they got of overpowering one another in war. And, above all, they loved the vainglory of their own words, *the pomp of argument and the vanity of ideas*.

So Pan became old and grey-bearded and goat-legged, and his passion was degraded with the lust of senility. His power to blast and to brighten dwindled. His nymphs became coarse and vulgar.

Till at last the old Pan died, and was turned into the devil of the Christians. The old god Pan became the Christian devil, with the cloven hoofs and the horns, the tail, and the laugh of derision. Old Nick, the Old Gentleman who is responsible for all our wickednesses, but especially our sensual excesses—this is all that is left of the Great God Pan.

It is strange. It is a most strange ending for a god with such a name. Pan! All! That which is everything has goat's feet and a tail! With a black face!

This really is curious.

Yet this was all that remained of Pan, except that he acquired brimstone and hell-fire, for many, many centuries. The nymphs turned into the nasty-smelling witches of a Walpurgis night, and the fauns that danced became sorcerers riding the air, or fairies no bigger than your thumb.

But Pan keeps on being reborn, in all kinds of strange shapes. There he was, at the Renaissance. And in the eighteenth century he had quite a vogue. He gave rise to an "ism," and there were many pantheists, Wordsworth one of the first. They worshipped Nature in her sweet-and-pure aspect, her Lucy Gray aspect.

"Oft have I heard of Lucy Gray," the school-child began to recite, on examination-day.

"So have I," interrupted the bored inspector.

Lucy Gray, alas, was the form that William Wordsworth thought fit to give to the Great God Pan.

And then he crossed over to the young United States: I mean Pan did. Suddenly he gets a new name. He becomes the Oversoul, the Allness of everything. To this new Lucifer Gray of a Pan Whitman sings the famous *Song of Myself:* "I am All, and All is Me." That is: "I am Pan, and Pan is me."

The old goat-legged gentleman from Greece thoughtfully strokes his beard, and answers: "All A is B, but all B is not A." Aristotle did not live for nothing. All Walt is Pan, but all Pan is not Walt.

This, even to Whitman, is incontrovertible. So the new American pantheism collapses.

Then the poets dress up a few fauns and nymphs, to let them run riskily—oh, would there were any risk—in their private "grounds." But, alas, these tame guinea pigs soon became boring. Change the game.

We still *pretend* to believe that there is One mysterious Something-or-other back of Everything, ordaining all things for the ultimate good of humanity. It wasn't back of the Germans in 1914, of course, and whether it's back of the bolshevists is still a grave question. But still, it's back of *us,* so that's all right.

Alas, poor Pan! Is this what you've come to? Legless, hornless, faceless, even smileless, you are less than everything or anything, except a lie.

And yet here, in America, the oldest of all, old Pan is still alive. When Pan was greatest, he was not even Pan. He was nameless and unconceived, mentally. Just as a small baby new from the womb may say Mama! Dada! whereas in the womb it said nothing; so humanity, in the womb of Pan, said nought. But when humanity was born into a separate idea of itself, it said Pan.

In the days before man got too much separated off from the universe, he was Pan, along with all the rest.

As a tree still is. A strong-willed, powerful thing-in-itself, reaching up and reaching down. With a powerful will of its own it thrusts green hands and huge limbs at the light above, and sends huge legs and gripping toes down, down between the earth and rocks, to the earth's middle.

Here, on this little ranch under the Rocky Mountains, a big pine tree rises like a guardian spirit in front of the cabin where we live. Long, long ago the Indians blazed it. And the lightning, or the storm, has cut off its crest. Yet its column is always there, alive and changeless, alive and changing. The tree has its own aura of life. And in winter the snow slips off it, and in June it sprinkles down its little catkin-like pollen-tips, and it hisses in the wind, and it makes a silence within a silence. It is a great tree, under which the house is built. And the tree is within the allness of Pan. At night, when the lamplight shines out of the window, the great trunk dimly shows, in the near darkness, like an Egyptian column, supporting some powerful mystery in the overbranching darkness. By day, it is just a tree.

It is just a tree. The chipmunks skelter a little way up it, the little black-and-white birds, tree-creepers, walk quick as mice on its rough perpendicular, tapping; the bluejays throng on its branches, high up, at dawn, and in the afternoon you hear the faintest rustle of many little wild doves alighting in its upper remoteness. It is a tree, which is still Pan.

And we live beneath it, without noticing. Yet sometimes, when one suddenly looks far up and sees those wild doves there, or when one glances quickly at the inhuman-human hammering of a woodpecker, one realizes that the tree is asserting itself as much as I am. It gives out life, as I give out life. Our two lives meet and cross one another, unknowingly: the tree's life penetrates my life, and my life the tree's. We cannot live near one another, as we do, without affecting one another.

The tree gathers up earth-power from the dark bowels of the earth, and a roaming sky-glitter from above. And all unto itself, which is a tree, woody, enormous, slow but unyielding with life, bristling with acquisitive energy, obscurely radiating some of its great strength.

It vibrates its presence into my soul, and I am with Pan. I think no man could live near a pine tree and remain quite suave and supple and compliant. Something fierce and bristling is communicated. The piny sweetness is rousing and defiant, like turpentine, the noise of the needles is keen with œons of sharpness. In the volleys of wind from the western desert, the tree hisses and resists. It does not lean eastward at all. It resists with a vast force of resistance, from within itself, and its column is a ribbed, magnificent assertion.

I have become conscious of the tree, and of its interpenetration into my life. Long ago, the Indians must have been even more acutely conscious of it, when they blazed it to leave their mark on it.

I am conscious that it helps to change me, vitally. I am even conscious that shivers of energy cross my living plasm, from the tree, and I become a degree more like unto the tree, more bristling and turpentiney, in Pan. And the tree gets a certain shade and alertness of my life, within itself.

Of course, if I like to cut myself off, and say it is all bunk, a tree is merely so much lumber not yet sawn, then in a great measure I shall *be* cut off. So much depends on one's attitude. One can shut many, many doors of receptivity in oneself; or one can open many doors that are shut.

I prefer to open my doors to the coming of the tree. Its raw earth-power and its raw sky power; its resinous erectness and resistance, its sharpness of hissing needles and relentlessness of roots, all that goes to the primitive savageness of a pine tree, goes also to the strength of man.

Give me of your power, then, oh tree! And I will give you of mine.

And this is what men must have said, more naively, less sophisticatedly, in the days when all was Pan. It is what, in a way, the aboriginal Indians still say, and still mean, intensely: especially when they dance the sacred dance, with the tree; or with the spruce twigs tied above their elbows.

Give me your power, oh tree, to help me in my life. And I will give you my power: even symbolized in a rag torn from my clothing.

This is the oldest Pan.

Or again, I say: "Oh you, you big tree, standing so strong and swallowing juice from the earth's inner body, warmth from the sky, beware of me. Beware of me, because I am strongest. I am going to cut you down and take your life and make you into beams for my house, and into a fire. Prepare to deliver up your life to me."

Is this any less true then when the lumberman glances at a pine tree, sees if it will cut good lumber, dabs a mark or a number upon it, and goes his way absolutely without further thought or feeling? Is he truer to life? Is it truer to life to insulate oneself entirely from the influence of the tree's life, and to walk about in an inanimate forest of standing lumber, marketable in St. Louis, Mo.? Or is it truer to life to know, with a pantheistic sensuality, that the tree has its own life, its own assertive existence, its own living relatedness to me: that my life is added to, or militated against, by the tree's life?

Which is really truer?

Which is truer, to live among the living, or to run on wheels?

And who can sit with the Indians around a big campfire of logs, in the mountains at night, when a man rises and turns his breast and his curiously smiling bronze face away from the blaze, and stands voluptuously warming his thighs and buttocks and loins, his back to the fire, faintly smiling the inscrutable Pan-smile into the dark trees surrounding, without hearing him say, in the Pan-voice: "Aha! Tree! Aha!

Tree! Who has triumphed now? I drank the heat of your blood into my face and breast, and now I am drinking it into my loins and buttocks and legs, oh tree! I am drinking your heat right through me, oh tree! Fire is life, and I take your life for mine. I am drinking it up, oh tree, even into my buttocks. Aha! Tree! I am warm! I am strong! I am happy, tree, in this cold night in the mountains!''

And the old man, glancing up and seeing the flames flapping in flamy rags at the dark smoke, in the upper fire-hurry towards the stars and the dark spaces between the stars, sits stonily and inscrutably: yet one knows that he is saying: "Go back, oh fire! Go back like honey! Go back, honey of life, to where you came from, before you were hidden in the tree. The trees climb into the sky and steal the honey of the sun, like bears stealing from a hollow tree-trunk. But when the tree falls and is put on to the fire, the honey flames and goes straight back to where it came from. And the smell of burning pine is as the smell of honey.''

So the old man says, with his lightless Indian eyes. But he is careful never to utter one word of the mystery. Speech is the death of Pan, who can but laugh and sound the reed-flute.

Is it better, I ask you, to cross the room and turn on the heat at the radiator, glancing at the thermometer and saying: "We're just a bit below the level, in here"? Then to go back to the newspaper!

What can a man do with his life but live it? And what does life consist in, save a vivid relatedness between the man and the living universe that surrounds him? Yet man insulates himself more and more into mechanism, and repudiates everything but the machine and the contrivance of which he himself is master, god in the machine.

Morning comes, and white ash lies in the fire-hollow, and the old man looks at it broodingly.

"The fire is gone," he says in the Pan silence, that is so full of unutterable things. "Look! there is no more tree. We drank his warmth, and he is gone. He is way, way off in the sky, his smoke is in the blueness, with the sweet smell of a pine-wood fire, and his yellow flame is in the sun. It is morning, with the ashes of night. There is no more tree. Tree is gone. But perhaps there is fire among the ashes. I shall blow it, and it will be alive. There is always fire, between the tree that goes and the tree that stays. One day I shall go—''

So they cook their meat, and rise, and go in silence.

There is a big rock towering up above the trees, a cliff. And silently a man glances at it. You hear him say, without speech:

"Oh, you big rock! If a man fall down from you, he dies. Don't let me fall down from you. Oh, you big pale rock, you are so still, you know lots of things. You know a lot. Help me, then, with your stillness. I go to find deer. Help me find deer.''

And the man slips aside, and secretly lays a twig, or a pebble, some little object in a niche of the rock, as a pact between him and the rock. The rock will give him some of its radiant-cold stillness and enduring presence, and he makes a symbolic return, of gratitude.

Is it foolish? Would it have been better to invent a gun, to shoot his game from a great distance, so that he need not approach it with any of that living stealth and preparedness with which one live thing approaches another? Is it better to have a machine in one's hands, and so avoid the life-contact: the trouble! the pains! Is it better to see the rock as a mere nothing, not worth noticing because it has no value, and you can't eat it as you can a deer?

But the old hunter steals on, in the stillness of the eternal Pan, which is so full of soundless sounds. And in his soul he is saying: "Deer! Oh, you thin-legged deer! I am coming! Where are you, with your feet like little stones bounding down a hill? I know you. Yes, I know you. But you don't know me. You don't know where I am, and you don't know me, anyhow. But I know you. I am thinking of you. I shall get you. I've got to get you. I got to; so it will be.—I shall get you, and shoot an arrow right in you."

In this state of abstraction, and subtle, hunter's communion with the quarry—a weird psychic connexion between hunter and hunted—the man creeps into the mountains.

And even a white man who is a born hunter must fall into this state. Gun or no gun! He projects his deepest, most primitive hunter's consciousness abroad; and finds his game, not by accident, nor even chiefly by looking for signs, but primarily by a psychic attraction, a sort of telepathy: the hunter's telepathy. Then when he finds his quarry, he aims with a pure, spellbound volition. If there is no flaw in his abstracted huntsman's *will,* he cannot miss. Arrow or bullet, it flies like a movement of pure will, straight to the spot. And the deer, once she has let her quivering alertness be overmastered or stilled by the hunter's subtle, hypnotic, *following* spell, she cannot escape.

This is Pan, the Pan-mystery, the Pan-power. What can men who sit at home in their studies, and drink hot milk and have lamb's-wool slippers on their feet, and write anthropology, what *can* they possibly know about men, the men of Pan?

Among the creatures of Pan there is an eternal struggle for life, between lives. Man, defenceless, rapacious man, has needed the qualities of every living thing, at one time or other. The hard, silent abidingness of rock, the surging resistance of a tree, the still evasion of a puma, the dogged earth-knowledge of the bear, the light alertness of the deer, the sky-prowling vision of the eagle: turn by turn man has needed the power of every living thing. Tree, stone, or hill, river, or little stream, or waterfall, or salmon in the fall—man can be master and complete in himself, only by assuming the living powers of each of them, as the occasion requires.

He used to make himself master by a great effort of will, and sensitive, intuitive cunning, and immense labour of body.

Then he discovered the "idea." He found that all things were related by certain *laws.* The moment man learned to abstract, he began to make engines that would do the work of his body. So, instead of concentrating upon his quarry, or upon the living things which made his universe, he concentrated upon the engines or instruments which should intervene between him and the living universe, and give him mastery.

This was the death of the great Pan. The idea and the engine came between man and all things, like a death. The old connexion, the old Allness, was severed, and can never be ideally restored. Great Pan is dead.

Yet what do we live for, except to live? Man has lived to conquer the phenomenal universe. To a great extent he has succeeded. With all the mechanism of the human world, man is to a great extent master of all life, and of most phenomena.

And what then? Once you have conquered a thing, you have lost it. Its real relation to you collapses.

A conquered world is no good to man. He sits stupefied with boredom upon his conquest.

We need the universe to live again, so that we can live with it. A conquered universe, a dead Pan, leaves us nothing to live with.

You have to abandon the conquest, before Pan will live again. You have to live to live, not to conquer. What's the good of conquering even the North Pole, if after the conquest you've nothing left but an inert fact? Better leave it a mystery.

It was better to be a hunter in the woods of Pan, than it is to be a clerk in a city store. The hunter hungered, laboured, suffered tortures of fatigue. But at least he lived in a ceaseless living relation to his surrounding universe.

At evening, when the deer was killed, he went home to the tents, and threw down the deer-meat on the swept place before the tent of his women. And the women came out to greet him softly, with a sort of reverence, as he stood before the meat, the life-stuff. He came back spent, yet full of power, bringing the life-stuff. And the children looked with black eyes at the meat, and at that wonder-being, the man, the bringer of meat.

Perhaps the children of the store-clerk look at their father with a *tiny* bit of the same mystery. And perhaps the clerk feels a fragment of the old glorification, when he hands his wife the paper dollars.

But about the tents the women move silently. Then when the cooking-fire dies low, the man crouches in silence and toasts meat on a stick, while the dogs lurk round like shadows and the children watch avidly. The man eats as the sun goes down. And as the glitter departs, he says: "Lo, the sun is going, and I stay. All goes, but still I stay. Power of deer-meat is in my belly, power of sun is in my body. I am tired, but it is with power. There the small moon gives her first sharp sign. So! So! I watch her. I will give her something; she is very sharp and bright, and I do not know her power. Lo! I will give the woman something for this moon, which troubles me above the sunset, and has power. Lo! how very curved and sharp she is! Lo! how she troubles me!"

Thus, always aware, always watchful, subtly poising himself in the world of Pan, among the power of the living universe, he sustains his life and is sustained. There is no boredom, because *everything* is alive and active, and danger is inherent in all movement. The contact between all things is keen and wary: for wariness is also a sort of reverence, or respect. And nothing, in the world of Pan, may be taken for granted.

So when the fire is extinguished, and the moon sinks, the man says to the woman: "Oh, woman, be very soft, be very soft and deep towards me, with the deep silence. Oh, woman, do not speak and stir and wound me with the sharp horns of yourself. Let me come into the deep, soft places, the dark, soft places deep as between the stars. Oh, let me lose there the weariness of the day: let me come in the power of the night. Oh, do not speak to me, nor break the deep night of my silence and my power. Be softer than dust, and darker than any flower. Oh, woman, wonderful is the craft of your softness, the distance of your dark depths. Oh, open silently the deep that has no end, and do not turn the horns of the moon against me."

This is the might of Pan, and the power of Pan.

And still, in America, among the Indians, the oldest Pan is alive. But here, also, dying fast.

It is useless to glorify the savage. For he will kill Pan with his own hands, for the sake of a motor-car. And a bored savage, for whom Pan is dead, is the stupefied image of all boredom.

And we cannot return to the primitive life, to live in tepees and hunt with bows and arrows.

Yet live we must. And once life has been conquered, it is pretty difficult to live. What are we going to do, with a conquered universe? The Pan relationship, which the world of man once had with all the world, was better than anything man has now. The savage, today, if you give him the chance, will become more mechanical and unliving than any civilized man. But civilized man, having conquered the universe, may as well leave off bossing it. Because when all is said and done, life itself consists in a live relatedness between man and his universe: sun, moon, stars, earth, trees, flowers, birds, animals, men, everything—and not in a "conquest" of anything by anything. Even the conquest of the air makes the world smaller, tighter, and more airless.

And whether we are a store-clerk or a bus-conductor, we can still choose between the living universe of Pan, and the mechanical conquered universe of modern humanity. The machine has no windows. But even the most mechanized human being has only got his windows nailed up, or bricked in.

Plight of the Ik and Kaiadilt is Seen as A Chilling Possible End for Man

John B. Calhoun

The Mountain—how pervasive in the history of man. A still small voice on Horeb, mount of God, guided Elijah. There, earlier, Moses standing before God received the Word. And Zion: "I am the Lord your God dwelling in Zion, my holy mountain."

Then there was Atum, mountain, God and first man, one and all together. The mountain rose out of a primordial sea of nothingness—Nun. Atum, the spirit of life, existed within Nun. In creating himself, Atum became the evolving ancestor of the human race. So goes the Egyptian mythology of creation, in which the Judaic Adam has his roots.

And there is a last Atum, united in his youth with another mountain of God, Mt. Morungole in northeasternmost Uganda. His people are the Ik, pronounced eek. They are the subject of an important new book, *The Mountain People,* by Colin M. Turnbull. They still speak Middle-Kingdom Egyptian, a language thought to be dead. But perhaps their persistence is not so strange. Egyptian mythology held that the waters of the life-giving Nile had their origin in Nun. Could this Nun have been the much more extensive Lake Victoria of 40 to 50 millennia ago when, near its borders, man groped upward to cloak his biological self with culture?

Well might the Ik have preserved the essence of this ancient tradition that affirms human beginnings. Isolated as they have been in their jagged mountain fastness, near the upper tributaries of the White Nile, the Ik have been protected from cultural evolution.

What a Shangri-la, this land of the Ik. In its center, the Kidepo valley, 35 miles across, home of abundant game; to the south, mist-topped Mt. Morungole; to the west the Niangea range; to the north, bordering the Sudan, the Didinga range; to the east on the Kenya border, a sheer drop of 2,000 feet into the Turkanaland of cattle herdsmen. Through ages of dawning history few people must have been interested in encroaching on this rugged land. Until 1964 anthropologists knew little of the Ik's existence. Their very name, much less their language, remained a mystery until, quite by chance, anthropologist Colin M. Turnbull found himself among them. What an opportunity to study pristine man! Here one should encounter the basic qualities of humanity unmarred by war, technology, pollution, over-population.

Turnbull rested in his bright red Land Rover at an 8,000-foot-high pass. A bit beyond this only "navigable" pass into the Kidepo Valley lay Pirre, a police outpost watching over a cluster of Ik villages. There to welcome him came Atum of the warm, open smile and gentle voice. Gray-haired at 40, appearing 65, he was the senior elder of the Ik, senior in authority if not quite so in age. Nattily attired in shorts and woolen sweater—in contrast to his mostly naked colleagues—Atum bounced forward with his ebony walking stick, greeted Turnbull in Swahili, and from that moment on took command as best he could of Turnbull's life. At Atum's village a plaintive woman's voice called out. Atum remarked that that was his wife—sick, too weak to work in the fields. Turnbull offered to bring her food and medicine. Atum suggested he handle Turnbull's gifts. As the weeks wore on Atum picked up the parcels that Turnbull was supplying for Atum's wife.

One day Autm's brother-in-law, Lomongin, laughingly asked Turnbull if he didn't know that Atum's wife had been dead for weeks. She had received no food or medicine. Atum had sold it. So she just died. All of this was revealed with no embarrassment. Atum joined the laughter over the joke played on Turnbull.

Another time Atum and Lojieri were guiding Turnbull over the mountains, and at one point induced him to push ahead through high grass until he broke through into a clearing. The clearing was a sheer 1,500-foot drop. The two Iks rolled on the ground, nearly bursting with laughter because Turnbull just managed to catch himself. What a lovable cherub this Atum! His laughter never ended.

New Meaning of Laughter

Laughter, hallmark of mankind, not shared with any other animal, not even primates, was an outstanding trait of the Ik. A whole village rushed to the edge of a low cliff and joined in communal laughter at blind old Lo'ono who lay thrashing on her back, near death after stumbling over. One evening Iks around a fire watched a child as it crawled toward the flames, then writhed back screaming after it grasped a gleaming coal. Laughter erupted. Quiet came to the child as its mother cuddled it in a kind of respect for the merriment it had caused. Then there was the laughter of innocent childhood as boys and girls gathered around a grandfather, too weak to walk, and drummed upon his head with sticks or pelted him with stones until he cried. There was the laughter that binds families together: Kimat, shrieking for joy as she dashed off with the mug of tea she had snatched from her dying brother Lomeja's hand an instant after Turnbull had given it to him as a last token of their friendship.

Laughter there had always been. A few old people remembered times, 25 to 30 years ago, when laughter mirrored love and joy and fullness of life, times when beliefs and rituals and traditions kept a bond with the "millions of years" ago when time began for the Ik. That was when their god, Didigwari, let the Ik down from heaven on a vine, one at a time. He gave them the digging stick with the instruction that they could not kill one another. He let down other people. To the Dodos and Turkana he gave cattle and spears to kill with. But the Ik remained true to their instruction and did not kill one another or neighboring tribesmen.

For them the bow, the net and the pitfall were for capturing game. For them the greatest sin was to overhunt. Mobility and cooperation ever were part of them. Often the netting of game required the collaboration of a whole band of 100 or more, some to hold the net and some to drive game into it. Between the big hunts, bands broke up into smaller groups to spread over their domain, then to gather again. The several bands would each settle for the best part of the year along the edge of the Kidepo Valley in the foothills of Mt. Morungole. There they were once again fully one with the mountain. "The Ik, without their mountains, would no longer be the Ik and similarly, they say, the mountains without the Ik would no longer be the same mountains, if indeed they continued to exist at all."

In this unity of people and place, rituals, traditions, beliefs and values molded and preserved a continuity of life. All rites of passage were marked by ceremony. Of these, the rituals surrounding death gave greatest meaning to life. Folded in a fetal position, the body was buried with favorite possessions, facing the rising sun to mark celestial rebirth. All accompanying rituals of fasting and feasting, of libations of beer sprinkled over the grave, of seeds of favorite foods planted on the grave to draw life from the dust of the dead, showed that death is merely another form of life, and reminded the living of the good things of life and of the good way to live. In so honoring the dead by creating goodness the Ik helped speed the soul, content, on its journey.

Such were the Ik until wildlife conservation intruded into their homeland. Uganda decided to make a national park out of the Kidepo Valley, the main hunting ground of the Ik. What then happened stands as an indictment of the myopia that science can generate. No one looked to the Ik to note that their hunter-gatherer way of life marked the epitome of conservation, that the continuance of their way of life would have added to the success of the park. Instead they were forbidden to hunt any longer in the Kidepo Valley. They were herded to the periphery of the park and encouraged to become farmers on dry mountain slopes so steep as to test the poise of a goat. As an example to the more remote villages, a number of villages were brought together in a tight little cluster below the southwest pass into the valley. Here the police post, which formed this settlement of Pirre, could watch over the Ik to see that they didn't revert to hunting.

These events contained two of the three strikes that knocked out the spirit of the Ik. *Strike No. 1:* The shift from a mobile hunter-gatherer way of life to a sedentary farming way of life made irrelevant the Ik's entire repertoire of beliefs, habits and traditions. Their guidelines for life were inappropriate to farming. They seemed to adapt, but at heart they remained hunters and gatherers. Their cultural templates fitted them for that one way of life.

Strike No. 2: They were suddenly crowded together at a density, intimacy and frequency of contact far greater than they had ever before been required to experience. Throughout their long past each band of 100 or so individuals only temporarily coalesced into a whole. The intervening breaking up into smaller groups permitted realignment of relationships that tempered conflicts from earlier associations. But at the resettlement, more than 450 individuals were forced to form a permanent cluster of villages within shouting distance of each other. Suppose the seven million or so inhabitants of Los Angeles County were forced to move and join the more than one million inhabitants of the more arid San Diego County. Then after they arrived all water, land and air communication to the rest of the world was cut off abruptly and completely. These eight million people would then have to seek survival completely on local resources without any communication with others. It would be a test of the ability of human beings to remain human.

Such a test is what Dr. Turnbull's book on the Mountain People is all about. The Ik failed to remain human. I have put mice to the same test and they failed to remain mice. Those of you who have been following SMITHSONIAN may recall from the April 1970 and the January 1971 issues something about the projected demise of a mouse population experiencing the same two strikes against it as did the Ik.

Fate of a Mouse Population

Last summer I spoke in London behind the lectern where Charles Darwin and Alfred Wallace had presented their papers on evolution—which during the next century caused a complete revision of our insight into what life is all about and what man is and may become. In summing up that session of 1858 the president remarked that nothing of importance had been presented before the Linnean Society at that year's meeting! I spoke behind this same lectern to a session of the Royal Society of Medicine during its symposium on "Man in His Place." At the end of my paper, "Death Squared: The Explosive Growth and Demise of a Mouse Population," the chairman admonished me to stick to my mice; the insights I had presented could have no implication for man. Wonderful if the chairman could be correct—but now I have read about the Mountain People, and I have a hollow feeling that perhaps we, too, are close to losing our "mountain."

Turnbull lived for 18 months as a member of the Ik tribe. His identity transfer became so strong that he acquired the Ik laughter. He laughed at seeing Atum suffer as they were completing an extremely arduous journey on foot back across the mountains and the Kidepo Valley from the Sudan. He felt pleasure at seeing Lokwam, local "Lord of the Flies," cry in agony from the beating given him by his two beautiful sisters.

Well, for five years I have identified with my mice, as they lived in their own "Kidepo Valley"—their contrived Utopia where resources are always abundant and all mortality factors except aging eliminated. I watched their population grow rapidly from the first few colonizers. I watched them fill their metal "universe" with organized social groups. I watched them bring up a host of young with loving maternal care and paternal territorial protection—all of these young well educated for mouse society. But then there were too many of these young mice, ready to become involved in all that mice can become, with nowhere to go, no physical escape from their closed environment, no opportunity to gain a niche where they could play a meaningful role. They tried, but being younger and less experienced they were nearly always rejected.

Rejecting so many of these probing youngsters overtaxed the territorial males. So defense then fell to lactating females. They became aggressive. They turned against their own young and ejected them before normal weaning and before adequate social bonds between mother and young had developed. During this time of social tension, rate of growth of the population was only one third of that during the earlier, more favorable phase.

Strike No. 1 against these mice: They lost the opportunity to express the capacities developed by older mice born during the rapid population growth. After a while they became so rejected that they were treated as so many sticks and stones by their still relatively well-adjusted elders. These rejected mice withdrew, physically and psychologically, to live packed tightly together in large pools. Amongst themselves they became vicious, lashing out and biting each other now and then with hardly any provocation.

Strike No. 2 against the mice: They reached great numbers despite reduced conceptions and increased deaths of newborn young resulting from the dissolution of maternal care. Many had early been rejected by their mothers and knew little about social bonds. Often their later attempts at interaction were interrupted by some other mouse intervening unintentionally as it passed between two potential actors.

I came to call such mice the "Beautiful Ones." They never learned such effective social interactions as courtship, mating and aggressive defense of territory. Never copulating, never fighting, they were unstressed and essentially unaware of their associates. They spent their time grooming themselves, eating and sleeping, totally individualistic, totally isolated socially except for a peculiar acquired need for simple proximity to others. This produced what I have called the "behavioral sink," the continual accentuation of aggregations to the point that much available space was unused despite a population increase to nearly 15 times the optimum.

All true "mousity" was lost. Though physically they still appeared to be mice, they had no essential capacities for survival and continuation of mouse society. Suddenly, population growth ceased. In what seemed an instant they passed over a threshold beyond which there was no likelihood of their ever recouping the capacity to become real mice again. No more young were born. From a peak population of 2,200 mice nearly three years ago, aging has gradually taken its toll until now there are only 46 sluggish near-cadavers comparable to people more than 100 years old.

It was just such a fading universe Colin Turnbull found in 1964. Just before he arrived, *Strike No. 3* had set in: starvation. Any such crisis could have added the coup de grace after the other two strikes. Normally the Ik could count on only making three crops every four years. At this time a two-year drought set in and destroyed almost all crops. Neighboring tribes survived with their cultures intact. Turkana herdsmen, facing starvation and death, kept their societies in contact with each other and continued to sing songs of praise to God for the goodness of life.

By the beginning of the long drought, ''goodness'' to the Ik simply meant to have food—to have food for one's self alone. Collaborative hunts were a thing of the past, long since stopped by the police and probably no longer possible as a social effort, anyway. Solitary hunting, now designated as poaching, became a necessity for sheer survival. But the solitary hunter took every precaution not to let others know of his success. He would gorge himself far off in the bush and bring the surplus back to sell to the police, who were not above profiting from this traffic. Withholding food from wife, children and aging parents became an accomplishment to brag and laugh about. It became a way of life, continuing after the government began providing famine relief. Those strong enough to go to the police station to get rations for themselves and their families would stop halfway home and gorge all the food, even though it caused them to vomit.

Village of Mutual Hatred

The village reflected this reversal of humanity. Instead of open courtyards around each group of huts within the large compound, there was a maze of walls and tunnels booby trapped with spears to ward off intrusion by neighbors.

In Atum's village a whole band of more than 100 individuals was crowded together in mutual hostility and aloneness. They would gather at their sitting place and sit for hours in a kind of suspended animation, not looking directly at each other, yet scanning slowly all others who might be engaged in some solitary task, watching for someone to make a mistake that would elicit the symbolic violence of laughter and derision. They resembled my pools of rejected withdrawn mice. Homemaking deteriorated, feces littered doorsteps and courtyard. Universal adultery and incest replaced the old taboo. The beaded virgins' aprons of eight-to-twelve-year-old girls became symbols that these were proficient whores accustomed to selling their wares to passing herdsmen.

One ray of humanity left in this cesspool was 12-year-old, retarded Adupa. Because she believed that food was for sharing and savoring, her playmates beat her. She still believed that parents were for loving and to be loved by. They cured her madness by locking her in her hut until she died and decayed.

The six other villages were smaller and their people could retain a few glimmers of the goodness and fullness of life. There was Kuaur, devoted to Turnbull, hiking four days to deliver mail, taunted for bringing food home to share with his wife and child. There was Losiké, the potter, regarded as a witch. She offered water to visitors and made pots for others. When the famine got so bad that there was no need for pots to cook in, her husband left her. She was no longer bringing in any income. And then there was old Nangoli, still capable of mourning when her husband died. She went with her family and village across Kidepo and into the Sudan where their village life turned for a while back to normality. But it was not normal enough to keep them. Back to Pirre, to death, they returned.

All goodness was gone from the Ik; leaving merely emptiness, valuelessness, nothingness, the chaos of Nun. They reentered the womb of beginning time from which there is no return. Urination beside the partial graves of the dead marked the death of God, the final fading of Mount Morungole.

My poor words give only a shadowy image of the cold coffin of Ik humanity that Turnbull describes. His two years with the Ik left him in a slough of despondency from which he only extricated himself with difficulty, never wanting to see them again. Time and distance brought him comfort. He did return for a brief visit some months later. Rain had come in abundance. Gardens had sprung up untended from hidden seeds in the earth. Each Ik gleaned only for his immediate needs. Granaries stood empty, not refilled for inevitable scarcities ahead. The future had ceased to exist. Individual and social decay continued on its downward spiral. Sadly Turnbull departed again from this land of lost hope and faith.

Last summer in London I knew nothing about the Ik when I was so publicly and thoroughly chastised for having the temerity to suspect that the behavioral and spiritual death my mice had exhibited might also befall man. But a psychiatrist in the audience arose in defense of my suspicion. Dr. Geoffrey N. Bianchi remarked that an isolated tribe of Australian Aborigines mirrored the changes and kinds of pathology I had among mice. I did not know that Dr. Bianchi was a member of the team that had studied these people, the Kaiadilt, and that a book about them was in preparation, *Cruel, Poor and Brutal Nations* by John Cawte (The University Press of Hawaii). In galley proof I have read about the Kaiadilt and find it so shattering to my faith in humanity that I now sometimes wish I had never heard of it. Yet there is some glimmer of hope that the Kaiadilt may recover—not what they were but possibly some new life.

A frail, tenacious people, the Kaiadilt never numbered more than 150 souls where they lived on Bentinck Island in the Gulf of Carpentaria. So isolated were they that not even their nearest Aboriginal neighbors, 20 miles away, had any knowledge of their existence until in this century; so isolated were the Kaiadilt from their nearest neighbors that they differ from them in such heredity markers as blood type and fingerprints. Not until the early years of this century did an occasional visitor from the Queensland Government even note their existence.

For all practical purposes the first real contact the Kaiadilt had with Western "culture" came in 1916 when a man by the name of McKenzie came to Bentinck with a group of male mainland Aborigines to try to establish a lime kiln. McKenzie's favorite sport was to ride about shooting Kaiadilt. His helpers' sport was to commandeer as many women as they could, and take them to their headquarters on a neighboring island. In 1948 a tidal wave poisoned most of the fresh-water sources. Small groups of Kaiadilt were rounded up and transported to larger Mornington Island where they were placed under the supervision of a Presbyterian mission. They were crowded into a dense cluster settlement just as the Ik had been at Pirre.

Here they still existed when the psychiatric field team came into their midst 15 years later. They were much like the Ik: dissolution of family life, total valuelessness, apathy. I could find no mention of laughter, normal or pathological. Perhaps the Kaiadilt didn't laugh. They had essentially ceased the singing that had been so much a part of their traditional way.

The spiritual decay of the Kaiadilt was marked by withdrawal, depression, suicide and tendency to engage in such self-mutilation as ripping one's testes or chopping off one's nose. In their passiveness some of the anxiety ridden children are accepting the new mold of life forced upon them by a benevolent culture they do not understand. Survival with a new mold totally obliterating all past seems their only hope.

So the lesson comes clear, and Colin Turnbull sums it up in the final paragraph of his book:

The Ik teach us that our much vaunted human values are not inherent in humanity at all, but are associated only with a particular form of survival called society, and that all, even society itself, are luxuries that can be dispensed with. That does not make them any the less wonderful or desirable, and if man has any greatness it is surely in his ability to maintain these values, clinging to them to an often very bitter end, even shortening an already pitifully short life rather than sacrifice his humanity. But that too involves choice, and the Ik teach us that man can lose the will to make it.

From Commodity to Community: Restoring the Soul of a De-sacralized Nature

The Role of the Humanities in Environmental Education

Carl P. Swanson

It is probably presumptuous for one trained in the biological sciences to discuss the role of the humanities in environmental education, but chances are it would be at least as presumptuous for a humanist to discuss the role of the environment in humanistic education. Be that as it may, I take some courage from the fact that what efforts have been made in the past to merge the scientific and humanistic aspects of man's endeavors, and with which I am familiar, are those that have been made by biological scientists: Julian Huxley (1964) has put his thoughts in terms of an evolutionary humanism, René Dubos (1965) has advanced the cause of humanistic biology, Van R. Potter (1971) speaks of bioethics, while Dobzhansky (1967) describes what he calls the biology of ultimate concern. The books and articles of Garrett Hardin are also threaded throughout with ethical and social implications, while the ethological writings of Lorenz, Tinbergen, and von Fritsch are gradually being interpreted in broader contexts, with the behavioral characteristics and idiosyncracies of gulls, fish, greylag geese, and bees being carried over into the realm of man, sometimes within a meaningful context, sometimes with unfounded enthusiasm and accompanying distortion. The insights of these writers, sharing commonalities within their individualistic presentations, do not offer any ultimate view of man, but we can today ignore their implications only to our own detriment.

I will not attempt to emulate these biologists, nor will I attempt to coin a well-turned phrase to describe what it is that I want to say; rather I would point out that just as there is a web of life in the biological realm, with every strand in the web connected directly or indirectly with every other strand and through which a flow of energy passes, so, too, is there a web of thought, experience, and action which, at any given point in time, is a reflection of the intellectual temper and accomplishments of that age, and which also determines man's relation to his environment and, consequently, his behavior and his outlook. Man, the value-forming and value-guided animal, is the central element in this web; the web changes with each age, as new discoveries, new ideas, new technology, and new ways of apprehending reality make their appearance and exert their effect. Through and along the strands of this web the intellectual, emotional, and societal energies ebb and flow, to mix and blend and emerge in new shapes, to be converted into other forms, and to produce new and often surprising effects. It is by being aware of, understanding, and making use of these energies that we can reassess and reshape the past in order to make better use of it in the present, and—hopefully—to mold the future to our needs as human beings.

Man—the Central Element

When thinking about the Humanities, spelled with a capital H, one intuitively thinks of the arts, language and literature, philosophy and some aspects of history—all familiar academic disciplines, segregated and compartmentalized in the several departments of our colleges and universities. It is from these disciplines that students generally gain an initial comprehension of aesthetics and ethics in a formal sense, acquire a sense of historical perspective, and begin to see man, both in a generic and an individual sense, living out his life in a thousand different ways. But whether the content and the manner of what is taught by the practitioners of these disciplines has meaning to education in general and to environmental education in particular, is as problematic and uncertain as it is in the sciences and engineering. As a casual perusal of humanistic journals will reveal, the so-called humanists can be as narrow, parochial, and unintelligible in their specialities as the most myopic of scientists. As the philosopher Ernst Nagel has somewhere said, "the capacity for making contributions to moral enlightment is not uniformly distributed," and, it might be added, neither is it limited to subject matter.

I would, therefore, shift my definition of the humanities by going from an upper to a lower case h, and embrace all of the disciplines, including the sciences and the practical arts which are approached in a humanistic manner; that is, which keep man as the central element in the web of history, and which give and always have given to man a sense of continuity, of individual worth and dignity, of animal antecedents as well as the heights of human achievement. If the humanities, including the sciences, can give us that, we need ask no more of them. The inner, private, and subjective world of the humanist can be (and all too frequently is) disjoined from the external, public, and objectified reality of the scientist, but only at a loss to both.

The several areas of learning were not always thus disjoined from each other, and once, in fact, were comfortably embraced within the designation "natural philosophy," a term which lost its meaning as the fragmentation of the disciplines took place in the 19th and 20th centuries. If we but scan the pages of the recent past we find that as the techniques and instruments for measurement and quantification became more and more perfected, and as the questions asked of nature and of man became more narrowly conceived, more sharply defined, and hence more readily answerable, the scholarly disciplines—particularly the sciences—have either dropped man out of the picture in order to bring accuracy and objectivity in, or have given him a universal but nameless face pieced together from computer cards, statistical tables, and projection graphs.

The individual man—and who among us is not an individual?—is lost in the process, and the unmeasurable qualities of man, his search for individual meaning and dignity, his value systems, his love for life itself and for beauty, form, and proportion—in a word, his human as opposed to his animal qualities—have been pushed aside to be handled as best they can be by the poet, the priest, or the philosopher, or they have been appropriated by the psychiatrist, to be dissected at times beyond recognition. Possibly this is the only way by which the burgeoning mass of humanity and its complex of problems can be handled and analyzed, but there can be little doubt that the leveling force of anonymity has been shattering.

What has all of this to do with environmental education? Very simply, I believe the question to be central and fundamental. Environmental problems arise because man is somewhere in the picture, and they must be defined in terms of man. When man makes use of an environment to maintain or improve his way of life, he does so within a system of ideas which reflects his attitude toward nature and himself. An environmental crisis is therefore a crisis of the human spirit, a crisis that arose because some judgmental facet of our rational, emotional, ethical, or moral being led to a past action, the consequences of which we are only now beginning to understand and to comprehend in terms of future restraints.

Every stable culture has its values that provide it with a sense of purpose, but the situation in which we find ourselves today suggests that the web of thought that can bind us together and help us to direct our activities wisely as human beings, that can enable us—individually and collectively—to reach full human potential in a congenial and sustaining environment, has been seriously distorted. The warning signals of impending danger that traverse the strands of the web have not been intercepted, or if intercepted, have been either misinterpreted or ignored. We are, of course, ringed about by things and experiences which have much to do with how we view the world about us, and external events over which we have no control—as well as those for which we are ourselves responsible—introduce discontinuties into the tenor of our ways, with the result that we come to view the past, the present, and the uncertain future not so much as a continuum of human endeavor as a series of ad hoc events unrelated to each other. Our lives become similarly episodic and fragmented, lacking the cohesiveness that provides us with a sense of shared goals and common ideals.

Ecology of the Human Spirit

In these days dominated by the brilliance, pervasiveness, and, oftentimes, perverseness of science and technology, man has been removed from the center of the web and replaced by something that we can define only with difficulty, but a "something" that has its own built-in autonomy and accelerator. This fact, we need to recognize, is one of the most insidious causes of environmental alteration. It is a displacement that, for the great masses of men, leaves little room for the sensibilities and sensitivities of the individual human spirit, and we find ourselves as ethical animals in a world that we have come to recognize possesses no ethical element of its own to comfort us. Thrown inward upon ourselves, we have now come to realize our dilemma. Overwhelmed by the rapidity and magnitude of intellectual and material change brought on by science and technology, we find that the stabilizing myths, the social structures, and the innermost and transcendent experiences of men of all ages are not sufficient to enable us to comprehend and to adjust to the kaleidoscopic and shifting scenes around us.

Change, of course, has always been one of the most difficult of phenomena to grasp and to manage. Our universities and our systems of religion, law, and government were once the great stabilizing forces of society, capable of modulating change and keeping it within human dimensions of manageability. Today they seem no longer equal to the task. The greatness that is man in his finer moments is lost in a vortex of fear and despair, rather than serving as a source of comfort, inspiration, and guidance. Granted that we can never be wholly prepared for that which is new (a circumstance which will arise more and more frequently as we move from a state of abundance and affluence into an economy of shortages), we nevertheless need to face the fact that every environmental crisis confronting us today stems from a value judgment made in the past—whether made consciously or unconsciously, whether made with all good intentions for all men or from a narrow parochial and partisan base.

I once heard a dean of an engineering school describe all environmental problems as engineering problems. Needless to say, I do not agree, for I believe that every environmental problem is, first and foremost, a problem of values; all other aspects are secondary. No one with any understanding of the significance of science and technology would deny that they are of central importance in helping us to solve many of our environmental problems; but the decisions as to the option to be selected, the direction in which to proceed, and the consequences of any action taken are fundamentally value judgments related to what we as human beings want out of life within the constraints imposed upon us by external considerations. It is our system of human values that is in need of reexamination far more than the ad hoc solution of any particular environmental problem. We need to understand the ecology of the human spirit as well as the ecology of the environment.

In times past, our several cultures included the shaman. He was, in a sense, a single-minded individual capable of blending the natural and the spiritual into a single encompassing entity and of carrying an individual or a culture through periods of crisis. Today, bereft of the gods who would sustain us, and lacking shamanistic intermediaries in whom we place our trust, we face an uncertain future with apprehension and foreboding. As we look into the mirror of the future, we see only ourselves, and we sense, as never before, our aloneness and our vulnerability.

The Price of Cultural Successes

There is little argument over the fact that man's animal needs of sustenance, protection, and propagation must be met before the human qualities of man can be nourished. As one humanist has pointed out, man must learn to "weave a coat before he makes a tapestry . . .he must learn the plain ways of communication before he writes a poem'' (Allen 1959). But man needs more than the animal requisites for the continuation of his cultures. He needs an inner as well as an outer world of reality. This need finds expression in the varied mythologies and arts of the world on the one hand, and in the structure, discoveries, and applications of science on the other. Man is also a creature of action in the pursuit of his cultural ways, an action that has put a greater and greater premium on the use of extrasomatic sources of energy and of the material resources of the environment.

We now recognize that our cultural successes have their costs as well as their benefits; the price we now pay is high, and presumably will mount higher in the years to come. The late 19th-century America saw the emergence of social Darwinism, an economic atrocity committed by man against man and justified in the name of evolution. Today we hear less of the philosophy and rhetoric of Darwinian individualism, but a collective or institutional Darwinism has sprung up in its stead, leading to a wholesale change in, or destruction of, the environment instead of an obvious exploitation of the masses (although in the final analysis it is always the masses of men who are the victims). Perhaps I can make my point more clearly by quoting a passage from Stephen Crane, author of *The Red Badge of Courage,* who wrote in the tradition of naturalism around the turn of the century. The passage is taken somewhat out of context, but not too much so. In Crane's short story, *The Blue Hotel* (in Stallman 1952), his main character was the Swede, searching for identity and recognition in a purposeless and deterministic world. The Swede was eventually and pointlessly killed in a poker game, and as Crane described the scene ''The corpse of the Swede, alone in the saloon, had its eyes fixed upon a dreadful legend that dwelt atop of the cash-machine: 'This registers the amount of your purchase.' ''

As environmental educators we have our eyes fixed on the cash-machine of the world, and we share with the dead Swede the difficulty of reading the purchase price of our way of life. We only know that the machine continues to ring up our purchases, and that the price increases as the resources of the environment are being constantly drained to scarcity levels. What is not so readily obvious is that, in the end, the purchase price must also include the cost of the impoverishment of the spirit, although we have no real way of ascertaining a quantitative figure for this side of the ledger.

Eric Hofer, I realize quite fully, would disagree with me. He sees nature as the enemy to be subdued if we are to know the full meaning of human freedom, and he equates that freedom with the feeling of having his feet on a paved road. ''If this nation declines and decays,'' he points out, ''it will be not because we have raped and ravaged a continent, but because we do not know how to build and maintain viable cities. America's destiny will be decided in the cities'' (Hofer 1971). And again, ''So true is it that the city is man's optimal creative milieu that even communion with the self is more attainable in the press and noise of the city than in the silence of the great outdoors. There is no genuine solitude outside the city.'' My own sympathies place me closer to the position expressed by Henry Beston, author of *Outermost House.* ''Nature is part of our humanity, and without some awareness and experience of the divine mystery man ceases to be man. When the Pleiades and the wind in the grass are no longer a part of the human spirit, a part of the very flesh and bone, man becomes, as it were, a kind of cosmic outlaw, having neither the

completeness and integrity of the animal nor the birthright of a true humanity"
(Beston 1971).

Refocusing on Man

It would be straining a point to maintain that it is our science and our technology that turn us into "cosmic outlaws." It is we who are the Frankensteins, we who have seemingly lost control of that which we have created. How then do we, as environmental educators, bring man back into central focus so that we can not only portray with reasonable accuracy the physical, biological, and social results of the man-environment interaction, but also point out the implications of these interactions to the intellectual, emotional, and social development of our students and ourselves?

I expect that most of us, as teachers, find it easier and more comfortable to be intellectual robber barons, dealing in profit-and-loss fashion with faceless graphs and figures in the interests of accuracy and objectivity, and when stress is brought to bear on an environmental system, to reconstruct our flow charts of energy and matter as we search for new levels of environmental equilibrium. The cold and depersonalized prose of our professional journals is a reflection of ourselves. The humanity of man is conspicuously absent in our teaching approach, but whether this absence is due to fear of sentimentality or egocentricity or to our own intellectual limitations is difficult to determine. But it is as biological for man to dream his dreams and to construct his heroic myths as it is for him to eat and to propagate, to hammer his Pietàs and Davids out of the chaos of life as it was for Michelangelo to hammer his out of formless blocks of Carrara marble. Only by recognition of the centrality of man in the environment and keeping him constantly in sharp focus can we begin to see our environmental problems in perspective; only then, as John Donne has written, can we begin to knit "the subtle knot that makes us men."

I am not so naive as to believe that alterations in life style more consistent with environmental constraints are easy to achieve, although I am optimistic enough to believe that they are attainable and realistic enough to know what they must change if we are not to be continuously confronted by traumatic crises. In this nation the affluent life that we lead is of relatively recent origin, a 20th-century phenomenon based on exploitation of the resources of the world rather than confining ourselves to what we have ourselves; but it would be arrogance indeed to believe that it can continue at the expense of the remainder of mankind, and in an age of emerging scarcities. It would be granted by all of us that the material benefits derived from this exploitive aspect of our culture have been enormous, and we would give them up only grudgingly and painfully. Changes, if they are to come and as I think that they must come, will take place slowly, but hopefully they will come as the result of conscious and deliberate planning rather than being crisis-induced by shortage economies. New geographical frontiers, so generative of human expansiveness, innovation, and optimism, are gone, but we have yet to plumb the depths and extent of the human mind and human behavior from which an altered environmental consciousness must emerge.

Environmental education, therefore, needs to embrace a consideration of the quality of life for all peoples as well as a knowledge of environmental parameters and an acquisition of the techniques for the solution of environmental problems. We must, I believe, broaden our teaching base and our environmental vision. Environmental literacy of the future must include the humane as well as the scientific, the artistic as well as the technological, the dreams and yearnings as well as the factual and the quantitative. All literature and all experience that is relevant should be explored, and that from history, religion, philosophy, and the arts should be included along with the scientific and the technological.

Each of us, if we subscribe to the view that we have a need to see man and his environments as total rather than fragmented systems, will approach our educational tasks in individualistic ways. But we will all cover a series of common problems: population, energy, resources, land use, pollution, and behavior, to list some of the more obvious. Most of us will have little difficulty with the scientific and technological aspects of these subjects; they are amply documented in the voluminous literature currently available. The broader and nontechnical aspects of these areas of concern—the humane aspects, if you will—require more than casual planning if they are to be an integrated feature of our discussions instead of being simply disruptive, diversionary, or platitudinous.

Humanistic Environmental Studies

When I seek to inject the human and the humane into the issues of environmental concern, I turn most naturally to the literary scene. It is the area, other than biology, that I know best and with which I am most at ease. I can see no reason, however, why other areas of human endeavor cannot be similarly explored—the arts, religion, economics, social phenomena—provided man, seen as living, breathing, dreaming, acting individuals, is kept in sharp focus. Let me illustrate by way of several examples. A humanist may very well disagree with my choices of literature from this field, but they are selected for their relation to particular environmental concerns.

Population

The "population problem" is one that concerns any thinking teacher. But it is also one within which the "numbers" game is so frequently played, often through the medium of "crisis" teaching, that the individual appears only as a statistic. It is furthermore a somewhat misleading term, for it is not just a single problem of worldwide dimensions but rather a multitude of smaller entities, each of which is peculiar unto itself and each of which may have a peculiarly unique solution. As teachers, we generally examine birth and death rates, make future projections on the basis of current or imagined trends, and judge these in terms of the capacity of the environment to sustain these numbers at various levels of sustenance. We have our students read those who express the "doomsday syndrome," and counterbalance these with the writings of those whose faith in our technological inventiveness to feed, clothe, and house the world is unbounded. We may point out that, in contrast to today, Europe had time during the 1800s and early 1900s to solve some of her population pressures through emigration to the Americas and to Australia. We document in grim terms the fact that the peoples of India and the sub-Sahara continue to face the specter of starvation through the crush of numbers, inadequate food supplies, and an out-dated or nonexistent technology. These are necessary pieces of information, and we cannot do without them if reasonable solutions are to be sought. But there is lacking an important human ingredient: compassion; and compassion is difficult to generate from the study of graphs and statistical tables. We need to turn to smaller problems which we can more readily grasp.

Not all population problems are necessarily related to number, they are not always solved by conventional means of population control such as birth control and abortion, and they are not peculiar to today. Vast areas of the Middle East, Greece of the Golden Age, and Rome of a later day, all felt the pressures of burgeoning growth. Theirs was a smaller world than that which we know today, and the tree-less, eroded hills of these areas bear mute testimony to the inability of the land to support these peoples. On a somewhat smaller scale, but closer in time to our own century, is the population problem of Ireland. In the 17th century, Jonathan Swift, in *A Modest Proposal* (see Wallace 1972), suggested in satiric terms one way to alleviate the Irish situation, but it took a fungus to do what man seemed incapable of doing. In mid-19th century, the potato blight ruined Ireland's basic food staple for a number of years and brought on starvation, massive emigration to America and Australia, and the institution of late marriages—all of which cut the population in half and brought about a measure of stability to an unhealthy and uneasy situation.

England has also had its problems although they are of a different character, as Thomas Malthus (1798), in his now famous essay, made clear in the late 18th century. Malthusian predictions of famine, disease, misery, and vice, stemming from inadequate food production, rising populations levels, and attendant social conditions, have been discredited by any number of scholars since that time; but such academic reassurances are of small comfort to the man who sees himself and his family disintegrating, physically and morally, because of insufficient diet. Malthusian ideas, if judged within the intellectual temper of his age, go far beyond the simple differences between arithmetic and geometric increases. Malthus needs to be read in the context of the rationalism of his time, the perfectibility of man as advocated by Godwin and Condorcet, Malthus' concept of moral restraint, the economic theory advanced earlier by Adam Smith in his *Wealth of Nations,* the poor laws of England and their background, and the effects of industrialism on the great masses of the cities as the energy of coal was harnessed to the newly developed steam engine. It is the latter situation which Charles Dickens depicts so well in his novel, *Hard Times.*

In our own century, and particularly during the first four or five decades, the more serious population problems were of a political, economic, and ethnic nature, and only incidentally numerical: the Russian pogroms, the extermination of the Jews by Nazi Germany, the plight of minority groups in this country, the agonies and problems of the emerging Third World nations. The humanistic literature available for incorporation into environmental education courses is enormous and varied, and of vital importance if we are to see man in his totality. In conjunction with such books as Karl Sax's *Standing Room Only,* Meadows et al. *The Limits to Growth,* and Paul Erlich's *The Population Bomb,* one should deal with *Humanae Vitae,* the papal encyclical of Pope Paul VI on the sanctity of life, Thoreau's *Life Without*

Principle, Alan Paton's *Tales from a Troubled Land,* James Baldwin's *Notes of a Native Son,* and Robert Frost's *The Death of the Hired Man.*

The point being made, therefore, is that the population problem is not just one of graphs, tables, and projections, with all of the dire consequences as these are extended into the future; it is also one of individual human beings and cultures caught up in events and circumstances larger than themselves and often not of their own making. It is the dilemma of man judged collectively and men judged individually. It is one thing to be viewed impersonally, even deterministically, in the monochromatic beam of scientific investigation, and quite another to be viewed sympathetically, emotionally, even autonomously, in the rainbow hues of the humanist. It is one thing to be a statistic, quite another to realize, belatedly and often without hope, that one could have lived a thousand lives and end up living only one, with the others dying unrealized as death intervenes. The scientific view is a valid one, but it is incomplete without the other.

Land Use

Let me touch upon another problem, one intimately related to that of population, and like it, deceptively complex. This is the question of the land upon which we live, from which we draw our sustenance, and which molds us even as we alter the landscape to human needs, proportions, and aspirations. We can all probably agree that a land and its people are inextricably intertwined; this holds true whether the land consists of the paved streets of a city lined with tenements or is the deep rich soil of western wheatfields.

Out of this interaction come many of the values that determine and define our attitudes and our life styles; but just as the interactions taking place at the landman interface are as varied as the landscape, its resources, and its inhabitants, so too are the values that emerge to characterize a culture. As a result there is probably no single land ethic which is universally applicable; the physical and psychological requirements of cultures, subcultures, and even individuals are too varied to be encompassed within a given ethic, and we have our different reasons for the preservation, alteration, utilization, or destruction of any particular landscape. We need constantly to be reminded, however, of the inescapable fact that there is no practical substitute for land surfaces, and however trite it may sound and however ingenious our science and technology, we are utterly dependent upon the ecosystem of which we are a part.

As with the population question, there is a wealth of readily available literature which deals with the land and its agricultural productivity, its yield of mineral and energy resources, its withdrawal from productivity for housing, industry, recreation, and the highways and power lines that spiderweb their way across the countryside. Central to a meaningful consideration of this immense topic is *Man's Role in Changing the Face of the Earth* (W. L. Thomas, editor), Henry Nash Smith's *Virgin Land,* and Leo Marx's *The Machine in the Garden*—the first covering a wide range of topics, the latter two related more specifically to an examination of a changing American ethic as our population moved westward. For those who would visualize a land being altered through the course of many centuries and as a result of many influences, W. G. Hoskins' *The Making of the English Landscape* is a splendid mixture of land, people, law, custom, industry, and poetry, with all elements threading their way through the text much in the manner of the hawthorn hedges meandering through the English countryside.

But there is a literature of another kind as well, a humanistic genre in which the land is the stage on which the human drama is enacted. It is a literature that is basically regional as though the land and its people breed a voice that speaks for them, a feature that should be taken advantage of for educational purposes. John Steinbach's *Grapes of Wrath* tells of those uprooted in the 1930s by the environmentally disastrous drought that created the Dust Bowl of the lower Midwest; Harry M. Caudill's two books, *Night Comes to the Cumberlands* and *My Land is Dying,* can be juxtaposed to *The Foxfire Books,* I and II, to gain an impression of the troubled, despoiled land of Appalachia and its gentle, but fiercly independent, inhabitants; Aldo Leopold's *The Sand County Almanac* depicts in a sensitive manner the history of a once-productive, but now abandoned, farm at the edge of the Wisconsin prairie, a farm now being recaptured by nature as the effect of the presence of man is lessened; Henry Beston's *Outermost House,* and John and Mildred Teal's *The Life and Death of a Salt Marsh* sense, each in its own way, the interactions that take place when men and the land impinge upon the margin of the sea, with the authors expressing their different value systems and images. In a wholly different manner, the deep psychological impact of a land on its inhabitants can be gained from Thomas Hardy's *The Return of the Native* and O. E. Rolvaag's *Giants in the Earth,* the former set in the English moors and the latter in the North Dakota prairies, and with both sensing the fraility of man in the presence of somber and foreboding natural forces. By way of contrast, one can turn to the many passages of celebration in Walt Whitman's *Leaves of Grass* or to certain of the poems of Wordsworth and Robert Frost; here the approach is that of a oneness with the land, and expression of belonging or of coming home rather than that of being an intruder.

Two short essays are worthy of final mention in this regard. They are less well known than Garrett Hardin's much reprinted "Tragedy of the Commons" (1968), and their approach is from a different vantage point, but they are of equal significance in gaining a sense of the interaction between man and his surroundings. The first is *The Westward-Moving House,* by L. B. Jackson, the second Hugh Raup's *The View from John Sanderson's Farm: A Perspective for the Use of the Land.* In both essays, the land is subordinate to the people who lived out their lives on it. As Raup (1966) has put it:

...the principal role of the land and the forests has been that of stage and scenery. The significant figures have always been the people, and the ideas they have had about what they might do at specific points in time with the stage properties at hand. At each such point in time an actor would play his role only by the rules he knew—in terms of his own conception of his relation to the play of which he was a part. He was always hampered by lack of precise knowledge of the stage and its properties, the land and the forests. Perhaps more important than this, he had severely limited knowledge of the changing rules by which he and other actors of his time were playing. Both of these failings are perennial and no doubt will continue to be....

John Sanderson's general attitude toward his farm and his land cannot be stated any more precisely than his planning horizons....For the early New England farmers the forested wilderness was an impersonal, physical barrier to be tamed and exploited to the hilt...

...Throughout most of the long period of his early experiments man was dealing with things and processes in wild nature that were entirely mysterious and potentially evil. Only in the last century or so, with the rise of conservation thought in all its manifestations, has he confronted himself repeatedly with the accusation of sin against the same "nature" and "land" that were for so long his arch enemies. This sin has had to be defended by whatever means came to hand—scientific research, favorable cost-benefit ratios, or simple economic necessity. Fortunately for John Sanderson he lived before his sense of sin against his land became popular, so it probably never occurred to him to defend it.

The Humanized Touch

The Museum of Fine Arts in Boston displays a Tahitian painting by Paul Gauguin. It is, to my relatively untrained eye, similar to other paintings that he has done, but it bears the enigmatic title *Whence do we come? What are we? Whither are we going?* In Ganguin's words, the title was added almost as an afterthought when "My eyes close in order to see without understanding the dream . . .that flies ahead of me, and I perceive the mournful procession of my hopes."

The recent flood of environmental literature is almost a dirge of the "mournful procession" of our values and actions. Looking back in time, one can say that the results were predictable. Our value systems, making use of the available science and technology, have wrought changes in the land and its meaning to which neither the land nor the human spirit could accommodate with ease, and crises of both an environmental and a spiritual nature are inevitable. John Platt (1966) has said that "The future is waiting to respond to a touch, if it is the right touch. It is ingenuity we need, not lamentations." As we seek solutions to environmental problems and attempt to adjust our way of life to an environment finite in space and resources, the "right touch" must be a humanized one, with kaleidoscopic man, existing in a kaleidoscopic environment, central in our thoughts and our teaching. And our image of this many-faceted individual is as much derived from the humanist as it is from the scientist and the engineer.

REFERENCES

Allen, D. C., ed. 1959. *A celebration of poets.* Johns Hopkins Press, Baltimore.
Beston, H. 1971. *Outermost house.* Holt, Rinehart & Winston, New York.
Dubos, R. 1965. Humanistic biology. *American Scientist* 53:4. (See also his books *The Dreams of Reason; So Human an Animal;* and *The God Within.*)
Dobzhansky, T. 1967. *The biology of ultimate concern.* New American Library, New York.
Hardin, G. 1968. The tragedy of the commons. *Science* 162:1243.
Hofer, E. 1971. *First things, last things.* Harper & Row, New York.
Huxley, J. 1964. *Essays of a humanist.* Harper & Row, New York.
Jackson, W. L. 1953. The westward-moving house. *Landscape,* vol. 2, no. 3. Also reprinted in *Landscapes,* by E. Zube. 1970. University of Massachusetts Press, Amherst, Mass.
Malthus, T. 1798. An essay on the principle of population. Reprinted in *Population, Evolution and Birth Control,* by G. Hardin. 1964. W. H. Freeman & Co., San Francisco.
Platt, J. 1966. *The step to man.* John Wiley & Sons, New York.
Potter, V. R. 1971. *Bioethics.* Prentice-Hall, Inc., Englewood Cliffs, N.J.
Raup, H. 1966. The view from John Sanderson's farm: a perspective for the use of the land. *Forest History* 10:2.
Stallman, R. W., ed. 1952. *Stephen Crane: an omnibus.* Alfred A. Knopf, New York.
Wallace, B. 1972. *Esays in social biology,* vol. 1. Prentice-Hall, Inc., Englewood Cliffs, N.J.

The Conservation of Non-Resources

David W. Ehrenfeld

Conservation cannot rely solely on economic and ecological justifications. There is a more reliable criterion of the value of species and communities.

Conservation is usually identified with the preservation of natural resources, and this was certainly the meaning intended by the person who probably coined the word, Gifford Pinchot. Resources can be defined very narrowly as reserves of commodities that have an appreciable money value to man, either directly or indirectly. Since the time that Pinchot first used the word, it has been seriously overworked. A steadily increasing percentage of "conservationists" has been preoccupied with preservation of natural features—species, communities, and ecosystems—that are not conventional resources.

An example of such a non-resource is an endangered amphibian species, the Houston toad, *Bufo houstonensis* (*1*). This animal (Fig. 1) has no demonstrated or conjectural resource value to man, other races of toad will replace it, and its passing is not expected to make an impression on the *Umwelt* of the city of Houston or its suburbs. Yet someone thought enough of the Houston toad to give it a page in the International Union for the Conservation of Nature's lists of endangered animals and plants (*2*), and its safety has been advanced as a reason for preventing oil drilling in a Houston public park (*3*).

The Houston toad has not claimed the undivided attention of conservationists, or they might by now have discovered some hitherto unsuspected value inherent in it; and this is precisely the problem. Species and communities that lack an economic value or demonstrated potential value as natural resources are not easily protected in societies that have a strongly exploitative relationship with nature. Many communities, probably the majority of plant and animal species, and some domesticated strains of crop plants fall in this category, at or near the non-resource end of a utility continuum. Those in favor of their preservation are often motivated by a deeply conservative distrust of irreversible change and/or a socially atypical attitude of respect for the components and structure of the natural world. These attitudes are not acceptable as a basis for conservation in Western-type societies, except in those few cases where preservation costs are minimal and there are no competing uses for the space now occupied by the non-resource. Consequently, defenders of non-resources generally have attempted to secure protection for their "useless" species or environments by means of a change of designation: a "value" is discovered, and the non-resource metamorphoses into a resource.

Perhaps the first to recognize this process was Aldo Leopold (*4*), who wrote in "The Land Ethic" that "one basic weakness in a conservation system based wholly on economic motives is that most members of the land community have no economic value. . . .When one of these noneconomic categories is threatened, and if we happen to love it, we invent subterfuges to give it economic importance."

David W. Ehrenfeld is Professor of Biology at Cook College, Rutgers University.

Economic Value of Non-resources

The values attributed to non-resources are diverse and sometimes rather contrived, hence the difficulty of trying to condense them into a list. In my efforts I have relied, in part, on the thoughtful analyses provided by several members of the Nature Conservancy (5). All values listed below can be assigned a monetary value and thus become commensurable with ordinary goods and services—although in some cases it would require a good deal of ingenuity to do this. All are anthropocentric values.

1. *Recreational and esthetic values.* This is one of the most popular ways of assigning value to non-resources, because although frequently quite legitimate, it is also easily fudged. Consequently, it plays an important part in cost-benefit analyses and impact statements, filling in the slack according to need. The category includes items that involve little interaction between man and environment: scenic views can be given a cash value. Less remote interactions are hiking, camping, sport hunting, and the like. Organizations such as the Sierra Club stress many of these qualities, in part because their membership values them highly. It is no coincidence, for example, that among the Australian mammals, the large, showy, beautiful, diurnal ones, those that might be seen on safari, are zealously protected by conservationists and are mostly doing well, while the small, inconspicuous, nocturnal marsupials include a distressingly large number of seriously endangered or recently exterminated species (6).

Some of the most determined attempts to place this recreational and esthetic category on a firm resource footing have been made by those who claim that the opportunity to enjoy nature, at least on occasion, is a prerequisite for sound mental and physical health. Several groups of long-term mental patients have supposedly benefited more from camping trips than from other treatments, and physiologically desirable effects have been claimed for the color green and for environments that lack the monotony of man-organized space (7).

2. *Undiscovered or undeveloped values.* In 1975 it was reported that the oil of the jojoba bean, *Simmondsia californica,* is very similar to oil of the threatened sperm whale in the stability of its responses to high temperatures and pressures. Overnight, this desert shrub of the American Southwest was converted from the status of a minor to a major resource (8). It can safely be assumed that many other species of hitherto obscure plants and animals have great potential value as bona fide resources once this potential is discovered or developed. Plants are probably the most numerous members of this category: in addition to their possibilities as future food sources, they can also supply structural materials, fiber, and chemicals for industry and medicine (9).

Animals have potential resource uses that parallel those of plants, but this potential is being developed at an even slower rate. The potential for domestication and large-scale production of the vicuña, the source of one of the finest animal fibers in the world, was only recognized after its commercial extinction in the wild had become imminent.

Some species are potential resources indirectly, by virtue of their ecological associations. Galston (10) has described one such case involving the water fern, *Azolla pinnata,* which has long been cultivated in paddies along with rice by peasants in northern Vietnam. This inedible and seemingly useless plant harbors colonies of nitrogen-fixing blue-green algae in pockets on its leaves. Not surprisingly, villages that have been privy to the secrets of fern cultivation have tended to produce exceptional quantities of rice.

Species whose resource possibilities are unknown cannot, of course, be singled out for protection, but most or all communities are likely to contain such species. Thus the undeveloped resource argument has been used to support the growing movement to save "representative," self-maintaining ecosystems in all parts of the world. Such ecosystems range from the stony and comparatively arid hills of Galilee, which still shelter the wild ancestors of wheat, oats, and barley, to the tropical forests of the world, whose timber, food, and forest product resources remain largely unknown even as they are destroyed (*11*).

3. *Ecosystem stabilization values.* This item is at the heart of the complex controversy that has arisen over the ecological theory of conservation. In its general form, Commoner (*12*) has stated it clearly:

The amount of stress which an ecosystem can absorb before it is driven to collapse is also a result of its various interconnections and their relative speeds of response. The more complex the ecosystem, the more successfully it can resist a stress. . . . Like a net, in which each knot is connected to others by several strands, such a fabric can resist collapse better than a simple, unbranched circle of threads—which if cut anywhere breaks down as a whole. Environmental pollution is often a sign that ecological links have been cut and that the ecosystem has been artificially simplified.

A more general, less controversial formulation of this "diversity-stability" concept is discussed separately under item 9.

One fairly specific (and less troublesome) derivation of the diversity-stability hypothesis concerns monocultures in agriculture and forestry. It has long been known that the intensive monoculture that characterizes modern farms and planted forests generates greater ease and reduced costs of cultivation and harvesting, and increased crop yields; but this is at the expense of higher risk of epidemic disease and vulnerability to insect and other pest attack (*13*). Here a reduction of species diversity results in much closer spacing of similar crop plants, which in turn facilitates the spread of both pests and disease organisms. It also eliminates plant species that constitute shelter for natural enemies of the specialized plant pests. Monocultures also create problems in ranching and fish farming, often because of incomplete use of available food resources by the single species involved.

4. *Examples of survival.* Communities and, to a lesser extent, species can have a value as examples or models of long-term survival. Humke et al. (*5*) observed that "most natural systems have been working in essentially their present form for many thousands of years. On the other hand, greatly modified, mandominated systems have not worked very reliably in the past and, in significant respects, do not do so at present." The economic value here is indirect, consisting of problems averted (money saved) by virtue of good initial design of mandominated systems or repair of faulty ones, based on features abstracted from natural systems. This viewpoint is becoming increasingly popular as disillusionment with the results of traditional planning grows. Thus it may make sense to look to successful natural communities for clues concerning the organization of traits

leading to persistence or survival. Wright (*14*) has stated this non-resource value in its strongest form in the final sentence of an interesting article on landscape development: "The survival of man may depend on what can be learned from the study of extensive natural ecosystems."

5. *Environmental baseline and monitoring values.* The fluctuation of animal or plant population sizes, the status of their organs or by-products, or even the mere presence or absence of a given species or group of species in a particular environment can be used to define normal or baseline environmental conditions and to determine the degree to which communities have been affected by extraordinary outside influences such as pollution or man-made habitat alteration. Biological functions such as species diversity (in the full sense of the term, which includes both richness and equitability measurements) are the best possible indicators of the meaningful effects of pollution, just as behavior is the best single indicator of the health of the nervous and musculoskeletal systems. Species diversity is a final common path, a resultant of all forces that impinge on ecosystems. It should also be noted that the traditional economic value of a species is of no significance in determining its usefulness as an environmental indicator—an important point if we are concerned with the metamorphosis of non-resources into resources.

With the exception of the biological monitoring of water pollution, this branch of conservation ecology is still in its infancy. In the case of water pollution, much of the pioneering work on algal and invertebrate communities has been done by Ruth Patrick and her associates (*15*). Lichens are sensitive indicators of air pollution, especially that caused by dust and sulfur dioxide (*16*). The common lilac, *Syringa vulgaris,* develops a disease called leaf roll necrosis in response to elevated levels of ozone and sulfur dioxide. The honey of honeybees can be used to monitor environmental heavy metal pollution (*17*). Organ analyses of snakes have been recommended as a way of following organochlorine pesticide and PCB residues in terrestrial environments (*18*). The presence of kinked or bent tails in tadpoles may be an indicator of both pesticides and local climatic change (*19*).

6. *Scientific research values.* Many creatures that are otherwise economically negligible have some unique or special characteristic that makes them extremely valuable to research scientists. Because of their relationship to man, orangutans, chimpanzees, and even the lower prosimians fall in this category. Squids and the sea hare, *Aplysia,* have nervous system properties that make them immensely valuable to neuroscientists. The identical quadruplet births of armadillos and the hormonal responses of the clawed toad, *Xenopus,* make them objects of special study to embryologists and endocrinologists, respectively. The odd life cycle of slime molds has endeared these fungi to biologists studying the chemistry of cell-cell interactions.

7. *Teaching values.* The teaching value of an intact ecosystem may be quantified by noting the economic value of displaced land-use alternatives. For example, a university administration may preserve a teaching forest if the competing use is as an extra parking lot for maintenance equipment, but it may not be so inclined toward conservation if the land is wanted for university housing.

In one case, in 1971, a U.S. Federal District Judge ordered the New York State National Guard to remove a landfill from the edge of the Hudson River and restore the brackish marsh that had occupied the site previously. One of the reasons he cited, although not the most important one, was the marsh's prior use by local high school biology classes (*20*).

8. *Habitat reconstruction values.* If we wish to restore or rebuild an ecosystem in what was once its habitat, we need a living, unharmed ecosystem of that type to serve as both a working model and a source of living components. This is tacitly assumed by tropical forest ecologists, for example, who realize that clear-cutting of very large areas of tropical moist forests is likely to be incompatible with maintaining a sustained yield of the full diversity of tropical hardwoods. In some north temperate forests, strip-cutting, with intervening strips of forest left intact for reseeding and animal habitat, is now gaining favor in commercial timber operations. Actual cases of totally rebuilt ecosystems are still rare: the best example may be the salt marsh reconstructions by Garbisch and his co-workers (*21*). If certain future endangered ecosystems are recognized as useful to man, then any remnant patches of these ecosystems will assume a special resource value.

9. *Conservative value: Avoidance of irreversible change.* This is a general restatement of a basic fear underlying every other item on this list; sooner or later it turns up in all discussions about saving non-resources. It expresses the conservative belief that man-made, irreversible change in the natural order—the loss of an evolved gene pool or community—may carry a hidden and unknowable risk of serious damage to humans and their civilizations. Preserve the full range of natural diversity because we do not know the aspects of that diversity upon which our long-term survival depends. This was Aldo Leopold's basic argument (*4*): "A system of conservation based solely on economic self-interest is hopelessly lopsided. It tends to ignore, and thus eventually to eliminate, many elements in the land community that lack commercial value, but that are (as far as we know) essential to its healthy functioning."

Without in any way impugning the truth of this statement, two serious oversights or omissions might be pointed out in Leopold's argument. First, Leopold provides no real justification for preserving those animals, plants, and habitats that are almost certainly not essential to the "healthy functioning" of any large ecosystem. This is not a trivial category, and includes, in part, the great many species and even communities that have always been extremely rare or that have always had very restricted distributions. Second, although Leopold rejected "economic self-interest" as a sole motive for conservation, he evidently did not realize that preserving the "healthy functioning" of land communities is also an economic self-interest argument, albeit one that manifests its resource benefits indirectly and over the long term.

In surveying the preceding list of reasons for valuing and hence preserving non-resources, the most striking feature is its practical political weakness. Regardless of the truth of these explanations of value, they are not as convincing as those that are backed by a promise of short-term economic gain. In a capitalist society, any private individual or corporation that treats non-resources as if they were resources is likely to go bankrupt. In a socialist society, the result will be nonfulfillment of growth quotas. People do not seem ready to assign resource values on the basis of long-term considerations or mere statistical probabilities of danger. As Matthews has pointed out (*22*), even "human health, especially in areas outside of cancer (for example, [sickness] from asbestos) and massive deaths (for example, from nuclear reactor accidents), is often given a second priority to the economic criteria [of GNP, employment, and the standard of living]."

If we examine the "conservative value" of non-resources discussed above, the difficulty immediately becomes plain. The economic value in this case is a remote and nebulous one: it is protection from the unknown dangers of irreversible change. An added problem is that if a danger materializes, it may be too late to reverse policy or it may be impossible to prove a connection with the initial loss of the non-resource. Even in those cases where loss of a non-resource seems likely to initiate long-term undesirable change, the argument may be too complex and technical to be widely persuasive among non-scientists or it may be contrary to popular belief. An excellent example has been provided by Owen (*13*) and by Ormerod (*29*) who have claimed that the tsetse fly, dread vector of African trypanosomiasis, may be essential to the well-being of large parts of sub-Saharan Africa.

In summary, the usual reasons that are advanced to persuade people to accept non-resources as resources are not very likely to convince them, regardless of their truth. When everything is called a resource, the word loses all meaning—at least in our value system.

One consequence of the failure to persuade is that conservationists are provoked into exaggerating and distorting the alleged values of non-resources. The most vexing and embarrassing example for conservationists concerns the diversity-stability issue. It is important to make clear at the outset that the necessity of maintaining diversity is not questioned. As one critical ecologist put it (*23*), "From a practical standpoint, the diversity-stability hypothesis is not really necessary; even if the hypothesis is completely false it remains logically possible—and, on the best available evidence, very likely—that the disruption of the patterns of evolved interaction in natural communities will have untoward, and occasionally catastrophic consequences."

The first comprehensive statement of the diversity-stability hypothesis was made by Margalef (*24*). In a classic paper he claimed that the successional drive toward a "climax" community ("mature" ecosystem in his terminology), which is characteristic of all natural ecosystems, is one of several strong pieces of evidence that the late stages of succession are more "stable" than earlier ones. These late ecosystems were also thought to be more diverse, and using information theory Margalef claimed to have demonstrated that the higher information content and greater number of interactions is responsible for the increased stability. This was widely interpreted to mean that mature ecosystems were better able to buffer their environments, were more resistant to man-made perturbations (such as chemical pollution), than were earlier and simpler stages. From this were derived analogies such as the one quoted above from Commoner, in which the strength of a late successional community was compared with that of a net. There is much intuitive support for this hypothesis. As Goodman has said (*23*), there is a "basic appeal of its underlying metaphor. It is the sort of thing that people like, and want, to believe."

Even as Margalef was refining his hypothesis, four lines of investigation and evidence were combining to undermine part of it. First, the results of many separate studies of terrestrial and aquatic ecosystems showed that diversity does not always increase with succession, particularly in the final phases. Second, investigations of plant associations by Whittaker and his colleagues (25) tended to show that the interdependence and interactions of the species found in mature communities had been exaggerated—at least if one looked at a single trophic level. Third, the mathematical analysis of May (26) failed to confirm the intuitively attractive notion stated by Commoner that the greater the number of interactions, or links, the greater the stability of the system. May's models worked the other way: the more elements (species and species interrelationships) there were, the greater the fluctuation of the populations in the system when a simulated external perturbation was applied. In theory, the most complex systems were therefore at the greatest risk of collapse. Fourth, the direct evidence of conservationists and ecologists was against the hypothesis: the diverse, mature communities were almost always the first to fall apart under heavy, man-imposed stress and were always the most difficult to protect (at least in the case of terrestrial systems). Indeed, Margalef's own description of early colonizing species (Hutchinson's "fugitive species") indicated that these immature community residents were usually resilient, opportunistic, genotypically and phenotypically plastic, and behaviorally adaptable, and had high reproductive rates. They are the vermin, weeds, and common game species, among others, and very few of them are exclusive residents of climax communities (27).

As May and others had perceived, the diversity-stability hypothesis, in the restricted sense described here, was a case of inverted cause and effect. The most diverse communities were those that had occupied the most stable environments for the longest period of time: they were dependent on stability—not the reverse.

The most comprehensive and lucid review of the diversity-stability controversy has been written by Goodman (23). Although Goodman may place too much emphasis on population fluctuation and not enough on persistence as a measure of stability (28), it does not alter the moral of the story for conservationists. In our eagerness to demonstrate a present "value" for the magnificent, mature, and most diverse ecosystems of the world—the tropical rain and cloud forests, the coral reefs, the temperate zone deserts, etc.—we stressed the role they were playing in immediate stabilization of their environments (including their own component populations). This was a partial distortion that not only caused less attention to be paid to the real, long-term values of these ecosystems but also helped to obscure, for a while, their extreme fragility in the face of human "progress."

Many different kinds of stability are indeed dependent on biological diversity. This is especially evident today in those places, often tropical, where soils are prone to erosion, nutrient loss, or laterite crust formation, and where desertification can occur (29); but none of these effects, however deadly and durable, is ever likely to be as easy to explain to laymen as the "stable net" hypothesis.

A much less complex example of an exaggeration or distortion that has resulted from the impulse to find values for non-resources concerns African game ranching. In the 1950s and 1960s it was first pointed out that harvesting the wild animals of the bush and savanna might produce at least as much meat per acre as cattle raising, without the reduction in carrying capacity that traditionally has been associated with cattle in Africa (30). This suggestion cannot be faulted in ecological theory, which recognizes that the phenomenon of niche specialization enables the dozens of species of native, large herbivores to utilize the primary productivity much more efficiently and completely than cattle alone.

The pitfalls in this straightforward plan have only recently made themselves felt. Apart from serious cultural problems, the major drawback is ecological. The early game ranching theory and the subsequent cropping programs of Parker tacitly assume that the animals to be cropped will replace themselves, or, to put it another way, that the populations of edible, wild herbivores will be able to adapt to a heavy, annual loss to market hunters. This is no doubt true of some of the r-selected species, but not all are likely to be r-selected. Hippopotamus and elephant supposedly have been cropped successfully in several places; nevertheless, the population dynamics and management ecology of nearly all species are still largely unknown (*31*), and exploitation, illegal and legal, is proceeding with little more than speculation about the long-term consequences. The issue here is the danger of assuming, with an air of infallibility, that one knows what the ecological effects of cropping will be. This point has been made repeatedly by Hugh Lamprey and others most knowledgeable about east African ecology, and is beautifully illustrated in an anecdote told by John Owen, the noted former park director at Serengeti (*32*). Owen was describing the controversy over the return of elephants, 2000 strong, to Serengeti and the alleged damage they were doing to the park ecosystem:

When I would come down from Arusha the wardens would take me around and show me the trampled acacias. Next day the scientists [from the Serengeti Research Institute] would take me out and show me the new acacia shoots blooming in another part of the park. Acacia seeds are carried and fertilized by elephant dung.

At this time, much of the trouble is with poachers, and there is admittedly the remote possibility that supervised game ranches and cropping schemes on a large scale will have the effect of making poaching (for cash sale) uneconomical. But there is also the possibility that game ranching and cropping will affect species diversity and ecosystem stability as much as poaching or even, in some cases, cattle raising. In our haste to preserve zebra, wildebeest, dik dik, and springbok by endowing them with tangible economic value, we may have exaggerated one type of resource potential (they have many others) and in the process endangered them further.

One of the lessons of the examples cited above is that conservationists should not assume that ecological theory will always support their cases, especially when these cases concern specific, immediate objectives and when the scope of the debate has been artificially restricted by a short-term, cost-benefit type of approach.

Another example of a situation where ecological theories, if viewed in a restricted context, do not support conservation practices was described by Janzen (*33*):

One possible remedy [for the year-round persistence of agricultural pests and diseases in the tropics] is unpleasant for the conservationist. The agricultural potential of many parts of the seasonally dry tropics might well be improved by systematic destruction of the riparian and other vegetation that is often left for livestock shade, erosion control, and conservation. It might be well to replace the spreading banyan tree with a shed. . . .Some studies even suggest that "overgrazed" pastures may have a higher overall yield than more carefully managed sites, . . .especially if the real costs of management are charged against the system.

What is important here is that Janzen has demonstrated that it is quite possible for ecological theory to endow non-resources with a negative value, to make them out to be economic liabilities. In this particular case, long-term ecological considerations (such as the ultimate costs of erosion, nutrient dumping, and factors related to all the other items on the list given above) would probably militate against the short-term ecological considerations described by Janzen. But the practical net result of any conservationist's attempt to demonstrate a resource value for natural riparian and other vegetation in the seasonally dry tropics, based on ecological theory, would be to expose the conservation position to unnecessary attack.

The point being made here is easy to misinterpret. At the risk of seeming obvious, I must make clear that the purpose of this paper is a restricted one; it is to identify the honest and durable reasons for saving non-resources. This does not mean that I reject resource arguments when they are valid. The Amazonian rain forest, the green turtle, and many other forms of life contribute heavily to the maintenance of human well-being. The prospect of their loss is frightening to anyone with ecological knowledge, and it is not my aim to make it appear less so. But this is only one of the rationales for conservation, and it should not be applied carelessly, if for no other reason than the likelihood of undermining its own effectiveness.

Even when it is quite legitimate to find economic values for quondam non-resources, it may be risky, from a conservation viewpoint, to do so. Gosselink et al. (34) have conducted an elegant and painstaking investigation of the value of tidal marshes along the coast of the southeastern United States which can serve as an illustration of these risks.

The purpose of the project was to establish a definite monetary value for tidal marsh based on tangible resource properties. Esthetic values were therefore not considered. The properties studied included the function of tidal marshes in removing pollutants from coastal waters (tertiary sewage treatment), sport and food fish production, potential for commercial aquaculture, and an assortment of other less quantifiable functions. The income-capitalized value of intact marsh, computed on the basis of its energy flow, amounted to $82,940 per acre. Although the validity of the energy/money conversion might conceivably be challenged, it is unlikely that more laborious methods of estimating value, if they were sufficiently inclusive, would change the results significantly. Salt marshes are valuable.

Is calling attention to this value the best way to conserve salt marshes? If a given marsh were worth less if put to competing use than in its intact condition, the answer might be yes, provided that the marsh were publicly owned. But discovering value can be dangerous. First, any competing use with a higher value, no matter how slight the differential, would be entitled to priority in the use of the marsh site. Because most competing uses are for all intents and purposes irreversible, future change in relative usage values subsequent to the alteration of the marsh would have no effect, even if a marsh usage later were able to claim higher value and priority. We do not generally tear down luxury, high-rise apartments.

Second, values change. If, for example, a new process is discovered and tertiary treatment of sewage becomes suddenly less expensive (or if the sewage acquires value as a raw material), then that component of the marsh value will decline proportionally.

Third, the implication of the study is that both the valuable and diseconomic qualities of the salt marsh are all known and identified. Conversely, this means that those qualities of the salt marsh that have not been assigned a conventional value are not very important. This is a dangerous implication.

Fourth, Clark (35) has shown that quick profits from immediate exploitation, even to the point of extinction, often are economically superior to long-term, sustained yield gains of the sort generated by intact marsh, provided that the profits and the discount rate are each sufficiently high.

Given these four objections, the hazards of even legitimate reassignment of non-resources as resources become quite plain, as do the hazards of overemphasizing the cost-benefit approach in conserving more traditional resources.

Another consequence of assigning resource value to non-resources deserves separate consideration: when real values are computed, it becomes possible to rank endangered ecosystems, or even species, for the purposes of assigning conservation priority. Because dollar values of the sort worked out for tidal marshes are generally not available, other ranking methods have been devised. These are meant to be applied in a mechanical, objective fashion.

Ranking systems based in large part on vegetation type have been devised for use in Wisconsin by Tans (36) and in Texas by Gehlbach (37). Properties that are scored and totaled in Gehlbach's system include "climax condition," "educational suitability," "species significance" (presence of rare, relict, peripheral, endemic, or endangered species), "community representation" (number and type of communities included), and "human impact" (current and potential), in order of increasing importance. Gehlbach evidently believes that the numerical scores generated by this system can be used, without additional human input, to determine conservation policy. He states that "it is suggested that if offered for donation [to the State of Texas], an area be accepted only when its natural area score exceeds the average scores of the same or similar community-type(s) in the natural area reserve system." Other ranking systems for both species and, more commonly, natural areas either exist in the literature or could be developed along the lines of the methods described above.

There are two fundamental problems with ranking systems that militate against their uncritical or mechanical use. First, there is the problem of incomplete knowledge. It is impossible to survey all the properties of any natural area (or species), and the dangers of overlooking value (positive or negative) are very great. Community descriptions, especially short ones, are largely artificial abstractions; they are designed to facilitate talking about vegetation, not deciding what to do with it. It is presumptuous to assume that any formal system of ranking can serve as a substitute for personal acquaintance with the land or informed human intuition about its meaning or value in the world of today or 100 years from now.

Second, formal ranking sets natural area against natural area in an unacceptable and totally unnecessary way. The need to conserve a particular community or species must be judged independently of the need to conserve anything else. Limited resources may force us to make choices against our wills, but ranking systems encourage and rationalize the making of choices. Ranking systems can be useful to conservationists as an adjunct to decision making, but the more formal and generalized they become, the more damage they are likely to cause.

There is only one account in Western culture of a conservation effort greater than that now taking place; it concerned endangered species. Not a single species was excluded on the basis of low priority, and by all accounts not a single species was lost. ("Of clean beasts, and of beasts that are not clean, and of fowls, and of everything that creepeth upon the earth, There went in two and two unto Noah into the ark, the male and the female, as God had commanded Noah" *Genesis* 7:8,9.) It is an excellent precedent.

When one is confronted with a "double bind" that resists attempts at solution, the only rational approach short of surrender is to alter both one's viewing perspective and the general statement of the problem until the double bind disappears (*38*). The attempt to preserve non-resources by finding economic value for them generates a double bind. Much of the value discovered for non-resources is indirect in the sense that it consists of avoiding costly problems that might otherwise appear if the non-resources were lost. On the one hand, if the non-resource is destroyed and no ecological disasters ensue, then the conservation argument loses all capacity to inspire credence. On the other hand, if disaster does follow extinction of a supposed non-resource, then it will usually be too late to do anything about it, and it may well prove impossible to prove a causal relationship between the initial loss of the non-resource and the subsequent disaster. Indeed, no one may even think of the connection.

A way to avoid the non-resource double bind is simply to identify the *non-*economic values inherent in all natural communities and species and to weight them at least equally with resource values. The first of these universal qualities might be described as the "natural art value." It has been best articulated by Carr (*39*):

It would be cause for world fury if the Egyptians should quarry the pyramids, or the French should loose urchins to throw stones in the Louvre. It would be the same if the Americans dammed the Valley of the Colorado. A reverence for original landscape is one of the humanities. It was the first humanity. Reckoned in terms of human nerves and juices, there is no difference in the value of a work of art and a work of nature. There is this difference, though. . . .Any art might somehow, some day be replaced—the full symphony of the savanna landscape never.

This viewpoint is not common but is apparently gaining in popularity. In an article on Brazil's endangered lion tamarins or marmosets, three species of colorful, tiny primates of the Atlantic rain forests, Coimbra-Filho et al. advanced the notion of natural art in a frank and thoughtful statement remarkably similar to the preceding quotation (*40*):

In purely economic terms, it really doesn't matter if three Brazilian monkeys vanish into extinction. Although they can be (and previously were) used as laboratory animals in biomedical research, other far more abundant species from other parts of South America serve equally well or better in laboratories. Lion tamarins can be effectively exhibited in zoos, but it is doubtful that the majority of zoo-goers would miss them. No, it seems that the main reason for trying to save them and other animals like them is that the disappearance of any species represents a great esthetic loss for the entire world. It can perhaps be compared to the destruction of a great work of art by a famous painter or sculptor, except that, unlike a man-made work of art, the evolution of a single species is a process that takes many millions of years and can never again be duplicated.

It should be noted that this natural art, unlike man-made art, has no economic worth, either directly or indirectly. No one can buy or sell it for its artistic quality, it does not always stimulate tourism, nor does ignoring it cause, for that reason, any loss of goods or services. It is distinct from the recreational and esthetic resource value described earlier and may apply to communities and species that no tourist would detour a single mile to see or to qualities that are never revealed to casual inspection.

Free as it is of some of the problems associated with resource arguments, the natural art rationale for conservation is nevertheless, in its own way, a bit contrived, and a little bit confusing. Do all ecological associations have equal artistic value? Most critics would say that El Greco was a greater painter than Stubbs, but is the African savanna artistically more valuable than the New Jersey Pine Barrens?

Even if we concede that the art rationale for conservation does not foster the kind of comparisons that are the essence of traditional art criticism, there is still something wrong: the natural art concept is still rooted in the same homocentric, humanistic world view that is responsible for bringing the natural world, including us, to its present condition. If the natural world is to be conserved because it is artistically stimulating to man, there is still a condescension and superiority implied in the attitude of man, the kindly parent, toward nature, the beautiful problem-child. This attitude is not in accord with humility-inspiring discoveries of community ecology or with the sort of ecological world view, emphasizing the connectedness and immense complexity of the man-nature relationships, that now characterizes a large bloc of conservationist thought (*41*). Nor is it in accord with the growing bloc of essentially religious sentiment that approaches the same position of equality in the man-nature relationship from a nonscientific direction.

The exponents of natural art have done conservation a great service, being the first to point out the unsatisfactory nature of some of the economic reasons advanced to support conservation. But something else is needed. Elton (*42*) has indicated another non-resource value, the ultimate reason for conservation and the only one that cannot be compromised:

The first [reason for conservation], which is not usually put first, is really religious. There are some millions of people in the world who think that animals have a right to exist and be left alone, or at any rate that they should not be persecuted or made extinct as species. Some people will believe this even when it is quite dangerous to themselves.

This non-economic value of communities and species is the simplest of all to state: they should be conserved because they exist and have existed for a long time. Long-standing existence in nature is deemed to carry with it the unimpeachable right to continued existence. Existence is the only criterion of value, and diminution of the number of existing things is the best measure of decrease of value. This is, as mentioned, an ancient way of evaluating "conservability," and by rights ought to be named the "Noah Principle" after the person who was one of the first to put it into practice.

Currently, the idea of rights conferred by other-than-human existence is becoming increasingly popular (and is meeting with increased resistance). I shall give only two examples. In a book entitled *Should Trees Have Standing?* Stone has presented the case for existence of legal rights of forests, rivers, etc. apart from the vested interests of people associated with these natural entities. Describing the earth as "one organism, of which Mankind is a functional part," Stone extends Leopold's land ethic in a formal way, justifying such unusual lawsuits as *Byram River, et al. v. Village of Port Chester, New York, et al.* If a corporation can have legal rights, responsibilities, and access, through its representatives, to the courts ("standing"), argues Stone, why not rivers? The merits and deficiencies of this notion are not important here, but its emergence at this time is a significant event (43).

The ultimate example, however, of the Noah Principle in operation has been provided by Dixon in a short but profound article on the case for the guarded conservation of *Variola,* the smallpox virus, as an endangered species (44):

If we experience twinges of guilt about the impending extinction of large creatures, why should we feel differently about small ones? Conservationists lavish just as much time and energy on butterflies as they do on elephants. Why discount the microbes?

Dixon, in other parts of the article, makes a strong case for preserving smallpox as a resource (not for biological warfare, though), but his non-resource, "existence" value argument is clearly stated:

Some of us who might happily bid farewell to a virulent virus or bacterium may well have qualms about eradicating forever a "higher" animal—whether rat or bird or flea—that passes on such microbes to man. . . .Where, moving up the size and nastiness scale (smallpox virus, typhoid fever bacilli, malarial parasites, schistosomiasis worms, locusts, rats . . .), does conservation become important? There is, in fact, no logical line that can be drawn.

It is not the purpose of this paper to discredit the economic and selfish uses of nature or to recommend the abandonment of the resource rationale for conservation. Selfishness in the sense of environmental exploitation, within bounds, is necessary for the survival of any species, ourselves included. Furthermore, should we rely exclusively on non-resource motivations for conservation, we would find, given the present state of world opinion and material aspirations, that there would soon be nothing left to conserve. But we have been much too careless in our use of resource arguments—distorting and exaggerating them for short-term purposes and allowing them to confuse and dominate our long-term thinking. Resource and non-resource reasons for conservation must always be presented together, and conservationists should make clear that the non-resource reasons are ultimately more significant in every case. If resource arguments seem legitimately strong there is no reason to ignore them, although they must be used with caution because of their potential to weaken the conservation position at unpredictable times and in unpredictable ways. Conversely, when a community or species has no known economic worth, there is no need either to trump up weak resource values for it or to abandon the effort to conserve it. Its non-resource value is enough to justify (but not necessarily to assure) its protection.

A number of years ago, Elton (42) proposed that there were three different reasons for the conservation of natural diversity: "because it is a right relation between man and living things, because it gives opportunities for richer experience, and because it tends to promote ecological stability—ecological resistance to invaders and to explosions in native populations.'' He stated that these reasons could be harmonized and that together they might generate a ''wise principle of co-existence between man and nature.'' Since these words were written, we have ignored this harmony of conservation rationales, shrugging off the first, or religious, reason as embarrassing or ineffective and relying on inadequate but ''hard scientific'' proofs of value.

Allen (45), for example, in summing up his resource-type arguments for preserving diversity, has said that the economic climate is now such that ''only the most severely practical arguments will prevail. Faint-hearted ecologists who fear that their favourite species *are* damned-well useless will just have to risk it. No doubt there is some redundancy in the system, but there are strong theoretical grounds for believing that most of the species on this planet are here for a better reason than that they are poor galactic map-readers.''

What Allen is saying is that everything—including nearly all species—is interconnected and nearly everything has its own part to play in maintaining the natural order: consequently, nearly all species are significant, have resource value. Remove a species, even a seemingly trivial one from a resource standpoint, and we are more than likely to feel the consequences somehow, somewhere, someday (46). But have there been permanent and significant effects of the extinction, in the wild, of John Bartram's great discovery, the beautiful tree *Franklinia alatamaha?* Or a thousand species of tiny beetles that we never knew existed before or after their extermination? Can we even be certain that our eastern forests suffer the loss of their passenger pigeons and chestnuts in some tangible way that affects their vitality or permanence?

As a faint-hearted ecologist, I am not so certain that Allen's ''strong theoretical grounds'' can protect the Houston toad, the cloud forests, and a vast host of other living things that deserve a chance to play out their evolution unhindered by us. Nor am I willing to ''risk it'' on behalf of other creatures and communities that will suffer the immediate consequences if the risk fails. There is no genuine responsibility (or feedback) when the consequences of risk-taking are not borne by those who make the decisions.

If non-resource arguments are ever to carry their deserved weight, cultural attitudes will have to be changed. Morally backed missionary movemens, such as the humane societies, are doing quite well these days, but I have no illusions about the chance of bringing about an ethical change in our Faustian culture without the prompting of some general catastrophe. What sort of change in world view would favor the conservation of non-resources? Nothing less than a rejection of the heroic, Western ethic with its implicit denial of man's biological roots and evolved structure.

Not all problems have acceptable solutions; I feel no constraint to predict one here. On the one hand, conservationists are unlikely to succeed in a general way using only the resource approach; and they will often hurt their own cause. On the other hand, an Eltonian combination of resource and non-resource arguments may also fail, and if it succeeds, as Mumford has implied, it will probably be because of forces that the conservationists neither expected nor controlled (47). But in this event we will at least be ready to take advantage of favorable circumstances—and will have had, whatever the outcome, the small, private satisfaction of having been honest for a while.

REFERENCES

1. I thank Walt Frey for first calling this notable non-resource to my attention.
2. R. E. Honegger. 1970. *Red Data Book III: Amphibia & Reptilia.* Morges, Switzerland: IUCN.
3. R. Sayre. 1976. Audubon action. *Audubon* 78:138-39.
4. A. Leopold. 1966. *A Sand County Almanac,* pp. 225-26. NY: Oxford Univ. Press.
5. G. A. Lieberman. 1975. The preservation of ecological diversity: A necessity or a luxury? *Naturalist* 26:24-31. J. W. Humke et al. 1975. Final report. The preservation of natural diversity: A survey and recommendations. Prepared for U.S. Dept. of Interior by the Nature Conservancy. Contract No. CX0001-5-0110.
6. R. Strahan. 1975. Status and husbandry of Australian monotremes and marsupials. In *Breeding Endangered Species in Captivity,* ed. R. D. Martin, pp. 171-82. NY: Academic Press.
7. H. H. Iltis, O. L. Loucks, and P. Andrews. 1970. Criteria for an optimum human environment. *Bull. Atomic Sci.* 26:2-6.
8. National Academy of Sciences. 1975. *Underexploited Tropical Plants with Promising Economic Value,* pp. 105-10. Washington, DC: National Research Council, Commission on International Relations.
9. S. Altschul. 1973. *Drugs and Foods from Little-Known Plants.* Cambridge: Harvard Univ. Press.
10. A. Galston. 1975. The water fern-rice connection. *Natural History* 84:10-11.
11. O. H. Frankel. 1970. Genetic conservation in perspective. In *Genetic Resources in Plants—Their Exploration and Conservation,* ed. O. H. Frankel and E. Bennett, pp. 469-89. Philadelphia: Davis.
12. B. Commoner. 1972. *The Closing Circle,* p. 38. NY: Knopf.
13. C. Yarwood. 1970. Man-made plant diseases. *Science* 168:218-20; D. Owen. 1973. *Man in Tropical Africa.* NY: Oxford Univ. Press.
14. H. E. Wright, Jr. 1974. Landscape development, forest fires, and wilderness management. *Science* 186:487-95.
15. R. Patrick. 1972. Aquatic communities as indices of pollution. In *Indicators of Environmental Quality,* ed. W. A. Thomas, pp. 93-100. NY: Plenum/Rosetta.
16. C. S. Brandt. 1972. Plants as indicators of air quality. In Thomas, ibid., pp. 101-7.
17. *New York Times,* 24 Sept. 1975, p. 41.
18. B. Bauerle, D. L. Spencer, and W. Wheeler. 1975. The use of snakes as a pollution indicator species. *Copeia* 1975:366-68.
19. J. Hillaby. 1975. Deformed froglets and walking catfish. *New Scientist* 67:32-33. The pH of rain may also be a factor: see F. H. Pough. 1976. Acid precipitation and embryonic mortality of spotted salamanders, *Ambystoma maculatum. Science* 192:68-70.
20. D. W. Ehrenfeld. 1972. *Conserving Life on Earth,* pp. 243-50. NY: Oxford Univ. Press.
21. E. W. Garbisch, P. B. Woller, W. J. Bostian, and R. J. McCallum. 1975. Biotic techniques for shoreline stabilization. In *Estuarine Research II,* ed. L. E. Cronin, pp. 405-26. NY: Academic Press.
22. W. H. Matthews. 1975. Objective and subjective judgements in environmental impact analysis. *Environmental Conservation* 2:121-31.
23. D. Goodman. 1975. The theory of diversity-stability relationships in ecology. *Quart. Rev. Biol.* 50:237-66.
24. R. Margalef. 1963. On certain unifying principles in ecology. *Am. Nat.* 97:357-74.
25. R. H. Whittaker. 1960. Vegetation of the Siskiyou Mountains, Oregon and California. *Ecol. Monogr.* 30:279-338; 1965. Dominance and diversity in land plant communities. *Science* 147:250-60; 1967. Gradient analysis of vegetation. *Biol. Rev.* 42:207-64. An excellent historical summary of the arguments of Gleason, Whittaker, and similarly minded plant ecologists against the organic ecosystem concepts of Clements, Margalef, E. Odum, and others is found in P. Colinvaux. 1973. *Introduction to Ecology,* esp. ch. 40. NY: Wiley.
26. R. M. May. 1973. *Stability and Complexity in Model Ecosystems.* Princeton Univ. Press.

27. A. S. Leopold. 1966. Adaptability of animals to habitat change. In *Future Environments of North America,* ed. F. F. Darling and J. P. Milton, pp. 66-75. Garden City, NY: Natural History Press.

28. L. B. Slobodkin. 1964. The strategy of evolution. *Am. Sci.* 52:342-57.

29. A. H. Westing. 1971. Ecological effects of military defoliation on the forests of South Vietnam. *BioScience* 21:893-98; J. Otterman. 1974. Baring high-albedo soils by overgrazing: A hypothesized desertification mechanism. *Science* 186:531-33; W. E. Ormerod. 1976. Ecological effect of control of African trypanosomiasis. *Science* 191: 815-21.

30. L. M. Talbot et al. 1965. The meat production potential of wild animals in Africa. *Commonwealth Agricultural Bureaux Technical Publications* 16; R. F. Dasmann. 1964. *African Game Ranching.* Oxford: Pergamon.

31. E. O. A. Asibey. 1974. Wildlife as a source of protein in Africa south of the Sahara. *Biol. Cons.* 6:32-39.

32. H. T. P. Hayes. In press. *The Last Place on Earth.* NY: Stein & Day.

33. D. Janzen. 1973. Tropical agroecosystems. *Science* 182:1212-19.

34. J. G. Gosselink, E. P. Odum, and R. M. Pope. 1974. The value of the tidal marsh. Baton Rouge: Louisiana State Univ. Center for Wetland Resources, LSU-SG-74-03.

35. C. W. Clark. 1973. The economics of overexploitation. *Science* 181:630-34; Profit maximization and the extinction of animal species. *Jour. Pol. Economy* 81:950-61.

36. W. Tans. 1974. Priority ranking of biotic natural areas. *Michigan Botanist* 13:31-39.

37. F. R. Gehlbach. 1975. Investigation, evaluation, and priority ranking of natural areas. *Biol. Cons.* 8:79-88.

38. G. Bateson. 1972. *Steps to an Ecology of Mind.* NY: Ballantine.

39. A. Carr. 1964. *Ulendo: Travels of a Naturalist in and out of Africa.* NY: Knopf.

40. A. F. Coimbra-Filho, A. Magnanini, and R. A. Mittermeier. 1975. Vanishing gold: Last chance for Brazil's lion tamarins. *Animal Kingdom,* Dec., pp. 20-26.

41. For an example of this viewpoint, see the critical comments concerning the life-support systems that have been proposed for orbiting space colonies, especially remarks by J. Todd. 1976. *Coevolution Quarterly,* Spring, pp. 20-21, 54-65.

42. C. S. Elton. 1958. *The Ecology of Invasions by Animals and Plants,* pp. 143-45. London: Methuen.

43. C. D. Stone. 1974. *Should Trees Have Standing?* Los Altos, CA: Wm. Kaufmann, Inc. It is my impression that Stone's argument is unlikely to make any significant headway in the courts unless the national value systems that ultimately mold judicial practice undergo a fundamental change.

44. B. Dixon. 1976. Smallpox—Imminent extinction, and an unresolved dilemma. *New Scientist* 69:430-32; but see also P. Razzell. 1976. Smallpox extinction—A note of caution. *New Scientist* 71:35.

45. R. Allen. 1974. Does diversity grow cabbages? *New Scientist* 63:528-29.

46. The scientific origins of this idea are contained in the nineteenth century writings of Babbage and Marsh: C. Babbage. 1838. *The Ninth Bridgewater Treatise,* 2nd ed., ch. 9. London: John Murray. Repr. 1967. London: Cass; G. P. Marsh. 1865. *Man and Nature; or, Physical Geography as Modified by Human Action,* pp. 548-49. NY: Scribner's.

47. L. Mumford. 1956. Prospect. In *Man's Role in Changing the Face of the Earth,* ed. W. L. Thomas, Jr., pp. 1142-43. Chicago Univ. Press.

Mighty, Like a Furbish Lousewort

Peter Steinhart

It must have been one thing for Noah to listen to the Lord's instructions and imagine the cows, camels, lions, and ostriches marching gaily into a freshly painted ark. The animals were all large, familiar creatures, with bright brown eyes right where you expected to find them. The ones Noah hadn't seen down on the farm, perhaps he'd seen at the circus. After all, the man was 600 years old. He'd been around.

It must have been something else again when the day arrived and Noah looked down past his sandals to see "every creeping thing that creepeth upon the Earth" creeping in pairs up his gangplank. What in his 600 years could have prepared Noah for the endless river of minute, faceless things—of weevils, sponges, snails, spittlebugs, fleas, and leafhoppers? Surely as he squinted at the teaming creation, it must have been a relief just to see the more familiar form of a scurrying lizard or a lugubrious newt. Where would he put all these things? Had he gotten into nature just a bit over his head?

We can understand Noah's apprehension today because lately we have undertaken to repeat his efforts. Again we are attempting to carry out the divine instructions to bring into the ark at least two of "every living creature of all flesh...to keep seed alive upon the face of all the Earth."

Such, in Biblical terms, is the purpose of the Endangered Species Act of 1973. It is a powerful statute, strong enough to help humble weeds topple huge concrete dams. Already it has lumped together with the timber wolf, panther, and other legendary savages such unlikely impediments to progress as the snail darter and the Furbish lousewort. Like Noah, we have moments of doubt when we consider the power we are bequeathing to seemingly trivial beings. And there are many who would cure their frustration by shortening the instructions and amending the Endangered Species Act.

The Endangered Species Act is a sweeping advance over earlier wildlife legislation. Previous endangered species acts in 1966 and 1969 centered their interests upon mammals, birds, and fish. The 1973 act offers protection to any member of the plant and animal kingdoms, including subspecies, races, and local populations. The endangered species list kept by the U.S. Fish and Wildlife Service might include the names of mud-dwelling clams, saltwater sponges, clubferns, and crabgrasses. Earlier laws assumed the government's duty to be a passive one, consisting chiefly of policing hunters and regulating trade in such things as exotic pets, eagle feathers, and alligator skins. The 1973 act views land development as a potent exterminator of wild creatures and turns the government's attention from hunters and furriers to miners, dam builders, loggers, and highway engineers. It is an activist measure. It calls not just for protection of a diminished population but for efforts to restore a species to the point at which it is no longer endangered. Finally, Section 7 of the act makes its provisions binding upon all the agencies of the federal government.

Section 7 is an unusual display of commitment to a legislative purpose. In it, all agencies are required to consult with and seek the assistance of the Secretary of the Interior and to use their authorities "to insure that actions authorized, funded, or carried out by them do not jeopardize the continued existence of [protected species] or result in the destruction or modification of habitat of such species which is determined by the Secretary...to be critical." The temporizing phrases of earlier acts, which bound agencies to conserve protected species only "insofar as is practicable given the primary purposes of such agencies," have been discarded. Congress was emphatic.

The concept of "critical habitat" in Section 7 is the act's sharpest cutting edge. If the Secretary of the Interior determines that a particular habitat is critical to the survival of an endangered species, Section 7 calls on all federal agencies to avoid modifications of the habitat that would disturb the species. It does not necessarily create a wilderness or a nature preserve. But it does prohibit interference with feeding, migration, and reproduction.

In 1973, Section 7 was not even controversial. Everybody agreed that saving individual species from extinction was a noble goal. And many endangered species, such as timber wolves, whales, and whooping cranes, had become popular causes. The act passed the House of Representatives with a near-unanimous 390-12 vote. Congress was so agreeable that it gave explicit authority to any person to file suit to enforce provisions of the act. Declared Michigan Congressman John Dingell, "Agencies of government can no longer plead that they can do nothing about it. They can, and they must. The law is clear."

The act incited few suspicions. People thought there were only a few endangered species, a pine marten in Minnesota and perhaps a salamander in California. In 1973 there were only 109 American species on the endangered list. They were regarded somewhat as curiosities in a nation traditionally blessed with abundance. And most of them were confined to small out-of-the-way places, to marshes and drylands not prized for commercial development.

But the act invited citizens to petition for the listing of other names, including those of plants and invertebrates. Within two years, there were 24,000 plants and animals suggested. There were tiny freshwater mollusks and idiosyncratic orchids, things so obscure that only the most sophisticated biologist would recognize them. There were enough creatures selected for consideration to keep the seven scientists of the Office of Endangered Species working for 450 years just deciding which ones were endangered. And the listing had just begun. There were nearly 100,000 insects in North America, none of which had yet been proposed. What would happen when the office got around to studying tiny aphids, nameless ichneumons, and provincial asters, creatures with fussy habits and half-acre distributions?

While federal agencies might in time accept Section 7, their clients in industry were bound to fear it. In their eyes, the act might create a host of biological Clark Kents—innocuous animals and plants which, when confronted with ecological injustice, would throw off scaly suits and pliant habits to display rippling legal muscles and a militant will. Any of thousands of faceless creatures might leap up from a crack in the Earth and devour a strip-mine, a four-lane highway, or a billion-dollar irrigation scheme. If the act worked that well, industry might insist that Congress call it in and discipline it, like a naughty child who has too successfully imitated an adult. Power breeds enmity.

It was not necessary to wait for a strange bug to walk through the planner's ink. A few months after the act became law, an ordinary timber sales contract was rejected by the Oregon Bureau of Land Management because it would eliminate nesting sites for the northern spotted owl. Timber companies sent their attorneys scurrying to study the act. Arizona Representative Sam Steiger attempted to persuade the House of Representatives to declare that "endangered or threatened species shall be given equal but no greater consideration than other uses in determining proper allocations" on public lands.

Fearing such amendments, the Department of the Interior has moved with extreme caution in implementing the act. Three years after passage, there were only 172 American species on the endangered list, nine on the threatened list, six designations of "critical habitat," and no regulations by which agencies might know what kinds of consultation and assistance they should seek and what they might do if their own experts disagreed with Fish and Wildlife Service experts. Critics charged the Fish and Wildlife Service with unconscionable delay.

The Office of Endangered Species replied that it simply had been careful. "I don't think slow is the word," says Keith M. Schreiner, Fish and Wildlife Service associate director and former endangered species program manager. "We have been moving legally and judiciously. We want to be very sure we're right about the biology, inform everybody openly of what we're doing, and then go ahead and do it. Because if we don't, we're going to have weakening amendments. It's a beautiful law if we can just hang on to it, establish a few precedents without getting it weakened, and show that it won't make the world stop."

If the Department of the Interior walked softly, environmental groups were anything but shy. In comments upon environmental impact statements, they warned federal agencies to avoid encroachments upon the habitats of listed species. Thus, through attorneys, the California condor asked the Bureau of Land Management to withhold permits for phosphate extraction from its refuge. The Yuma clapper rail protested a planned resort development on public lands in Nevada. The palila urged the Hawaii Department of Land and Natural Resources to stop keeping goats for the benefit of hunters inside its fragile habitat. Peregrine falcons have cautioned the Bureau of Reclamation over plans to develop the Snake River plain. Grizzlies in Montana, whooping cranes in the Dakotas, bald eagles on the Potomac, and pine martens in Minnesota have all flexed the legal muscle given them by Section 7.

These comments are merely administrative actions, but they move inexorably toward courtroom tests of the Endangered Species Act. One prime candidate for a courtroom appearance was discovered recently in northern Maine, where the U.S. Army Corps of Engineers proposes to build large dams at Dickey and Lincoln Schoolhouse on the St. John River. At a cost of $670 million, Dickey–Lincoln would dam the last free-flowing river in the Northeast, flood 120,000 acres of forest, and provide a small amount of hydroelectric power to northern New England. Last summer, the Corps discovered a cluster of small yellow snapdragons on the banks of the St. John and identified them as Furbish lousewort. Thought to be extinct decades ago, the Furbish lousewort grows only in the St. John Valley. It is a partial parasite whose host is unknown, so it cannot be transplanted. Said Richard Dyer, a botanist working for the Corps of Engineers, "There will be a definite confrontation with the Endangered Species Act."

In court, legal arguments will turn upon the strength of Section 7. Does it apply to projects already under construction? Does the act permit trade-offs between environmental and economic benefits? Does it apply to overseas projects, say to foreign aid in development of a dam that jeopardizes the red-faced malkoha in Sri Lanka or Mrs. Morden's owlet in Kenya?

So far, the courts have smiled upon Section 7. In 1975, the National Wildlife Federation sued the Department of Transportation over plans to build a section of interstate highway through a proposed refuge for the last 40 Mississippi sandhill cranes. The Fish and Wildlife Service advised highway engineers that excavation techniques would lower the water table inside the cranes' marshy nesting area and that a planned interchange would lead to commercial development and housing. Either of those effects would doom the cranes. On the eve of the trial, the Fish and Wildlife Service declared Jackson County, Mississippi, to be "critical habitat." The court held that Section 7 of the act required the Federal Highway Administration not only to consult with the Secretary of the Interior but to "insure that the highway did not jeopardize the cranes or modify their habitat."

The Mississippi sandhill cranes did not demolish the highway. The court merely ordered elimination of the proposed interchange and care during construction to protect the water table. However, not all projects are as easily modified as a highway. Some projects are all-or-nothing. Dams, which are planned on enormous scale to fit the ponderous logic of cost-benefit analyses, tend to fall under this heading. When an endangered species comes up against a dam, it is almost sure to be one of those clashes between impetuous force and immovable object from which only one party limps away.

The snail darter, a small fish that feeds on snails in the clear, gravelly shallows of the Little Tennessee River, has become just such an impetuous force. The fish is found in no other river and, in fact, was not known to science until 1973. Six years earlier, however, Congress had authorized the Tennessee Valley Authority to construct Tellico Dam on the lower reaches of the river. Filling of the 30-mile reservoir would silt the gravelly bottom and reduce oxygen in the water. The snail darter would be destroyed. The last seventeen miles of the river were declared "critical habitat," and the snail darter went to court.

TVA argued that Congress had spent over $100 million on Tellico and that it was already 80 percent completed. To stop the project now would be "absurd" and "irrational." But the court replied, "Whether a dam is 50 or 90 percent completed is irrelevant in calculating the social and scientific costs attributable to the disappearance of a unique form of life." The court forbade closure of the dam and declared, "Only Congress or the Secretary of the Interior can properly exempt Tellico from compliance with the act." As things now stand, either TVA must prove the snail darter can be transplanted to the Hiwassee River, allowing the Secretary of the Interior to reconsider its "critical habitat," or Congress must vote to override the act to permit Tellico to be filled, or there will be an unused $100 million concrete wall—in one man's view, the world's largest drive-in movie screen—across the Little Tennessee.

It is just this predicament that worries modern-day Noahs. For just how mighty is a snail darter or a lousewort? Probably no mightier than the political sentiment it can muster. Not only is the immovable project an expensive one, but the impetuous force turns out to be something much less endearing than a porpoise or a timber wolf. Will Congress allow an economically insignificant fish to stop a $100 million dam? William Brown, consultant to the Fish and Wildlife Service, says, "Congress tends to like warm-blooded, big things. When we get to talking about snail darters and louseworts, that really worries me." Christian A. Herter III, executive director of the Maine Natural Resources Council and vigorous opponent of Dickey–Lincoln, says, "We can't believe that this dam is going to be stopped by a lousewort."

There is yet a fourth course of action, and that is outright emasculation of Section 7. Sooner or later, a lousewort or something more appealing is going to force Congress to choose between it and energy. Some legislators do not want to wait for such a contest but wish to abort Section 7 before it produces a popular plant or animal martyr. A bill introduced by Idaho Senator James A. McClure and Wyoming Senator Clifford P. Hansen would delay determination of "critical habitat" by requiring the Fish and Wildlife Service to prepare an environmental impact statement for each determination. Both senators fear that proposed grizzly "critical habitat" in their states could forestall prospecting for natural gas and recreational developments. Tennessee Senator Howard Baker has shelved TVA requests for a special exemption for Tellico and called instead for a review of the entire Endangered Species Act. Hearings in the summer may center upon amendments aimed either at making the listing of endangered species and determination of "critical habitat" discretionary rather than mandatory or exempting certain kinds of federal projects from the act. Either kind of amendment would divest Section 7 of its authority.

Attempts to amend the act make sense chiefly if one wants to shield projects from public scrutiny. Override votes are most likely to focus upon older projects, dams and irrigation schemes which have been sitting on the books for decades quietly soaking up small change while Congress or the Office of Management and Budget holds up the big construction fees. Such projects were seldom planned to meet today's environmental standards, and new public discussions might prove embarrassing to sponsor agencies. Would Congress blithely reauthorize California's gigantic Auburn Dam, which appears to be headed for a shaky seismic future? And if Congress does make individual overrides, it is likely to impose new environmental safeguards upon old projects, as it did when it overrode the National Environmental Policy Act to permit construction of the trans-Alaska pipeline.

Supporters of the act hope it can withstand attempts to amend Section 7. Says Keith Schreiner, "Our record is good. We haven't acted in a flippant manner. We hope that Congress will see that we've acted judiciously and honestly and will let us go ahead and see if the problems are really that great. We want an opportunity to consult with federal agencies before they're locked in, with huge amounts of money being spent, their opinions in concrete, and the public divided. Given the chance, we can do the job for endangered species without making the world stop."

If it comes down to a choice between amendment of the act and individual overrides, it is clear which is the lesser of two evils. Says Schreiner, "I'd rather lose the species. The act has the potential to save many species over time in its present form. I'd rather lose one than many."

Modern-day Noahs haven't the certainty of divine revelation to rest upon. They cannot tell whether they are engaged in revolution or mere rebellion. But it is certain that we, as a people, are undergoing a profound change. Before midcentury, we spoke of conservation as a means of deciding how we should distribute our resources. Today, we are demanding that some resources be left undistributed and instead allowed to serve unseen purposes and embody spiritual values. So new is this outlook that we haven't yet agreed upon ways to describe it. Our legislation is written with vague purpose clauses, whose voices trail off into uncertain dedications to "unquantified environmental amenities," "esthetic values," and "other intangibles."

Nevertheless, there is a general goal visible beneath this change. We wish to place man in a new perspective—to reject the badly battered view of man as Earth-pilot, firmly in control of nature and his own emotions. We seek rather to see man as a talented subject, capable of greatness but limited by dependencies upon lifeforms and processes he only begins to perceive. We would rid the world of conquerors and make it safe from dictators. While liberating humans from tyranny, we would also restore other creatures to their own innate capacities for survival. One attempt has been the Endangered Species Act. Perhaps the best reason to save the act is that not everybody has yet discovered its larger goal.

Legal power grows in strange places. It has risen from the backs of slaves to free them. It has crawled out from the shadows of racial segregation to gather voting rights and fair employment standards. It is collecting in suburban kitchens and juvenile prisons to create new rights for women and children. Sometimes its emergence seems silly, as when someone wins the right to run naked on a beach or to make insulting gestures at policemen—or to halt a half-billion-dollar dam in the name of the lousewort. But it is always serious business, for it indicates what we see and what we value. Frequently, that is wiser than we know.

The Ecological Conscience

Aldo Leopold

Conservation is a state of harmony between men and land. Despite nearly a century of propaganda, conservation still proceeds at a snail's pace; progress still consists largely of letterhead pieties and convention oratory. On the back forty we still slip two steps backward for each forward stride.

The usual answer to this dilemma is 'more conservation education.' No one will debate this, but is it certain that only the *volume* of education needs stepping up? Is something lacking in the *content* as well?

It is difficult to give a fair summary of its content in brief form, but, as I understand it, the content is substantially this: obey the law, vote right, join some organizations, and practice what conservation is profitable on your own land; the government will do the rest.

Is not this formula too easy to accomplish anything worth-while? It defines no right or wrong, assigns no obligation, calls for no sacrifice, implies no change in the current philosophy of values. In respect of landuse, it urges only enlightened self-interest. Just how far will such education take us? An example will perhaps yield a partial answer.

By 1930 it had become clear to all except the ecologically blind that southwestern Wisconsin's topsoil was slipping seaward. In 1933 the farmers were told that if they would adopt certain remedial practices for five years, the public would donate CCC labor to install them, plus the necessary machinery and materials. The offer was widely accepted, but the practices were widely forgotten when the five-year contract period was up. The farmers continued only those practices that yielded an immediate and visible economic gain for themselves.

This led to the idea that maybe farmers would learn more quickly if they themselves wrote the rules. Accordingly the Wisconsin Legislature in 1937 passed the

Soil Conservation District Law. This said to farmers, in effect: *We, the public, will furnish you free technical service and loan you specialized machinery, if you will write your own rules for land-use. Each county may write its own rules, and these will have the force of* law. Nearly all the counties promptly organized to accept the proffered help, but after a decade of operation, *no county has yet written a single rule.* There has been visible progress in such practices as strip-cropping, pasture renovation, and soil liming, but none in fencing woodlots against grazing, and none in excluding plow and cow from steep slopes. The farmers, in short, have selected those remedial practices which were profitable anyhow, and ignored those which were profitable to the community, but not clearly profitable to themselves.

When one asks why no rules have been written, one is told that the community is not yet ready to support them; education must precede rules. But the education actually in progress makes no mention of obligations to land over and above those dictated by self-interest. The net result is that we have more education but less soil, fewer healthy woods, and as many floods as in 1937.

The puzzling aspect of such situations is that the existence of obligations over and above self-interest is taken for granted in such rural community enterprises as the betterment of roads, schools, churches, and baseball teams. Their existence is not taken for granted, nor as yet seriously discussed, in bettering the behavior of the water that falls on the land, or in the perserving of the beauty or diversity of the farm landscape. Land-use ethics are still governed wholly by economic self-interest, just as social ethics were a century ago.

To sum up: we asked the farmer to do what he conveniently could to save his soil, and he has done just that, and only that. The farmer who clears the woods off a 75 per cent slope, turns his cows into the clearing, and dumps its rainfall, rocks, and soil into the community creek, is still (if otherwise decent) a respected member of society. If he puts lime on his fields and plants his crops on contour, he is still entitled to all the privileges and emoluments of his Soil Conservation District. The District is a beautiful piece of social machinery, but it is coughing along on two cylinders because we have been too timid, and too anxious for quick success, to tell the farmer the true magnitude of his obligations. Obligations have no meaning without conscience, and the problem we face is the extension of the social conscience from people to land.

No important change in ethics was ever accomplished without an internal change in our intellectual emphasis, loyalties, affections, and convictions. The ptoof that conservation has not yet touched these foundations of conduct lies in the fact that philosophy and religion have not yet heard of it. In our attempt to make conservation easy, we have made it trivial. When the logic of history hungers for bread and we hand out a stone, we are at pains to explain how much the stone resembles bread. I now describe some of the stones which serve in lieu of a land ethic.

One basic weakness in a conservation system based wholly on economic motives is that most members of the land community have no economic value. Wildflowers and songbirds are examples. Of the 22,000 higher plants and animals native to Wisconsin, it is doubtful whether more than 5 per cent can be sold, fed, eaten, or otherwise put to economic use. Yet these creatures are members of the biotic community, and if (as I believe) its stability depends on its integrity, they are entitled to continuance.

When one of these non-economic categories is threatened, and if we happen to love it, we invent subterfuges to give it economic importance. At the beginning of the century songbirds were supposed to be disappearing. Ornithologists jumped to the rescue with some distinctly shaky evidence to the effect that insects would eat us up if birds failed to control them. The evidence had to be economic in order to be valid.

It is painful to read these circumlocutions today. We have no land ethic yet, but we have at least drawn nearer the point of admitting that birds should continue as a matter of biotic right, regardless of the presence or absence of economic advantage to us.

A parallel situation exists in respect of predatory mammals, raptorial birds, and fish-eating birds. Time was when biologists somewhat overworked the evidence that these creatures preserve the health of game by killing weaklings, or that they control rodents for the farmer, or that they prey only on 'worthless' species. Here again, the evidence had to be economic in order to be valid. It is only in recent years that we hear the more honest argument that predators are members of the community, and that no special interest has the right to exterminate them for the sake of a benefit, real or fancied, to itself. Unfortunately this enlightened view is still in the talk stage. In the field the extermination of predators goes merrily on: witness the impending erasure of the timber wolf by fiat of Congress, the Conservation Bureaus, and many state legislatures.

Some species of trees have been 'read out of the wide limits. All gains from density are subject to a law of diminishing returns.

Whatever may be the equation for men and land, it is improbable that we as yet know all its terms. Recent discoveries in mineral and vitamin nutrition reveal unsuspected dependencies in the up-circuit: incredibly minute quantities of certain substances determine the value of soils to plants, of plants to animals. What of the down-circuit? What of the vanishing species, the preservation of which we now regard as an esthetic luxury? They helped build the soil; in what unsuspected ways may they be essential to its maintenance? Professor Weaver proposes that we use prairie flowers to reflocculate the wasting soils of the dust bowl; who knows for what purpose cranes and condors, otters and grizzlies may some day be used?

A land, ethic, then, reflects the existence of an ecological conscience, and this in turn reflects a conviction of individual responsibility for the health of the land. Health is the capacity of the land for self-renewal. Conservation is our effort to understand and preserve this capacity.

Conservationists are notorious for their dissensions. Superficially these seem to add up to mere confusion, but a more careful scrutiny reveals a single plane of cleavage common to many specialized fields. In each field one group (A) regards the land as soil, and its function as commodity-production; another group (B) regards the land as a biota, and its function as something broader. How much broader is admittedly in a state of doubt and confusion.

In my own field, forestry, group A is quite content to grow trees like cabbages, with cellulose as the basic forest commodity. It feels no inhibition against violence; its ideology is agronomic. Group B, on the other hand, sees forestry as fundamentally different from agronomy because it employs natural species, and manages a natural environment rather than creating an artificial one. Group B prefers natural reproduction on principle. It worries on biotic as well as economic grounds about the loss of species like chestnut, and the threatened loss of the white pines. It worries about a whole series of secondary forest functions: wildlife, recreation, watersheds, wilderness areas. To my mind, Group B feels the stirrings of an ecological conscience.

In the wildlife field, a parallel cleavage exists. For Group A the basic commodities are sport and meat; the yardsticks of production are ciphers of take in pheasants and trout. Artificial propagation is acceptable as a permanent as well as a temporary recourse—if its unit costs permit. Group B, on the other hand, worries about a whole series of biotic side-issues. What is the cost in predators of producing a game crop? Should we have further recourse to exotics? How can management restore the shrinking species, like prairie grouse, already hopeless as shootable game? How can management restore the threatened rarities, like trumpeter swan and whooping crane? Can management principles be extended to wildflowers? Here again it is clear to me that we have the same A-B cleavage as in forestry.

In the larger field of agriculture I am less competent to speak, but there seems to be somewhat parallel cleavages. Scientific agriculture was actively developing before ecology was born, hence a slower penetration of ecological concepts might be expected. Moreover the farmer, by the very nature of his techniques, must modify the biota more radically than the forester or the wildlife manager. Nevertheless, there are many discontents in agriculture which seem to add up to a new vision of 'biotic farming.'

Perhaps the most important of these is the new evidence that poundage or tonnage is no measure of the food-value of farm crops; the products of fertile soil may be qualitatively as well as quantitatively superior. We can bolster poundage from depleted soils by pouring on imported fertility, but we are not necessarily bolstering food-value. The possible ultimate ramifications of this idea are so immense that I must leave their exposition to abler pens.

The discontent that labels itself 'organic farming,' while bearing some of the earmarks of a cult, is nevertheless biotic in its direction, particularly in its insistence on the importance of soil flora and fauna.

The ecological fundamentals of agriculture are just as poorly known to the public as in other fields of land-use. For example, few educated people realize that the marvelous advances in technique made during recent decades are improvements in the pump, rather than the well. Acre for acre, they have barely sufficed to offset the sinking level of fertility.

In all of these cleavages, we see repeated the same basic paradoxes: man the conqueror *versus* man the biotic citizen; science the sharpener of his sword *versus* science the searchlight on his universe; land the slave and servant *versus* land the collective organism. Robinson's injunction to Tristram may well be applied, at this juncture, to *Homo sapiens* as a species in geological time:

Whether you will or not
You are a King, Tristram, for you are one
Of the time-tested few that leave the world,
When they are gone, not the same place it was,
Mark what you leave.

Toward An Ecological Ethic

Toward an Ecological Ethic

Wes Jackson

Those of us who think about the need for an ecological or environmental ethic should take seriously the wise words of Aldo Leopold who said, "...nothing so important as an ethic is ever 'written.' Only the most superficial student of history supposes that Moses 'wrote' the Decalogue; it evolved in the minds of a thinking community, and Moses wrote a tentative summary of it for a 'seminar.'"[1]

No ethic written this evening or tomorrow concerning the environment will be widely accepted. Rather it is for us as colleagues in the "thinking community" Leopold mentioned to do lots of hard thinking about that ethic.

Sizing Up the Problem

I will avoid a re-statement of the problems of the environment in checklist fashion. I will also refrain from presenting an extensive literature review of opinion on the causes. Nevertheless, there are a few rather widespread notions of where to lay the blame that we might consider for a moment.

Most of you are familiar with the now-classical paper by the historian Lynn White, "The Historical Roots of Our Ecological Crisis." White takes the philosophical position that "Human Ecology is deeply conditioned by beliefs about our nature and destiny—that is by religion." Christianity doesn't come out so well in that paper for, according to White, we must "reject the Christian axiom that nature has no reason for existence save to serve man."[2]

A more thorough-going treatment of the subject was attempted by Theodore Roszak who posited tandem culprits: Christianity *and* Science. Christianity is blamed because of its insistence that all other myths be excluded in favor of one great myth. Science is criticized because it explains objects in the environment as "nothing but." The mystical essence of objects was removed as Nature was turned over and over in the palm of the hand, in the test tube and on the lab bench. Once the mystical essence had been destroyed or reduced, our old animistic faith with the environment had been broken. The pursuit of reason and objectivity granted mankind power over Nature.[3]

The following poem by Galen Rowell is about a bristle cone pine. Named "WPN-114" by a scientist, it illustrates the attitude of which Roszak writes. The pine began life in 2880 B.C. and ceased to exist as a tree on 1964 A.D.—a span of 4844 years.

The ex-Oldest Living Thing on Earth—
Was ancient when Cortez Conquered Mexico,
Was bent with years when Caesar entered Gaul,
Was old beyond memory when Moses delivered the Law,
Was Time's patient watchman when Cheops built his pyramid,
Was sliced by a chainsaw to see how old it was.

Requiescat in Pacem[4]

It is the pursuit of reason and objectivity which made this tree just an object, in Roszak's analysis. It is a small wonder that an alien and distanced relationship with our environment has developed.

Science is only one culprit. Christianity helped by placing emphasis on the "word," making the "word" central. The altar was symbolically pushed to the side and replaced by the pulpit. The scientific revolution was thus inevitable. In the wake of this revolution, Roszak contends, we find humans stripped of their "sacramental awareness" of nature and their "energies of transcendence" gone. Reason now rules. Reason dictates our politics and economics. The whole man is destroyed and the man of "single vision" reigns.[5] The reward for the destroyed communion with nature has been power, both power over nature and power over other humans. So goes the Roszak thesis.

Thomas J. Lyon has suggested that the root of our crisis may be a psychic split, actually a problem of brain anatomy.[5] His touchstone is the somewhat popular book, *The Psychology of Consciousness* by Robert Ornstein, who, in summarizing much research, describes the bilateral specialization of the cerebral cortex.[6] The left hemisphere of the brain processes information in orderly sequence. Language and logic are at home here. So are our sense of time, our ability to plan, to write, to verify, to reason and to read. On the right side we find specialization for our intuitive sense and altogether non-linear understanding. Our sense of place, ability to see, sing and dream are associated with this right side.

We recognize right away that Western civilization has placed a premium on the things which the left side does well and has diminished the importance of the intuitive and space senses of the right half. Perhaps in our hunting-gathering days, there was more balance in our psychic activity in order to survive in such an environment. But when we began to manage ecosystems through agriculture, more time during the day had to be devoted to the rational, logical side. Lyon suggests that this psychic split and over-emphasis of one side may be construed as responsible for the human condition of alienation from the environment.

These are but three accounts of the many efforts to size up the problem. Personally, I would be somewhat reluctant to blame either the Judaeo-Christian ethic or Science for the demise of the planet. The Genesis statement on dominion does appear early in the *Holy Bible* and therefore likely was read more often than statements which spoke to alternative relationships to nature. To be sure, scientists have treated objects in the environment as "nothing but," taking a very mechanistic view of nature, but destruction was underway before either the Judaeo-Christian influence or science as we know it came on the scene. After all, Plato lamented the sorry condition of the mountains of Attica, a once prosperous region only "fit for bees" by his time.[7] Finally, to explain the whole of the human condition as the consequence of a fragile connection between the brain hemispheres seems a bit much.

A Look to Some Eastern Religions for Help

Whatever the cause of our growing alienation from nature, many in our society are responding by developing an interest in some of the religions of the East, religions which we faintly recall have a strong dose of nature worship and are therefore worthy of examination. To be sure, the Shinto religion of the Japanese was originally a form of nature worship. But Buddhism is especially attractive to many environmentalists, particularly those who see consumerism as the heart of the ecological problem. Buddhists believe we are sad because we thirst for things, and when we have accumulated things we become their slaves. So long as we desire possessions, we are prevented from attaining knowledge and insight. (For a splendid treatment of Buddhist economics, see the now popular book, *Small is Beautiful, Economics as if People Mattered,* by the British economist, E. F. Schumacher.)[8]

The religion of the East of which we seem to hear more and more in our search is Taoism, one of the three great religions of China. Tao rules heaven, heaven rules earth, and earth rules man. All are designed to move in harmony, except that man has upset this harmony by substituting his own designs. Tao is "the way" which man can only know if he returns to a life of humility and simplicity. He can find peace and harmony only by returning to nature.

So it would seem that we could take our pick of the ethical systems already instituted long ago by the religions of the East. Perhaps there is no need for a "thinking community" to evolve an ecological ethic. Like most solutions, however, there is at least one major flaw. For in spite of the fact that Eastern cultures often did practice their beliefs, and that officials did encourage harmony with nature, they did so when in Tuan's words, "it did not conflict with the urgent needs of the moment."[9] Rene Dubos goes so far as to say that the "Chinese attitude of respect for nature probably arose, in fact, as a response to the damage done in antiquity."[10] The British scientist and historian, Joseph Needham, has shown how the Chinese used technology destructively long before the West had equaled China in scientific and technological development, which wasn't until the 17th century.[11] Even the Buddhists contributed to deforestation to build their temples. In some places they used more than half the available timber.[12] Finally, the classic nature poets of China, writing as though they had achieved identification with the cosmos, were, it turns out, retired bureaucrats living on estates in which gardeners trimmed and managed local nature.[10]

Since these religions arose after much destruction, their relative ineffectiveness when "urgent needs were upon the people," causes one to wonder how much they have to contribute to our "thinking community," only lately worrying about similar problems in the West. I believe we *cannot* turn exclusively to the religions of the East for profound guidance; we must do some creative thinking on our own.

The Fall of Man Revisited

To begin this creative process, I suggest a revisit of the "fall of man." The Genesis account, you will recall, is one in which an explicit commandment was given by God. The first humans disobeyed, and, according to some, for that error we still pay. Much of the human condition is the consequence of this act.

There is another "fall of man" story—a modern one—relevant to our situation. A few years ago on the last page of *Life Magazine,* I saw a memorable photograph of a near-naked and well-muscled tribesman of Indonesian New Guinea, staring at a parked airplane in a jungle clearing. The caption read something to the effect that the Indonesian government was attempting to bring these savages into the money economy. They had set up a stand on the edge of the jungle and reportedly were doing a brisk business in beer, soda pop and tennis shoes.

We can imagine what must have followed, what the wages of their sin, *their* fall, must have been—decaying teeth, anxiety in a money system, destruction of their social structure. If they were like what we know of most so-called primitive peoples, in spite of a hierarchial structure, they had a much more egalitarian society than industrialized people today.[13]

The New Guinea tribesmen did not receive an explicit commandment to avoid the "goodies of civilization," unlike Eve, and later Adam, who partook of the tree of knowledge (something for us academics to ponder). They were simply *unwittingly accessible* to the worldly items of beer, soda pop and tennis shoes.[14] In the Genesis version, the sin involves disobedience, an exercise of free will. In the latter, the "original sin" is our very nature, our unwitting accessibility to the material things of the world.

And now, for a third rendition of the fall of man. This is another modern story, perhaps a parable for our time. Several years ago, I saw a newspaper account of the recent life of Edwin "Buzz" Aldrin, Jr., an astronaut who walked on the moon. After his adventures, he told of pressure to accomplish and excel in the space program. He discussed the anxieties, the rivalry, the internal politics, all the common human problems which became exacerbated among those attempting the greatest technological adventure of all time. "Our profession requires constant study and work. It was too competitive to get behind," Aldrin said. Some time after his return and the around-the-world public relations trip, Aldrin recognized that his mental health was in jeopardy and spent a month in a hospital undergoing psychiatric treatment. But there is a stunning end to the story. In spite of the terrific psychological turmoil, he has said that he would do it all over again.

In the Genesis account, Eve and Adam and all of humanity to follow had no choice as to their way of life after the forbidden fruit was taken. The New Guinea tribesmen, unwittingly accessible and lacking much of an overall perspective, doubtlessly became technological junkies with all the attendant problems. They likely stayed hooked. Is the story of Buzz Aldrin the analog for modern humanity? We know we have broken from an intimate association with nature. As a people we associate less with trees, grass, pure water, things warm and human, and more and more with cars, TV sets and chemical feasts. We make the comparison, acknowledge the psychological turmoil of the modern way and say it is too bad. But the TV set gets a higher rating than a sunset and all that remains healthy is the GNP.

What Kind of a Creature is This?

When we think about our problem with ourselves and with nature, we become perplexed and ask, "What kind of a creature is this?", almost within a mood that suggests we aren't talking about humans, but about some other species. And of course, as soon as we ask that question, we have asked the oldest religious question, "What is man?"

There are lots of answers to this question, and they have to do with where we begin in time, and what dimension of humanity we speak about. If we go way back into our origins, we can picture ourselves as beautiful children of the universe along with all other living things. Here is how Nobel laureate and biologist George Wald describes us:

We living things are a late outgrowth of the metabolism of our Galaxy. The carbon that enters so importantly into our composition was cooked in the remote past in a dying star. From it at lower temperatures nitrogen and oxygen were formed. These, our indispensable elements were spewed out into space in the exhalations of red giants and such stellar catastrophes as supernovae, there to be mixed with hydrogen, to form eventually the substance of the sun and the planets, and ourselves. The waters of the ancient seas set the pattern of ions in our blood. The ancient atmosphere molded our metabolism.[15]

Beautiful! What a beginning!

We don't fare so badly either when we describe ourselves as higher primates, having been around some 2 to 3 million years or so. We have had this large brain for some 200,000 years. Continuing forward, Cro-magnon was here by 30,000 years ago. Indeed, we were hunters and gatherers until some 8 to 10 thousand years ago. Think of it: for some 95% of our total evolutionary history with the big brain, we gathered and hunted and fished in what we would recognize today as mature ecosystems. Aside from causing the extinction of some significant megafauna,[16] we were a species pretty well-integrated with our surrounding environment. To this point we still might regard ourselves as that innocent child of the universe.

Our age of innocence ended with the advent of agriculture, that period 8 to 10 thousand years ago when the greatest set of revolutionaries the earth has known began to change the face of the earth. The revolutionaries gave us essentially all of our crops and domesticated animals. Since then, very few ones have been added. With that revolution came the large immature ecosystems, the monoculture, and maybe for the first time, the epidemic. Because immature ecosystems have an excess of potential energy, that revolution eventually gave us civilizations which ran along on what Georgescu-Roegen[17] calls our "terrestrial dowery," usually with a decline in that dowery.

However it began, it seems likely that the agricultural enterprise began unwittingly with no explicit warning that some agriculture promotes more agriculture in the same way that some consumer items such as beer, soda pop and tennis shoes promotes the need for more beer, soda pop and tennis shoes. Eventually man took over much of the role of nature and now a new thing had appeared on the earth, at least in a magnitude unknown till now: the substitution of enterprise for patience. Man began to reward enterprise as nature continued to reward patience. Innocence now began to fade. From agriculture on, the slide toward mine dependence was simply a matter of enterprising man using his clever brain—usually with more cleverness than wisdom.

I think it is important for us to remember that it all began in innocence rather than sin. If modern day tribesmen were accessible to the beer, soda pop and tennis shoes, even while they were living within the context of the system which had shaped both their bodies and their psyches, why should it be at all surprising that "out-of-context" hunters and gatherers with backs bent by agriculture would be accessible to the promises of coal, oil and natural gas?

And now I must pause, for if the description of what we are stops here, *Homo sapiens* is only half-described. The other half, of course, is that we are a species capable of creating and manipulating symbols, a creature who, William Blake insisted, "must and will have some religion."[18] We are a species whose existence seems to be as dependent upon the opportunity to rise to creative and religious heights as it is dependent upon the opportunity to breathe good air and drink good water. And then there is the most sobering thought of all; we seem to be matter's way of having gained self-recognition, at least for this solar system. If we fashion a do-it-yourself extinction, it will be a long time before matter can recognize itself again, at least in this part of the universe.

What kind of creature are we? Hunters and gatherers out of context. Enterprising! (Perhaps enterprising because we are out of context.) What is man? A creature born more in innocence than in sin. Accessible to the products of the earth that our clever minds can fashion. A symbol-maker and manipulator of symbols. A creature who "must and will have some religion."

Four Proposals

All of these considerations must be background for a "thinking community" out of which an ecological ethic can evolve. No modern day or future Moses, conducting a seminar in which our ethic becomes summarized, dares ignore this totality.

I have four proposals to contribute to this segment of the "thinking community"—proposals which I think can help us toward the evolution of an ecological ethic. These four proposals very much involve us both as individuals and as biologists. I have stressed that our fall with agriculture and our continued tumble into the making of civilizations and the exploitative industrial state happened innocently. *I have not done this for the purpose of suggesting that we return to hunting and gathering.* Far too much has gone through the turbines for that to happen.

In spite of my contention that we were born in innocence, we need to remember that there comes a time in the life of an innocent child when innocence leads to disruption or destruction in the home that parents will not tolerate. Eventually, the child must develop the point of view of the parents.

The age of innocence for humanity is over. It is time to ask, almost prayerfully, "What would the system have us do in order to preserve and maintain the long-term ability of the system to support a variety of life and culture and maximize options for future generations?" So my first proposal is that we begin to develop the point of view of the life support system.

I first began to think about this in earnest after reading Aldo Leopold's essay on "Thinking like a mountain."[1]

"A deep chesty bawl echoes from rimrock to rimrock, rolls down the mountain, and fades into the far blackness of the night. It is an outburst of wild defiant sorrow, and of contempt for all the adversities of the world.

"Every living thing (and perhaps many a dead one as well) pays heed to that call. To the deer it is a reminder of the way of all flesh, to the pine a forecast of midnight scuffles and of blood upon the snow, to the coyote a promise of gleanings to come, to the cowman a threat of red ink at the bank, to the hunter a challenge of fang against bullet. Yet behind these obvious and immediate hopes and fears there lies a deeper meaning, known only to the mountain itself. Only the mountain has lived long enough to listen objectively to the howl of a wolf.

"Those unable to decipher the hidden meaning know nevertheless that it is there, for it is felt in all wolf country, and distinguishes that country from all other land. It tingles in the spine of all who hear wolves by night, or who scan their tracks by day. Even without sight or sound of wolf, it is implicit in a hundred small events: the midnight whinny of a pack horse, the rattle of rolling rocks, the bound of a fleeing deer, the way shadows lie under the spruces. Only the ineducable tyro can fail to sense the presence or absence of wolves, or the fact that mountains have a secret opinion about them.

"My own conviction on this score dates from the day I saw a wolf die. We were eating lunch on a high rimrock, at the foot of which a turbulent river elbowed its way. We saw what we thought was a doe fording the torrent, her breast awash in white water. When she climbed the bank toward us and shook out her tail, we realized our error: it was a wolf. A half-dozen others, evidently grown pups, sprang from the willows and all joined in a welcoming mêlée of wagging tails and playful maulings. What was literally a pile of wolves writhed and tumbled in the center of an open flat at the foot of our rimrock.

"In those days we had never heard of passing up a chance to kill a wolf. In a second we were pumping lead into the pack, but with more excitement than accuracy: how to aim a steep downhill shot is always confusing. When our rifles were empty, the old wolf was down, and a pup was dragging a leg into impassable slide rocks.

"We reached the old wolf in time to watch a fierce green fire dying in her eyes. I realized then, and have known ever since, that there was something new to me in those eyes—something known only to her and to the mountain. I was young then, and full of trigger-itch; I thought that because fewer wolves meant more deer, that no wolves would mean hunters' paradise. But after seeing the green fire die, I sensed that neither the wolf nor the mountain agreed with such a view."

Mountains can relate part of the opinion of the life support system. So can rivers in their angry, muddy, churning every spring when they raise their backs, and within widening and caving banks carry a rich plasma, the ecological capital, the terrestrial dowery, all the way from my area in Kansas to New Orleans and the Gulf. With the prairie sponge nearly gone, thousands of tons of this ecological capital disappear into the Gulf in a year.

The air of our Earth Mother testifies about the earth's condition to the passengers of a jet who look out the window and to the inhabitants of our large industrial cities whose eyes begin to water when they walk out the doors of their homes. The Mother seems to say, "This air sink is too full." And, as if this message is not direct enough, our very cells, having had no evolutionary experience with large numbers of various man-made chemicals, often go wild when Mississippi water is consumed in New Orleans.

We can even say that Mother Earth is telling us through species extinctions and declining populations. These species are like mine canaries to us, as Roger Tory Peterson has said. This is so, of course, because the redwood and the whale, the sunflower and the osprey, and essentially all the rest of the living creation possess the same blueprint approach through the DNA's and the RNA's in assembling the same 20 amino acids. In mechanistic language, the canary is sent into the mine as a highly sensitive instrument. Its similarity to us is what makes it reliable as an instrument, not its difference. Any atmosphere, sufficiently noxious to be wrong for the canary is eventually wrong for us. Through our awareness of this similarity of life forms, Mother Earth effectively says that whatever it is that threatens other species with extinction or serious population decline is also a threat to humans. It is the role of biologists to make this clear to all our students and to a listening public. I happen to agree with Schumacher that the primary purpose of education is for the transmission of values.[8]

Unwittingly and innocently accessible to our clever devices we have been, and now the message comes back in a thousand ways; however beautiful we children of the earth are, we products of the simian line, however tender a carnivore we claim to be, the Earth Mother simply will not stand much more in the way of extensive species truncation and extinctions for the sake of further increasing the amount of human biomass and wasteful livelihood.

The beautiful child of the home has learned that it is tenderness and not greed which enhances her stature in the family. The beautiful child has learned that it is service to others within the family which generates stability, not exploitative demands. All humans must eventually learn, that this is also the proper relationship with our Earth Mother.

We *can* learn from the earth. So in developing an ecological ethic, we should first develop the point of view of the life-support system. Any standards of conduct which are set by an ecological ethic must be with this point of view in mind.

My second proposal may be highly controversial because of the current disagreement about the value of Sociobiology between Harvard colleagues E. O. Wilson and Richard Lewontin. Nevertheless, I propose that we learn as much as we can about human activity in the environment which shaped us. We spend most of our time peeking into our past through written history, mainly because the history of agricultural man, civilized man, is easily available. But if we take the 5 to 6 thousand years of recorded history and compare it to the 200,000 years that man has existed with the big brain, we are talking about some 2 to 3 percent of the total. I jokingly remind my historian friends that written history is an account of humans during the most abnormal years of the species. If one is interested in abnormal social psychology, he or she studies history.

I think we can learn much about our current and otherwise unexplainable behavior by studying our paleolithic rootedness, the pattern of events in the day and the year in the life of those intelligent hunters and gatherers. Please understand, this is not for the purpose of discovering a primitive ''Be Kind to Nature'' ethical system. In fact, I sometimes wonder how important an ecological ethic was for our ancestors, or for that matter how important it is for the few tribes left.

The Kalihari Bushmen are hunters and gatherers, and we can learn about ourselves by observing their lives. Bushmen of the Kalihari like to eat a rather large nocturnal mammal called the springhaas.[19] Capturing and killing this animal causes a complete destruction of the immediate area. When two hunters discover a burrow, they position themselves at opposite ends and begin to dig furiously with long sticks, throwing dirt in every direction. They have only one thing in mind, to capture and kill this animal.

How about an environmental impact analysis with a paragraph or two on impact mitigation for this area? It isn't necessary, of course, for nature does have redemptive powers, and for that area, redemption is carried out by the reproductive pressure of the springhaas population and ecological succession of the vegetation. By the time these or other tribesmen come that way again, the local area likely will have healed. And here is the point: they can afford to take without thought for the morrow, because the long-term ability of the system to support a variety of life and their culture has not been destroyed. The local terrestrial dowery is still there. Even the nutrients tied up in the springhaas will be returned to the general area for recycling. No ecological ethic is necessary so long as the energy input into an area is spent through the arms and legs of the people of the area.

Why should we be so surprised then that the environment takes such a beating? We simply take, as we always have, from the environment, usually without thought. This pattern of behavior is likely deep within our psychological meat and will not be mitigated without internalized pressure from an ethic. Before the fall, when our numbers were few and our tools simple, like the Bushmen, such an ethic was not necessary.

But to return to the main point of this second proposal. Is it not likely that there are some paleolithic urges which need to be satiated, played out, bled off—*now that we are out of context*—and others which need to be amplified? The total ensemble of our daily activities, I would think, could be enhanced by a discovery of their analogs in the past.

Is it possible that we will one day see our drive to attain status in a hierarchy in order to obtain big cars, big houses, and multitudes of consumer goods as ways of playing out the urges which were needed for survival in our paleolithic past? And isn't it possible that we might invent games or activities to satiate those urges and thereby make the big car and the heavy consumption unnecessary? But I realize that I am treading on dangerous ground. Yet, as the debate about Sociobiology continues, I shall maintain this second proposal: to learn as much as possible about life in the environment which shaped us.

My third proposal involves the heart of the ethic. This proposal is to place ourselves in positions to maximize our sense of organic interrelatedness both among members of our own species and other species so that we can know and feel our rootedness in the land.

Guilt and fear may be good motivators for initiating action, but in the midst of seeming plenty they do a poor job at sustaining that action. Shortly before and after Earth Day, 1970, we saw a flourish of eco-activity throughout the "respectable" society that, at best, bordered on tokenism. Housewives changed their soaps, hauled their cans and papers to the re-cycling center, turned the thermostats down a little in winter and up a bit in summer. Here and there, a few car pools were tried. School kids pulled old tires out of streams and vowed to have "no more than two." Finally, it mostly died down. Guilt had been satiated, and fear turned to fatalism. Those with "mature judgement" in the society dismissed the whole thing as a fad and let it go at that. It was "business as usual," even in the midst of it all.

During that period, almost every environmental speech ended with "what the individual can do," partly because the guilty and fearful wanted to know. Most of those speeches contained a statement to the effect that the quality of life can improve with a decrease in the consumption of material goods. However, this was such a new idea that it was not really understood or seriously tried by many. Now we have citizens who are beginning to understand the need for the U.S. to conserve resources but are not personally motivated to decrease their consumption of material goods. And so we are at a new point of departure. From now on, any suggestion as to what the individual can do must have an appeal more like the proverbial carrot before the donkey, rather than the switch behind his rump. We have had, almost exclusively, the negative motivations of fear and guilt before us, but with little success. Maybe it is because the guilty and fearful have caught on that their resource savings will simply get blotted up by the non-guilty and non-fearful.

If we are to try the "carrot" approach, the heaviest burden is on the environmentalist who must suggest alternatives which favorably compete with the large single-unit campers, high-powered motorboats, entire evenings of TV with its advertisements that whet and give license to consumptive appetities, the shopping trips to huge discount shopping centers to "buy a few items" as a way of dealing with off-hour boredom, and all the forms of recreation which are resource-expensive.

This third proposal focuses on off-work hours for a very good reason. Very few of us will be able to make even minor changes on the job. Activity on that job is keyed to accommodating the system which is inherently exploitative to some degree of both people and resources. Because the individual must sell his or her body to the job for the purpose of keeping the kids in food and clothing and paying the mortgage, any boat-rocking on the job can place individuals in a vulnerable position. Any time that belongs to the individual is during off hours, though even then some time has to be set aside to "putting things in order."

But we still face a practical problem. When I say that we seek a sense of inter-relatedness and rootedness in the land, I seem to be describing lofty and vague goals. As we begin to think how this is to be translated into action during our daily lives, I know that we need something to maximize that sense of inter-relatedness and to know that rootedness. That "something" must not be a cheap gimmick, but must be a "to-the-marrow" recognition of a personal need or purpose. We need a religious purpose to sustain our action. I think that purpose simply involves a decision *to take more control over our own lives,* with the added spinoff being a reduction of our vulnerability and a higher expression of our innate potentialities.

How can a person, who wants to take more control over his own life, especially in off-work hours, position himself to maximize his sense of inter-relatedness with members of his own species and other species and feel his rootedness in the land? The suggestions I will make to answer this question will be directed to those people in suburbia, where 55% of the American population lives. Here reside the so-called affluent, middle-class Americans, from blue to white collar workers, who are the largest consumers.

My first suggestion for the suburbanite is for him to try to grow most of his own vegetables. Two practical reasons for growing vegetables are to save money and to eat safer, more healthful food. However, the monetary savings is not great, especially at first. Compared to most countries, food is a relatively inexpensive item in the household budget for Americans. But there is also the possibility that the overall health and longevity of the family could improve. We don't really know the effects of all the pesticide residues, preservatives and other chemical additives in our commercially-produced food, but we have good reason to be uneasy about them. But let us discount health as a significant factor, just as we discounted the monetary saving. What is left?

What is left is a symbolic gesture with a purpose. Symbolic gestures which are meaningful must ultimately be associated with the physical world. Sometimes the chain between the symbol and the physical world is so long that it takes a philosopher to explain the relationship. But this is not so with food production. The garden is a statement that the individual is seizing more control over his or her own life, is taking a step away from such complete vulnerability, is getting more in touch with the earth.

After people in the suburbs have begun to overcome the spiritual danger of believing that food comes from a grocery store, they can then strive to overcome the second spiritual danger described by Aldo Leopold, the belief that heat comes from a stove.[1] This can be accomplished relatively inexpensively by those who build solar collectors for space heating and water heating. The Association of Home Appliance Manufacturers has estimated that some 60% of home energy is consumed for space heating and 15% for water heating. The family that installs solar collectors to provide 75% of their home energy needs would be taking a significant step towards gaining even more control over their own lives.

Solar heating systems can now be purchased from many companies. However, individuals can build their own. Literature on solar energy systems is available at the elementary level, and the technology is not complicated.

Materials that go into the collector can be purchased or scavenged and the collectors can be assembled slowly. Collectors can be mounted on roofs, integrated as patio covers, or simply positioned in yards if space is available and safety is taken into consideration. This activity, which is bound to attract the attention of the neighborhood, is a very significant statement. It shows further progress toward gaining control over one's own life. Like the garden, the solar collector can help us get in touch with the world.

Several of my California students have reminded me about the Mormon practice of storing up a two-year supply of food, pointing out how the Mormons will be in great shape in the event of food scarcity. My reply has always been that if I am hungry, I am liable to "hunt me up a Mormon." All the old visions of defending the bomb shelter with a machine gun come to mind. As a boy I wondered how Noah managed to keep the unbelievers off the ark in the last moments of rising water. That's more of a miracle than the flood itself. My point is that our salvation lies in being one of the community, not in being the only one with foresight to develop alternate food and energy sources. Why would anyone want to be an isolated "have" in the midst of "have-nots"?

Although a person may have placed himself in a position where he can feel his rootedness in the land and can take more control over his own life, he is still a part of a community. A healthy interdependence is possible if others in the community also adopt the religious purpose of taking more control over their own lives. This could result in a charming variety within the suburbs. Homesites might be surrounded with gardens, greenhouses and possibly small livestock. Solar collectors, windmills, and methane generators would be part of the scene. Some homes could be turned into small shops. With necessities closer to home, fewer automobiles would be needed, and this would surely change the face of the community for the better. Such changes are difficult to imagine for the Rosemonts, Winding Hills, Oak Acres and Ridgewoods. But most important changes are difficult to imagine.

My fourth proposal is that we begin to assemble and cannonize an ecological Bible, a mutable *Whole Earth Book*. The *Whole Earth Book,* not to be confused with the *Whole Earth Catalogue,* would have a symbolic acronym, WEB. Our

WEB might contain Wald's version of the genesis of the earth. There might be a Book of Proverbs, a Book of Songs. Parts would be light and joyful; parts would be solemn. The WEB would celebrate the earth and life on the earth through song, poetry and prose, painting and photography. The WEB would help Americans begin to establish a common covenant with nature.

There could be many potential contributors, such as Loren Eisley, Roger Tory Peterson, John Muir, George Perkins Marsh, John Burroughs, Sigurd Olsen and the Odum Brothers. But there is one contributor to the environmental movement who stands above everyone else, and without whose writing no *Whole Earth Book* would be complete. That man is Aldo Leopold. On the need for a land ethic, Leopold seems to have said it all, and well. Perhaps our WEB should have a Book of Leopold. But we must be careful, for it is not in the nature of an ecological ethic to make room for sainthood. Nature is mutable and knows few if any absolutes. Besides, Leopold himself would have resisted any attempt to make him a patron saint. Our best tribute to Leopold would not be to sanctify him in a *Whole Earth Book,* but to include him as one of the people in the "thinking community" who contributes toward the evolution of an ecological ethic.

References and Notes

1. Aldo Leopold, *A Sand County Almanac,* Oxford University Press, N.Y., 1949.
2. Lynn White, Jr., "The Historical Roots of Our Ecological Crisis," Science 155: 1203-1207. 10 March 1967.
3. Theodore Roszak, *Where The Wasteland Ends,* Doubleday, Garden City, N.Y., 1973.
4. Galen Rowell, "The Rings of Life," Sierra Club Bulletin, 59: No. 8, Sept. 1974.
5. Thomas J. Lyon, "John Muir, The Physiology of the Brain and the Wilderness Experience," *The Living Wilderness* 38: 25-30, Summer, 1974.
6. Robert E. Ornstein, *The Psychology of Consciousness,* W. H. Freeman, S.F., 1972.
7. Plato, Critias, translated by Arnold Toynbee in *Greek Historical Thought,* pp. 146-47.
8. E. F. Schumacher, *Small Is Beautiful,* Harper & Row, New York, 1973.
9. Yi-Fu Tuan, "Discrepancies between Environmental Attidude and Behaviour: Examples from Europe and China," The Canadian Geographer, 12, 176-191, 168.
10. René Dubos, "Franciscan Conservation versus Benedictine Stewardship," in *A God Within,* Charles Scribner's Sons, 1972.
11. Joseph Needham, *Science and Civilisation in China,* 4 vols., Cambridge: University Press, 1954-62.
12. Yi-Fu Tuan, "Our Treatment of the Environment in Ideal and Actuality," American Scientist, 58, p. 248, 1970.
13. James V. Neel, "Lessons from a 'Primitive' People," Science 1970: 815-821, 20 November 1970.
14. This expression "unwittingly accessible" appears in *Tales of Power* by Carlos Casteneda, Simon and Schuster, New York, 1974.
15. Quoted in article by S. I. Rasool, "Evolution of the Earth's Atmosphere," Science 157: 1466-1467, September, 1967.
16. See John D. Buffington, "Predation, Competition, and Pleistocene Megafauna Extinction," BioScience, 21: 167-170. Also, Daniel A. Guthrie, "Primitive Man's Relationship to Nature," BioScience, 21: 721-723, 1971.
17. Nicholas Georgescu-Roegen, "Entropy the Measure of Economic Man" in Science 190: 447-450.
18. *Blake: Complete Writings,* edited by Geoffrey Keynes, Oxford University Press, 1969.
19. The Time-Life Book on *Early Man,* 1965 by F. Clark Howell contains some superb sequence photographs of Bushmen digging for and capturing the springhaas on pages 186-187.
20. Prepared for the general session at the meeting of the Association of Southeastern Biologists, Braniff Place, New Orleans, La., April 22, 1976.

The Human Enterprise

George Wald

We have come to a time of great decision not only for man but for much of life on the earth. We are in a period of great crisis, in fact, of many crises. John Platt has spoken of them as a "crisis of crises." They are all coming upon us at once, all coming to a head within the next fifteen to at most thirty years; and this, of course, faces us with multiple problems. We have very hard decisions to make.

The things we need to face and try to do are terrifying in their complexity and their difficulty. We need in fact a revolution. I use the word in its literal sense, a turn-about. We here in America, living in a democracy, still hope that we can *vote* ourselves that revolution; but vote it or not, that revolution must come if we are to survive.

Nor can it be done piecemeal. Most of our problems are closely interrelated, so that we have to deal with them together, each one dependent upon the others. That calls for a tremendous effort that involves not only the people of this country but to a great degree of the globe. That means that we will have somehow to learn to move and work together; and that in turn calls for some sort of common acceptance of the questions that men have always tried to answer throughout their history: Whence they come, what kind of thing they are, and out of these realizations at least some hint of what is to become of us.

Those are the age-old questions. Men have always tried to answer them, and all the traditional religions try to answer them. Fortunately for us at this time one can find a kind of answer in the world view of science, an answer that presents an astonishingly unified view of the universe, the place of life in it, and the place of man in life. In that unified view I think we can find new sanctions for our beliefs in the sanctity of life and in the dignity of man, more credible and more reliable than any that the older traditions offered us.

What is that unified view? We know now that we live in a historical universe, one in which not only living creatures but stars and galaxies are born, come to maturity, grow old and die. That universe is made of four kinds of elementary particles: protons, neutrons, electrons, and photons, which are particles of radiation. If not the whole universe then surely large parts of it began in a kind of gas, a plasma, of such elementary particles, filling large sections of space. Here and there, quite by accident, within that plasma an eddy formed, a little special concentration of material, and this, through the ordinary forces of gravitation, began to pull in the stuff around it, to pull in the particles out of the space around it. So it grew, and the more that there was, the harder it pulled. It swept the material out of larger and larger sections of space and grew and grew, a condensing mass of elementary particles. As that mass condensed, as all such masses in condensation do, it heated up. When the temperature in the deep interior reached about five million degrees, something new began to happen.

That new thing was that one of these particles, the protons—a proton is the nucleus of a hydrogen atom, so that one speaks of them as hydrogen—the protons began to join together, four protons condensing to make a nucleus of the atom helium, four protons, each approximately of mass 1, condensing to make a helium nucleus of mass approximately 4.

But in that transaction a little mass is lost: and that little bit of mass is converted into radiation, according to Einstein's famous formula. $E = mc^2$, in which E is the energy of that radiation, m is the little bit of mass, and c is a very big number, the speed of light, 186,000 miles a second, 3×10^{10} centimeters per second. Multiply even a little bit of mass by that big a number and you get an awful lot of energy. That energy beginning to be poured out in the deep interior of what had been a condensing mass of particles backs up the condensation, and this mass comes into an uneasy steady state, in which its further impulse to collapse through gravity is held back by the outpouring of energy inside. What I have just described, of course, is the birth of a star. Our own star, the sun, was born in that way about six billion years ago. It is just an ordinary run of the mill, middle-aged star. It has approximately another six billion years to run.

Stars live by this process. They live by the so-called "burning" of hydrogen to helium. Inevitably the time comes when every star begins to run out of hydrogen. With that, it begins to produce less energy; and with that it begins to collapse again. With that, it heats up again. When the temperature in the deep interior reaches about one hundred million degrees, something new begins to happen.

That is the "burning" of helium. Those helium nuclei of mass 4 begin to unite with one another. It's all simple arithmetic. Two helium nuclei condense: four and four make eight. That is beryllium 8, an atomic nucleus so unstable that it disintegrates within so small a fraction of a second that it has never been measured. Yet always at these enormous concentrations of matter and enormous temperatures there are a few beryllium atoms; and here and there a beryllium nucleus captures another helium nucleus. Eight and four make twelve, and what is twelve; *Carbon;* and that is where carbon comes from in our universe. And when you have got the carbon, that carbon 12 can capture another helium nucleus: twelve and four make sixteen, and what is sixteen? *Oxygen;* and that is where oxygen comes from. And when you have some carbon, that can do another thing. The carbon itself can begin to pick up protons, hydrogen nuclei. And carbon 12 plus two protons make fourteen, and what is fourteen? That is *Nitrogen.*

These processes produce a new enormous outpouring of energy in the deep interior of the star, enough energy not only to back up the further condensation but to puff it out to enormous size. It is now a red giant, a dying star, gigantic because it has been puffed up to enormous size, and red because it has cooled off somewhat in its outermost layers. A red giant, a dying star.

Those red giants are in a delicate condition. They are always distilling a lot of stuff off their surfaces into space. Every now and then a great streamer of material goes shooting off into space: a flare. Every now and then a whole star threatens to blow up: a nova. Every now and then it does blow up: a supernova. And in all these ways the stuff of which red giants are made is spewed out into space to become part of the huge masses of gases and dust that fill all space. It is sometimes estimated that as much as half the mass of our universe is in the form of gases and dust.

Then here and there in the gases and dust a new eddy forms, a new little knot of material, that once again by gravitation begins to pull in the stuff from all around it; and a new star is born.

But those later generation stars, unlike the first generation of stars made entirely of hydrogen and helium, contain the carbon and nitrogen and oxygen; and we know that our sun is such a later generation star, *because we are here*—because we, as all other living creatures we know, and I am sure, though that is another story, that must be true everywhere that life occurs in the universe, because 99 percent of our living substance is made of just those elements I have been naming: hydrogen, carbon, nitrogen, and oxygen. It is a moving realization that stars must die before organisms may live.

Stars are at too high temperatures for the atomic nuclei to gather the electrons about themselves in orderly ways. That can happen only in the cooler places of the universe, on the planets. There, where the electrons can be brought into orderly ways around the atomic nuclei, those electrons can begin to interact with one another, and so become the first molecules.

Molecules are a great new thing in the universe, for until there are molecules nothing has a shape or size. We are still in the world of Heisenberg's Indeterminancy Principle. So long as one is in the world of elementary particles, even atoms, there are no shapes or sizes of even definable positions and motions. All those things come into the universe with the first molecules.

So molecules are a great thing. As soon as the earth was formed, some four and a half billion years ago, the molecules began to form. In the primitive atmosphere of the earth there were such molecules as hydrogen, ammonia, water and methane; and in the upper layers of the atmosphere, sparked by sunlight and electric discharges, those and other molecules began to interact to form that which would eventually give rise to life, the so-called *organic* molecules, the molecules made of hydrogen, carbon, nitrogen and oxygen. Over the ages they were leached out of the atmosphere into the seas. About three billion years ago somewhere, sometime, or perhaps several times in several places, an aggregate of such molecules in the ocean reached a condition that a competent biologist, had he been present, would have been willing to concede to be alive.

Life, too, was a great new thing in our universe. I have heard life called disparagingly a disease of matter. No, it is no disease of matter. It is a *culmination* of matter. Give matter a chance, and give it that chance for long enough, and life appears inevitably. It is a culmination of matter, so far as we know the most complex state of organization that matter achieves in our universe.

And life, since it appeared on the earth, has transformed the whole environment. Even biologists still occasionally make the mistake of thinking that the environment is something given for life to fit itself into or perish; that it is the environment that plays the tune to which life must dance or die.

But it isn't that way at all. The early atmosphere of this planet in which those first organic molecules appeared that led to life, contained no oxygen gas, O_2, the stuff with which all animals and all higher plants respire. There was no oxygen gas in the early atmosphere of the planet. It was put into the atmosphere by living organisms, by plants in the process of photosynthesis; and it is now held in the atmosphere entirely by that process.

All the molecular oxygen in our atmosphere comes out of plants in the process of photosynthesis and goes into plants and animals in the process of cellular respiration, and so is completely renewed, about every two thousand years.

Two thousand years is just a moment in geological time. With carbon dioxide it is still more strange. All the carbon dioxide, not only in the atmosphere but dissolved in all the waters of the earth, goes into photosynthesis and comes out of respiration and so is completely renewed every three hundred years.

Life is a great thing on this planet. Two-thirds of the planet is covered with water; yet all the water on the earth goes in and out of living organisms and is completely renewed every two million years; and two million years is just a day in geological time. We have had men on the earth for that long.

The appearance of oxygen through the process of plant photosynthesis did another very strange thing for life on the earth. You see, the radiation from sunlight produced in the way I have described, by turning hydrogen into helium, contains short wavelength ultraviolet components that are incompatible with the existence of life, that no life or even such large molecules as proteins, or nucleic acids can tolerate. So long as that radiation poured onto the surface of the earth, life could not exist on the surface. It had to stay under water.

But there in the ocean photosynthesis began. About four-fifths of all the photosynthesis on the earth still occurs in the upper layers of the ocean. The photosynthesis poured oxygen into the atmosphere; and in the uppermost layers of the atmosphere, sparked by sunlight, some of the oxygen formed a little *ozone*. (Oxygen gas is O_2, ozone is O_3.) That little ozone absorbed and still absorbs those ultraviolet radiations out of sunlight that are incompatible with life. It is only because of that little ozone in our upper atmosphere that animals and plants were able to come out from under water and populate the earth and the air.

How much ozone? The whole story represents a delicacy, a sensitivity of control almost beyond belief. The only thing that lets us survive outside of water on the surface of the earth is that ozone; yet all the ozone in the upper atmosphere, if brought to 1 atmosphere pressure—ordinary air pressure at the surface of the earth—and zero degrees centigrade, would form a layer only three millimeters thick, about one eighth of an inch.

And so, particularly after the oxygen and the ozone had arrived, life flourished on the earth and populated every corner of the earth with a most extraordinary ingenuity—every corner. Every place where a little energy can be obtained that makes life possible, you find life there, fitting itself into the most extraordinary conditions.

About two million years ago, man appeared. Man too is a great new thing, man and his like, a great new thing in the universe. You see, you have to wait a long time, all those things have had to happen, and then at last—and I think, given enough time, inevitably—a creature appears who begins to know; a science-and art-making animal, who begins to cast back on this whole history, and begins for the first time to understand it.

You may have heard it said that a hen is only an egg's way of making another egg. In just the same sense a man is the atom's way of knowing about atoms. If you wish, a man is the star's way of knowing about stars—a great new thing.

But in his knowing, man also begins inevitably, as part of that knowing, going hand in hand with that knowing, to breed a technology. The technology isn't artificial; it is part of nature, since it is part of human nature. The technology comes along with that kind of knowing on the part of any such creature, wherever he arose.

I have heard the silly question asked, "Why is the earth about five billion years old?"—and the silly answer—a silly question always deserves a silly answer: Because it took that long to find that out. That is the way it is. Now we are coming to ask another curious question: When you have come to the point of finding that out, can you go much further? Is such a development self-limiting?

I am sure that there is not only life in very many places in the universe, but there are also man-like creatures; not men, but similarly contemplative, technology-making creatures, in many other places in the universe. I see no reason offhand why many of them shouldn't be far ahead of us.

We are beginning to develop our technology very rapidly, and at an increasing pace. If that kind of thing is true for us, it might well be true for them. If they have had another thousand years—and a thousand years is nothing—why not a hundred thousand, a million years, why indeed not a billion years—where might they have reached by now?

Think of where we might reach in even another hundred years if we survive, if we manage well. One has to begin to ask, are there such highly superior technological civilizations elsewhere in the universe, or is there not only a time in which such a creature arrives, but a somewhat later time, perhaps not very much later, in which he departs? That problem now very much concerns us.

Because we have reached a point suddenly in which our very existence and continuance, not only as a civilization but as a species, is threatened by wholly new problems. One of the most important of those problems is overpopulation. It is entirely new. Darwin gave us the phrase, "the survival of the fittest"; and biologists, who like to measure all things, long ago began asking how we were to measure fitness. Long ago we decided that the measure of fitness would be reproductive success—that we could consider those lines of organism most fit that breed the largest number of offspring that themselves survive to sexual maturity and reproduce. I suppose that man is the first species on earth, animal or plant, to be threatened by his own reproductive success.

As everyone knows, by all present indications, unless we can bring something different to happen very quickly, the present world population of something over three and a half billion will have increased by the end of the century to perhaps double that number. Long before that we expect famine in many parts of the world on an unprecedented scale. Yet those famines aren't the heart of the problem. If they were, one could even feel slightly optimistic, because in the last decade the world production of food has increased a little faster than the world population; but that isn't the heart of the problem.

The heart of the problem, as of all human problems, is one of *meaning*. It would be altogether meaningless and bankrupt now to make of the human enterprise a simple exercise in production, an attempt to see how many people one could keep alive on the surface of the earth. Our problem isn't one of numbers, but of the *quality* of human lives. What we need to do is to produce that size of population in which human beings can most fulfill their potentialities.

From that point of view—some may disagree with me and quite properly—in my opinion we are already overpopulated, not just in such places as India, China, and Puerto Rico, but here and in Western Europe. With that overpopulation in our

Western world there has been, I think, a signal deterioration in our culture all through the last century.

I think that though this period is kinder to the sciences than to the arts, the life of the individual scientist is nothing like it was. It has deteriorated enormously. I look back a century and envy those scientists who lived then—the way they lived, the way they made their science, the amount of science they succeeded in making, and its quality. All those things have gone badly downhill.

And then we have a closely related problem, also enormously threatening and important, and that is the way we are wasting all our remaining resources and polluting the surface of the earth—a terrible problem, and to an extraordinary degree an American problem.

We are the worst offenders—not *they, we*. We with six percent of the world's population are said to consume about forty percent of the world's irreplaceable resources, and to account for about fifty percent of the world's industrial pollution. It is we Americans who do those things not only to this country but to all the world.

And then there is a third gigantic problem. We have come into the nuclear age. I should like to say something about that, because what should have come to humankind as a promise of a new degree of freedom such as men on earth and life on earth had never experienced before, comes upon us instead as a threat, perhaps the most serious threat we now have to face.

Why do I say a promise? It is very simple. You see, there came a point for life on earth that was absolutely critical and revolutionary. (The big revolutions are the revolutions of nature. The big revolutions among men are the revolutions of science. Make no mistake about that. Darwin nursing his dyspepsia in a garden in Cambridge was a much greater revolutionary than Karl Marx. He changed our world.)

Life first arose on the earth out of that aggregation of organic molecules leached out of the atmosphere into the seas over ages of time. Having arisen, it lived on those molecules. That is a losing game, because just so many of those molecules had accumulated, and living organisms had begun to use and destroy them, just as we have almost finished by now using and destroying our accumulations of fossil fuels.

Eventually that process would have had to come to an end, and life would have come to an end. All of it would have had to begin again from the beginning. But before that happened something else took place: living organisms invented photosynthesis, by which using the energy of sunlight, they could begin to make their own organic molecules. That made them independent of their previous history, of the stores of organic molecules that had accumulated over previous ages on the earth.

Now with the coming of the nuclear age we have a similar opportunity, one of those things that happen only once in several billion years, if then. Because, you see, all life up until now has lived on sunlight, the plants directly, the animals by eating the plants.

Now we can begin to make our own sunlight. That process that the sun lives by, turning hydrogen into helium, is the same process that goes on in a hydrogen bomb. What a disgrace! Think of it! A nuclear reaction which could mean that we could shortly make our own sunlight, that we could make a new basis for life on the earth, that we could make our own energy—that reaction is turned mainly into a weapon that threatens our lives, that promises to become the biggest polluter of our environment, and that now threatens our existence and much of the rest of life on the earth.

It is a symptom of the illness of our society that people think of that as inevitable. Of course one makes a bomb as fast as one can. But there is nothing inevitable about it. That is just our present way of life. It is our western culture at work, our western culture with its beautiful Judeo-Christian ethic. It is our culture alone among the cultures of the earth that sees it that way, that has brought the technology of killing and destruction much further than any culture on the earth ever dreamed of doing before.

It was the Chinese who invented gunpowder. And what did they do with it? They used it for firecrackers. Poor people! All of us know, we are all being told, that the Chinese are crazy. They can't be trusted, they didn't know what to do with gunpowder as we did. But we have taught them.

And the space program: The next person who says to me that we can solve the population problem because we can now get to the moon, I think I will kick him. That is the wrong model, and if we follow it we will be in terrible trouble. That trip to the moon was an exercise in what you can do with lots of wealth and power. The scientific content was trivial and negligible. It was an exercise of power; and as for its technology, that is expected to be very useful in our future weaponry.

There is no inevitability about using all our technology for killing and destruction. We have just taken the wrong turn. So I should like to end with a parable—not a Biblical parable, a biological parable.

Some 200 million years ago we were in the Age of Reptiles. The dinosaurs were the lords of the earth. They looked very fine, those dinosaurs. They were big, the biggest land animals that have ever existed. They were well-armed: horns, teeth, claws. They were well protected: scales, armor plate. They looked awfully good, those dinosaurs.

And back in the shadows, hiding among the roots of the trees was a small, tender, defenseless group of animals. They were the first mammals. They had little to offer, but one thing. They had rather large brains for their size. The dinosaur had a very small brain for its size. The proportion of brains to brawn in a dinosaur was very low. The mammals were doing better in that regard.

And pretty soon there were no more dinosaurs. The Age of Reptiles had given way to the Age of Mammals.

And the mammals kept working on the beautiful brain. Two million years ago they gave rise to man.

Man, as I have been telling you, is a wonderful thing. A man, standing on his own two feet, with that wonderful brain—gentle, harming no one and nothing, altogether in control—a beautiful creature, something one could love. But put him in a car! Now he is making a roar and a stink through the streets. You hardly see the man. It's hard to love a man in a car. And the proportion of brains to brawn has again sunk very low. He has become a kind of medium sized dinosaur.

And dangerous. Cars kill more than 50,000 Americans per year. Please notice one says that cars kill those Americans, not men in cars; because we realize all too well that the man isn't altogether in control. While we weren't watching, we've become dinosaurs again. And cars are just the beginning of it. There are trucks and trains and planes and hydrogen bombs—the proportion of brains to brawn has sunk terribly low, and it is going down fast. And this time if we have an extinction it will be a do-it-yourself extinction. And this time there is no other creature to take over.

Mammals brought another thing into life on earth, infinitely precious. Mammals take care of their young. Dinosaurs laid their eggs and left them. That was the way it was with all the previous creatures: the fishes, the amphibia, the reptiles. Not mammals. Mammals carry their young inside them, and after they have given birth to them they nurse them for months more (that is where the word "mammal" comes from, the nursing); and after that they watch them play in the sun, and protect them, and feed them, and teach them the ways of life.

That is another of our problems. We are no longer taking good care of our young. We have introduced them into a world that offers them little that they want and threatens their very existence. We have become dinosaurs again, and that is our problem.

So what are we to do? Please realize where we are, because whatever we do now we have to try somehow to do as men and not as dinosaurs. The temptation is great to do those things as dinosaurs. That is true every way one turns now. There are traps besetting us now in everything we try to do.

Take the population problem, for example. We are being told from some quarters that the attempt to control population is an attempt to commit genocide, an attempt on the part of the well-to-do to limit the numbers of the poor, an attempt on the part of the well-to-do nations to limit the numbers in the under-developed nations. Yet the only hope of the poor and of the underdeveloped nations is to limit population.

So what is wrong? One has to couple that attempt to limit population with a genuine and effective taking care of all the people there are. To do the one without the other would be conscienceless. We need to limit population, but we need meanwhile to take care of people better than we do now, and most of all we need to take care of children, all children everywhere, very much better than we are doing.

So I have almost done, because it is that way with the pollution problem, too. That, too, is beset with such traps, two of them rather obvious. One trap is to try to make of pollution, of our new concern with the environment, an issue that will distract people, mainly young people, from all the other problems that now properly concern them. The second trap is to turn pollution into a new dinosaur, to turn pollution into the new multi-billion dollar business. The only way to deal with pollution that really would mean anything is to stop it at its source; but that is difficult, and very strongly opposed by some powerful forces. The temptation is great to let the pollution go right on, but to superimpose on it a new multi-billion dollar business of anti-pollution; and in these days of conglomerates it would be the same business: one division would pollute, the other division would clean up; and both would make a lot of money.

So here we are at the crossroads. We have to make hard choices. We have not only to try to do, but to succeed in doing those fantastically difficult things, so difficult that if there were any alternative we would be well advised to avoid them. But there is no alternative. Those are the things that *must* be done, for us, and much more for our children. For it is they who must inherit a good earth, a decent place in which they can live their lives—they and their children, and their children's children.